introduction i

BUSINES
MANAGEMENT

7th EDITION

introduction to

BUSINESS
MANAGEMENT

7th EDITION

Editors
Prof GS du Toit
Prof BJ Erasmus
Prof JW Strydom

Authors
Prof JA Badenhorst-Weiss
Prof MC Cant
Prof GS du Toit
Prof BJ Erasmus
Prof PA Grobler
Prof LP Krüger
Mr R Machado
Prof J Marx
Prof R Mpofu
Prof S Rudansky-Kloppers
Prof R Steenkamp
Prof JW Strydom

Contributors
Prof T Brevis
Ms L Coetzee
Ms S Cronjé
Dr D Geldenhuys
Dr C Mischke
Prof C Nieuwenhuizen
Prof K van der Linde
Ms M Vrba
Mr R Wordsworth

Consulting editors
Dr MDC Motlatla
Prof GJ de J Cronjé

OXFORD
UNIVERSITY PRESS
Southern Africa

OXFORD
UNIVERSITY PRESS
Southern Africa

Oxford University Press Southern Africa (Pty) Ltd

Vasco Boulevard, Goodwood, Cape Town, Republic of South Africa
P O Box 12119, N1 City, 7463, Cape Town, Republic of South Africa

Oxford University Press Southern Africa (Pty) Ltd is a subsidiary of
Oxford University Press, Great Clarendon Street, Oxford OX2 6DP.

The Press, a department of the University of Oxford, furthers the University's objective of
excellence in research, scholarship, and education by publishing worldwide in

Oxford New York

Auckland Cape Town Dar es Salaam Hong Kong Karachi
Kuala Lumpur Madrid Melbourne Mexico City Nairobi
New Delhi Shanghai Taipei Toronto

With offices in

Argentina Austria Brazil Chile Czech Republic France Greece
Guatemala Hungary Italy Japan Poland Portugal Singapore South Korea
Switzerland Turkey Ukraine Vietnam

Oxford is a registered trade mark of Oxford University Press
in the UK and in certain other countries

Published in South Africa
by Oxford University Press Southern Africa (Pty) Ltd, Cape Town

Introduction to Business Management
Seventh edition
ISBN 978 0 19 576688 2

© Oxford University Press Southern Africa (Pty) Ltd 2007

The moral rights of the author have been asserted
Database right Oxford University Press Southern Africa (Pty) Ltd (maker)

First published 2007
Seventh impression 2010

Publishing Manager: Alida Terblanche
Project Manager: Ulla Schreuder
Editor: Patricia Myers Smith, Ethné Clarke
Designer: Brigitte Rouillard
Cover Photo: Great stock

Set in Photina 10pt on 12pt by Mckore Graphics
Reproduction by Mckore Graphics

Printed and bound by ABC Press, Cape Town
113546

ABRIDGED TABLE OF CONTENTS

CONTENTS

Preface

This book focuses on the management of business organisations in the South African business environment. It describes how managers should manage resources and activities in such a way that organisations can operate as profitably as possible, thereby increasing the wealth of society and the country in general.

This seventh edition of *Introduction to Business Management* marks a milestone in introductory business management texts in South Africa as it is one of a few introductory business management texts that have shown consistent growth over an extended period. The first edition was published in 1984 and now 22 years later the seventh edition sees the light! Since the publication of the first edition nearly half a million students at many universities and other institutions have used *Introduction to Business Management* as the cornerstone of their careers in business.

Organisation of the text

The first part of the book introduces the reader to business management. It describes the role of the entrepreneur and manager in the business world, the business organisation as the subject of study and the South African business environment.

Part two contains an exposition of the management process and a survey of general management principles on which the functional management areas discussed in part three are based.

Part three deals with marketing management, financial management, operations management and purchasing management.

In part four a number of contemporary management issues, such as productivity, globalisation and knowledge management are briefly discussed.

Changes from previous editions

The seventh edition follows a value chain approach where some of the supply chain concepts are used. Supply chains and value chains are complementary and focus on the flow of products and services in one direction and the value that is generated in the eyes of the customer flowing back. Creating a profitable value chain requires a careful alignment between what the customer wants (through the demand or value chain) and what is delivered via the supply chain.

In this edition the authors have endeavoured to retain all the elements that have contributed to the success of the book. Comments by students and academics were extremely useful and were incorporated where possible, in the new layout and contents.

The seventh edition of *Introduction to Business Management* offers many improvements in style, content and presentation to make the text even more effective and enjoyable. This edition includes substantial new and improved material. Each chapter commences with a case study that places the core elements in a practical perspective and integrates theory and practice. Chapters also include challenges in the form of short case studies that require students to think critically about the concepts and the applications thereof. Key terms and questions for discussions are included at the end of every chapter.

In addition to the textual revisions two new editors have been added to the editorial panel and new authors have contributed to the contents. The combined experience of the editors and new authors further enhance the quality and the relevance of the text.

Acknowledgements

This book benefited from the ideas contributed by a wide range of colleagues who teach from it in a number of tertiary institutions. Their ideas and suggestions were extremely useful and were incorporated, where possible, in the new layout and contents.

We continue to welcome constructive comments from colleagues at universities, as well as from managers in business practice, in an attempt to make future management education in South Africa even more relevant and meaningful.

We also thank Prof GJ de J Cronjé, former HOD of the Department of Business Management for his contribution as consulting editor of the seventh edition. We furthermore acknowledge the work done by Dr MDC Motlatla in insuring that the text is Africa oriented and culture sensitive.

We specifically want to cite the contributions of the following colleagues who contributed to the updating of certain chapters:

Prof T Brevis
Ms L Coetzee
Ms S Cronjé
Dr D Geldenhuys
Dr C Mischke
Prof C Nieuwenhuizen
Prof K van der Linde
Ms M Vrba
Mr R Wordsworth

The editors

Prof GS Du Toit
Prof BJ Erasmus
Prof JW Strydom

introduction to
BUSINESS MANAGEMENT

The seventh edition of the textbook *Introduction to Business Management* follows a value chain approach. In this process we considered some of the supply chain concepts that are used today. Supply chains and value chains are complementary views that focus on the flow of products and services in one direction and the value that is generated in the eyes of the customer flowing back. Creating a profitable value chain therefore requires a careful alignment between what the customer wants (through the demand or value chain) and what is delivered via the supply chain.

The value chain model used for this book is depicted in the figure below and indicates the relationship between the different areas of the book which builds up the value chain concept as we understand it.

The value chain distinguishes between the types of activities in an organisation, namely primary and secondary activities. The primary activities are those involved in the physical production of the product, while the secondary activities provide the infrastructure that allows the primary activities to take place.

As can be seen from the model we have the support activities that are grouped in chapters 1, 2, 3, 5, 7, 8, 9, 10, 11, 12 and 24. As in any organisation we need to do a strategic evaluation of the business environment in which the business operates (chapter 4). Having done this, we move on to the primary activities of the value chain which are covered in chapters 13, 14, 15, 16, 17, 18, 19, 20, 21, 22 and 23. This model will be shown in each part of the book to indicate the progress of the student in understanding the value chain concept.

Chapter 1: The business world and business management **Chapter 2:** Entrepreneurship **Chapter 3:** The establishment of a business		Flows
Chapter 24: Contemporary management issues		Products
Chapter 4: The business environment		Services
Chapter 5: Introduction to general management **Chapter 6:** The basic elements of planning **Chapter 7:** Organising	**Chapter 13, 14, 15 and 16:** Marketing and public relations management	Information
	Chapter 17, 18, 19: Financial management	Financial
Chapter 8: Leadership **Chapter 9, 10, 11:** Human resources management **Chapter 12:** Controlling the management process	**Chapter 20 and 21:** Operations management	Resource
	Chapter 22 and 23: Purchasing and supply management	Demand

Customer satisfaction and value

Source: Adapted from: Mentzer, J. T. (ed.), *Supply Chain Management*, Sage, London, 2001 pp. 22–23.

THE BUSINESS WORLD AND BUSINESS MANAGEMENT

The purpose of this chapter

This is the introductory chapter of a textbook that introduces the student to the science of business management. It discusses the role of business in society and explains how a business organisation in a market economy employs the various resources of a nation – its natural resources, human resources, financial resources and entrepreneurship – in order to satisfy the need for products and services. This chapter gives an overview of the prevailing economic systems in the world and explains how the business organisation functions in a market economy.

It is against this background that the purpose and nature of business management are examined, particularly with regard to the task of business management, which involves studying the factors, methods and principles that enable a business to function as efficiently as possible. Some of these factors, methods and principles are highlighted in the case study on page 5 about the airline industry. A classification of the study material of business management is also presented.

Learning outcomes

The content of this chapter will enable learners to:

- Appreciate the role of the business organisation in making available the products and services society must have to exist and thrive
- Describe the needs of society and how a business organisation satisfies those needs in a market economy
- Distinguish between the three main economic systems in the world
- Explain the interface between a business organisation and a market economy
- Describe the nature and purpose of business management as a science, that is, to study the factors, methods and principles that enable a business to function efficiently
- Comment on the development of business management as a science
- Distinguish and comment on the different management functions

1.1   Introduction

In a market economy the business world can be seen as a complex system which involves transforming resources into products and services. These products and services must meet the needs of people in exchange for a profit. This description of business emphasises four different elements:

- Human activities
- Production
- Exchange
- Profit

We shall discuss these elements in detail in section 1.2, but first consider the case study on page 5. This case study provides an illustration of how, in a market economy such as that of South Africa, businesses can grow into industries with their own sets of rules and dynamics, all with the view of striving for the ultimate business goal, namely making a profit.

1.2   The role of business in society

The business world is a complex system of individuals and business organisations that, in a market economy, involves the activity of transforming resources into products and services in order to meet the needs of people. These products and services are offered to the market in exchange for a profit. This description of business we introduced in section 1.1 emphasises four different elements:

- **Firstly, business activity involves human activities.** Business organisations are managed by people. While businesses may own property, machines and money, all of these are managed or operated by people.
- **Secondly, business activity involves production.** Production is the **transformation** of certain resources into products and services, as illustrated in figure 1.1. This may be, for example, the conversion of flour, sugar and butter into bread, or the conversion of bricks, sand, cement, wood and steel into a house. Indeed, even services are produced. A hospital provides an example of this: labour, beds and medicine are converted into a health service. The South African airline industry offers another example: passengers are transported safely and efficiently to their required destinations, and as this happens the passengers (consumers) become part of the transformation process.
- **Thirdly, business involves exchange.** Businesses produce products and services, not for their own use, but to exchange for money or for other products and services.
- **Finally, business involves profit.** Neither individuals nor business organisations could continue producing products and services without earning a profit. **Profit** is the reward for meeting the needs of people,

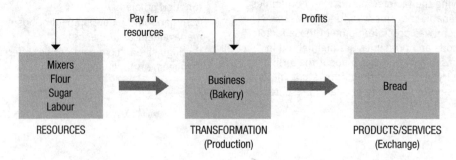

Figure 1.1: The transformation of a nation's resources into products and services by entrepreneurs

Case study

The South African airline industry flying high

The terrorist attacks on the World Trade Centre in the USA, which took place on 11 September 2001, resulted in a global downturn in air travel and had a significant impact on the American and European airline industries. US airlines posted net losses in excess of $7 billion and 80 000 jobs were lost in the US alone as a direct result of the attacks. Amidst this global downturn, air travel to and from South Africa increased as tourists' and business people's perceptions of what constituted a "safe destination" changed.[1] In 2005 in excess of seven million tourists visited South Africa.

The growth in the South African airline industry has been phenomenal over the five years since 2002. At nearly 8% per annum, this growth has been far faster than GDP growth, which has averaged in the region of 3% to 4% per year.

South Africa's largest domestic and international airline, state-owned South African Airways (SAA), flies more than six million domestic, regional and international passengers a year. Although SAA has benefited from the growth in air travel to and within South Africa, it is not "business as usual" at South Africa's largest carrier as the airline faces stiff competition. SAA's net profit for 2005 was R65 million down from over R2 billion in 2001.[2] While still having to compete with traditional rival airlines such as British Airways and Lufthansa in the international arena, SAA faces a new and growing challenge in the domestic airline market. Following considerable deregulation of the South African airline industry, a number of smaller low-cost domestic airlines entered the market, the first of which was kulula.com in July 2001, followed by 1time Airlines in 2004.

In a very small amount of time the smaller airlines were able to leverage their resources, particularly technological resources, and capitalise on the opportunities presented in South Africa's ever increasing market economy. Kulula.com was the first airline in South Africa to introduce the concept of e-ticketing, allowing for savings in commission and agents fees of between 12% and 15%. Further savings were achieved through the airline's "no frills" strategy. Other low-cost carriers followed suit with similar "least cost systems". Within a few short years, the smaller airlines revolutionised the way South Africans book and pay for their air tickets, and at the same time changed the competitive dynamics of the South African airline industry. Particularly in domestic air travel, it would appear as though price is fast becoming one of the main decision-making criteria for many price-sensitive consumers. So much so that SAA probably can't believe it ever made the following statement to *Business Day* in 2003[3]: "SAA is not a low-cost carrier and therefore has no reason to change its market positioning. Most of its passengers are discerning business people who value the frequency, convenience, punctuality and reliability of flights the most."

In November 2006, SAA introduced, amidst a cloud of controversy, its own low-cost carrier, Mango, to compete directly with kulula.com and 1time. While domestic travellers are smiling, only time will tell how long the South African airline industry will be able to keep up such an aggressive and sustained price war. Or will the 2010 Soccer World Cup come just in time to give further impetus to the race for profits?

and it enables businesses to pay for resources and to make a living. That is why the airline industry case study ends by raising the question of how long the price war between the various airlines can be sustained. Without profits being generated from operations, brought about by such fierce competition and price wars, eventually some of the airlines might cease to exist.

The **business world** is therefore a system of individuals and business organisations that produces products and services to meet people's needs. Some businesses produce tangible products such as cars, bread, houses or bicycles. Other businesses produce services such as transport (see the airline industry case study at the start of this chapter), communication, television entertainment, insurance or lottery services. Business is the means by which society endeavours to satisfy its **needs** and improve its standard of living. At the heart of all business activity are entrepreneurs, who start new ventures and thereby create jobs, economic growth and, it is hoped, prosperity. No one invented the business world. It is the result of activities related to meeting the needs of people in a market economy.

The most important characteristic of the business world in the **developed** countries of the West and Asia is the freedom of individuals to establish any business of their choice and to produce, within limits, any product or service the market requires. This system, in which individuals themselves decide what to produce, how to produce it, and at what price to sell their product, is called the **market system** or a **market economy**. This is the prevailing economic system in South Africa.

The market economy is a complex system comprising various types of small and large business organisations that collectively mobilise the resources of a country to satisfy the needs of its inhabitants. These businesses group together to form industries. Figure 1.2 shows the composition of the South African

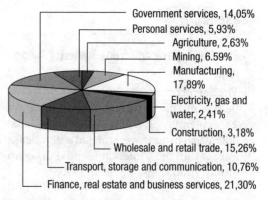

Government services, 14,05%
Personal services, 5,93%
Agriculture, 2,63%
Mining, 6.59%
Manufacturing, 17,89%
Electricity, gas and water, 2,41%
Construction, 3,18%
Wholesale and retail trade, 15,26%
Transport, storage and communication, 10,76%
Finance, real estate and business services, 21,30%

Figure 1.2: The composition of the South African business world in terms of contribution to gross domestic product (GDP)

Source: Statistics South Africa, "Gross Domestic Product", *Statistical release P0441, 2006.*

business world in terms of major industry sectors and their contribution to the economy.

The business world or economic structure of South Africa resembles that of many industrialised countries. Large businesses (such as Eskom, Standard Bank, Vodacom, Anglo American, Barloworld, and many other large public corporations, over 400 of which are listed on the Johannesburg Securities Exchange (JSE), are responsible for most of South Africa's economic activity.

Large businesses contribute 65,2% to GDP, while small and medium-sized enterprises (SMEs), which are mostly family or individually owned, produce about 30% of products and services. Micro-enterprises consisting of one-person businesses contribute 5,8% of economic activity. Strictly speaking, micro-enterprises (the informal sector) are not regarded as part of the formal economy because the people involved in these enterprises live primarily on a subsistence or survival basis. Moreover, such people put pressure on the infrastructure of inner city areas and contribute nothing in the form of income tax.

The variety of needs that a country has determines the complexity of its business environment. In First World countries businesses

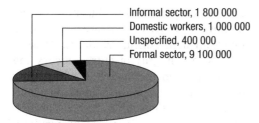

Informal sector, 1 800 000
Domestic workers, 1 000 000
Unspecified, 400 000
Formal sector, 9 100 000

Figure 1.3: The contribution of business to employment in South Africa

Source: Statistics South Africa, *Labour Force Survey*, 2004.

are the primary source of products, services and employment. Figure 1.3 shows the importance of the South African business world in providing employment in South Africa.

Business creates wealth, is a catalyst for economic growth, and is credited with bringing about the high standard of living in developed countries. Take for example the role business has played in the USA. In the space of two centuries the USA went from being a relatively undeveloped nation to a leading industrial nation, owning nearly 40% of the world's wealth with only 6% of the world's population. Business also serves the community indirectly by means of technological innovation, research and development, and improvements to infrastructure. It plays a crucial role in supporting, in various ways, education, the development of human resources, the arts, conservation and sport, and other activities that improve the quality of life of a community.

The business world and society both depend on and influence each other. At the heart of the business world is the entrepreneur or businessperson. In the pursuit of profit, entrepreneurs constantly search for new ideas, new products and new technologies. In so doing, they initiate innovation and bring about change. Their decisions on investment, production and employment influence not only the state of the economy, but also the prosperity of whole communities. Consider, for example, the influence of the Enron

(once tipped as the "corporation of the new millennium") and WorldCom accounting scandals on world economies in 2002. Because of such scandals caused by some of the most eminent entrepreneurs in the USA, stocks in New York fell to seven-year lows, thousands of employees lost their jobs, pensions evaporated, and investors lost confidence in corporate America, not to mention the fact that the former CEO of Enron was sentenced to 24 years in jail in October 2006. The scandals also had a ripple effect in Europe and Japan.

Conversely, society exerts its influence on business in a number of ways. If businesses fail to abide by the expectations and desires of the community – for instance by employing fraudulent or unethical practices, by polluting or degrading the environment, or by indulging in profiteering and monopolistic exploitation – the community will often react by instituting regulations and legislation to curb such practices. Consider an example relating to the airline industry case at the beginning of the chapter: at OR Tambo International Airport in Johannesburg in November 2006, more than a million litres of jet fuel was accidentally allowed to leak from the airport into the nearby Blaauwpan Dam. Residents in the neighbouring suburbs did not sit by idly, but rather chose to put pressure on the Airports Company of South Africa (ACSA) to take responsibility for the disaster.

Moreover, the attitude of society towards the business world is by no means consistent, for in a changing environment the community will, at different times, have different expectations of the business world. If the business world fails to respond to the expectations of the community, the attitude of the community towards the business world is likely to change. Consider, for example, the issue of equity in South African organisations. When South Africa became a democracy in 1994, businesses were obliged to include black people in their organisations. Because of the slow rate of response to this call, however, society reacted through government by instituting legislation that forces the business world to transform its organisations so that black people are included at all levels. The Employment Equity Act 55 of 1998, as well as the Broad-Based Black Economic Empowerment Act 53 of 2003, are examples of society's response to the exclusion from business of people of colour, women and people with disabilities.

Most Western countries have, over the years, come to regard the business sector as a valuable social institution because it has helped to realise society's needs and also to raise the standard of living. In the closing decades of the twentieth century, however, most Western nations decided that a high standard of living amid a deteriorating physical environment and inadequate social progress does not make sense. The business world is, thus, under continuous and often increasing pressure with regard to the following factors:

- **Social responsibility.** The **social responsibility** of business is a concept that originated in media revelations of malpractice by businesses and the resultant insistence of society on restricting such malpractice through regulation. Historically, social responsibility has been measured by the contribution of a business towards employment opportunities and its contribution to the economy. While profits and employment remain important, many other factors are nowadays included in assessing the social performance of a business. These other factors are equity or the empowerment of previously disadvantaged individuals, both economically and managerially; environmental awareness; the provision of housing and a responsible and safe workplace; concern about health issues; and involvement with community issues. Social responsibility will be discussed in more detail in chapter 4.
- **Business ethics.** As a concept, this is closely related to social responsibility[4], except that business ethics focuses specifically on the ethics or the ethical behaviour of managers

and executives in the business world. Managers, in particular, are expected to maintain high ethical standards. At issue here is the integrity of entrepreneurs and managers, and the degree to which their decisions conform to the norms and values of society. Business ethics revolves around the trust that society places in people in business, and the obligations people in business have towards society. Factors such as greed, the exploitation of workers and consumers, and the abuse of positions of trust have often resulted in the business ethics of entrepreneurs being deplored.
- **Affirmative action or equity regarding an organisation's workforce.** This affirmative action or equity is aimed at creating equal employment opportunities for all by ensuring that workforces are composed in roughly the same proportions as the groups that make up the population as a whole. In South Africa, the Employment Equity Act became law in 1998. The stated intention of the Act is to eliminate unfair discrimination, ensure employment equity, and achieve a diverse workplace that is broadly representative of the country's demographic realities. The inclusion of black people and other designated groups at management level is of crucial importance to South Africa's economy. According to the South African government's Accelerated and Shared Growth Initiative for South Africa (AsgiSA) strategy, economic growth of 4,5% per year for 2005–2009 is targeted (thereafter 6% per year). The economy can grow at the much-needed growth level of 4,5% or higher only if there are enough skilled managers to drive the economy. It is widely recognised that a moderate real economic growth rate of 2,7% per year will require an additional 100 000 managers each year for the foreseeable future. In 2006 South Africa's gross domestic product grew by approximately 4,5%.[5] Since the traditional source of managers, namely the population of

white males, has been exhausted, most of the managers required will have to come from the black population. Since 1994 there has been a steady increase in the number of black people in management, yet, despite this, white people, especially white males, remain over-represented in management. At the time of publication of this book, white people represented 72,4% of South African senior management. African people accounted for 14,5%, coloured people for 6% and Indian people for 7%. At the same time males accounted for 76,3% of senior management and females for only 23,6%.[6]

The growth of broad-based black economic empowerment in South Africa

The research group Empowerdex has examined a broad spectrum of empowerment issues. An important finding is that in the six years to 2006 at least 10% of South Africa's top 40 companies have sold in excess of 25% of their shares to black shareholders. In the decade to 2006 approximately 1 360 BEE transactions have taken place, worth R285 billion.

A further indicator of the impact of broad-based black economic empowerment in South Africa, as highlighted by Empowerdex, is witnessed in the number of black directors on the boards of JSE-listed companies.

In 1992 South Africa had 15 black directors on the boards of JSE-listed companies. In 1997 there were 98. In 2003 that increased to 207 and in 2006 there were more than 400 black directors holding 556 board seats at JSE-listed companies.

In 2006 the top five empowerment companies, according to Empowerdex, were as follows. Company Empowerment score:
1. Sekunjalo Investments – 76,44%
2. The Don Group – 74,07%
3. Sun International – 70,04%
4. Enaleni Pharmaceuticals – 69,88%
5. Telkom – 67,16%

Source: Empowerdex, *Top Empowerment Companies Survey*, 2006.

- **Environmental damage.** Citizens often form pressure groups to protect the environment. Businesses are frequently responsible for air, water and soil pollution, and for the resultant detrimental effects on fauna and flora. For example, because of pressure from the community, the construction of a new plant that Iscor had planned to establish at Saldanha was delayed for 17 months. Iscor eventually had to build the plant eight kilometres away from the initial site, so as to avoid possible damage to the ecology. Another more recent South African example is the 2006 jet fuel leak from OR Tambo International Airport, mentioned earlier. This leak resulted in massive ecological damage to aquatic and bird life.
- **Consumerism.** This is a further social force that protects consumers against unsafe products and malpractice by exerting moral and economic pressure on businesses. In South Africa the South African National Consumer Union acts as a watchdog for consumers. Social pressure on businesses often results in increased government regulation to force compliance with social requirements and norms. Ultimately, the will of the community is seen to prevail.

The business world is so interconnected with society that the business world may be defined as a process that uses the means of production of a country to produce products and services to satisfy the needs of the people. The primary purpose of business in a free-market system is to make a profit while satisfying the needs of the people. A brief overview of the needs of communities, and of the means of satisfying these needs, is given on page 10 to explain not only the purpose of business in a market system, but also the extent of the field of business management, which is the focus of this book.

1.3 Needs and need satisfaction

1.3.1 The multiplicity of human needs

The continued existence of humans depends upon the constant satisfaction of numerous **needs**, both physical and psychological. The work that every member of a community performs is directly or indirectly related to need satisfaction. There is, even in the most remote inhabited areas, a need for certain goods and services. These needs may be very simple and few, as in the case of a rural and underdeveloped community in which individuals or families, with the help of nature, find the resources necessary to satisfy a simple need structure. The traditional way of life of the Kalahari San people, for example, depends on the satisfaction of the most basic necessities for survival. However, in highly industrialised communities, needs may be numerous and may therefore require large and complex organisations to satisfy them.

A need may have a physical, psychological or social origin, but no matter what form it takes, it requires satisfaction. The number of identifiable needs is infinite. Some needs, particularly those that are physiological, are related to absolutely basic necessities, such as the satisfaction of hunger and thirst. These needs have to be satisfied for the sake of survival. Other needs, particularly those that are psychological, are merely to make life more pleasant – without their being essential to survival. Such needs include holidays, video machines, dishwashers, tennis courts, luxury cars, and innumerable products and services of a similar nature.

Basic physical and psychological needs may also overlap. For example, people do not wear clothes merely for warmth and protection, but also to be fashionable. Some people enjoy expensive delicacies, accompanied by fine wines, in luxurious restaurants, and in this way simultaneously satisfy survival needs and psychological needs.

Abraham H. Maslow (1908–1970) was an American clinical psychologist who explained variable and unlimited human needs by means of a sequence or **hierarchy of needs**. According to Maslow, human needs range, in a definite order, from the most essential for survival to the least necessary. Figure 1.4 shows this hierarchy of needs.[7]

It is clear from figure 1.4 that the need hierarchy is composed in such a way that the order of importance ranges from basic physiological needs, which have to be satisfied for survival, to psychological needs, with which the higher levels of the hierarchy are mainly concerned. Because humans are social beings who live in communities, they also have collective needs, such as protection

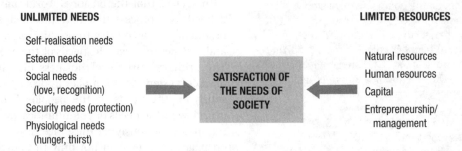

Figure 1.4: The needs and resources of the community

Source: Based on *The pyramid of human needs* from: Maslow, Abraham H., Frager, Robert D., Fadiman, James, *Motivation and personality*, 1954, New York: Harper, pp. 35-47 based on "A Theory of Human Motivation". Adapted by permission of Pearson Education Inc., Upper Saddle River, NJ. As dealt with in Griffin. R. W., *Management*, Houghton Mifflin Co., Boston, 1987, p. 440.

and education. An individual, a family or a community first satisfies the most urgent needs, and then, when this has been done, moves up to the next level until the higher psychological levels are reached. With changing circumstances, individuals not only desire more possessions, but also continually want still newer and better products and services. For example, radio offers entertainment, but black-and-white television is believed to offer better entertainment, and colour television still better entertainment. Once these have been acquired, however, the need arises for a DVD player, more television channels – as evidenced in the phenomenal growth of DSTV – and more and better programmes. And so it goes on. As society satisfies one need, a new one comes into existence, and there is no end to the constantly increasing number of human needs.

Table 1.1 indicates some of the needs people have. It is interesting to note that in 2001 South African households spent 30,3% of their income on food, which satisfies one of the most basic needs.

Table 1.1: Expenditure patterns of South African households 2001

Product and service needs	Total expenditure %
Food, drink and tobacco	30,3
Clothing and shoes	5,1
Housing and household goods	21,2
Transport and communication	14,8
Medical	7,1
Education, recreation and relaxation	2,2
Other	19,3
Total expenditure	100,0

Source: Quarterly Bulletin, South African Reserve Bank, June 2001.

1.3.2 Society's limited resources

If one considers the multiple and **unlimited needs** of humans, especially in highly developed societies, it is clear that there are only **limited resources** available to satisfy all their needs. Although Western countries, most notably the USA, possess very impressive means of production, they do not have unlimited resources. Consider for example the increases in crude oil prices that have occurred over the past few years. These increases have been brought about by the fact that the world has a limited supply of oil. It is estimated that there were originally around 2 000 gigabarrels of oil on earth. Society has already used up 45% to 70% of this precious resource, half in the last 40 years.[8] The impact of these increases also hit the airline industry hard: in 2005 SAA's fuel bill increased from R1,7 billion to R4,9 billion. A country has only a certain number of people in its workforce to operate a certain number of machines, and a certain number of factories, hospitals and offices to produce a certain quantity of products and services. In other words, the **resources** of any community are **scarce**, and can easily be exceeded by its needs. Resources are therefore the basic inputs in the production of products and services – they are also known as **production factors**. Figure 1.4 shows those resources society possesses in limited quantities only, and which it uses to satisfy its needs: natural resources, human resources, capital and entrepreneurship:

- **Natural resources**, often known as "land", include agricultural land, industrial sites, residential stands, minerals and metals, forests, water, and all such resources that nature puts at the disposal of humankind. The most important characteristic of natural resources is that their supply cannot be increased. In other words, the amount of natural resources any one country possesses is given, and therefore in most cases is scarce. Moreover, human effort is usually necessary to process these resources into need-satisfying products, for example, in the transformation of forests into timber and paper, or, in the case of the airline industry, the refining of oil to produce the jet fuels that aeroplanes need to fly.

- **Human resources**, also known as the production factor of labour, include the physical and mental talents and skills of people employed to create products and services. People receive wages for their labour. The size of the labour force of any country, and therefore, in a sense, the availability of that production factor, is determined by, among other things, the size of the population, the level of its education and training, the proportion of women in the labour force, and the retirement age. For the manufacturing processes of a country to be of any value, the country's labour force has to be trained for certain periods and to certain levels of skill to be able to produce the products and services required. The training of a petrol pump attendant, for example, will be considerably shorter than that for a brain surgeon. The combination of human skills is of particular importance, for without this combination natural resources and capital cannot be productively utilised. Consider again the airline industry: SAA employs close to 12 000 people worldwide, including 3 600 at SAA Technical, 2 800 flight attendants and more than 800 pilots.
- **Capital** is represented by the buildings, machinery, cash registers, computers, and other goods produced, not for final human consumption, but for making possible the further production of final consumer products. Capital products usually have a long working life, for example office buildings, factories, machinery and other equipment used over and over again in the production process. In the airline industry capital usually has an exceptionally long working life, but also comes at a very high price. The reason for the scarcity factor of capital is that a community takes years to build up its stock of capital. Every year it spends a certain amount on things such

as roads, bridges, mineshafts, factories and shopping centres, and there is always a shortage of such things. The owners or suppliers of capital are usually remunerated in the form of interest or rent.

- **Entrepreneurship** is the fourth production factor. It refers to the collective capacity of entrepreneurs – those individuals in the community who accept the risks involved in providing products and services for society. The airline 1time, mentioned in the airline industry case study at the start of this chapter, was started by four entrepreneurs, Gavin Harrison, Glenn Orsmond, Rodney James and Sven Petersen. Entrepreneurs are rewarded with profits for the risks they take and the initiative they show, but they suffer losses for errors in judgement. The production factor of entrepreneurship is scarce in the sense that not everybody in a community is prepared to take the risks that are inevitable when providing products or services, or has the ability to manage an organisation successfully. Although the contemporary focus on entrepreneurship is mainly on small and medium businesses, entrepreneurs are not limited to these. A large or corporate business is also a place for entrepreneurship.

1.3.3 Need satisfaction: A cycle

To be able to satisfy the needs of the community, entrepreneurs have to utilise these scarce resources in certain combinations in order to produce products and services. Economic value is created in the course of the production process by combining production factors in such a way that final products are produced for consumers. A nation's survival depends on the satisfaction of its people's needs. Striving for need satisfaction with the limited resources available is an incentive for economic progress.

Given its unlimited needs but limited resources, society is confronted with a fundamental economic problem: how to ensure the highest possible satisfaction of needs with these scarce resources. This is also known as the **economic principle**.

Society cannot always get what it wants, so it must choose how it will use its scarce resources to the maximum effect in order to satisfy its needs. In short, it has to make a decision about solving the following fundamental economic problems:

- **Which products and services should be produced, and in what quantities?** What are the numbers and amounts of capital products, and what are the numbers and amounts of consumer products? Should railways or trucks, houses or flats be built? If flats are chosen, how many?
- **Who should produce these goods?** The state or private individuals? In the case of the airline industry, this responsibility is shared by the state and private individuals.
- **How should these products and services be produced and what resources should be used?** There are various methods of production, and different combinations of the production factors can be applied to create products and services.
- **For whom are these products and services to be produced?** For rich or poor people? Old or young people? Families or individuals? Business or leisure passengers?

The answers to the fundamental economic problems listed above are given by the community. The **community** decides which **institutions** should be responsible for the production and distribution of products and services, as well as the role that each institution has to play. Figure 1.5 on the next page shows how, against the background of its needs, and by means of its political process, the community determines the **economic system** in which the necessary need-satisfying institutions are established.

In a more or less free-market system, need-satisfying institutions, including business organisations, offer products and services on the market in return for profit. If the community is not satisfied with the way

> **Example**
>
> The needs of society ultimately culminate in products or services that satisfy particular needs. A case in point is cell phones. People have a basic need to communicate, and where this is possible, to communicate with individuals over distance. During most of the last century the only way this could be done was by means of the telephone, where the caller first had to phone to a specific building (house or office) and then wait for the relevant person to be found by whoever answered the phone. The cell phone was, therefore, a response to the need to communicate immediately with a specific individual, without the inconvenience of having to locate the person first, or the frustration of dealing with inoperative telephone lines.

in which these organisations provide for its needs, it will change the economic system or choose a new need-satisfying system. The appearance of new businesses and the disappearance of others are examples of this cycle of need satisfaction in the community. With the large-scale urbanisation of South African society and the participation of women in the labour market, especially during the late 1960s and 1970s, shopping hours increased to allow for Saturday afternoon and Sunday shopping. This proved extremely successful, because there was a communal demand for longer shopping hours. The community therefore got what it wanted!

Over the years, different communities have developed different approaches to the satisfaction of their needs, and different **economic systems** have been tried and tested.

Each of these systems, as chosen by various communities to satisfy specific needs, has its own approach to the fundamental economic problem of what products and services should be provided by whom and for whom. The study of these systems constitutes the field of economics as a social science and examines the means used to

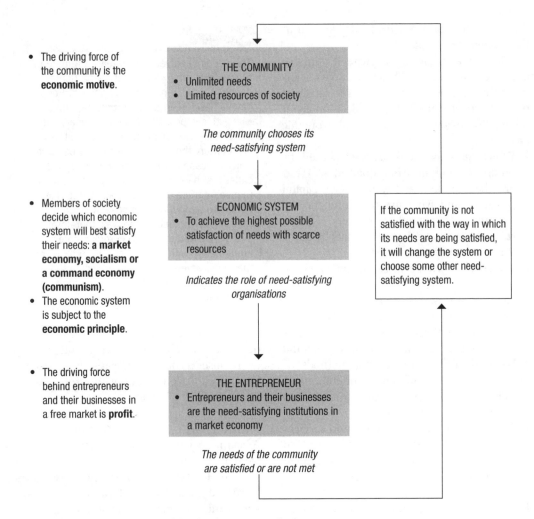

Figure 1.5: The cycle of need satisfaction in a community

satisfy innumerable human needs with limited resources. Business management, in contrast, is concerned with the institutions that are created in the economic system to satisfy the needs of a community, and these are mainly business organisations.

To provide some necessary background to the study of business management and the role of business organisations in society, a brief overview of the different economic systems now follows.

1.4 The main economic systems

1.4.1 The community and its economic system

As was stated earlier, every community is engaged in a struggle for survival, and that struggle originates in, and is necessitated by, scarcity. Therefore every community needs to have a complex mechanism that is constantly occupied with the complicated tasks of ensuring the production and distribution of products for the survival of the community. A country is therefore confronted with the fundamental economic problem, and it has to decide on some system to solve that problem. Which economic system should a country choose to solve the problem of what products should be produced and marketed by which producers for which consumers?

Over the years, countries and communities have approached need satisfaction in different ways. There are three main approaches that are still followed by present-day communities for the solution of their fundamental economic problems. They are the **free-market economy**, the **command economy** and **socialism**. While these economic systems are often incorrectly referred to as political ideologies, they should rather be described as economic systems influenced by politics. It is necessary to take a brief look at these systems to understand the origin and role of business organisations in society. As none of these economic systems is ever found in a pure form, the discussion that follows is merely an exposition of the basic premises of each system, and is not a theoretical debate.

1.4.2 The free-market economy

One of the economic systems adopted by humans for the solution of their economic problems is the **market economy**, also known as the **free-market economy** or **free-enterprise system**. It is a system in which most products and services demanded by a community are supplied by private organisations seeking profits. It functions on the assumption that:

- Members of a community may possess assets and earn profits on these
- The allocation of resources is affected by free markets
- Members of the community have free choice of products, services, places of residence and careers
- The state keeps its interference in the system to a minimum

In the free-market economy, particular value is attached to the right of individuals to possess property such as land, buildings, equipment or vehicles, including the right to earn an income from them. This right is also the driving force of the free-market economy: it stimulates individuals and entrepreneurs to acquire more and to make a profit through the productive utilisation of their assets or their capital. In seeking maximum profits, this **capital**, which is nothing other than the resources of the community, is applied as productively as possible. This aspect also affects the second basic premise of the free-market economy, namely the **distribution of resources through free markets**. The private possession of capital has an important influence on the manner in which resources are allocated or employed in a free-market economy. The decisions about what products should be produced by which producers therefore rest with those who own the resources.

This means that farmers, factory owners, industrialists and individuals are free to do what they like with their assets. In their decisions concerning production and marketing, however, they have to take account of the tastes, preferences and other demands of consumers if they want to make a profit. Thus, the question of which consumers (for whom?) is also solved. Such decisions in a free-market economy are not taken by some central body but by a system of free markets (market economy), which puts a price on every production factor or consumer product.

Free markets also imply the third characteristic of this system, namely **freedom of choice**. The producers are able to decide whether or not they can profitably produce their products at the prices set by the market. This is the producers' free choice. Likewise, the consumer is free to choose whether to buy the product at that price. A system of free markets therefore necessarily entails freedom of choice. Private owners of property are free to own what they like, and to do with it as they please: whether to rent it out, sell it, exchange it, or, even, give it away. People with businesses are free to produce what they wish and to employ whoever they choose. Similarly, owners of the resource of labour – that is, workers – can use their resources as they choose. Consumers, again, are free to buy what they like, to live where they wish, to follow whatever career they choose. In this way, **competition** comes into operation in a system of free markets.

The final characteristic of a free-market economy is **minimum state interference** in markets. The assumption is that the state should merely ensure the proper maintenance of the system without excessive regulation of, or even participation in, the business world.

1.4.3 Command economy or centrally directed economic system

The second type of economic system, adopted by some countries as an alternative to a free-market economy, is a **command economy**, which until recently was known as **communism**. Its main characteristic is that the state owns and controls the community's resources or factors of production.

In a command economy the state provides the answers to the fundamental economic questions. A command economy is a system of communal ownership of the production factors of a country in which the individual owns no property, with the exception of private domestic assets. This means that individuals own no land, factories or equipment. The state assumes complete responsibility for the production and distribution of products and services, and all decisions about what should be produced – and about how, by whom, and for whom it should be produced – rest with a central government.

The choices of products and services are therefore limited to what the state offers; they fall entirely outside the control of ordinary individuals. It is the state that decides what the needs of the community are, how and where the goods desired will be obtainable, and in what quantities they may be used. In the absence of free consumer choice, the profit motive is also absent, as is the competition factor, because, as mentioned above, the state owns the organisations that produce the products and services.

A free economy creates wealth

The fewer restrictions on economic activity, the wealthier a country's citizens. The Heritage Foundation/*Wall Street Journal*'s 1998 Index of Economic Freedom measures how well 156 countries score on a list of ten broad economic factors. These factors include trade policy, taxation, government intervention in the economy, monetary policies, capital flows and foreign investment, banking and exchange controls, wage and price controls, property rights, regulation, and black market activities. Taken cumulatively, these factors offer an empirical snapshot of a country's level of economic freedom. The results demonstrate beyond doubt that countries with the highest levels of economic freedom also have the highest living standards.

The 2006 study rates South Africa a relatively poor 50th, with a rating of 2,74 out of 5, where 5 represents absolute economic repression. This places South Africa on a par with Kuwait and Madagascar, and ahead of some Eastern European and most African countries, but well below established industrial economies and certain Far East high fliers.

Countries with high scores on the Economic Freedom Index (for example the USA) have an average per capita income of US$30 607, while those with lower scores, such as South Africa, earn a mere US$3 026 per capita. It is also quite clear that a country's level of economic freedom has a direct impact on its standard of living, as is clear from figure 1.6 on the next page.

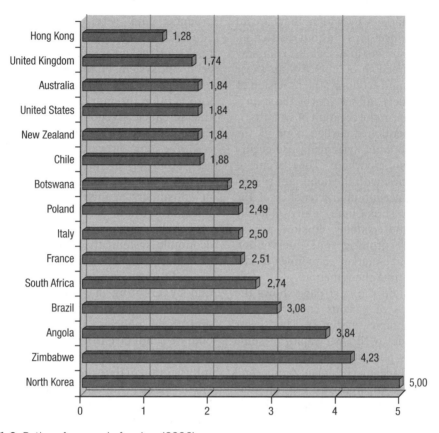

Figure 1.6: Rating of economic freedom (2006)

Source: Index of Economic Freedom, 2006

The command economy has failed in most countries that have adopted it because it robbed individuals of the initiative to produce goods and services, and it prevented the creation of wealth. Proof that the system cannot create wealth was the poverty and the collapse in the early 1990s of communism in the former Soviet Union and other East European countries. Command economies are, nevertheless, still officially adhered to in China, Cuba and some African states.

1.4.4 Socialism

Socialism may be taken as the third economic system proposed as a solution to a society's fundamental economic problems. Under this system, which may be regarded as a **compromise** between a pure market economy and a pure command economy, the state owns and controls the principal (generally strategic) industries and resources, such as manufacturers of steel, transportation, communications, health services and energy. Less important and smaller matters such as trade and construction, and the production of materials and services of lesser strategic importance, are left to private initiative. In socialism, the fundamental assumption is that strategic and basic resources should belong to every member of the community. For the rest, businesses and consumers operate within free markets in which they are at liberty to make decisions without restriction. Although consumers in a socialist economy have greater freedom of choice than those under a command economy, the provision of the basic products and services by the state is a limiting factor in the creation of wealth.

As was mentioned earlier, none of the three main economic systems in use occurs in a pure form anywhere. They occur as **mixed economies**, with the dominant system incorporating certain characteristics of the other systems. Thus China, which officially has a command economy, employs private initiative, while growing state intervention in the major free-market economies of the world is no strange phenomenon.

Figure 1.7 on the next page shows the relative success of various countries with different economic systems. The gross national product (GNP) per capita of some of the world's poorest countries – namely Mozambique, Tanzania, Ethiopia, Zambia and Zimbabwe – is compared with that of some of the richest – namely Switzerland, Japan, Germany, the USA and the United Kingdom.

Countries such as South Africa, Brazil, Hungary, Namibia and Argentina, each of which has a unique economic system, rate about midway between the richest and poorest countries of the world. Several factors, including education, culture and work ethic, affect the prosperity of any particular country, but Figure 1.7 shows that countries with free-market economies are wealthier than others.

1.4.5 The state and economic systems

The fact that under both the free-market system and socialism the state intervenes to help solve the economic problem does not mean that there is necessarily a tendency to move to the direction of a command or centrally controlled economy. Any intervention by the state should be seen as necessary, to provide the essential collective products and services such as roads, education, water, power, health care and justice, on the one hand, and to maintain the economic system, on the other.

In particular, this means government intervention in market mechanisms and the so-called freedom of entrepreneurs. Examples here are the protection of natural resources by preventing pollution, the restriction of monopolistic practices by ensuring competition, and the protection of consumers against false or misleading information and exploitation. The state also helps business by stimulating the economic system, through the promotion of exports, by encouraging the creation of small businesses, by assisting research, and by granting subsidies. Furthermore, through the application of its monetary and fiscal policies, the state creates a climate conducive to economic growth and productivity. In a nutshell, government intervention in the economic system aims at encouraging economic growth and stability by managing recession and inflation, and effecting greater equity in the distribution of incomes.[9]

A much debated form of government intervention takes place when the state does not limit itself to the above-mentioned activities, but acts as an entrepreneur in its own right. The state does this in the areas of transport services, electricity supply, arms manufacture, broadcasting and television services, and many other industries in South Africa. The main reason usually advanced for government intervention in these spheres is that the free or private entrepreneur is not interested in these activities and, perhaps, is not even capable of carrying them out. This situation arises because of the enormous scale of the businesses – for instance power supply, transport and the production of arms – and the corresponding risks attached to them.

It is also argued that some government organisations are of such strategic importance to the community that they

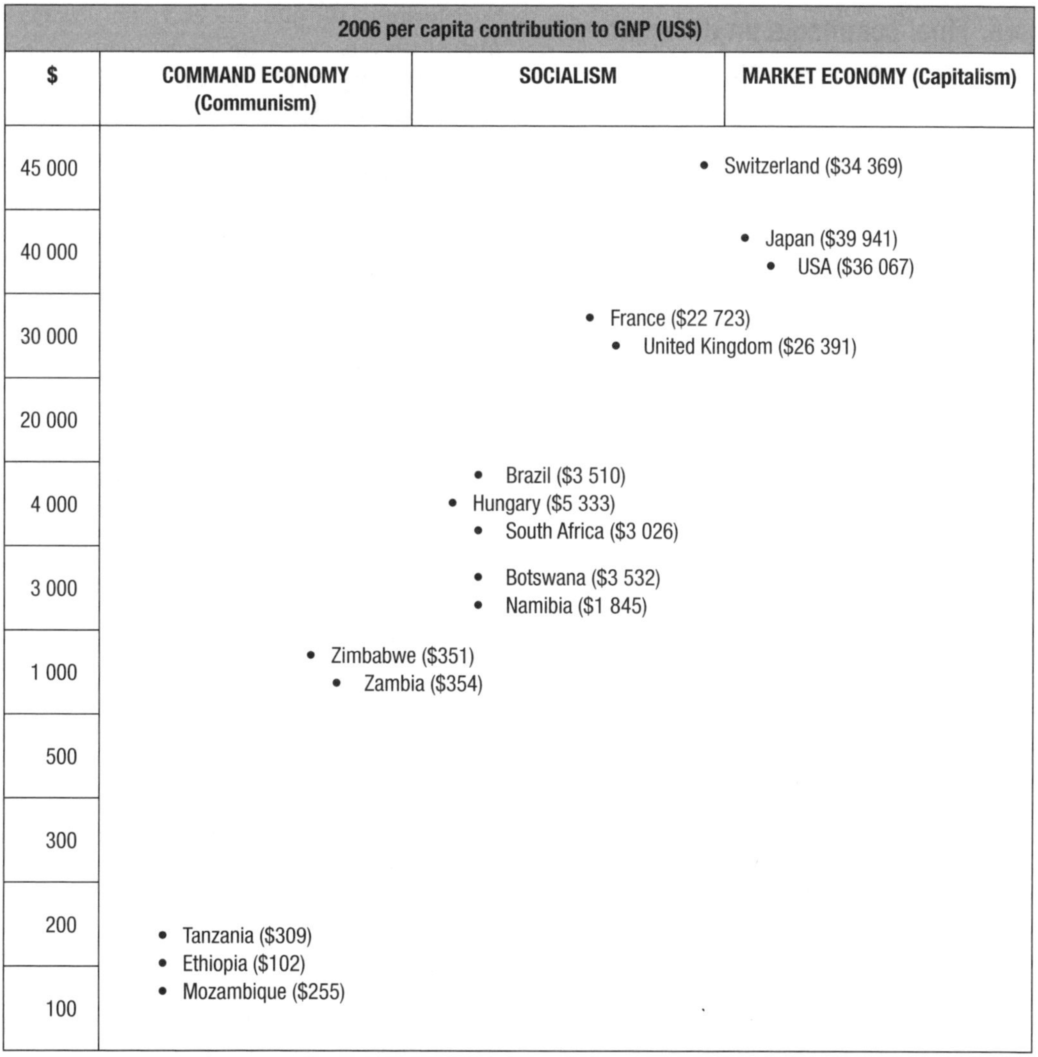

2006 per capita contribution to GNP (US$)			
$	COMMAND ECONOMY (Communism)	SOCIALISM	MARKET ECONOMY (Capitalism)
45 000			• Switzerland ($34 369)
40 000			• Japan ($39 941) • USA ($36 067)
30 000		• France ($22 723) • United Kingdom ($26 391)	
20 000			
4 000		• Brazil ($3 510) • Hungary ($5 333) • South Africa ($3 026)	
3 000		• Botswana ($3 532) • Namibia ($1 845)	
1 000	• Zimbabwe ($351) • Zambia ($354)		
500			
300			
200	• Tanzania ($309) • Ethiopia ($102) • Mozambique ($255)		
100			

Figure 1.7: Alternative economic systems

Source: Adapted from *World Bank Development Report*. By permission of Copyright Clearance Center Inc.

cannot be left to profit-seeking private entrepreneurs. However, these arguments do not entirely justify a regular and continuous entrepreneurial role by government. If any such intervention by the state is carried to excess, the result is a bureaucracy that affects national productivity adversely by limiting private competition.

The purpose of this overview has been to give a brief exposition of the basic economic systems and the role of government in them, rather than an evaluation of the divergent opinions about what the proper role of government in the economy of a country should be.

1.4.6 Final comments on different economic systems

Different communities use different economic systems to meet their needs with their available resources. Each system thus has its own peculiar characteristics (as can be seen from table 1.2), and each country arranges its economic system in such a way that it solves its wealth problem as effectively as possible in accordance with the wishes of its inhabitants. Bearing in mind the fact that pure forms of the different economic systems almost never exist, the most appropriate description of the prevailing economic system in South Africa is that it is a mixture between the free-market system and the socialist system. More precisely, the South African economic system can be defined as moving towards a market-oriented economy yet with a high degree of government participation and control in the economy.[10]

South African consumers thus enjoy a high degree of freedom to buy what

Table 1.2: A comparison of the main economic systems

	Free-market economy	Socialism	Command economy
Main characteristics	Private ownership of production factors. Freedom of choice.	Basic industries owned by state. Freedom of choice.	State owns and controls all industries and agriculture.
Markets	Free competition.	Limited competition as a result of state industries.	No competition.
Driving force	Profit and reward according to individual ability.	Profit motive recognised. Employees' pay in state-owned concerns based on workers' needs.	Profit not allowed. Workers urged to work for the glory of the state.
Management	Management environment is private businesses. Free to choose career. Free to make decisions.	Management environment state-owned as well as private businesses. Decisions restricted to government policy in state-owned organisations.	Management environment is the state. No freedom of decision. Managers also party members.
Labour	Workers independent and free to choose job and employer. Free to join union and to strike.	Free to choose job and employer. Limited right to strike in state organisations.	Limited choice of job. State-controlled unions.
Consumers	Freedom of choice in free markets. Spending limited only by income.	Freedom of choice, except in respect of products of state organisations, the prices and quality of which have to be accepted.	Rationing of products. Very limited choice. Prices of goods and income levels set by state.
Advantages	Private initiative. Economic freedom.	Possibility of full employment. State stabilises economic fluctuations.	State can concentrate resources towards particular ends.
Disadvantages	Unstable environment. Cyclical fluctuations. High social costs.	Little incentive in state organisations. Unproductive state organisations.	Low productivity. Low standard of living. Planning difficult or impossible.

they want, and where. Consequently, the responsibility rests with the individual entrepreneur to judge which products and services the consumer wants, and then to offer these products and services at a price the consumer is prepared and able to pay. A complex network of organisations evolves out of the interaction between needs and the entrepreneurs who satisfy these needs, and this network constitutes what is known in a free-market economy as the **business world**.

1.5 The need-satisfying institutions of the free market

1.5.1 Business organisations

From the discussion of contemporary economic systems it is clear that the economic systems of Western countries, with which South Africa associates itself, arc combinations of a free-market economy and socialism. Despite the defects and shortcomings of the more or less free-market order in South Africa, most inhabitants believe that this economic system satisfies their needs better than any that might be based on pure socialism or a command economy.

Critical thinking

In section 1.4.6 we stated that the prevailing economic system in South Africa is a mixture between the free-market system and the socialist system, and that, more precisely, the South African economic system can be defined as moving towards a market-oriented economy yet with a high degree of government participation and control in the economy. While this is indeed true, since 1994 South Africa has steadily moved to an increasingly market-oriented position with less and less government intervention and control. This move has undoubtedly had a positive effect on the South African economy, as can be seen in the figures below.

In 2004 South Africa's GDP figure stood at R1 404 billion and GDP per capita was R30 129. Consumer price inflation was at its lowest level in 40 years – 3,4% – and producer price inflation was even lower at 1,9% – a 58-year low.

South Africa's exports were valued at R292,3 billion and its imports at R304,7 billion, with major exports being minerals, precious metals, machinery, vehicles, automotive components, pulp and paper.

South Africa has more telephones, cellphones, autobanks, and computers than the rest of the countries in the continent of Africa together. South Africa also has more than 15 times the African average of paved roads, and half the electricity and energy capacity in the whole of Africa.

What are some of the factors that make South Africa a favourable investment destination and what are some of the factors that deter investors from the country?

Positive factors include:

- A stable political environment
- Sound macro-economic policies
- 100% ownership permitted
- A large, growing domestic market in South Africa
- Modern transport and communication systems
- Rich natural resources
- Modern banking and financial services

Some negative factors include:

- High rates of crime
- Extensive exchange controls, although these are being eased
- Major skills shortages, particularly in management roles

The workings of a free-market economy are affected by the need-satisfying institutions created by the system, that is, the private business organisations which, for the most part, satisfy the needs of the community. The business world therefore consists of a complex system of interdependent organisations that mobilise the resources of a country to satisfy the country's needs at the risk of a loss and in seeking profit.

The emphasis is on the opportunity to make a profit as well as the risk of a loss. Such are the conditions under which a private business exists in a free-market economy. Under such a system, an organisation has to make a profit to be able to survive. This can happen only if it satisfies the needs or wishes of the consumer, and hence the community.

Business organisations therefore solve the fundamental economic problem, that is, which goods and services, how and for whom, should be produced, by meeting the wishes of the consumer.

Figure 1.8 on the next page shows how businesses, as the main need-satisfying institutions under this system, use the resources of society to produce products and services for consumers.

Consumers' needs culminate in the demand for consumer products and services offered on the market (in department stores, boutiques, car salesrooms, pharmacies, and so on) by businesses. Therefore, consumer demand helps to determine what products and services need to be provided, and for whom. To be able to produce products and services, business organisations need resources, so a demand arises for production factors, which are offered in the factor market by the community. Business organisations pay salaries and wages to the community in exchange for production factors, and consumers in turn pay for their products and services with that money. Competition in both markets determines how the products and services are to be produced so that the entrepreneur can continue to make a profit.

In order to make **a profit**, the enterprise must therefore take the initiative and accept certain risks in mobilising the resources of the community before things – for example a single loaf of bread, or bicycle or house – can be produced or built. The owner of a bicycle factory, for example, has to erect or rent a building, install machinery, buy raw materials and components, and employ people to manufacture bicycles as productively as possible to satisfy the needs of consumers. The transport contractor has to transport goods to places where there is a need for them. The retailer has to present a range of products conforming to consumers' needs in as convenient a way as possible. A banker does not produce a physical article, but provides – also at a risk and in pursuit of profit – a service in the form of finance placed at the disposal of manufacturers, dealers and numerous other entrepreneurs and consumers. These are but a few examples of the innumerable activities carried out in the business world by business organisations – for example Toyota, SABMiller, Pick 'n Pay, Standard Bank, and many others, large and small, local and multinational – that play an indispensable part in South African society. Moreover, as will be discussed in greater detail in chapter 3, business organisations assume different forms: a sole-proprietorship, a partnership, a close corporation, a private company, or a public company.

The **business organisations** we have examined may be defined as those private need-satisfying institutions of a free-market economy that accept risks in pursuit of profit by offering products and services on the market to the consumer. They constitute the main subject of the study of management and are therefore the major topic of research and study in business management. Businesses do not function in isolation, but in a business environment that influences their operation, and which is at the same time influenced by the businesses. Therefore an overview of certain aspects of the environment also falls within the field of study of management.

DEMAND   SUPPLY

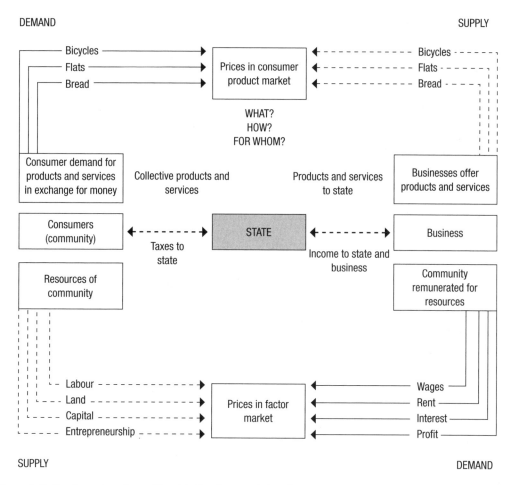

Figure 1.8: Goods and services offered in the free-market system

Source: Adapted from Samuelson, P., *Economics*, McGraw-Hill Company, 1980, p. 41.

It should be clearly understood that when we speak of a business organisation we mean a **private enterprise** – that is, one owned by private entrepreneurs. (In a mixed market economy, there are state-owned and non-profit-seeking organisations in addition to the profit-seeking businesses that the community establishes as need-satisfying organisations. For the sake of completeness, a few observations about such organisations are now discussed.)

1.5.2 Government organisations

In the discussion of the various economic systems, several principles of a free-market economy were identified. One principle identified was the condition that government should intervene as little as possible with market mechanisms, and when it does, it should confine itself to the protection and creation of collective non-profit-seeking facilities and services such as those concerned with health care, education, justice and defence. The government departments responsible for such state functions may themselves be regarded as need-satisfying organisations. Because the profit motive is absent and the services provided are collective, such institutions fall under the subject of Public Administration as an independent science.

The discussion of the various economic systems also mentioned that the pure free-market economy exists only in theory, and that several mixed systems are in fact to be found, including the South African system, which was defined as a market-oriented economy with a high degree of state intervention. The intervention specifically indicates the large number of government organisations (also known as state-owned enterprises or SOEs, parastatals, or public corporations) in South Africa which – unlike the collective systems that produce products and services on a non-profit-seeking basis – offer products and services for profit, and sometimes in competition with other businesses in the market. Sometimes these public corporations may be regarded as business organisations, but with this difference: they are owned and controlled by the state and not by a private entrepreneur. Eskom, Transnet and SAA are examples of such public corporations, and there are many others.

These public corporations may also be regarded as need-satisfying institutions through which the state creates products and services believed to be of strategic, economic or political importance to the community, especially as regards self-sufficiency in transport, energy, military equipment and armaments. There is, however, a growing trend in South Africa towards the privatisation of major SOEs. The first of an important example of such privatisation was in 1979, when state-owned SASOL was sold. More recently telecommunications giant Telkom listed on the JSE and New York Stock Exchange in 2003. An example from the South African airline industry is ACSA, which was also an SOE prior to privatisation in 1998.

Although the productivity levels of government organisations are suspect, those that seek profits, and in which the state is the exclusive shareholder, also fall within the scope of business management.

1.5.3 Non-profit-seeking organisations

These organisations are the final group of need-satisfying institutions that offer services, and, to a lesser extent, products not provided by private enterprise, government organisations or the state. Examples of non-profit-seeking organisations are sports clubs, cultural associations and welfare organisations, and associations of organised business such as the National African Federated Chamber of Commerce (Nafcoc) and the South African Chamber of Business (Sacob). These organisations differ from other need-satisfying organisations in that they provide their services without seeking profit.

The continued existence of such organisations therefore depends on the financial support of those members of the community who require their services. Although such organisations do not set profit making as their primary objective, they often function on the same basis as a business organisation, seeking a surplus of income over expenditure, or at least a balance of income and expenditure. These organisations – especially the larger ones – therefore employ management principles. And despite their small share in the economy, the study of such organisations also falls within the field of business management.

Against the background of this exposition of the various economic systems, and in the light of various need-satisfying institutions, especially private businesses of the mixed market economy as found in South Africa and other countries, we will now examine the purpose and task of business management more closely.

1.6 The nature of business management

1.6.1 Economics and business management as related sciences

As was explained earlier, human survival is closely linked to the problem of scarcity, that is, satisfying the unlimited needs of a community with limited resources. Moreover, a society is constantly faced with the problem of how to use these scarce resources so as to satisfy its needs as efficiently as possible. **Economics** as a social science studies how humans and society exercise choices concerning different ways of using their scarce resources for products and services. It is therefore a study of the economic problems and variables of the community as a whole, with the improved well-being of the community as its preconceived goal. Economics as a science, on the one hand, studies variables including prices, money, income and its distribution, taxes, productivity, government intervention, and economic growth, as well as many other economic questions affecting the well-being of a country.

Critical thinking

Students often ask these questions: "How is it possible that government organisations act as need-satisfying institutions?" and "How is it possible for government organisations and private businesses to service similar needs of society?"

The answer to the first question is that government organisations very definitely act as need-satisfying institutions in that they provide an array of both products and services to the citizens of the country. In most cases the exchange for these products and services is generally in the form of rates and taxes. The key difference between government organisations and private businesses lies, however, in the fact that private businesses seek to make profits through the fulfilment of society's needs, whereas this is not the case with government institutions.

The second question can be answered using two examples that are particularly relevant in the South African situation:

- The first example is society's need for a safe and secure environment. South Africa has a particularly high crime rate compared to those of other developed countries. In response to this, both government organisations and private businesses seek to address society's security needs. Government does this through the provision of policing services, an efficient judicial system and effective correctional services

facilities. In doing this government seeks to address society's needs, although not with a profit orientation. At the same time, in South Africa many business organisations provide products and services to address the security needs of society. Examples of these products include electric fencing, burglar alarms, and security gates (think of a company such as Trellidor), while examples of services include private security, vehicle tracking, and short-term insurance. In contrast to the government organisations, businesses providing these products and services do so in exchange for profits.

- Another good example in South Africa is health care. Both government and private businesses seek to address society's need for health care. Government seeks to provide health care services to its citizens through public hospitals, clinics and emergency services, without a focus on profit. At the same time private companies – such as Netcare, Medi-Clinic and Afrox Healthcare – seek to offer the same services, but with the goal of providing quality services in exchange for profit.

Many more examples exist in South Africa in the areas of education, transport and social security.

Business management as an applied science, on the other hand, is concerned with the study of those institutions in a particular economic system that satisfy the needs of a community. In a mixed market economy, as is found in South Africa, private business organisations are therefore the main area of study. Economics examines the entire economic system of a country, while business management limits its studies to one component of the economic system, namely the individual organisation, whether it be a private business, a government corporation or, to a lesser extent, a non-profit-seeking organisation. For example, economics examines the problem of inflation against the background of its implications for the national economy, while business management is more concerned with the effects of inflation on individual businesses. The main link between economics and business management as independent sciences is that one studies the economic system as a whole, while the other studies a single component of that system.

1.6.2 The purpose and task of business management

The discussion of the cycle of need satisfaction indicated that the primary human endeavour is to achieve the highest possible satisfaction of needs with scarce resources. This endeavour is known as the economic principle, and every economic system is subject to it. That being the case, it follows that any component of an economic system, including a business organisation, is also subject to the economic principle. Where the individual business organisation is concerned, this entails achieving the highest possible output with the lowest possible input of means of production.[11] This is the **purpose of business management**: to produce the highest possible number or units of products and services, at the lowest possible costs.

The **task of business management** emerges from this, namely to determine how an organisation can achieve the highest possible output (products and services) with the least possible input (labour, capital, land). More specifically, it entails an examination of the factors, methods and principles that enable a business to function as efficiently and productively as possible in order to maximise its profits. In short, it is a study of those principles that have to be applied to make a business organisation as profitable as possible. It may also include a study of the environmental factors that could have an effect on the success of an organisation, its survival or its profitability.

The study of business management entails comprehensive and ongoing research and the examination of management problems, the testing of approaches and principles, experimentation with methods and techniques, and the continuous weighing up of environmental variables. The result is an applied science that indicates how business organisations can best be directed towards realising their objectives. Therefore, in the case of business organisations, the economic principle is defined as the endeavour to achieve the highest possible income in the market at the lowest possible cost, with profit as the favourable difference between the two.[12] This principle is also applicable to state-owned enterprises and non-profit-seeking organisations. The only difference is that in the case of state-owned enterprises and non-profit-seeking organisations, the difference between inputs and outputs is not measured in profit, but rather in terms of surplus, savings or higher productivity.

In a business organisation the economic principle and the profit motive coincide, making profits the driving force, and so the task of business management becomes one of maximising profits.[13] This does not mean, however, that the task of business management is to maximise profits at the cost of everything else, especially the well-being of society. In today's business environment the objective is rather to maximise profits through good management and care of employees, customers, investors and society in general.

To summarise, the task of business management is to study those factors, principles and methods that will lead a business organisation, as a component of the prevailing economic system, to reach its objectives. In a mixed market economy this primarily – though not exclusively – means making a profit. Having clarified the field of study and the task of business management as an independent discipline, we shall now discuss its development and how it relates to some other disciplines.

Examples of approaches, principles and methods studied by business management with the purpose of making an organisation function as productively as possible

- General approaches to management methods, tested over the years, include the following:
  - The **mechanistic approach**, introduced at the turn of the century, emphasises mass-production, especially under the management of engineers.
  - The **human relations management approach** originated in the 1930s, and puts emphasis on the motivation of workers.
  - The **contingency approach** of the 1950s argues that the management approach is prescribed by the prevailing situation.
  - **Strategic management**, the most recent approach, makes a special study of how management should act in an unstable environment.
  - Various supplementary approaches and developments, such as **organisation design, the management of change, information management, corporate culture** and the **management of diversity** are still being studied.
- In the field of marketing management, research into experimentation with approaches and methods has also contributed to the more productive operation of businesses. These include the following:
  - The **marketing concept** replaced the **production approach** in management philosophy to enable businesses to adjust their resources more effectively to the needs of consumers.
  - **Market research**, as an instrument of marketing philosophy, has developed many methods of studying the needs of consumers.
  - Methods of studying and determining consumer habits and segmenting markets, as well as strategic management aids, have also stimulated marketing management to higher productivity.
- **Financial management** as an area of business management has also tested many methods, especially financial ratios. The following are some examples:
  - The development of ratios to access the financial performance of businesses.
  - Capital budgets and capital budget techniques in particular to evaluate potential investment possibilities.
  - Approaches to dividend policy.
  - Approaches to and methods of financing growth and expansion as profitably as possible.
- In the same way, numerous methods, principles, approaches and problems in other areas of business management, such as production and operations, purchasing, human resources management, and external relations, have been researched and tested.

The sum total of this sustained study of, and experimentation with, management approaches and methods, and research on management problems, constitutes the **body of knowledge** known as business management.

The purpose and task of business management

- The economic principle consists of the human endeavour to satisfy unlimited needs with limited resources. All economic systems are subject to it.
- In a mixed market economy, a business organisation as a need-satisfying institution is a **component** of the economic system and is therefore also subject to the economic principle.
- According to the economic principle, a business organisation always has to endeavour to obtain the highest possible output (product and services) at the least possible input (lowest cost). This is the **purpose** of business management.
- The business organisation is the **subject** studied by business management.
- The **task** of business management is to examine factors, methods and principles that enable a business organisation to maximise its profits and achieve its objectives.

1.7 The development of business management

1.7.1 The course of development of business management

In the previous sections we discussed in detail the nature of business management and its role in the business world, and we also mentioned various interfaces between business management and other independent disciplines. Throughout, we defined business management as a science in its own right. It is probably not incorrect to refer to business management as a science, but in an introductory work such as this, it is pertinent to pause and consider its status. Before deciding whether any given field of study is a science or not, we should look at its origins and history.

Although the origins of business man-agement can be traced back to the age of mediaeval mercantilism or even earlier, we shall not present a comprehensive historical survey of a subject that really developed into a science only in the 20th century. Nevertheless, the events leading up to the development of business management, as it now exists, deserve a brief mention.

Up until the Industrial Revolution, which was in full swing by the end of the 19th century, the economic systems of communities consisted of simple structures which aimed to satisfy the needs firstly of the individual, and secondly of the community. The early Middle Ages, from about the year 1000, were characterised by subsistence economies that included craft, in a feudal and manorial system. A manor consisted of a number of families living in small villages or communities and working for the lord of the manor, with mere survival and shelter as their main objectives.

The voyages of the explorers in the time of the Renaissance stimulated trade and industry and resulted in the birth of mercantilism during the later Middle Ages. The infant business era saw the rise of simple urban industries, territorial specialisation, and the development of banking and book-keeping, also known as accounting. The latter was probably the earliest management problem to be studied. Early capitalism followed the Renaissance and was characterised by the work of theorists such as Adam Smith, and the growth of cities, a middle class and world markets. It was during the Industrial Revolution that entrepreneurs first made their appearance. At that stage all economic activities took place on a small scale, both technically and financially. Business operations were carried out by individual entrepreneurs or one-person businesses.

Entrepreneurs risked their own money in ventures that they managed themselves. In other words, the business was financed almost exclusively by the owner, though

Example

Adam Smith, the father of capitalism, published his classic manifesto on the capitalist or market order in 1776, under the title *The wealth of nations*. In doing so, he gave form to what is now accepted as the free-market economy, and to economics as an independent science.

That period marks the beginning of the Industrial Revolution of the 18th and 19th centuries. The number of patents registered in the 18th century in Britain alone, and the rate at which they increased, shows the expansion of technological innovation.

Periods	Number of patents
1700–1730	149
1730–1760	230
1760–1790	976

This increase in technological innovation, together with the discovery of new sources of power and raw materials, and the invention of new means of communication and transport, provided the driving force of the Industrial Revolution.

Source: Viljoen, S., *Capitalism: A historical survey*, HAUM, Cape Town, n.d.

supplemented by bank loans and, in the case of larger undertakings, by partners or members of the family. The one-person business was typical of how capitalism was organised, not only in commerce and industry, but also in mining, shipbuilding and banking. In this form of business, the independent entrepreneur was the self-appointed manager who bore all the risks and to whom all profits accrued. The requirements for success were sound intelligence, common sense and an intimate knowledge of technical production. In a nutshell, experience, and not scientific management, was the prerequisite for a successful business.

Since the end of the 19th century, however, capitalism, or the free-market economy, has changed radically. The technological innovations of the Industrial Revolution, which made mass production possible, not only gave rise to population growth and higher living standards but also created an almost insatiable demand for products. This convergence of factors then required a new form of organisation, much larger than that of the small entrepreneur, to make possible the extensive financing necessary for large-scale production. The company or corporation, with its great number of shareholders or suppliers of capital, now made its appearance. This form of business resulted in a dichotomy between suppliers of capital and management. The result was suppliers of capital who did not manage, and managers who did not provide capital.

From this unique convergence of circumstances in the market economies of the world there arose a need for professional management, for it soon became evident that the problems of management in the new form of organisation could not be solved by experience alone.[14] Following the demand for professional management, business management came into being as a discipline to examine how a business should best be managed. At the beginning of the 20th century the current stage of business management as a discipline was introduced. As a discipline, business management is therefore roughly 100 years old.

Since then it has followed a course of pragmatic empirical development, through which certain approaches, methods and functional areas have taken shape in conformity with practical needs. For example, during the early decades of the 1900s, production management was emphasised as a means of satisfying an almost insatiable mass demand for products. During the 1930s over-production caused the emphasis to shift to sales management in an attempt to get rid of the excess. The marketing concept of the 1950s and 1960s followed. And in the 1970s and 1980s, a period marked by a turbulent business environment, the emphasis shifted to strategic management. In the 1990s it moved again to the globalisation of business management as business activities across national boundaries increased. Coca-Cola, for example, is sold in 195 different countries and is a truly global product. Over 80% of Coca-Cola's annual profits come from international sales.

As the emphasis in management shifted from production to marketing to global management, different management theories were shaped. The existing knowledge of management and perspectives on management stem from a combination of sustained research and practical experience. These perspectives or theories on management are classified into different schools of thought, namely the **scientific school**, the **classical school**, the **human relations school**, and **contemporary management thinking**, which includes downsizing, outsourcing, change management, the management of technology, total quality management, and the management of diversity. The management of diversity is of special importance to South African managers. Over many decades business management developed a body of knowledge that is constantly improved by research, management education and training, mentoring and practical experience.

Against this background of the development of business management, we may now consider whether or not business management may be regarded as a science.

> **Business management education in South Africa**
>
> In South Africa it is estimated that some 12 000 students per year qualify for the various specialised BCom and BTech degrees, and some 1 600 advanced management education students per year complete the MBA/MBL degree. A feature of the MBA market in South Africa is its extraordinary growth. In 1997 the industry produced 689 MBA graduates from 9 schools. A year later, there were 12 schools and they produced 909 graduates. The following year saw an increase of 38% to 1 254 graduates, and 2002 saw a total of 1 853 enrolments from 18 schools.

1.7.2 Is business management an independent science?

As we have mentioned, business management is a young subject, and its scientific basis is still the subject of lively debate. There are certain considerations that have to be met in order for a specific field of study, discipline or body of knowledge to be regarded as a **science**. There is no easy answer to the question in the title of this section, because there are many diverse opinions as to what exactly constitutes a science.

The most common definitions of a science emphasise different characteristics. Business management is continually being tested in the light of these definitions to determine whether it merits the status of a science.

- The most outstanding characteristic of an independent science is a **clearly distinguishable subject of study** that forms the nucleus of a discipline.[15] Business management completely satisfies this condition, particularly with regard to the business organisation, which, as a component of the free-market economy, is its subject of study.
- A fundamental characteristic of a science, which supplements the one mentioned above, is that it should be **independent**

of other sciences. As we have already pointed out, business management has its own identifiable subject of study, and from this point of view may be regarded as a science. However, it should be clearly understood that a business organisation can be studied by other sciences for other reasons. People are social animals who organise themselves into groups to fulfil purposes that are too big or too complex for a single individual. A business organisation comprises people who wish to attain certain personal and organisational goals. Business organisations may also, therefore, form a subject of study for sciences such as sociology, psychology and medicine. However, the way in which business management views an organisation is indicated by the purpose of the study, which is to examine those things that may guide businesses as effectively as possible towards their objective, which is primarily to make a profit. This essential characteristic also allows business management to qualify as a science because, unlike other sciences, it is concerned mainly with ways of maximising the profitability of a business.

- A third consideration is the definition of a science as a **uniform, systematised body of knowledge of facts and scientific laws**, and the existence of laws and principles that are constantly **tested in practice**.[16] In this regard business management encompasses a great deal of systematised knowledge found worldwide in the comprehensive literature on the subject. It also contains numerous rules and principles that may successfully be applied in practice, even though they are not as exact as those in the natural sciences. This leads to the view that management is a normative science, which means that it constantly endeavours to establish norms or guidelines for management with a view to maximising profits.
- It is also said that the final purpose of a science should be to produce a **generally accepted theory**. In this regard, business management does not yet satisfy the requirements of an independent science. Because of the rapidly changing environment in which business organisations exist, it is doubtful whether this stage will ever be reached. It should also be borne in mind that the involvement of people in the management process, and the influence of uncontrollable variables make it difficult, if not impossible, to explain management problems with any single uniform theory.

Although we have not come to a perfectly clear conclusion as to whether business management can be regarded as an independent science, this examination at least provides an insight as to its nature. To summarise, we may say that business management is a young applied science that sets out to study the ways in which a business can achieve its prime objective, which is to make a profit. However, this does not mean that the application of management principles and approaches should always be done in a scientific way, nor does it require that the "feel" and experience of managers should be summarily dismissed. For this reason, successful management is often regarded as an art as well as a science.

1.7.3 The interfaces between business management and other sciences

Throughout the discussion of the scientific status of business management, it was held that the business organisation, as the subject of study, is the most important entity. However, one should bear in mind that businesses are also studied by other disciplines for other reasons. Business management, in its task of studying and examining those things that help a business to attain its goals as efficiently as possible, constitutes a young, developing science that frequently makes use of the knowledge gathered by other disciplines on the functioning of the business organisation, even though these disciplines may not be interested in the profitability of organisations. In short, business science takes from other disciplines what it can use to help businesses as much as possible to accomplish their goals.

Many current management concepts originated in other sciences and now form an integral part of the body of knowledge of business management. For example, the concept of strategy was borrowed from military principles; sociological knowledge and principles enable us to explain the behaviour of an organisation; engineering principles are applied to improve productivity in the manufacture of products; and mathematical models and computer science are used to help management make decisions. Furthermore advertising frequently uses psychology, the arts and communication principles and techniques – all, of course, from the viewpoint of profitability. Table 1.3 on the next page provides a self-explanatory exposition of the multidisciplinary nature of business management. In view of the constantly changing environment in which contemporary businesses operate, business management is likely to make more, rather than less, use of other sciences in future.

1.8 Classification of the study material of business management

Against the background of the above introductory discussion of the business world, the economic systems that people institute to solve their welfare problems, the business organisation as a component of the free-market economy, and the task of business management as a young science, we shall now explain how the study material and the contents of this book have been organised.

In order to decide on appropriate study material as well as identify problems relating to business management – especially in view of its multidisciplinary character – a definite **guideline** must be followed. A business

organisation, as a component of the economic system, is subject to the economic principle; therefore it can be said that all internal or external phenomena that exert an influence on lower costs or increased profits can be viewed as **questions** within the field of business management. This guideline not only creates a broad basis upon which knowledge of business management can be built, but also indicates the task of business management, which is to examine those things that will best improve the profitability of the business organisation.

In this endeavour certain activities in the organisation have to be carried out by management:

- Markets must be researched to determine whether there is a need for a particular product.
- Raw materials must be purchased to produce such products.
- Staff and equipment must be acquired to manufacture the products.
- Money has to be obtained to pay for the materials and the equipment, as well as to remunerate staff.
- Moreover, these often disparate activities have to be coordinated or managed.

These different activities, which together make the business organisation work, constitute the field of business management. To give scientific direction to the study of these interrelated activities, the total field of business management is divided into seven **functions** (see table 1.3 and the discussion that follows). These functions, which are also known as **management areas**, comprise all aspects of a specific group of activities.

The main reason for dividing the field of study of business management into different functional areas of management is the need to systematise the large body of knowledge. The multidisciplinary nature of the subject also makes division necessary. The training and skills required for the various functions are highly diverse, and each function on occasion makes use of different disciplines to

Table 1.3: Interfaces between business management and other sciences

Business management/ Other sciences	General management	Marketing management	Financial management	Production and operations management	Purchasing management	Human resource management	Public relations management
Anthropology	• Cultural relationships and organisational behaviour • Management of diversity	• Cultural determinants of demand • Behavioural structures				• Employee behaviour • Diversity	• Behaviour of external groups
Economics	• Environmental scanning	• Market analysis of, for example, consumer expenditure	• Influence of financial strategy • Behaviour of financial markets	• Location problems	• Market analysis of availability and stockpiling • Evaluation of competition in the market	• Labour market analyses • Remuneration structures	• Economic influence of external groups
Engineering		• Product development		• Erection of factories • Factory outlay	• Value analysis	• Safety of employees	
Law (especially Mercantile law)	• Format of an organisation	• Misleading practices • Product safety • Packaging	• Takeovers • Mergers	• Pollution by factories	• Representations • Law of contracts	• Conditions of employment • Negotiation with unions • Labour laws	• Misleading messages • Sponsorship contracts
Computer science	• Information management • Planning models	• Marketing research • E-marketing	• Financial models	• Optimal outlays	• Materials requirement planning • Manufacturing resource planning	• Labour information systems • Labour research	• Public relations research
Accounting	• Control systems • Budgets	• Marketing audit • Sales and cost analyses	• Interpretation of financial statements	• Cost analysis	• Valuation of inventory • Cost analysis	• Human asset accounting	• Budgets
Psychology	• Leadership • Motivation • Negotiation	• Consumer behaviour • Communication			• Negotiation	• Testing • Performance analysis	• Communication • Persuasion
Sociology	• Organisational behaviour • Interfaces between the organisation and the environment	• Socio-demographic classification • Group influences			• Business ethics	• Organisational behaviour	• Group influences
Mathematics and statistics	• Decision models • Planning models	• Market research • Market forecasting • Market measuring	• Financial models • Deviations		• Inventory forecasting	• Human resource planning models	• Pre- and post-testing of programmes

achieve its management purpose. Financial management makes use of computer science, risk management and accountancy concepts, while human resource management uses a great deal of psychological knowledge and social theory.

Because of the broad basis of the body of knowledge, some degree of specialisation in a specific management area is necessary to make management as productive as possible. In this book, however, the functions are distinguished only for analytical purposes, to provide a better understanding of each and to explain its relation to the others. Ultimately, they form a synergistic whole to direct the business organisation towards its goal and objectives.

The functional areas to be examined may be summarised as follows:

- **The function of general management.** This includes an examination of the management process as a whole: the planning that management has to do, the organisation that it has to establish to carry out its plans, the leadership needed to get things done and the control that has to be exercised over the whole process. This requires a survey of the different management approaches that may be adopted. As will be shown in chapter 5, this embraces the overall function through which top management develops strategies for the whole business, and it cuts through all the other functions because such functions as planning and control are carried out not only at top level but also in each functional area. In chapter 5 we shall review the management process, developments in management theory and some of the approaches to management. Planning and organising, in chapters 6 and 7, form the starting point for the management process. In chapter 8, leadership is discussed. Chapters 9 and 10 deal with people in the organisation. These chapters discuss the function of human resources, namely the appointment of the organisation's employees. Chapter 11 discusses the legal environment of human

resources. Chapter 12, which discusses control, is the final chapter of part 2. Part 3 examines the functional areas of business management.

- **The marketing function.** The marketing function is responsible for marketing the products or services of the business. This includes assessment of the market and the needs of consumers, as well as the development of a strategy to satisfy those needs profitably. Chapter 13 provides a brief overview of the marketing process. Chapter 14 deals with marketing instruments, while chapter 15 focuses on an integrated marketing strategy.

- **The public relations function.** The aim of the public relations function in a business organisation is to create a favourable and objective image of the business, and to promote good relations and goodwill between those businesses and external groups directly or indirectly involved in the business, its products or services. This is examined in chapter 16.

- **The financial function.** The financial function includes the acquisition, utilisation and control of the money the business needs to finance its activities, raw materials and equipment in such a way that its profits are maximised without endangering its liquidity or solvency. Chapter 17 introduces financial management, while chapter 18 examines the management of investment. Chapter 19 discusses financing decisions.

- **The production and operational function.** The production and operational function includes that group of activities concerned with the physical production of products, namely the establishment and layout of the production unit, the conversion of raw materials and semi-finished products into finished products, and the scheduling of services that are produced for the market. Chapter 20 provides an introduction to operations management, while chapter 21 focuses on operational management activities, techniques and methods.

- **The purchasing function.** The purchasing function is responsible for the acquisition of all products and materials required by the business to function profitably – raw materials, components, tools, equipment and, in the case of wholesalers and retailers, the inventory to be purchased. Purchasing managers have to be in contact with suppliers, so that they are aware of new products and know the prices at which goods can be bought; they also have to keep inventory up to date, to ensure continuity of functioning. Chapter 22 gives an overview of the purchasing and supply function, while chapter 23 focuses more specifically on sourcing activities.

Following on from the analysis of the functional areas in parts 2 and 3, part 4 deals with various contemporary management problems that accompany these functions, and briefly surveys some of the contemporary issues confronting business. Part 4 considers such matters as productivity, globalisation and knowledge management. These matters cannot be discussed under each function because of limited space.

In completing part 1 (the introduction to business management), chapter 2 discusses the entrepreneur, chapter 3 examines the establishment of the business organisation in greater detail, and chapter 4 examines the environment within which a business operates.

1.9 Summary

This chapter is the first of four that form the introduction to business management. We have explained the role of the business organisation in society, and we have considered the interaction between society and the organisation as a social process that transforms the means of production of a country, so that products and services can be produced that will satisfy the needs of society. This process was explained in greater detail in the discussion of a business organisation as a component of the economic system, where it was specifically shown how, as a need-satisfying institution of the free-market economy, it provides for the needs of people. In conclusion, we examined the task of business management.

 Key terms

Business world	Institutions
Capital	Market economy
Command economy	Market system
Community	Maslow's hierarchy
Competition	Needs
Developed	Profit
Economic principle	Resources
Economic system	Science
Entrepreneurship	Social responsibility
Free market	Socialism
Industries	Transformation

 Questions for discussion

Reread the case study on "The South African airline industry flying high" at the beginning of the chapter and answer the following questions:

1. Do you think the fact that South Africa is moving more towards a free-market economy has had an impact on the South African airline industry? If you do, give your reasons by saying how.
2. An airline is a different type of business from a production company, for example SAPPI. How might the resources, transformation process and outputs of SAA and SAPPI differ?
3. It is clear from the case study that price is one of the key competitive factors in the airline industry. Do you agree that, however, price need not be the only factor on which airlines compete? Give reasons for your answer.
4. Do you think ACSA should be held responsible for the fuel leak that took place at OR Tambo Airport? Comment by stating

what you think would be suitable actions to rectify the situation.

5. Is increased competition the only reason for SAA's declining profit? Can you think of other reasons why an airline's profit might decrease so sharply? (You might want to do a little extra reading and research to answer this question. A good place to start would be the company's annual reports from the past few years.)

References

1. Morrell, P.S. & Alamdari, F., *The impact of 11 September on the aviation industry: Traffic, capacity, employment and restructuring*, International Labour Office, Geneva, 2002.
2. SAA, *Annual report*, 2006.
3. Phasiwe, K., "New no-frills no competition says SAA", *Business Day*, 11 November 2003.
4. Cowan, K.R., "Business ethics in South Africa: An investigation of managerial perceptions and attitudes", Paper presented at the 4th Conference of the SA Institute of Business Scientists, Vista University, Bloemfontein, June 1992.
5. Statistics South Africa, "Gross Domestic Product", *Statistical release P0441*, 2006.
6. Department of Labour, *Commission for Employment Equity Annual report for 2005–2006*, Pretoria, 2006.
7. Based on Maslow, A.H., "A theory of human motivation", as dealt with in Griffin, R.W., *Management*, Houghton Mifflin Co., Boston, 1987, p. 440.
8. British Petroleum, *BP Statistical Review of World Energy (XLS)*, BP, 2006, http://www.bp.com (8 December 2006).
9. Lombard J.A., Stadler J.J. & Haasbroek, P.J., *Die ekonomiese stelsel van Suid-Afrika*, HAUM, Pretoria, 1987, p. 34.
10. *Ibid.*, p. 17.
11. See also Radel, F.E. & Reynders, H.J.J. (Eds), *Inleiding tot die bedryfsekonomie*, J.L. van Schaik, Pretoria, 1980, p. 2.
12. Radel & Reynders, op. cit., p. 4.
13. *Ibid.*, p. 5.
14. *Ibid.*, p. 3.
15. Lucas, G.H.G. et al., *Die taak van bemarkingsbestuurder*, J.L. van Schaik, Pretoria, 1979, p. 11.
16. Radel & Reynders, op. cit., p. 2. See also Marx, F.W. & Churr, E.G., *Grondbeginsels van die bedryfsekonomie*, HAUM, Pretoria, 1981, p. 24.

ENTREPRENEURSHIP

The purpose of this chapter

This chapter examines entrepreneurship as the driving force behind the business organisation. It is basically the entrepreneur who decides what, how, by whom and for whom products and services should be produced to satisfy the needs of society. This chapter also examines the nature of entrepreneurship and the role of entrepreneurs and small businesses in the economy. In addition, it looks at the entrepreneurial process or the way in which one becomes an entrepreneur, as well as the different ways of entering the business world: by starting a new business, by growing a business, by buying an existing business and growing it, by entering into a franchise agreement or corporate entrepreneurship or intrapreneurship. Finally, aspects of new venture opportunities are discussed.

Learning outcomes

The content of this chapter will enable learners to:
- Explain the concept of entrepreneurship and the entrepreneurial process
- Define an entrepreneur
- Describe the roles of entrepreneurs and small businesses in the economy
- Describe how to become an entrepreneur
- Comment on the skills and resources required to become an entrepreneur
- Identify and describe the different ways of entering the business world
- Present recommendations on the choice of a business opportunity

2.1 Introduction

In the previous chapter our introductory discussion revolved around the role of the **business** organisation in society. We explained how business organisations, large and small, transform a nation's resources (land, labour, capital, and entrepreneurship) into products and services to meet the needs of its people.

We also explained that the purpose of business management as a science is to examine ways and means of improving the performance of a business organisation.

However, in order to understand how the business organisation satisfies the needs of a nation in a market economy, one needs to understand the driving force behind the business organisation, namely the **entre-**

preneur. It is the entrepreneur who decides what, how, by whom and for whom products and services should be produced. The entrepreneur is, moreover, the source of one of the four main factors of production, discussed in chapter 1: natural resources (land), human resources (labour), financial resources (capital) and entrepreneurship.

The case study on the next page shows entrepreneurship in action.

Entrepreneurship is the factor that mobilises the other three resources (land, labour and capital) and harnesses them in different combinations to meet the needs of society. The case study shows an example of this: Mr Ebrahim managed to raise R3 million seed capital to start his own business, an investment company, by selling his shares in Naspers and involving his brothers, who also made capital available from their savings, in the business. In addition, he appointed at first too many employees at too high a cost, but managed to set this right and ensure the involvement of productive and knowledgeable employees. In spite of many regulations and restrictive rules regarding investments for his market, he managed to identify investments complying with the requirements of his clients.

Entrepreneurship is the fourth factor of production and includes those individuals in society who take the initiative and **risk** by harnessing the factors of production to produce products and services. The entrepreneur's reward for taking initiative and risk is profit. Loss is the punishment for taking the wrong decision. Entrepreneurship is, moreover, a scarce resource since not everyone in a country has the skills or is prepared to take risks in generating products and services. In South Africa, for example, only 5,29% of the population is involved in early-stage entrepreneurial activity, compared to an average of 9,43% for all countries.[1] Total early-stage entrepreneurial activity (TEA) is the percentage of people aged between 18 and 64 actively involved in **starting a business** or

managing a business which they wholly or partly own and which is less than three-and-a-half years old. It is a measure of the national rate of new business formation.[2]

By understanding what it is that drives entrepreneurs, how they identify and assess business opportunities and enter the business world, the student of business management will better understand how business organisations function. An **entrepreneur** is someone who starts a business and assumes the risk of losing all of his or her resources if the venture fails. This process of starting a new business, of sometimes failing and sometimes succeeding, is **entrepreneurship**. Entrepreneurs risk their resources to make a profit. Managers, in contrast, are not entrepreneurs for they assume relatively little risk for the success or failure of the business. However, managers play a key role in the success or failure of the business organisation, and need to know how the **entrepreneurial process** works. A brief overview of the rediscovery of entrepreneurship will help explain its nature and importance to society.

2.1.1 The rediscovery of entrepreneurship

Entrepreneurs throughout the world are stirring up a revolution that is revitalising economies, because the establishment of new businesses and the growth of existing ones are responsible for most of the products and services that are changing people's lives. These new products and services are generated by entrepreneurs. Furthermore, entrepreneurs create jobs. The traditional providers of job opportunities, namely large enterprises and government organisations, have been replaced by small businesses as the main provider of jobs. In the USA, the world's most successful economy, small and medium-sized enterprises (SMEs) employ 85% of the workforce, and in Central and Eastern Europe millions of new entrepreneurs are endeavouring to reform

Case study: Entrepreneurship in action

Exploiting restrictive rules

Buying shares in a company run by one of the finalists in this year's World Entrepreneur Awards helped finalist Adam Ismail Ebrahim – CEO and CIO of Oasis Group Holdings – fund his company.

"In 1997 – when I realised that my time as an employee was coming to an end – I sold shares that I had bought in Naspers a year before its listing at R1,45, for R50," says Ebrahim, whose brothers, Mohamed Shaheen (chairman) and Nazeem (deputy chairman), pooled resources with him to start an investment company.

They wanted to provide a particular service not previously offered to Muslims, both in terms of savings and retirement. Muslims have the dilemma that their religious rules prohibit them from benefiting from the proceeds of companies involved in alcohol, tobacco, financial services, entertainment and pork products as well as companies that are highly leveraged. The use of derivatives is also prohibited.

Oasis began with R3m seed capital, with a strong focus on developing the niche market of investments that complied with Shari'ah religious law. It has since grown to be the leader worldwide in Shari'ah-compliant investments and both its global funds were rated AA by Standard & Poor's and its Crescent Global Fund received a five-star rating from MorningStar.

Ebrahim, who hails from District Six, holds a BSoc (Hons) from UCT. He later studied accounting, completed his articles at Deloitte and was seconded to the firm's London office in September 1986.

"It was an interesting time, with new regulations being implemented in the financial services sector. On top of first-hand experience of changes in the regulatory environment, I witnessed the stock market crash the following year," says Ebrahim, who gained insight into the world of investment while witnessing the contrast between "absolute euphoria caused by booming market conditions and utter depression" when the tide turned.

He returned to SA in 1988 and joined Allan Gray as an analyst, but was soon promoted to partner responsible for training managers. "Until 1996 things went very well and I felt that I was living my dream," says Ebrahim, who later found it "increasingly difficult to get motivated by my environment".

"When I resigned to start out on my own, Allan Gray offered to fund my business. However, I felt that it would be inappropriate and that I wouldn't really be independent. I wanted the freedom to paddle my own boat, to follow my own philosophy and target untapped markets with my own resources. Thus we became competitors after I had eight good years with Allan Gray gaining confidence and understanding of the industry.

"But then I made a huge mistake," says Ebrahim. "I believed people who made promises of vast amounts of money that they'd invest in the new business. On the strength of that I made the next mistake: I hired 16 people – six being highly paid CAs.

"We had no revenue, no assets, a very expensive salary bill and a very expensive cost structure – and the losses just kept mounting. To make matters worse, two weeks after getting our first institutional client, markets were hit by the Asian crisis. I know it has since become a sensitive image to use, but it was like a toddler taking his first steps along the beach just when a tsunami hits ...

"But we survived – on the foundations of an investment philosophy of no volatility, which, combined with our ethical offering, proved to be a very definite and successful niche.

I fired everybody after realising they were having a ball doing nothing. We started managing the money we did have very strictly, our performance improved, losses disappeared and the company – and each of its operating subsidiaries – has never made a loss again," says Ebrahim.

"After having made every mistake possible, and having learnt very expensive lessons, performance started picking up and we decided to enter the retail market, which provided the breakthrough the company needed. People started coming to us, whereas before we had to call on people trying to convince them to invest R300 a month. Up to 65% of our sales were based on that direct model, which has led to our having the lowest churn ratio in the industry and proving how important personal relationships are in business. We now have 30 000 direct retail clients."

The Oasis Crescent Equity Fund, its flagship fund, has been the best performing equity fund since its inception in August 1998: R100 000 invested in that fund is now worth more than R1,1m and the fund has now crossed the R2bn mark.

December 2000 was another land-mark for the group, when it registered its first global fund, the Crescent Global Equity Fund. That has since established itself as the world's best performing Shari'ah-compliant equity fund.

The retail retirement business was launched in 2002, providing all investors access to Shari'ah-compliant and ethical retirement savings not previously available. "We find that 30% of our clientele aren't Muslims," says Ebrahim. Oasis also launched the first Shari'ah-compliant prudential unit trust in April last year and the first listed Shari'ah-compliant property fund in November last year.

Ebrahim ascribes the success of the business – voted best collective investment scheme manager in SA for the past two quarters – to an owner-based culture and adherence to global regulatory and ethical standards. He says the Oasis model is also built on selling a product tailored to what people need and not so much on what they want, a result of building up a personal relationship with a client.

Oasis has more than R25bn of assets under management, employs 140 people in SA and Ireland and will shortly launch operations in Dubai. Through a joint venture in Malaysia, the group has exposure to Singapore, Indonesia and Brunei.

"We see SA as a great investment destination and intend to run our global business from our head office in Cape Town," says Ebrahim.

Source: Naudé, C., "Exploiting restrictive rules", *Finweek*, 9 November 2006, p. 69.

and transform the liberated communist economies. Entrepreneurs are also transforming China and Cuba, the last bastions of communism.

Worldwide, countries are debating ways and means of addressing the problems of unemployment. Statistics show that the more flexible the labour market – in other words, the more free it is from government intervention – the lower the unemployment rate.

Employment is closely linked to the state of the economy. When there is no growth in the economy, fewer employment opportunities are available. Employment in South Africa is low, with an approximate unemployment rate of 25,6%.[3]

High-potential entrepreneurs intend to grow their businesses. They are responsible for growth and employment creation in the economy. The results of the *Global Entrepreneurship Monitor: South African Report 2004* indicate that the small and medium enterprise sector employs in excess of four million people in South Africa.[4]

The combination of all businesses – namely **small, medium and micro-enterprises (SMMEs)** and large national and international businesses – determines the state of the economy. Growth in the South African economy has declined over the past 20 years. In the 1960s the gross domestic product (GDP) growth averaged nearly 6% per year. During the 1980s the GDP growth decreased to only 2,2%, with no growth in the 1990s and an average of 3,8% growth between 2000 and 2004 and 4,9% in 2006. The aim in South Africa is to reach 6% growth again within the next few years to sustain and improve the economic development of the country. The contribution of entrepreneurs will be relied on for a large part of the prospective 6% growth. An economic growth rate of about 12% per year is needed to achieve an employment growth rate of 3%.

There are many reasons for South Africa's high unemployment levels. One reason in particular is the labour laws, but another important reason is that South Africa does not have enough businesspeople involved in small businesses to create employment. The current interest in the question of entrepreneurship is therefore only too clear, but various questions concerning the entrepreneur need to be answered: "What is an entrepreneur?", "Is there a difference between an entrepreneur and a manager?" and "Are entrepreneurs found only in the form of small business enterprises?"

The answers to these and other questions will help not only to clarify the nature of entrepreneurship, but also to explain the interest that is being shown in it, and its importance. An examination of the concept of entrepreneurship is therefore important.

2.1.2 What is entrepreneurship?

The first question that arises in the quest for a scientifically based definition of the notion of "entrepreneur" concerns identity: "Who or what is an entrepreneur? Is the owner of a suburban filling station, or an estate agent, or the local butcher, or the owner of a Fastfit or Nando's franchise an entrepreneur? Are there entrepreneurs in schools, government enterprises and large enterprises?" There is no hard-and-fast rule here – nor is there a formal classification or register of entrepreneurs. Moreover, scientists have different views on whom or what exactly an entrepreneur is.

- Economists subscribe to the view that entrepreneurs combine different resources in specific combinations to generate products and services at a profit. Their focus is what entrepreneurs do. Entrepreneurs, to them, are people who are driven primarily by the profit motive.
- Behaviourists tend to see entrepreneurs from the behavioural perspective: for who the entrepreneurs are. Behaviourists are specialists in human behaviour – for example psychologists and sociologists. Their objective is to describe entrepreneurs according to their characteristics, for example the achievement-orientation of entrepreneurs and their propensity towards creativity and risk taking.
- Marxists regard entrepreneurs as exploiters.
- Corporate managers, in contrast, see entrepreneurs as small operators who lack the potential to manage a large enterprise.
- Proponents of a market economy see entrepreneurs as the economic force responsible for the prosperity of a country.

Many more views may be added to the above list. Writers on management and entrepreneurship also have different views on the concept of entrepreneurship. This results in as many definitions of an entrepreneur as there are writers on the subject. Entrepreneurs have been described as persons who:

- Have innovative ideas (because business involves new products, new processes, new markets, new materials and new ways of doing things)
- Identify opportunities (created by the unlimited needs of people and trends that appear in the environment)
- Find resources (capital, natural resources, human resources and entrepreneurship) to pursue these opportunities for personal gain (profit)

- Take financial risk (run the risk of potential loss or failure of the businesses they start)
- Bring about change, growth and wealth in the economy (winning nations have entrepreneur-driven economies)
- Re-energise economies and create jobs (desperately needed in South Africa)
- Start, manage and grow small businesses (the owner of a business starts and manages the business and re-allocates the business resources in such a way that the business makes a profit and grows)

It is important to remember that the word "entrepreneur" is associated with founding a new business or owning and managing a small one.

Critical thinking

Who is an entrepreneur?

At the end of this section the following question arises: "Who is an entrepreneur?"

Entrepreneurship is the process of mobilising and risking resources (land, capital, human resources) to utilise a business opportunity or introduce an innovation in such a way that the needs of society for products and services are satisfied, jobs are created, and the owner of the business profits from it. This process includes new as well as existing businesses, but the emphasis is usually on new products or services and new businesses.

An **entrepreneur** is a person who engages in entrepreneurship. He or she is usually a creative person with high achievement motivation who is willing to take a calculated risk and who views new opportunities as a challenge. The fact that the word "entrepreneur" is associated with founding a new business or owning and managing a small one does not mean that entrepreneurs are not found in large corporations. In fact, most of South Africa's large corporations were

started from small beginnings by people who went on to become illustrious entrepreneurs.

The following people are well-known entrepreneurs:

- Anton Rupert, founder of Rembrandt, Remgro and Richemont
- Raymond Ackerman, founder of Pick 'n Pay
- Patrice Motsepe of African Rainbow Minerals, Armgold
- Tokyo Sexwale of Mvelaphanda Holdings
- Mark Shuttleworth of Thawte
- Annetjie Theron, founder of Annique Skin Care and Cosmetic range
- Bill Venter of Altech and Altron
- Herman Mashaba, founder of Black Like Me

However, these "captains" of South African business number but a few of the thousands of entrepreneurs, in large as well as small businesses, who drive the South African economy. A brief look at what they do will bring us closer to understanding entrepreneurship.

2.2 What entrepreneurs and SMMEs do and why they do it

Entrepreneurs establish and grow businesses but all SMMEs are not necessarily entrepreneurial. There is a distinct difference between entrepreneurial businesses and some, or perhaps even the majority of, SMMEs that are not entrepreneurial. SMMEs often exist as an alternative to earning income instead of working as an employee; due to the need of the owner for independence or the orientation towards a career that satisfies the lifestyle needs of the owner.

2.2.1 The role of entrepreneurs in society

In chapter 1 we described how businesses, owned and driven by entrepreneurs, satisfy needs by mobilising a country's national, financial and human resources to produce much-needed products and services. In the process, wealth is created for society (in the form of jobs) and for the entrepreneur (in the form of profits). Entrepreneurial activity is the essential source of economic growth and social development, and the key role played by this factor of production was underestimated for many decades. Entrepreneurship is the spark that brings the other factors of production into motion. However, it is also important to realise that entrepreneurship itself is, in turn, mobilised by the confidence, creativity, skills and expectations of individuals. If the entrepreneurial spirit is absent, the production machine does not go into action.

People with entrepreneurial talents and skills and leanings are able to achieve more than others in mobilising productive resources by starting enterprises that will grow. People with entrepreneurial qualities are rare and valuable. They constitute a resource that greatly contributes to, if not causes, the production of goods and services. They set in motion the creation of employment opportunities. They differ dramatically from small business owners who are satisfied with some autonomy and earning a reasonable income for themselves and perhaps a few employees, but who have no intention of **growing** and developing their business entrepreneurially.

Mr Ebrahim, the subject of the case study at the start of this chapter, is a true entrepreneur. He not only started his own business in 1997, but also managed to grow it over fewer than ten years to become a medium to large business, and he still remains entrepreneurial. He continuously adds new products and services, such as the Oasis Crescent Equity Fund in 1998, the Crescent Global Equity Fund (Oasis's first global fund) in 2000, and Oasis's retail retirement business in 2002, and a prudential unit trust as well as a property fund in 2005. Oasis plans to launch operations in Dubai, a further growth and expansion opportunity it has identified.

Opportunity and high growth entrepreneurs are of major importance to any economy, but this does not mean less entrepreneurial SMMEs are not also important. SMMEs form 97,5% of all businesses in South Africa and generate 35% of the GDP. Although the SMMEs employ 55% of all the formal private sector employees, more than 90% of SMMEs employ fewer than 20 people, with the average business in South Africa employing 13 people. In the USA, Japan and Germany, small businesses contribute more than half the GDP in each country. However, in developed economies, small businesses employ up to 500 people. In South Africa the upper limit of small businesses is 50 employees and for medium businesses it is 200 employees.[5]

Figure 2.1 illustrates that over 80% of businesses in the most successful economy in the world – that of the USA – have fewer than 100 employees. In fact, 50% of the businesses employ between one person and four people only.

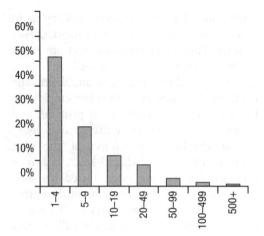

Figure 2.1: Employment size of business in the USA

Source: US Small Business Administration, as shown in Hatten, T. S., *Small Business: Entrepreneurship and beyond*, Houghton Mifflin Company, 1997, p. 5.

The above brief overview of what entrepreneurs do – namely produce products and services and create wealth in the form of economic growth, jobs and profits – sheds further light on the concept of entrepreneurship and the difference between entrepreneurs and SMME owners.

2.2.2 Why do entrepreneurs do what they do?

In endeavouring to explain the concept of entrepreneurship we have briefly examined what an entrepreneur is and what it is entrepreneurs do. A brief overview of why entrepreneurs enter the world of business will add to an understanding of this complex concept.

The question of why entrepreneurs do what they do has eluded researchers for many years. What is it about the entrepreneur that causes him or her to enter into the world of business? Comparative studies have indicated that roughly one-third of a nation's people enter into business, while the other two-thirds are professionals, government em-

ployees, employees of businesses, and the unemployed.

The question of why entrepreneurs initiate new ventures or have a desire to own and manage their own business is a complex one. The decision to enter into business is influenced by many variables, which differ from country to country. Three broad categories of determinants or reasons for individuals initiating ventures are discussed in the three sections below.

2.2.2.1 Outsourcing

The success of leading countries such as the USA, Japan and England has proved that the only growth sector in the economy is the SMME sector, driven by entrepreneurs. This means that SMMEs become established and grow. In contrast, employees of large businesses are often laid off or become self-employed. They also become employed by new SMMEs formed as some of the activities of large businesses are contracted out. In addition, some of the sections of these large businesses are closed down or sold off to function as SMMEs. Once again, entrepreneurs play an important role. They are responsible for the formation of new businesses, to which non-core functions are **outsourced**, to take over or to buy the sections that would have been closed down. For example, three employees of a large mining group that unbundled a few years ago bought two mines that would have been closed down. They had experience in the mining industry, developed a plan, took some risks, started off with a loan, took over the operations, restructured and made some crucial changes. They've been extremely profitable, are growing and are in the process of buying additional mines and providing employment to many.

The worldwide privatisation of government organisations has also resulted in employees becoming entrepreneurs. This is especially true in the case of outsourcing: government organisations and large businesses outsource many of the services and

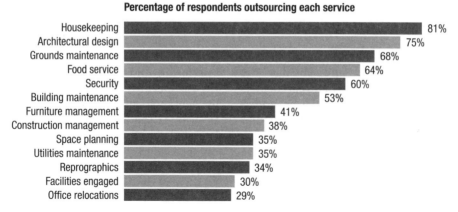

Percentage of respondents outsourcing each service

Service	Percentage
Housekeeping	81%
Architectural design	75%
Grounds maintenance	68%
Food service	64%
Security	60%
Building maintenance	53%
Furniture management	41%
Construction management	38%
Space planning	35%
Utilities maintenance	35%
Reprographics	34%
Facilities engaged	30%
Office relocations	29%

Figure 2.2: Services most often outsourced

Source: International Facility Management Association, *Research Report*, No. 10, p. 6

components they need. In this way they reduce personnel costs and gain access to special skills. Figure 2.2 illustrates the services most often outsourced. These environmental trends are only a few of the reasons for people becoming entrepreneurs. In South Africa, due to Labour Laws and other complicated issues in the environment, human resource functions are also often outsourced, more specifically by SMMEs.

2.2.2.2 Experience in a particular industry or possession of particular skills

Some people can exploit certain opportunities more successfully than others. **Skills** and knowledge, an identified opportunity and the quest for independence are among the most important reasons for people becoming entrepreneurs. Other reasons include events such as job termination and job dissatisfaction. In South Africa the experience of not having a job may trigger some people into becoming entrepreneurs. These entrepreneurs are known as **necessity entrepreneurs** and are usually less successful than **opportunity entrepreneurs**. **Experience**, training and education in a specific field contribute to the success of an entrepreneur in identifying

an opportunity, establishing a business and managing it. It is unfortunately an unrealistic expectation that entrepreneurship is an opportunity for the unemployed. Very few unemployed people have the four main factors of production, namely natural resources (land), human resources (labour), financial resources (capital) and entrepreneurship. Experience, access to resources and an identified opportunity (which usually comes with experience and exposure in business) are essential for successful entrepreneurship.

For example, Mr Ebrahim, featured in the case study at the start of this chapter, is qualified in accounting and knew the financial services sector well due to extensive exposure and employment for ten years. He also had access to capital (his own savings in shares and that of his brothers) and, most importantly, he had the desire and ability to create a new business instead of continuing to be employed.

2.2.2.3 Traits or psychological variables that distinguish some individuals as entrepreneurs

By examining what motivates people to become entrepreneurs, more people might be motivated to establish businesses. Consider the following **traits** or characteristics of entrepreneurs.

(a) Achievement motivation

The most researched, and possibly the most important, trait of an entrepreneur is **achievement motivation**. In pioneer studies done by researchers such as McClelland,[6] Murray and Gould, entrepreneurs are described as people with a higher need to achieve than people who are not entrepreneurs have. Achievement motivation is characterised by actions of intense, prolonged and repeated effort to accomplish something that is difficult. The person with achievement motivation will also work single-mindedly towards his or her goal and will have the determination to win, do everything well and enjoy competition. Achievement motivation goes hand-in-hand with ambition and competitiveness. People with a high need to achieve are attracted to jobs that challenge their skills and their problem-solving abilities. They avoid goals that they think would be almost impossible to achieve or ones that would guarantee success. They prefer tasks in which the outcome depends upon their individual efforts. Entrepreneurs or would-be entrepreneurs have a high need for achievement and this need includes the need:

- To be personally responsible for solving problems
- To set their own goals and reach these goals through their own effort
- To have feedback on the degree of success with which they accomplish tasks
- To have personal accomplishments
- To have control over their own time and to use time and money creatively. Those who start a new business usually desire independence and do not want to be controlled by someone else.

Mr Ebrahim of Oasis Group Holdings, the subject of the case study at the start of this chapter, has a need for achievement. He realised his dream changed once he had reached it as an employee who had became a partner in Allan Gray. He realised he had other goals to achieve and started his own business. He indicated a definite need to be independent by refusing funding from his former employer. He used his own time and money (resources) in new markets, indicating his creativity. He wanted the freedom "to paddle my own boat, to follow my own philosophy and target untapped markets with my own resources".

(b) Locus of control

The second important characteristic of an entrepreneur is a strong internal **locus of control** as opposed to an external locus of control. An **internal locus of control** indicates the need of a person to be in charge of his or her own destiny, whereas an external locus of control indicates that a person believes that the outcome of an event is primarily out of his or her personal control. People with an external locus of control regard luck and fortune, rather than personal ability and hard work, as the reasons for success. People with a strong internal locus of control believe that the outcome of an event is determined by their own actions. They believe that they have control over their own behaviour, are successful in persuading and motivating other people, actively seek relevant information and knowledge, are well informed about their careers, perform well on skills-related tasks and process information efficiently. Luck or change of fate is therefore of little importance to an entrepreneurial personality.

In the case study, Mr Ebrahim clearly acknowledged his own mistakes, for example believing in promises made by people and hiring a workforce that was too expensive. He took personal control by getting rid of superfluous employees, personally started to manage the money in the company and initiated an investment policy of no volatility.

(c) Innovation and creativity

Successful entrepreneurs and owners of small businesses are innovative and creative.

Innovation, or the production of something new or original, results from the ability to see, conceive, and create new and unique products, processes or services. Entrepreneurs see opportunities in the marketplace and visualise creative new ways to take advantage of them. Innovation is usually included in any definition of creativity. Although not all entrepreneurs find new products or services or discover new resources, every person who establishes an enterprise, who adds value and who sets out to ensure that an enterprise continues to exist and thereby develops job opportunities, is involved in economic creation.

Creativity can involve the adjustment or refinement of existing procedures or products and the identification of opportunities and solutions to problems. Basically, it involves new ideas. Any application of new ideas is based on innovation. Although entrepreneurs understand the importance of innovation, they often view the risk and the high investment that the development of innovative products or services requires as being out of proportion to the profit potential. This explains why entrepreneurs often creatively adapt innovations of competitors by, for example, product adjustments, marketing and client service. Thus their creativity finds expression on the continuum of innovation and adaptation.

Creativity also refers to the creation of something new, for example the creation of a new business by developing a new product or service, building an organisation by financial manipulation, reshaping an existing business, creating a business that will survive on its own and a financial fortune as testimony to the entrepreneur's skill.

In the case study at the start of this chapter, Mr Ebrahim was innovative. He developed a savings and retirement service, equity fund, prudential unit trust and property fund not previously offered to a particular target market, namely Muslim people. By ensuring compliance to shariah religious laws (that prohibit Muslim people from benefiting from proceeds of companies involved in alcohol, tobacco, financial services, entertainment, pork products, high-leverage operations and the use of derivatives), he made it possible for this target market to save and invest for retirement.

(d) Risk taking

Most researchers agree that entrepreneurship behaviour involves the **taking of risks** in one way or another. In the business world there are variables such as interest rates and currency fluctuations, new laws, and so on, which are beyond production and control. The successful entrepreneur correctly interprets the risk situation and then determines actions that will minimise the risk; he or she does not take chances, but sometimes feels it is necessary to take calculated risks. Unsuccessful entrepreneurs, in contrast, do not take any risks, or else they take expensive, impulsive decisions that they don't think through. Entrepreneurs investigate the situation and calculate the probable results before they take decisions. Successful entrepreneurs avoid opportunities where there is a high probability that they will be unsuccessful, regardless of the reward.

Entrepreneurs manage the risk of their enterprises by accepting control and being involved in the basic aspects of the enterprise. They control their enterprises by getting access to information. They reduce their exposure to financial loss by involving investors, often with the risk of losing control. They shorten the period between the conceptualisation of an idea and the making of the product or service available in the market. In this way they often limit the risk of competition.

The conclusion can be drawn that successful entrepreneurs take calculated risks, based on information gathered and analysed and on applicable research and investigation of the probable results of an opportunity, before venturing into something. They undertake such things as **feasibility** studies, market research and research and development.

In the case study at the start of the chapter, Mr Ebrahim knew that he had experience in the business that he planned to pursue. He was also willing to invest his own money, by the sale of his shares in another company, as well as money provided by his brothers, who were to become shareholders in the business. He determined the cost, his available funds and his own knowledge before starting the business. Yet this was not sufficient proof that the business would be a success. He first had to learn various other lessons in the business before he became successful. The establishment of any business involves some risks. Personal mistakes, as well as environmental factors such as volatile financial markets, contributed to the risks in the business, but Mr Ebrahim overcame them through entrepreneurial skills and knowledge of the industry.

(e) Other traits

These include a high level of energy, confidence, orientation towards the future, optimism, the desire for feedback, high tolerance for ambiguity, flexibility/adaptability and commitment.

The brief overview given above of some of the most important reasons for people becoming entrepreneurs does not, however, cover the exhaustive list of traits that may be found in many textbooks. It must also be

remembered that entrepreneurs and owners of small businesses come in every shape, size and colour and from all backgrounds.

Figure 2.3 indicates the various reasons people in the USA have for going into business.

2.2.3 The small business

Because the concept of entrepreneurship is so strongly associated with the establishment of a small business or owning one, a few remarks about what is meant by SMEs is important at this stage.

2.2.3.1 Definition of a small business

It is difficult to formulate a universal definition of a small business, because the economies of countries differ and people adopt particular standards for specific purposes. The following are typical examples of small businesses in South African towns – the local hairdressing salon, greengrocer, video shop and hardware store. A local supermarket regarded by some people as big may actually be small in comparison with a business such as Pick 'n Pay. Likewise, medium and, even, large businesses in South Africa may be small in comparison with their overseas counterparts. In most countries it is therefore accepted

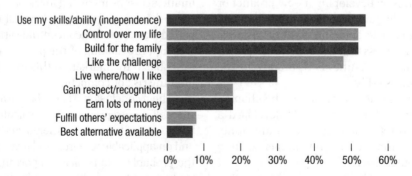

Figure 2.3: Reasons for going into business in the USA

Source: Hatten, T. S., *Small business: Entrepreneurship and beyond*, Houghton Mifflin Company, p. 37.

practice to make use of quantitative and qualitative criteria when attempting to define a small business enterprise.

Examples of quantitative criteria in defining a small business are:
- Number of employees
- Sales volume
- Value of assets
- Market share

In the National Small Business Amendment Act 26 of 2003, micro-businesses in the different sectors, varying from the manufacturing to the retail sectors, are defined as businesses with five or fewer employees and a turnover of up to R100 000. Very small businesses employ between 20 and 50 employees, and small businesses employ between 21 and 50 employees. The upper limit for turnover in a small business varies from R1 million in the Agricultural sector to R13 million in the Catering, Accommodation and other Trade sector as well as in the Manufacturing sector, with a maximum of R32 million in the Wholesale Trade sector.

Examples of small businesses are an employee at a restaurant who learns and gains knowledge about the restaurant business and then eventually starts her own restaurant specialising in a gap or a need for a specific type of restaurant identified, for example one specialising in organic food. She is however satisfied with the success of her restaurant and the income she earns from it and has no plans or inclination to expand or open other restaurants.

Medium-sized businesses usually employ up to 200 people (100 in the Agricultural sector), and the maximum turnover varies from R5 million in the Agricultural sector to R51 million in the Manufacturing sector and R64 million in the Wholesale Trade, Commercial Agents and Allied Services sector.

A comprehensive definition of an SME in South Africa is therefore any enterprise with one or more of the following characteristics:

- Fewer than 200 employees
- Annual turnover of less than R64 million
- Capital assets of less than R10 million
- Direct managerial involvement by owners

For the purposes of this discussion, it is not important to adhere to any particular definition. It is far more important to know that an enterprise that is not classified as large in South Africa is one which the owner owns and controls independently, and in the management of which the owner is directly involved. The concepts "small" and "large" may differ from one industry to the next.

Oasis, the subject of the case study at the start of this chapter, is an example of an entrepreneurial business that began as a small business with limited funds but that, through the entrepreneurial flair of Mr Ebrahim, developed and grew to be a medium-sized to large business.

2.2.3.2 The strategic role of small business in the economy

In advanced nations the entrepreneur is recognised as a key factor in the process of economic development. Entrepreneurs innovate, take risks and employ people. They create markets and serve consumers by combining materials, processes and new products in new ways. They initiate change, create wealth and develop new enterprises. More specifically, the strategic role of small business in any economy revolves around the following:

- **Producing products and services.** Small business combines the resources of society efficiently to produce products and services for the society in which it operates. Small businesses are less inhibited by large bureaucratic decision-making structures and are more flexible and productive than many large firms are. In advanced economies they not only employ the majority of the workforce, but also produce most of the products and services.
- **Innovation.** Small businesses have been

responsible for most of the innovation worldwide. Statistics show that many scientific breakthroughs in the USA originated with small organisations, and not in the laboratories of large businesses. The following are some examples of the new products created by entrepreneurs:

- Photocopiers
- Jet engines
- Insulin
- Helicopters
- Vacuum tubes
- Colour film
- Penicillin
- Ballpoint pens
- Zips
- Personal computers
- Velcro

More recently, mostly technology related, products and services created by entrepreneurs include:

- Cellphones
- The Internet
- Search engines such as Google
- Microchips
- MP3 Players such as the iPod
- Internet safety software
- MXIT, cellphone-based chat rooms
- Drag and draw digital paint sets
- **Aiding big business.** Any successful country needs large enterprises to be able to function competitively in local and, especially, international markets. The Japanese mega-corporations, for example, compete internationally as world players and have conquered markets that earn them billions in foreign currency for domestic development. In the process, they provide millions of local suppliers with orders. It is the efficiency of the local suppliers, however, that enables the big corporations to compete internationally. Small businesses not only act as suppliers to large businesses, but also distribute their products and services.
- **Job creation.** As was previously stated, small businesses provide many of the new

job opportunities needed by a growing population. In fact, they create jobs, whereas large corporations are shedding jobs.

The small business is often entrepreneurially driven. It is this entrepreneurial spirit encountered in the smaller enterprise in particular that is the catalyst for economic development and job creation. Small businesses tend to stimulate competition and thereby improve productivity.

We have now clarified what an entrepreneur is, and we have discussed some of the reasons for people becoming entrepreneurs, including a brief overview of what a small business is, and its role in the economy. The entrepreneurial process may now be examined more closely.

2.3   The entrepreneurial process

Entrepreneurship is the process of identifying, creating or sensing an opportunity where others do not see it, and of finding and combining resources (often owned by someone else) to pursue the opportunity until it becomes a successful established business. Of the thousands of business ventures that entrepreneurs launch every year, many never get off the ground, while others have a spectacular start. Much of the success in establishing a new business depends on how well the entrepreneur has done his or her homework. This is a difficult process because the range of problems and options confronting the entrepreneur is vast, and differs from one opportunity to the next. For example, although Holiday Inn and City Lodge compete in the same industry, they did not evolve in the same way. The options appropriate for one entrepreneurial venture may be completely inappropriate for another. Entrepreneurs must make a bewildering number of decisions – and they must make the right decisions or perish.

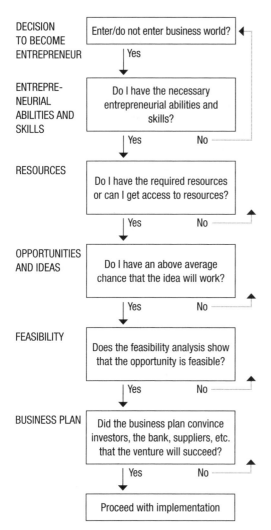

Figure 2.4: The entrepreneurial process: A framework for new venture decision making

By following a scientific decision-making framework as illustrated in figure 2.4, the entrepreneur has a better chance of success. This framework or entrepreneurial process of entering the business world follows a logical sequence and clarifies many of the questions the entrepreneur is faced with. The entrepreneurial process involves the following phases or clusters of problems and questions which the entrepreneur must clarify and solve:

- **Abilities and skills.** The personal charac-teristics, abilities and skills of the new owner of a business have a profound influence on the success or failure of the new venture. Before entering the business world, any potential entrepreneur should first clarify whether he or she has what it takes to do so.
- **Access to resources.** Another key factor in new venture creation is the question of **resources**, or rather access to resources. Without capital or the other resources necessary for the establishment of a business, the new venture is doomed.
- **Opportunity.** A further important aspect of the entrepreneurial process is the assessment of the opportunity that the entrepreneur is pursuing.
- **Feasibility.** Once the opportunity has been identified and defined, the entrepreneur needs to find out if it can be turned into a successful venture. This calls for a feasibility study.
- **Business plan.** Once the entrepreneur has some certainty about the feasibility of the venture, he or she needs to compile a business plan.
- **Manage the business.** Once feasibility has been established and resources have been acquired, the entrepreneur launches and manages the new business.

The above-mentioned phases of what is popularly called the entrepreneurial process can also be perceived as a framework for decision making. At each of the phases in the process the entrepreneur is faced with many questions that must be clarified before he or she can proceed to the next phase. The framework given above does not guarantee that a new venture will be successful. Rather, it provides a logical sequence of steps or phases in the entrepreneurial process. In each phase there is a multiplicity of issues that need to be carefully assessed if the new idea is to be implemented successfully.

We shall now undertake a closer exa-mination of the above-mentioned phases of the entrepreneurial process.

2.3.1 Skills required for entrepreneurship

A **skill** is simply knowledge that is demonstrated through action. Potential entrepreneurs therefore need knowledge about the particular environments and industries in which they want to operate, plus considerable management skills, such as the following:

- **Strategy skills.** These involve the ability to consider the business as a whole and to understand how it fits within its market place, how it can organise itself to deliver value to its customers, and the ways in which it does this better than its competitors.
- **Planning skills.** These involve the ability to consider what the future might offer, how this will impact on the business, and what needs to be done now to prepare for it.
- **Marketing skills.** These involve the ability to see past the offerings of the business and their features, how these satisfy the customer's needs, and why the customer finds them attractive. In the case study at the start of this chapter, Mr Ebrahim invested in a model of direct selling based on a personal relationship with investors. This model ensured the lowest churn ratio in the investment industry, with 30 000 direct retail clients. The product was tailored to what people needed and not so much to what they wanted. This was determined by Oasis through the personal relationship with clients.
- **Financial skills.** These involve the ability to manage money – to be able to keep track of expenditure and to monitor cash flow – but also to assess investments in terms of their potential and their risks.
- **Project management skills.** These involve the ability to organise projects, to set specific objectives, to draw up schedules, and to ensure that the necessary resources are in the right place at the right time.
- **Human relations skills.** These involve the ability to deal with people, and include leadership skills, motivational skills and communication skills.

The above-mentioned management skills are discussed in parts 2 and 3 of this book.

Figure 2.5 illustrates how entrepreneurial performance is influenced by a combination of industry knowledge, management skills, people skills and achievement motivation. The successful entrepreneur must know how to use these skills and learn from using them.

All these determinants of entrepreneurship are important, and the more favourably a person is endowed with these determinants, the greater his or her chances for success.

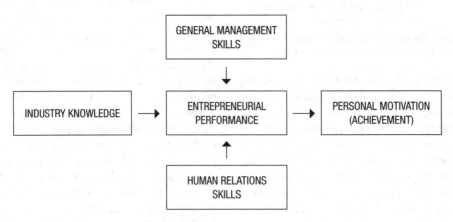

Figure 2.5: Factors influencing entrepreneurial performance

Source: Wickham, P., *Strategic entrepreneurship*, Pearson Education, UK, 1998, p. 43.

2.3.2 Resources needed to start a business

An entrepreneur must have some resources to start a business. Alternatively, he or she must have access to resources to be able to enter into business. In many ventures entrepreneurs do not necessarily want to own the resources that will enable them to start a business, but they may seek control of the resources they use. The emphasis is therefore not on what resources the entrepreneur owns, but rather on what access to and control of resources he or she has.

We stated in the introductory remarks that entrepreneurs acquire resources from the economy and transform these into need-satisfying products and services for the community. **Resources** are therefore the inputs that the business combines to create the outputs it delivers to its customers. In broad terms, there are three kinds of resources that entrepreneurs need to build their ventures, namely:

- **Financial resources.** An opportunity can be exploited only if the entrepreneur has money or has access to it. Financial resources can take the form of cash, a bank overdraft, loans, outstanding debtors or investment capital. Financial resources include basic resources that can readily be converted into cash.
- **Human resources.** Examples are the management team, lawyers, accountants, and technical and other consultants. Human resources basically include people with knowledge and skills that contribute to the success of the venture.
- **Operating resources** or **physical resources**. These are assets such as office or other equipment, a delivery vehicle, raw materials and, in the case of larger small businesses, buildings, machinery and the plant.

Prospective entrepreneurs must realise that the acquisition of resources implies a risk, especially if the expected profits and return on investments do not materialise. Prospective entrepreneurs must know that investors always compare alternative investments to anticipated return on investment and the risks involved. The entrepreneur is the one who carries the risk, and who stands to lose personal savings or, even, the house he or she lives in, by acquiring resources for an unsuccessful venture.

Despite the fact that a prospective entrepreneur may have the right experience and the right personal traits to become an entrepreneur, he or she cannot successfully exploit an opportunity without the necessary resources, or without access to these resources. This is the most difficult hurdle to cross in becoming the owner of a small business.

2.3.3 New business opportunities

Establishing a new business usually involves an idea that the entrepreneur pursues enthusiastically. Finding a good idea is therefore a first step in converting an entrepreneur's creativity into a business opportunity. The danger, however, is that the importance of the idea is often overrated. In other words, having the best idea is by no means a guarantee of success. Unless the entrepreneur has the capacity and capability to transform the idea into a product or service that captures a significant share of the market, the idea is of little value.

But where do new ideas for a business start-up come from? Research in both the USA and other countries points to the fact that prior work experience, an understanding of the industry, and knowledge of the market account for most new venture ideas. In the case study at the start of the chapter, we saw that Mr Ebrahim had extensive experience in the financial services industry and he also had a very good knowledge of the market, namely the people of the Muslim community and their needs, as well as the shariah restrictions that apply to them. This knowledge and experience ensured that 30% of the clients of Oasis are not Muslims or bound by shariah, but nevertheless have confidence in the excellent service provided and ethical considerations of the business.

The scientific way to search for ideas involves a thorough search of the business environment for ideas and patterns that emerge from the various trends in the environment. The business environment is examined in more detail in chapter 4.

2.3.3.1 Searching for new venture ideas in the environment

The environment referred to includes everything that happens around the entrepreneur. **Trends** in the environment include economic, political and social trends; fashions that change over time; new ways in which goods are distributed; new services that are offered; and so on. In South Africa some of these trends include the following:

- **Economic trends.** The relatively low exchange rate of the rand makes South Africa a very attractive tourist destination, and almost everything associated with tourism could provide entrepreneurial opportunities.
- **Social trends.** The high unemployment rate, as well as a police force that appears incapable of enforcing the law, makes violent crime the most prominent trend in South Africa. This trend threatens, for example, foreign investment and tourism, but offers many ideas and opportunities for the protection of individuals and their property. Because of this trend, businesses that install burglar bars, security fences, security gates, alarm systems and security services such as guards cannot cope with the demand. Changing social trends over the past decade include food consumption and distribution patterns, with the proliferation of fast-food outlets and pubs. Among the new services that have sprung up in the wake of privatisation are mail and courier services, as well as services that are outsourced by large organisations

to SMEs. Examples include human resource and labour services as well as payrolls (due to extensive labour laws), garden services, cafeteria services, maintenance services, and so on.

In searching the environment for entrepreneurial ideas, entrepreneurs must remember that industries, like fashions, go through various life cycle stages, as illustrated by figure 2.6 on the following page.

Virtually everything changes and goes through the stages of **introduction (embryo), growth, maturity** and **decline**. It is important to know in what life cycle stage a new venture idea falls, because each cycle needs a different strategy. Industries in the maturity stage are, for example, very competitive, and this requires high marketing costs. It is clear from the life cycle diagram that the car (automobile) industry as a whole is very mature. Nonetheless, some of its segments are in a developing phase, for example, mini-vans, sports models, and upmarket imports. Convertibles are back in fashion, and in the suburbs young mothers drive around in 4x4s. Despite increasing traffic jams, people still drive, and the cars they drive reflect changing lifestyles.

Where can you find gaps in the life cycle diagram in figure 2.6? Ideas can be generated at any point in the life cycle stages of industries. They may emerge even in those industries that fall into the decline category, as is evident from the revival of cigar smoking. There is even a magazine in South Africa that specifically targets cigar smokers!

South African industries also fall into the categories that appear in figure 2.6, but prospective entrepreneurs should take a close look at the following industries, which could, in the African landscape, be **labelled embryo industries or growth industries:**

- The government's main priority is to educate all South Africans. Proof of this is the fact that the budget for education comprises the largest portion of the annual budget. Because of the importance of education and the inability of the government to reach its educational objectives, there are many opportunities in **private education**, from elementary education to technical and tertiary education.

- A second important industry in South Africa is **health care**. Because most government hospitals perform poorly, numerous opportunities exist for entrepreneurs to start health care ventures, especially home health care. In addition, opportunities such as the development of generic medicine and other health care products exist.

- A third important South African industry is **tourism**, which could provide thousands of new jobs. Very little start-up capital is needed to become a tour guide, for example, or to establish a Bed and Breakfast in an existing personal residence. Many opportunities exist due to South Africa's becoming a destination for international conferences and sporting events. Examples include visits by international hockey and other sports teams, design and academic conferences, and the Soccer World Cup planned for in 2010.

- The **privatisation** of government and semi-government services is another priority of the South African government. Many changes are currently taking place, since government services are being privatised worldwide. In many countries, for example, the government has been one of the principal markets in respect of programmes such as defence, energy, transport, cleaning services and building projects.

Other sources of ideas include advertisements, retailers, competitors, trade shows, industry associations, contracts, consultants, patents and research institutes. An important aspect in the generation of new ideas is the creative ability of the prospective entrepreneur. A truly creative person will find useful ideas in a variety of different ways and by various means. Ideas, however, have to be transformed into opportunities if they are to result in the creation of small businesses.

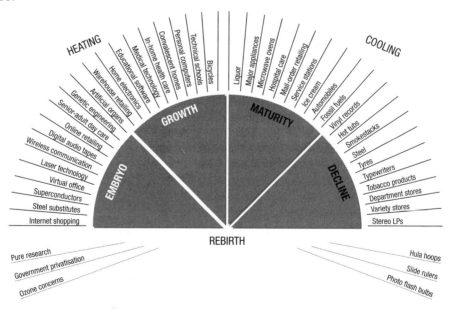

Figure 2.6: The life cycle stages of industries

Source: Ryan, J.D., Eckert, L.A. and Ray, R.J., *Small business*, South-Western Publishing, by permission of Thomson Learning, 1998, p. 29.

Critical thinking

Different industries offer different levels and types of opportunities, which are often determined by environmental factors and the economy. The following question arises: "What is an example of an entrepreneurial opportunity in the health care industry?"

An example of an entrepreneurial opportunity in the health care industry

Pharma Dynamics is a business that Paul Anley established.

Pharma Dynamics is very strong in the field of generic medicines for chronic cardiovascular illnesses, especially hypertension.

Anley says: "We benefited hugely by entering a very young industry with an experienced management team and sales force." He says that was a definite contributing factor to the company being profitable from day one.

Based on research by IMS, the world's leading provider of business intelligence and strategic consultancy services for the pharmaceutical and healthcare industries, Pharma Dynamics has since its inception in 2001 been SA's fastest growing pharmaceutical company: more than 50% for 2005, with the same projected growth for 2006 to an expected turnover of R80m. And Anley is confident that it will achieve a figure of R270m by 2010.

The company, with its head office in Cape Town and a regional office in Sandton, north of Johannesburg, employs 53 people, 33 being sales staff who sell to 2 500 retail pharmacies, private practitioners and specialist physicians, especially in the cardiovascular field, throughout SA.

Anley says: "One of our strengths is the fact that we focus on 17 products instead of hundreds, which means that the reps can spend quality time with doctors. It's also

important to be first to market with a new product, and this we achieve by obtaining the SA marketing rights for every pharmaceutical product expiring over the next three years.

"In the early days it was difficult for us as a small company to be first to market with generics, because you're constantly coming up against huge multinationals," says Anley, who had to mortgage his house "to the hilt" to get seed capital. "However, it also helped that I cashed in some Warner Lambert share options granted in US dollars in the days when the rand traded at US$1/R12."

Apart from its strength in the field of cardiovascular generics, Pharma Dynamics also focuses on the growth of biogenerics. Because a very large portion of the population of SA suffers from diabetes, it has formed a joint venture with Wockhardt, a leading biopharmaceutical company in India. After its products have been submitted to the necessary regulatory procedures, the first generic insulin products will hopefully be brought to SA in the next couple of years.

Mr Anley is an entrepreneur who identified an opportunity in a growth industry.

He identified an opportunity in a young field in the health industry, namely generic medicines for cardiovascular illnesses.

He is a true entrepreneur as he not only established Pharma Dynamics in 2001 but also consistently ensured growth in the business and it is the fastest growing pharmaceutical company in SA.

Pharma Dynamics employs 53 people, and has 17 products with a turnover of R80 million for 2006. It is still a medium business but with the projected growth it will soon be a entrepreneurial large business.

The business also focuses on new developments such as biogenerics for diabetes indicating that entrepreneurial growth will continue.

Source: Naudé, C., "A dose of confidence", *Finweek*, 9 November 2006, http://www.fin24.co.za/articles/print_article.asp?aricleid=_2025855 (22 February 2007).

2.3.3.2 Opportunities

Good ideas can be turned into successful new ventures. But a good idea is not necessarily the same thing as a good **opportunity**. It may be a good idea, for example, to freeze a swimming pool during the short South African winter to save pool chemicals and to provide a home ice-rink for children. But the idea cannot be transformed into a new venture opportunity because research has shown that South African pool owners do not find the idea persuasive (pool surfaces are too small); moreover, because of the costs involved, the idea is not feasible.

A good idea is also not necessarily a good **investment opportunity**. Many people tend to become infatuated with an idea and to underestimate the difficulty involved in developing it into a product or service that will be desirable to the market. Ultimately, the market determines whether an idea has potential as an investment opportunity. The following are some of the fundamental requirements for a good investment opportunity:

- There must be a clearly defined **market need** for the product. The most successful entrepreneurs and investors are **opportunity focused**; they start with what customers and the market wants, and they do not lose sight of this.
- The opportunity must be able to achieve a **sustainable competitive advantage**.
- The opportunity must have the **potential to grow**.
- The opportunity must be **rewarding** to the investor and/or the entrepreneur.
- The **timing** of the opportunity must be right. A window of opportunity must exist. The window of opportunity for delivery of a wedding cake, for example, closes on the day of the wedding. If the wedding cake is delivered on the morning after the wedding, it is worthless.

Good opportunities therefore satisfy a market need and also reward the entrepreneur. It is important that they be well timed.

However, generating a good idea and starting a new venture from scratch is not the only way to enter the business world. Buying an existing business or procuring a franchise can reduce many of the uncertainties faced when starting a business.

2.3.3.3 Buying an existing business

There are several advantages to buying an existing business when compared with other

Table 2.1: Advantages and disadvantages of buying an existing business

Advantages	Disadvantages
1. Customers familiar with location	1. Business location may be undesirable – or threatened with becoming undesirable
2. Established customer base at present location	2. Image difficult to change
3. Experienced employees	3. Employees are inherited rather than chosen
4. Planning can be based on known historical data	4. Possible difficulties in changing the way the business is run
5. Supplier relationships already in place	5. Potential liability for past business contracts
6. Inventory and equipment in place	6. Possible obsolete inventory and equipment
7. Possible owner financing	7. Financing costs could drain cash flow and threaten the survival of the business

strategies for entering the business world. Since customers are used to doing business with the company at its present address, they are likely to continue doing so once it has been taken over by a new owner. If the business has been making money, the new owner will break even sooner than if he or she started the business from scratch. Planning for an ongoing business can be based on previous financial records, rather than having to rely on projections, as with a start-up. An inventory, equipment, and suppliers are already in place, and the business is managed by employees who know from experience how to keep the business going. In addition, it may be possible to obtain financing from the previous owner.

If the timing of the deal occurs when the entrepreneur is ready to buy a business and the owner needs to sell for a legitimate reason, this may be the best way of entering the business world. There may be disadvantages, however, in buying an existing business, as table 2.1 on the previous page shows.

One cannot simply buy an existing business in the hope that it is or will be an ongoing success. The business remains an opportunity for which a feasibility analysis will be necessary.

2.3.3.4   Franchising

Another way of entering the business world is through the acquisition of a **franchise**. The franchise concept gives an entrepreneur the opportunity of starting a business that has been proven in the marketplace. The entrepreneur then becomes a **franchisee**. The **franchisor** gives the franchisee the right to operate a business, using the franchise company's name, products and systems. In return, the franchisee pays the franchise company for this right on an ongoing basis.

The franchisor is an entrepreneur, whereas a franchisee should rather be seen as an **intrapreneur**, possibly initiating innovative ideas in the franchise system. Franchisees do not have the freedom to experiment, operate

and market their businesses based on their own vision of how things should be done. Instead, they must usually adhere strictly to the plans of the franchisor. However, a recent study proved that franchisees do show an entrepreneurial orientation in certain situations, such as multiple-outlet franchisees.[7] Franchisors in many sectors have recognised the benefit of multiple-unit franchisees,[8] and this is seen as an entrepreneurial continuation of the franchise trend.

Franchisors usually fall in the medium-sized to large business category, as the more successful franchisors usually manage large numbers of franchises as part of their business, apart from the overall management of the franchise group. In South Africa there are 391 franchise systems, of which 90,5% originated and developed in South Africa. International franchise systems in South Africa account for 37. The franchise systems combined are responsible for 22 825 outlets employing 284 447 people, according to the 2004 census by Franchise Advice and Information Network (FRAIN). The contribution of the franchise industry to GDP is 11%.[9]

In South Africa most reputable franchises are registered with the Franchise Association of Southern Africa (FASA). The purpose of this organisation is to ensure that franchising in Southern Africa is a quality concept that can enable entrepreneurs to start new businesses. FASA is an excellent source of information on franchises.

2.3.3.5   Corporate entrepreneurship

Corporate entrepreneurship is entrepreneurship in an existing business. It happens when a person or team develops a new corporate business within a business through identification of a new opportunity or business idea. Corporate entrepreneurship is a method by which a corporation or large business introduces new and diversified product(s) or service(s) to an existing business. This is done through internal processes and use of the corporation's resources. It creates opportunities for diversification for a corporation as well as for the creation new industries. In addition, corporate entrepreneurship enables investment and profits through the establishment of new businesses within a business.

Corporate entrepreneurs are also valuable wealth creators in an economy. The advantage of new businesses established in this manner is that sufficient funding or seed capital is usually available for the capital intensive establishment phases and following growth phase.

As explained in the box below, Koos Bekker initiated a totally new concept in the 1980s: pay television in the form of M-Net, within an existing company Naspers,

a conventional publishing house responsible for publication of newspapers and magazines.

Thus an existing business diversified by adding a totally new product, pay television.

The new product was a new concept that developed into MultiChoice, which developed and now provides pay television to 50 African countries.

Through corporate entrepreneurship, in the form of Mr Bekker, who is a true corporate entrepreneur, another new and diversified product was added, namely cellular phones when MTN was established.

MWeb, an Internet company was also launched through corporate entrepreneurship by Naspers.

Critical thinking

We may now ask "What exactly does corporate entrepreneurship mean?" The following is an example:

The advantages of corporate entrepreneurship: The Naspers example

Mr Koos Bekker, currently CEO of Naspers, and two friends approached Ton Vosloo, chairman of Naspers, a publishing company, in the mid 1980s to determine whether he would be interested in the concept of pay television. It was at the time of the start of pay television in America but television was still relatively new in South Africa. Eventually a consortium of all publishers of daily newspapers was established to finance M-Net, which was started in September 1986. Initially it was catastrophic as most knew nothing about television and nobody knew anything about business. The initial target market of M-Net, namely hotels and flat complexes, was not interested and neither were advertisers. Six months later the business was losing R3,5 million per month on a turnover of R500 000.

When decoders were introduced to single

houses it started to sell. Two years later the company started to break even and then it became profitable. M-Net then led to the establishment of various companies such as MultiChoice, which was born out of it in 1990 and today provides pay television channels to 50 African countries. Apart from pay television, MultiChoice also introduced the cellphone concept to South Africa. Mr Bekker and his team presented a business plan to the entire board of Telkom's predecessor, which saw it as ridiculous to hope that 300 000 people would buy cellphones. Nevertheless MultiChoice proceeded with the development of the project. After many delays the government and ANC decided that two licences would be granted: one to MultiChoice and its partners Nail and Transnet, and another to Telkom and associates (Vodacom). In retrospect, the figures of MultiChoice were just as limited as those of Telkom's. Today more than 20 million people own cellphones in SA.

MultiChoice also established M-Web when the role of Internet in the economy became clear.

Source: Naude, C., "Die begin is die lekkerste", *Finweek*, 9 November 2006, p. 70,
http://www.fin24.co.za/articles/print_article.asp?aricleid=_2025855 (22 February 2007).

Thus, from within a publishing business various other business opportunities were identified and established.

2.3.4 The feasibility of the idea or opportunity

Many small businesses result from an idea that has been converted into a useful application. Ideas have little value until they are converted into new products, services or processes. But, as was discussed in previous sections, not all ideas can be converted into feasible ventures. An idea must therefore be subjected to a feasibility test to prove that it has value. Aspiring entrepreneurs often find that the idea has already been developed or that competitors already exist. The same applies to opportunities that entrepreneurs may recognise. The entrepreneur should therefore also do a feasibility analysis of any apparent opportunity.

Buying an existing business or recognising a franchise opportunity does not necessarily mean that the new or existing venture will be an instant success. No matter how promising the idea or opportunity may appear, the entrepreneur should as soon as possible determine whether it is feasible. Doing a feasibility analysis in good time may prevent the entrepreneur from losing valuable resources on an idea or opportunity that in fact offers little hope of success.

A **feasibility study** is the collection of data that helps forecast whether an idea, opportunity or a venture will survive. The feasibility study gives the entrepreneur an information profile that should enable him or her to take a definite decision on whether or not to go ahead with the venture. A feasibility study is not the same as a **business plan**. It precedes the business plan and consists mainly of gathering data to enable the entrepreneur to take a decision on whether to go ahead with the idea, opportunity or new venture. Once the feasibility of an idea has been assessed, the

entrepreneur can commit to implementing the idea or abandon the idea altogether, depending on the outcome.

Upon deciding that an idea appears feasible, and therefore to proceed with it, the entrepreneur has then to decide how to make the idea work. In other words, the entrepreneur must now decide how to translate the idea into reality. This stage entails the drawing up of a business plan. Because of its importance to the entrepreneurial process, the business plan will be discussed more fully in the following chapter.

2.4 Summary

In this chapter both the concept of entrepreneurship and the idea that the entrepreneur is the driving force behind the business organisation were dealt with. The role of entrepreneurs in the economy was examined, as were the reasons for people becoming entrepreneurs. Following this, the various aspects and phases of the entrepreneurial process were examined, including an assessment of the entrepreneur's unique abilities and skills, access to resources, the search for opportunities, the feasibility study, and, finally, the business plan. The business plan will be dealt with in detail in chapter 3, as will the professional management of the new venture.

 Key terms

Achievement motivation	Life cycle stages
Business	Locus of control
Business plan	Managing a business
Capital	Marketing skills
Corporate entrepreneurship	Necessity entrepreneur
Creativity	Operating resources
Economic trends	Opportunities
Employment	Opportunity entrepreneur
Entrepreneur	Outsource
Entrepreneurial process	Physical resources

Experience	Planning skills
Feasibility	Project management skills
Financial resources	Resources
Financial skills	Risk orientation
Franchise	Skills
Growing a business	Small, medium and micro-enterprises (SMMEs)
Human relations skills	Social trends
Human resources	Starting a business
Innovation	Strategy skills
Intrapreneurship	Traits
Job creation	

? Questions for discussion

Reread the "Entrepreneurship in action" case study at the beginning of the chapter and answer the following questions:

1. What do you regard as the primary reasons for the success of Oasis? Give and discuss three reasons.
2. Do you think Mr Ebrahim was an entrepreneur or an owner of a small business after he started the business? Give reasons for your answer.
3. How do Mr Ebrahim and his company contribute to the economy of South Africa?
4. Do you think Mr Ebrahim is a necessity entrepreneur or an opportunity entrepreneur? Give reasons for your answer.
5. Why was Mr Ebrahim's business idea a good opportunity? Discuss and give reasons for your answer.

References

1. Maas, G. & Herrington, M., *Global Entrepreneurship Monitor, South African Report*, University of Cape Town, 2006, p. 15.
2. Maas, G. & Herrington, M., *Global Entrepreneurship Monitor, South African Report*, University of Cape Town, 2006, p. 14).
3. Statistics South Africa, *Labour Force Survey*, Statistical release P0210, March 2006.
4. Orford, J., Herrington, M. & Wood, E., *Global Entrepreneurship Monitor: South Executive African Report 2004*, University of Cape Town, Graduate School of Business, Centre for Innovation and Entrepreneurship, Cape Town, 2004, p. 25.
5. "National Small Business Amendment Act 26 of 2003", *Government Gazette*, Vol. 461, No. 25763, 26 November 2003.
6. McClelland, D.C., "Characteristics of successful entrepreneurs", *Journal of Creative Behavior*, Vol. 21, No. 3, 1986, pp. 219–233.
7. Maritz, P.A., Entrepreneurial service vision in a franchised home entertainment system, Unpublished DCom thesis (Business Management), University of Pretoria, 2005.
8. Johnson, D.M., "In the mainstream, multi-unit and multi-concept franchising", *Franchising World*, April 2004.
9. Franchise Advice and Information Network (FRAIN), *Franchise Census 2004*, CSIR, Pretoria, 2004.

THE ESTABLISHMENT OF A BUSINESS

The purpose of this chapter

This chapter focuses on the different forms of enterprise or legal ownership that are available to the entrepreneur. It covers the characteristics, advantages and disadvantages of the sole proprietorship, the partnership, the close corporation, the business trust and the company. Each of these forms is discussed in order to enable learners to compare them and make informed decisions. Once the entrepreneur knows what the available options are, he or she will be able draw up a business plan for the new business. The location factors are also discussed here.

Learning outcomes

The content of this chapter will enable learners to:
- Understand and discuss the key considerations that are applicable when a form of business has to be chosen
- Distinguish the different forms of enterprise found in South Africa
- Explain the objectives, importance and need for a business plan
- Evaluate a business plan
- Give an overview of a business plan
- Identify the location factors of a business

3.1 Introduction

This chapter will focus on the different enterprise forms that are available to the entrepreneur. It will explain the factors that should be taken into account in selecting the appropriate form of enterprise for a particular business. The characteristics of the sole proprietorship, the partnership, the close corporation, the company and the business trust will be explained and the relative advantages and disadvantages of

each will be highlighted. An entrepreneur who is aware of the various enterprise forms and their implications can make an informed decision regarding the structure of his or her business. A brief overview of the proposed amendments to the Companies Act 61 of 1973 is also included in section 3.2.10.

Once the entrepreneur knows what the available options are, he or she can put everything together by drawing up a business plan for the new business. This will also be discussed in this chapter. The location factors of a business will also briefly be discussed.

3.2 The legal form of ownership[1]

3.2.1 Introduction to the legal form of ownership

An entrepreneur can conduct business through various forms of enterprise. An enterprise is an organisational structure through which business is conducted. Several options are available to the entrepreneur, but there are also many issues that should be considered when deciding on the form of ownership. To what extent does the entrepreneur want to be liable for financial and legal risk? Who will have a controlling interest in the business? How will the business be financed?

It is clear that one of the first issues facing an entrepreneur about to enter the business world is choosing a form of enterprise. This decision can have a tremendous impact on almost every aspect of the business. As a business changes over time, a different form may become more appropriate. Knowledge of the different enterprise forms is thus also necessary in order to plan for the possible future expansion or transfer of a business.

Many factors influence the entrepreneur's decision about what form of enterprise to use for the businesses. Some considerations are the size of the business, the nature of the proposed business activities, the participation style, the management structure, the financing needs, the accountability of participants, and tax and legal implications. The key to choosing the "right" form of ownership is understanding how the characteristics of each enterprise will influence an entrepreneur's specific business and personal circumstances. A characteristic regarded as a decisive advantage in one business may be seen as a distinct disadvantage in another. Although, generally speaking,

Case study: Entrepreneurship in action

The importance of location

Thabang Molefi is a young up-and-coming entrepreneur from Soweto. Thabang used all the money she saved while working as a beauty therapist on a passenger liner to open a beauty spa in a township. Her Roots Health and Beauty Spa in Diepkloof was so successful that she decided to open another spa in Spruitview. The R190 000 that she won in the SAB Kickstart entrepreneurship competition provided the funding to open four more Roots Health and Beauty spas in other townships, four years after the first spa was opened in Diepkloof in 2002.

"One of the most important factors of a successful venture, particularly in my business, is a good location. I was very fortunate to have obtained such a position when I started. It is a lesson which I still remember," says Thabang.

As so many young entrepreneurs do, Thabang found it difficult to obtain financing from conventional sources and she admits that the prize money from the SAB Kickstart competition saved her business.

"It was impossible to obtain finance from anybody when I started because the business was considered to be too risky and unconventional," she says.

Today she has three investors, two with a share of 10% each and one with a 5% share, who provide in her financing needs.

Source: Finweek, 11 January 2007, p. 48.

there is no best form of enterprise, there may well be one form best suited to each entrepreneur's specific circumstances.

The characteristics of each of the enterprise forms will be explained with reference to a number of key considerations. These are independence, liability, control, compliance, taxation and transferability. These considerations will be explained below.

3.2.2 Considerations in choosing a form of enterprise

From a legal point of view the most important consideration is whether or not the enterprise has **legal personality**. A **juristic person** exists independently from its members. It is recognised as a legal subject alongside natural persons or individuals. It has its own rights, assets and obligations. As its existence is not affected by changes in its membership, it provides continuity and can potentially exist forever. The members are usually not liable for the debts or obligations of the juristic person. This feature is called **limited liability**, because the members stand to lose only the capital they have contributed to the entity. Although closely associated with separate legal personality, limited liability is not an automatic consequence of a juristic person. Companies and close corporations are juristic persons while sole proprietorships, partnerships and business trusts are not.

Critical thinking

In considering the case study at the start of this chapter, assume that Thabeng is married to an up-and-coming businessman, JJ, who owns two business properties in the CBD area of Johannesburg. The couple also own a house which is registered in JJ's name. They are married in community of property.

How will this information affect Thabeng's choice of the form of enterprise for her beauty spas?

The extent of the **liability of the business owner** is a very important consideration. Ideally an entrepreneur would like to insulate his or her personal assets from the business creditors so that he or she will not lose everything if the business is unsuccessful. The members of companies and close corporations are usually not liable for the debts of the enterprise. In contrast, sole proprietors and partners are liable in their personal capacities for the debts of the business. Although the parties to a trust are personally liable for trust debts, they effectively enjoy limited liability because their liability is restricted to the trust assets.

Another factor is the **degree of control or management authority** the entrepreneur will be able to exercise over the activities of the business. A broad range of options exists in this regard. At one end of the scale is the sole proprietor who enjoys total management autonomy with respect to the business he or she owns. At the other end of the scale is the company, characterised by a formal division between ownership and control. The participative management structures of partnerships and close corporations fall in between these two. Although a business trust is administered or managed by the trustee, the trust deed can apportion control between the trustee, the establisher of the business trust and trust beneficiaries.

The **potential for capital acquisition** is also relevant. Some businesses are extremely capital intensive and this factor may be decisive. In other businesses capital may be of lesser importance due to the business activities involved. A public company is ideally suited to the raising of large sums of capital. In other enterprise forms the capital is provided by a limited number of persons and their own financial positions are thus important. Factors such as the number of participants, their exposure to risk and their say in the management play a role in financing decisions.

Compliance with legal formalities and regulation can impose a considerable administrative and financial burden on an enterprise. The requirements for and the cost of the establishment, management and dissolution of each form of enterprise differ. Irrespective of the particular enterprise form adopted, a business can be subject to a multitude of other **legal and regulatory requirements** that often depend on size-related factors such as turnover and number of employees.

Taxation is also an important consideration. The rates for income tax, capital gains tax and transfer duty vary depending on the kind of taxpayer. Value added tax (VAT) is, however, neutral as to enterprise form. At the time of writing, companies and close corporations are taxed at a fixed rate of 29% on their taxable income, while secondary tax on companies (STC) is payable at a rate of 10% on the net dividend distributed to members. Individuals are taxed on a sliding scale, with the maximum marginal rate set at 40%. Business trusts are taxed at a flat rate of 40% on the income retained in the trust. Capital gains tax is charged on the net capital gain of a taxpayer in the tax year. In the case of natural persons, a primary exemption applies, after which 25% of the net capital gain is included in the taxable income of the individual and taxed at the normal rates. The inclusion rate for companies, close corporations and business trusts is 50% of the net capital gain. This included part will be taxed at the normal rates for companies, close corporations and trusts.

Transfer duty is levied at a flat rate of 8% on the value of fixed property acquired by companies, close corporations and trusts. Natural persons pay no transfer duty in respect of property up to a value of R500 000, thereafter 5% of the value between R500 000 and R1 million. On property above R1 million in value, natural persons pay R25 000 plus 8% of the value above R1 million.

Many factors will influence the total income tax burden of an enterprise and there is thus no single enterprise form that can be said to be the most advantageous from a tax perspective. The total income tax will depend on the amount of the taxable income (or loss) generated in the business (whether or not the enterprise is a separate taxpayer), the tax status and taxable income of the business owners and the extent of distributions made to them. It is sometimes said that double taxation arises with respect to companies and close corporations. Although it is true that income which has already been taxed in the hands of the company or close corporation is taxed again when it is distributed to members as dividends or payments, the effect is offset by the specific tax rates imposed on income and distributions respectively. The income of a sole proprietorship and a partnership is taxed in the hands of the sole proprietor or partners. The income retained in a business trust is taxed in the hands of the trustee as representative taxpayer while the beneficiaries are taxed on the income distributed to them during the tax year.

The ease with which the business or the entrepreneur's interest in the business can be **transferred** should also be considered when the most appropriate enterprise form is being selected. There may be many reasons why an entrepreneur may wish to, or have to, transfer his or her business or parts of it. Shares in public companies, especially if they are listed on an exchange, are very easily transferable and the most liquid form of investment in a business. In private companies, close corporations and partnerships, the transfer of an interest is dependent on the approval of the remaining members or partners. Beneficiaries of a business trust may transfer their rights in accordance with the trust deed.

In the paragraphs that follow we shall discuss the main characteristics of sole proprietorships, partnerships, close corporations, companies and business trusts in terms of these key considerations.

Critical thinking

Recall the case study at the start of this chapter. Taking tax considerations into account, which form of enterprise would you recommend as most suitable for Thabeng's Beauty Spas?

3.2.3 The sole proprietorship

The **sole proprietorship** is a business that is owned and managed by one individual. This is by far the most common type of business. It is a simple enterprise form that is very easy and inexpensive to set up.

A sole proprietorship does not have an independent **legal personality**. It cannot exist independently of the owner or proprietor. The **lifespan** of the business is linked to the lifespan or the **legal capacity** of the owner. (The owner's legal capacity is his or her capacity to act under the law, for example to enter into contracts.) If the owner dies, becomes insolvent, or otherwise legally incapable, this usually means the end of the business. If the business is discontinued, even temporarily, following the death or incapacity of the sole proprietor, it can be difficult for the heir or transferee to resume the business.

There is no legal separation of the personal and business assets of the owner. Practically it is preferable to keep separate books in respect of the business, but all the assets used in the business belong to the owner alone. Any profit of the business belongs to the owner in his or her personal capacity, even if it is kept in a separate business account or invested in business assets.

The owner does not enjoy any limitation of liability and could therefore lose all his or her personal possessions if the business is unable to meet its obligations. The owner is **personally liable** for all the debts and claims arising from the business operations. Personal creditors can claim against business assets and vice versa.

The owner has direct control and authority over the activities of the business. The owner usually manages the business and is free to take decisions concerning the running of the business. The business is therefore able to adjust readily to changes. However, a sole proprietorship can, depending on the circumstances, make exceptionally high demands on the management ability and personal freedom of the owner. The proprietor may delegate some or all management functions or decisions to employees or agents.

The **capital acquisition potential** of the sole proprietorship depends on the owner's financial strength and creditworthiness. The owner may already have sufficient assets or could rely on debt financing (loans). A sole proprietor may encounter difficulty in obtaining sufficient funds, especially when the business reaches a stage of expansion. Financiers often limit their risk by insisting on some measure of control or supervision over the business operations. The sole proprietor may thus have to relinquish authority and freedom in exchange for funding.

There are very few formalities and legal requirements for the establishment of a sole proprietorship. As a result, it is the least expensive enterprise form. Apart from the prescriptions of the Business Names Act 27 of 1960, there are no particular legal requirements for the establishment, management or dissolution of a sole proprietorship.

As far as **tax liability** is concerned, we have already mentioned that the entire income of the business belongs to the owner even if the income is kept in the business. Accordingly, the income is taxable in the hands of the owner as an individual taxpayer. Depending on the owner's taxable income and the tax rates at any given time, the sole proprietorship can therefore be an advantage or disadvantage compared to other enterprises. If the business operations resulted in a loss, this can be set off against other income of the proprietor, thus reducing the total taxable income.

The **transfer of ownership** of a sole

proprietorship is fairly simple from a legal perspective. The owner can decide at any time to sell the business, to close down, or to transfer the business or assets to someone else. However, it may be a problem to find a buyer. The business may be so closely associated with the personality of the proprietor that it may be difficult to place a value on the goodwill of the business. In some instances the proprietor or executor may have to sell the business assets individually at a price that compares very unfavourably to the value of the business as a going concern.

A sole proprietorship offers the following **advantages**:

- It is simple to create.
- It is the least expensive way of beginning a business.
- The owner has total decision-making authority.
- There are no special legal restrictions.
- It is easy to discontinue.

The **disadvantages** of a sole proprietorship are the following:

- The owner is personally liable without limitation.
- Limited diversity in skills and capabilities is available.
- The owner has limited access to capital.
- There is lack of continuity.

In the course of time, it has become evident that if two or more sole owners join forces, they are able to bring about a stronger unit, because their combined financial and other resources are then at their disposal. This has led to the development of the partnership as another form of business available to the entrepreneur. The partnership is possibly one of the oldest commercial institutions known to humankind. We shall discuss the partnership in the next section.

3.2.4 The partnership

In many respects, a **partnership** is similar to a sole proprietorship, and many of the disadvantages of the sole proprietorship apply to partnerships as well. The partnership may be described as a contractual relationship between 2 or more – but usually not more than 20 – persons (called partners) who operate a lawful business with the object of making a profit. Partners may be natural or juristic persons. Each partner has to contribute something to the partnership, the partnership must be carried on for the joint benefit of the partners, and each partner should have the expectation of sharing in the profit. The partners have to act in good faith towards each other.

A partnership does not have a **legal personality**, and it is the partners in their personal capacity, rather than the partnership as such, who jointly enter into all transactions or contracts. The assets contributed to or accumulated by the partnership belong to all the partners jointly as co-owners. The partners are also **jointly liable** for all the partnership debts. Although a partnership is not a juristic person, the law nevertheless regards a partnership as an entity for certain limited purposes:

- Firstly, the partners may institute legal proceedings in the name of the partnership rather than all the partners jointly. The partners may also be sued in the name of the partnership, for example "Du Buisson and partners" or "Smith and Brown Financial Advisers".
- Secondly, the law treats the partnership estate as a separate estate for purposes of sequestration. Although the estates of the partners will also be sequestrated when the partnership estate is sequestrated, the partnership creditors will have to prove their claims in the partnership estate and not against the estates of the individual partners.

The continued existence of a partnership depends on the continued involvement of the partners. Whenever there is any change in the membership of the partnership, for example through the death or withdrawal of a partner or the admission of a new partner, the partnership dissolves automatically. However, the remaining partners can form a new partnership and, in most cases, a partnership agreement will provide for the "continuing" of a partnership between the partners.

During the existence of the partnership the partners are **jointly liable** for all claims against the partnership, regardless of who was responsible for bringing about the claim. A creditor must either sue all the partners jointly or sue in the name of the partnership. If the partnership assets are insufficient to meet the claim of the creditor, the partners are liable for the debt out of their personal estates. The personal possessions of the partners are therefore not protected against any claim. Once a partnership has been dissolved, the partners are jointly and severally liable for partnership debts. This means that a creditor can recover the full debt from one partner only, leaving it to the partner to claim the necessary proportionate contributions from his co-partners.

The partners have **joint control and authority** over the business. The partners can, however, adjust the control and authority aspect in their partnership agreement, for example by excluding one or more partners from representing or managing the partnership. But even if the partnership agreement excludes a partner from participating in the management of the partnership, the partnership may still be bound to contracts concluded on its behalf by such an excluded partner, provided the contract falls within the scope of the partnership business. Such a partner will, however, be in breach of his fiduciary duty to his co-partners. The joint management of the partnership can lead to problems if the partners have different opinions, and in this respect the partnership is less adaptable to changing circumstances than is the sole proprietorship. However, the partnership's broader authority can mean improved management ability, because the

business draws on the knowledge, experience and expertise of a greater number of people. It also allows for division of labour and specialisation, with the additional advantage that individual partners are exposed to less pressure than a sole proprietor is.

A partnership usually has better **capital acquisition potential** than a sole proprietorship because there are more people who can contribute and who can provide security for credit. It is a requirement for a valid partnership that each partner must make an initial contribution to the partnership. A contribution can consist of anything that has a monetary value, for example money, property, services, knowledge or skill. If the partnership contract does not specify how the profits will be divided, the division will be done in proportion to the value of each partner's contribution.

There are no formal requirements for setting up a partnership. A partnership is established by contract. A partnership contract may be concluded orally, in writing or, even, tacitly (that is, through certain behaviour). However it is customary and preferable for the contract to be in writing. The contract makes provision for matters such as the nature and goals of the business, capital contributions by individual partners, profit sharing, management and dissolution.

A partnership is **not a taxpayer**. Since the partnership income belongs to all the partners jointly in specific proportions, each partner is taxed on his or her share of the income. The partners also deduct the partnership expenses in the same proportion as the income. The income tax payable on each partner's share of the partnership income will depend on his or her tax status and other income.

In general, **transfer of ownership** is more complicated in partnerships than in sole proprietorships because more people are involved and because the stipulations or provisions of the partnership contract have to be complied with. However, it can be easier for a partner to sell his or her interest in a partnership than it is to sell a sole pro-prietorship. One reason for this is that the remaining partners may buy the partner out. Often partners take out life insurance policies that will enable the remaining partners to acquire a deceased partner's interest. Some entrepreneurs may also prefer to buy an interest in a business rather than buy a whole business.

To summarise, the partnership offers the following advantages:

- Ease of formation
- Diversification of skills and abilities of partners
- Increased opportunity for accumulation of capital
- Minimal legal formalities and regulation

The partnership has the following disad-vantages:

- The personal liability of partners
- The relative difficulty in disposing of an interest in the partnership
- The potential for conflict between partners
- Lack of continuity (can be overcome by agreement)

3.2.5 The close corporation

A **close corporation** has characteristics of both a partnership and a company and has the advantage of being a **legal person** that exists separately from its members. A close cor-poration may have one or more members, but not more than ten. Juristic persons may not be members of a close corporation, except in certain very limited circumstances, specified in the Act, where they may be members in an official representative capacity. The core characteristic of the close corporation is that it is "closed" in the sense that the members both own and control the close corporation. The interest of a member is expressed as a percentage, and the total interest of members must always amount to 100%. The **name** of a close corporation must end with the abbreviation CC or its equivalent in any other official language of the Republic of South Africa.

As a **juristic person**, a close corporation has its own rights, assets and liabilities. A close corporation has the capacity and powers of a natural person of full capacity in so far as this may apply to a juristic person. A close corpo-ration is thus even entitled to certain funda-mental rights set out in the Constitution. Because the close corporation has legal perso-nality, its continued existence is not influenced by the withdrawal or entry of members.

The members of a close corporation are **generally not liable** for the debts and liabilities of the close corporation. Their personal assets are thus not at risk of being lost in the business. However, the Close Corporations Act 69 of 1984 imposes **personal liability** on members for cer-tain violations of its provisions. Personal liabi-lity is also imposed for carrying on the business of the corporation recklessly, fraudulently or with gross negligence, or for abusing the juristic personality of the corporation.

The members share the management and control of a close corporation on an equal basis. The Act regulates the internal operation of the close corporation and further provides that certain persons, such as minors or insolvents, may not participate in the management of a close corporation. Decisions are generally taken by majority vote, but in some specific instances a majority of 75% or, even, the consent of all the members is required.

If the corporation has two or more members, they may enter into an **association agreement** that alters certain aspects of the internal functioning of the corporation. An association agreement may, for example, provide that only certain members will manage the corporation or that authority will depend on the percentage of each member's interest. In relation to contracts concluded with non-members of the close corporation, every member is regarded as an agent who is able to bind the close corporation to contracts, regardless of whether or not such contracts fall within the scope of business of the corporation.

The close corporation will not be bound, however, if the non-member knew or should reasonably have known that the member did not have the authority to represent the corporation. This arrangement protects third parties contracting with the corporation, but it exposes the members of the corporation to risk. Although the member who acted without authority will be liable to the corporation, the corporation will still be bound to the contract. It is thus important that members are carefully selected. Members of a close corporation have a **fiduciary relationship** with the corporation, which means that they are expected to carry out their duties honestly and in good faith and not to exceed their powers.

The **capital acquisition potential** of a close corporation is higher than that of a partnership mainly because members may be more inclined to contribute to a corporation knowing that they do not stand to lose more than what they have invested. Each person who becomes a member of a close corporation must make a contribution of money or property. When a close corporation is first formed, a contribution may also consist of services in connection with the formation of the corporation. Services are not an acceptable contribution for a new member joining an existing corporation. The members' contributions and their interest in the corporation need not be in direct proportion to one another. Two members who have contributed the same amount of money to a corporation may, for instance, agree that one of them will hold a 60% member's interest and the other one 40%. A close corporation can also use loan capital and members are often required to bind themselves as sureties for credit incurred by the corporation. Although this in effect removes the advantage of limited liability, it enables the corporation to obtain increased funding.

A close corporation may not make any payments to members in their capacity as members (for example profit distribution or repayment of contributions) unless the solvency and liquidity tests are satisfied.

- The **solvency test** means that after payment the corporation's assets must still exceed its liabilities, based on a reasonable valuation.
- A corporation meets the **liquidity test** if, after the payment, it will still be able to pay its debts as they become payable in the ordinary course of business.

Close corporations are regulated by the Close Corporations Act 69 of 1984. The legal prescriptions with which the members of a close corporation must comply are not strict, and the corporation can be registered at very little cost. A close corporation is created by the registration of a **founding statement**, which contains details such as the proposed name of the corporation, the nature of the business, and the personal details of members and their interests in the corporation. The founding statement can be compared with the memorandum of association of a company. Although a founding statement is registered, it is not open for public inspection and nobody is considered as knowing its contents.

Unlike a company, a close corporation is not expected to appoint an auditor, but it does have to appoint an accounting officer. Financial statements must be drawn up within nine months of the corporation's year end, and must be approved and signed by all the members or on their behalf.

A close corporation is a **separate taxpayer**. For purposes of the Income Tax Act close corporations are treated as companies and the distributions they make to their members are regarded as dividends. The taxable income of a close corporation is therefore taxed at a fixed rate. STC is payable on the net "dividend" distributed to members. The total income tax payable by the corporation and by the members on the profits generated by the corporation will thus be influenced by the extent to which income is retained in the close corporation or distributed to members. This flexibility can be used to the advantage of members.

The member's interest can be **transferred** to another individual who will then become a member of the corporation. New members can also acquire a members' interest directly from the corporation by making a contribution, followed by an adjustment to the percentages held by the other members. A member may also sell his or her member's interest to the corporation if the corporation satisfies the solvency and liquidity criteria. In such a case the relative percentages of the remaining members will also be adjusted. Transfers or acquisitions of members' interests must be in accordance with the **association agreement** or, if there is no such agreement, with the approval of all the members of the corporation. A transfer of member's interest does not affect the existence of the corporation. A member's interest is thus more easily transferable than a partnership interest. Unrestricted transferability is, however, limited by the "closed" nature of a close corporation.

The advantages of a close corporation are the following:
- The relative ease of formation
- The limited liability of the members
- Increased capital acquisition potential
- Continuity

A close corporation has the following disadvantages:
- Membership is limited to ten.
- Juristic persons may not be members.

3.2.6 The company

The **company** developed to meet business-people's need to obtain more capital than they could through a sole proprietorship or partnership, and also because the partnership still had certain deficiencies and undesirable features as a form of business. People eventually came to accept the idea that, from a legal point of view, there could be a fictitious person having rights and duties, being able to participate in commercial life, and whose existence would not depend upon the life of a natural person or persons. Businesspeople could obtain large sums of money through

such a separate legal entity, so that they could undertake commercial ventures that individuals could not afford, to the benefit of the entire community.

The company is characterised by the separation of ownership and control. This means that a formal distinction is made between the owners or members and the managers or directors.

The Companies Act provides for the incorporation of two types of companies, namely:
- Companies with a **share capital**
- Companies **limited by guarantee**

An incorporated association not for gain, or a section 21 company as it is commonly known, is a type of company limited by guarantee. The members of a company limited by guarantee agree to contribute a specific amount if the company is liquidated. Such companies are not often used for carrying on a business. The most common type of company is the company having a share capital and our discussion will be restricted to this type. A company with a share capital can be either a **public company** or a **private company**.

A company is a **juristic person** and thus has its own rights, assets and liabilities. A company exists independently from its members or shareholders and has the potential for perpetual existence. The personal possessions of the shareholders are thus not involved when claims are instituted or made against a company. Unlike a close corporation, which has unlimited capacity and powers, a company exists only for the purpose for which it is formed, as determined by the main object set out in the **memorandum of association**. However, it has become practice to formulate the main object very widely so that capacity does not present a problem.

The shareholders and directors are **not personally liable** for the debts of the company. The shareholders enjoy limited liability as they stand to lose only the consideration they paid in exchange for their shares. In exceptional circumstances the directors and controlling shareholders may be held personally liable for debts of the company if the juristic personality of the company has been abused or if the company's business has been conducted recklessly.

As has been stated, a distinction is made between **ownership** and **control**. A company has two organs:

- **The general meeting of members.** The general meeting makes broad policy decisions and exercises control over the company's affairs through its right to appoint and remove directors and to amend the company's articles of association, which govern the internal operation of the company. The voting rights of shareholders are linked to the number of shares they hold in the company, and decisions at meetings are normally taken by means of a vote.
- **The board of directors.** The Act entrusts the administration of the company to its directors. The precise division of powers between the board of directors and the general meeting is determined by the articles of association. The day-to-day management of the company is usually delegated to the board of directors. Directors are usually appointed by the general meeting, and their functions and powers are defined in the articles of association. These functions are jointly exercised by the directors (as the board of directors) by means of a majority vote. The board can, if it is empowered to do so by the articles of association or the general meeting, delegate some of its functions and powers to a managing director.

The structure of a company facilitates the appointment of specialised managers with diverse areas of expertise and experience. This is usually an advantage, but there is always a risk of decision making being delayed due to differences of opinion.

A company's capital is made up of share capital, representing the consideration the company receives in exchange for the shares it issues, as well as accumulated funds and loan capital. As far as the **potential for capital acquisition** is concerned, the company, and particularly the public company, has a distinct advantage over the sole proprietorship, partnership and close corporation. This is because the general public can be invited to invest capital and acquire shares in a public company. The features of limited liability, free transferability of shares and the existence of specialised management all facilitate diversification of shareholders. The shares of public companies may further be listed on a stock exchange, which increases the ability to raise capital even further. The strict regulation of companies, coupled with compulsory financial disclosure, also makes financial institutions more willing to provide loan capital to a company than to other forms of enterprise. The capital acquisition potential of a company can be further enhanced if shareholders or directors are prepared to provide additional loan security in their personal capacities. This often happens in practice, especially in the case of private companies.

A shareholder's interest in the company is represented by the number of shares he or she holds in the company. Shareholders share in the profits of a company when a dividend is declared or a payment by virtue of shareholding authorised. Distributions by the company are subject to compliance with the criteria of solvency and liquidity.

A company is subject to many more **legal prescriptions** than the other forms of enterprise, which translates into increased costs as well.

Companies are **regulated** by the Companies Act 61 of 1973. The Securities Services Act of 36 of 2004 regulates aspects of listed companies. A company has to have a constitution, which has to be registered with the Registrar of Companies. The constitution is made up of two documents, namely the memorandum of association, which governs the external relationships of the company, and the articles of association, which govern the internal affairs of the company. These documents also contain the name, main objectives and internal management rules, among other things. Any person dealing with the company is presumed to be aware of the contents of these public documents.

A company has to comply with **requirements** concerning accounting records, financial reporting, auditing, minutes, registers of shareholders, annual returns, and so on.

A company is a **taxpayer**. It is taxed at a fixed percentage on its taxable income. STC is payable on the net dividend distributed by a company (STC is currently being phased out).

In public companies the **transfer of ownership** takes place through the unlimited and free transfer of shares. Ownership is transferred through the private sale of shares or, in the case of a listed company, through transactions on the stock exchange. The transfer of shares usually has no influence on the activities of the company, and the company therefore has an **unlimited lifespan**.

Shares in a private company are not freely transferable, and the method of transfer is laid down in the company's articles of association. Transfer is usually subject to the approval of the board of directors: a shareholder who wants to sell his or her shares therefore has to find a buyer who is acceptable to the board. In most instances a shareholder has to offer the shares to the remaining shareholders first in proportion to their existing shareholding and may transfer them to an outsider only if the other members are not prepared to acquire them at the same price. Despite these limitations the transfer of shares in a private company is also unlikely to influence its activities, or the continued existence of the business.

To summarise, the advantages of a company are:
- Limited liability
- The ability to raise large amounts of capital

- Separation of ownership and control
- Continuity
- Transferability of shares

The disadvantages are:
- A high degree of legal regulation
- High operation costs

3.2.7 Differences between the public company and the private company

The main differences between a private company and a public company are as follows:
- The number of members (**shareholders**) of a private company ranges from 1 person to 50 people. A public company must have at least seven members, but there is no maximum, provided the number of shares authorised in the memorandum at any given time is not exceeded.
- A private company must have at least one **director**, and a public company must have at least two directors.
- The articles of association of a private company must contain some restriction on the **transfer of its shares**. The shares in a public company are freely transferable.
- The **general public** cannot subscribe to the shares of a private company. Public companies may raise capital by issuing shares to the public. The public can be invited to buy shares in the company by means of a prospectus.
- The **name** of a private company must end with the words (Pty) Ltd or (Proprietary) Limited, for example Maxi Removals (Pty) Ltd. There is also another type of private company, the incorporated company or section 53(b) company, the name of which ends in the word Incorporated (Inc.), for example Andersons Incorporated. Certain professions allow their members to form this type of company instead of practising in a partnership. The members, who usually have to be directors as well, are jointly and

individually liable for the contractual debts of the company. The name of a public company must end in Ltd or Limited, for example Moroko Traders Limited.

- While both types of company are subject to a number of **legal regulations**, a private company is not as strictly controlled as a public company.

3.2.8 The business trust

The **business trust** is becoming an increasingly popular enterprise form. It developed out of the ordinary trust. A trust is established when the **founder** of the trust places assets under the control of a **trustee** to be administered for the benefit of the **beneficiaries**. The trust assets and the beneficiaries must be clearly identified. There is no limit on the number of beneficiaries, who may be natural or juristic persons. A business trust has the object of conducting a business for profit.

A trust is **not a juristic person**. The trustee owns the trust assets in an official representative capacity and is also **liable** for the debts of the trust in his or her capacity as trustee. However, since the trustee is liable only out of the trust assets and not in his or her personal capacity, the effect is similar to limited liability. A trust can be set up for any period of time and is thus capable of **perpetual existence**. The existence of a trust does not depend on the identity of the trustee or of the beneficiaries.

The management of a trust is in the hands of the trustees who have to exercise their duties in accordance with the trust deed and in good faith. The trust founders are able to exercise control over the trustees by their right to amend the trust deed. In a private business trust the same persons are usually founders, trustees and beneficiaries of the trust. This means the management structure is similar to that of a partnership.

The capital of a trust is provided by the trust founder or founders. A trust has limited **potential for capital acquisition**.

Loan capital may be obtainable, usually in exchange for security provided by the parties to the trust. The distribution of profits to members will usually be left to the discretion of the trustees, affording the parties maximum flexibility with regard to retention or distribution of funds.

It is easy and cheap to establish a trust. All that is required is a **trust deed** identifying the trust property, trustees and beneficiaries, and setting out the powers of the trustees. There is very little **regulation** of trusts compared with regulation of other enterprise forms. Trusts that take investments from the public, for example unit trusts, are, however, subject to specific regulation. The lack of regulation of trusts can be a disadvantage if the trust deed has not been formulated properly and if trustees are not selected carefully.

A trust is regarded as a **separate taxpayer**. The trustee is seen as a representative taxpayer. Income tax on trust income is allocated according to the **conduit principle**. Income that accrues to the beneficiaries is taxed in their hands while income retained in the trust is taxed in the hands of the trustee as representative taxpayer. Where the entitlement of beneficiaries to income is not predetermined in the trust deed but left to the discretion of the trustees, great flexibility in tax planning and structuring is possible. **Transfer of the interest** of a beneficiary can be achieved by a variation of the trust deed.

The **advantages** of a private business trust are the following:
- Ease of formation
- Limited liability
- Extreme flexibility
- Absence of legal regulation
- Continuity

The **disadvantages** of a business trust are:
- Limited access to capital
- Potential for conflict between parties

3.2.9 Other forms of enterprise

Various other enterprise forms are possible in South Africa, although the forms that have been discussed are the most common.

Cooperative societies should be mentioned briefly. Although some cooperatives are restricted to agriculture and farming activities, trading cooperatives can be used for various kinds of businesses. Cooperative societies are similar to private companies in many respects. The Cooperatives Act 91 of 1981 applies to cooperatives, but is to be replaced by the Cooperatives Act 14 of 2005, which has not yet been put into operation. Cooperatives attempt to achieve certain economic advantages for their members through joint action on the members' part. In South Africa cooperatives are found mainly in farming communities as organisations selling and/or supplying products or goods and services. Because of their distinctive features, cooperatives are not usually real alternatives to the forms of business we have mentioned.

Mention should also be made of **joint ventures**. "Joint venture" is a generic term designating some sort of cooperation between persons or businesses. It does not refer to a specific legal construction with unique consequences. In each instance the legal consequences will depend on the specific agreement between the parties. The term is most often used to denote a partnership between two or more companies, in which case ordinary partnership principles apply to the joint venture.

3.2.10 Law reform

Corporate law in South Africa is being reformed and the Companies Act 61 of 1973 will be replaced by new legislation. Although the reforms have not been finalised at the time of writing, some proposals have been published. All indications are that substantive changes will be introduced. It is not possible to deal with all the proposals, but some important aspects will be referred to:

- The distinction between public and private companies will be replaced by a distinction between **widely held** and **closely held** companies.
- For purposes of financial reporting, a distinction between **public interest** and **limited interest** companies will be introduced. Public interest companies, which will include all widely held companies and certain closely held companies, will be subjected to stringent financial disclosure measures, while the requirements for limited interest companies will be made less burdensome than the current position applicable to private companies.
- It will become easier to **register** a company.
- It is envisaged that close corporations may eventually be phased out if the **simplifications** introduced prove workable for smaller businesses.

It can be expected that the promulgation of the new legislation will be followed by a reasonable transitional period during which existing companies will be able to adapt to the new rules and procedures.

3.2.11 Summary of legal forms of ownership

Once entrepreneurs have identified their opportunity and evaluated it, they basically have three options for entering the business world (as discussed in chapter 2), namely:

- Entering into a franchise agreement
- Buying an existing business
- Establishing a business from scratch

In all these cases the entrepreneur's choice of a form of business is very important.

In choosing a form of enterprise, entrepreneurs must remember that there is no single "best" form of enterprise. Each form has its own advantages and disadvantages. An entrepreneur's choice must reflect his or her particular situation: there may be a business form that is best for the entrepreneur's individual circumstances. Understanding the forms of enterprise, and the characteristics, advantages and disadvantages of each one, is the entrepreneur's key to selecting the form of ownership that best suits him or her.

In this section we have discussed the different forms of enterprise available to the entrepreneur. We have compared the characteristics, advantages and disadvantages of the sole proprietorship, the partnership, the close corporation, the company and the business trust. Once the entrepreneur knows what the available options are, he or she can put everything together by drawing up the business plan for the new business.

3.3   Developing the business plan for the new business

In this section the development of the business plan for the new venture will be examined.

3.3.1   The objectives of a business plan

For the entrepreneur starting a new venture, a **business plan** is a written document that accomplishes certain basic objectives. The most important objective is to **identify** and **describe the nature** of the business opportunity or the new venture.

The second objective is to present a written plan of how the entrepreneur plans to **exploit the opportunity**. Here, the business plan explains the key variables for the success or failure of the new venture: it is a guideline to the things that must be done to establish and operate the new venture. It provides a large number of instruments – such as the mission, goals, objectives, target markets, operating budgets, financial needs, and so on – which the entrepreneur and managers can draw on to lead the venture successfully. These instruments, which help managers to keep the venture on track, constitute the key components of the

business plan. A business plan is therefore also a valuable managerial tool that helps the entrepreneur and his or her team to focus on charting a course for the new business.

A third objective of the business plan is to **attract investors**, or to persuade a bank or other institution or person who provides financial resources, to lend the entrepreneur the money he or she needs to establish the new business. Careful preparation can make the difference between success and failure when shopping in the capital market.

Apart from the above-mentioned main objectives, a business plan provides many other benefits, such as the following:

- Systematic, realistic evaluation of the new venture's chances of success in the market
- A way of identifying the key variables that will determine the success of the new venture, as well as the primary risks that may lead to failure
- A game plan for managing the business successfully
- A management instrument for comparing actual results against targeted performance
- A primary tool for attracting money in the hunt for financial resources

3.3.2   Importance and necessity of the business plan

The overall importance of the business plan lies in its planning activities. Planning is the fundamental element of management that predetermines what the business organisation proposes to accomplish, and how this is to be accomplished. Planning, and thus the idea of a business plan, is hardly something new. Big businesses have long been turning out annual business plans by the thousands, especially for marketing new products, buying new businesses or expanding globally. What is new, however, is the growing use of such plans by small entrepreneurs. These entrepreneurs are, in many cases, forced by financial institutions to draw up a business plan before any financial support will be considered.

The business plan is important not only to the entrepreneur, but also to his or her employees, potential investors, bankers, suppliers, customers, and so on. Each group of "stakeholders" in the business plan will study the plan from a different perspective. It is therefore clear that any business, but especially a new venture, needs to have a business plan to answer questions that various stakeholders in the venture may raise.

There are eight reasons for an entrepreneur to write a business plan:

- **To sell the business to him- or herself.** The most important stakeholders in any business are its founders. First and foremost, the entrepreneur needs to convince him- or herself that starting the business is right for him or her – from both a personal point of view and an investment viewpoint.
- **To obtain bank financing.** Up until the late 1980s, writing a business plan to obtain bank financing was an option left up to the entrepreneur. Bankers usually took the approach that a business plan helped the entrepreneur to make a better case, though it was not an essential component in the bank's decision-making process. However, banks now require entrepreneurs to include a written business plan with any request for loan funds. As a consequence, obtaining money from a bank is tougher than it has ever been, and a business plan is an essential component of any campaign to convince banks about a new business.
- **To obtain investment funds.** For many years now, the business plan has been the "ticket of admission" to venture capital or "informal" capital from private investors.
- **To arrange strategic alliances.** Joint research, marketing, and other efforts between small and large companies have become increasingly common in recent years, and these require a business plan.
- **To obtain large contracts.** When small companies seek substantial orders or ongoing service contracts from major corporations, the corporations often respond – perhaps somewhat arrogantly – as follows: "Everyone knows who we are. But no one knows who you are. How do we know you'll be around in three or five years to provide the parts or service we might require for our product?" For this reason entrepreneurs are required to have a business plan.
- **To attract key employees.** One of the biggest obstacles that small, growing companies face in attracting key employees is convincing the best people to take the necessary risk – that the company will thrive and grow during the coming years.
- **To complete mergers and acquisitions.** No matter which side of the merger process the entrepreneur is on, a business plan can be very helpful if he or she wants to sell the company to a large corporation.
- **To motivate and focus the management team.** As smaller companies grow and become more complex, a business plan becomes an important component in keeping everyone focused on the same goals.

3.3.3 Stakeholders in a business plan

There are internal as well as external stakeholders. Each category is discussed in the sections that follow.

3.3.3.1 Internal stakeholders

(a) New venture management

A written business plan is essential for the systematic coverage of all the important features of a new business. It becomes a manual to the entrepreneur and his or her management team for establishing and operating the venture. The following are of primary importance to the entrepreneur and his or her team:

- The vision that the entrepreneur has for the new business
- The mission that defines the business
- An overview of the key objectives (this is derived from the mission statement)
- A clear understanding of the overall strategy

to accomplish the objectives, as well as a clear understanding of the functional strategies (marketing strategy, financial strategy, human resource strategy, etc.), which form substantial parts of the business plan.

(b) Employees

From the employees' point of view, there is also a need for a business plan. More specifically, employees also need to have a clear understanding of the venture's mission and objectives to be able to work towards attaining the objectives. A business plan also serves to improve communication between employees and to establish a corporate culture. A well-prepared plan provides employees with a focus for activities. The business plan also helps prospective employees to understand the emerging culture of a young business. It is important that managers and employees contribute to the development of the business plan to establish "ownership" of the plan among them.

Critical thinking

Consider the case study at the start of this chapter. Who are the internal stakeholders in Thabang Molefi's Roots Health and Beauty Spa?

3.3.3.2 External stakeholders

The business plan is even more important to outsiders, on whom the entrepreneur depends for the survival and success of the venture. Indeed, the importance of the business plan may be said to revolve around "selling" the new business to outsiders, who may include the customers, investors and banks.

(a) Customers

When small businesses seek substantial orders or ongoing service contracts, major customers always want assurance that the business will still be around in three or five years' time to provide the parts or service they as customers might require for the product. Customers are almost always impressed by a business plan, since it proves to them that the entrepreneur has thought about the future.

(b) Investors

Almost everyone starting a business faces the task of raising financial resources to supplement their own resources (personal savings, investment in shares or property, etc.). And unless the entrepreneur has a wealthy relative who will supply funds, he or she will have to appeal to investors or bankers to obtain the necessary funds. Very few investors or financial institutions will consider financial assistance without a well-prepared business plan.

Investors have a different interest in the business plan to the interest of other stakeholders, and if the entrepreneur intends to use the business plan to raise capital, he or she must understand the investor's basic perspective. A prospective investor has a single goal: to earn a return on the investment, while at the same time minimising risk. While many factors may stimulate an investor's interest in the venture, certain basic elements of a business plan attract (or repel) prospective investor interest more than others.

The matrix in figure 3.1 presents an evaluation of business plans from the investor's point of view. Certain basic indicators only have been included.

(c) Banks

Banks are a common source of debt capital for small businesses. To improve the chance of obtaining bank loans or what is known in South Africa as "overdraft facilities", the entrepreneur should know what it is that banks look for in evaluating an application for such a loan. Most banks look at the four Cs by which an application for a loan is evaluated, namely capital, collateral, character and conditions.

- **Capital.** A small business must have a stable equity base of its own before a bank will grant a loan. The bank expects the small business to have an equity base of

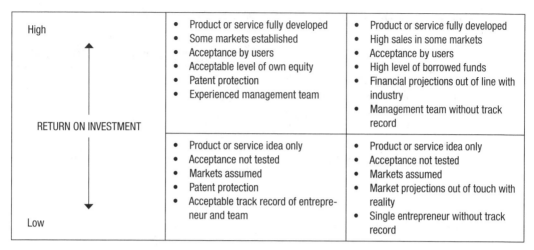

High	• Product or service fully developed • Some markets established • Acceptance by users • Acceptable level of own equity • Patent protection • Experienced management team	• Product or service fully developed • High sales in some markets • Acceptance by users • High level of borrowed funds • Financial projections out of line with industry • Management team without track record
RETURN ON INVESTMENT		
Low	• Product or service idea only • Acceptance not tested • Markets assumed • Patent protection • Acceptable track record of entrepreneur and team	• Product or service idea only • Acceptance not tested • Markets assumed • Market projections out of touch with reality • Single entrepreneur without track record

Figure 3.1: Matrix for the evaluation of business plans

investment by the owner(s) before it will make a loan. South African banks generally insist on at least 50% equity.

- **Collateral.** This includes any assets the owner pledges to a bank as security for repayment of the loan. Bankers view the owner's willingness to pledge collateral (personal or business assets) as an indication of the entrepreneur's dedication to making the venture a success.
- **Character.** Aspects of the owner's character – such as honesty, competence, determination, ability and a good track record – play a critical role in the bank's decision to grant a loan.
- **Conditions.** The conditions surrounding a loan request also affect the bank's decision. Banks will consider factors relating to the business operation, such as potential market growth, competition and form of ownership, as well as the current state of the economy.

3.3.4 The scope of the business plan: How much planning is needed?

The level of commitment to the writing of a business plan varies greatly among entrepreneurs. Once the preparation of the business plan is under way, the question remains as to the level of effort to be given to the plan. Should it be 1 page or 100 pages long? Considerations that determine the amount of planning include the following:

- Style and ability
- The preferences of the management team
- The complexity of the product or service and of the business
- The competitive environment
- The level of uncertainty

The depth and detail in the business plan therefore depend on the size and scope of the proposed new venture. An entrepreneur planning to market a new portable computer nationally will need a comprehensive business plan, largely because of the nature of the product and the market pursued. In contrast, an entrepreneur who wants to manufacture burglar bars and steel gates for the local market will not need such a comprehensive plan. The difference in the scope of the business plan may depend on whether the new venture is a service, involves manufacturing, or is an industrial product or consumer goods. The size of the market, competition, and many other environmental factors may also affect the scope of the business plan.

3.3.5 Components of the business plan

While it is important that the primary components of a solid business plan be outlined, every small entrepreneur must recognise that such a plan should be tailor-made, emphasising the particular strengths of the new venture. Two issues are of primary concern when preparing the business plan, namely:

- The basic format of the written presentation
- The content or components of the business plan

3.3.5.1 The format of the business plan

The first question that comes to mind in writing the business plan is "Who should write the plan?" Many small business managers employ the professional assistance of accountants, attorneys and marketing consultants. However, experts agree that the entrepreneur may consult professionals, but should in the end write the plan him- or herself. To help determine whether or not to use a consultant, the entrepreneur may use a table like table 3.1 to make an objective assessment of his or her own skills.

Through such an assessment the entrepreneur can identify what skills are needed and who should be consulted to help prepare the business plan.

There are no rigid rules regarding the format of the business plan. However, whatever format is eventually decided on, it should at all times be of a good appearance.

The length of the business plan will depend on the venture, but it can vary from 5 to 20 pages, excluding annexures and substantiating documents.

3.3.5.2 The content of the business plan

As has already mentioned, the business plan for each venture is unique. Although

Table 3.1: Skills assessment for writing a business plan

Skills	Excellent	Good	Fair	Poor
Planning				
Market research				
Forecasting sales				
Accounting charges				
Operational issues				
Labour law				
Management issues				
Product design				
Legal issues				

no single standard list of business plan components exists, there is considerable agreement as to what the content of the business plan should be. The following are the most important components of the business plan:

- The executive summary
- The general description of the venture
- The products and services plan
- The marketing plan
- The management plan
- The operating plan
- The financial plan
- The supporting materials

By now it may be assumed that the value of a business plan is understood and the entrepreneur is ready to prepare one.

Apart from the fact that the business plan begins with the cover page, the huge amount of information that has been collected makes it difficult to decide what to include under the headings of the various business plan components listed above. The beginner needs a conceptual scheme to identify the important segments of a good business plan. Table 3.2 on the next page provides an overview of such a plan.

Table 3.3 on the next page provides a more detailed outline for each section of a good business plan. Once each of these phases has been completed by the entrepreneur, he or she will have a simple but complete draft of a business plan.

In developing a comprehensive plan, the simple plan will be supplemented by an exhaustive set of questions that should be considered. The examination and consideration of each component of the comprehensive business plan will be discussed in more detail below.

Critical thinking

Consider once again the case study at the start of this chapter. Given the nature of the business of Roots Health and Beauty Spa, which component of the business plan should Thabeng pay the most attention to when preparing a business plan?

3.3.6 Description of a new venture

With the introductory concepts of the business plan as well as an outline of the main components behind us, it may be said that step 1 of the business plan has been completed. More specifically, step 1 included an overview of the cover page and the preparation of the executive summary as well as the outline of the business plan.

Step 2 concerns a description of the venture – this is dealt with in this section. This step is actually an extension of the feasibility analysis discussed in chapter 2. The entrepreneur analyses the entrepreneurial environment to assess the new idea or venture as well as the factors that might improve his or her chances of success and factors that could work negatively against the proposed venture. This analysis of the environment assists the entrepreneur in taking a rational

decision about whether to implement the idea or abandon it. If the entrepreneur decides to implement the idea, he or she must describe it in detail and prepare a business plan for the new idea or venture.

3.3.6.1 A general description of the new venture

Bearing in mind the needs and requirements of banks and investors for a successful business plan, namely that it should not be too long and that it should be concise and accurate, a brief but accurate description of the new venture is necessary.

The body of the business plan begins with a brief description of the new venture itself. If the business is already in existence, its history is included. By examining this section, the reader will know, for example, whether the business is engaged in tourism, retailing, construction, or some other line of business, and also where the business is located and whether it serves a local or an international market. In many cases, issues noted in the legal plan – especially the form of organisation – are incorporated into this section of the plan. Some important questions to be addressed in this section of the plan may include the following:

- Is this a start-up, buyout, or expansion?
- Has this business begun operation?
- What is the firm's mission statement?
- Where was this business started?
- What are the basic nature and activity of the business?
- What is its primary product or service?
- What customers are served?
- Is this business in manufacturing, retailing, service, or another type of industry?
- What are the current and projected states of this industry?
- What is the business's stage of development? For example, has it begun operations? Is it producing a full product line?
- What are its objectives?
- What is the history of this company?

Table 3.2: Overview of a business plan

Executive summary	A one- to three-page overview of the total business plan. Written after the other sections are completed, it highlights their significant points and, ideally, creates enough excitement to motivate the reader to read on.
General company description	Explains the type of company and gives its history if it already exists. Tells whether it is a manufacturing, retail, service, or other type of business. Shows the type of legal organisation.
Products and services plan	Describes the product and/or service and points out any unique features. Explains why people will buy the product or service.
Marketing plan	Shows who will be your customer and what type of competition you will face. Outlines your marketing strategy and specifies what will give you a competitive edge.
Management plan	Identifies the "key players" – the active investors, management team, and directors. Cites the experience and competence they possess.
Operating plan	Explains the type of manufacturing or operating system you will use. Describes the facilities, labour, raw materials, and processing requirements.
Financial plan	Specifies financial needs and contemplated sources of financing. Presents projections of revenues, costs and profits.

Table 3.3: Outline of a simple business plan

General company description	Name and location Nature and primary product or service of the business Current status (startup, buyout, or expansion) and history (if applicable) Legal form of organisation
Products and/or services	Description of products and/or services Superior features of advantages relative to competing products or services Any available legal protection – patents, copyrights, trademarks Dangers of technical or style obsolescence
Marketing plan	Analysis of target market and profile of target customer How customers will be identified and attracted Selling approach, type of sales force, and distribution channels Types of sales promotions and advertising Credit and pricing policies
Management plan	Management-team members and their qualifications Other investors and/or directors and their qualifications Outside resource people and their qualifications Plans for recruiting and training employees
Operating plan	Operating or manufacturing methods used to produce the product or service Description of operating facilities (location, space, equipment) Quality-control methods to be used Procedures used to control inventory and operations Sources of supply and purchasing procedures
Financial plan	Revenue projections for three years Expense projections for three years Necessary financial resources Sources of financing

- What achievements have been made to date?
- What changes have been made in the structure or ownership of the existing business?
- What is the firm's distinctive competence?

Again, there are no fixed issues that should be considered in the general description of the new venture. Some entrepreneurs may emphasise a successful history, while others may concentrate on the new venture's competitive advantage. The following, which is a sample of a general description based on a business called Calabash Guided Tours and Transfers, highlights four cri-

tical aspects that should be included in the general description.

3.3.7 Analysing the market

Certain activities that form the basis of the business plan take place simultaneously. Strictly speaking, the description of the new venture's strategy can be finalised only once the entrepreneur has completed a market analysis to find out if a market for the product exists and, if so, how he or she will exploit the market. In other words, once the entrepreneur is convinced that there is good market potential in a particular segment of the market, he or she will have to work out

---

Description of Calabash Guided Tours and Transfers

Name and location of the new venture
Calabash Guided Tours and Transfers is a proposed extension of a successful existing small venture called Tswane Airport Shuttle. Tshwane Airport Shuttle has been operating for three years, transferring mainly tourists from Johannesburg International Airport to Pretoria and back. It now wants to expand into guided tours for tourists. Calabash Guided Tours and Transfers will be a partnership between Mthombeni Mahlangu and Jacques du Toit. They can both be contacted at 444 Nicolson Street, Brooklyn, Pretoria, 0181, which is also the existing premises of Tswane Airport Shuttle. Tel. (012) 444-4444.

Nature and primary product or service of the business
During the past twelve months the two partners have studied trends in the transfer and transportation of tourists in mainly the Gauteng area of South Africa. They have identified a strong need by tourists for "safe" transfers, safe day-trips and longer tours in a crime-ridden South Africa, where tourists have come to be included in robbery and

murder statistics. Because of their three years of experience in transferring tourists and businesspeople from OR Thambo International Airport to Pretoria, offering guided transfers, trips and tours will form a natural extension of their existing small business. They expect to fully satisfy their customers by providing a safe and quality guided tour service in the upmarket segments of the tourism industry in Gauteng.

Current status
The new business, Calabash Guided Tours and Transfers, will be started at the beginning of the new year, assuming that adequate funding will be found in the next four months.

Legal form of organisation
The new business will begin operation as a partnership between Mthombeni Mahlangu and Jacques du Toit. Both partners agree to entering into a formal partnership agreement based on a 50–50 decision concerning workload, profits and responsibilities, and how the new venture is funded. Should the source of funding necessitate a close corporation or a limited company, the two persons also agree to restructure the legal form of the new venture to accommodate any requirements a bank or private investor may have.

how the product will reach the market and what marketing strategy to adopt.

Entrepreneurs often run the risk of becoming infatuated with their product or service and consequently they simply believe or hope that there is a market for their product. This euphoria can be very costly, if not devastating, to the new venture with its limited resources. The analysis of the new venture's market and the development of a marketing strategy involve the following key items:

• Concepts
• The identification of a target market
• Research and forecasting in the target market
• A marketing plan or strategy for the selected market segment(s)

Chapters 13 to 15 deal with these aspects in detail.

3.3.8 Determining the financial needs of the new venture

The entrepreneur or potential investors need answers to certain crucial financial questions to determine whether the new venture is not only attractive, but also feasible. The financial analysis constitutes a further crucial component of the business plan. The entrepreneur's projections of a new venture's profits, its required assets, and its financial requirements over the next one to five years should be supported by substantiated assumptions and explanations regarding how the costs, profits, and financial requirements are determined. In order to make the necessary financial projections, the entrepreneur must first have a good understanding of financial statements and how to interpret them.

The key issues in this section are therefore:

• An understanding of how financial statements work
• An understanding of how profitability is assessed
• An ability to determine a venture's financial requirements

Chapters 17 to 19 deal with these aspects in detail.

3.4 The location of the business

3.4.1 The choice of location

The choice of geographical location for premises is of extreme importance for all kinds of businesses, although for some it may be more important than for others. For certain businesses, location may be a crucial factor. Depending on the nature of the proposed product or service to be offered, the entrepreneur should decide, for example, whether the business needs to be located either near its market, near its sources of raw materials, near to other competitors, in the city centre, in the suburbs, in a rural area, in existing industrial areas, or according to personal preference.

The location factors that have to be considered when making this choice are briefly analysed in section 3.4.2.[2]

3.4.2 Location factors

The most important **location factors** are the following:

• **Sources of raw materials.** Where, in what quantity and of what quality, and at what prices, can these materials be obtained?
• **Availability of labour.** Where, and at what cost, is the required labour available in terms of, for example, quantities, levels of training, development potential and productivity?
• **Proximity of, and access to, the market.** This includes aspects such as the potential advantages over present competitors; the current extent and potential development of the market; the perishability of products; the needs of consumers and users regarding, for example, delivery, after-sales services and personal contact; and the possible entry of competitors into the market.

- **Availability and cost of transport facilities.** This includes aspects such as the availability of rail, air, road, and water transport facilities; the transport costs of raw materials in relation to finished products; and the possibility of using one's own transport (road links and limitations on private transport).
- **Availability and costs of power and water.** These must satisfy the needs of the prospective business.
- **Availability and costs of a site and buildings.** Buildings need to comprise units of the required size and appearance, with the necessary facilities and expansion possibilities. Consideration should also be given to accessibility for raw material suppliers, customers and employees.
- **Availability of capital.** This does not necessarily affect the choice of a specific location, but can still play a role when the suppliers of capital set specific conditions or express certain preferences in this regard, for example, or when capital is such a limiting factor that it necessitates the choice of the cheapest location.
- **Attitude, regulations and tariffs of local authorities.** These comprise, for example, the attitude of local authorities to industrial development, including possible concessions that encourage location; health regulations; building regulations; property rates; water and electricity tariffs; and the availability and costs of other municipal services.
- **The existing business environment.** This could influence the establishment of the proposed business by, for example, the provision of repair and maintenance services, as well as the availability of spares and banking, postal and other communication facilities.
- **The social environment.** This concerns the provision of satisfactory housing and educational, medical, recreational and shopping facilities for employees of the proposed business.

- **Climate.** Some production processes require a particular type of climate. Climate can also influence the acquisition, retention and productivity of personnel.
- **Central government policy.** This may encourage or discourage the establishment of certain types of businesses in specific areas in a direct or indirect manner through, for example, tax concessions.
- **Personal preferences.** These relate to the area or areas that entrepreneurs and their families prefer to live in.

Critical thinking

Recall the case study at the start of this chapter. Should Thabeng extend her business into the CBD of Johannesburg? Would she be just as successful?

3.5 Summary

In this chapter the legal forms of a business that are available to the entrepreneur were discussed. This discussion covered the characteristics, advantages and disadvantages of the sole proprietorship, the partnership, the close corporation, the company and the business trust. In addition, the development of the business plan for a new venture was examined. The final section dealt with the most important location factors.

 Key terms

Sole proprietorship	Business trust
Partnership	Business plan
Close corporation	Location factor
Company	

? Questions for discussion

1. What is the need for a business plan from the perspectives of both internal and external users?

2. What are the key sections of a business plan?
3. What are the factors to consider in choosing among the legal forms of organisations?
4. What are the advantages and disadvantages of a business trust?
5. What are the factors to consider when deciding on the location of a new family restaurant?

References

1. Havenga, P.H., *General principles of commercial law*, 3rd edition, Juta, Cape Town, 1997.
2. Cronje, G.J.deJ., Du Toit, G.S. & Motlatla, M.D.C., *Introduction to business management*, 5th edition, Oxford University Press, Cape Town, 2000, p. 42.

THE BUSINESS ENVIRONMENT

The purpose of this chapter

The previous chapter focused on the establishment of a business and the different forms of legal ownership available to the entrepreneur. An important consideration subsequently facing entrepreneurs and established organisations alike is the internal and external environmental factors that can either help or hinder the development of business. These environmental factors are the fundamental foundation of strategies formulated and implemented by the organisation.[1] Ideas and trends discussed in this chapter shape our thinking about business and stimulate our thinking about the kinds of strategies that are likely to be effective. The purpose of this chapter is to introduce the reader to the environment in which a business functions and to explain how the environment influences the development of a business organisation. This includes treatment of the following related topics:

- The concept of environmental change which, in the case study on page 89, forces De Beers to rethink its business model
- The composition and characteristics of the business environment (De Beers's business environment, for example, is composed of the micro, market and macro sub-environments) – the entry of many new competitors is an example of change in the market environment)

- The impact of the different environmental variables (components of the sub-environments) on the daily operation of business (the De Beers example in the case study illustrates how changes in exchange rates can lead to increases or decreases of millions of rands in annual profit)
- Threats and opportunities that transpire due to an interaction of the variables in the external environment (new technology holds opportunities for De Beers, while increased competition poses a threat to the group)

The chapter concludes with a brief discussion on how management should monitor the environment and how a business organisation can respond to the influences of the environment. (De Beers's Board realises that it should consider all the internal and external environmental variables before it makes a multi-billion rand decision. This is especially important in the diamond industry, since this industry has seen many changes in the last few decades.)

Learning outcomes

The content of this chapter will enable learners to:

- Understand the meaning of environmental change

- Explain the composition and characteristics of the business environmental model
- Discuss each of the sub-environments of the environmental model
- Explain how each of the environmental variables in the micro, market and macro environments can influence an industry or individual business
- Explain the difference between opportunities and threats in the external environment
- Discuss environmental scanning as a means of managing (measuring, projecting and evaluating) change in the business environment

4.1 Introduction

In Chapter 1 the interdependence between a business organisation and the environment within which it operates was briefly discussed. It was pointed out that society depends on business organisations for most of the products and services it needs, including the employment opportunities which businesses create. Conversely, business organisations are not self-sufficient, nor are they self-contained. They obtain resources from the society and environment in which they operate. Business organisations and society, or, more specifically, the environment in which they function, therefore depend on each other. This mutual dependence entails a complex relationship between the two. This relationship increases in complexity when certain variables in the environment – such as technological innovation, economic events or political developments – bring about change which impacts in different ways on the business organisation. The importance and influence of environmental change on the successful management of an organisation became acutely apparent in the last few decades when environmental forces brought about un-foreseen change.

The 1970s were characterised by oil price and energy shocks. The 1980s experienced a shift from local to global business, and fierce competition from Japan and other Asian countries. In turn, the 1990s heralded a new age of connectivity, with the emergence of the Internet and the World Wide Web, both

of which revolutionised the operations of business organisations. Businesses could now take their digital documents and material and send them anywhere at very little cost. The spread of the commercial web browser allowed individuals or companies to retrieve documents or web pages stored in websites and display them on any computer screen in an easy to use manner.[2] During the latter part of the 1990s western countries enjoyed the longest ever economic boom, which ended on 11 September 2001 with the terrorist strike on the World Trade Centre in New York. This incident heralded a new era in world history, introducing a new world order with new alliances and new enemies.

In South Africa, similar and other complicated environmental factors (that is, political and cultural changes) make the management environment more difficult and tougher.[3] Decades of instability and a new era of rapid change and uncertainty have increased business organisations' need to stabilise the impact of environmental change. The result of this is a greater awareness of environmental influences on management decisions, and the development of an approach to investigate and monitor change in the environment.

4.2 The organisation and environmental change

It has been said that change has become the only constant reality of our time and is the only definite phenomenon in management.[4]

Case study: The business environment in action

The case study below illustrates how the three components of the environmental model are relevant in a South African context.

De Beers faces challenges before going ahead with new diamond mine in Cullinan

De Beers was established in 1888 and is today the world's leading diamond company, producing approximately 40% of the world's supply of rough diamonds. In its early years, when the company produced over 90% of the world's diamonds, it was able to control the production and hence the supply of diamonds almost at will. Then, from the early 1900s, when competitors began to challenge its prominence, De Beers used its position to coordinate and regulate the supply of diamonds in pursuit of price stability and consumer confidence. During the 1990s the diamond industry experienced dramatic swings in the supply of diamonds, the world economy moved onto a low inflationary path and the industry experienced a period of pricing pressure. It was clear that De Beers would have to rethink its business model and strategy.

One key challenge the De Beers Board faced was the decision of whether or not to go ahead with the R7 billion Centenary Cut diamond mine project in Cullinan, near Pretoria. The cut will create a new mine underneath the existing 100-year-old mine and will extend mining operations for another 30 years, producing more gems of astonishing quality. The old mine produced diamonds of outstanding quality, for example the flawless 545,67 carat Golden Jubilee diamond and the 530 carat Cullinan 1 – the latter now a part of the Crown Jewels in England.

It is an important decision to be made taking into account an industry that has changed radically in the last few decades. The South African mines were once the leading producers in the world but now only produce marginal quantities of diamonds in comparison to mines in other African countries. The Orapa mine in Botswana, for example, produces 12 million carats a year compared to the 1,5 million carats produced by the Cullinan mine. Under the leadership of general manager Hans Gastrow, the old Cullinan mine has been able to reduce costs and increase productivity drastically. The strength of the rand has however nullified the gains and the mine may be nearing the end of its working life – unless De Beers decides to go ahead with the Centenary Cut. New technology and engineering processes will allow the company to mine deeper. The production level for the first block in the new mine will be 932 metres below the surface. In the second stage of development, production will be at the 1 153 metre level.

"All development and production activities will be mechanised and the use of automated systems will be applied where possible. This hands-off process allows for maximum efficiency and security. When the Board makes the R7 billion decision on the Centenary Cut they will be mindful of the increased competition from Australia, where the Argyle mine produces huge quantities of small diamonds, and Canada, with its fine Arctic diamonds. If De Beers is to stay ahead of the game it needs to produce the best diamonds and in substantial quantities. The most likely source of such gems is the proven Cullinan mine. On the other hand, new legislation would mean that De Beers would have to pay an 8 percent royalty to the South African government on all diamonds found, on top of the standard range of corporate taxes" (Robinson, 2004). Whether to go ahead with the project or not is a multifaceted decision, but De Beers is fully aware of and ready to face the numerous internal and external challenges.

Sources: Robinson, T., "The double-decker diamond mine", *South African Process Engineer*, No. 6, Johnnic Communications, Cape Town, 2004, p. 36 and The De Beers Group, "Group history", 2007, http://www.debeersgroup.com/debeersweb/About+De+Beers/De (16 February 2007).

In the management sciences particularly, change is a difficult concept to define. The *South African Pocket Oxford Dictionary* defines change as moving from one system or situation to another.[5] Expressed simply, change refers to any alteration in the status quo. This implies a change from a condition of stability to one of instability, a shift from the predictable to the unpredictable or from the known to the unknown. Change cannot be measured, and it causes insecurity. No single factor can be held responsible for it and it occurs in different ways and at a different rate depending on place and community. Moreover, the rate of change often has a greater effect on the environment than the direction of change. Change is therefore a process of constant renewal and regeneration in every conceivable sphere of society.

To understand the rapid rate of change, consider the extract in the box alongside. It comes from a famous speech by former US president John F. Kennedy in 1962.

At the beginning of the 21st century the rapid rate of change is even more staggering. Today the rise of a "knowledge economy", often described in terms of globalisation, is characterised by an explosion of technologies (for example blogging, online encyclopaedias and podcasting), with knowledge and resources connecting all over the world. Computers, e-mail, fibre-optic networks, teleconferencing and dynamic new software allow more people than ever before to collaborate and compete in real time with other people on different kinds of projects from different corners of the planet and on a more equal footing than at any previous time in history.[6]

Environmental variables that are constantly at work changing the environment in which business organisations operate include **technological innovations** (for example those mentioned above); **economic fluctuations** in emerging markets, which result in high interest rates and falling currencies; **new laws**, such as South Africa's labour laws; and **social factors** such as increased urbanisation and changing social values. During the past 15

> ## "We choose to go to the moon"[7]
>
> *No man can fully grasp how far and how fast we have come, but condense, if you will, the 50 000 years of man's recorded history in a time span of but a half-century. Stated in these terms, we know very little about the first 40 years, except at the end of them advanced man had learned to use the skins of animals to cover them. Then about 10 years ago, under this standard, man emerged from his caves to construct other kinds of shelter. Only five years ago man learned to write and use a cart with wheels. Christianity began less than two years ago. The printing press came this year, and then less than two months ago, during this whole 50-year span of human history, the steam engine provided a new source of power. Newton explored the meaning of gravity. Last month electric lights and telephones and automobiles and airplanes became available. Only last week did we develop penicillin and television and nuclear power, and now if America's new spacecraft succeeds in reaching Venus, we will have literally reached the stars before midnight tonight.*

years the structure of South African society and its lifestyles, values and expectations have changed visibly, in particular since 27 April 1994, when a "new" South Africa was formally established.

For the first time in its history South Africa has a democratically elected government and this has brought about drastic changes. The democratisation of South Africa normalised international relations, but at the same time exposed South African businesses to a borderless world in which they have to compete. A notable transformation is the steady economic growth to which President Thabo Mbeki and Finance Minister Trevor Manual have led South Africa in the past ten years. By December 2006 economic confidence in South Africa soared on forecasts of a firmer rand and tamer inflation.[8] Conversely, southern Africa experiences accelerating urbanisation and increased poverty, an influx of unskilled immigrants and high crime rates.

Business organisations, as the central component of the business environment (see Figure 4.1), are naturally subject to change. Environmental variables increasingly affect the environment in which business organisations operate and make decisions regarding investments and strategies to pursue.

In the case study at the beginning of this chapter it was noted that the diamond industry has experienced radical changes in the last few decades. Dramatic swings in the supply of diamonds, the world economy's move onto a low inflationary path and a period of pricing pressure forced De Beers to rethink its business model. De Beers's South African mines no longer produced the majority of diamonds in the world and De Beers subsequently had to rethink its strategy for, and investment in, one of the old mines in Cullinan.

Worldwide, business organisations are restructuring, outsourcing and trimming workforces. Without these major changes, business organisations will not be able to align themselves with the realities of the changing external environment. And without adapting to these changes, they will not be fit to compete in the new global economy. Other changes that affect the business organisation include those in monetary and fiscal policy, which impact on financial management. Changing consumer needs, often the result of economic and technological change, make new demands on marketing management. Existing methods of production can change suddenly because of technological advances (as in the De Beers example in the case study at the beginning of the chapter), and the introduction of new raw materials can cause established industries to disappear. Moreover, trade unions, through strikes and forced absenteeism, are making increasing demands on human resources management.

The interaction between the environment and a business organisation is an ongoing process that often results in a new environment

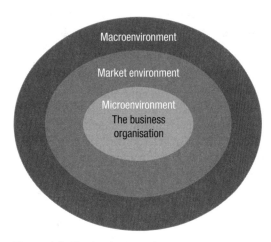

Figure 4.1: The business environment

Critical thinking

In this section on environmental change it is important to ask, "Why is environmental change so important in a business context?" If you scrutinise the chairman's report/statement in an annual report of your choice, you will find various trends mentioned. Some of these trends or changes have had a positive impact on the business's operations, while others might have affected performance in a negative way. To illustrate this point, consider the following excerpt.

Challenges faced during the year – FirstRand Group's chairman report 2006
One of the most significant challenges facing financial services globally is ever-increasing regulation and South Africa has not escaped this trend, in both the banking and insurance sectors. Banks worldwide regard excessive regulation as the most important risk factor facing the banking industry. The reasons include cost, diversion of management time and the sheer volume of regulatory initiatives.

Source: Ferreira, G.T., "Chairman's Report", *FirstRand Group Annual Report 2006*, 2007, pp. 4–7, http://www.firstrand.co.za/AnnualReport2006/chairmans_report.pdf (28 March 2007).

with new threats and new opportunities. Management should align its organisation with the environment in which it operates in such a way that it can identify in advance the opportunities and threats environmental change brings. It is only when management is fully prepared that an organisation can fully utilise the opportunities and deal with possible threats. To be able to do this, managers must first understand the composition and nature of the business environment. The composition of the business environment will be discussed below.

4.3   The composition of the business environment

4.3.1   The three sub-environments

The importance of environmental change to the effective management of the business organisation became apparent in the second half of the 20th century. This was partly the result of the **systems approach to management**, which argued that an organisation is an integral part of its environment, and that management should therefore adopt a policy of "organisational Darwinism" to ensure that its business does not become extinct in a rapidly changing world in which only the fittest can survive.

The rising instability in the environment, as discussed in the previous section, made it increasingly necessary to study environmental change and influences. The question was what exactly to look for in the environment. It would have been hopelessly confusing to have to take every single factor into consideration without any framework to organise information. A variety of influences, ranging from spiritual and cultural values to purely natural influences, may be identified as determinant variables in the business environment.[9]

The **business environment** is therefore defined as all the factors or variables, both inside as well as outside the business

organisation, which may influence the continued and successful existence of the business organisation. In other words, the business environment refers to the internal as well as external factors that impact on the business organisation, and that largely determine its success.

In order to recognise the environmental variables that influence a business, a realistic classification is necessary. Classification makes it possible to identify distinct trends for further analysis in each group or sub-environment. Figure 4.2 on the next page shows the composition of the business environment with its various sub-environments. It is a visual model of the interaction between a business organisation and its environment.

According to this model, the business environment consists of the three distinct environments described below.

4.3.1.1   The microenvironment

The **microenvironment** consists of the business itself, over which management has complete control. This includes variables in this environment, such as the **vision** of the business organisation, the various **business functions**, and the **resources** of the business, which are under the direct control of management. The decisions made by management will influence the market environment through the strategy employed to protect, maintain or increase the business's share of the market. For example, management might apply a marketing strategy, in which pricing and advertising can be applied, to increase market share. In the case study at the start of this chapter, general manager Hans Gastrow followed a strategy to reduce costs and increase productivity.

An analysis of the microenvironment allows managers to determine the capabilities – the strengths and weaknesses – of the organisation.[10] Knowing the organisation's strengths and weaknesses allows management to utilise opportunities and counter threats in the external environment. The microenvironments of many

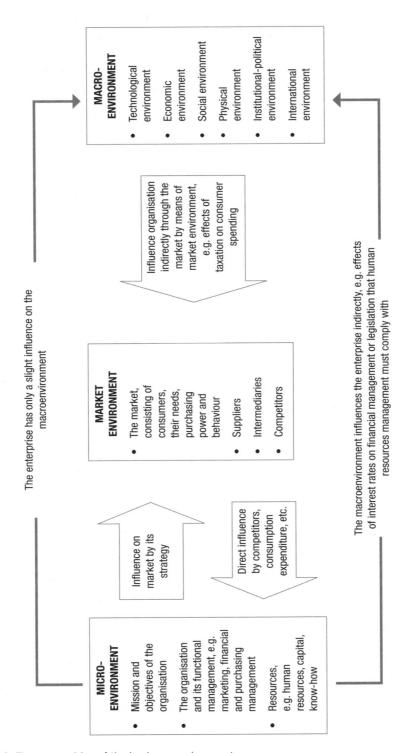

Figure 4.2: The composition of the business environment

business organisations worldwide have been subjected to changes relating to re-engineering, restructuring and trimming workforces. Without these major changes, businesses would no longer be able to align themselves with a changing environment.

4.3.1.2 The market environment

The **market environment** is encountered immediately outside the business organisation (refer to figure 4.1). In this environment all the variables depicted in figure 4.2 become relevant for every organisation, because they determine the nature and strength of competition in any industry. The key variables in this environment are **consumers** with a particular buying power and behaviour; **competitors** in the market, including new and potential competitors who want to maintain or improve their position; **intermediaries** who compete against each other to handle the business's product; and **suppliers** who supply, or do not wish to supply, products, raw materials, services and finance to the business organisation.

All these variables give rise to particular **opportunities** and **threats**. It is in the market environment that management finds its most important tasks: to identify, assess, and take advantage of opportunities in the market, and to develop and adapt its strategies to meet competition. For these reasons the market environment is often called the **task environment**. Management has no control over the components of the market environment, although management may influence the variables concerned through its strategy. The market environment continually influences a business. For example, a new competitor with sufficient resources could start a price war, or a competitor could market a new product protected by patents. In the case study at the start of this chapter, the De Beers Board has to be mindful of the increased competition from Australia and Canada before it makes

the R7 billion decision on the Centenary Cut. Similarly, conditions such as consumer buying power and consumer boycotts can affect a business. The commercial movie *Blood Diamond* reflects an increased consumer awareness regarding the unethical trading of diamonds sourced from wartorn countries. At the same time, the market environment and, subsequently, the microenvironment are affected by developments in the macroenvironment – the third component of the business environment.

4.3.1.3 The macroenvironment

The **macroenvironment** is external to both the organisation and the market environment, and consists of six distinct sub-environments or variables:

- The **technological environment**, which continuously brings change and innovation
- The **economic environment**, in which such factors as inflation, exchange rates, recessions, and monetary and fiscal policy influence the prosperity of the business organisation
- The **social environment**, in which consumer lifestyles, habits and values, formed by culture, make certain demands on the business organisation, particularly through consumerism
- The **physical environment**, which consists of natural resources such as mineral wealth, flora and fauna, and manufactured improvements such as roads and bridges
- The **institutional environment**, with the government and its political and legislative involvement as the main components
- The **international environment**, in which local and foreign political trends and events affect the business organisation (microenvironment) as well as the market environment

Threats and opportunities may also occur in the macroenvironment that is external to the business organisation. The individual business organisation therefore has very little or no control over the macroenvironment, and its influence on these variables is insignificant.

Each of these sub-environments – the microenvironment, the market environment and the macroenvironment – is characterised by interplay of the variables peculiar to the particular environment (for example the interplay between the technological and social sub-environments), while at the same time there is interaction between the various environments. These interactions will be elaborated on in the discussion of the various sub-environments. In the foregoing discussion we have described the composition of the business environment. We shall now examine the characteristics of the business environment.

4.3.2 Characteristics of the business environment

Before the various sub-environments are discussed in greater detail, a brief survey of the most important characteristics of the business environment will help to show why it is necessary for management to continuously monitor the business environment.

The following are a few of the main characteristics of the business environment:
- **The environmental factors or variables are interrelated.** A change in one of the external factors may cause a change in the microenvironment and, similarly, a change in one external factor may cause a change in the other external factors. For example, the crash in August 1998 of the Johannesburg Securities Exchange (JSE) – Africa's largest stock exchange – caused a 30% decline in the value of the rand against foreign currencies. This, in turn, resulted in more economic change, including extremely high interest rates, which reduced the purchasing power of consumers and, in turn, led to depressed property and car sales. Export businesses benefited from this change in the macroenvironment.
- **Increasing instability.** One of the consequences of interdependence in the environment is increasing instability and change. Although the general rate of change in the environment accelerates, environmental fluctuation is greater for some industries than for others. For example, the rate of change in the pharmaceutical and electronics industries

---

Critical thinking

In considering the characteristics of the business environment the economic variable inflation serves as a good example to illustrate the interrelatedness, uncertainty, instability and complexity of the business environment. Can you think of the various environmental variables that might influence inflation?

Variables influencing inflation
Inflation in South Africa is being influenced by the following environmental variables:[11]
- **Physical environment.** Billions of rand are being invested in the economy to bolster South Africa's infrastructure capacity (for

example, R25 billion for the Gautrain and 2010 soccer stadiums alone).
- **Consumer buying power.** A massive increase in consumer spending, which is, in turn, a result of economic growth, low interest rates and the growth of the black middle class (the Black Diamonds).
- **Physical environment.** Rising oil prices and food prices.
- **Economic environment.** A depreciation of the rand's exchange rate.

All of the variables listed above are likely to lead to acceleration in inflation in the short term.

may be higher than in the automobile component and bakery industries.

- **Environmental uncertainty.** Uncertainty about the environment is dependent on the amount of information about environmental variables and on the confidence that management has in such information. If there is little information available, or if the value of the information is suspect, the uncertainty of management about the environment will increase, and vice versa.
- **The complexity of the environment.** This indicates the number of external variables to which a business organisation has to respond, as well as variations in the variables themselves. A bakery, for example, has fewer variables in its business environment to consider than a manufacturer of computers has, and therefore has a less complex environment. It is one of the advantages of businesses with less complex environments that they need less environmental information to make decisions.

These few exceptional characteristics of the environment show how important it is for management to know and understand the environment within which the business organisation operates. With these facts in mind, we will now consider the various business sub-environments referred to above in greater detail.

4.4   The microenvironment

As explained earlier, the microenvironment comprises the internal environment of the business. The microenvironment may be viewed as an environment with three sets of variables:

- The vision, mission and objectives of the business
- Its management
- Its resources[12]

These variables are responsible for the outputs of the business, and they are under the direct control of management. As discussed, an analysis of these variables will lead to the identification of the organisation's strengths and weaknesses. Each of the variables in the microenvironment is linked to the external environment in some way.

The **vision, mission** and **objectives** of the enterprise are the reason for its existence. A vision statement answers the question "What do we want to become?" A mission statement is developed after the vision statement. A mission statement is an "enduring statement of purpose that distinguishes one business from other similar firms" – the mission answers the question "What is our business?"[13] The mission statement, in turn, serves as the foundation for the development of long-term objectives, which are specific results an organisation seeks to achieve.[14] Without definite goals and objectives to strive for, there would be no need for an organisation. Examples of a mission statement and strategic objectives are given on the next page.

An organisation's objectives and mission statements, for example those given on the next page, are influenced by the external environment. For example, a drastic decrease in the demand of beer, due to changes in South African consumer preferences (unlikely as it now may seem) would force SABMiller to reconsider its mission. If this turned out to be a prolonged social trend, the organisation might shift its strategic focus to hotels and gaming.

The different areas of **management** or business **functions**, and the way in which an organisation is structured – that is, its **organisational structure** – constitute another set of variables in the microenvironment that have certain interfaces with the external environment. For example, marketing is the business function which is in close contact with the market: marketing management keeps an eye on consumers and their preferences as well as on the activities of competitors so that it can develop strategies to counter any influences from the market environment. Similarly, financial management keeps an

The mission statement and strategic objectives of SABMiller

Mission statement

SABMiller plc is an international company committed to achieving sustained commercial success, principally in beer and other beverages, but also with strategic investments in hotels and gaming. We achieve this by meeting the aspirations of our customers through quality products and services, by sharing fairly among all stakeholders the wealth and opportunities generated, and by seeking business partners who share our values. Thereby, we fulfil our goals of business growth and maximised long-term shareholder value, while behaving in a socially responsible and progressive manner.

Strategic objectives

Our success will depend on the rigorous implementation of four strategic priorities:
- *Creating a balanced and attractive global spread of business*
- *Developing strong, relevant brand portfolios in the local market*
- *Constantly raising the performance of local businesses*
- *Leveraging our global scale*

Source: SABMiller, "Our strategy", 2007, http://www.sabmiller. com/sabmiller.com/en_gb/Our+business/About+SABMiller (16 February 2007).

eye on levels of taxation and rates of interest that could influence the financial position of the business. Human resources management may influence the environment through its employment policy, just as trade unions, strikes, the availability of skilled labour, wage demands and new labour laws may affect its decisions. A business organisation should be structured in such a way that it is able to deal with influences from the environment and still operate productively within the environment, especially the market environment.

The **resources** of a business comprise the

last set of internal variables that have certain interfaces with external environments. Resources include the following:
- **Tangible resources**, such as production facilities, raw materials, financial resources, property and computers
- **Intangible resources**, which include brand names, patents and trademarks, company reputation, technical knowledge, organisational morale and accumulated experience
- **Organisational capabilities**, which refers to the ability and ways of combining resources, people and processes in a particular way[15]

For example, an important tangible resource, such as a particular production process, may be threatened by a new technology or new invention. Alternatively, special skills or knowledge (intangible resource) can be employed to exploit an opportunity in the environment – for example, a business with knowledge and experience of exporting will take advantage of a devaluation in the rand, making it a profitable opportunity. In the case study at the start of this chapter, the skills of Hans Gastrow served as an intangible resource to De Beers; Gastrow used his skills and knowledge to reduce costs and increase productivity at the old Cullinan mine.

The purpose of this brief survey of the microenvironment and its variables has been to indicate possible interfaces between the business organisation and its environment. However, it should be remembered that the microenvironment varies from one business organisation to the next.

4.5 The market or task environment

The market environment is immediately outside the business organisation, as shown in figures 4.1 and 4.2, and consists of the market, suppliers, intermediaries and competitors,

---

Critical thinking

How does a mission statement differ from vision and objectives? Study the information about Apple Computer Inc. below and see if you can answer this question.

Vision and Mission of Apple Computer Inc.
Vision statement
Apple is committed to bringing the best personal computing experience to students, educators, creative professionals, and consumers around the world through its innovative hardware, software, and Internet offerings.
Mission statement
Apple Computer is committed to protecting the environment, health and safety of our employees, customers, and the global communities where we operate. We recognise

that by integrating sound environmental, health, and safety management practices into all aspects of our business, we can offer technologically innovative products and services while conserving and enhancing resources for future generations. Apple strives for continuous improvement in our environmental, health and safety management systems and in the environmental quality of our products, processes and services.

In theory, a vision statement and objectives, on the one hand, focus on the future and answer the question "What do we want to become?" The mission statement, on the other hand, concerns the present, the reality of daily operations, and answers the question "What is our business?"

Sources: David, F.R., *Strategic management: Concepts and cases*, 11th edition, Pearson, NJ, 2007, pg. 3 and Ehlers, T. & Lazenby, K., *Strategic management: Southern African concepts and cases*, Van Schaik, South Africa, 2004, p. 56.

which are sources of both opportunities and threats to a business. More precisely, this environment contains those variables that revolve around competition. In order to understand clearly the interaction between the enterprise and its market environment, it is necessary to examine the variables in the market environment more closely.

4.5.1 The market

Several meanings can be attached to the term "market", and we shall discuss the subject more fully in chapter 13. Briefly, we can say that the market consists of people who have needs to satisfy and have the financial means to do so. In other words, the market, as a variable in the market environment, consists of people with particular demands who manifest certain forms of behaviour in satisfying those demands. If a business wants to achieve success with a strategy of influencing consumer decisions in its favour

in a competitive environment, management needs to be fully informed on all aspects of consumer needs, purchasing power, and buying behaviour.

Management also has to understand that these conditions are directly influenced by variables in the macroenvironment: demographic trends influence the number of consumers, economic factors such as high interest rates determine the buying power of consumers, and cultural values exert certain influences on the buying behaviour. Management should also understand that this continuous interaction between market variables and the variables in the macro-environment gives rise to changes in both environments.

South African businesses operate in a complex market environment, characterised by a heterogeneous population. Besides the total number of consumers in a specific area or market segment analysed by management to determine the market for its market offering,

Purchasing power and consumer spending in South Africa[16]

In part due to stable economic growth, consumer spending in South Africa seems to be growing exceptionally fast at a rate of between 6% and 7% per year. This, in turn, influences buying behaviour – in August 2006 almost 45 000 new passenger vehicles were sold and annual sales were up more than 17%. Flat screen televisions were selling just as fast.[17] In February 2007, *Finweek* reported the following: "The stereotype of the typical SA consumer is one of a highly geared spendthrift whose love of flat screen televisions is matched only by his [sic] low propensity to save."[18]

An increase in purchasing power and consumer spending seems to be bolstered by the inexorable march of black families up the income ladder. In 2005, the black middle class (also called the" Black Diamonds") grew by 30%. The black middle class can be defined as black people in Living Standards Measures (LSMs) 7–9, which correlates to an average monthly income ranging from R6 444 to R11 864. Each LSM category includes a wide range of incomes. What they measure is the possession of durable products and the associated buying behaviour. During the same period LSM 10 (income above R12 000/month) experienced the fastest growth in new black members of any LSM category since 2001, an increase of over 200% or a total gain of 81 000 people. The result of black households increasingly entering income ranges that were once almost exclusively white has seen a dramatic increase in the black consumer base in various product types.

the purchasing power of consumers is also a significant component of the **consumer market**. **Purchasing power** is represented specifically by consumers' **personal disposable income**. Personal disposable income is the portion of personal income that remains after direct taxes plus credit repayments (loans from banks, shops and other institutions) have been deducted, and is available for buying consumer products and services. Purchasing power therefore also serves as an interface between the macroenvironment and microenvironment.

Only two of the main characteristics of the consumer market, namely number of consumers and the purchasing power of consumers, were mentioned above. However, numerous other characteristics, such as language, age structure, gender distribution, marital status, size of family, and literacy influence the purchasing patterns or buying behaviour of the consumer market. These factors are discussed in more detail in chapter 13.

The consumer market can further be subdivided into **durable products** (for example furniture, domestic appliances and motorcars), **semi-durable products** (for example food, tobacco) and **services** (for example insurance, rental, communication). This classification enables management to analyse specific segments of the market.

Besides the market in consumer goods, there are also **industrial markets** in which products and services are supplied by manufacturing enterprises for the production of further products and services. **Government markets** involve the purchase of products and services by the central government, provincial governments and local authorities. **International markets** relate to foreign buyers, including consumers, manufacturers, resellers and governments.

It is clear from the foregoing discussion of different markets why the market environment is of such importance to management. Without an ongoing assessment and analysis of this component, a business organisation cannot function successfully. Moreover, variables in the macroenvironment, such as economic factors, political trends and upheavals, as well as population growth and urbanisation, also influence the market environment and, eventually, the products and services which the business offers to the market.

4.5.2 Suppliers

According to the systems approach, a business organisation is regarded as a system that receives inputs from the environment and converts them into outputs in the form of products or services for sale in the market environment. The inputs required are mainly materials, including raw materials, equipment and energy, and capital and labour. Suppliers provide these items to businesses. If one considers that approximately 60 cents out of every rand spent goes into purchases from suppliers, the importance of suppliers in the market environment becomes clear. If a business cannot obtain the right inputs of the necessary quality, in the right quantity and at the right price, for the production of its products, then it cannot achieve any success in a competitive market environment. The interaction between a business organisation and its supplier network is a good example of the influence of environmental variables on the business.

In the case of materials, practically every business, whether it is in manufacturing, trading or contracting, depends on regular supplies. The whole question of materials management, the scanning of the environment with regard to suppliers, and relations with suppliers as environmental variables is dealt with in chapters 22 and 23. A business organisation depends not only on suppliers of raw material, but also on suppliers of capital. Banks and shareholders are such suppliers. They are discussed in chapter 18. Small businesses in particular find it difficult to raise capital. Another supply which businesses need is the provision of labour. Trade unions and other pressure groups can also be regarded as "suppliers" of labour. Enterprises, especially in the manufacturing and mining sectors, have complex relations with these "suppliers". The scanning of the environment, with particular regard to labour, or rather human resources problems, is discussed in greater detail in chapters 10 and 11.

4.5.3 Intermediaries

Apart from the consumers and competitors with whom market management has to deal in the market environment, intermediaries also play a decisive role in bridging the gap between the manufacturer and consumer. Intermediaries include wholesalers and retailers, agents and brokers, representatives and, in townships, spaza shops. They also include bankers, asset managers, and insurance brokers, who, from a financial perspective, are also involved in the transfer of products and services.

Decision making by management in respect of intermediaries is complicated by the following:

- **The dynamic and ever-changing nature of intermediaries.** New trends and markets are responsible for the development of new kinds of intermediaries. Contemporary trends in South Africa in this regard are, for example, extended shopping hours, the shift of power from the manufacturer to large retailers because of bar coding and own brand names (the retail chain stores such as a Pick 'n Pay, Woolworths and Shoprite/Checkers are well known for their "no-name" or generic brands), increased advertising by shopping centres themselves, the escalating importance of black retailers in black residential areas, and the increase in the number of franchises and in spazas.
- **Relationships with intermediaries.** This means entering into long-term agreements that, again, may have certain implications for marketing strategy. The power of large retailers also has certain implications for price and advertising decisions.

New trends among intermediaries provide management with certain opportunities, but also hold out the possibility of threats.

4.5.4 Competitors

Since the fall of communism, most organisations operate in market economies that are characterised by competition in a market environment. This means that every business that tries to sell a product or a service in a market environment is constantly up against competition, and that it is often competitors which determine how much of a given product can be sold, and what price can be asked for it.

Moreover, businesses compete for a share of the market and also compete with other businesses for labour, capital and materials. As a variable in the market environment, **competition** may be defined as a situation in the market environment in which several businesses, offering more or less the same kind of product or service, compete for the patronage of the same consumers. The result of competition is that the market mechanism keeps excessive profits in check, stimulates higher productivity, and encourages technological innovation. Although the consumer benefits from competition, the latter is, nevertheless, a variable that management has to take into account in its entry into, and operations in, the market.

In the assessment of competition, marketing management should bear in mind that the nature and intensity of competition in a particular industry are determined by the following five factors (also see Figure 4.3):
- Possibility of new entrants (or departures)
- Bargaining power of clients and consumers
- Bargaining power of suppliers
- Availability or non-availability of substitute products or services
- Number of existing competitors

Figure 4.3 illustrates the five **competitive forces** responsible for competition in a particular industry. The collective strength of these five forces determines the competitiveness in the industry and therefore the profitability of participants in the industry. Competition varies from intense, in industries such as tyres and retailing, to moderate in the mining and cold drinks industries. The weaker the five forces are, the better the chances are of survival and good performance. Digital technologies and the Internet, although not yet in full swing in South Africa, have also contributed to an increase in competition. E-commerce reduced entry barriers and widened the geographical span of markets and increased price transparency. It is

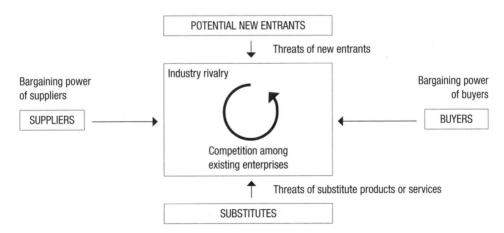

Figure 4.3: The competitive forces in an industry

Source: Griffin, R.W., *Management*, Houghton Mifflin Company, 1999, p. 87.

therefore an important task of management to find a position in the market where the business organisation can successfully defend itself against the forces of competition. The alternative would be to find a position where the business can influence the forces of competition in its favour. This is, for example, the position in which De Beers finds itself, even though it needs to be mindful of new Australian and Canadian competitors (refer to the case study at the beginning of the chapter).

Continuous monitoring of competition provides the basis for the development of a strategy. It emphasises the critical strengths and weaknesses of the business, gives an indication of the positioning strategy that should be followed, singles out areas in which strategy adjustments can contribute to higher returns, and focuses on industry trends in terms of opportunities and threats.

The scanning of the market environment for opportunities and threats entails an examination of such variables as the economy and technology in the macroenvironment, as well as trends in the variables within the market environment, namely those factors that influence consumer spending, suppliers and competition in the market.

4.5.5 Final comments on the market environment

The market environment entails an inter-action between a business and its suppliers, consumers, and competitors with alternative market offerings. This interaction can result in opportunities or threats to a business, and these require on the part of management awareness of trends in the market environment. Awareness of this sort is required so that management can exploit opportunities profitably and avoid threats in good time. Environmental scanning, market research and information management are the proper instruments to do this, as discussed elsewhere in this book.

4.6   The macroenvironment

4.6.1 The composition of the macroenvironment

Apart from the market environment, which has a direct influence on the fortunes of a business, there is a wider macroenvironment within which a business also operates. This wider macroenvironment has variables that directly or indirectly exert an influence on a business and its market environment. These variables constitute the uncontrollable forces in the external environment that are sometimes referred to as **megatrends**.

As figure 4.2 shows, the macroen-vironment is divided into six variables or sub-environments – technological, economic, social, physical, institutional or political, and international – which a business organisation has to observe and respond to.

Macrovariables have an effect not only on the market environment and on decision-making by management, but also on one another, and this constantly causes change in the business environment. In a democratically elected state, the community (which is also the consumer), with its particular culture and values, decides what government it wants, and gives the government a mandate to form a certain political structure, which in turn determines the affairs of the community. Therefore, politics is interwoven with the economy and is influenced by the policies adopted and the economic measures taken to achieve political ends. The result is a certain standard of living for the community.

Stimulated by the needs of the com-munity, and with the support of the eco-nomy and the government, technology is mainly responsible for the rate of change in the business environment. Social trends also influence politics and the economy. The international environment acts as a considerable force for change in the other variables, and therefore in the total business environment. The result of this interaction is often a new business environment, with new opportunities and new threats.

In studying the macroenvironment, the emphasis is on change caused by the uncontrollable macrovariables and the implications for management. Earlier in the chapter the acceleration of the rate of change was illustrated by John F. Kennedy's speech.

The macrovariables and changes caused by these variables will now be discussed in greater detail.

4.6.2 The technological environment

Change in the environment is generally a manifestation of technological innovation or the process through which human capabilities are enlarged. Technological innovation originates in research and development (R&D) by, mainly, business, universities and government. This technological innovation results not only in new machinery or products, but also in new processes, methods, services and, even, approaches to management, which bring about change in the environment. Table 4.1 illustrates how the moving assembly line in car manufacturing (a new production process) enlarged human capabilities and brought about widespread change.

The introduction of the moving assembly line by Henry Ford in 1913 resulted in a radical reduction in manufacturing effort. Improved productivity enabled Ford to

A rapidly changing macroenvironment

With the exception of a few basic products, most of the things bought and sold today came into existence in the last 60 years. Aeroplanes, radio, television and nuclear power were unknown in the time of Dingane, while Albert Luthuli never knew antibiotics, personal computers, photostat machines or space flights. Steve Biko did not know of robot factories, ordinary citizens as space travellers, or the silicon protein molecules that have already made the silicon chip obsolete. And when former president Nelson Mandela was inaugurated as State President, cellphones were not yet in operation. One reason for the constant rate of acceleration of technological innovation is the fact that 90% of all the scientists who have ever lived are alive today!

reduce dramatically the price of his Model-T car from $850 to $360 between 1908 and 1913. The car was no longer only available to a small number of the wealthy elite, but also to a broader section of society.

Technological innovation also affects other environmental variables. The economic growth rate (measured in terms of Gross Domestic Product) is influenced by the number of new inventions. Social change, in which the appearance of a new product – such as satellite television, the Internet, or cellphones – brings about a revolution in people's way of life, is also partly the result

Table 4.1 Craft versus mass production at Ford (1913–1914)

Assembly time	Craft production 1913 (minutes)	Mass production 1914 (minutes)	Reduction in effort (%)
Engine	594	226	62
Magneto	20	5	75
Axle	150	26,5	83
Components into vehicle	750	93	88

Source: Smith, D., *Exploring innovation*, McGraw-Hill Education, Maidenhead, Berks., 2006, p. 25.

The Sony Walkman and social change

The Walkman, when it first came out, was a highly innovative product. It was a audio product, a personal stereo, that enabled its young, mobile users to listen to music whenever and wherever they wanted to, without being harassed by older generations concerned about noise. The Walkman was a huge commercial success, selling 1,5 million units in just 2 years. As well as securing Sony's future as a consumer electronics manufacturer, it had a much wider impact on society. It was soon copied by other manufacturers, but, more significantly, it changed the behaviour of consumers. Young people found they could combine a healthy lifestyle while continuing to listen to music. So the Walkman may be said to have helped promote a whole range of activities, including jogging, walking and use of the gym.

Consumer needs evolve and change is inevitable. CDs wiped out the market for cassette tapes. Portable audio tape players were replaced by portable audio CD players. Then came the iPod and iTunes. Apple Computer Inc. is revolutionising the music industry through integrating technology, music, images and animation. Apple introduced the popular iPod digital music player and the iTunes website for the sale and download of music. It seems that the Walkman is forever a thing of the past.

of technology. Conversely, these variables influence technology, and so the process of innovation and change is repeated. The Sony Walkman example above illustrates how innovation and change is repeated and how an innovation can bring about social change.

Technological breakthroughs such as cell-phones, fibre optics and arthroscopic surgery, bullet trains, voice recognition computers, and the Internet result in new products and services for consumers, lower prices, and a higher standard of living. But technology can also make products obsolete, as seen in case of the Sony Walkman.

Every new facet of technology and every innovation creates opportunities and threats in the environment. Television was a threat to films and newspapers, but at the same time it presented opportunities for instant meals, satellite communications and advertising. The opportunities created by computers and the Internet in banking, manufacturing, transport, and practically every other industry are innumerable. Moreover, technological innovation often has unpredictable consequences. For example, the contraceptive pill meant smaller families, more women at work, and therefore more money to spend on holidays and luxury articles that would previously not have

Technology and changes in lifestyle

- Early in the 19th century, railways opened up the hinterlands of America and England.
- In the 19th century, electricity revolutionised people's lifestyles. Today electricity supply in informal settlements in South Africa is changing people's lifestyles.
- Since the beginning of the 20th century, the motorcar has brought radical changes to the development of cities and the workplace.
- The advent of the passenger jet in the 1950s transformed tourism within two decades into the world's major industry.
- People are now experiencing the impact of micro-electronics. What used to be a room-sized computer is now a pocket model. The effect of micro-electronics is that it results in ever-smaller units of production that nevertheless yield the same returns.
- Advances in nanotechnology are dramatically changing industries such as health care and mining.
- Cellphones have revolutionised communication.

been affordable. The most outstanding characteristic of technological innovation is probably the fact that it constantly accelerates the rate of change.

A further characteristic of technological innovation that impacts on management is the fact that inventions and innovations are unlimited. Technology influences the entire organisation. The most basic effect is probably **higher productivity**, which results in keener competition. The ability to produce more and better products threatens organisations with keener competition, compelling them to reassess factors such as mission, strategy, organisational structures, production methods, markets and other functional strategies. Superior management of technology within the organisation can be an important source of competitive advantage. Continued assessment of the technological environment should include the following:

- The identification of important techno-logical trends
- An analysis of potential change in import-ant current and future technology
- An analysis of the competitive impact of important technologies
- An analysis of the organisation's tech-nological strengths and weaknesses
- A list of priorities that should be included in a technology strategy for the organisation

In a developing country such as South Africa, managers should continually assess technology trends that revolve around the following:

- **Water technology.** South Africa's water resources can sustain only 80 million people.
- **Mineral technology.** South Africa has vast mineral resources and new ways to improve the processing of its mineral treasures should continually be assessed.
- **Marine technology.** This is needed to utilise South Africa's vast coastal and oceanic resources.

- **Agricultural and veterinary technology.** South Africa is one of a few countries that allow the genetic modification (GM) of crops. GM maize and corn, for example, can make crops more drought resistant, but they also pose threats to biodiversity. Technology in this area therefore needs to be assessed continually to find a balance between providing food to the African continent while still preserving Africa's wildlife and tourism.
- **Medical technology.** This is needed to prevent epidemics and to support the sports industry.
- **Transport technology.** This is needed provide transport for people. Transport in South Africa is an increasingly important issue, especially as the 2010 Soccer World Cup approaches.
- **Power technology.** This is needed to harness cheaper and environmentally friendly forms of power, such as solar power. The need for power or electricity in South Africa

Nanotechnology

It is said that, in advanced form, nano-technology will have significant impact on almost all industries and all areas of society. According to the Centre for Responsible Nanotechnology, it will offer "better built, longer lasting, cleaner, safer, and smarter products for the home, for communications, for medicine, for transportation, for agriculture, and for industry in general".

Consider the following: "Imagine a medical device that travels through the human body to seek out and destroy small clusters of cancerous cells before they can spread. Or a box no larger than a sugar cube that contains the entire contents of the Library of Congress. Or materials much lighter than steel that possess ten times as much strength" (U.S. National Science Foundation).

Source: Anon, 2006, "General purpose technology", *Centre for Responsible Nanotechnology*, http://www.crnano.org/whatis.htm (28 March 2007).

has increased exponentially since the 1994 election. South Africa's current infrastructure cannot support the increased demand; power failures have become a standard occurrence in Cape Town and surrounding regions. Gauteng is also predicted to be affected heavily during coming winters. Apart from causing inconvenience, power failures cause losses of millions of rands to businesses.

Technological progress therefore affects a business as a whole, including its products, life cycle, supply of materials, production process and, even, its approach to management. These influences all require management to be increasingly on the alert for technological change.

4.6.3 The economic environment

After technology, which is primarily responsible for change in the environment, there is the economy, which is influenced by technology, politics and the social and international environments, while in turn also influencing these variables. These cross-influences continuously cause changes in, for example, the economic growth rate, levels of employment, consumer income, the rate of inflation, interest rates, and the exchange rate. Ultimately, these economic forces have implications for management.

The economic well-being of a country, or its **economic growth rate**, is measured by the range and number of products and services produced. Expressed in monetary terms, this standard is known as the **Gross Domestic Product** (GDP) – in other words, the total value of all goods and services finally produced within the borders of a country in a particular period (usually one year).[20] A high economic growth rate of around 7% to 8% per year in real terms, on the one hand, signals an economy which grows fast enough to create jobs for its people, one which exports more products than it imports to sustain a positive

trade balance and a stable currency, and one which can provide its people with an improved standard of living. A low economic growth rate, on the other hand, especially one that is below the population growth rate, usually lowers the people's standard of living.

Between 1999 and 2006, South Africa saw the longest period of uninterrupted economic growth in its history – a trend that is still continuing. The GDP grew at an annualised 4,9%, one of the highest rates in the world, in the second quarter of 2006. Although South Africa needs a growth rate of over 7% per year in real terms to provide jobs for the millions in the unemployment queue, the economic story over the last 12 years is overall a good one to tell.[21]

It is important to realise that a country's economic growth rate influences consumers' purchasing power, which can, in turn, give rise to changes both in spending behaviour and in the type of products or services purchased (also see previous section).

Management must take note of structural changes in the incomes of different consumer groups and adjust its strategies accordingly. In addition to monitoring the economic growth rate, management must also monitor the business cycle very carefully. The correct assessment of upswing and downswing phases in the economy is essential to the strategy of any business. If management expects a recession, it can, for example, reduce its exposure by decreasing inventory, thereby avoiding high interest costs. Any plans for expansion can also be deferred. In an upswing (or boom period) the right strategy may be to build up sufficient inventory in good time and to carry out whatever expansion is necessary.

Inflation, like economic growth, is an economic variable that affects the decisions management has to make. During the 1960s South Africa had a very low inflation rate, but from the mid-1970s double-digit inflation became a regular phenomenon. From 1974 to 1992 the average annual rate of consumer price increases amounted to 13,8%. Since 1993, however, single-digit price increases, comparable to those of the early 1970s, have again been recorded because of improved monetary discipline. Consider the following facts regarding inflation in South Africa.

Although South Africa is experiencing its lowest consumer inflation rate in 25 years, the costs and effects of inflation on a business need to be analysed and managed on a permanent basis. Due to rising oil prices and depreciation of the rand's exchange rate, inflation is set to break out of the 3% to 6% target range for 2007.[22] Inflation increases costs for exporting industries and also local industries competing against imported goods. When a country's inflation rate is higher than that of its major trading partners and international competitors, there is a reduction in its international competitiveness. This is still the case with South Africa, because its inflation rate is still higher than most of the world's important trading countries.

Another economic variable affecting a business and its market environment is the government's **monetary policy**. This affects or influences the money supply, interest rates, and the strength of the currency, and therefore has important implications for management. High interest rates result in a high cost of credit, which tends to modify behaviour and results in a subsequent decline in consumer spending and fixed investment. Consider the critical thinking feature on the following page.

The government's **fiscal policy**, in contrast, affects both businesses and consumers, through taxation and tax reforms. The fiscal policy is also reflected in the annual National Budget, which is normally communicated in February of each year. In the 2007/2008 National Budget, Finance Minister Trevor Manuel announced that the Secondary Tax on Companies is to be lowered from 12,5% to 10% and eventually phased out. This will clearly have a major impact on business. Tax relief is also provided to individuals; the reduction amounts to approximately R4 billion and will, it is hoped, lead to an improvement in household savings.[24] Education has the largest share of expenditure (R105,5 billion), which communicates the importance of skills development to the government; R8,1 billion is to be set aside to hire teachers and improve wages, and R700 million is set aside for bursaries for teachers.

The economies of surrounding countries also affect the economic variables of a country. The South African economy operates in a region where most of the world's poor people live on less than US $1 per day. Of Africa's 49 states, 24 are among the poorest in the world. In addition, Africa has 11% of the world's population but produces only 0,5% of world GDP.

The economic trends discussed above demand constant examination by management and regular consideration of the influences of economic variables.

Facts regarding inflation in South Africa[23]

- From 1946 to 1997 the average level of consumer prices rose by 4 638% over the entire period, or an average rate of 8,7% per annum.
- This means that an item that cost R100 in 1946 cost R4 638 in 1997.
- Expressed in terms of purchasing power, R1 in 1997 could purchase only about one-fiftieth of the goods and services it could buy in 1946.
- The average inflation rate of 6,9% in 1998 was the lowest since 1973, when it was 6,5%.
- The average annual rate of consumer price increases from 1974 to 1992 was 13,8% – at this rate, prices doubled every 5 years.
- In 2006 consumer inflation was within the South African Reserve Bank's range of 3% to 6%.

Critical thinking

Can you explain the important implications of economic variables for management? Consider the following:

A rise in interest rate bound to curb consumer spending[25]

High interest rates that surpass 25% – as the rate briefly did in 1998 – seem to be a thing of the past. Over the past few years, South Africa has experienced low interest rates. Of growing concern, however, is the high growth in consumer spending and consumer indebtedness. Consumer spending hikes up the inflation rate. Consumer indebtedness, which can be defined as household debt relative to annual income, grew to 68% (the highest in South African history) in 2006. In an attempt to curb consumer spending the South African Reserve Bank raised the repo rate by 0,5% to 7,5 % in June 2006 and then to 8% in August 2006. Another one percentage point rise is expected in 2007 and this would take the prime lending rate (interest rates experienced by the end consumer) to 12,5%. Increased interest rates send a signal to the market that the cost of credit is rising. This, in turn, restrains consumer spending, and purchases in certain product categories, such as cars, might decrease.

4.6.4 The social environment

The environmental variable probably most subject to the influence of other variables – especially technology and the economy – is the socio-cultural dimension of a nation. This affects management indirectly in the form of consumers, and directly in the form of employees.

Humans are largely products of their society. As members of a particular society, they accept and assimilate their society's language, values, faith, expectations, laws and customs. A culture, or the way of life of a group of people, influences the individual's way of life, and so consumption cannot be explained solely in economic terms. Consumption is also a function of culture and social change.

South Africa: A mixed society[26]

South Africans are a complicated combination of races, languages, religions, colours and cultures. South Africa's indigenous cultures include those of the Basotho, Tswana, Xhosa, Swazi, Ndebele, San, Venda, Nama, Zulu, Pedi and Tsonga people. Apart from the majority of indigenous cultures, there are also three other large groups, namely Indian people, white people and coloured people.

However, a culture is not static. Over time, a society's values, expectations, habits and way of life change. We will now briefly examine the influence of some observable social trends.

4.6.4.1 Demographic change

Demographic change – that is, change in the growth and composition of populations – is probably the social variable that causes the most change in the market. It does so by altering people's way of life. Societies in the developed world are characterised by falling population growth rates and shrinking families, with the emphasis on smaller consumer units. There are growing numbers of one-person households, and consequently a growing demand for services. There is also a growing population of ageing, and more affluent, persons and families over the age of 65, who create special marketing opportunities. For example, affluent people of that age like to travel. South Africa should target these markets internationally by presenting itself as an attractive tourist destination.

Internationally, the question of population growth and poverty in developing countries is causing great concern to politicians and environmentalists. The following excerpt illustrates international population patterns.

Population patterns in developed and developing countries

In 2003, the world's population stood at 6,3 billion. More than half of all people live in six countries: China, India, the USA, Indonesia, Brazil and Pakistan. Eighty per cent of the world's population lives in developing countries – and 95% of births are in developing countries. The total is still rising, but there are signs that worldwide growth is slowly coming under control. The average annual population growth rate in developed countries is 0,2% per year, while 1,5% in less developed countries and even as high as 2,5% in Africa. Developed regions also have a lower fertility rate – averaging 1,6 children per woman, less than the "replacement level" target of 2. In the developing world this rate is 2,9 and can even increase to 8 in the poorest of countries.

Source: Translated from *Wêreld-Atlas vir Suid-Afrikaners*, Jonathan Ball, South Africa, 2004, p. 11–12.

The concerns surrounding high population growth rates in developing countries revolve around poverty, pollution and degradation of the environment, as well as illness and famine. A third of the world's population (two billion people) is in danger of starving. All of these concerns have a profound effect on business, especially in Africa, where 55 million people (including a large percentage of employees) are expected to die of Aids by 2020.

The total population of South Africa is expected to increase at 1,5% per annum, from 45,3 million in 2001 to 52 million in 2021. The proportion of black people, which was 69,5% in 1951, will increase to 79,6% in 2021, while that of white people, at 19,1% in 1951, will decrease to 9,7% in 2021. The number of illegal immigrants in South Africa is a controversial issue; figures as high as 12 million immigrants have been quoted. Overall, the projected growth rates of the various population groups in South Africa are due to decline, with the rate of decline greatest among white people, followed by Asian people, coloured people and black people. At 0,18% annual growth, the white population will be approaching zero population growth by the year 2011. This has many implications for producers of products and services for traditionally white market segments.

Changes in population growth patterns, as well as age and composition patterns, have an effect on the needs, income and behaviour of consumers and also on employment patterns. This will be discussed in greater detail in section 4.6.4.7.

4.6.4.2   Urbanisation

Changes in population growth patterns are changing trends in the geographical distribution and mobility of the population. The movement of people from rural areas towards cities is known as **urbanisation**. Urbanisation is one of the foremost trends of the world population. Estimates of the future spread of urbanisation are based on the observation that in Europe, North America and South America, the urban share of the total population is approximately 70%. Although Africa and Asia compare weakly with 38%, the highest growth rate in urban populations is found in developing regions.[27] It is expected that in the next decade an extra 100 million people will join the cities of Africa and by 2030 nearly two-thirds of the world's population will be urban. Urbanisation therefore affects businesses in many ways, especially in the areas of housing, sanitation, slum-control, and health services.

4.6.4.3   Level of education

Another social trend that will greatly affect management is the **level of education** of the population. This will influence, on the one hand, the level of skills of both managers and workers and on the other, books, magazines and newspapers as higher education will result in new demands for quality literature and articles. This trend will also influence the tourism industry.

Furthermore, better education and training will mean a more sophisticated consumer, with definite demands being made on management regarding quality of goods, advertisements and working conditions. In South Africa, the educational level of all consumers is rising, with a matric pass rate of 68,9% in 2002 (5% higher than 2001). Rob Hart, editor of *South African Process Engineer*, clearly illustrates, however, the problems regarding skill shortages in South Africa. He indicates that South Africa needs to produce approximately 300–350 engineers for every 1 million people. In 2004, the Engineering Council of South Africa had only 3 037 candidates registered for the year.[28]

4.6.4.4 The changing role of women

Another social variable with clear implications for management is the **changing role of women in developed societies**. As recently as 15 years ago, 60% of American women believed that a woman's place was in the home. Now only 22% are of that opinion.

The proportion of economically active white South African women increased from 19% in 1960 to 36,7% in 2004. The proportion of economically active coloured women stands at 34,6% in 2007. The involvement of Asian women in economic activities also increased sharply, from 1 in every 20 in 1960 to about 1 in every 4 in 2004. The proportion of economically active black women has nearly doubled to 27,3% in 2007; only 17% of black managers are women, but this percentage is expected to show a marked rise.

4.6.4.5 Consumerism

A further social trend to be considered is **consumerism** – the social force that protects the consumer by exerting legal, moral, economic and even political pressure on management. This movement is a natural consequence of a better educated public that resists such things as misleading advertisements, unsafe products, profiteering and other objectionable trade practices, and presses for the so-called rights of the consumer. In a market system, these rights are generally recognised as the following:

- **The right to safety.** This entails protection against products that may be dangerous or detrimental to life or health.
- **The right to be informed.** This means the provision of objective information to enable the consumer to make rational choices.
- **The right to freedom of choice.** This entails giving the consumer access to competitive products or substitutes. It is a protection against monopolies.
- **The right to be heard.** This means that consumers are given the assurance that their interests will receive attention from government and related parties.

The South African Consumer Union endeavours to protect the consumer, to act as a watchdog, and to be in direct contact with manufacturers, suppliers and distributors of consumer goods wherever this may be in the consumer's best interests. The Union also monitors legislation that may affect the consumer and, where necessary, campaigns for the amendment of existing laws or advocates for new legislation to protect the consumer.

4.6.4.6 Social responsibility and business ethics

Another important aspect of the social environment is the pressure that society exerts on business organisations, forcing them to seek legitimacy by being **socially responsible**. This means that business organisations should not only seek shareholder value maximisation, but also constantly consider the consequences of their decisions and actions on a broader society. Well-known management scholars Ghoshal, Bartlett and Moran maintain that organisations should seek compatibility of their own interests with the interests of society while striving for overall value creation.[29] Consumers are realising that although businesses produce much of what is good in our society, they also cause great harm. Management is mostly criticised for misleading advertising, dangerous products, pollution of the environment, layoffs, industrial accidents, exploitation of the consumer and other consequences.[30] Organisations are therefore called upon to be socially responsible.

Corporate social responsibility (CSR) can be defined as "the broad concept that businesses are more than just profit-seeking entities and, therefore, also have an obligation to benefit society".[31]

While profits and employment remain important, many other factors are today included in assessing the performance of a business, namely equity or the empowerment of designated groups economically and managerially, housing, response to environmental concerns, provision of a responsible and safe workplace, care

Table 4.2: The social responsibility of business

Area of social responsibility	Issues in social responsibility	Laws/regulations pertaining to social responsibility issues
SOCIAL RESPONSIBILITY TO EMPLOYEES (Workplace responsibility)	• Equal employment opportunities • Developing a quality workforce (training and the skills levy) • Gender inclusion • Access for disabled persons • Sexual harassment awareness • Respect for diversity • Safe working conditions	• Employment Equity Act 55 of 1998 • Skills Development Act 97 of 1998 • Gender Equality Act 39 of 1996 • Health and Safety Act 29 of 1996
SOCIAL RESPONSIBILITY TO THE CONSUMER AND CUSTOMERS	• Safe products and services • No misleading advertising and communication • Proper information about products and services	• Consumer Protection Measures Act 95 of 1998
RESPONSIBILITY TO THE INVESTOR AND FINANCIAL COMMUNITY	• No deceptive accounting reports • Accuracy of financial reporting • No insider trading • No bribes to customs or other government officials	• South African Statement of Generally Accepted Accounting Practice (GAAP) as approved by the Accounting Practice Board • The King Code, i.e. the Code of Corporate Practices representing the principles of good governance as set out in the *King Report 2* of 2002, which supersedes the *King Report* of 1994
SOCIAL RESPONSIBILITY TO THE GENERAL PUBLIC	• Natural environment issues, including conservation and the preservation of the ecology, and pollution control • Public health issues such as HIV/Aids • Housing for the poor • Philanthropic donations • Social welfare • Avoiding unlawful competition	• World Heritage Convention Act 49 of 1999 • Housing Act 107 of 1997 • Welfare Laws Amendment Act 106 of 1996

about health issues, and involvement with community issues. Some businesses perform an annual social audit to measure their social performance. Based on the results of the social audit, a business can review its social responsibility. The crux of social responsibility is, however, the insistence of the community that business should in every respect be a "good corporate citizen", one that produces profit for owners and investors, but simultaneously markets safe products, combats pollution, respects the rights of employees and consumers, and assists the disadvantaged. In short, businesses are expected to promote the interests of society.

In South Africa, corporate social responsibility seems to play an especially important role. Government alone cannot be expected to rectify the inequities of the past at a rate fast enough to alleviate poverty. Though South African business spends millions on social investment, it remains under pressure to uplift the disadvantaged. In future, in South Africa and elsewhere, pressure will intensify and may even give rise to a more regulatory environment. Table 4.2 on page 111 shows the various aspects according to which society judges the social performance of a business.

As a concept, **business ethics** is closely related to social responsibility, except that business ethics has specifically to do with the ethics or the ethical behaviour of managers and executives in the business world.

Ethics can be defined as " a guide to moral behaviour based on culturally embedded definitions of right and wrong".[32]

Managers, in particular, are expected to maintain high ethical standards. At issue here are the integrity of entrepreneurs and managers, and the degree to which their decisions conform to the norms and values of society. Business ethics revolves around the trust that society places in people in business and the obligations these people have towards society.

Greed, the exploitation of workers and consumers, and the abuse of positions of trust have caused the business ethics of entrepreneurs and managers to be criticised. In 2002, for example, only 17% (down 8% from 2001) of Americans regarded business executives' ethics as high or very high.

In South Africa, examples of unethical and corrupt conduct by executives include the controversial arms deal, the Saambou affair and the misuse of funds at LeisureNet. Corporate governance was institutionalised by the publication of the *King Report on Corporate Governance* in November 1994, which has since been superseded by the *King Code* of 2002. The purpose of the Code of Corporate Practices and Conduct contained in the *King Report* is to promote the highest standards of corporate governance, and therefore business ethics, in South Africa.

Many South African organisations have

SABMiller supports sustainable development

We believe that our sustainability framework is more than just an ethical duty, it's key to sustained growth and superior shareholder returns.

- *Responsible drinking – We want to discourage irresponsible drinking within our sphere of influence.*
- *Our commitment – We believe that behaving responsibly contributes towards profitability and economic growth.*
- *Our priorities – We've outlined 10 sustainable development priorities to focus our efforts and make a difference, such as reducing our environmental impact and investing in communities where we operate.*
- *Our performance – We ensure our sustainable development priorities are transparent and measurable so you can check the facts and details behind our performance.*

Source: SABMiller, "Our responsibility", http://www.sabmiller.com/sabmiller.com/en_gb/Our+responsibility/ (16 February 2007).

responded to the call for socially responsible and ethical behaviour. SABMiller, for example, has a sustainability framework and clearly communicates its responsibility towards the communities in which it operates. Consider the excerpts from its website (see page 112).

4.6.4.7 HIV/Aids

A particular social problem that concerns and influences all South African (and other African) businesses is the curse of HIV/Aids. In sub-Saharan Africa it is devastating families and communities and destroying hope. So far, 17 million people have died of Aids. At least 25 million may follow in the next few years. South Africa now has the largest number of people living with HIV/Aids in the world: about 20% of South Africa's adult population, up from 13% in 1997. Table 4.3 on page 115 shows the frightening statistics of HIV prevalence, both around the globe and in South Africa.

The concerns that potential investors, and especially human resources managers, have about the epidemic revolve around the fact that organisations will soon have to deal with a workforce of which one-third is infected with HIV/Aids, and with a situation in which an organisation could lose key people, as well as 25% to 50% of its workforce. Because organisations are legally obliged to support HIV/Aids-positive employees, few investors are interested in entering labour-intensive industries such as transport, mining and manufacturing. The total cost to the South African economy could soon be a reduction in the economic growth rate of between 0,3% and 0,4%, at a cost of R167 billion per year. To individual businesses, the cost of Aids includes the costs of absenteeism, lost productivity, hospitalisation, and the replacement of workers. These are currently costing businesses between 2% and 6% of salaries a year. Management urgently needs to develop strategies and programmes to deal adequately with HIV/Aids in the workplace.

4.6.4.8 Culture

Culture is another social variable that influences organisations in a number of ways. In South Africa new cultural values are emerging among young urban black people. For example, the extended family living under one roof is viewed with disfavour, women have become more independent, and negative attitudes towards marriage and large families are frequently expressed. The shape of the market, the influence of the culture that currently enjoys political power, and the attitude of the workforce are only a few of the numerous ways in which culture can affect an organisation.

Social problems such as the HIV/Aids epidemic and poverty bring about developments that, in turn, effect change in the environment. Management cannot afford to ignore these social influences.

4.6.5 The physical environment

The **physical environment** refers to the physical resources that people (and businesses) need to support life and development, such as water, air, climate, the oceans, rivers, forests, and so on. Environmentalists warn that if the biomass, which maintains a destructible balance in sustaining life, is damaged beyond repair, planet earth will simply shake us off, as it has shaken off countless species before us. With approximately 6,3 billion people relying on the resources of the same planet, government and business are now beginning to realise that the plundering of physical resources may endanger countries and even continents.

Currently, the numbers of domestic stock the planet's people keep are too high, and the amount of crops and other biomaterial that people extract from the earth each year exceeds by an estimated 20% what the planet can replace. Issues of most concern, regarding the physical environment, include:[33]

- **Population and health patterns.** Despite a slow-down in population growth, the number of people on earth is still rising. In poor countries, mostly in Asia and Africa, population growth leads to land degradation, pollution, malnutrition and illness.
- **Food.** Two billion people – one-third of the planet's population – are in danger of starving.
- **Water.** Within the next 25 years, two-thirds of humanity may live in countries that are running short of water. Only 2,5% of the earth's water is fresh, and only a fraction of that is accessible, despite the fact that each person needs 50 litres per day for drinking, cooking, bathing and other needs. At present, 1,1 billion people lack access to clean drinking water and 2,4 billion people lack adequate sanitation.
- **Energy and climate.** The demand for energy is growing worldwide. Since the 1970s, US oil consumption has grown by 25%, while about 2,5 billion people still have no access to modern energy sources. Most of South Africa's power is provided by Eskom, whose production increased by 4,5% in 2006. In general, the world is overly dependent on fossil fuels, such as oil and coal, which result in heavy air pollution. Air pollution promotes global warming and climate disruptions. The realisation that people need a safe, clean, affordable, diverse supply of energy has led to billions being invested in energy research and development.
- **Biodiversity.** More than 11 000 known species of animals and plants are threatened with extinction. Many vanishing species provide humans with both food and medicine.

The physical environment influences business simply because it is the environment from which business obtains its physical resources. It is also the environment into which business discharges its waste. The following interfaces with the physical environment present opportunities as well as threats to a business organisation:

- **The cost of energy.** Oil prices have a direct bearing on the environment and dramatically affect the political and economic landscape. This presents, as a consequence, threats to, and opportunities for, business. The increasing cost of energy has launched the most widespread drive for technological innovation the energy sector has ever seen.[34] Research on solar power, wind power and nuclear power has been intensified, and offers many op-

---

Critical thinking

How do social trends influence management decision making? Before answering this question, consider the following information.

Convenience a main driver of food consumption in South Africa

Social trends play an important role in consumers' focus on convenience. The Bureau for Food & Agricultural Policy, in a report entitled *SA Agricultural Outlook*, found that the main requirements are for portable and prepared food products and for availability at convenient shopping locations. These needs are driven by social changes such as longer working hours, more women entering the workforce and the lack of efficient public transport in South Africa.

To meet the growing demand for convenience, 1 500 service station stores and about 550 new stores in the grocery retail sector opened between 1994 and 2004. As an example of the convenience trend, the report cites 24,5% growth in the sale of prepared baby foods during 2003/2004.

Source: Adapted from Sherry, S., "Consumer trends – the quick and the healthy", *Financial Mail*, 28 July 2006, http://secure.financialmail.co.za/06/0728/business/cbus.htm (25 February 2007).

Table 4.3: Regional HIV and AIDS statistics and features for 2003 and 2005

Country	Adults (15+) and children living with HIV	Adults (15+) and children newly infected with HIV	Adult (15–49) prevalence (%)	Adult (15+) and child deaths due to AIDS
Sub-Saharan Africa				
2005	24.5 million	2.7 million	6.1	2.0 million
2003	23.5 million	2.6 million	6.2	1.9 million
North Africa and Middle East				
2005	440 000	64 000	0.2	37 000
2003	380 000	54 000	0.2	34 000
Asia				
2005	8.3 million	930 000	0.4	600 000
2003	7.6 million	860 000	0.4	500 000
Oceania				
2005	78 000	7 200	0.3	3 400
2003	66 000	9 000	0.3	2 300
Latin America				
2005	1.6 million	140 000	0.5	59 000
2003	1.4 million	130 000	0.5	51 000
Caribbean				
2005	330 000	37 000	1.6	27 000
2003	310 000	34 000	1.5	28 000
Eastern Europe and Central Africa				
2005	1.5 million	220 000	0.8	53 000
2003	1.1 million	160 000	0.6	28 000
North America, Western and Central Europe				
2005	2.0 million	65 000	0.5	30 000
2003	1.9 million	65 000	0.5	30 000
Total				
2005	38.6 million	4.1 million	1.0	2.8 million
2003	36.2 million	3.9 million	1.0	2.6 million

Source: UNAIDS, "Overview of the global Aids epidemic," *2006 Report on the global AIDS epidemic,* 2006, pg. 13, http://data.unaids.org/pub/GlobalReport/2006/2006_GR_CH02_en.pdf www.unaids.org(28 March 2007).

Destruction of natural vegetation in South Africa

- Roughly 11 million tons of firewood is used every year in South Africa – more than all the wood commercially harvested in the same period. At least 12 million people – one-third of the population – still rely on firewood as their main source of energy. This not only has far-reaching consequences for the environment, but the daily gathering of wood is uneconomical and time consuming.
- Mainly indigenous and natural vegetation is destroyed in this way, and such vegetation is not regenerated.
- The destruction of the natural habitat has had dire consequences all over South Africa. Soil erosion is one of the most visible results of the over-exploitation of natural resources.

portunities to entrepreneurs. South African farmers are currently investigating the production and use of ethanol – using surplus maize yield – as an alternative energy source.

- **The growing cost of pollution.** Pollution costs the community a great deal in terms of destroyed living space, as well as expenses related to the prevention and remedying of pollution and compliance with laws designed to minimise it. Here opportunities present themselves, for example, in the form of new methods of producing and packaging goods to keep pollution to the minimum.
- **Environmentalism.** Many opportunities for entrepreneurs exist in the fields of conservation and ecotourism.
- **Scarce resources.** A broad range of resources that are becoming increasingly scarce – for example raw materials, energy and foodstuffs – are a matter of concern to entrepreneurs. Shortages affect the supply of products and can cause severe price rises. However, shortages also create

opportunities, since they often necessitate different methods of production or substitute products.

Business should respond to the vulnerability of the physical environment by taking timeous steps to limit any harmful effects on the community. If management does not show clear signs of a sense of social and environmental responsibility, managers should not be surprised if hostile relations develop that may threaten the survival of the business. Changes in the energy sector have already been discussed. The fast-food industry is responding by developing containers to minimise pollution, the soap industry is carrying out research on less harmful chemicals, and the motor industry is being compelled by legislation to design emission systems to minimise pollution.

4.6.6 The institutional–governmental environment

Management decisions are continually affected by the course of politics, especially the political pressures exerted by the ruling administration and its institutions. As a component of the macroenvironment, government affects the business environment and business enterprise in a regulating capacity, as explained in chapter 1. The government intervenes in the macroenvironment on a large scale and influences it by means of legislation, the annual Budget, taxation, import control (or a lack of it), promotion of exports, import tariffs to protect certain industries against excessive foreign competition, price controls for certain goods and services, health regulations, incentives to encourage development in a specific direction, and so on.

Furthermore, the government influences the market through government expenditure. Whenever the government acts as a producer, as in the case of numerous businesses, for example Eskom, it competes with private enterprise for labour, materials and capital. To an increasing extent, it is the task of man-

An overhaul for South Africa's corporate law[35]

For over three decades companies in South Africa felt that they were being regulated by legislation that was described as being out of touch with the needs of a modern business. The philosophical approach spelt out by the Department of Trade and Industry (DTI) is that "company law should promote the effectiveness and development of the South African economy". The new bill aims to increase flexibility and efficiency in South Africa's company law, while at the same time strengthening transparency, corporate governance and protection for stakeholders, according to Astrid Ludin, deputy-general at the DTI.

agement to study the numerous and often complex activities of government, as well as legislation and political developments, to determine their influence on the profitable survival of the business. The new political dispensation in South Africa, with its new form and philosophy of government, resulted in new power bases, with far-reaching consequences

for the South African business environment. The new labour laws and the Employment Equity Act 55 of 1998 are examples of how the government influences the management of businesses. One of the most critical tasks facing businesses is to retain well-qualified, skilled employees in order to carry out the Employment Equity Act (EEA). Tito Mboweni, the current governor of the Reserve Bank, points out the difficulty of this in the following reported comment: "I have sought to recruit many competent black people, and no sooner have we trained them than they leave."[36]

A major development in the institutional environment was the release, in February 2007, of a draft bill that proposes to replace the Companies Act of 1973.

4.6.7 The international environment

While each of the factors so far discussed exerts – to a greater or lesser extent – an influence on the business environment, the situation is rendered even more complex, with even more opportunities and threats, if an international

Critical thinking

After reading the information below, see if you can answer the questions that follow it:

Environmental influences

Toyota South Africa is one of the country's largest car manufacturers. It is exposed to influences from the environment on a daily basis. Internally, management has to deal with problems ranging from its mission and objectives to marketing strategies, internal conflict and retrenchments.

Toyota South Africa is directly affected by the market environment through the needs, preferences and purchasing power of consumers, and consequently has to produce vehicles to satisfy these demands. The access segment of the market, which developed during the last decade, is an example of a shift in consumer needs. The Toyota Tazz was developed for this market segment.

Management also has to take into account suppliers of components, particularly with regard to availability, quality and cost. In addition, management must keep an eye on competition to ensure Toyota's leadership in the market. (The Tazz was replaced in 2006 with the Toyota Yaris.)

Indirect factors or, more specifically, variables in the macroenvironment – such as technological innovation in production processes, inflation, or high interest rates – can also create opportunities or threats for Toyota South Africa. Toyota is also influenced by the new labour laws, including the Employment Equity Act 55 of 1998.

1. What other variables in the market environment could influence Toyota's management?
2. What further variables in the macro-environment might influence Toyota's management?

dimension is added to each. Businesses that operate internationally find themselves in a far more complex global business environment because every country has its own peculiar environmental factors, technology, economy, culture, laws, politics, markets and competitiveness, and each is different from those of every other country.

International and multinational organisations, for example De Beers (discussed in the opening case study), are susceptible to all kinds of international currents and trends. De Beers is vulnerable to changes in the market environment of the countries in which it mines and sells diamonds. The De Beers group was, in the case study, exposed to price pressures and increased competition.

The new economic order taking shape worldwide is indicative of the increasing globalisation of the world economy. Globalisation and the trend towards a borderless world continually affect businesses in new ways. However, globalisation does not only present opportunities – it also poses threats. Management must therefore constantly assess possible global threats to its markets and product.

4.6.8 Final comments on the macroenvironment

Under the free-market system, a business exists in a dynamic environment in which technological innovation, economic fluctuations, changing ways of life, and political trends are continually altering the environment. Insight into trends and events in the environment, and an ability to foresee how these will affect decision making, are now assuming great importance for management. In a rapidly changing environment, experience of the past is often of little help in solving the latest problems.

4.7 Opportunities and threats in the market environment and macroenvironment (external environment)

The changes brought about in the market environment by the respective variables and their interactions, and the trends that constantly develop in the macroenvironment, may be classified into two groups:

- Changes that offer an opportunity
- Changes that pose a threat

An **opportunity** may be defined as a favourable condition or trend in the market environment that can be exploited to advantage by a deliberate management effort. However, it should be clearly understood that the possibilities inherent in an opportunity always have to be assessed against the background of the organisation's resources and capabilities (microenvironment). Without the necessary capabilities and resources, an opportunity cannot be properly exploited. The success of a business in making good use of an opportunity therefore depends on its ability to satisfy the requirements for success in that particular market. In the case study at the beginning of this chapter, technological innovation in production processes hold an opportunity for De Beers. If De Beers has adequate financial resources the opportunity can be exploited; it will allow De Beers to establish a whole " new" mine under the old one.

In contrast to an environmental opportunity, an environmental **threat** may be defined as an unfavourable condition or trend in the market environment that can, in the absence of a deliberate effort by management, lead to the failure of the business, its product or its service. In view of the constant changes in the market environment, it is the task of management to identify such threats, both actual and potential, and to develop a counterstrategy to meet them. The De Beers case study clearly shows that increased international competition poses a threat to the Centenary Cut project.

Knowledge of trends in the environment, along with the identification of those issues that largely determine the course of development of a business, is also necessary to make the decisions that will maximise profitability. For this, scanning the environment is a necessary management task. It enables management to identify threats and demands from the environment and, wherever possible, to turn these into opportunities.

4.8   Environmental scanning

The degree to which the environment influences the management of a business depends largely on the type of business and the goals and objectives of its management. Moreover, environmental influences differ from one management area to the next, and even at different levels of management. This means that the importance, scope and method of **environmental scanning** – that is, the process of measurement, projection and evaluation of change in the different environmental variables – differs from one organisation to the next.

The importance of environmental scanning may be summarised as follows:[37]

- The environment is continually changing – therefore purposeful monitoring is necessary to keep abreast of change.
- Scanning is necessary to determine what factors and patterns in the environment pose threats to the present strategy of a business.
- Scanning is also necessary to determine what factors in the environment present opportunities for the more effective attainment of the goals and objectives of a business.
- Businesses that systematically scan the environment are more successful than those that do not.
- In the 50 years between 1920 and 1970, almost half of the 100 largest organisations in the USA failed because they did not scan the environment adequately and adapt themselves to change accordingly.

The extent of environmental scanning is determined by the following factors:
- The nature of the environment within which a business operates, and the demands made by the environment on a business. (The more unstable the environment, and the more sensitive the business is to change, the more comprehensive the scanning has to be. Increasing instability usually means greater risk.)
- The basic relationship between a business and its environment
- The source and extent of change. (The impact of change is rarely so compartmentalised that it affects only one or two areas of an organisation; change has an interactive and dynamic effect on several aspects of a business.)

The best method of environmental scanning is a much-debated subject. It will largely be determined by the importance the business attaches to the environment, and by the amount of scanning required. The following are a few guidelines that may be followed:
- The most elementary form of scanning is to update relevant secondary or published information obtainable from a wealth of sources such as the media, the organisation's own data, professional publications, financial journals, statistics, associates in other organisations, banks, research institutions, records in the organisation's own filing system, and, even, employees.
- The more advanced form of scanning is the addition of primary information, or special investigations on particular aspects of the environment. Such investigations can be carried out by members of the organisation's own staff or by outside consultants.
- Scanning at a much more advanced level could mean the establishment of a scanning unit within the business. The unit should have its own staff, who monitor a broad

range of environmental variables and make forecasts about some of these. Economic predictions by economists using a number of models, assessments of the market and of competition by market researchers, and technological predictions by industrial analysts are only a few examples. Such a scanning unit is usually located in management's planning department.

The question that arises is how all the collected information can be brought to the attention of the relevant manager. There are many different opinions about this, the most common being that information about the environment forms the foundation of strategic planning since it influences the types of strategies likely to be successful. Strategic planning is the responsibility of top management and will be discussed in greater detail in chapter 6.

4.9 Summary

A business and the environment in which it operates, including the community that it serves, depend on each other for survival. Together they form a complex dynamic business environment where change in the environmental variables continually determines the success or failure of a business. Because these variables are often beyond the control of management, it is management's task to adapt the organisation to change in the environment. At times, management acts proactively by anticipating events, thereby also accelerating change. Knowledge of a changing environment by means of sustained environmental scanning is a prerequisite for taking advantage of opportunities, as well as averting threats.

 Key terms

| Business environment | Macroenvironment |
| Competitive forces | Management functions |

Competitors	Market environment
Consumer market	Microenvironment
Consumerism	Mission
Corporate social responsibility	Monetary policy
Economic environment	Objectives
Environmental change	Opportunity
Environmental scanning	Organisational capabilities
Environmental variables	Personal disposable income
Environmentalism	Physical environment
Ethics	Purchasing power
Fiscal policy	Social environment
Gross domestic product	Suppliers
Industrial market	Systems approach to management
Inflation	Tangible resources
Institutional environment	Task environment
Intangible resources	Technological environment
Intermediaries	Threat
International environment	Urbanisation

? Questions for discussion

Read the case study at the beginning of the chapter again. Now answer the following questions:

1. Discuss the most dramatic changes that forced De Beers to reconsider its business model. Can you think of any other changes in South Africa that might influence De Beers's strategic decision?

2. Discuss the variables in the microenvironment that influenced the operation of the old mine. Which other variables in the microenvironment will influence the management of the new Centenary Cut?

3. Do an internal and external environmental analysis on De Beers in the following areas:
    a. *Microenvironment*
    b. *Market environment*
    c. *Macroenvironment*

4. Do you think De Beers wields some bargaining power as a supplier of diamonds?
5. What is the competitive situation in the diamond industry (refer to the remaining four competitive forces in the market)?
6. What is the difference between an opportunity and a threat (use examples from the case study)?
7. What is the scope of environmental scanning that a company such as De Beers needs? Also discuss the various methods of environmental scanning and suggest one method to the De Beers board.

References

1. David, F.R., *Strategic management: Concepts and cases*, 11th edition, Pearson, NJ, 2007.
2. Friedman, T.L., *The world is flat: The globalised world in the twenty-first century*, Penguin Books, England, 2006.
3. Ehlers, T. & Lazenby, K., *Strategic management: Southern African concepts and cases*, Van Schaik, South Africa, 2004.
4. *Ibid.*
5. Soanes, C. (Ed.), *South African Pocket Oxford Dictionary*, 3rd edition, Oxford University Press, South Africa, 2002, p. 141.
6. Friedman, T.L., *The world is flat: The globalised world in the twenty-first century*, Penguin Books, England, 2006.
7. Lowne, C. (Compiler), *Speeches that changed the world*, Bounty Books, China, 2005, p. 73.
8. Anon., "Economic confidence soars – but HSBC bearish on the FSE", *Sunday Times Business Times*, 14 January 2007, p. 2.
9. Van Wyk, R.J., "Environmental change and the task of the human resource manager", *SA Journal of Business Management*, Vol. 16, No. 2, 1985, p. 72.
10. Smit, P.J., *Strategic management: Study Guide for STRBES-C*, University of South Africa, Pretoria, 2003.
11. Van den Heever, J., "A good story to tell", *Finweek, Survey*, 21 September 2006, p. 10; Fife, I, "Dubai Property", *Financial Mail*, 12 January 2007, http://www.fm.co.za/cgi-bin/pp-print.pl (25 February 2007).
12. See also Hodge, B.J. & Anthony, W. P., *Organization theory*, Allyn & Bacon, 1984, chapter 3.
13. David, F.R., *Strategic management: Concepts and cases*, 11th edition, Pearson, NJ, 2007, pg. 11.
14. *Ibid.*
15. Pearce, J.A. & Robinson, R.B., *Strategic management*, 9th edition, McGraw-Hill, New York, 2005, p. 151.
16. Bisseker, C., "The black middle class", *Financial Mail*, 16 December 2005, http://secure.financialmail.co.za/051216/ecomark/ecomark.htm.
17. Els, F., "Tito, please don't let the wheels come off", *Finweek*, 21 September 2006, p. 89.
18. Theunissen, G., "Not quite profligate nation: Structural improvement in household disposable income", *Finweek*, 15 February 2007, p. 50.
19. Bureau for Market Research, *The advertising and marketing environment in the new South Africa*, UNISA, Research Report no. 213, 1994, p. 2.
20. Mohr, P.J., Fourie, L.J. & Associates, *Economics for South African students*, J.L. van Schaik, Pretoria, 1995, p. 91.
21. Van den Heever, J., "A good story to tell", *Finweek, Survey*, 21 September 2006, p. 10.
22. Van den Heever, J., "A good story to tell", *Finweek, Survey*, 21 September 2006, p. 10.
23. *Quarterly Bulletin of the South African Reserve Bank*, South African Reserve Bank statistics, September 1998, http://www.resbank.co.za/Economics/stats.html; Van den Heever, J., "A good story to tell", *Finweek, Survey*, 21 September 2006, p. 10.
24. Laubscher, J., 2007. "The 2007//2008 National Budget", *Sanlam Economic commentary*, 21 February 2007, http://www.sanlam.co.za/eng/economicinsight/economiccommentary/economic+commentary+21+february+2007.htm (25 February 2007).
25. Van den Heever, J., "A good story to tell", *Finweek, Survey*, 21 September 2006, p. 10.
26. *Wêreld-Atlas vir Suid-Afrikaners*, Jonathan Ball, South Africa, 2004, pp. 11–12.
27. *Wêreld-Atlas vir Suid-Afrikaners*, Jonathan Ball, South Africa, 2004, p. 49.
28. Hart, R. "Editor's note", *South African Process*

Engineer, No. 6, Johnnic Communications, Cape Town, 2004.

29. Ghoshal, S., Bartlett, C.A. and Moran, P., "A new manifesto for management", *Sloan Management Review*, Spring 1999, pp. 9–20.

30. Werther, W.B. Jr. & Chandler, D., *Strategic corporate social responsibility: Stakeholders in a global environment*, Sage, USA, 2006.

31. Werther, W.B. Jr. & Chandler, D., *Strategic corporate social responsibility: Stakeholders in a global environment*, Sage, USA, 2006, p. 7.

32. Werther, W.B. Jr. & Chandler, D., *Strategic corporate social responsibility: Stakeholders in a global environment*, Sage, USA, 2006, p. 7.

33. "Special report: How to save the earth", *Time*, 2 September 2002, pp. 18–22; Bodman, S.W.,

"This needs to change", *Newsweek Special Issue*, December 2006–February 2007, p. 20.

34. Yergin, D., "A great bubbling", *Newsweek Special Issue*, December 2006–February 2007, p. 30.

35. McNulty, A., "Corporate Law: Back in touch with business", *Financial Mail*, 23 February 2007, http://www.fm.co.za/cgi-bin/pp-print.pl (25 February 2007).

36. Israelstam, I. " Employees are victims of 'Affirmative Auction' ", *The Star*, 16 October 2006, http://www.ioljobs.co.za/ (25 February 2007).

37. Glueck, W.F., *Business policy and strategy management*, McGraw-Hill, Tokyo, 1980, pp. 89–93.

PART 2

General
MANAGEMENT PRINCIPLES

Chapter 1: The business world and business management		Flows	
Chapter 2: Entrepreneurship			
Chapter 3: The establishment of a business			
Chapter 24: Contemporary management issues		Products	
Chapter 4: The business environment		Services	
Chapter 5: Introduction to general management	Chapter 13, 14, 15 and 16: Marketing and public relations management	Information	Customer satisfaction and value
Chapter 6: The basic elements of planning	Chapter 17, 18, 19: Financial management	Financial	
Chapter 7: Organising			
Chapter 8: Leadership	Chapter 20 and 21: Operations management	Resource	
Chapter 9, 10, 11: Human resources management	Chapter 22 and 23: Purchasing and supply management	Demand	
Chapter 12: Controlling the management process			

Source: Adapted from: Mentzer, J. T. (ed.), *Supply Chain Management*, Sage, London, 2001 pp. 22–23.

INTRODUCTION TO
GENERAL MANAGEMENT

The purpose of this chapter

Entrepreneurs identify opportunities and establish businesses to produce the products and services that the market needs. Entrepreneurs are the driving force behind the venture, but they are not necessarily the only key success factor. Businesses, or the ideas and new ventures of entrepreneurs, need to be managed. That is, the **resources** deployed in the business – such as people, money, equipment and knowledge – must be managed in such a way that the business reaches its profit and other goals. This means that the resources must be planned, organised, led and controlled so that the business maximises its profits.

This chapter describes the role of management in the business organisation and examines the four fundamental management tasks of the management process, namely planning, organising, leading and control. It also explains the different levels and kinds of management in the business and gives an overview of the development of **management theory**.

Learning outcomes

The content of this chapter will enable learners to:

- Give an overview of the role of management in businesses
- Describe the four fundamental management tasks, namely planning, organising, leading and control
- Explain the management process
- Comment on the different levels and kinds of management in the business organisation
- Describe the various schools of thought in management

5.1 Introduction

In chapter 3 we discussed the entrepreneur who initiates new ventures and establishes new business organisations. We also examined the different types of business organisations, such as a partnership, a closed corporation, a private company, and so on. These different organisations, like the many other kinds of organisations such as hospitals, schools and sports clubs, which serve society, need to be managed. The purpose of this chapter is to examine the general principles involved in the management of a business.

The case study on the next page provides an illustration of how these management tasks are applied in a real-life situation in South Africa.

5.2 The role of management

An organisation may be described as consisting of people and resources, and certain goals that have to be reached. These predetermined goals, which may differ from one organisation to the next, constitute the purpose of an organisation, because humans, as social beings, arrange themselves in groups to achieve goals that would be too difficult or too complex for an individual to achieve alone. For this reason, a squash club endeavours to get to the top of the league, a hospital tries to make its services as productive and efficient as possible, a political party tries to win an election, and a business endeavours to make a profit and achieve its goals, to mention but a few examples.

However, organisations do not achieve their goals automatically. In addition to the people, **physical resources, financial resources** and knowledge in an organisation, a further element is necessary to direct all these resources and activities effectively toward goals. That indispensable element is management. Without this, no purposeful action is possible. All members of the organisation would pursue their own ends in their own ways, and the result would be a waste of time and valuable resources, and the organisation would ultimately fail.

Consider the case study presented on the next page. As much as Vodacom's history appears to be an easy story of success, its success can be attributed to its sound management principles, practices and managers at all levels of the organisation.

One of the commonest causes of failure in a business, especially a small one, is poor management. Table 5.1 indicates the main causes of business failure.

It is becoming more and more widely recognised and accepted that the performance and success of an organisation – whether large or small, profit-making or non-profit-making, private or public – depends on the quality of its management.

Management is therefore indispensable to any business for the following reasons:

- **Management directs a business towards its goals.** Without the input of managers, the resources of the business would not be channelled towards reaching its goals, and in a market economy few businesses are able to reach their profit objectives without managers. No business can survive if it cannot make a profit. In short, a business cannot maintain the purpose for its existence without effective management.

Table 5.1: Causes of business failure

Percentage of business failure	Cause of failure	Explanation
40%	Managerial incompetence	Inability to run the business, either physically, morally or intellectually
30%	Lack of leadership	Inability to think strategically and to bring about change in the organisation
20%	Lack of managerial experience	Little, if any, experience managing employees and other resources before going into business
10%	No industry experience	Little, if any, experience in the product or service before going into business

Case study: Management in action

Vodacom: South Africa's leading cellular company

It is difficult to imagine that in the mid-1990s South African company Vodacom had some 40 employees, 1 of the 2 GSM network licences awarded in September 1993 and not much else except a market of potential cellphone subscribers, financial backing from its shareholders, an entrepreneurial leader with a vision for a leading cellular network and a belief that Vodacom would seek out impossible tasks.

In 2007, Vodacom boasts net profits after taxation of approximately R5,1 billion and 23,5 million customers in Africa. The Vodacom services are distributed through a vast network consisting of Vodaworld (the world's first dedicated cellular mall), dealers and franchises that include Vodashop, Vodacare, Vodacom 4U and Vodacom active stores in addition to 9 870 retail outlets in national chains. By March 2006, Vodacom had a total of 5 459 employees, of which 4 302 were based in South Africa and 1 157 in other African countries. Behind Coca-Cola and SAB, Vodacom is South Africa's third favourite brand and one of South Africa's favourite advertisers.

Since its inception, Vodacom has con-sistently achieved its goals and targets, improved its market share, seen substantial growth in revenues and profits, continuously developed new products and technologies, and remained at the leading edge of information and technology communications in line with worldwide trends. It has pursued a strategy of constant innovation and product develop-ment as well as market development. But how has Vodacom managed to build and sustain its success? A part of the Vodacom Group (Pty) Ltd's success can be attributed to its Chief Executive Officer, Alan Knott-Craig. Holding both engineering and business degrees, Alan Knott-Craig is both a technical and a managerial expert. In the corridors of Vodacom he is well known for being an ambitious though humble perfectionist and a motivator who fills his employees with inspiration and enthusiasm. He is also a much admired business leader in the mobile communications community and has re-ceived one of only ten GSM Association golden awards ever handed out for his inno-vation and the pivotal role he has played in the democratisation of mobile commu-nications in Africa.

But ask any of the Vodacom top mana-gement executives where the real secret of success lies and they will answer that people play a significant role in business success and that Vodacom would not be where it is today without its employees, their expertise and their commitment to doing everything to the best of their ability. Vodacom seeks to be an employer of choice through its recruitment and succession planning, reward systems and belief in diversity. By 2006, 80% of the employees were from historically disad-vantaged groups and quite a few key executive positions were held by women. Vodacom is committed to ensuring that its employees have the right skills and knowledge to service customers' needs and believes that its future success relies on having strong and diverse management teams across all its operations.

What does the future hold? For Vodacom the key to customer satisfaction is to continue to provide services that consumers need. It believes that it is in a good position to take advantage of new opportunities that new developments in information and com-munication technology bring. It hopes to supplement growth in the South African market with more investments in Africa. At the same time Vodacom is committed to black economic empowerment and to playing a leading role in the democratisation of telephony in Africa. It has a high regard for corporate social responsibility and good corporate governance practices.

Source: The Vodacom Group (Pty) Ltd, *Annual Report*, 2006, www.vodacom.co.za (9 January 2007).

- **Management sets and keeps the operations of the business on a balanced course.** In the microenvironment – that is, within the business itself – a balance must be maintained between the goals of the business, the resources it needs to realise those objectives, the personal goals of the employees, and the interests of the owners. Table 5.2 shows four basic kinds of resources found in organisations, namely human resources, financial resources, physical resources such as equipment and raw materials, and information or knowledge resources. Management is necessary to combine and direct the resources of different organisations so that each can achieve its goals as efficiently or productively as possible.

    To Vodacom, the primary goal may be to increase market share and number of customers. Sasol's primary goal may be a certain profit margin or return on investment, while the management of the

Typical management tasks

- Who determines where Vodacom should next set up cellphone towers in South Africa to ensure widespread cellphone reception for its customers? Management.
- Who decides where the next Standard Bank branch will be established? Management.
- In a modest restaurant, who sees that there are adequate funds, equipment, raw materials and staff available to perform the various functions? Management, even if the manager is also the owner of the business.
- Who decides whether South African Airways will increase or reduce the number of its flights to London? Management.

University of South Africa will see its goals as improving its teaching through more student support, and better research and service to the community. The management of the City of Tshwane may have as its goal

Table 5.2: The basic resources used by an organisation

Organisation	Human resources	Financial resources	Physical resources	Information resources
Vodacom	Managers, engineers, technical and administrative staff	Equity provided by shareholders such as Telkom and Vodafone, profits, loans	Cellphone towers and base stations, Vodacom Office Park	Market research reports, forecasts
Sasol	Managers, engineers, technical and administrative staff	Profits, shareholders' equity, loans	Refineries, coalfields, plant	Forecasts, market information
University of South Africa	Teaching and administrative staff	State subsidies, contributions from the private sector	Buildings, libraries, computers	Research reports, annual reports, calendars
City of Tshwane	Engineers, lawyers, doctors, technicians, administrative staff	Municipal rates and taxes, fines	Buildings, cleaning services, waterworks	Various population statistics, annual reports, budgets
Kgomotso's Bed & Breakfast	Owner-manager, workers	Profits, owner's equity	House, furniture	Hospitality industry magazines, tourism association membership

making Pretoria a safer and cleaner city, while the owner-manager of a small bed-and-breakfast establishment may be in business to maintain a standard of living for his or her family. For these goals to be reached, management has to strike a proper balance between resources, interests and goals.

- **Management keeps the organisation in equilibrium with its environment**. On the one hand, management adapts the organisation to environmental change, for example by aligning its employment policy with the requirements of the Employment Equity Act 55 of 1998, or increasing advertising in African languages to communicate with the increased number of black consumers in the market. Recall the case study at the start of this chapter: new developments in information and telecommunications technology provided Vodacom with an opportunity to increase its range of services. On the other hand, management may try to achieve a better equilibrium with the environment by trying to change the environment itself, in an attempt to reach the organisation's objectives. Vodacom's development of prepaid pay-as-you-go product offerings, which it introduced in 1996, changed the cellphone market significantly.
- **Management is necessary to reach the goals of the organisation at the highest possible level of productivity**. In chapter 1 we indicated that the economic principle, namely to ensure the greatest possible output with the least possible input, is the reason for the existence of business management.

Thus far, we have shown that management is an indispensable component of the successful functioning of an organisation, especially the business organisation. In the following sections, we shall provide a more comprehensive overview of the task of management.

5.3   A definition of management

Management can be defined, quite simply, as the process followed by managers to accomplish a business's goals and objectives. More precisely, it may be said that management is a process of activities that are carried out to enable a business to accomplish its goals by employing human, financial and physical resources for that purpose. Therefore management may be formally defined as the process whereby human, financial, physical and information resources are deployed in order to reach the goals of an organisation.

Much has been said about the goals and resources of a business, and the fact that management directs the resources to reach the goals. But how does this process manifest itself? What form and sequence does the process or activities assume for the accomplishment of business goals?

Although there is general agreement that management is necessary to direct a business toward its goals, the many definitions offered in the literature on management demonstrate the wide differences of opinion among writers and experts about exactly what the activities of management should be. Most experts, however, single out four fundamental activities as the most important tasks of the management process.

Management does four things: it decides **what** has to be done; it decides **how** this should be done; it **orders** that it be done; and, finally, it **checks** that its orders have been carried out. As we have noted, the management terms used to define these fundamental tasks are **planning**, **organising**, **leading** and **control**. These are the basic tasks of a manager, and they are linked in the sequence shown in figure 5.1. It would not make sense to perform them in any other sequence, for managers cannot decide to do something unless they know what should be done; they cannot order a task to be done until they have decided how it should be done, and

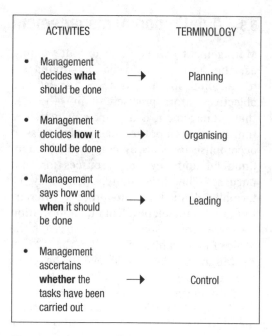

Figure 5.1: Basic tasks of management

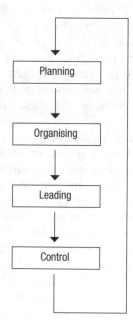

Figure 5.2: The four fundamental management tasks represented as a process

they cannot check the results before the orders have been given.

It should be clear at this stage that the fundamental management activities and the resources of a business, as well as its goals, should not be viewed as separate entities, but rather as an integrated process which has to do with the following: planning the goals and the resources to accomplish them, organising the resources and people, leading the people, and, lastly, controlling the resources and the activities of the people.

Figure 5.2 shows management as an integrated process.

The following brief description of the fundamental management activities eluci-dates the concept of management and the management process:

- **Planning** determines the mission and goals of the business, including the ways in which the goals are to be reached in the long term, and the resources needed for this task. It includes determining the future position of the business, and

guidelines or plans on how that position is to be reached.

- **Organising** is the second step in the management process. After goals and plans have been determined, the human, finan-cial and physical resources of the business have to be allocated by management to the relevant departments or persons, duties must be defined, and procedures fixed, to enable the business to reach its goals. Organising therefore includes developing a framework or organisational structure to indicate how people, equipment and materials should be employed to reach the predetermined goals. Because the goals and resources of different businesses differ greatly, it makes sense that each must have an organisational structure suited to its own peculiar needs.
- **Leading** entails directing the human resources of the business and motivating them. Leaders align the actions of subordinates with the predetermined goals and plans. The part played by leadership

in getting and keeping things going, in motivating and influencing staff through good communication and relations between management and staff, and among staff, has a decisive effect on the culture prevailing in a business. Managers do not only give orders. As leaders, they collaborate with their superiors, equals and subordinates, as well as with individuals and groups, to reach the goals of the business.

- **Control** means that managers should constantly establish whether the business is on a proper course towards the accomplishment of its goals. At the same time, control forces management to ensure that activities and performance conform to the plans for reaching predetermined goals. Control also enables management to detect any deviations from the plans and to correct them. It also obliges management to constantly reconsider its goals and plans.

Figure 5.2 illustrates the management process as a logical sequence of actions. It is, important, however, to realise that the functions of management do not occur in a tidy, step-by-step order. Managers do not plan on a Monday, organise on a Tuesday, lead on Wednesday and control on Friday. At any given time a manager is likely to be engaged in several management activities simultaneously.

The management process and the four elements that it comprises are encountered at all levels and in all departments of the business. These will now be examined more closely.

5.4 The different levels and types of management in businesses

Managers are found not only at the top of a business hierarchy, but at all its levels.

Critical thinking

How do the management activities of planning, organising, leading and controlling take place in practice? Consider the following information about Kate Mahlangu and advise Kate on planning, organising, leading and controlling.

Kate Mahlangu completed her BCom at Unisa and was working for a retail store in the make-up and cosmetics department. She was frustrated because her supervisor told her that her degree would not be of any advantage since there were no management positions open to which she could be promoted. Moreover, she had been in her position for six years.

So, when Kate's aunt asked her to come and help her build up the very successful little knitting company her aunt had started three years earlier, Kate was interested. Her aunt told her that since Malome (her uncle) had died the previous year, it had become very difficult for her to keep the staff together and to process the many orders they received for

jerseys. Despite the demand for their quality products at a very reasonable price, her aunt was unable to keep things running as smoothly as before.

Kate accepted the position as assistant manager and joined the business at the beginning of March – when the first deliveries of orders for winter stock had to be made. Kate found the little factory in disarray: no one knew what objectives to achieve, who to turn to for advice and authority, what quantities to deliver, or what standards to adhere to. She observed that they were not planning what needed to be done, that resource allocation was haphazard, that no one was taking on leadership, and that there was virtually no control over any activities. She decided that the most important problem was the lack of a proper management process, and that such a process should be implemented immediately.

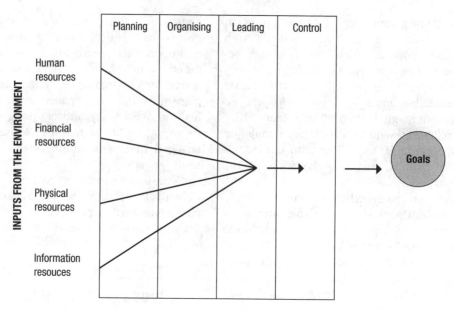

Figure 5.3: The integrated management process

Source: Griffin, R.W., *Management,* Houghton Mifflin Company, 1990, p. 7.

Thus, each manager is in charge of a number of managers under him or her. They, in turn, are in charge of a number of subordinates. A business also has different **types of managers**, each responsible for the management of a more or less specialised group of activities. Figure 5.3 indicates the integrated management process.

5.4.1 The different levels of management

As shown in figure 5.4, several **levels of management** may be identified. For the sake of convenience and ease of explanation, however, only three levels, namely top, middle and lower management, are represented.

    Top management comprises the relatively small group of executives who control the business and in whom the final authority and responsibility for the execution of the management process rests, for example the board of directors, the partners, the managing director and the

chief executive, as well as any management committees consisting mainly of members of top management. Top management is normally responsible for the business as a whole and for determining its mission and goals. It is concerned mainly with long-term planning, with organising insofar as the broad business structure is concerned, and with providing leadership and controlling the business by means of reports and audits. Top management also monitors the environment within which the organisation operates. At the Vodacom Group featured in the case study at the start of this chapter, for example, top management consists of the board of directors as well as Alan Knott-Craig (Group CEO), the Chief Financial Officer (CFO), the Chief Operating Officer (COO) and so forth. In a government department, top management typically consists of the Minister, the director general and the deputy directors general.

    Middle management is responsible for certain functional areas of the business and is primarily accountable for executing the policies, plans and strategies determined by top management. Normally, middle management consists of functional heads, such as the marketing manager, the purchasing manager, the personnel manager, and so on. Middle management is therefore responsible for medium- and long-term planning and organising within its own functional areas, as well as for control of its management activities. It should at all times also monitor environmental influences that may affect its sphere of operations.

Lower management, also referred to as supervisory management, is responsible for still smaller segments of the business, for example the various subsections that form part of a department. For instance, the marketing department may have a product manager, a promotions manager or a sales manager for certain areas. Supervisors and foremen are included in lower management. Their duties mainly involve the day-to-day activities and tasks of a particular section, short-term planning, and implementing the plans of middle management. Lower management supervises the finer details of

organising, such as allocating tasks on a daily basis. These managers guide staff in their own subsections and keep close control over their activities. Lower management is often called line management; it is the first management level to which subordinates from operational ranks are promoted. They then devote most of their time to supervising their subordinates.

For the sake of simplicity and convenience, we have distinguished only three levels of management, but in practice the number of levels is determined largely, though not exclusively, by the size of the organisation. The main reason for this is a limit on the number of people whom one person can manage effectively. A one-person business, for example, has only one level of management, in which the functions of upper, middle and lower management are combined in the person of the owner. A very large business employing thousands of workers may well comprise many more than three levels.

In chapter 7 we shall discuss this question further in our examination of organisational structures.

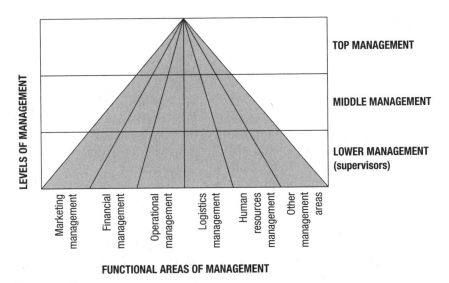

Figure 5.4: Different levels or types of management in a business or organisation

5.4.2 The different types of managers in a business organisation

Figure 5.4 on the previous page showed the different levels of management and the different types, or functional areas, of management that may be distinguished, irrespective of level. **Functional management** refers to specialised managers who are necessary for the different functions of the business. Functional managers are responsible for only the specified management activities of their functions or departments.

Marketing management, for example, is responsible for the following:

- **Planning the activities of the marketing department.** This means that marketing objectives, for example a 10% increase in market share by 2009, are carried out in accordance with the goals and objectives of the business as a whole, and plans are devised to reach those goals.
- **Organising marketing activities.** An example is the allocation of tasks to persons so that certain objectives can be attained.
- **Assumption of leadership of marketing activities.** This entails motivating and giving orders to marketing staff in order to accomplish the goals and objectives, and if necessary, providing guidelines.
- **Controlling marketing activities.** An example is measuring the results and costs of a campaign against its objectives

In the same way, **financial management, human resources management, logistics management**, and other functional managements plan, organise, lead and control their departments. Many organisational functions may be identified, depending on the required number of specialist areas that a business may need. In practice, the number and importance of these specialised areas vary from business to business. There is, however, only one organisational function – general management – that is universally encountered, and that has a definite part to play in every organisation. Some examples of management levels are given in the box below.

> **Management levels: Some examples**
> - Before privatisation in 1991, Telkom (then part of the old Department of Posts and Telecommunications) had more than 20 management levels or hierarchical layers and some 65 000 telecommunications employees. By 2003, Telkom had 27 000 employees and only 9 management levels.
> - Sasol has ten management levels.
> - The University of South Africa has approximately 8 management levels and some 4 500 employees.
> - Small business ventures such as bed-and-breakfast establishments typically have one level of management.

5.4.3 The function of general management

One function not shown vertically in figure 5.4, but which is nevertheless identified as a separate function in the literature and occurs in every business, is **general management**. General management differs from other specialised functions in that it integrates all the others. It deals particularly with the activities of top management, while at the same time manifesting itself in other functions, as in the case of marketing management. General management is therefore the overriding function that controls the management process and the general principles of management as applied by top management.

The same elements of the management process and the general principles of management also affect the other functions, however. This means that all managers in the business should have a thorough knowledge of the management process and its general principles in order to be able to manage their own specialised functions more efficiently.

For this reason, general management is discussed as an introduction to the other functions in this chapter, and again in chapters 6, 7, 8 and 12.

This question may justifiably be asked: "Is there any difference between business management as a subject of study and the management process?" The answer is, decidedly, yes. Business management is the science that examines all the things that affect the productive and profitable operations of a business. It considers not only the management process, but also the external environmental factors that can influence it, as well as the specialised management areas and various disciplines and techniques. In contrast, the study of the actual management process of a business is only one component of business management. It examines only the management process and the general management principles that enable the business to accomplish its goals and objectives as effectively as possible.

We have described the management process, the levels of management, the functions in which the management process takes place, and the unique position and nature of general management. The skills required of managers in executing the management process, and the roles they play in the business, will now be considered in greater detail.

5.5 Skills needed at different managerial levels

Although management is found at all levels and in all functions of a business, the personal skills needed to do the job differ at each level. Figure 5.5 depicts the different skills.

The skills and abilities necessary for top management to carry out the functions of general management are different from those required by lower management. Three key skills are identified as prerequisites for sound management:[1]

- **Conceptual skills**, that is, the mental capacity to view the business and its parts in a holistic manner. Conceptual skills involve the manager's thinking and planning abilities.
- **Interpersonal skills**, or the ability to work with other people. Since management is about dealing with people approximately 60% of the time, it is obvious that a manager

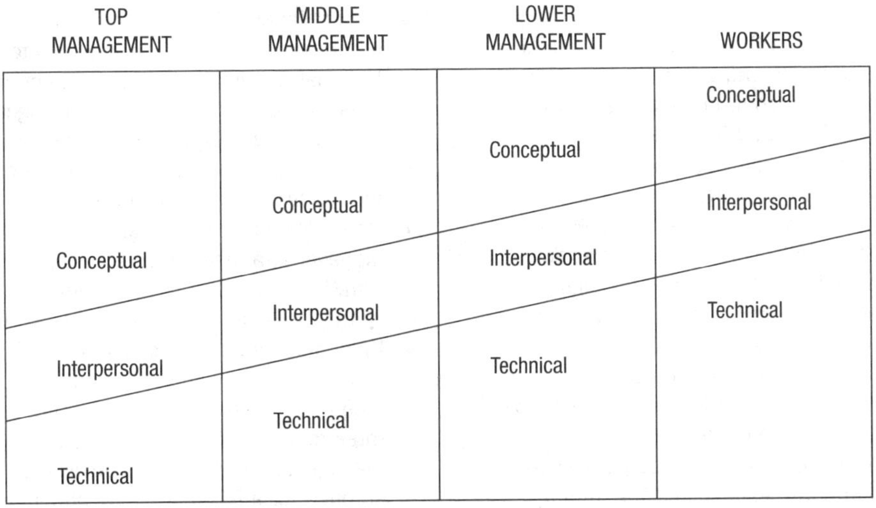

TOP MANAGEMENT	MIDDLE MANAGEMENT	LOWER MANAGEMENT	WORKERS
			Conceptual
		Conceptual	
	Conceptual		Interpersonal
Conceptual		Interpersonal	
	Interpersonal		Technical
Interpersonal		Technical	
	Technical		
Technical			

Figure 5.5: The skills needed at various managerial levels

should be able to communicate with and motivate groups as well as individuals.[2]

- **Technical skills**, that is, the ability to use the knowledge or techniques of a particular discipline. Knowledge of accountancy or engineering or economics is an example of a technical skill that is required to perform a specified task. Managers at lower levels, in particular, should have sufficient knowledge of the technical activities they have to supervise. However, the time spent on technical activities decreases as managers move up the managerial ladder, where conceptual and analytical skills assume more importance.

Where do managers acquire these skills? One source is management education at schools, technikons and universities. Some businesses also provide their own management training. Worldwide there is currently a strong tendency to consider formal academic education in management as a prerequisite for success in business.

Another source of managerial competence is practical experience. A natural aptitude for management, as well as self-motivation and ambition, plays a considerable part in the development of managerial skills.

5.6   The role of managers

Every manager must fulfil a specified role, irrespective of the managerial level or area he or she occupies. A manager, after all, performs

---

Critical thinking

What type of skills do South African managers have? How do their educational backgrounds and experience relate to the three key skills required for sound management?

- The CEO of Vodacom Group (Pty) Ltd, Alan Knott-Craig, holds a BSc degree in electrical engineering and a Master's in Business Leadership. He also serves as a Commissioner on the Presidential National Commission on Information Society and Development for ICTs.
- Vodacom's CFO, Leon Crouse, holds a BCom degree and a Certificate in the Theory of Accounting and is a Chartered Accountant (South Africa).
- The formal qualifications of Vodacom's COO, Pieter Uys, include both BSc and MSc degrees in engineering as well as a Master's in Business Administration.
- Shameel Aziz-Joosub, the managing director of Vodacom (Pty) Ltd and Vodacom Service Provider Company (Pty) Ltd, holds a Bachelor of Accounting Science Honours degree as well as a Master of Business Administration degree.
- Entrepreneur Patrice Motsepe, law graduate and attorney, established the mining company ARMgold in 1997. He currently serves as executive chairman to ARM.
- Mangisi Gule, CEO of ARMplatinum, has qualifications in business management and has extensive experience in the field of management, training, human resources, communications, corporate affairs and business development.
- Maria Ramos, Group CEO of Transnet Ltd, holds a banking diploma, a BCom Honours degree, and an MSc degree in Economics.
- Trevor Manuel, the South African Minister of Finance since 1996, has completed a National Diploma in Civil and Structural Engineering and an executive management programme and holds no less than seven honorary doctoral degrees in commerce, technology, economics and law.
- Nancy Naidoo, the Human Resources Manager at a medium-sized advertising firm, holds a BCom Honours degree in Human Resources Management.
- Kgomotso Sedibe is a school teacher who started her own venture in 2003, a bed-and-breakfast establishment with three rooms. She has completed two management certificate courses and enrolled for a BCom in Hotel and Tourism Management last year.

certain functions, meets certain needs and assumes certain responsibilities for the business. Mintzberg studied the behaviour of a group of managers and concluded that they fulfilled about ten different roles.[3]

As figure 5.6 shows, the roles of managers can be placed in three overlapping groups, namely interpersonal, information and decision-making roles:

- Three groups of activities constitute the **interpersonal role** of managers:
  - Acting as the **representative figure** who attends charity dinners, meets visitors, attends a colleague's wedding, or opens a new factory
  - **Leading** in the appointment, training, performance, promotion, and motivation of subordinates
  - **Maintaining good relations** within the organisation and with its public (this role can occupy up to 50% of a manager's time): internal relations involve other managers and individuals; external relations involve suppliers, banks customers, and so on.
- The **information role** enables managers to obtain information from colleagues, subordinates, superiors and people outside the business, to help them make decisions. This role focuses on monitoring or gathering information about change, opportunities or threats that may affect their department. Managers analyse this information and pass relevant data on to colleagues, superiors and subordinates. In this way, they constitute an important link in the business's communication process. The information role also demands that managers act as spokespeople in their departments or businesses, both internally as well as with the outside world.
- The **decision-making role** involves the gathering and analysis of information. In this respect, managers may be regarded as entrepreneurs who use the information at their disposal to achieve positive change in the form of a new product or idea, or the restructuring of their business. An example from the case study at the start of the chapter is that Vodacom's management decided to expand Vodacom's operations to Lesotho and Tanzania, based on market research reports. Managers also have to deal with and solve problems such as strikes, shortages and equipment breakdowns. Managers have to decide how to allocate the resources of the business. These include funds, human resources

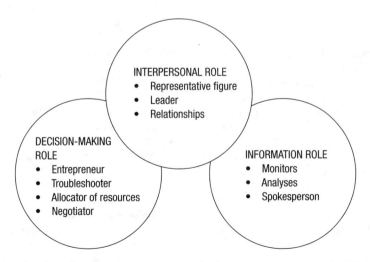

Figure 5.6: The overlapping roles of managers

and equipment, and the allocation of these is often a critical management decision. In their role as negotiators, managers regularly interact with individuals, other departments or businesses to negotiate goals, performance standards, resources and trade union agreements.

By viewing managers from a perspective of the different roles they play in a business organisation, we gain insight into the manager's tasks. This is important for the following reasons:[4]

- The concept of a **manager's roles** creates an awareness of what a manager does, and hence what skills are required.

- A manager's seniority in the business largely determines his or her role, and how much time is spent on each activity.
- The concept of role distribution explains why managers cannot systematically move from planning to organising to leading and, eventually, to control. The complexity and turbulence of their environment requires a more flexible approach.

The above discussion regarding the management skills required for different management activities, and the role of managers, aims at explaining how management works, and should not be viewed as an exact exposition of a management process, because

---

Critical thinking

At the end of this section on the roles managers play, we can ask ourselves the question "How do the different roles managers play overlap?"

Gavin Rajah as an example of a South African manager

Gavin Rajah, a Cape Town based fashion designer famous for his feminine evening and cocktail wear, was the first South African fashion designer to have been invited to show a collection at the prestigious Paris Fashion Week, in July 2006.

Rajah started selling clothes when he was at university when he was enrolled for a law degree. Friends increasingly started asking him for modifications and eventually he started making dresses from scratch for special occasions. He abandoned his law degree for fashion, but admits that he had to learn how the fashion industry and seamstresses work in order to turn his venture into a sustainable business.

Today he has a thriving business and works from a shop in a tourist area of Cape Town. He is well known for using magnificent fabrics, which he sources from all over the world. He concentrates on evening and cocktail wear and special accessories and in order to ensure further exclusivity he limits his ranges and employs only eight people.

Showcasing his designs during the Paris Fashion Week required extensive planning. There are only 24 couture shows, which are attended by 6 000 members of the media. Each designer had to choose his or her own location and use his or her own production company. Gavin's show was a great success and he now has a showroom in Paris and has appointed an agent to build awareness of his brand. He is also in the process of appointing an agent in London in order to serve the needs of different buyers in different regions.

Some of the roles that Gavin Rajah plays include:

- An interpersonal role. He liaises with employees, clients and his agents.
- An information role. He obtains information from industry specialists and agents and acted as a spokesman for his own venture during the Paris Fashion Week.
- A decision-making role. He gathers and analyses information to design and develop his new 2007/2008 collection.

Source: Adapted from Fornby, H. "Swatch this space: Profile Gavin Rajah", *Financial Mail*, 28 July 2006.

Table 5.3: The development of management theory

State of management until early 1900s	State of management during 20th century	The 21st century: What will the state of management be?
A few large organisations, but no mega-organisations	Many huge and powerful organisations in both the private and public sectors	Emphasis on corporate governance and corporate social responsibility
Comparatively few managers – no middle management	Many managers – a comparatively large middle management group	Influence of rise of emerging markets such as China on development of management theory
Managerial activities not clearly distinguished from activities of owners	Well-defined managerial activities clearly separated from non-managerial activities	
Succession to top management based primarily on birth	Promotion to top management on a basis of qualifications, competence and performance	
Few decision makers		
Emphasis on command and intuition	Many decision makers	
	Emphasis on leadership, teamwork and rationality	

the variables differ from one business to the next. In addition, the four management tasks discussed in table 5.3 above are supplemented by various other activities that also have to be performed by management, again depending on the nature of the business.

Besides a knowledge of, and skills in, the four fundamental management elements, management also requires a basic knowledge of supporting management activities.

Although many activities may be identified, four main supplementary or supporting management activities are normally distinguished, namely:
- The gathering and processing of information to make decisions possible
- Decision making
- Communication
- Negotiation

These supplementary activities are not grouped under any of the four management elements because they occur in each element – for example, information is necessary not only for planning but also for organising, and even

more so for control. Similarly, management communicates while planning and organising. Communication is an essential component of leadership. In chapter 8 these activities are examined in greater depth.

The nature of management may further be explained by examining the evolution of management thought over the past few decades. This will also help to explain the present status of management and the approach followed in this book.

5.7 Development of management theory

Because management experience and knowledge of the past are important both to present and future management success, it is necessary to provide a brief overview of the development of management theory over the 20th century. In chapter 1 we briefly outlined the development of business management as a science. The emphasis there was mainly on business management in past centuries, when the entrepreneur both owned and managed his or her business. In contrast to this, the 20th century saw the emergence of the professional manager paid by the owners to manage the business. The manager's level of remuneration often depends on his or her success in managing the business profitably. Table 5.3 on the previous page gives an exposition of the state of management in previous centuries as opposed to management in the 20th century. It also raises some questions as to the future state of management in the 21st century.

The concept of the professional manager resulted in, among other things, a number of theories or approaches to management. Management scholars as well as practitioners researched management issues, postulated theories about how best to manage a business organisation, and published their theories or approaches to management.

Although professional management as we know it today is a product of the 20th century, during its early years there was much uncertainty about what the activities and elements of management actually were. It was only in 1911, with the publication of F.W. Taylor's *Principles of scientific management*, that management was at last placed on a scientific footing.[5] Since then, theories and approaches to management have developed unevenly, with a good deal of overlapping at times. This fitful progress is no doubt attributable to the uneven development of such supplementary disciplines as psychology, sociology and mathematics. With each wave of development in these subjects, new developments and theories in management evolved, which were in turn followed by more knowledge about the factors that determine the success of a business. At the same time, changes in the business environment resulted in the development of new perspectives on existing management theories.

Most of the approaches to management in the literature of even the recent past reveal a great deal of diversity and overlapping of the views of writers and scholars about what can

properly be regarded as managerial activities. The inadequacy of academic research during the formative years of management has in recent decades been amply compensated for by an abundance of research and literature. Scholars are all too ready to put forward a wide range of opinions about management. Behaviourists, for example, inspired by the human relations approach of the 1930s, see management as a complex system of interpersonal relations, and psychology as the basis of management theory. Others, again, see sociology as the basis. Some maintain that the essence of management is decision making, with mathematics playing a central role, while others argue that accounting should be the basis of all management principles and theories. The different viewpoints and approaches towards a theory of management are a reflection of the political, economic, social, technological and environmental issues of the time.

It is often asked whether the various theories and viewpoints of the past have any relevance for the contemporary organisation. Among the many theories about how to improve the performance of the organisation, some aspects of each have survived and, indeed, contributed to contemporary theories on management. In this way, the legacy of past successes and failures becomes part of present and future management approaches. A brief examination of the different theories of management is therefore necessary.

5.7.1 The main schools of thought on management

The existing body of knowledge on management theory or management approaches has emerged from a combination of ongoing research on management issues and the practical experience of certain scholars of management. The management theories that have evolved over many decades are grouped into a number of schools of thought. Each school believed at some stage that it had found the key to management success in terms of productivity and profitability. Later assessments of the various approaches to management, however, demonstrated that these so-called answers to the problems of management were at best only partially correct. Yet, each has made some contribution to the theoretical body of knowledge on management.

The theories of management can be classified into two main schools of thought, namely:

- The **classical** approaches (+1910–1950)
- The **contemporary** approaches (+1960–present)

Figure 5.7 illustrates the development path of management theory.

5.7.1.1   The scientific school

The contribution of the **scientific school** is especially associated with the work of F.W. Taylor (1856–1915). He was an engineer at a steelworks in Philadelphia, and believed that a scientific approach to any task would greatly increase the productivity with which it was carried out. Through the scientific application of observation, job analysis, job measurement, the redesign of jobs, and financial incentives (by paying workers according to their output), he and his colleagues proved that the productivity of a business could indeed be increased.

Although research was confined to workers and lower management levels, this school made a valuable conceptual contribution in that managers and academics became convinced that scientific approaches and methods could be applied in productive ways to attain the goals of an organisation.

5.7.1.2   The management process school

The **management process school**, by contrast, concentrated on top management. Its method was to identify the most important functions in a business and the most important elements of management, so that universal principles of management could be developed for each function and element. The theory was that the application of universal management principles would take any business towards its goals.

Henri Fayol (1841–1925) was the originator of this approach. His personal con-

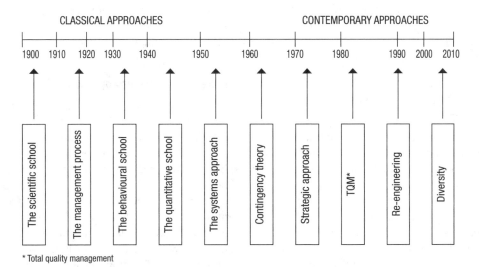

* Total quality management

Figure 5.7: The evolution of management theory

tribution included the identification of six functions of a business:

- The technical (production-operational management) function
- The commercial function (purchasing and marketing)
- The financial function
- An accountancy function
- A security function (protection of property)
- The function of general management

This functional approach, albeit in a modified form, still receives wide support and offers the following advantages:

- It systematises the great variety of activities and problems in a business.
- It facilitates the internal organisation of a business by classifying activities into departments according to their functions.
- It facilitates management by making it possible to appoint people with the right qualifications to the various functional departments.
- It makes the study of management science considerably easier by grouping similar problems. (This book, for example, is classified functionally.)

Fayol also identified the following fundamental elements of the management process: planning, organising, leading, coordinating and control. This description of the management process is still accepted today.

5.7.1.3　The human relations or behavioural school

The **human relations** or **behavioural school** came into being because of the failure of the scientific and classical management process schools to make an adequate study of the human element as an important factor in the effective accomplishment of the goals and objectives of a business. Elton Mayo (1880–1949) found that increased productivity was not always attributable, as the scientific school believed, to a well-designed task and sufficiently high wages. It could also be attributed to such factors as the relationship between people in the business – between management and workers, and between workers themselves in a particular group.

The basic premise of this school is that psychological and sociological factors are no less important than physical factors in the attainment of the goals of a business. Research into social interaction, motivation, power relations, organisational design and communications forms the basis for the contributions by this school, which are particularly valuable in the area of personnel management.

5.7.1.4　The quantitative school

The **quantitative school** sees management primarily as a system of mathematical models and processes. It is largely composed of operational researchers or decision experts who believe that if management or any elements of it are at all a logical process, then this should be expressible as mathematical relations.

The contribution of this school, particularly in the development of models for the running of complex processes, is important. However, this school should be regarded as an aid to management rather than as a separate school of management theory.

5.7.1.5　The systems approach

The **systems approach** to management developed in the 1950s. This approach compensated for the main limitations of the previous approaches. These limitations were, firstly, that they ignored the relationship between the organisation and its external environment, and secondly, that they focused on only one aspect of the organisation at the expense of other areas. Some managers would, for example, focus only on financial aspects and neglect the organisation's market and customers. To overcome these shortcomings, management scholars developed systems theory, which views the organisation as a group of interrelated parts with a single purpose, where the actions of one part influence the other parts.

Managers cannot therefore manage the separate parts independently, but should rather manage them as an integrated whole. This approach was the forerunner of the concept of **strategic management**.

5.7.1.6 The contingency approach

The **contingency approach** seeks to eliminate the defects of other theories. Like the systems approach, it attempts to integrate the ideas of the different schools. The basic premise of the contingency approach is that the application of management principles depends essentially on a particular situation confronting management at a particular moment. In a given situation, management will decide to apply the principles of the functional, quantitative or behaviourist school, or combinations of these. In other words, the contingency approach attempts to adapt the available techniques and principles provided by the various management approaches to a given situation, so as to reach the objectives of the business as productively as possible. It may be said that this approach does not really recognise the existence of universal principles of management, but instead concentrates on whatever means are available to solve problems.

5.7.2 Some contemporary approaches to management

During the second half of the 20th century the environment in which business organisations operated began to change at an increasing rate, as explained in chapter 4. Because of the rapidly changing environment, new issues and challenges emerged, and so, too, did new approaches to management. The contemporary schools of thought were ushered in by the concept of strategic management, followed by a number of contemporary approaches, which we shall outline below.

5.7.2.1 Strategic management

Strategic management as an approach to organisational success evolved from the turbulent environments of the 1960s and 1970s. The pace of technological change, the emergence of Japan and other new post-World War II economies, and demographic change, as well as other political and social trends, forced management to align the goals and objectives of their organisations with trends in the business environment. By focusing on the threats and opportunities in the environment, and evaluating its strengths and weaknesses in order to overcome the threats and exploit the opportunities, the organisation builds a distinct competence in a particular market.

During the early years of the strategic management approach, large organisations had to make big strategic planning decisions. Since the 1980s, however, many of these decisions have been abandoned because today every manager in the organisation is required to think and act strategically. Today, businesses involve managers from all levels of the organisation in the strategic planning process.

5.7.2.2 Total quality management

Total quality management (TQM) is one of the contemporary management approaches that evolved during the late 1980s and the 1990s and revolves around the matter of quality. American managers examined the success of their German and Japanese counterparts in the American market, and found that the latter were obsessed with quality. What further inspired management scholars was the fact that Japanese and German managers not only delivered top quality products and services, but did so at a higher rate of productivity.

5.7.2.3 The learning organisation and the re-engineering of businesses

The management theories that evolved in the 1990s relate to the concepts of the **learning organisation** and the **re-engineering of businesses**.

- The **learning organisation** is a management approach that requires learning individuals. The inability to learn can cripple an organisation.
- **Re-engineering** is a management approach that forces the organisation to focus on its core business and to outsource those activities that do not relate to the core business. Since the 1990s, most organisations have reduced the size of their workforces by outsourcing activities such as the company cafeteria, garden services, maintenance, and a host of activities that are unrelated to the organisation's core business. Telkom reduced its workforce from 67 000 employees in the early 1990s to approximately 28 000 by 2007.

5.7.2.4 Diversity management

Diversity management is another important challenge in contemporary management. In South Africa, the management of diversity is partly enforced by the Employment Equity Act 55 of 1998. Management in Africa will, in due course, develop a management approach with a body of knowledge that is peculiar to the needs and cultural diversity of the continent.

Contemporary business issues that could shape management theory in the 21st century include **corporate governance**, **corporate social responsibility** (also referred to as **corporate citizenship**) and **knowledge management**. Management approaches and theories are important instruments in broadening knowledge about management. The student of management will, accordingly, be equipped to take a critical view of new ideas and new approaches to management.

5.7.3 Conclusion

The above examination of how management theory has evolved and contributed to the broader body of knowledge on management clearly shows that there is no single uniform and consistent theory of management that may be universally accepted and applied. However, understanding the historical context provides us with a broad perspective on the vastness of the body of knowledge, particularly with regard to the research, principles, problems and approaches to management, which managers can draw on.

We have adopted the process paradigm

Ubuntu: an African perspective

The upbringing and socialisation of individuals in African society have always emphasised interpersonal, informational and decision-making roles. Interpersonal roles are subsumed in the notion of *ubuntu* in Zulu and Xhosa, *unhu* in Shona, *botho* in Tswana, *broederbond* in Afrikaans, *bunhu* in Tsonga, *vhuthu* in Venda, and *brotherhood* in English. Thus, *ubuntu* is a literal translation of the notion of collective personhood and collective morality.

Therefore, a leader (*mutugamir* in Shona, and *umukhokheli* in Zulu) guided by the *ubuntu* philosolophy is expected to inform and communicate with his or her own group and to be its mouthpiece in external communication. Decision making is the hallmark of leadership, which involves analysis of the situation at hand, in consultation with others, and guiding the process until a course of action is selected.

Source: Mbigi, L, *Ubuntu: The African dream in management*, Knowledge Resources, Randburg.

Management in the new millennium

Businesses today are exposed to a number of revolutionary forces: technological change, global competition, demographic change and trends towards a service society and the information age. Forces like these have changed the playing field on which businesses must compete. In particular, they have dramatically increased the need for businesses to be responsive, flexible and capable of competing in a global market. To be able to do this, management experts have predicted that the "new organisation" will have the following characteristics:

- The average business will be smaller and employ fewer people.
- The traditional pyramid-shaped business will give way to new organisational structures. In the boundaryless business, employees will no longer identify with separate departments, but instead interact with whoever they need to in order to get the job done.
- Employees at all levels will be called on to make more and more decisions.
- "Flatter" organisations will be the norm.
- Work will be organised around teams and processes, rather than specialised functional sections.
- The basis of power will change. Competency and knowledge, not titles, will be the basis of power.
- The new business will be knowledge based.
- Management will empower employees.
- Managers will have to become agents of change.

Source: Dessler, G., *Managing organisations*, The Dryden Press, Fort Worth, 1995, pp. 16–18.

in this chapter because it offers a conceptual framework for the study of management, it simplifies the subject, and it favours the development of a universal theory of management.

5.8 Summary

This is the first of eight chapters dealing with general principles of management. We have learned that management is an indispensable component of any organisation, without which the orgainsation's resources cannot be properly utilised to reach its goals and objectives. In addition, we have defined management as a process that consists of four fundamental elements or management activities: planning, organising, leading and controlling.

Management – that is, the process of planning, organising, leading and controlling – also represents a distinct function, namely general management, which, at the top level, predominates, and also coordinates other management areas. At middle and lower management levels the management process is evident in every business function. Each level of management requires certain skills, and the roles played by managers differ from one level to the next.

Our examination of the evolution of management theory and the various approaches to it has shown how the different schools of thought have contributed to the vast body of management knowledge. The process approach, which distinguishes four elements of management and seven functions within a business, forms the basis of this book. In the next seven chapters the various elements of the management process will be examined more closely.

 Key terms

Conceptual skills	Lower management
Contemporary approach	Management
Contingency approach	Management principles
Controlling	Management process school

Corporate governance and citizenship	Management process
Decision-making role	Management theory
Diversity management	Marketing management
Financial management	Middle management
Financial resources	Organising
Functional management	Physical resources
Human relations or behavioural school	Planning
Human resources	Quantitative school
Human resources management	Re-engineering of a business
Information resources	Resources
Information role	Scientific school
Interpersonal role	Strategic management approach
Interpersonal skills	Systems approach to management
Leading	Technical skills
Learning organisation	Top management
Levels of management	Total quality management approach
Logistics management	Types of management

? Questions for discussion

Reread the "Management in Action" case study at the beginning of the chapter and answer the following questions:

1. What (use examples) resources did Vodacom have when it was established?
2. How did Alan Knott-Craig apply the management process at Vodacom in order to achieve the goals of the business?
3. What skills should Alan Knott-Craig have as CEO of Vodacom?
4. What roles do the managers at Vodacom play? How do these roles differ from management level to management level?

References

1. Griffin, R.W., *Management*, Houghton Mifflin Co., Boston, 1990, pp. 18–23.
2. *Ibid.*, p. 19.
3. Mintzberg, H., "The nature of managerial work", as quoted in Donnely, J. H., Gibson, J. C. & Ivancevich, J. M., *Fundamentals of management*, Business Publications, Plano, Texas, 1987, p. 28.
4. Griffin, *op. cit.*, p. 18.
5. Mescon, M. H., *Management*, Harper & Row, New York, 1985, p. 43.

THE BASIC ELEMENTS OF PLANNING

The purpose of this chapter	Learning outcomes
This chapter gives an overview of the first fundamental element of the management process. In fact, planning predetermines what the business proposes to accomplish (the development of the mission and goals), and determines how this will be achieved by making and implementing various plans. Chapter 6 covers the importance of planning, the planning process, goals and the development of goals, as well as the development of plans. The different types of plans, from long-term or strategic plans to functional and operational plans, are examined. Some elementary strategies are also explained.	The content of this chapter will enable learners to: • Explain the nature of planning as a management task • Describe the importance of planning as the first step in the management process • Describe the planning process • Interpret meaningfully the importance of goals • Describe the different organisational goals • Depict the hierarchy of goals • Differentiate between strategic, functional and operational planning • Recommend different strategies to accomplish different goals

6.1   Introduction

In chapter 5 we identified planning as the starting point of the management process. Planning is the fundamental element of management that predetermines what the business proposes to accomplish and how it intends realising its goals. In other words, **planning** involves those activities of management that determine the mission and goals of an organisation, the ways in which these are to be accomplished, and the deployment of the necessary resources to realise them. In short, planning entails a systematic and intelligent exposition of the direction a business organisation must follow to accomplish predetermined goals. Planning encapsulates the following three dimensions:

- **The determination dimension.** The business must determine what it wants to achieve by a specified date in the future. This means that goals have to be formulated that will serve as guidelines for the business and its various departments and sub-departments.
- **The decision-making dimension.** These goals determine the actions that are necessary, or the way in which they might be accomplished. In other words, management has to decide what resources (human, financial, knowledge) should be deployed in order to reach these goals, in what combinations, and over what period. This primarily means a choice between alternative ways of accomplishing the goals.
- **The future dimension.** A goal is something to be accomplished in the future. Planning establishes a connection between the things that have to be done now to bring about a certain situation in the future. This future dimension of planning is also intended to cope with change in the business environment. This dimension enables the organisation to be proactive in its interaction with its external environment.

As a fundamental element of management, planning is not only the starting point of the management process, but in a sense also the point around which management activities revolve. The goals and the plans determine the type of organisation needed, the leadership required, and the control to be exercised to steer the business as productively as possible towards its goals.

The case study below provides a glimpse of planning in action at the Verge Hotel Group.

Case study: Planning in action

Background to the Verge Hotel Group (a ficticious organisation)

The Verge Hotel Group (Pty) Ltd was established in 2003 and opened the doors of its first three hotels simultaneously in Cape Town, Durban and Johannesburg on 1 January 2004. Rapid expansion in 2006 saw the group also open hotels in Bloemfontein, Port Elizabeth and Tshwane. The Verge Hotels are small, boutique hotels that each have 20–25 rooms and target young upcoming managers and executives who travel extensively for business. The Verge Hotels seek to create a relaxing yet inspiring working/sleeping environment away from the office/home. The architecture and interior design of the hotels is high-tech and minimalist with open spaces and lots of natural light.

The rooms are not traditional hotel rooms and are instead studio or loft-type rooms that have a sleeping area, a working area and time-out area. The working areas are fitted with adjustable desks and office chairs as well as the latest in information technology applications. The name of each regional hotel reflects the group's awareness of catering to the young, upcoming technology savvy business executive and are known as, for example, verge@jozi, verge@ct, verge@pe, verge@bloem, verge@dbn and verge@tshwane. Verge Group CEO Johnston Luhabe says that from its inception, the mission of the Verge Hotel Group has been "to provide the travel weary executive with an inspirational working/sleeping space that supports productivity whilst minimising the stress of extended business trips".

The importance of planning

Many factors contribute to the Verge Group's success. Luhabe cites one of these factors as the Verge's Group's ability to plan in detail and to execute plans successfully. Detailed strategic, tactical and operational plans ensure that every manager and employee knows exactly what the group as a whole, each hotel and each employee has to achieve. Luhabe emphasises that, through the focus on rigorous planning, the Verge group remains aware of the opportunities and threats that the hospitality industry brings, as well the unique requirements of its target market.

All planning, be it strategic or operational planning, is based on the mission of the group. Long-term goals for the group as a whole were derived from the mission statement and each hotel has a set of tactical goals that are based on the group's overall strategic goals, which are translated into more detail with operational goals.

Once a year, the general managers of all the hotels, together with the board of directors and the chief executives, meet for a three-day planning session. The first step at the planning session is to review progress, in other words, the extent to which the previous year's goals have been achieved. Time is also spent on analysing both the internal and external environments of the Verge Group. The tactical goals are then reviewed, adjusted or reformulated, ensuring that the new set of tactical goals remains aligned with the strategic goals of the Verge Group and the mission of the Verge Group.

Once the tactical goals have been agreed on, tactical plans are developed. Each general manager then returns to his or her hotel, where these tactical plans are discussed in detail with the employees of each hotel. Operational goals are then developed and detailed operational plans and initiatives are then developed for each hotel's tactical plan to ensure that the tactical goals are achieved, which in turn contributes to the achievement of the strategic goals of the Verge Hotel Group.

Mission statement of the Verge Hotel Group

Firstly, we provide the travel weary executive with an inspirational working/sleeping space that supports productivity and minimises the stress of extended business trips; secondly, we seek to become an employer of choice; and lastly we will earn above average returns for our shareholders.

Through our mission we are committed to our strategic goals:
- Offer shareholders returns of 19% over the next 10 years.
- Expand market share from 10% to 20% over the next 5 years.
- Establish Verge hotels in Tanzania, Botswana and Nigeria in the next 6 years.

6.2 **The importance of planning**

It is clear that planning forms the basis of all the tasks of management, because it gives the business its direction and determines the actions of management. Without planning, organising would be haphazard, and it would be extremely difficult to lead subordinates and explain clearly where the business is heading. Moreover, any control measures would only be subjective, as there would be no norms or standards against which to judge actual performance. Planning is indispensable for the following reasons:

- **Planning gives direction.** Probably the most important contribution that planning makes to the managerial process is that it gives direction to the organisation in the form of goals, on the one hand, and in the form of plans indicating how to set about achieving them, on the other. At the same time, it clarifies the goals and determines their feasibility. In short, planning shows whether the business is doing the right thing. In the process, it eliminates all uncertainties and guesswork, thereby reducing risks.

Getting it right

Many businesses impress with their ability to turn out large quantities of products at a low unit cost and in a short time. That is, they do the thing right. Yet it is often these very businesses that fail to show profit – probably because they are not in fact doing the right thing, although they are perfectly capable of getting it right.

- **Planning promotes coordination between the various departments and people in the business.** Once goals have been clearly formulated and plans have been developed, tasks and resources can be allocated so that everybody involved is able to contribute effectively to the realisation of the goals. Scarce resources can be channelled and utilised rationally, which is absolutely necessary for the productivity and ultimate profitability of the business.

- **Planning compels managers to look to the future.** It eliminates crisis management by obliging future-oriented management to anticipate threats in the environment, and to take steps in time to avert them. By looking back over the past and forward to the future, management can organise the present so that the future will be as prosperous as possible.

Looking to the future

Too many managers are so obsessed with the present that they spend too little time contemplating the future. They are like a woodcutter who has no time to sharpen his or her axe because he or she is too busy cutting down trees.

- **Planning ensures that businesses keep abreast of technology.** The influence of modern technology on contemporary businesses, especially in the development of complex products using complicated processes, makes heavy demands on planning. Large projects, for example the building of the Gautrain, take several years. It is very expensive in terms of both time and money to launch such a project, and proper planning is critical to its success.

- **Planning ensures cohesion.** The increasing complexity of businesses and the interdependence of various functional management areas – such as marketing, finance and production – where decisions cannot be made in isolation, also emphasise the necessity of planning. Planning enables top management to see the business as a total system in which the objectives of different functions are reconcilable with one another as well as with the primary endeavours and objectives of the business as a whole.

- **Planning promotes stability.** Probably the most important single factor – even in smaller or less complex businesses – that makes planning indispensable is rapid change in the business environment. Indeed, strategic planning has its origins in the very instability that has been one of the main characteristics of the business environment since the 1960s. Planning, therefore, encourages proactive management. In other words, management plays an active part in the future of the business.

Stressing the importance of planning as the point of departure in the management process helps to explain its nature. We shall now consider it as a process.

6.3   The planning process

A goal or objective is a desirable state of affairs that a business aims to achieve at some point in the future. A plan is the means by which the goal is to be realised. Planning is therefore a complex process consisting of various activities.

As a process in its own right, planning may be seen as the identification and formulation of the goal of a business, followed by decision making to choose the right plan to achieve the goals, and then the implementation of the selected plan. **Implementation** of the plan means putting it into operation by organising tasks and departments for the purpose, taking the lead to set the plan in motion, and, finally, exercising control. In short, implementation means the execution of the plan throughout the management process. Figure 6.1 below illustrates the planning process.

What has to be clearly understood is that, although planning is a process in its own right, it does not take place in isolation, but rather in close relation to the other elements

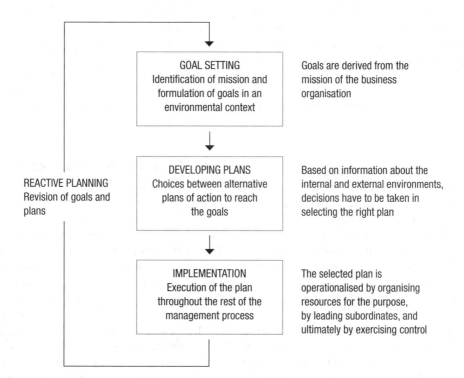

Figure 6.1: The planning process

of the management process. Consider the following:

- Without planning, the next step in the management process, organising, cannot be taken. This is so because without definite goals and plans to reach the goals, the human and physical resources of the business cannot be deployed in the most effective way to produce its products or services as profitably as possible.
- Effective leadership is also not possible unless the necessary planning has been done, for without goals and plans to accomplish them, people cannot be instructed and encouraged to carry out their tasks as productively as possible.
- Control, the last element in the management process, is closely related to planning. A good plan can achieve nothing by itself, and depends not only on effective organisation and leadership in order to be carried out, but also on effective control. If there is deviation from the plan, control will reveal this, and then **reactive planning** is necessary – that is, the goal and the resources required have to be reconsidered. Planning is therefore intimately bound up with organising, leading and controlling, though there is a particularly close connection between planning and control.

Planning does not take place in isolation; it is a dynamic process in which the deployment of the resources of the business and the influences of the business environment are constantly scrutinised. It is important to know that all organisations engage in a planning process, but no two organisations plan in the same way.

Figure 6.1 represents the planning process that most organisations follow. Against this background, the planning process can now be examined at greater length. We shall begin with the setting of the mission and goals of the business organisation.

6.4   Organisational goals

6.4.1   The importance of goals

An **organisational goal** may be defined as a particular future state of things to be achieved by the business. Goals serve various important purposes:

- **Firstly, they provide direction for everyone in the organisation.** Goals can help everyone understand where the organisation is going. A university or bank or clothing manufacturer, for example, that does not know where it wants to be in three or five years will not be able to formulate any plan to get there.
- **Secondly, goals affect other aspects of planning in the organisation.** A strong growth goal, for example, encourages marketing management to look for new marketing opportunities.
- **Thirdly, goals serve as motivation for people to achieve.** This is especially the case if people are rewarded when they achieve the goals for which they are responsible.
- **Finally, goals provide a benchmark for performance measurement and control purposes.** It is not possible to measure goal achievement if no goals have been set or if the goals are not clear.

6.4.2   The formulation of goals

Goals are not set in isolation, but in relation to the four factors that form the basis of planning, namely the **mission** of the organisation (which describes the organisation's purpose), the **environment** in which the organisation operates, the **values** held by management, and the **experience** that management has gained. These four factors are relevant in setting realistic organisational goals. A change in any of them influences the organisation's goals.

- The **mission** of an organisation is a statement made by the owners and managers of the organisation that defines the purpose of the organisation in terms of the product or service it produces, the market it serves and the technology it applies in serving the market. The mission therefore describes those characteristics of the business that set it apart from other business organisations. The mission gives direction to the activities of the business and is a concise organisational outline of what its nature is, what it does and where it is heading. Sun International's mission, for example, stresses Sun International's superior entertainment facilities as the factor that sets it apart from City Lodge, which focuses instead on a "no frills" concept and tariffs that are below those of full-service hotels. It is clear that any goal that is set should be derived from the mission.

- The business **environment**, as discussed in chapter 4, impacts in various ways on organisations, and therefore on the goals that organisations set. The current focus of society on gender equality has forced many South African organisations to reconsider their employment goals. Although it has no control over the environment, an organisation nevertheless has to assess environmental trends carefully in order to plan realistically, and this obviously includes periodically revising its mission and goals in terms of changes in the environment. Anticipating change in the environment results in proactive planning.
- Managerial **values** have an important influence on the formulation of goals. The values of management may vary from the ethical standards held, to how the organisation treats its employees, to its position on social welfare. The mission statements of Sun International and City Lodge, for example, reflect divergent managerial values. Whereas the management of Sun International sees gambling as an important facility it offers its customers, City Lodge does not pursue this line of business. Values therefore have a profound effect on the goals of an organisation.

- The **experience** of management is a further factor that influences the formulation of goals. The experience management has of a specific market or industry will affect the formulation of goals relating to that market.

With the above-mentioned factors in mind, management can now formulate goals for the organisation. It is, however, important to know that organisations establish different kinds of goals. These goals vary according to organisational level and time frame.

6.4.3 The different organisational goals

There are basically two sets of goals in any organisation. One set of goals may be described as **organisational goals** that include the mission, long-term strategic goals, and tactical and operational goals. These goals form the basis of organisational planning and direct the organisation towards the accomplishment of its mission. However, the organisation consists of people who have their own private aspirations and **personal goals**. Although personal goals in an organisation are of no direct concern to management, they nevertheless have an enormous influence on the accomplishment of the organisational goals, and management should be aware of this.

Organisational goals should flow directly from the mission statement of an organisation. If, for example, the mission statement or **overall strategic goal** of a hospital is to offer a full range of medical services to the northern suburbs of Johannesburg within six years, the following goals would be appropriate:
- To increase the number of beds by 180 within the next 3 years
- To increase operational productivity by 20% over the next 2 years
- To install surgery units, which will include a full range of heart surgery, within 5 years

More specific short-term goals should then be formulated to accomplish the above longer-term goals. Figure 6.2 depicts the different kinds of goals and the levels at which they are encountered in the organisation.

According to figure 6.2, the following kinds of goals are encountered at various levels in the organisation:

- The **mission** of the organisation is formulated by the owners and top management. The mission or overarching goal defines the organisation in terms of its unique combination of products, markets and technology, which sets it apart from other organisations operating in the same industry. Long-term strategic goals are derived from the mission and are formulated by the top management. These long-term goals are more specific than the broad guidelines implicit in the mission. For example, the mission of the Verge Hotel Group featured in the case study at the beginning of this chapter is to provide the travel weary executive with an inspirational working/sleeping space, to become an employer of choice and to earn above average returns for its shareholders. From this mission, more precise and detailed long-term goals are derived, for example to expand its share of the market over the next 5 years from 10% to 20%, to produce return on investment of 19% for the next 10 years, and to establish Verge Hotels in other African countries. In considering **long-term or strategic plans**, top management usually includes goals in such critical areas as profitability, productivity, competitive position, human resources development, human relations, technological leadership, and social responsibility. The strategic goals must be clear, since the tactical goals are derived from them.

- **Tactical or functional goals.** These refer particularly to those set at middle management level and by managers in each functional area. Tactical goals focus on how to carry out tasks necessary to the achievement of strategic goals. They are, by their very nature, medium-term or short-term goals derived from the long-term objectives, for example in order to increase market share from 10% to 20% over the next 5 years, sales will have to be increased in urban areas by 18% a year, occupancy rates will have to be increased

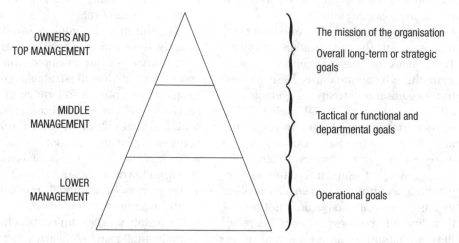

Figure 6.2: Different organisational goals and the levels at which they occur

to 70%, new services may have to be added and additional staff will have to be appointed.

- **Operational goals.** Operational goals are set by lower level management. These are short-term goals concerning such matters as a special for a particular month or quarter, or additional temporary workers

to cope with peak travelling periods, for example. A retail shop may, for example, decide to employ extra salespeople over the Christmas period.

Table 6.1 provides examples of missions and long-term (strategic), functional (tactical) and operational goals.

Table 6.1 Examples of mission and long-term (strategic), functional (tactical) and operational goals

Type of goal	Verge Hotel Group	Hospital	University
Mission	To provide an inspirational working/sleeping space for travel weary executives, to become an employer of choice and to earn above average returns for its shareholders	To provide a complete range of medical services to patients	To provide academic tuition and research to serve the needs of the community
Long-term (strategic or overall) goals (5–10 years)	Offer shareholders returns of 19% over the next 10 years Expand market share from 10% to 20% over the next 5 years Establish Verge Hotels in Tanzania, Botswana and Nigeria	Achieve return on total capital of 16% p.a. Establish image as best provider of medical services	Create facilities to accommodate growth of 8% p.a. over the next 5 years Raise contributions by private sector by 10% p.a. over next 6 years
Tactical or functional goals (1–3 years)	Increase room occupancy rates to 70% over the next 2 years (marketing goal) Increase profit margin by 3% in the next year (financial goal) Reduce staff turnover by 3% over next 3 years (human resources goal)	Increase number of beds by 175 over next 2 years (production goal) Limit increase in patient costs to 5% next year Repay short-term loan over next 18 months (financial objective)	Raise teaching productivity by 3% p.a. over the next 3 years Establish image of academic excellence over the next 36 months Build up research fund to R50m over the next 2 years
Operational short-term goals (1 year at most)	Develop promotional campaign aimed at corporate travel agents Extend restaurant hours during conferences Establish supply partnerships with local laundromats and dry cleaners	Take on additional temporary nursing staff for Easter weekend Increase supply of blood plasma by 30% for Christmas weekend	Keep library open until 22h00 during examination periods Next January provide additional student guidance during registration

The second set of objectives within the business comprises the personal goals of employees, that is, the goals that employees hope to accomplish as a result of their activities and involvement in the business. Examples are a basic salary and a particular status or opportunity for self-development. Conflict may arise if organisational and personal goals cannot be reconciled. Employees working for financial benefits, and who realise that it is possible to achieve a higher income if the business is successful, will work harder to meet organisational objectives so that their personal goals can be accomplished.

Critical thinking

Which of the following objectives are strategic goals, which are tactical goals and which are operational goals?

- To increase customer satisfaction by 15% by the end of the year
- To decrease customer complaints by 5% in the next month
- To have more customer care specialists available for queries over weekends
- To employ 10 additional clerks in the next 6 months for the Financial Department
- To identify a successor to the CFO by the end of next year
- To build 25 new cellphone towers per year for the next 5 years
- To establish three hotels in Nigeria in the next 5 years
- To develop 3 advertising campaigns in the next 2 years
- To obtain financing of R15 million in the next 2 years.

With these different types of objectives in mind, we shall now briefly consider the setting of goals.

6.5   Setting goals

6.5.1   Satisfying initial requirements

In formulating goals for a business organisation or a department or a particular project, management first has to satisfy these requirements:

- Management must clearly understand the **importance of goals** because:
  - **Goals provide guidance and unanimity.** They spell out to everyone the direction of the business and the importance of achieving goals. Without goals, a business is like a ship without a rudder.
  - The setting of realistic goals facilitates planning.
  - Goals can inspire and motivate subordinates, especially if their achievement is linked to remuneration.
  - Goals provide an effective means of evaluation and control.

> "If you do not know where you're going, any road will take you there"
> *Thedore Levit*

- Goals should accurately represent the details of what is being pursued. This means that goals have to be **measurable**, so that managers can check whether the goals are being accomplished when comparing results with predetermined goals. This is especially true for tactical and functional goals. To say, for example, "Market share should be increased" is too vague and not measurable, whereas to say "Market share should be increased by 10% over the next 2 years in Gauteng" is precise and measurable.
- Not only should goals be precise, but the **responsibility** for reaching them should be clearly assigned to specific individuals. Each manager, however, generally has responsibilities for setting goals at his or her level in the organisation. This means that the relation between the expected

results and the persons responsible for the results should be clearly stated, so that managers fully understand the aims and goals and are in no doubt about what they have to do to achieve them.

- Goals should be set consistently, that is, not conflict with one another.
  - **Horizontal consistency** refers to the compatibility of the objectives of various departments with one another. If, for example, the marketing department proposes to extend its line of products, the costs of production will increase, and therefore the production division will find it difficult to embark on cost cutting as one of its goals.
  - **Vertical consistency** means that departmental goals are compatible with those of subsections. For example, an increase of 8% in sales set by marketing has to be compatible with the sales objectives set for certain geographical markets of the business – in other words, the total increase in sales for the particular regions should add up to 8%.
- Goal setting must be **integrated with the remuneration system** in order to provide subordinates with a means of realising both business and personal goals. Employees who realise that their personal goals, for example a higher income or more status and power, can only be achieved if the business's goals are achieved, will set more realistic goals and work much harder to achieve them.
- Management must ensure that **subordinates accept the goals** and are willing to cooperate in achieving them. People who share in formulating goals more readily associate themselves with their achievement.

6.5.2 Two basic approaches to setting goals

There is some argument about the way in which management should ensure the effective setting of goals. There are two basic approaches:

- **The hierarchical approach.** This approach is one whereby managers at upper levels determine the goals to be worked for by their subordinates. Figure 6.3 on the following page shows this schematically. The advocates of this approach argue that it is the proper and obvious way because top management knows exactly the direction the business should take to achieve its long-term goals, due to top managers' involvement in formulating its mission. The problem with this approach, however, is that top management does not always possess the information required by the lower ranks to perform a particular task.
- **Bottom-up** or the well-known **management by objectives.** This technique is sometimes referred to as a distinct management approach because it facilitates the setting of goals and the planning and controlling that follows from this. Management by objectives[1] entails the setting of goals and objectives that are considered jointly by superiors and subordinates. This method may be used at any level of management, and the goals set for employees can be linked to a given remuneration for their achievement. The advantage of this method lies mainly in its motivation of employees – they tend to work harder and more purposefully when they have had a part in the formulation of objectives. It also makes performance management possible.

The choice of a particular approach, however, is limited by such factors as the size of the business, its organisational structure, its corporate culture, the prevailing situation, and the leadership style of top management.

Management has to take into account the personal objectives of individuals, and coordinate and integrate them in such a way

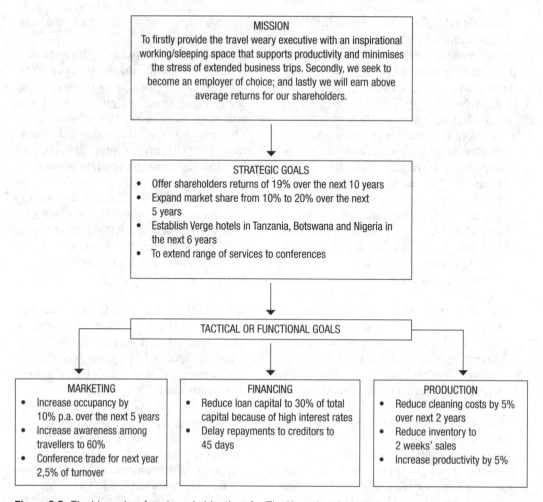

Figure 6.3: The hierarchy of goals and objectives for The Verge hotel group

---

Critical thinking

How would you advise the following manager regarding the formulation of goals for his organisation?

John du Toit, a senior civil servant, was offered an early retirement package in 2002. He accepted the offer. A few weeks into retirement, however, he felt that he was too young to simply stop working, so he started looking for a small business to invest in. With South Africa being a popular tourist destination and being awarded the 2010 Soccer World Cup, he decided to qualify as a tour guide and purchased a minibus. His business grew and he purchased another two minibuses and now has three tour guides working for him. Demand for his services is growing and he wants to get a short-term loan from the bank to expand his venture once again. As part of the business plan that he has to present to the bank manager, he has to set specific goals.

that the purpose and mission of the business are fulfilled as productively as possible.

The next step in planning, namely the development of actual plans, will now be considered.

6.6 Developing plans: The choice of alternatives

Planning has already been defined as the fundamental element of management that determines what a business proposes to achieve and how it should go about it. The importance of goals and goal formulation discussed in the previous section indicates what the business organisation intends to achieve, and, to an extent, how this should be done. In other words, the goals themselves implicitly indicate the combination of resources – people, equipment and money – that need to be employed, as well as the ways of realising the goals, or plans to be followed in achieving them. In planning, it should also be made clear who is to do what, and when. In a nutshell, the second phase of planning – **developing plans** – includes the consideration of several alternative plans of action, and ultimately the selection of the alternative or plan that will lead to the achievement of the predetermined goals.

If an existing plan of action does not succeed in accomplishing the predetermined goals, or if some new goal is established, then management has to develop alternative plans from which a new plan can be selected. In developing such alternative plans, management must constantly bear in mind the following:

- **The influence of external factors** – such as market factors, legislation or economic trends – on the business environment for the achievement of goals, and hence the level of action. Such environmental influences occur in the form of opportunities that may be exploited or threats that must be averted and should be considered in the development of alternatives. Environmental scanning was discussed in chapter 4.
- **The strong and weak points of the business.** When alternative plans of action to achieve some purpose are being developed, the strong points – for instance a particular skill, a patent, possession of a raw material source or a marketing channel, capital, or, even, the image of the business – should always be taken into account. At the same time, alternative plans should not expose the weak points of the business to threats.
- **The costs of each alternative** plan should be weighed against the advantages offered by it. In this way, a more or less rational plan of action may be developed. Rational decision making plays a vital role in the choice of an optimal plan of action that has evolved against the backdrop of environmental influences, been assessed in accordance with costs and benefits, and will stand the best chance of achieving its purpose.

This process of devising plans, in which several alternatives are developed and an optimal plan decided on, indicates that different kinds of plans may be developed to make the accomplishment of different kinds of goals possible. An overview of the types of plans originating at different levels of management makes the **planning process** clearer.

6.6.1 Types of plans: The levels and time frames of planning

Just as different kinds of goals and objectives are encountered at each level of a business, so different kinds of plans originate on different levels of management (see figure 6.2 on page 154). It follows that certain objectives can be attained only by means of specific actions or plans. For this reason, particular plans have to be formulated at the different levels to achieve the different objectives. Figure 6.4 on the next page shows the kinds of plans encountered at various levels. Each merits a brief overview.

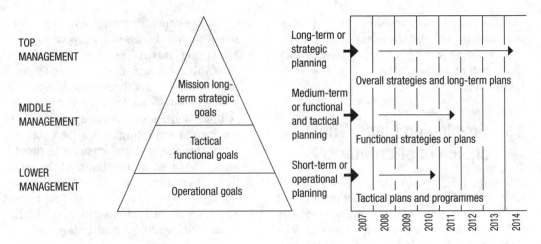

Figure 6.4: The levels and time frames of different kinds of plans

6.6.1.1 **Strategic planning**

Strategic planning, or **long-term planning** as it is sometimes called, is the development of a broad long-term overall strategy to realise the mission of the business. In figure 6.4 the following characteristics of strategic planning are apparent:

- It is carried out by top management, which normally devotes most of its time to strategic or long-term planning.
- It has a time frame of three to ten years or more.
- It is focused on the business as a whole.
- It is future-oriented and is at all times on the lookout for changes in the environment.
- It includes constant adaptation to the environment.
- A long-term or strategic plan is not concerned with details, but is in the form of broad general guidelines to keep the business on its course.
- Management constantly endeavours to use it to deploy the resources and skills of the business among the opportunities and risks in the business environment, and to steer the business as profitably as possible towards its mission.

These characteristics distinguish strategic planning from functional and operational planning (also known as conventional planning), in which the emphasis falls more on short-term and comprehensive plans for particular departments.

The first half of the 20th century was characterised by stable business environments with low and stable rates of interest, few raw material shortages, a slow and steady rate of technological innovation, and a general economy in which inflation was practically unknown. In such a stable environment businesses were able to sell their products or services without being too concerned about the future. It was assumed that future environments would be more or less the same as prevailing ones, so that a mere extension or projection of old plans was perfectly adequate to ensure profitable survival.

However, since the 1950s, as discussed in some detail in chapters 4 and 5, the business environment has been changing at an unprecedented rate. Management has had to look for new approaches, because old ones – such as budgeting, management by objectives, and policy formulation – have proved to be of little use in an unstable environment. At the same time, businesses have become larger and more complex. In these circumstances, long-term planning came into being during the late 1950s in an attempt to take countermeasures against instability in the business environment. In the 1960s and 1970s especially, the general concept of strategic planning was deployed to try to keep abreast of change in the business environment, and various concepts were developed to enable managers to develop long-term or strategic plans. After the turbulent 1990s, strategic planning remains a popular management tool and is increasingly used by government departments as well as not-for-profit organisations. Strategic planning therefore gives long-term direction to a business, with its mission as the ultimate aim to be achieved. Various long-term strategies can be devised to accomplish the mission. The following are typical examples:[2]

- **A concentration strategy.** This is the most popular long-term strategy, and normally entails a business directing all its resources and skills to the profitable growth of a single product in a single market – in short, concentrating all that it has on what it does best to realise its mission. In the case of Avis, for example, the business concentrated on car hire and got rid of businesses for which it did not have the necessary expertise and skills.

- **Market development.** This means that existing markets for the present products of the business are developed more intensively, or else new markets are developed for existing products. In the latter case, new regions or even an export market can be considered. Recall the case study at the start of this chapter. The Verge Hotel Group's decision to establish its hotels in other African countries is an example of a market development strategy.

- **Product development.** This type of strategy is closely related to market development, and involves new products being developed for existing markets, or existing products being modified to win greater approval among consumers. For example, in the 1990s, Castle Lite was introduced to the existing market by South African Breweries to satisfy the needs of beer drinkers who preferred a light beer. By the late 1990s beverage companies such as South African Breweries expanded their product ranges to include alco-pops and ciders, such as Brutal Fruits and Redds.

- **Innovation.** This is a long-term strategy that entails constantly changing and improving products to take advantage of the initial high profitability of a new improved product in order to achieve the mission. This strategy is especially popular in the motor vehicle industry, with the underlying idea of creating a new life cycle for the product with each innovation, and so making competitive products obsolete. It is also effective in other markets. Polaroid, for example, markets each new camera intensively until competitors have caught up with it technologically. By that stage, Polaroid usually has an advanced new product ready for the market.

- **Horizontal integration.** This is a long-term growth strategy in which similar

Example

In the 1970s, Avis, the multinational car rental organisation, was a conglomorate with businesses involved in car rental, motels, hotels, travel agencies and tourism. For many years it operated at a loss, until Robert Townsend was appointed chief executive and gave it a much-needed sense of direction. He formulated Avis's mission as follows: "We want to be the fastest growing organisation with the highest profit margins in the business of renting cars without drivers." Three years later, Avis was number two in the industry. To achieve this, Townsend had to develop and implement various strategies, including selling off related but money-losing businesses. But most importantly, he focused on the core business of Avis, namely renting out cars.

businesses are taken over. This strategy gives access to new markets, on the one hand, and gets rid of competition, on the other.

- **Vertical integration.** This occurs when the business's strategy is to take over suppliers, such as those providing raw materials, or businesses that buy from it. It can be used to ensure a source of supply or a distribution channel to ensure an outlet.
- **Joint venture.** A joint venture is a strategy for two or more firms to embark on some project that is too big for one to tackle on its own. The advantage of such a strategy lies mainly in the pooling of resources and skills.
- **Diversification.** This strategy represents a positive departure from existing activities by the takeover of other firms, or the setting up of a completely new entity by the business itself. The objectives of such a strategy include distribution of risk, synergy, a more rapid rate of growth, or higher profits. If the Verge Hotel Group, for example, decided to open a series of restaurants, this would be an example of a diversification strategy.

- **Rationalisation.** In difficult times businesses may find that their profits decline and they are compelled to cut costs drastically by terminating unprofitable products, getting rid of unprofitable assets, and, in particular, improving ineffective management.
- **Divestiture.** This is closely related to the foregoing strategy, and may lead to the selling off of a business or parts of it to make it possible for it to fulfil its mission. Transnet, for example, has sold one of its valuable assets, the Victoria and Alfred Waterfront in Cape Town, as part of its turnaround strategy.
- **Liquidation.** This is a final strategy, and amounts to the discontinuation of the whole business because it cannot be successfully sustained.

The following question now arises: "How should a business decide on one of these strategies?" Several advanced techniques – such as the well-known PIMS (profit impact of market share) studies, the BCG (Boston Consulting Group) portfolio matrix, the GE (General Electric) matrix, and many others – have been developed for this purpose. Table

Table 6.2: Choice of alternative strategies

Strategic options						
	1	2	3	4	5	6
Opportunities in the business environment	Western Cape markets offer very little competition		Present market sensitive to prices		Business offers too narrow a range of products	
Long-term goals derived from mission						
• Average investment over five years	15%	19%	13%	17%	23%	19%
• Sales over five years	+50%	+40%	+20%	+0%	+35%	+25%
Overall strategy	Horizontal integration	Market development	Concentration	Selective retrenchment	Product development	Concentration

6.2 shows a simple matrix that management can use to make use of opportunities in the environment for the accomplishment of its mission and long-term goals.

Strategic planning – that is, the development of a mission and long-term goals in a business and the choice of one or more long-term strategies to realise them – depends on functional planning or the development of functional plans to put the overall or grand strategy into effect.

6.6.1.2 Functional planning

As shown in figure 6.4 (see page 160), **functional and tactical planning** refers to **medium-term planning** carried out by middle management (in cooperation with top management) for the various functional departments to realise their goals (which are themselves derived from the long-term strategic goals). Table 6.3 provides examples of functional strategies or functional plans. Functional plans may sometimes be of a long-term nature, although they are normally designed for the medium term, and are therefore more tactical than strategic. Most

medium-term plans are components of long-term strategies and plans. Because long-term strategies and plans are exposed to many uncertainties and changes in the business environment, medium-term planning, especially in very turbulent environments, forms the nucleus of the planning activities of some businesses.

6.6.1.3 Short-term planning

Short-term planning, also referred to as **operational planning**, is done for periods of not longer than a year. It is developed by lower management to achieve operational objectives (which are derived from the functional and tactical goals), and may therefore be regarded as a component of functional plans. Short-term plans are concerned with the day-to-day performance of tasks and the allocation of resources to particular persons in accordance with particular programmes, schedules or budgets to fulfil certain aims. Budgeting is the main method used by management in planning the allocation of resources to alternative plans of action. Moreover, planning is carried out in accordance with a particular policy or set of procedures that gives direction to routine activities, thereby facilitating plans.

Many factors may disturb the planning process: unrealistic objectives, environmental influences, financial constraints, and a host of others. Management can take various actions to overcome these disturbances, but should start by setting realistic objectives that are precise, clear and achievable. Top management should take responsibility for planning and allied activities. Communication with subordinates and the gaining of their participation promotes good planning. People who are informed and share in decision making are likely to cooperate in making the plans succeed. Management should also realise that planning is subject to certain limitations, and should be revised from time to time.

Table 6.3: Functional strategies and plans

Functional management areas	Key aspects to be considered
Marketing	Product line, market position, distribution channels, market communication, prices
Finance	Policy on debtors, dividends, asset management, capital structure
Production and operations	Improvement of productivity, locational problems, legislation
Human resources	Labour relations, labour turnover, training of human resources, equity considerations
Purchasing	Suppliers, policy on creditors, sources of raw materials

6.6.2 Implementation of the selected plan

During the first two phases of the planning process – while objectives are being formulated and plans devised – management must decide who is to be responsible for the activities to be carried out, and what means or resources are to be used in doing so. Obviously, therefore, even at the planning stage, attention is given to some aspects of the other three elements of management, namely organising, leading and control. This confirms, once again, the interdependence of the four fundamental elements of management, and reminds us that none of them can be carried out in isolation. The implementation of the chosen plan therefore involves the development of a framework for its execution, leadership to set the plan in motion, and the exercise of control to determine whether the performance of the activities is going according to plan. In short, the third phase of planning – that is, the implementation of the plan – forms part of the other three elements of the management process.

6.7 Summary

Planning is the starting point of the management process – it determines what an organisation proposes to achieve and how it is to be done. The "what" refers to the various goals to be formulated prior to different strategies and plans being devised so as to realise them. The "how" is the plan, which describes how the goals should be achieved. The plan can be strategic, tactical or operational. To implement the plans, the tasks and activities must be organised and leadership must be applied to achieve the goals. Plans are finally controlled to establish if the goals have been achieved.

The development of an organisational structure is the second fundamental task of the management process which needs to be examined.

Critical thinking

Which of the following are examples of strategic planning? Give reasons for your answer.

- Standard Bank has decided to open several branches in Tanzania in the next five years in order to introduce its existing products into new markets.
- Kgomotso has decided to add a restaurant to her bed-and-breakfast establishment in the next year.
- Vodacom has decided to develop a marketing campaign in the next six months to increase its number of subscribers.
- The Integrated Human Resource Management and Development programme of the Department of Public Service and Administration seeks to ensure the effective and appropriate use of human resources through targeted interventions that improve management and overall capacity of government departments in South Africa.[3]
- Melissa's fine foods will employ three new employees in its Cape Town factory.

 Key terms

Bottom-up	Management by objectives
Concentration strategy	Measurable goals
Decision-making dimension	Medium-term or functional and tactical planning
Determination dimension	Mission
Developing plans	Operational goals
Diversification	Organisational goals
Divestiture	Overall long-term or strategic goals
Future dimension	Personal goals
Goal setting	Planning
Hierarchical approach	Planning process
Horizontal consistency	Product development
Horizontal integration	Rationalisation
Implementation	Reactive planning

Innovation	Short-term or operational planning
Joint venture	Tactical or functional goals
Liquidation	Vertical consistency
Long-term or strategic planning	Vertical integration

? Questions for discussion

Reread the Verge Hotel Group case study at the beginning of the chapter and answer the following questions:

1. What are the various dimensions that planning encapsulates?
2. Imagine that the CEO of the Verge Hotel Group has invited you as a guest speaker to open its annual strategic planning session. He has asked you to discuss the importance of planning for the Verge Hotel Group as well as the components of the planning process. What would the key points of your presentation be?
3. What might the tactical and operational goals for the Verge Hotel Group be?
4. What are the different types of plans? Distinguish between them.

References

1. Drucker, P., *The practice of management*, Harper & Row, New York, 1954, p. 62.
2. Pearce, J.A. & Robinson, R.B., *Strategic management*, 9th edition, McGraw-Hill, New York, 2005, pp. 189–203.
3. Department of Public Service and Administration. Medium-Term Strategic Plan.

ORGANISING

The purpose of this chapter

Once management has devised a plan to achieve the organisation's goals, it must deploy resources such as people, equipment, money and other resources. In addition, it must design jobs; assign tasks, duties and responsibilities to people; coordinate activities; and establish lines of communication and reporting. This is called organising. This chapter examines organising as the second fundamental task of management. An overview of the importance of organising is provided, followed by an examination of the fundamentals of organising. An exposition is given of how an organisation evolves from a one-person business to a large business organisation with many departments. Authority relationships and reporting relationships are explained, and thereafter coordination is discussed. A brief overview of the informal organisation is also given. Finally, the factors influencing the design of an organisation's structure are discussed. It is emphasised that such a structure must enable the people concerned to work effectively towards the organisation's mission and goals.

Learning outcomes

The content of this chapter will enable learners to:
- Explain the concepts of organising and organisational structure
- Describe the importance of organising
- Discuss the fundamentals of organising
- Explain how an organisation evolves from a single-entrepreneur organisation to a large one
- Present viewpoints regarding the factors that influence organising

7.1 Introduction

Planning, the first fundamental element of the management process, is defined as the setting of goals and the development of a plan of action to achieve the goals as productively as possible. Planning, however, is only one component of the management process, and it alone cannot guarantee that the goals of the business organisation will be accomplished. Once the plan to achieve certain goals has been selected, management must combine human and other resources – such as money, machines, raw materials and information or knowledge – in the best possible way to achieve the organisation's goals. The most important of these tasks is the task of grouping people into teams or departments to perform the activities that will convert the plan into accomplished goals. In the Edcon case study on the next page we shall see the grouping of people and other resources in three divisions, namely the department store division, the discount store division and the financial services division. The structured grouping and combination of people and other resources, and the coordination of them to achieve organisational goals, constitute the second fundamental element of management, namely organising.

Organising means that management has to develop mechanisms in order to implement the strategy or plan. Arrangements have to be made to determine what activities will be carried out, what resources will be employed, and who will perform the various activities. These arrangements involve the distribution of tasks among employees, the allocation of resources to persons and departments, and the giving of the necessary authority to certain people to ensure that the tasks are in fact carried out. Above all, there must be communication, cooperation and coordination between the people and the departments or sections performing the tasks.

A business's **organisational structure** therefore indicates the work to be done and the connections between various positions and tasks. Organising, or the design of a framework of how the work must be done to accomplish the goals, is an indispensable step in the management process of any business, whether existing or new.

In a newly established business, decisions have to be taken regarding equipment, supplies, processes to be followed, and people who must perform the tasks. In addition, the structure indicating the distribution of tasks among departments and individuals has to be drawn up, indicating the responsibilities and lines of authority and communication. In an existing business, organising has to be constantly reviewed and adapted to accommodate new products and new processes or any organisational changes which affect

the activities. In line with the strategy or plan, management still arranges what needs to be done so as to reach the objectives.

Organising the activities that must be performed to achieve the goals is like building a toy castle. Imagine giving a child a pile of coloured wooden blocks of different shapes and asking him or her to build a castle. The child might then select some square blocks, some round blocks, some red blocks and a combination of other wooden blocks, and build a castle. Ask another child to do the same, and a different selection of shapes and colours will be combined differently and will produce a different castle. Choosing certain combinations of blocks and putting them together in unique ways is, in a sense, like trying to organise or choose certain combinations of resources and people and putting them together in unique ways. Just as children select different building blocks to build a castle, managers choose the building blocks of an organisation. And no two teams of managers will put the same organisational structure together. Managers can use various basic building blocks to construct an organisation. Examples of these basic building blocks are job design, the grouping of jobs (also called departmentalisation), the establishment of chains of command, the assigning of authority, and the establishment of coordination mechanisms to link activities between jobs.

The case study on the next page provides an illustration of how the principles of organising are applied to a real-life situation in South Africa.

7.2   The importance of organising

Organising, like planning, is an integral and indispensable component of the management process. Without it, the successful implementation of plans and strategies is out of the question because of the absence of a systematic allocation of resources and people

Case study: Organising in action

Edgars Consolidated Stores Ltd (Edcon)

Since its founding in 1929, Edgars Consolidated Stores Ltd (Edcon) has established itself as one of the leaders in South Africa's clothing, footwear and textile retail arena. Edcon is organised in three divisions, namely the department store division (encompassing Boardmans, CNA, Edgars, Prato, Red Square and Temptations), the discount store division (encompassing Jet, Jet Mart, Jet Shoes and Legit), and the financial services division.

Edcon's biggest plus is a management team that lends visible support to all human resources initiatives. It believes that the key to sustainable business development lies in successfully addressing people issues. The group's biggest minus is that regular perception surveys suggest that career development programmes have been neglected in the recent past and require some extra attention.

People who thrive at Edcon are those who are not prepared to accept the status quo. They are creative thinkers and hard workers – retail is a challenging environment, and that means long hours. The company boasts 9 retail brands with over 900 stores in South Africa, Botswana, Namibia, Swaziland and Lesotho. Edcon has eight pillars on which it focuses its attention: culture, company reputation, work environment, learning, compensation, community, employee care and leadership. Its culture is one of inclusiveness, built on the organisation's values of people, integrity, performance and professionalism.

Edcon's focus on building a reputation as an employer of choice means that the organisation has a number of thorough HR policies and procedures in place. Examples are a talent acquisition programme and the establishment of Edcon Academy, which provides training related to merchandising and operations. The company has excellent labour relations and it offers above-market guaranteed pay. With 57% of management and 87% of the total workforce comprising previously disadvantaged individuals, the success of Edcon's employment equity programme is self-evident.

Edcon has identified education, social development and health as the key areas for investment. The company also donates clothes, books and general merchandise to communities in need. In future, the group is seeking to achieve further profits through organic growth in the Edgars and Jet Stores, while improving productivity in both the department store and discount divisions.

Source: Brevis, T., "Best companies to work for in 2005", *Management Today*, Vol. 21, No. 10, 2005, pp. 50–55.

to execute the plans. Leadership and control are not possible if the activities of management and subordinates are not organised, or if the business does not clearly designate the individuals responsible for specific tasks.

More specifically, organising is important for the following reasons:

- **Organising entails a detailed analysis of work to be done and resources to be used to accomplish the aims of the business.** It is through organising that tasks and resources, and methods or procedures, can be systematised. Everyone should know their duties, authority and responsibility, the procedures they must follow or the methods they have to adopt, and the resources they can use. Proper organising ensures that the joint and coordinated efforts of management have a much greater and more effective result than the sum of individual efforts.

- **Organising divides the total workload into activities that can comfortably be performed by an individual or a group.** Tasks are allocated according to the abilities or qualifications of individuals, thus ensuring that nobody in the business has either too much or too little to do. The ultimate result is higher productivity.
- **Organising promotes the productive deployment and utilisation of resources.** Related activities and tasks of individuals are grouped together rationally in specialised departments such as marketing, personnel or finance departments, in which experts in their particular fields carry out their given duties.
- **The development of an organisational structure results in a mechanism that coordinates the activities of the whole business into complete, uniform, harmonious units.**

Successful organising, then, makes it possible for a business to achieve its goals. It coordinates the activities of managers and subordinates to avoid the unnecessary duplication of tasks, and it obviates possible conflicts. It also reduces the chances of doubts and misunderstandings, enabling the business to reach its goals efficiently. Against this background, we shall now examine the building blocks or fundamentals of organising.

7.3   The fundamentals of organising

Building an organisational structure revolves around the building blocks or the fundamentals of organising, namely:
- Designing jobs for employees
- Grouping employees into teams or departments based on commonalities
- Assigning authority
- Establishing a command structure
- Establishing coordinating mechanisms

7.3.1 Designing jobs

Job design is the determination of an employee's responsibilities in an organisation and the compilation of a job specification that explains what he or she must do and what performance standards are expected. The job design and description of a sales manager of the department store division of Edcon, for example, would give a detailed exposition of sales objectives per week, month and year.

The point of departure of designing jobs for employees is to determine the level of specialisation or the degree to which the overall task of the organisation is broken down into smaller, more specialised tasks. Specialisation is the way in which a task is broken up into smaller units to take advantage of specialised knowledge or skills to improve productivity. The best example of specialisation or division of labour is still the assembly line, a production method usually attributed to the inventive mind of Henry Ford. His pioneering work opened the way to mass production, which, in the early decades of this century, had a profound effect on Western societies. The division of a task into smaller units, however, means that the various units have to be coordinated. Coordination is therefore an indispensable part of organising.

> **Specialisation**
>
> The principle of specialisation or the division of labour is generally ascribed to Adam Smith. In his famous enquiry into the wealth of nations, he described how specialisation was applied in a pin factory so as to increase productivity. One man unrolled the wire, another straightened it, a third cut it, a fourth sharpened the tip, and so on. In that way, said Smith, 10 men could produce 48 000 pins a day, while 1 man on his own could make only 20 a day![1]

The way in which the principle of **work specialisation** operates may be illustrated by means of the hypothetical example in figure 7.1.

Suppose an amateur inventor designs a machine in his or her garage. First of all, he or she builds it at home, sells it him- or herself, keeps a set of accounts him- or herself, and also buys the parts required. If he or she is successful, the business will soon become too big for him or her to do all these things alone. At this stage, as phase 2 in the figure 7.1 shows, the inventor has a small business with a part-time bookkeeper who relieves him or her of part of the total workload. Therefore, in phase 2, the inventor is beginning to specialise. As the business grows, the inventor is compelled, in phase 3, to get help with the production of the machine. At the same time, he or she employs somebody else to help to sell it, and the part-time bookkeeper is appointed on a full-time basis so that the inventor can devote more time to the general management of the business. Eventually the inventor arrives at phase 4, at which point the business is becoming a large business.

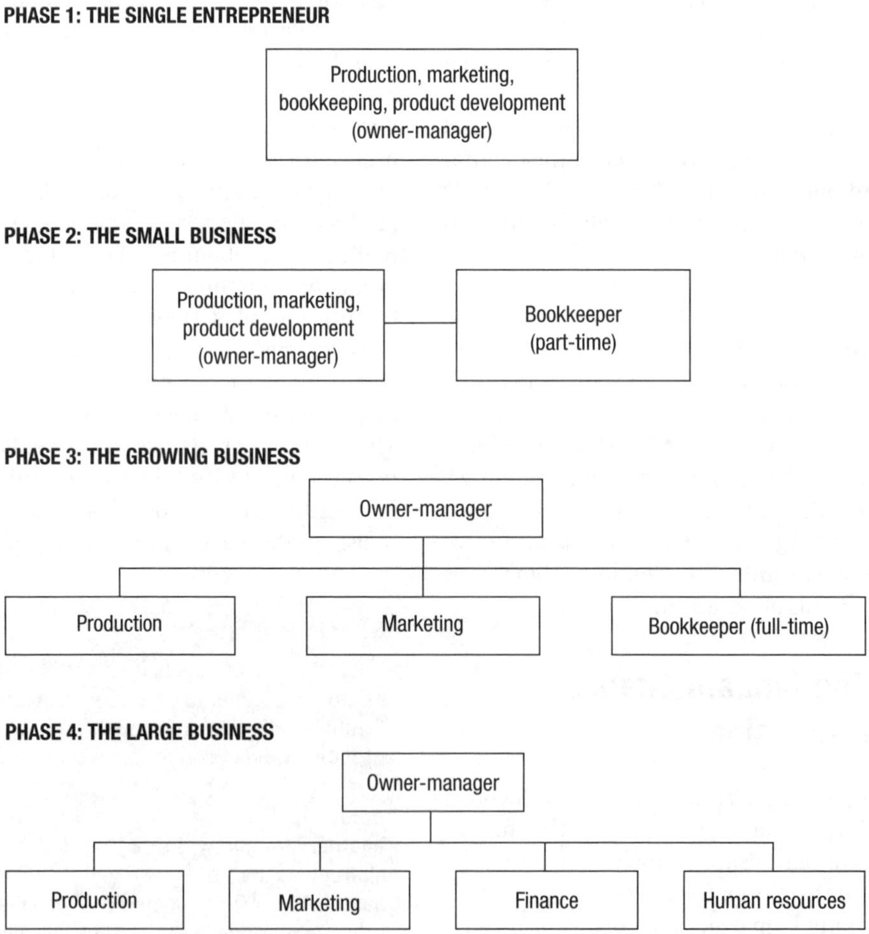

PHASE 1: THE SINGLE ENTREPRENEUR

Production, marketing, bookkeeping, product development (owner-manager)

PHASE 2: THE SMALL BUSINESS

Production, marketing, product development (owner-manager) — Bookkeeper (part-time)

PHASE 3: THE GROWING BUSINESS

Owner-manager

Production | Marketing | Bookkeeper (full-time)

PHASE 4: THE LARGE BUSINESS

Owner-manager

Production | Marketing | Finance | Human resources

Figure 7.1: The evolution of specialisation

The growth of the business, as depicted in the model in figure 7.1, is characterised by two developments in particular:

- The growing total task of the business
- Constant pressure to split the total task into smaller units

Put differently, the growing business is continually compelled to apply specialisation or the division of labour. Besides this evolutionary pressure, there are other reasons that justify specialisation, including the following:

- **Individual ability.** If individuals concentrate on some simple small task, they acquire a certain degree of skill in that area and can perform the task as a specialist more quickly and better than anybody else. This has obvious advantages for the business.
- **Reduced transfer time.** Workers who do several jobs lose time when they switch from one job to another. Specialisation eliminates such non-productive transfer time.
- **Specialised equipment.** Specialisation leads to the development of specialised equipment, which increases the productivity of each worker.
- **Reduced training costs.** Division of labour reduces the costs of training, because workers are trained in a particular part of the total task.

The main purpose of specialisation is to increase productivity. Although specialisation has traditionally been applicable mostly at the operational level, it is increasingly being applied at managerial levels also. However, one should not lose sight of the fact that excessive specialisation may have a negative effect on productivity.

The main criticism of specialisation is that workers who perform highly specialised jobs may become bored and demotivated. Managers should be sensitive to over-specialisation and should also consider such approaches as **job enrichment**, **job enlargement** and **job rotation** to counter the negative effects of specialisation.

7.3.2 Departmentalisation

A second principle underlying organising is **departmentalisation**, the formation of departments. While this is a result of specialisation, it also promotes specialisation, since it is necessitated by the logical grouping of activities that belong together. By grouping financial services activities into one division, Edcon's employees can specialise in this field and also contribute to Edcon's overall performance. The reasons for departmentalisation are therefore inherent in the advantages of specialisation and the pressure in a growing business to split the total task of management into smaller units. As soon as a business has reached a given size, say phase 4 in figure 7.1, it becomes impossible for the owner-manager to supervise all the employees. So it becomes necessary to create new managerial positions according to departments based on a logical grouping, in manageable sizes, of the activities that belong together.

The various departments created constitute the organisational structure of the business as they appear on the organisation chart. Depending on such factors as the size and kind of the business, and the nature of its activities, various organisational structures may be developed through departmentalisation. We shall now discuss some basic forms of organisation.

7.3.2.1 Functional organisational structure

The **functional organisational structure**, as shown in figure 7.2, is the most basic type. Here, activities belonging to each management function are grouped together. Activities such as advertising, market research, and sales, for example, belong together under the marketing function, while those concerned with the production of goods are grouped under operations.

7.3.2.2 Product departmentalisation

Product departmentalisation is illustrated in figure 7.3. Departments are designed so that all activities concerned with the manufacturing of a product or group of products are grouped together in product sections, where all the specialists associated with the particular products are grouped.

In the case study at the start of this chapter, Edcon applied product departmentalisation by grouping all its activities and resources into three divisions. Edcon's personnel, financing and marketing needs for the various divisions differ. For example, the personnel, marketing and financing needs for its department store division differ from those in the financial services division. This is a logical structure for large businesses providing a wide range of products or services. The advantages of this structure are that the specialised knowledge of employees is used to maximum effect, decisions can be made quickly within a section, and the performance of each group can easily be measured. The disadvantages are that the managers in each section concentrate their attention almost exclusively on their products and tend to lose sight of those of the rest of the business. Moreover, administrative costs increase, because each section has to have its own functional specialists, such as market researchers and financial experts.

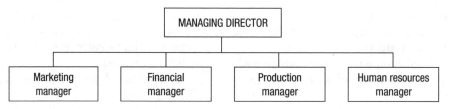

Figure 7.2: A functional organisational structure

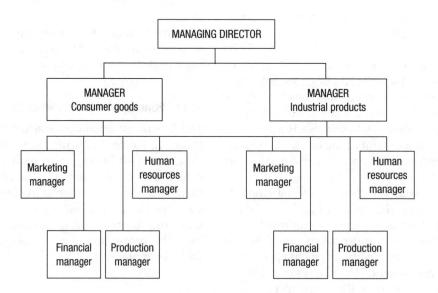

Figure 7.3: Departmentalisation according to product

7.3.2.3 Location departmentalisation

Location departmentalisation is illustrated in figure 7.4. This is a logical structure for a business that manufactures and sells its goods in different geographical regions, for example SABMiller, which operates and markets its range of products all over South Africa as well as internationally. This structure gives autonomy to area managements; this autonomy is necessary to facilitate decentralised decision making and adjustment to local business environments. This structure is also suitable for a multinational business.

7.3.2.4 Customer departmentalisation

Customer departmentalisation is adopted particularly when a business concentrates on some special segment of the market or group of consumers or, in the case of industrial products, when it sells its wares to a limited group of users. Figure 7.5 illustrates this structure.

Departmentalisation according to customer has the same advantages and disadvantages as departmentalisation according to product and location or geographical area. A bank, for example, can have various departments servicing private and corporate clients.

Unlike a functional structure in which activities are grouped according to knowledge, skills, experience or training, a section based on product, location or customers resembles, in some ways, a small privately owned business. It is more or less autonomous, and is accountable for its profits or losses. However, unlike an independent small business, it is subject to the goals and strategies set by top management for the business as a whole.

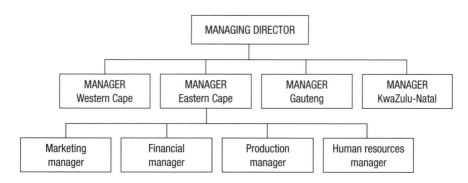

Figure 7.4: Departmentalisation according to location

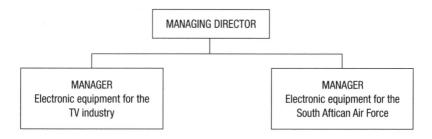

Figure 7.5: Departmentalisation according to customer

7.3.2.5 Matrix organisational structure

The **matrix organisational structure** is important because no organisational structure, whether designed according to function, product, location or customer, will necessarily meet all the organisational needs of a particular business. When departments are formed according to function, there is sophisticated specialisation, but coordination remains a problem. If they are formed according to product, location or customer, certain products or regions may be successful, but the rest of the business does not reap the benefits of good organisation.

To overcome these problems, which mainly occur in large businesses and in those handling specific projects, the matrix organisational structure has been created to incorporate the advantages of both structures discussed earlier. As indicated in figure 7.6, horizontal (staff) and vertical (line) authority lines occur in the same structure so that project managers (horizontal) and functional managers (vertical) both have authority.

The matrix organisational structure is particularly suited to ad hoc and complex projects requiring specialised skills. For example, IBM created a matrix structure for the development of its personal computer, and it disbanded the team when the product had successfully been launched. However, in other businesses the matrix structure may be permanent; for example, a car manufacturer that continually develops certain models as projects may retain this structure. The major advantage of the matrix structure is that specialist project managers can help manage complex projects while the advantages of functional specialisation are retained. The

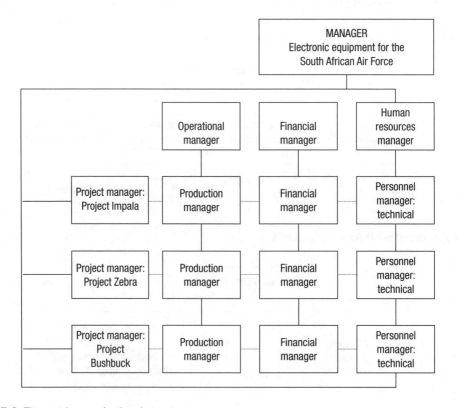

Figure 7.6: The matrix organisational structure

disadvantage is divided authority. Both project leader and departmental head can exercise authority over the same subordinates. The unit of command is therefore affected, and there is a serious risk of soured relations between the project and functional executives. In addition, the position of subordinates may be difficult in the case of having to satisfy two bosses.

7.3.3 Authority relations

In the previous section we discussed the process of task distribution, which, as we stated, includes the breaking up of the total task of the business into smaller specialised units, and the allocation of these units to certain departments and persons. However, this is not the end point of organising. The assignment of tasks to sections and members of staff also entails the assignment of responsibility and authority to each post in an organisational structure. This further entails the creation of organisational relations, that is, stipulating the persons from whom subordinates receive instructions, to whom they report, and to whom and for what they are responsible.

Responsibility, on the one hand, is a particular obligation or commitment on the part of managers (especially at middle or lower level) and, to a more limited degree, their subordinates, to carry out tasks in accordance with instructions they have received. This also means that subordinates should be able to account for what they have done.

Authority, on the other hand, is the right to command or to give orders. Authority is power that has been legitimised by the organisation. It also includes the right to take action to compel the performance of duties and to punish default or negligence. In the formal business structure, several examples of which have been discussed, the owners of the business possess the formal authority. They appoint directors and give them authority, and these directors, in turn, appoint managers, who assign a certain authority to subordinates. In this way authority flows down the line.

This formal authority passed down from above is known as **delegation of authority**. Delegation can be viewed as the main source of authority. However, according to the acceptance theory of authority, authority originates from lower levels, because no one has any authority unless subordinates accept instructions and carry them out. Other sources of authority are, or may be, the personality of the manager, or his or her style of leadership or exceptional knowledge of some particular job or situation.

Responsibility and authority go hand in hand. No one can take responsibility without the authority necessary to enable him or her to compel action. The centralisation of authority means the concentration of power in the hands of top management, with little delegation to middle and lower managements, as is the case with decentralisation of authority.

In our discussion of authority, the terms "line authority" and "staff authority" require some clarification.

7.3.3.1 Line authority

Line authority is authority delegated down through the line of command. In figure 7.7 on the next page, the managing director has line authority over the financial, human resources and marketing managers, while the marketing manager has line authority over the advertising manager, and so on, down the line of command. The managers in this line are directly responsible for achieving the goals of the organisation.

7.3.3.2 Staff authority

Staff authority is an indirect and supplementary authority. Individuals or sections with staff authority – for example, the legal adviser and the marketing research section shown in figure 7.7 – assist, advise and recommend. Their source of authority is usually their special knowledge of a particular field.

Once the distribution of tasks and authority has been completed, management has to design an organisational structure that will enable the various jobs to be done in a coordinated fashion.

7.3.4 Reporting relationships

A further fundamental element of organising is the establishment of **reporting lines** among departments and positions in departments. For example, in the case study at the start of this chapter, will the marketing manager of Edcon's department store division report to the operations manager, or will the operations manager report to the marketing manager? Or should both report to the general manager? Furthermore, who should report to Edcon's Chief Executive Officer?

The first step in establishing reporting lines is to determine who reports to whom. Clear and precise reporting lines are important, so that everybody knows who is in charge of what activities. This is called the **chain of command**. The second part of establishing reporting lines is to determine the **span of management**, that is, the number of subordinates who report directly to a manager. Figure 7.8 on the next page illustrates this concept schematically.

A narrow or high structure may mean that managers are being underutilised, and that there is excessive control over subordinates. At the same time, it may be difficult to coordinate the tasks of a large number of managers. The converse is true of a broad or flat structure, in which management has little time to spare for individuals. The ideal span of management, however, exists only in theory. In practice, factors such as the complexity of the business and the degree of supervision and planning that are necessary determine the span. However, the trend is that structures are becoming flatter as re-engineering and outsourcing result in the need for fewer middle managers, and, consequently, the emergence of leaner organisational structures.

Managers should understand the variables that affect the span of management, as well as the implications of a taller or flatter organisation.

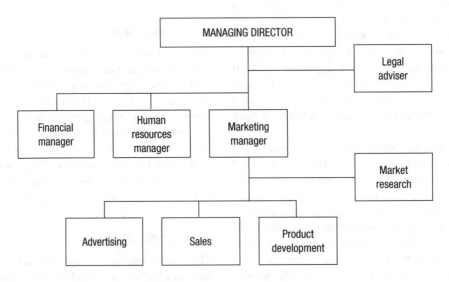

Figure 7.7: Line and staff authority in the organisational structure

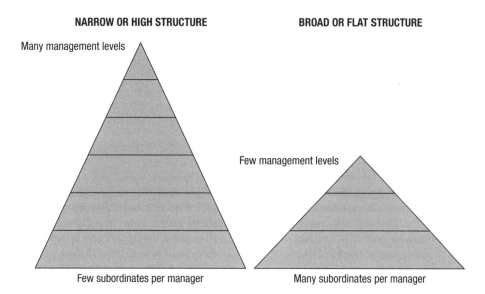

NARROW OR HIGH STRUCTURE

Many management levels

Few subordinates per manager

BROAD OR FLAT STRUCTURE

Few management levels

Many subordinates per manager

Figure 7.8: The span of management

7.3.5 Coordination

Yet another fundamental element of organising is **coordination**. Organisation means dividing up the total task of the business into smaller units so as to take advantage of specialisation and achieve the goals of the business as productively as possible. However, this division of work into smaller jobs immediately raises the problem of **cooperation**, or the coordination of divided tasks and various departments into an integrated whole to achieve the goals of the business.

The key to keeping each department focused on the organisation's goals is **coordination** or the process of linking the activities of the various departments in the organisation into a single integrated unit. The primary reason for coordination is that departments and groups are interdependent. They depend on each other for resources in order to be able to perform their activities. The greater the interdependence between the departments, the more coordination the organisation acquires.

In the case of Edcon in the case study at the start of this chapter, the various sections in its department store division are interdependent. Furthermore, all three divisions of Edcon are also interdependent. The combined performance of the three divisions will determine the overall performance of Edgars Consolidated Stores Ltd.

Without coordination, individuals and departments lose sight of the organisation's primary goals and of their part in that effort. Coordination is the synthesis of separate parts into a unity, and, as such, it is the binding factor in the managerial process. It means the integration of goals and tasks at all levels, and also of all departments and functions, to enable the business to work as a whole. In addition, an element of timing is necessary, because various smaller tasks have to be scheduled to mesh with one another.

Hence, coordination is an endeavour by management to develop congruence, or harmony of goals, through organising. Other mechanisms that promote coordination are the organisation chart, the budget, a committee, the broad policy and procedures in accordance with which tasks are carried out, and the information system of the business.

Once management has deployed all the building blocks of the organisation, it can finalise the formal structure of the organisation. Besides the formal organisation of a business, there is also an informal organisation that often supplements it and helps it to run smoothly.

7.4   The informal organisation

So far, only the formal organisation has been considered. However, relations within a particular business are not confined to those prescribed by the formal organisation chart. Alongside the formal structure there is also an

---

Critical thinking

At the end of this section on the fundamentals of organising, we may ask ourselves the question "Why is organising and creating an effective organisational structure so important?" The following excerpt provides an example of the importance of organising.

Flight Centre Limited

The Corporate Research Foundation (CRF) invited an expert panel to determine the top ten best employers in South Africa for 2005. Flight Centre Limited was amongst the top ten.

Flight Centre Limited, an Australian-based company, established its South African operation in 1994. The company has opened branches in many of the country's major centres, its growth spurred by an innovative approach to selling value-for-money travel solutions. Its ability to offer discounted international and domestic flights, accommodation and holiday packages, together with its unique "Price Beat Guarantee", has ensured it a significant share of the South African market. Flight Centre intends to entrench its favourable position by consolidating its travel brands in the wholesale, leisure and corporate markets.

Flight Centre's biggest plus is a corporate culture that focuses on empowering its people, providing them with the tools to become successful.

Flight Centre sells discount airfares, accommodation and holiday packages. Its organisational structure is based on product departmentalisation. The company opened its doors in South Africa in 1994 and operates

from more than 100 stores in Johannesburg, Pretoria, Richards Bay, Cape Town, Port Elizabeth, East London and Bloemfontein.

The factor that most contributes to Flight Centre's success is its unique structure: each operation is made up of business teams of no more than seven people. These teams form families, which unite to form a village. In essence, a village comprises all families in one area. The spirit of friendly "competition" exists between teams and villages.

A career development programme and detailed job description provide each employee with a detailed needs analysis, based on the position he or she ultimately hopes to achieve and the tools needed to get there. Training, and especially leadership training, are priorities. Flight Centre does not recognise agreements with any trade unions. It rather prefers an open door policy and staff members usually resolve their own disagreements. The impressive earning potential of Flight Centre contributes to the company's reputation as an excellent employer. Rewards and recognition are firmly embedded in its culture.

Flight Centre's ultimate goal is to dominate all aspects of the South African travel market – wholesale, leisure and corporate. This will be done not only through business and organic growth, but also through growing Flight Centre's people. Specific future goals include taking advantage of technological advances and establishing an even greater presence. It reveals that 10 to 15 new stores will open within the next year, along with up to 3 new corporate travel outlets.

Source: Brevis, T., "Best companies to work for in 2005 ", *Management Today*, Vol. 21, No. 10, 2005, pp. 50–55.

informal organisation, which may be defined as the interpersonal relations in a business that are not defined by the formal organisational structure.

Because there is regular interaction between people, social relations that assume a definite form are established. This interaction is achieved by informal communication, also known as "the grapevine". Moreover, these relations exist not only between individuals, but also between groups – though on an informal basis. If sound, these relations can support the formal structure. However, if they are unsound, they may include activities not in harmony with those envisaged in the formal structure. Rather than trying to suppress the informal structure, management should encourage it, for the following reasons:

- Informal communication takes place at a much more rapid pace than formal communication, and therefore decision making could be expedited.
- The informal organisation promotes teamwork within departments, as well as cooperation between departments.
- The informal organisation supports the formal organisation.

Having considered the basis of the task of organising, we shall now examine some of the factors that may influence the organisational structure.

7.5 Factors that influence organising (organisation design)

Organising can be effectively carried out only if the organisational structure has been developed to optimise the execution of strategies and plans. In other words, plans can be successfully implemented only if the organisational structure makes this possible. Planning, leading and control are facilitated if management has an effective and dynamic organisational structure. This raises the question "Which organisational structure is the best?" There is no definite answer, and a business must choose a structure that is best suited to its particular activities or may be adapted to its strategy and requirements.

Organising is carried out in a context where many different factors need to be taken into account. Each of these factors may provide input in the design of the organisational structure.

Some experts believe that the environment in which a business operates is a decisive factor. Others emphasise the connection between strategy and structure. Obviously, the size and complexity of the business, the competence of its employees, and the nature of the product and the market all play important parts. Moreover, the organisational climate or corporate culture should not be ignored in the design of the structure and in the formation of departments and distribution of tasks. Above all, according to modern management theory, whatever structure is designed should be adaptable to changes in the business environment. We shall now briefly examine the above-mentioned factors as we complete our study of organising.

7.5.1 The environment in which a business operates

The environment in which a business operates may be taken as a basis for designing an organisational structure, since it is the starting point for the development of strategy, on the one hand, and because the organisational structure is the mechanism that should keep the business in touch with its environment, on the other. As we have already said, a business has to adapt to its environment to survive. There are various types of environment.

7.5.1.1 Stable environment

A **stable environment** is one that does not change much or is not subject to unexpected change. Here, product changes are the exception rather than the rule. When a change does occur, plans can be made to cope with it in good time. Demand for the product is regular, with only slight fluctuations. New technological changes are small or unlikely. A foundry manufacturing manhole covers and a workshop making violins, for example, operate in stable environments. In a stable environment the functional structure is suitable, because there is little in the way of innovation and no great need for coordination and cooperation between departments. Similarly, businesses with fewer competing markets, which are under little pressure regarding product development to satisfy consumers' needs (for example, a manufacturer of nuts and bolts), will have functional structures with few specialists such as market researchers and advertising experts. Decision making takes place mainly at the top level.

7.5.1.2   Turbulent environment

A **turbulent environment** is one in which changes are the norm rather than the exception; competitors unexpectedly bring out new products and technological innovations cause revolutionary changes in the manufacturing process or the product itself. The pharmaceutical industry is an example of such an environment, which necessitates many specialists for market research, product development and production, and close coordination and communication between them. In such a business, departmentalisation according to product is especially suitable, as this speeds up decision making. More decisions are made in the separate departments than by top management.

The retail environment in which Edcon operates is an example of a challenging environment. Edcon boasts 9 retail brands with more than 900 stores. Product departmentalisation is therefore also suitable for Edcon. Businesses in stable environments are less differentiated in structure than those in turbulent environments.

7.5.1.3   Technologically dominated environment

A **technologically dominated environment** – that is, one in which a particular technology forms the basis for a business's product – organisational design will be influenced by the level of technological sophistication. Technologically complex firms tend to have more managers and more levels of management because specialised technicians work in small groups with a narrow span. Technology, and especially technological innovation, requires an adaptable organisational structure based on one or other form of departmentalisation.

7.5.2   The relationship between strategy and structure

The close relationship between the strategy of a business and its organisational structure is well known. The implication is that the strategy provides a direct input in the design of the organisational structure, and that the structure cannot be separated from the strategy. Structure should always follow strategy.

7.5.3   The size of the business

It is equally obvious that the structure also depends on the number of employees and managers to be coordinated. An increase in the size of the business also creates a need for greater specialisation, more departments, and more levels of management. The danger of bureaucratic management, as a result of detailed procedures, strict job demarcation and, consequently, less emphasis on initiative and regeneration, is always present in large businesses.

7.5.4   Staff employed by the business

There is also a close relationship between an organisational structure and the competence and role of staff, whether this competence is a result of training or experience, availability or attitude. Edcon, for example, has established the Edcon Academy, which provides training related to merchandising and operations to employees. In this way, Edcon improves the competence of its staff.

In management, especially in top management, the structure influences both the choice of strategy and the preferences as to how things should be done. Most managers have a personal preference for a particular organisational structure and for the type

Critical thinking

At the end of this section on factors that influence organisation design, we may ask ourselves the question "Which factor plays a decisive role in organisational design?" Some experts believe that the environment in which the business operates is a decisive factor. The following excerpt provides a practical example of changes that occurred in Discovery's environment, and how these changes influenced Discovery's organisational design.

Environmental changes at Discovery

Discovery comprises five companies operating in the international health and life insurance markets: Discovery Health, Discovery Vitality, Discovery Life, Destiny Health (US) and PruHealth (UK). The core purpose of the group is to make people healthier and to protect and enhance their lives. Its relatively short history is characterised by continual innovation and a spirit of entrepreneurship. The organisation's various companies and products are all at different stages of their life cycles, which make for an extremely dynamic and complex environment. Discovery serves more than two million people, most of whom subscribe to more than one Discovery product.

Discovery's greatest plus is a business philosophy which believes that through an insightful understanding of socio-economic trends and innovative thinking, the group is able to provide solutions that have a profound effect on clients and, in turn, offer excellent business opportunities.

Discovery's biggest challenge is the fact that it faces a highly regulated business environment. High demands on innovation place pressure on the company's people and

systems to keep up with constant change.

When Discovery Health was established in 1993 it identified two trends in the private healthcare market: rising medical inflation and increasing consumerism. The medical savings account was launched as an antidote to rising medical inflation, leveraging the trend towards consumerism by placing money used to pay for these expenses directly into the hands of the consumer.

In 1997, Discovery identified the rapid development of preventive screening and an increasing focus on wellness, in particular on longevity. Discovery Vitality was an innovative solution – a rewarding mechanism to engage clients in the management of their health and well-being.

In 2000, Discovery Life was set up as a unique pure-risk life insurance company offering flexible life insurance products separating out investment products, focusing on risk benefits only – which had never been done before. In the same year, Destiny Health was initiated as the first of its kind providing consumer-driven healthcare cover for 60 000 lives in the USA. In late 2004, PruHealth was born and within a few months, gained the status as one of the top two providers of private healthcare in the UK.

Discovery's strategy is one that analyses social trends in order to identify opportunities to come up with something completely new, and make positive and significant impact on the people it serves. Discovery's culture is best described by a "can do, will do" attitude.

For Discovery, the key to the future is exciting new business opportunities which are evident for each company.

Source: Brevis, T., "Best companies to work for in 2005", *Management Today*, Vol. 21, No. 10, 2005, pp. 50–55.

of relations with subordinates, and also a personal attitude to formality and authority. The tendency is to move away from the strictly formal bureaucratic structure.

7.5.5 The organisational culture

The final factor that plays an important part in organisational design is **organisational culture**. This culture is a concept that may be defined as the beliefs and values shared by people in a business. It is the "personality" of the business. Unless management analyses this concept correctly, it will never know why employees do, or do not do, certain things. Corporate culture comprises basic values reflected not only in organisational behavioural patterns, but also in aspects such as the business's architecture, office decor, dress regulations, and the general way things are done. Edcon's culture is one of inclusiveness built on the organisation's values of people, integrity, performance and professionalism.

The type of structure that leads to the successful implementation of tasks also depends on the culture of the business. The structure of a business with a formal culture will differ from one with a more informal culture.

The above-mentioned considerations are some of those that may influence the design of an organisational structure. They are, however, no more than guidelines for organising. It should, moreover, be understood that the organising process is not used only for a new structure. Organisational structures should be revised whenever strategies or plans change.

7.6 Summary

The setting in motion of the planned activities is part of the organising task of management. Organising is the development of a structure or framework within which the tasks to be performed for the accomplishment of goals, and the resources necessary for the performance of these tasks, are allocated to particular individuals and departments. This division of labour may be done in various ways and ultimately be coordinated to make concerted action possible. Someone, however, has to take the lead in setting in motion the activities involved in the various phases of planning, organising and control. We will deal with the third fundamental element of management in chapter 8.

 Key terms

Authority	Matrix organisational structure
Chain of command	Organisational culture
Coordination	Organisational structure
Customer departmentalisation	Organising
Departmentalisation	Product departmentalisation
Functional organisational structure	Reporting lines
Informal organisation	Responsibility
Job design	Span of management
Job specification	Work specialisation

 Questions for discussion

Reread the "Organising in action" case study and answer the following questions:

1. Do you agree that departmentalisation according to product is the most suitable for Edcon? Substantiate your answer.
2. What are the various authority relations that could exist in the Edcon group?
3. Do you think that a narrow or high organisational structure would be appropriate for Edcon? Substantiate your answer.
4. What factors could influence the organisation design of Edcon?

Reference
1. Smith, A., *The wealth of nations*, J.M. Dent & Sons, New York, 1960, p. 5.

CHAPTER

8

LEADERSHIP: LEADING PEOPLE IN THE ORGANISATION

The purpose of this chapter

If organisations were comprised solely of machines that could implement plans predictably and with precision, only the planning, organising and control functions of management would be necessary to achieve an organisation's goals. However, organisations employ people to activate the financial, physical and informational resources of the organisation. In order to manage the important human resource, managers perform the third management function, namely leading to influence, guide and direct the organisation's employees towards achieving its goals. This chapter deals with the nature of the leading function. We shall discuss the difference between leadership and management. We shall examine the components of the leading function, namely influence, authority, power, delegation, responsibility and accountability. We shall briefly examine the major leadership

theories and investigate the importance of motivation, groups and teams, and communication as elements of the leading function.

Learning outcomes

The content of this chapter will enable learners to:

- Define the concept of leadership
- Differentiate between leadership and management
- Describe the components of leadership
- Discuss the major leadership theories
- Identify contemporary leadership issues
- Explain why managers should understand what motivates their employees' behaviour
- Differentiate between groups and teams in organisations
- Describe a simple communication model

8.1 Introduction

In the introductory discussion on general management in chapter 5, we said that organisations use physical, financial, informational and human resources in order to achieve their goals. Organisations employ

people (the human resources) to activate the other resources of the organisation. The next set of chapters deals with managing the human resources of organisations. Chapter 9 deals with attracting people to the organisation, chapter 10 with motivating and managing human resources, and chapter 11 with the legal environment of human resources. In this chapter we shall examine the nature of the leading function.

8.2 The nature of leadership

Leadership is one of the most researched and

most controversial topics in management. Many researchers[1] have attempted to define it during the past fifty years, using various variables such as traits, behaviour, influence, interaction patterns and role relationships, but it remains an elusive concept. A popular contemporary definition of leadership, from

Case study

Bill Lynch, CEO, Imperial Holdings

Imperial Holdings's chief executive Bill Lynch has become the first South African to win the prestigious Ernst & Young World Entrepreneur Award. Lynch won the award for 2006 at a glittering ceremony in Monte Carlo. The Ernst & Young programme celebrates those who are building and leading successful, growing, and dynamic businesses, recognising them through regional, national, and global awards programmes in over 115 cities and more than 30 countries. The international recognition of the award positions recipients as world-class entrepreneurs and provides a benchmark for entrepreneurial excellence. Winners are much admired leaders in their industries and are important role models. Lynch built South Africa's largest transport and mobility group, Imperial Holdings. Today, he is chief executive of a business with market capitalisation of €4 billion.

The company follows a strict policy of decentralisation, which enables each of the company's divisions to develop as a unique business unit.

"We give all our executives a co-equal measure of authority and responsibility. We provide them with a reasonable definition of the job to be done and give coaching and guidance as required," says Lynch. The result, he believes, is an empowering

working environment, where employees are armed with an arsenal of tools to do their jobs well.

Lynch believes his management style is influenced by a strong belief in honesty, sincerity and openness. Lynch believes in seeking out and observing the greatness of others.

"This doesn't necessarily pertain to high-powered, sophisticated employees only," he points out. "We believe that all our staff members are blessed with diligence, intelligence and commitment, which are extraordinary qualities. We give people leeway to develop themselves without being stifled by bureaucracy. More importantly, we talk to our employees and give recognition where it is due."

This approach seems to encourage employees to give their best of their own accord, but perhaps the strongest motivator at Imperial is the fact that employees take a proprietary interest in their departments. Lynch believes this attitude leads to good decision making.

"Our people look on their departments as belonging to them, and it is therefore their responsibility to make them a success," he explains.

This mindset is actively cultivated.

"We encourage our people to be in the centre of the field and not to sit on the fence," he says.

Source: Adapted from "South Africa's leading managers", CRF Publishing, 2003 pp 10–13 http://www.imperial.co.za/ImperialNews.aspx (Accessed 2007-03-29.)

a managerial point of view, describes it as "the process of influencing employees to work willingly toward the achievement of organisational objectives".[2]

In the preceding chapters, we have discussed the first two management functions, namely planning and organising, and in chapter 12 we shall discuss control, the final function. Planning and organising set the wheels of the management process in motion, but the process is by no means complete, since the plans formulated to achieve the goals must still become a reality. Thus the third fundamental function of management comes into play – leading.

In order to influence their subordinates to achieve goals, managers should understand what motivates their employees' behaviour and they should create working environments where their employees are motivated to work productively. We shall discuss motivation in section 8.4.

In modern organisations, managers manage individuals, as well as groups or teams. Groups do much of the work in organisations and may consist of task groups, command groups and informal groups. Managers manage these groups – for example the legal section, the purchasing department, the production section, or salespersons – towards reaching the organisation's goals and objectives. Increasingly, managers in contemporary organisations need to build teams that perform a variety of tasks. Managers should understand the dynamics of teams and know what **team leadership** entails. We shall examine the functioning of groups and teams in section 8.5.

Managers communicate their organisations' visions, missions, goals, strategies, plans, problems and expectations to employees. They also listen to the employees' problems and aspirations. The ability to communicate effectively is an important element of leading. We shall examine a simple communication model in section 8.6.

When they perform the leading function,

managers take the lead to bridge the gap between formulating plans and reaching goals. They transform plans into reality by influencing individuals, groups and teams in the organisation, by communicating with them and by ensuring that they are motivated.

8.2.1 Leadership and management

Leadership is not the same as **management**. Management is broader in scope, comprising four management functions; leading is only one of them.[3] People can work as managers without being true leaders if they do not have the ability to influence others. Conversely, there are leaders in organisations who are not managers. The informal leader of a group, for example, may have more influence in the group than the manager, because of his or her ability to influence group members. Influencing[4] is the process leaders follow when communicating ideas, gaining acceptance of them, and inspiring followers to support and implement the ideas through change. Influencing is also about the relationship between leaders and followers. Managers may coerce employees to influence their behaviour, but leaders do not. In the case study at the start of this chapter, Imperial Holdings's chief executive, Bill Lynch, says, "We give people leeway to develop themselves without being stifled by bureaucracy. More importantly, we talk to our employees and give recognition where it is due." This approach seems to encourage Imperial's employees to give their best of their own accord.

Clearly, leadership is not the only ingredient of organisational success, but it is one of the most important variables influencing this success. Indeed, in the South African business context there are innumerable examples of success (or failure) of organisations attributed to a particular leader. For example, the late Dr Anton Rupert built the Rembrandt Group into an international organisational empire. In less than 25 years, Raymond Ackerman

Top 5 most CEOs/directors in 2006

Jacko Maree – Standard Bank	11,4
Brian Joffe – Bidvest	10
Johann Rupert – Remgro	4,5
Maria Ramos – Transnet	3,5
Laurie Dippenaar – FirstRand	3
Stephan Koseff – Investec	3
Mark Lamberti – Massmart	3
Raymond Ackerman – Pick 'n Pay	3

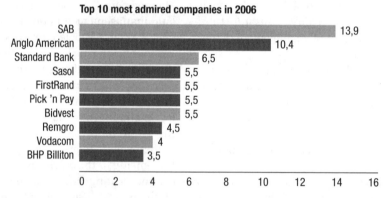

Top 10 most admired companies in 2006

SAB	13,9
Anglo American	10,4
Standard Bank	6,5
Sasol	5,5
FirstRand	5,5
Pick 'n Pay	5,5
Bidvest	5,5
Remgro	4,5
Vodacom	4
BHP Billiton	3,5

Figure 8.1: Top five most admired CEOs/directors in 2006 and the top ten most admired companies in 2006

Source: "Ask Africa Most Admired Companies", *Finweek*, 21 September 2006, pp. 11–14.

established Pick 'n Pay as the largest retail organisation in South Africa. Within a few years of the dismantling of apartheid, Dr Nthato Motlana developed the Metlife Group into an organisational giant. Business leaders such as Tokyo Sexwale and Don Ncube have had similar successes.

In the 2006 "Ask Africa Most Admired Companies"[5] survey, a strong link emerged between South Africa's most admired companies and their CEOs' ratings as the most admired CEOs. In determining the winners, CEOs were rated on six drivers of admiration: trust, brand, leadership, competence, financial governance and social responsibility. Figure 8.1 shows the results of the 2006 survey.

In the dynamic and fast-changing business environment of the 21st century, organisations

need managers who are also strong leaders. The existing extensive body of knowledge on leadership is used by organisations worldwide to improve the leadership skills of managers. Figure 8.2 illustrates the process of developing managers into leaders.

8.2.2 The components of the leading function

In chapter 7, we discussed organisational structures and the authority relations they create in organisations. These authority relations relate strongly to the leading function of managers, because the leading function gives managers the right to use authority, power, responsibility, accountability and delegation to influence employees to

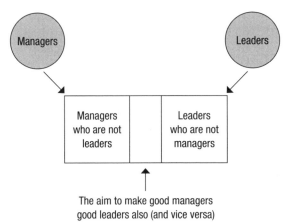

The aim to make good managers
good leaders also (and vice versa)

Figure 8.2: The integration of leadership and management

achieve the organisation's goals.[6] In the case study at the start of this chapter, the chief executive of Imperial Holdings, Bill Lynch, says: "We give all our executives a co-equal measure of authority and responsibility. We provide them with a reasonable definition of the job to be done, and give coaching and guidance as required." The result, he believes, is an empowering work environment, where employees are armed with an arsenal of tools to do their jobs well.

The leadership components of leadership entail the following:

- **Authority** denotes the right of a manager to give commands to, and demand actions from, employees.
- **Power** is a manager's ability to influence his or her employees' behaviour.
- **Responsibility** is the obligation to achieve organisational goals by performing required activities. Managers are responsible for the results of their organisations, departments or sections.
- **Delegation** is the process of assigning responsibility and authority for achieving organisational goals. Managers delegate responsibility and authority down the chain of command. Delegation refers to giving employees new tasks, which may become part of a redesign job, or may simply be a one-time task.

- **Accountability** is the evaluation of how well individuals meet their responsibilities. Managers are accountable for all that happens in their sections or departments. Managers can delegate authority and responsibility, but they can never delegate their accountability.

Authority and power are probably the most important components of leading and therefore deserve a few further remarks.

8.2.2.1 Authority

Managers are responsible for ensuring that employees work together to achieve the organisation's goals. Without authority, managers are unable to manage, initiate or sustain the management process. Authority therefore revolves around obtaining the right to perform certain actions (within specified guidelines), to decide who does what, to demand the completion of tasks, and to discipline those who fail to do what the organisation expects of them. In short, this entails the right to demand action from employees and the right to take action.

Final authority rests with the owners or shareholders of an organisation, who transfer or delegate authority to the board; the board, in turn, delegates it to top management, top management to middle management, and so on, to the lowest levels. Managers, in turn, delegate authority to employees to enable them to execute tasks. For example, certain bank officials have the authority to enter the bank's vault, certain managers have the authority to sign cheques in the organisation's name, and others have the authority to negotiate and conclude contracts on behalf of the organisation – the organisation confers this formal authority on them.

A clear manifestation of formal authority is evident in an army, wherein those with specific powers wear insignia to indicate their authority or rank: captains have authority over lieutenants, lieutenants over sergeants, and so on. Although managers do not wear insignia, their organisations confer authority in the same way on a specific position or rank. The organisation confers on a manager the right to expect action from employees. Members of groups in organisations also confer authority on a manager if they accept him or her as their leader. Authority and leadership are therefore closely related – the organisation grants authority to particular managers to lead individuals and groups in achieving the organisation's goals.

8.2.2.2 Power

Managers who are strong leaders influence their employees because they possess power and therefore are able to exercise their authority fully. Leadership and power go hand in hand. Without power, a manager would not be able to influence employees sufficiently towards achieving organisational goals. Leaders have two types of power, position power and personal power. Top management delegates position power down the chain of command. Managers have personal power when their followers bestow it on them. Figure 8.3 shows the power continuum from position power to personal power:

- **Coercive power** is the power to enforce compliance through fear, whether psychological, emotional or physical. Criminals often make use of such power through physical force or violence. Modern organisations do not use physical force, but the psychological or emotional fear of employees that the organisation will retrench them or the social exclusion from a group constitute a form of power that managers could exercise to put pressure on employees.
- **Reward power** is based on the manager's ability to influence employees with something of value to them. It concerns the power to give or withhold rewards. Such rewards include, for example, salary raises, bonuses, praise, recognition and the allocation of interesting assignments.

The more rewards a manager controls, and the more important these rewards are to employees, the greater reward power a manager possesses.
- **Legitimate power** is the power an organisation grants to a particular position. Accordingly, a manager has the right to insist that employees do their work and the right to discipline or dismiss them if they fail to comply.
- **Referent power** refers to a manager's personal power or charisma. Employees obey managers with referent power simply because they like them, respect them, and identify with them. In other words, the leaders' personal characteristics make them attractive to others.
- **Expert power** is the power that a manager's expertise, knowledge and professional ability give him or her, particularly over those who need the knowledge or information. The more important the information, and the fewer the people who possess it, the greater is the power of the person who commands it.

A manager who commands all five types of power is a strong leader. However, it is not only managers who possess power. Occasionally employees possess it too, for example when a manager is dependent on a subordinate for information or for social influence. Managers should be aware that their employees also possess power, and they should use their own power judiciously, and only to the extent necessary to accomplish the organisation's goals. Table 8.1 provides a useful perspective on how managers may wield power.

Position Power				Personal Power
Coercive	Reward	Legitimate	Referent	Expert

Figure 8.3: The power continuum

Source: Adapted from Lussier, R.N. & Achua, C.F., *Leadership: Theory, application, skill development*, South-Western College Publishing, Cincinnati, 2001, p. 342.

Table 8.1: Uses and outcomes of power

Source of leader influence	Type of outcome		
Referent power	**Commitment** *Likely* If request is believed to be important to leader	**Compliance** *Possible* If request is perceived to be unimportant to leader	**Resistance** *Possible* If request is for something that will bring harm to leader
Expert power	*Likely* If request is persuasive and subordinates share leader's task goals	*Possible* If request is persuasive but subordinates are apathetic about leader's task goals	*Possible* If leader is arrogant and insulting, or subordinates oppose task goals
Legitimate power	*Possible* If request is polite and highly appropriate	*Likely* If request or order is seen as legitimate	*Possible* If arrogant demands are made or request does not appear proper
Reward power	*Possible* If used in a subtle, very personal way	*Likely* If used in a mechanical, impersonal way	*Possible* If used in a manipulative, arrogant way
Coercive power	*Very unlikely*	*Possible* If used in a helpful, non-punitive way	*Likely* If used in a hostile or manipulative way

Source: Griffin, R.W. & Moorhead, G., *Organisational behaviour*, Houghton Mifflin Company, 2001, p. 370.

Effective managers use their power in such a way that they maintain a healthy balance between their own power and that of employees. Figure 8.4 illustrates such a balance.

In order to identify the influences that create effective leaders, various researchers have studied, developed and tested a variety of leadership theories to determine the key characteristics and behaviour patterns of a good leader. We shall examine some of the major leadership theories in the next section.

8.3 Leadership theories

The major leadership theories, which we shall briefly summarise below, are trait theory, behavioural theory and contingency theory.[7]

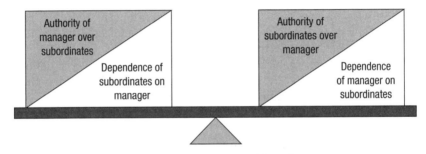

Figure 8.4: Equilibrium between the power of management and that of employees

Early research into leadership involved the identification and analysis of the **traits** of strong leaders. The assumption was that strong leaders have certain basic traits that distinguish them from followers and unsuccessful leaders. Many researchers tried to list the distinctive characteristics of effective leaders. The results of these research efforts have been largely inconclusive because traits vary from one leader to another and some traits develop only after a leader assumes a leadership position. Research interest then turned towards investigating how successful leaders **behave**.

An assumption of the **behavioural approach** to leadership is that successful leaders behave differently from unsuccessful leaders. Researchers tried to determine what successful leaders *do* – how they delegate, communicate and motivate their employees. The belief was that managers could learn the "right" behaviour. Research conducted at the University of Iowa, the Ohio State University, the University of Michigan, and the work of Blake and Mouton support the behaviour approach to leadership.

Researchers at the University of Iowa identified three basic leadership styles, namely **autocratic**, **democratic** and **laissez-faire** leadership styles. The researchers concluded that the laissez-faire style, whereby leaders leave all decisions to their employees and do not follow up, was ineffective on every performance criterion when compared to the other two styles. The researchers found that the democratic leadership style (the style of a leader who involves employees in decision making, delegates authority, encourages participation in deciding work methods and goals, and gives feedback) was the most effective style. Imperial Holdings's Bill Lynch, for example, believes that all Imperial staff members are blessed with diligence, intelligence and commitment, which are extraordinary qualities, and therefore he delegates responsibility and authority to them to take decisions without being stifled by bureaucracy.

Researchers at the Ohio State University identified two leadership styles, namely initiating structure and consideration:

- **Initiating structure** is the extent to which a leader defines and structures his or her role and the roles of employees to attain goals.
- **Consideration** is the extent to which a leader has job relationships characterised by mutual trust, respect for employees' ideas, and regard for their feelings.

According to the researchers, effective leaders exhibit both dimensions strongly in their leadership style. At the University of Michigan, researchers distinguished between the following:

- **Production-oriented leaders**, who emphasise the technical or task aspects of a job
- **Employee-oriented leaders**, who emphasise interpersonal relations

In these studies, employee-oriented leaders were associated with higher group productivity and higher job satisfaction.

Blake and Mouton developed the "**Managerial Grid**" – an instrument that identifies various leadership styles on a **two-dimensional grid**. They used a questionnaire to measure **concern for people** and **concern for production** on a scale of one to nine. The researchers identified the "ideal" leadership style as the "team management style" where a manager is strong on both dimensions (9,9). The behavioural theories in general had little success in identifying consistent patterns of leadership behaviour and successful performance, because results varied over different ranges of circumstances. This led researchers to investigate the effect of the **situation** on effective leadership styles.

The **contingency** or **situational** approach to leadership acknowledge that predicting leadership success is more complex than examining the traits and behaviours of successful leaders. Contingency theory attempts to determine the best leadership style for a given situation. In the development of contingency theories, researchers considered variables such as how structured the task is, the quality of the relationship between the leader and employees, the leader's position power, the employees' role clarity and the employees' acceptance of leader's decisions.

Fiedler's contingency theory of leadership proposes that effective group performance depends on the proper match between a leader's style of interaction with employees, and the degree to which the situation gives control and influence to the leader. Fiedler developed an instrument to measure whether the leader is task oriented or relationship oriented and he identified three situational criteria that organisations can manipulate to create a proper situational match with the behaviour orientation of the leader. According to Fiedler, an individual's leadership style is fixed. If, for example, a situation requires a task-oriented leader and the person in the leadership position is relationship-oriented, the organisation must either change the situation or move the leader to another situation where his or her leadership style is compatible with the situation.

Robert House developed the **path–goal model**, asserting that it is the leader's responsibility to help employees to achieve their goals. Leaders should provide the necessary direction and support to ensure that employees' goals are in line with the organisations' goals and objectives. House identified four leadership behaviours (directive, supportive, participative and achievement-oriented), which managers can use in different situations. The majority of research evidence supports the logic of the theory: if the leader counteracts the employee's limitations in the work situation, this will probably influence the employee's performance positively.

The premise of **Hersey and Blanchard's situational leadership model** is that the work maturity of employees determines the best leadership style for a particular situation. Work maturity is determined by the employee's

need for achievement, willingness to accept responsibility and task-related ability and experience. The manager uses one of four leadership styles (telling, selling, participating and delegating) to match the employees' maturity level in a given situation.

8.3.1 Contemporary issues in leadership

In a worldwide business environment often rocked by scandals involving business leaders who have acted in dishonest ways and betrayed their organisations and their followers, **trust** is becoming a vital component of effective leadership. Managers cannot be effective leaders if their employees do not perceive them as being trustworthy. The five dimensions of trust include the following:

- **Integrity** – a manager's honesty and truthfulness
- **Competence** – a manager's technical and interpersonal knowledge and skills
- **Consistency** – a manager's reliability, predictability and good judgement in handling situations
- **Loyalty** – a manager's willingness to protect another person
- **Openness** – one can rely on a manager to tell the whole truth[8]

The recipient of the prestigious Ernst & Young World Entrepreneur Award, Bill Lynch, says his management style is influenced by a strong belief in honesty, sincerity and openness.

The discussion on leadership theories in the previous section defined leadership as leaders' ability to influence their employees to achieve organisational goals. More recently, the focus has shifted and leaders are increasingly described as "individuals who define organisational reality through the articulation of a vision".[9] This view of leadership is not confined to top managers – managers at all levels are stronger leaders if they can convey the vision of their section, department, group or team to their employees.

Visionary leaders, charismatic leaders and transformational leaders have the ability to communicate and share their vision for their organisations.

8.3.1.1 Charismatic leadership

A strong positive relationship is perceived between **charismatic leadership** and the employees' performance and satisfaction. Charismatic leaders often have traits such as selfconfidence, vision, the ability to articulate the vision, strong convictions about the vision, unconventional behaviour and environmental sensitivity. Charismatic leadership may be most appropriate when the followers' task has an ideological component, perhaps explaining why charismatic leaders most often appear in politics, religion or unusual business organisations.

8.3.1.2 Visionary leadership

Visionary leadership goes beyond charisma. Visionary leaders have the ability to create and articulate a realistic, credible, attractive vision of the future of the organisation; this vision grows out of and improves on the present. Such a vision creates enthusiasm and brings energy and commitment to the organisation. Visionary leaders exhibit certain skills: the ability to explain the vision to others, the ability to express the vision through the leaders' behaviour, and the ability to extend the vision to different leadership contexts.[10]

8.3.1.3 Transactional and transformational leadership

The behavioural and contingency theories, which we discussed in the previous sec-

---

Critical thinking

Leadership is a fascinating topic that has generated great interest. In recent years, studies of visionary leadership have created excitement amongst researchers. Are visionary leaders best suited to lead their organisations through the major changes contemporary organisations face? The excerpt below offers some food for thought on this question.

End of worship of visionary leadership

The visionary leader has become the hero of the business myth, but most organisations do better in the long term by hiring solid performers strong on consistency rather than charisma and celebrity status.

   The test of effective leadership is what the leader achieves with the organisation, not what was once envisioned. By emphasising the performance qualities that make a great visionary, a senior executive can neglect the development of the practical attributes that will get the job done.

   Often business leaders do not learn the basic functional skills that will enable them

to execute the vision. If they are lucky, they work in an organisation whose culture enables them to learn the implementation basics of the job. Most organisations do not have this cultural predisposition to prompt execution. The danger is then that a leader who believes his or her job is purely the development of strategy will take the organisation precisely nowhere. Case studies cited in the book *Good to Great* by Jim Collins confirm this. Collins identified the US organisations that had been consistently successful for the longest period. The results were heartening for the vast majority of executives who lack star quality: the case studies showed that leaders who consistently achieved their organisational goals without fanfare achieved long-running success.

   These uncelebrated leaders set out clear strategic ambitions, lay down a change agenda that can be implemented, put together a strong leadership team and develop a process to ensure that the job is done.

Source: Adapted from *Business Day Management Review*, January 2007, p. 15.

tion, view leaders as transactional leaders. Transactional leaders appeal to their employees' self-interest, for example, managers exchanging pay and status for work effort. The distinction between transactional leadership and transformational leadership is as follows:

- **Transactional leadership** is viewed as leaders' exchange of rewards for employee compliance.
- **Transformational leadership** is viewed as leaders' effect on followers in that the followers feel trust, admiration, loyalty and respect for their leader and are motivated to do more than is expected of them.[11]

In most organisational contexts, transformational leadership is desirable because it improves employee satisfaction, trust and commitment.[12] Research findings indicate that it consistently promotes greater organisational performance.[13] Furthermore, transformational leaders are effective in organisations where major change and transformation are taking place.

From the discussions in the previous section and above, it is obvious that leadership has been studied in different ways, depending on the researchers' preferences and the research time line. Clearly, researchers have made some progress in probing the "mysteries"[14] surrounding leadership, but many questions remain.

8.4 Motivation

The second component of the leading function of managers is **motivation**. Employees (the human resources) influence the organisation's productivity and profitability directly. In order to manage employees effectively, managers should understand what motivates the behaviour of their employees.

"Motivation is an inner desire to satisfy an unsatisfied need."[15] It is an intrinsic process and therefore managers cannot "motivate" their employees. However, they can create a working environment where their employees will be motivated to achieve the organisation's goals. Consider an example from the case study at the start of this chapter: at Imperial Holdings employees are motivated because the company allows them to take responsibility for the success of their departments. Thus, from an organisational perspective, motivation is the willingness of an employee to achieve the organisation's goals.[16]

The motivation process moves in a certain sequence and commences with an unsatisfied need.[17] For example, an employee has an unsatisfied **need** for higher status in the organisation. Her **motive** is the desire to advance to a first-line managerial position, which leads to certain **behaviour**, such as working overtime or enrolling for a management course. The **consequence** of the behaviour might be that she receives a promotion (or does not receive a promotion), which will lead to the **satisfaction** (or **dissatisfaction**) of her need. If dissatisfaction occurs, the need remains unsatisfied, and the motivation process will start all over again. Satisfaction is usually short-lived because people have many needs, and as soon as one need is satisfied, another need will surface. If the person in the example advances to a first-line management position, she may very soon want a further promotion to a middle management position. This will again cause dissatisfaction and the motivation process will start all over again.

If managers understand what motivates the behaviour of their employees, they can influence the employees' work performance. It is important to note that motivation is not the only factor that influences work performance. The variables that determine performance are motivation, ability (training, knowledge and skills) and the opportunity to perform:[18]

$$Performance = ability \times motivation \times resources$$

Effective managers understand that employees must possess a high level of motivation plus the appropriate training, knowledge, and skills that are necessary to perform effectively in a given work situation. If employees lack the skills they need to perform, they will not be able to do their work properly, no matter how motivated they are. Employees should also have the opportunity to perform, which means that they must have adequate resources, such as tools, equipment, materials, and supplies, to be able to do the work.

From the above discussion, it is clear that managers have a major role to play in terms of the work performance of their employees.

The value of leadership and motivation theories is that they provide managers with a better understanding of how to manage their employees in order to get the best performance from them. At the same time, these theories ensure that the organisation creates an environment where employees can satisfy their needs. In chapter 10 we shall discuss the motivation theories.

8.5 Groups and teams in organisations

The employees of modern organisations do not work merely as individuals with individual needs and goals, but also as members of groups and teams. Managers lead individual employees, as well as groups and teams to achieve the organisation's goals.

Many writers use the words "group" and "team" interchangeably, but recent management literature makes a definite distinction between them, saying that all teams are also groups, but not all groups are teams. A **team** is a special kind of group. Changing groups into teams is a process that requires special management skills. In this section, we shall first focus on groups in general and then discuss work teams as an integral part of successful contemporary organisations.[19]

8.5.1 Informal and formal groups

A **group** comprises two or more individuals who regularly interact with one another and who work for a common purpose. People

---

Critical thinking

At the end of this section on motivation, we may ask ourselves the question "How much do South African bosses really know what motivates employees and makes them want to come to work in the morning?" The following excerpt shows that they know very little.

Best company to work for 2006
Research from the 2006 *Financial Mail* "Best companies to work for" survey shows a growing gap between how well managers think they are looking after employees and how the "troops" themselves see the results of company initiatives.

The following is a list of ways to ensure that employees are motivated, based on

interviews with a group of HR specialists, employees and responses to the 2006 Best Company questionnaires:

"Top 10 ways to turn your staff on":
1. Development and career opportunities
2. Fair reward and recognition
3. Leadership by example and through vision
4. Open two-way communication
5. Treat staff as individuals and with respect
6. Trust your staff
7. Staff must understand how their job contributes to business
8. A clear performance management system
9. Team spirit and a common goal
10. Ensure a healthy work/life balance

Source: Adapted from "Is that all?", *Financial Mail*, 29 September 2006, pp. 32–33.

join groups for a variety of reasons, ranging from satisfying their social needs to achieving goals impossible to achieve as individuals. Some people join groups to achieve some level of prestige or status. Others feel that they enhance their self-worth by belonging to a specific group. Individual group members often feel they have more power by joining a group because group action can achieve more than individual action. In organisations, there are informal and formal groups.

8.5.1.1 Informal groups

Informal groups can be either of the following:

- **Interest groups.** In interest groups group members usually share a common interest. For example, a group of employees might campaign for better cafeteria facilities at their workplace. When the organisation provides better facilities, the group will disband.
- **Friendship groups.** The groups usually exist to satisfy the social needs of members. For example, a group of employees might play bridge once a week.

8.5.1.2 Formal groups

Formal groups are either of the following:

- **Command groups.** Command groups are characterised by a formal organigram and line of authority, for example managers and their employees. The organisation's structure defines formal groups in terms of allocated work assignments which determine tasks and the formation of work groups.
- **Task groups.** Task groups are created to complete a specific task or project in the organisation. When the task is done the group disbands. Organisations can create task groups across hierarchical boundaries. For example, the dean of the College of Management Sciences of a university might appoint a committee comprising staff

members from the production department and the editorial department and junior and senior academics to investigate the quality of study material produced for all departments in the college. On completion of the project the group will disband.

8.5.2 The characteristics of groups

Every group in an organisation is different in terms of its structure or a set of characteristics – for example the size of the group, the composition of the group, group norms and cohesiveness – that shapes the behaviour of both the group and the individual group members.[20]

Group **size** affects the group's overall performance. If the group is too big, social loafing occurs. **Social loafing** refers to the tendency for individuals to put in less effort when working in a group than when working individually. Thus group size has an influence on the productivity of groups.

Group **composition** can influence a group's performance. Heterogeneous groups, with members diverse in terms of, for example, gender, race, and nationality have more difficulty working together at first, but they outperform homogeneous groups over time.

Status in groups can be formal or informal, meaning that groups sometimes give higher (informal) status to group members who are relatively low on the hierarchical level of the organisation. Such status derives from factors such as the age or experience of a group member or the social influence of a group member.

Norms are standards shared by members of a group and develop from interaction between the members. Norms can be positive or negative. Managers should manage group norms. An example of a positive norm is that the group strives to outperform other groups; a negative norm is "We only do what is asked from us – no more, no less".

In groups the formal **leader** is usually identified by a title such as section or department manager, supervisor, foreman, project leader, task force head, or committee chair. However, sometimes an informal leader has more influence in a group, which may influence the performance of the group positively or negatively.

Cohesiveness refers to the way a group stands together as a unit rather than as individuals in a group. There is a strong relationship between performance norms and cohesiveness, which can either be beneficial or detrimental to the organisation. If a group is very cohesive, the members' adherence to group norms will be stronger.

In order to manage groups in an organisation effectively, managers should understand how groups are structured and how the various characteristics of specific groups influence the organisation's performance.

8.5.3 Teams

As we stated previously, groups and teams are not the same – while all teams are also groups, not all groups are teams. A **work group** is "a unit of two or more people who interact primarily to share information and make decisions that will help each group member perform within his or her own area of responsibility".[21] Work groups have skills that are random and varied. Usually there is a leader, such as a manager, appointed by the organisation. Individual members of work groups are accountable and rewarded for their own performance. For example, an administrative clerk's manager assesses her performance and rewards her accordingly if she has reached her performance goals. Her performance appraisal and rewards are not dependent on the performance of the other administrative clerks. Furthermore, the group's performance is the sum of the group members' individual performances – the output of the group of clerks in the office where the clerk works is the sum of all their performances.

A **work team** "comprises a small number of employees with complementary competencies who work together on a project, are committed to a common purpose, and are accountable for performing tasks that contribute to achieving an organisation's goals".[22] Clearly work teams differ from work groups. Work teams perform collectively and members are dependent on each other to complete their work, while work group members only share information. For example, in a team tasked with developing a new product from its conception to completion, all the members are dependent on one another because the output of one member becomes the input of another member.

Work teams have positive synergy, meaning that the performance of an effective team can be greater than the sum of the performance of individual team members – work groups have neutral and sometimes negative synergy. If we take the example cited above a little further, it is clear that the efforts of the team tasked with developing a new product amount to more than the sum of their individual performances because they are creating something new. Furthermore, team members are individually and mutually accountable for the performance of the team, whilst group members are only accountable for their own performance. In our example, the team members are mutually responsible and accountable for the new product, but the individual members are also individually accountable for their own inputs.

Lastly, the skills of members are complementary in work teams because of the interdependent nature of their work; in work groups the members' skills are random and varied.[23]

Teams are sometimes upheld as a cure-all solution to organisational problems. However, teams are not suitable in all organisational settings. Teams are effective only in organisations where the organisational culture is conducive to teamwork. Furthermore, the organisation's reward system must be designed to reward team performance, the commitment and support of top management for teams must be evident throughout the organisation and the organisation's work must be suitable to perform in a team environment. Despite these considerations, teams are gaining popularity throughout the world, and complex global organisations cannot function without effective teams.

The different types of teams are the following:[24]

- **Problem-solving teams.** These comprise employees from the same department who meet regularly to discuss ways of improving quality, efficiency and the work environment.
- **Self-managed work teams.** These take on the responsibilities from their former managers, including tasks such as planning, scheduling and control. Team members address problems in the work process, sometimes, even, team member selection and discipline.
- **Cross-functional teams.** These comprise employees at the same hierarchical level, but from different work areas, who come together to accomplish a task. These teams are effective in allowing people from diverse areas in an organisation to exchange information, develop new ideas, solve problems and coordinate complex projects. Task forces and committees are common examples of cross-functional teams.

High-performance teams have a number of characteristics in common, including a clear understanding of the team's goals and relevant technical skills and abilities to achieve the goal. Individuals are capable of readjusting their skills and there is high mutual trust among members, unified commitment and good communication. Team members possess adequate negotiating skills. Team leaders encourage team members by clarifying goals and they help members to realise their potential.[25]

Using teams in an organisation is a challenging managerial task, involving the selection and training of potential and current employees to become effective team members. It is also important that the organisation's

---

Critical thinking

Teams have been touted as the miracle solution to organisational problems in recent years. But do teams work in all organisations?

In certain situations it is not advisable to use teams

The answer is that in certain situations it is not advisable to use teams. The following guidelines are suggested by Wageman for the effective use of teams.

Use teams when:

- There is a clear, engaging reason or purpose
- People must work together to get the work done
- The organisation rewards teamwork and team performance

- Ample resources are available
- Teams will have clear authority to manage and change the work they are doing

Do not use teams when:

- There is not clear purpose
- People working independently can do the work
- The organisation rewards individual effort and performance
- The necessary resources are not available
- Management will continue to monitor and influence the work they are doing

---

Source: Wageman, R., "Critical success factors for creating superb self-managing teams", *Organisational Dynamics*, Vol. 26, No.1, 1997, pp. 49–61.

performance and reward systems should encourage team effort.

Managers should not underestimate the role of groups and teams in the overall accomplishment of organisational goals. They should understand group dynamics and manage groups and teams in their organisations.

8.6 Communication

A common thread in the discussion on the leading function of managers is that effective leadership depends on constant communication between leaders and their employees. Good communication is conducive to good relations between managers and individual employees, groups, teams and, ultimately, the organisation and its environment. A considerable proportion of a manager's time is devoted to communicating with the organisation's stakeholders, both inside and outside the organisation. Furthermore, the management process is dependent on effective communication.

Theoretically, communication is the transfer of information or messages from one person to another. Figure 8.5 illustrates a simple communication model.

The **sender** is the source of a message. To communicate effectively, the sender should know exactly what the message is that he or she wishes to transmit. The sender should take care with his or her choice of words and their meaning and encourage two-way communication by showing insight into the receiver's perceptions.

The **message** may convey ideas, opinions, plans, orders, or explanations. In the interest of effective communication, the message should be simple and clear.

The **communications channel** is the manner in which the message reaches the receiver. It may assume any form perceptible to any of the recipient's senses, as long as it is comprehensible. For example, the recipient can hear spoken language, see or feel gestures and read the written word.

The **receiver** of the message should absorb the message and show that he or she has received and understood the message (listening skills are important here).

For communication to be effective, the recipient should receive the message unimpeded, meaning that the recipient should understand the message in accordance with the sender's intentions. Because effective communication is so important in leadership, managers should remove all hindrances that may affect the clarity of their messages, such as obscurity, language differences, erroneous perceptions, doubts about the source or sender and ambiguities. Managers should promote effective communication by encouraging feedback and by using face-to-face communication wherever possible. Managers can enhance their communication by using simple language. They should contemplate any symbolic content in their communication before sending the message.

Communication is an essential element of leading. It is important in building and sustaining relationships between managers

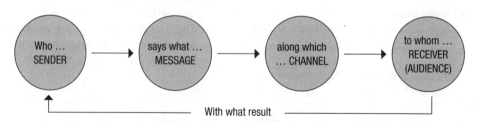

Figure 8.5: A basic communication model

Critical thinking

Communication is an essential part of leading. Listening is an important component of effective communication. How well do you listen? Good listeners do the following – do you do the same?

Good listeners do the following

- Stop what you are doing and give your complete attention to the speaker.
- Avoid distractions such as fiddling with pens or papers.
- Stay "tuned in" – do not let your mind wander.
- Do not assume you know what the speaker is going to say and jump to conclusions.
- Listen to the entire message without interrupting the speaker.
- Watch for non-verbal cues such as body language and eye expression – sometimes people say one thing and mean something else.
- Ask questions if you feel you have incomplete information.
- Take notes to help you remember the message later and to document it, if necessary.
- Convey meaning, for example use verbal clues to let the speaker know that you are listening. For example, say "I see" and "I understand" or nod your head and make eye contact.

---

and employees and between individuals and groups in an organisation. The communication model provides a basis for understanding the key elements of interpersonal communication.

8.7 Summary

Organisations need managers who are also good leaders in order to be successful. Managers perform the leading function to manage effectively the human resources in their organisations. They use authority and power to influence their employees to strive willingly to achieve organisational goals. Leadership theories help managers understand what leadership entails. In this chapter we examined the most important categories of leadership models as well as contemporary issues in leadership. Effective managers should understand how their employees' behaviour is motivated. We touched on the topic in this chapter, but chapter 10 deals in detail with the motivation theories. Modern organisations use work groups and work teams extensively – managing them is an added responsibility of contemporary managers. Communication is a crucial element of the leading function without which a manager will not be a good leader.

Key terms

Accountability	Management versus leadership
Authority	Managerial grid
Autocratic leadership style	Path–goal model
Behavioural leadership theories	Power
Charismatic leadership	Production-oriented leadership style
Coercive power	Referent power
Concern for people	Responsibility
Concern for production	Reward power
Democratic leadership style	Team leadership
Employee-oriented leadership style	Trait theory
Expert power	Transactional leadership
Fiedler's contingency theory of leadership	Transformational leadership
Hersey and Blanchard's model	Trust
Laissez-faire leadership style	Two-dimensional leadership
Leadership	Visionary leadership

Legitimate power	

? Questions for discussion

1. How would you define the leading function of managers and describe how the leader in the opening case study sees his leadership role?
2. Are managers also leaders? Explain the differences.
3. How would the behaviour of a manager who is a strong leader compare with that of a manager who is not a strong leader? Describe managers known to you, or use information from the Internet or newspapers to answer the question.
4. What are the components of leadership?
5. Why are managers who use power effectively strong leaders?
6. What are the shortcomings of the trait theory and the behavioural theories?
7. Compare work groups and work teams. Why are work teams not always appropriate to use?

References

1. Yukl, G., *Leadership in organizations*, 4th edition, Prentice-Hall, Upper Saddle River, 1998, p. 2.
2. Lussier, R.N., *Management fundamentals*, South-Western College Publishing, Cincinnati, 2000, p. 452.
3. *Ibid.*, p. 453.
4. Lussier, R.N. & Achua, C.F., *Leadership: Theory, application, skill development*, South-Western College Publishing, Cincinnati, 2001, p. 7.
5. "Ask Africa Most Admired Companies", *Finweek*, 21 September 2006, pp. 11–14.
6. Lussier & Achua, 2001, *op. cit.*, p. 187.
7. This section is based on Lussier, 2001, *op. cit.*, pp. 453–457 and Robbins, S.P., *Organizational behavior*, 10th edition, Prentice-Hall, Upper Saddle River, 2003, pp. 316–328.
8. Robbins, *op. cit.*, p. 336.
9. Robbins, *op. cit.*, p. 340.
10. Robbins, *op. cit.*, p. 344.
11. Bass, B.M., "Leadership and performance beyond expectations", 1985, in Yukl, *op. cit.*, p. 325.
12. Barling, J., Slater, F. & Kelloway, E.K., "Transformational leadership and emotional intelligence", *Leadership and Organizational Development Journal*, Vol. 21, No. 3, 2000, pp. 157–161.
13. Lowe, K.B. & Kroeck, K.G., "Effectiveness correlates of transformational and transactional leadership: A meta-analytic review", *Leadership Quarterly*, Vol. 7, 1996, pp. 385–426.
14. Yukl, *op. cit.*, p. 14.
15. Lussier, 2000, *op. cit.*, p. 420.
16. *Ibid.*
17. Smit, P.J., Cronje, G. de J., Brevis, T., Vrba, M.J., *Management principles: A contemporary edition for Africa*, Juta, Cape Town, 2007, pp. 338–339.
18. Robbins, *op. cit.*, pp. 173–174.
19. Robbins, *op. cit.*, p. 258.
20. Based on Robbins, *op. cit.*, pp. 226–238.
21. Robbins, *op. cit.*, p. 258.
22. *Ibid.*
23. *Ibid.*
24. Robbins, *op. cit.*, pp. 260–270.
25. Robbins, S.P. & Decenzo, D.A., *Fundamentals of management*, 3rd edition, Prentice-Hall, Upper Saddle River, 2001, p. 290.

MEETING HUMAN RESOURCE REQUIREMENTS AND DEVELOPING EFFECTIVENESS IN HR

The purpose of this chapter

The purpose of this chapter is to introduce the issues relating to the management of human resources within an organisation.

Learning outcomes

The content of this chapter will enable learners to:

- Describe the basic steps involved in human resource planning

- Explain how companies use recruiting to find qualified job applicants
- Describe the selection techniques and procedures that companies use when deciding which applicants should receive job offers
- Describe how to determine training needs and select the appropriate training methods
- Discuss how to use performance appraisal to give meaningful performance feedback
- Describe basic compensation strategies and how they affect human resource practice

9.1 Introduction

Internationally renowned HR consultant Jeffrey Pfeffer contends in *Competitive advantage through people*[1] that what separates top performing companies from their competitors is the way they treat their workforces. He goes on to argue that companies that invest in their employees create long-lasting competitive advantages that are difficult for other companies to duplicate. However, the process of finding, developing and keeping the right people to form a qualified workforce remains one of the most difficult and important of all management tasks.[2] To assist in this regard, this chapter is structured around the four parts of the human resource management process shown in figure 9.1: determining human resource needs, and finding, developing and keeping a qualified workforce.

Accordingly, we shall begin this chapter by reviewing how human resource planning determines human resource needs, such as the kind and number of employees a company requires to meet its strategic plans and objectives. Next, we shall explore how

Figure 9.1: The HR cone

companies use recruiting and selection techniques to find and hire qualified employees to fulfil those needs. The following section will review how training and performance appraisal can develop the knowledge, skills and abilities of the workforce. The last part will conclude with a review of compensation, that is, how companies can keep their best workers through effective compensation prac-

tices.[3] However, before we look at each of these aspects in detail, it is necessary for us to find out who will take responsibility for these tasks.

The case study below provides an indication of how these activities can be applied within an organisation.

9.2 The relationship between line management and the HR department

It is important to understand that managing people is every manager's business.[4] However, successful organisations are those that combine the experience of line managers with the expertise of HR specialists to develop and utilise the talents of employees to their greatest potential. Addressing HR issues is thus rarely the exclusive responsibility of HR departments acting alone.[5] Instead, HR managers work side by side with line managers to address the people-related issues of the organisation, as indicated at Sunnyside University in the

Case study

Managing HR at Sunnyside University

Barry manages the human resource department at Sunnyside University. Everyone in his department works hard at servicing their customers (faculty, students and staff), but their reputation is only average, even though the compensation paid to the staff in HR is above the industry average. Through the HR planning process, Barry recognised that he needed both more staff and more talented staff. He lobbied for, justified and gained approval for seven additional employees, including two managers. Even though he

needed these people quickly, he took the time to determine exactly what characteristics were required for each job, then recruited and interviewed candidates against these traits. At the end of three months, he had hired seven exceptional employees. He invested the time in training them properly for a period of six months. After a further three months he undertook his first performance appraisal of the new staff and is very satisfied with the outcome. The restructured department is perceived as one of the highest performing departments in the university.

Source: Adapted from White, D., *Coaching leaders: Guiding people who guide others*, Jossey-Bass, San Francisco, 2006, pp. 43–44. Used with permission.

case study. Although line managers and HR managers need to work together, their responsibilities are different, as are their competencies and expertise. According to Bohlander, Snell and Sherman,[6] the major activities for which an HR manager is typically responsible are the following:

- **Advice and counsel.** The HR manager often serves as an in-house consultant to supervisors, managers and executives on issues such as HR policies, labour agreements, past practices and the needs of employees.

- **Service.** HR managers also engage in a host of service activities, such as HR planning, recruitment, selection, the conducting of training programmes and compensation.

- **Policy formulation and implementation.** HR managers generally propose and draft new policies or revise existing ones to cover recurring problems or prevent anticipated ones.

- **Employee advocacy.** Another HR responsibility is being an employee advocate, that is, listening to employees' concerns and representing their needs to managers.

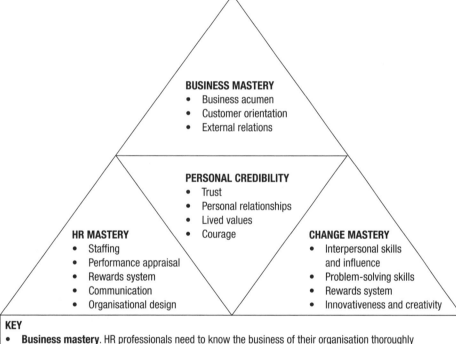

Figure 9.2: Human resource competency model

Source: Yeung, A., Brockbank, W. & Ulrich, D, "Lower cost, higher value: Human resource function in transformation", in Bohlander, G., Snell, S. & Sherman, A., *Managing human resources*, 12th edition, South-Western Publishing, by permission of Thomson Learning, 2001, p. 30.

To execute these roles successfully, HR managers must assume a broader role within the organisation and acquire a complementary set of competencies, as shown in figure 9.2.[7]

Thus, by helping their organisations build a sustained competitive advantage, and by learning to manage many activities well, HR professionals can become full business partners. The first step towards making this process a reality is to establish a company's human resource needs.

9.3   Human resource planning

Human resource planning is the process of using an organisation's goals and strategy to forecast the organisation's human resource needs in terms of finding, developing and keeping a qualified workforce. HR planning can be divided into three specific steps:
- **Step 1:** Identify the work being done in the business at present (job analysis and job description).
- **Step 2:** Identify the type of employees needed to do the work (job specification).
- **Step 3:** Identify the number of employees who will be needed in the future (human resource forecasting and planning).

9.3.1   Job analysis

The first step in HR planning is to determine the nature of the work being done, as Barry did at Sunnyside University in the case study at the start of this chapter. **Job analysis** is the process of describing and recording information about job behaviours and activities.[8]

The following questions might be asked when undertaking a job analysis:
- What is the employee responsible for?
- What tasks are performed?
- What decisions are made?
- What information is needed to enable the work to be done?
- Under what conditions is the job performed?

There are various ways in which this information can be collected. One method is observation by a qualified job analyst. The job analyst observes the employee working and records all the relevant information. Observation may also include videotaping, audiotaping and electronic monitoring. This method is especially suited to manual labour, where it is easy to see exactly what the employee is doing. However, administrative work is more difficult to observe.

The method generally followed for administrative work is interviewing, where the job analyst interviews an employee and asks for a description of responsibilities and tasks.

Questionnaires may also be used. Here the employee (and sometimes his or her immediate superior) answers a number of specific questions about the tasks and responsibilities of the job. Questionnaires may be developed for specific circumstances, or standardised questionnaires (which are more economical) may be purchased from external vendors.

9.3.2   Job description

Whatever method of data collection is used for job analysis, the information is put in writing in a certain format – a **job description** – so that other people, who are not involved in the job analysis, can nevertheless gain thorough insight into the contents of the job.

A job description does not merely list a number of facts. It is usually prepared in a predetermined format so that it is easily readable. It generally starts with a summary of the job, followed by a brief description of each main task, with more detail and practical examples as subdivisions. A description of the kind of decisions that need to be taken by the employee may follow.[9]

The job description format generally differs from business to business. The important point, however, is that the content of jobs must be put on record in an understandable way.

9.3.3 Job specification

The personal qualifications an employee must possess in order to perform the duties and responsibilities depicted in the job description are contained in the **job specification**.[10] Typically, job specifications detail the knowledge, skills and abilities relevant to a job, including the education, experience, specialised training, personal traits and manual dexterity of the person doing the job. This was a very important issue at Sunnyside University in the case study at the start of this chapter. At times, an organisation may also include the physical demands the job places on an employee. These might include the amount of walking, standing, reaching, or lifting required of the employee.[11]

9.3.4 Human resource forecasting

A further step in human resource planning is to conduct regular forecasts of the quantity and quality of employees the business is going to need in the future. As indicated in figure 9.3, the purpose of **HR forecasting** is to balance **HR supply** and **HR demand**. Demand is affected by business objectives – the number of people needed to attain the objectives. Supply is affected by the HR programmes providing the human resources. Factors to be kept in mind during forecasting are as follows:

- **Economic growth.** This involves forecasting the expected growth (or shrinkage) of the business in view of probable economic developments. For example, will there be a recession or growth in the near or distant future?
- **New developments in the business.** These include planned physical extensions, the establishment of new branches, and technological changes (especially those that will affect staff, for computerised machinery might create a greater need for technically skilled employees). This became a very important issue at Sunnyside University in the case study.

- **The labour market.** Important questions in this regard include: Are there sufficient opportunities in the labour market, or is there a high level of unemployment? What will the nature and scope of labour turnover in the future be? Will there be a shortage of a certain type of skilled employee? Will employees be readily available?

9.3.5 The human resource plan

Using the information obtained thus far, the HR manager can compile an **HR plan**, the final step in the process. The purpose of this plan is to provide concrete guidelines and steps that indicate how the business's short-, medium- and long-term human resource requirements can be provided for. In other words, it answers the question "What must we do today to be prepared for tomorrow?" The HR plan should dovetail with the strategic plan of the business, as mentioned earlier. In the case study at the start of this chapter, through the HR planning process, Barry at Sunnyside University determined that he needed a further seven additional staff.

Such an HR plan might, for example, make provision for an active recruiting campaign, emphasise the need for intensive training programmes, or, even, make a strong recommendation to automate because of a possible shortage of human resources.

This stage concludes the process of HR planning. The next activity in the process is finding qualified workers.

9.4 Finding qualified workers

9.4.1 Recruiting

The express purpose of **recruiting** is to ensure that a sufficient number of applicants apply for the various jobs in the business as and when required. Therefore, as soon as vacancies occur, the HR manager must decide from where suitable candidates for the job will be obtained. There are two basic sources from

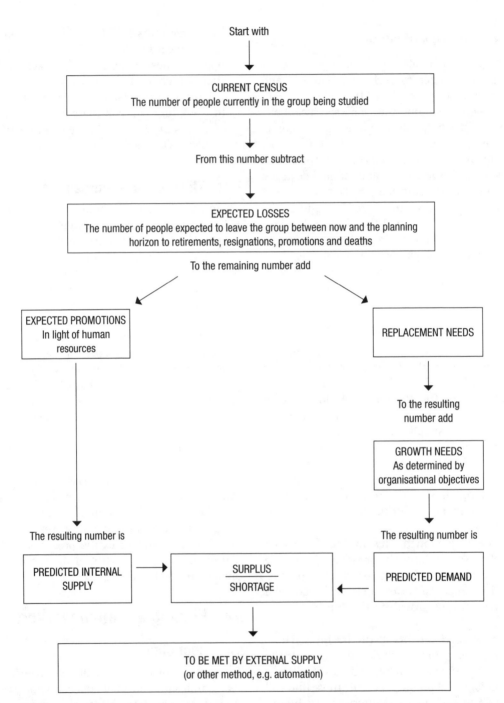

Figure 9.3: A procedure for estimating the human resource shortage or surplus for a job or occupational category

Source: Anthony, W.P., Kacmar, K.M. & Perrewé, P.L., *Human resource management: A strategic approach*, 4th edition, South-Western Publishing, by permission of Thomson Learning, 2002, p. 127.

Critical thinking

At the end of this section we may ask ourselves the question "Do we really need HR planning?" The following hypothetical situation may help to answer this question.

A building contractor compares present workforce capabilities with future demands

Imagine that you are a building contractor who has been contracted by a family to build their new home in a complex. The developers provide you with a plan of the house and request that you manage the whole project, including purchasing and ordering the materials. It seems very daunting but you realise that you firstly need to establish whether the plans have been approved by the local authorities and when the project needs to be completed. Secondly, you need to look at the plans and calculate how long the project will take to complete, how much and what kinds of material and people (skills) you will need to finish the project and whether there is water and electricity at the premises. Once this has been completed you need to draw up a schedule for obtaining quotations from different suppliers to ensure that you do not exceed the allocated budget. You will also have to provide for unforeseen delays. To do proper planning you firstly have to gather all the relevant facts and assess the current situation. You then need to consider what you require to complete the project successfully (material and people). Another aspect that you have to consider is the fact that you need specific material and people with particular skills at a specific time.

This scenario also applies to any organisation. Most organisations employ many people, who occupy different positions. As conditions change, the need often arises to employ more people (as in Sunnyside University's case) and as the organisation's goals change the organisation also needs to make provision for its changed needs to ensure that it can continue to function successfully in future. A comparison of the present workforce capabilities with future demands is necessary; this is what is called human resource planning.

Source: *Only Study guide for Human Resource Management (MNH202-C)*, University of South Africa, Pretoria, pp. 19–20. Used with permission.

which potential employees can be recruited: inside the business or external sources.

9.4.1.1 Recruitment from inside

Recruitment from inside (**internal recruiting**) means trying as far as possible to fill vacant positions with existing staff members, except for jobs on the lowest levels. In practice, it means that people from outside are appointed only at the lowest level, and that all more senior jobs in the hierarchy are filled by means of promotion (or sometimes lateral transfers) of existing staff. This was unfortunately not possible at Sunnyside University in the case study at the start of this chapter. Where a job at a very senior level becomes vacant, this leads to a whole series of promotions. Whatever a business decides, it will also have to take into account labour legislation such as the **Employment Equity Act 55 of 1998** and the **Labour Relations Act 66 of 1995 (as amended).**[12]

The advantages of a policy of recruiting from inside are the following:

- Career planning becomes possible, in that individual employees see a future for themselves in the business. This has a positive effect on morale.
- Assessment of applicants is easier because the business already has considerable information on the possible candidates' abilities, work performance and potential.

The cost of recruitment is low because advertising, travel, and board and lodging expenses are largely eliminated.

However, there are also three disadvantages connected with such a policy:

- The business tends to stagnate because staff members often think like their predecessors. There are therefore no new ideas.
- Staff appointed at lower levels do not necessarily have the potential to fill senior management posts. If people with high potential are appointed at the lowest levels, they might not be prepared to wait long for promotion opportunities.
- There can be a lot of personal competition among colleagues, to the detriment of cooperation among them.

9.4.1.2 Recruitment from outside

Recruitment from outside means looking for suitable applicants outside the business when a post becomes vacant (**external recruiting**). This was the case at Sunnyside University in the case study.

This has the following two advantages:

- An active effort is made to obtain the right person for the job, that is, someone with the most suitable qualifications and experience.
- The opportunity is created for bringing in new ideas, schools of thought and approaches, which considerably increase the possibility for innovation in the business.

However, the disadvantages must also be taken into consideration:

- Recruiting costs are considerably higher for items such as advertising and travelling expenses to enable applicants to come from elsewhere for the interview, and the reimbursement of successful applicants' moving costs.
- It is risky because the assessment of applicants can never be perfect. The possibility therefore exists that the successful applicant will not be successful in the job.

The morale of existing personnel can be negatively influenced. Employees with high potential will not be prepared to stay indefinitely at the same level and might consider resigning.

It is especially for the last reason that most businesses do not follow a policy of recruitment only from outside. Most businesses apply both approaches in one of two ways:

- Some businesses first look inside – and only when they cannot find a suitable candidate do they recruit outside.
- Some businesses advertise all jobs above a certain level, but encourage existing personnel to apply. In this way, management tries to find the most suitable candidate, regardless of whether the person comes from inside or outside.

9.4.1.3 The recruiting procedure

If a business recruits from inside, the HR manager must ensure that an efficient HR record system exists. Such a record system – which is now available in a computerised form known as a **human resources information system (HRIS)**[13] – should contain information on each employee's qualifications, training and experience, as well as an assessment of achievements and interests. When a job becomes vacant, the HR manager should be in a position to identify the most suitable candidates.

Recruitment from outside the organisation is much more complex, and it is important that the HR manager knows exactly whom to recruit, where to recruit from, and how the people should be recruited. Successful recruitment does not only mean that enough people apply for a job. If too many applicants apply for a job, selection will be a very time-consuming process. The ideal is therefore that only those suitable for the job apply.

To begin with, recruitment from outside requires a thorough labour market analysis. A **labour market** can be defined as the social or geographical area from which a business draws its employees. Certain mines in South Africa draw most of their staff from neighbouring countries. Their labour market is, for example, Lesotho or Malawi (that is, a geographical area). Other businesses, again, might employ mainly women who want to work half-days. This market can be regarded as a social area.

Every labour market has unique characteristics. A characteristic of the South African labour market is that the relationship between skilled and unskilled workers is relatively unbalanced. Obtaining unskilled labour does not appear to be a big problem, whereas this is not the case for skilled and professional people, who are exceptionally scarce. Human resource managers must therefore know the composition of their company's labour market as well as that of the South African labour market as a whole, if they are to recruit effectively.

9.4.1.4 Recruiting techniques

The HR manager can employ various **recruiting techniques:**[14]

- **Recruitment through advertisements.** This is probably the most common form of recruiting, in spite of its high cost. The compilation and placement of an advertisement is a specialised task and because it can cost thousands of rands, some companies use professional advertisement compilers. With the implementation of the Labour Relations Act 66 of 1995 (as amended), as well as the Employment Equity Act 55 of 1998, it is crucial that the advertisement be neutrally worded. If a requirement is set which may preclude one of the disadvantaged groups, then it must be a genuine prerequisite for the performance of the job. It has been found that the more specifically the responsibilities for the job are defined, the better are the chances of drawing the "right" applicants. Qualifying requirements, such as a certain academic qualification, or language ability, must be included to limit unsuitable applications

to a minimum. An indication of the remuneration offered is also important, firstly to draw the right applicants and secondly to eliminate potential applicants who already earn more. General requirements in the advertisement, such as "loyalty", "initiative", "sense of responsibility" and "drive" are totally superfluous, because they never deter a person from applying for a job. Advertisements may be placed in journals and newspapers or on bulletin boards.

- **Recruitment through consultants and labour agencies.** This approach is becoming increasingly prevalent in South Africa. The use of HR consultants is especially suitable for smaller businesses for which the services of a full-time HR manager cannot be justified. Such businesses inform a consulting firm of their needs, and the latter undertakes all the recruitment, including preliminary selection and recruitment administration for the business. In most cases (depending on the job level), the consultant recommends two or three applicants to the business, which must then make the final choice.

- **Recruitment through existing employees.** Existing employees are asked to recruit friends or acquaintances for the business. The rationale of this approach is that if members of staff feel positively about their work, they will more easily persuade others to apply. This method obviates the necessity for advertisements.

- **Recruitment through personal approach.** Using this method (often called **headhunting**), an individual personally known to the management of a business or consulting firm is approached and offered a job. This saves a lot of recruiting costs but has the disadvantage that the person cannot be weighed objectively against other applicants. This means that the selection process takes place before the recruitment process, in that the business first decides to appoint an individual to a specific job, and then asks him or her to consider the appointment.

- **Recruitment through radio, TV and the Internet.** Using this type of media is costly and still in its infancy in South Africa. However, following international trends, the approach should become more popular in the future, especially via the Internet.
- **Sundry recruiting strategies.** Visits to schools and universities to draw students' attention to employment opportunities are often used by businesses – not so much to recruit for specific jobs, but with long-term objectives in mind. The allocation of study bursaries with a compulsory period of service linked to them is a further method of drawing candidates with high academic potential. Participation in career exhibitions and the distribution of general recruitment brochures are other techniques available to the HR manager to ensure a sufficient flow of suitable applicants from whom appointments to the business can be made.

After applicants have been recruited, the next step is to select the best candidates.

9.4.2 Selection

The **selection** process can vary from a very short interview, to obtain a general impression of the applicant, to an intensive assessment process. However, this differs from business to business and depends especially on the level of the appointment.[15] In figure 9.4 on the next page, nine steps in a typical selection process are depicted.

The process described below, however, is the more intensive approach followed in the selection of applicants for senior management posts. For this reason, not all the steps indicated in figure 9.4 are followed in this discussion. The selection process to be used for senior management posts can be divided into the following three phases:

- Preliminary screening

- Intensive assessment
- Final selection

With the implementation of the Labour Relations Act and the Employment Equity Act, a number of important components of the selection process – that is, the application form, the interview and the tests used – have been affected. For example, the application form must not contain discriminatory questions such as "Are you married, divorced, single?" Moreover, these types of question may not be asked during the interview, and the various tests used must not be culturally biased.

9.4.2.1 Preliminary screening

The most efficient method for separating undesirable candidates from potential applicants is to compare the application with the job specification (step 1 in figure 9.4). This is a process that Barry followed at Sunnyside University in the case study at the start of this chapter.

A great deal of information can be included on the application form. What is asked depends largely on the needs of the specific business and the nature of the selection process. Information that is usually requested on an application form is **personal detail** (for example, name, address, educational qualifications) and **work history** (for example, jobs held in the past, reasons for resignation, and salary progress). Also, references are usually requested, that is, persons or institutions are approached to support the information given on the form (step 5 in figure 9.4).

Questions can also be asked about the applicant's significant achievements, disappointments, career expectations and communal and leisure-time activities. What is important is that the application form should serve as a preliminary selection instrument. In this preliminary selection, the HR manager should learn the following:

- Does the applicant comply with the minimum requirements as given in the job specification?
- What type of jobs did the applicant hold in the past?
- How quickly did he or she progress?
- How often has he or she changed jobs?

After the above-mentioned activities have been completed, the next step is to have a short interview with the applicants who are, according to information in the application form, suitable candidates (step 2 in figure 9.4). This interview provides the HR manager with the opportunity to form a general opinion of the applicant, based on appearance, articulateness and self-confidence. It also gives the applicant the opportunity to obtain more information about the business and the specific job.

A preliminary interview is usually not practical for applicants who would have to travel far. They would instead be invited to report for a more intensive assessment.

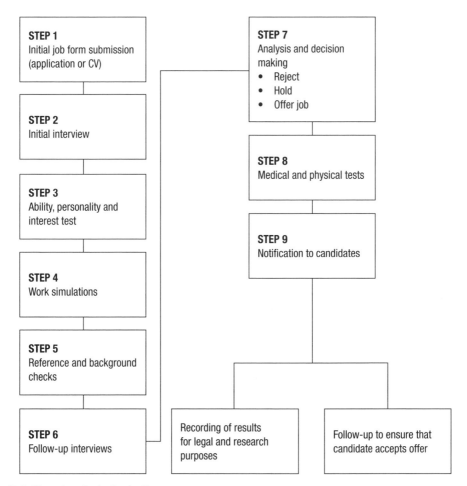

Figure 9.4: Steps in a typical selection process

Source: Adapted from Jackson, S.E. & Schuler, R.S., *Managing human resources: A partnership perspective*, 7th edition, South-Western Publishing, by permission of Thomson Learning, 2000, p. 315.

9.4.2.2 Intensive assessment

Intensive assessment basically involves two steps, namely **psychological testing** and **diagnostic interviewing**. Although medical selection usually forms part of the final selection process (step 8 in figure 9.4), it is advisable to have the applicant first assessed medically if the job has stringent physical requirements, for example, in the case of an airline pilot. However, the use of general medical tests in South Africa could have legal implications for the business, depending on the results of the medical examination and any hint of discrimination in their interpretation or use. Businesses therefore need to act with caution in this regard.

- **Psychological testing** can provide valuable information on an applicant. Tests usually involve a measurement of the applicant's personality, abilities and management skills (steps 3 and 4 in figure 9.4). An important aspect here is to take care that the tests used are not culturally biased, as mentioned earlier. Some HR managers have the required qualifications for doing testing themselves, while others have the testing done by professionals. The important point to remember is that a test can never predict accurately whether an applicant will be successful or unsuccessful. Test results give only a general indication that must be considered together with other factors.
- A **diagnostic interview** is used to obtain information that was not highlighted in the tests or on the application form (step 6 in figure 9.4). A good interviewer looks for certain characteristics by asking specific questions about the applicant's past performance. It seems from the information provided in the case study at the start of this chapter that at Sunnyside University this process was done thoroughly. For instance, an applicant's initiative can be assessed by asking about new projects that he or she may have initiated in previous jobs. The interview also gives the HR manager a chance to delve deeper into

possible shortcomings indicated by tests. If, for example, the interviewer suspects that the applicant does not always have good relationships with other people, more can be asked about interpersonal relationships. However, as mentioned previously, questions of a discriminatory nature must be avoided, such as any about the person's religious convictions or sexual preferences.

The key to good interviewing is to ask questions that give no indication of what answer is expected.

Some HR managers prefer to do diagnostic interviews alone, without involving the line functionaries under whom the applicant will work. Others, however, find it useful to include line functionaries at this stage and sometimes, even, to have them take part in the interview.

9.4.2.3 Final selection

At the stage of **final selection** there is usually enough information available about the applicants to compile a **shortlist** of, at most, three persons.

Before the applicants on the shortlist are finally weighed against each other, the HR manager must consult their **references** to confirm the information they have provided. (In figure 9.4 this was done before the diagnostic interview. However, there is no right or wrong stage at which to consult references.) Some HR managers do not attach much value to references because applicants would not refer HR managers to people who did not have a high regard for them. Therefore it is not, in fact, worth very much simply to ask referees for an opinion about the applicant's suitability. However, if the referees are asked to confirm information (whether positive or negative) obtained in the intensive assessment phase, they can make a very valuable contribution to the selection process.

In the final **comparison of applicants** it

may be useful to interview all three (or two) again briefly. What is essential, however, is to record the strengths and weaknesses of each of the final applicants in writing before the final decision is made (step 7 in figure 9.4). These documents must be kept for record purposes should a problem arise in the future.

After the most suitable applicant has been decided on, the person concerned is offered the job (step 9 in figure 9.4). This is the time to explain what is expected of the person in the job and to advise what the conditions of employment are. The applicant can then decide whether to accept the job or not.

If the job is accepted, the applicant usually has to be **medically examined** to ensure that there are no serious health problems.

9.4.2.4 Placement and induction

Once the job offer has been accepted, the new employee must report for duty as soon as possible. This process seemed to have taken approximately three months in the case study about Sunnyside University. With the placement of the person in the job a number of outstanding matters can be finalised. For example, in some cases arrangements must be made for the transport of furniture, provision of temporary housing, collection of missing information (for example copies of education certificates) and the completion of forms authorising tax and medical aid contribution deductions.

The new employee must also go through a process of **induction** (also known as **orientation** or **socialisation**). Experience has shown that when employees do not do this, it takes much longer for them to start working productively.

An induction programme will achieve the following:[16]

- Introduce new employees to their colleagues and facilitate and expedite the socialising process
- Explain to them the business's policy, procedures and rules, so that they are aware of the environment in which they will work
- Inform new employees about the business's history, products and services, as well as its reputation in the market, not only to fix their attention on their futures, but also to make them aware of the contribution they might make to the realisation of the business's objectives
- Inform employees about practical arrangements, for example payment procedures, overtime payment, incentive systems, eating arrangements and leave benefits
- Inform them about the organisational structure of the business and show them where they fit in and which communication channels are available to them

Once employees have been recruited, selected and placed in their jobs, the next step is training. This involves providing them with the skills, knowledge and abilities necessary to perform their jobs successfully.

9.5 Developing qualified workers

9.5.1 Human resource development (HRD)

It is the task of the human resource manager not only to ensure that the company employs sufficient staff but also to create opportunities for the employees to make themselves more valuable to the company. This activity can be subdivided in several ways, but a good method is to distinguish firstly between **training** and **development**, and secondly between **technical** training and **management** training.

Training typically involves providing employees with the knowledge and the skills needed to do a particular task or job, although attitude change may also be attempted (for example in sexual harassment awareness

Critical thinking

Employee selection seems simple enough, but as the discussion in section 9.4 shows, the human resource manager faces enormous challenges in choosing the right person for a specific job. The question that must be asked is "What other issues can assist this in this regard?" The excerpt below provides some answers.

What people tend to forget during selection

Why is it that the highly skilled and competent employee that you've hired is not performing well or, worse, still seems to be unable to work with others?

Many of the human capital problems that organisations are facing could have been prevented, directly or indirectly, if only more time and energy had been invested in selecting the "right" person. In this context, the word "right" means not only the person with the job-related knowledge, skills, and abilities derived from education, experience, and specific identifiable skills, but also the person with the right set of character attributes. Research studies by Hunter and Schmidt indicate that, on average, education has a predictive validity of only .10, while experience has an unimpressive predictive validity of .18 when linked to job performance.

The importance of selecting the right

person (in the sense just outlined) for your company is reinforced by Jim Collins in his book, Good to Great, *when he states that leaders of companies who have really made a success did not begin by setting a new vision and strategy; they first got the right people on the bus, the wrong people off the bus, and ensured that the right people were in the right seats. Only then did they figure out where to drive. Collins emphasises that people are not your most important asset, but that the right people are.*

Getting the right people on the bus places more emphasis on identifying the "right" character attributes of individuals and less emphasis on the specialised knowledge they possess. Given time, most people can learn the skills you may require them to have or acquire the knowledge you need them to acquire over time, but they may not possess the essential character traits that make them right for your team or organisation. In other words, they do not have the potential imbedded in their character that you're looking for in order to make your department, team or organisation successful.

Character attributes that may be considered when selecting prospective employees are self-efficacy, hope, optimism, resilience, and an internal locus of control.

Source: Adapted from Pienaar, C. & Bester, C. "What people tend to forget during selection", *People Dynamics*, Vol. 24, No. 5, 2006. pp. 3–4. Used with permission.

training). From the case study at the beginning of this chapter it is clear that Barry pursued this process seriously at Sunnyside University. **Developmental** activities, in contrast, have a longer-term focus on preparing for future work responsibilities, while at the same time increasing the capacities of employees to perform their current jobs.[17]

While the methods used for training and development are basically the same, the purpose differs. Thus, one person may attend a course on marketing because he or she currently fills a marketing post, whereas another person may be sent to the same course because management wants him or her to fill a marketing post at some future point. Similarly, a superior may spend time teaching a subordinate how to do his or her work correctly, but may also spend time teaching the subordinate to do the superior's work with a view to future promotion.

For our purposes, we will speak of **development** as the overall concept, with the understanding that it includes both training and development in the narrower sense of the word. We can thus define **human resource development** as a set of systematic and planned activities designed by an organisation to provide its members with the opportunities to learn necessary skills to meet current and future job demands. Consequently, learning is at the core of all human resource development activities.[18]

The word "technical" means not so much tasks performed in a workshop, but any task that has to be performed physically. Accordingly, the keeping of journals is just as technical as the repair of a machine. In its wider sense, we use the word "technical" to refer to all non-management tasks. By "management work" we mean tasks such as planning for, organising, controlling and, especially, managing people.

HRD activities should begin when an employee joins an organisation and continue throughout his or her career, regardless of whether that employee is an executive or a worker on an assembly line. HRD programmes must respond to job changes and integrate the long-term plans and strategies of the organisation to ensure the efficient and effective use of resources.

The HR manager does not have to train other employees personally (usually there are HRD professionals to do this) but he or she is primarily responsible for providing development facilities and courses. The HR manager must ensure that the employees are given an opportunity for training and development and that they are encouraged to develop to higher levels of competence.

9.5.2 Development methods

The development activities can be executed in four basic ways, namely:[19]
- Informally within the work situation
- Formally within the work situation
- Informally outside the work situation
- Formally outside the work situation

9.5.2.1 Informal development inside the work situation

In this situation the employee does not follow an official training programme. He or she is put to work immediately and expected to learn in due course. It might also happen that a newcomer works with an experienced employee for a while to give him or her time to "find his or her feet".

Informal development within the work situation can also occur through coaching by the employee's immediate superior. The superior may, for example, give his or her subordinate certain responsibilities and show the employee how to perform certain tasks.

Another common form of informal internal development is job rotation. This means that a staff member is moved to a new job as soon as he or she knows the current job well. The rotation could be short term, for example, two weeks in every job, or long term, for example, one year in every job. The latter usually applies to more senior management jobs and is often preparation for a general management position. What is important, however, is that the development does not take place at random. The HR manager can make an important contribution in this regard by:
- Keeping a careful record of each employee's development progress
- Encouraging line managers to establish this type of development (the HR manager does not usually have the official authority to enforce the development described)
- Discussing the progress and prospects of individual staff members with those individuals themselves

Often, when an employee resigns, he or she is informed for the first time of all the development plans that the company had for him or her. In most cases, however, it is then too late. The HR manager can prevent many resignations by ensuring that individuals are kept informed of the career path planned for them in the enterprise.

9.5.2.2 Formal development within the work situation

By "formal development" we mean a training process in which the employee receives a formal qualification. The most common form of this type of development is a learnership. The subordinate is allocated to a qualified artisan and so provided with the necessary practical training. From time to time, the subordinate must attend a few block courses, usually at a technical institution. After a certain period (the time varies according to the nature of the training) the subordinate receives a certificate if he or she has passed the compulsory examination. Other examples of this type of training are the qualifying exams for promotion in the South African National Defence Force and banking exams. The purpose of this type of training is not only to equip employees for their present jobs, but also to give them a wider perspective and background on the work situation in which they find themselves.

9.5.2.3 Informal development outside the work situation

In this sort of training an employee does not receive a qualification, although a certificate is sometimes issued to indicate that he or she has attended a particular training programme.

Probably the most common form of this type of development is a **training course** offered inside the company. Many companies (especially larger ones) have training centres where staff members receive training in a variety of subjects, for example interpersonal relationships, sales techniques, secretarial skills, supervision techniques, communication techniques, and planning techniques.

An **induction course** would also fall into this category. These courses are sometimes presented by the HR manager or by a HRD manager specially appointed for the job. The courses can also be presented by outsiders who specialise in presenting this type of course.

The advantage of courses presented within a company is that the training material is aimed specifically at the circumstances and operations of that particular company. This type of course is not meant only for workers at the lowest level of the company, but also for managers.

There are many courses in which managers can learn skills for handling and motivating subordinates. By arranging for managers in the company to attend such training programmes, the HR manager can make a big contribution towards line managers' optimal utilisation of employees.

Another form of informal development outside the work situation is the public seminar presented by an outside institution (for example a consultant or professional institution). Such courses are normally attended by a variety of employees from various companies. This type of course is valuable especially to smaller companies that want to expose only a few staff members to this type of training and can therefore not present the course within the organisation. The disadvantage here is that training material becomes generalised because it must apply to a number of widely divergent companies.

The above-mentioned courses normally last a few days or weeks, full-time. However, staff members might also attend a training session one morning a week, for example, and such a programme could last for a number of months.

Some companies use **programmed instruction** (PI) as a training method. Here, the instructional material is broken down into frames and programmed for the computer. Each frame represents a small component of the entire subject to be learned, and each frame must be successfully completed before the next one can be tackled. An advantage of PI is that large numbers of employees can be trained simultaneously, with each learner free to explore the material at his or her own pace. In addition, PI includes immediate and individualised feedback. A disadvantage is that development costs are high, especially for computerised PI.[20]

Another form of informal development is a fixed **reading programme**. For example, an employee may undertake to study certain books before a certain date, or to become a regular subscriber to a professional journal. If such a programme is agreed on, the HR manager must follow it up regularly, otherwise it is likely to peter out in the course of time.

9.5.2.4 Formal development outside the work situation

By this we mean formal study programmes presented by educational institutions, for example universities and colleges. What mainly contributes to the employee's general development is extensive and general training, rather than being equipped for the specific job he or she is currently doing. Many companies encourage their employees to attempt this type of development and even offer to pay the fees if the employee is successful in his or her studies.

9.5.3 The danger of the "shotgun" approach to development

As is clear from the above, there are many development possibilities that the HR manager can use. However, a problem is that many HR managers are of the opinion that "any training is valuable". They therefore encourage employees to attempt extramural studies, and they arrange for a certain number of employees to attend some training programmes every year. They aim, as if with a shotgun, in a general direction and hope to hit something.[21]

The successful HR manager, however, attempts to obtain as much value as possible from development programmes. Firstly, he or she will make a thorough analysis of the development needs that exist within the company and then choose training programmes on the basis of how specific programmes comply with these needs. Secondly, he or she will ensure that training money is spent only on members of staff who show a potential for further development. This is the case at Sunnyside University, as the statement in the case study about "exceptional employees" shows. Thirdly, the HR manager will make plans with the immediate superior of the employee concerned to utilise the new skills or insight in the work situation. Lastly, the HR manager will undertake follow-up studies to determine whether the training programmes have had the desired results.

We have focused thus far in this chapter on some of the most effective methods available to managers for finding and developing top-notch employees. However, having talented employees is not enough – successful organisations are particularly adept at engaging their workforces to achieve goals that benefit the organisation as well as the individual. One of the most helpful tools a company can use to maintain and enhance productivity and facilitate progress towards strategic goals is performance appraisal programmes.[22]

9.5.4 Performance appraisal

The purpose of a **performance appraisal** is to determine in which aspects the employee has:

- Performed exceptionally well (that is, surpassed the requirements for the job)
- Complied with the requirements for the job
- Not complied with the requirements for the job

Such appraisal has also been called **employee rating, employee evaluation, performance review, performance evaluation** and **results appraisal**.[23] Performance appraisal can be done by anyone who is familiar with the performance of individual employees, including supervisors who rate their employees, employees who rate their superiors,

Critical thinking

Organisations spend a substantial amount of their human resource budgets on the training and development of their employees. In order to convince top management that this amount is being well invested, the HR manager will have to convince management of the contributions proper training and development can make to organisational goal achievement. The question thus is "What focus should the training have to achieve this goal?" The excerpt below provides some answers in this regard.

Real time training for real time issues

Gone are the days of training being an expense – a great idea with the hope of making participants better at what they do that fails to become real beyond the four walls of the training room. With the new business reality involving concepts, products and solutions that need to be swiftly taken to market under greater pressure and with greater risk than ever before, the call is for training to facilitate this process. This picture of success demands building the skill and confidence that enables individuals and teams to positively deal with their company's real time issues successfully, in a lasting and tangible way, beyond the training manual that gets filed away in the cabinet with the comment, "it was thought provoking while it lasted".

It's the "Cinderella complex": everything seems value-adding until the training clock strikes twelve, and what seemed initially like a worthwhile training investment leaves the business feeling disenchanted soon after, pumpkin-style. Companies determined to find the right "fit" are therefore having to look beyond what training providers can do WITHIN training time, but how they can assist individuals and teams in effecting business change AFTER.

The reality is that employees already HAVE the knowledge. If you take the average sales team, chances are they would score 100% in a product knowledge multiple choice test, so to what degree would booking 30 of them on to a generic "sales impact" course

assist them when they have to talk a new product to a challenging client the next day? No one wants a walking brochure, they want an indispensable business partner and trusted advisor, and only the former is found frolicking in the traditional training set-up.

The issue is that most training initiatives focus on telling people what they already know instead of addressing the implementation gap between what we know versus what we do.

The new ... interventions that are making an impact are those that don't undermine participants by assuming that their know-how isn't in place but focus instead on using training sessions as realistic problem solving sessions with a bias to action. Knowledge is base camp. The summit lies in creating a discipline of execution: this could be where the company's brand and service promise is pro-actively taken from the "walls to the halls" internally, or when a product is taken to market by participants who have had the experiential opportunity of refining skills in fluently talking the client's language around their specific products – communicating solutions to clients in a way that gets their buy-in.

Be practical

Powerful business outcomes based training therefore starts with a strong practical component during sessions as its foundation. It doesn't matter whether participants staple themselves to their process in service initiatives, track their service processes through the eyes of the client, ensure a benchmark level of service excellence and value-driven actions at all critical touch points. It could also be strategising how to bring brand values to life through concrete behaviours at critical touch points in values initiatives or "real-playing" how to leverage their technical and product knowledge – translating it into marketing and sales opportunities to grow the profitability of their existing client base and acquire new clients in solutions based selling and presentation workshops – the experiential opportunity to rehearse for business relevant realities is key. And just like relationship loses its lustre when the intention doesn't exist in those involved to actively work on it, the planning component is key to the sustainable success of any intervention aiming to achieve business results.

It's essential that whatever the nature of the training, participants take the initiative as they leave the session, having committed to a gutsy personal and business unit action plan, which translates training into tangible results around the desired outcomes set by the client. This challenges the dominant logic of feel-good inspirational sessions, which may leave you with a short term high, but a famously low impact in the long term.

So think twice before you "okay" the next training day. Your training spend should be value adding enough that your end clients feel its resonance. Ask yourself, "Am I training merely for training's sake? Or am I unleashing a new energy and imagination in my team, with training as a powerful vehicle to establish momentum, to participatively plan to translate the way forward into a high impact reality?"

It's not about filling out definitions in a training manual, or about exploring the five new sales techniques to close the deal. It's about a customised process that aligns strongly with business objectives – an investment that can give birth to sustained and measurable confidence and competence in teams to impact the bottom line.

Source: © Bluen V. from *HR Future*, Osgard Media through DALRO 2008.

team members who rate each other, employees who do self-appraisal, or outside sources. At Sunnyside University in the case study at the start of the chapter, the performance appraisal took place after the employees had been working for three months on the job.

The more **objective** this appraisal is, the more successful it is likely to be. It is therefore important for the HR manager to ensure that there are objective criteria against which the performance of the individual or team can be measured. Thus, an ideal performance appraisal involves the comparison of work results with quantitative objectives.[24] For example, a salesperson's actual sales are compared with a sales target; a truck driver can be appraised against, amongst other things, the maintenance costs of his or her truck; and a teller's performance may be measured against the number of times he or she did not achieve a balance.

Some performance appraisal methods also provide for the assessment of an employee's **characteristics**, such as attitude, enthusiasm, initiative and neatness. However, this type of assessment is much more subjective than the

comparison of results with objectives because it depends mainly on the opinion of the immediate superior.

The least effective form of performance appraisal is that whereby employees are compared with each other in general. In this approach the employee is assessed mainly on the basis of the **impression** the superior has of him or her – and the risk of prejudice (positive or negative) is much greater.

As a result of the numerous problems that arise out of traditional performance appraisal methods, a new approach, namely the **360° system**, was developed some years ago. This multi-source rating recognises that the manager is no longer the sole source of performance appraisal information. Instead, feedback from various colleagues and constituencies is obtained and given to the manager, who then interprets the feedback from the various sources.[25]

In practice, and for a number of reasons, formal performance appraisal programmes sometimes yield disappointing results.

Primary causes include a lack of top-management information and support, unclear performance standards, rater bias, too many forms to complete, and the use of the programmes for conflicting purposes.[26] The **results** of a performance appraisal can be used for three basic purposes, namely:

- To provide a basis for financial rewards
- To determine whether the employee should be promoted to a higher level of work
- To provide the employee with feedback on how well he or she is doing

It is not possible for the HR manager to do the performance appraisal him- or herself (except where employees – that is, the HR officers – fall directly under his or her control, as is the case at Sunnyside University in the case study). Therefore the HR manager must ensure that performance appraisal is done by the line managers and must help them to do it, especially by providing them with suitable instruments for doing appraisals.

A critical aspect in performance appraisal is **feedback** to the individual or team concerned. In order to be effective, feedback should possess characteristics other than timeliness – for example, it must be concise (not too lengthy), specific (examples must be provided), relevant (it must be job related) and supportive (offer suggestions for positive change).[27]

Rewarding those employees whose performance appraisals are excellent is important and necessary. However, organisations also use compensation to attract the quality and quantity of employees needed, retain those employees, and motivate them towards organisational goal achievement. In the following section, the important role played by compensation within an organisation will be discussed.

9.6   Keeping qualified workers

9.6.1 Compensation of employees

Compensation refers to all forms of financial returns and tangible services and benefits employees receive as part of an employment relationship.[28] It is one of the most important

factors that motivates an individual to seek employment with a specific company. The other is the nature of the work. If an employee is dissatisfied with his or her compensation, there is a good chance that the employee will not remain with the company for long. The HR manager must therefore ensure that the compensation policy does not lead to a high staff turnover. From the case study at the start of this chapter it is clear that above average salaries are paid to the HR employees at Sunnyside University. It is also evident that there is not a high staff turnover in HR at the University.

Thus, the establishment of a compensation policy is an absolute necessity.[29] Although the HR manager, in most companies, does not have the final say in the compensation policy, it must nevertheless be initiated by him or her. Regarding this policy:

- Firstly, a decision must be made about how the company's compensation in general should compare with that of the labour market. Will it be the same? A little higher? Considerably higher? Or a little lower? What form should the compensation take? How much will be in the form of direct financial compensation? And how much in the form of fringe benefits? The fringe benefits of some companies do not involve more than 30–40% of the total compensation, while those of others are as high as 50%.
- Secondly, a policy must be determined on a cost-of-living adjustment. Does every employee automatically receive an increase that corresponds with the Consumer Price Index (CPI), or does each receive a larger or smaller increase?
- Thirdly, the compensation policy must determine what form rewards will take. Most companies reward by means of salary increases. Other companies, however, only give salary increases in accordance with the rise in the cost of living, and then give cash bonuses to reward good work performance.

9.6.2 Types of compensation

Compensation can be regarded as the output an employee receives for the input (work) he or she produces. **Direct compensation** is the basic salary or wage an employee receives, while **indirect compensation** refers to the fringe benefits an employee receives, such as leave, medical aid and a pension scheme.[30] The other aspect of compensation is **reward**, that is, the recognition of good work performance.

9.6.2.1 Direct compensation

A person who is paid monthly receives a **salary**, whereas someone who is paid daily or weekly receives a **wage**. Most employees' salaries or wages are based on the period of time they have worked for the company, measured by days, weeks or months. Thus, there is no direct relationship between the compensation they receive and the amount of work that they perform. Such a system is simple to administer but has the disadvantage that, for remuneration purposes (in the short term, at any rate) there is no distinction between productive and unproductive workers. To overcome this problem, some companies use a **piece** wage system. Here, the employee is compensated for the amount of work he or she performs, regardless of the time used to perform the work.

Example: Time wages and piece wages

A vegetable farmer in KwaZulu-Natal pays the labourers R30 per day (that is, time wages) but at harvesting time the farmer pays them R6,00 for every bag of peas they pick (that is, piece wages). If they pick only 3 bags a day, they receive R18,00 for the day's work. If they pick 8 bags, they receive R48,00 for the day's work.

9.6.2.2 Indirect compensation

The **benefits** an employee receives from his or her membership of an organisation are called **fringe benefits**. These increase in size and scope as the employee moves to higher levels in the organisation.

Fringe benefits generally provided are:

- **Leave benefits**, for holidays, illness, studies, etc.
- **Insurance benefits**, for example against medical costs, injury, and unemployment; these also include life cover and pension benefits
- **Housing benefits**, in the form of free housing, housing at a low rental, or loan subsidies for buying a house
- **Car benefits**, which can vary from a free car with all expenses paid to financial assistance in buying a car

There are also other types of fringe benefits. These differ from company to company. The important point, however, is that fringe benefits are a form of compensation linked to the hierarchical level of the employee. For example, only staff members above a certain status level enjoy cars as a fringe benefit, and the higher the level, the more expensive the car.

9.6.2.3 Reward

In most cases, neither direct nor indirect compensation is linked to an individual's work performance, and both forms of compensation are therefore regarded as "rights" by most employees. Both forms of compensation therefore have very little influence on the motivation of employees. The fact that an employee receives an end-of-year bonus (often equivalent to a month's salary) will not cause him or her to work twice as hard to merit this in future.

The HR manager must therefore ensure that there are other ways of rewarding an individual's work performance. Such rewards can take various forms, a few of which are as follows:

- The most common form of reward is a **salary increase** based on the individual's work performance (that is, a merit award). A distinction must be made here between the **cost-of-living adjustment** (given to all employees to adjust to the inflation rate) and **merit increases** given in recognition of the individual's achievement.

- Some companies give **financial bonuses** to those employees who have performed exceptionally well.
- Other companies reward outstanding employees with a **paid holiday** or an **overseas trip** with all expenses paid.

To summarise: **compensation** is part of an agreement and is given to the employee for satisfactory performance. It can therefore correctly be regarded as a **right** because the company is **committed** to paying it. A **reward**, however, is not a commitment on the part of the company – it is, instead, the company's **voluntary** acknowledgement of an individual's good work performance.

9.6.3 The amount of compensation

The question that now arises is "How much should a specific staff member be paid by way of compensation (salary and fringe benefits)?" We know that a factory manager will probably earn more than a machine operator, but how large ought the difference to be, and how much should each receive?

The first step in deciding on compensation is to make an **external comparison**. How much

do factory managers at other companies earn? What is the nature and scope of their fringe benefits? The HR manager must do a **salary survey** to obtain this information.

Salary surveys are undertaken country-wide by different institutions, and the HR manager may choose to use such surveys rather than do his or her own survey. However, it is important in such a survey that equivalent jobs are compared with each other. The mere fact that two people have the job title "factory manager" does not necessarily mean that they do the same type of work. So, for example, a person in control of a small workshop where hand-made chairs are manufactured by three artisans might carry the title "factory manager", but it is obvious that this job is not equivalent to that of a factory manager in a large motor manufacturing plant.

The second step is to make an **internal comparison**.[31] This means that the value of jobs must be compared with each other in terms of the demands they make on the employee. Accordingly, it may be said that the demands made on an accountant are higher than the demands made on an accounting clerk.

This internal comparison is known as **job evaluation**,[32] and there are various methods of undertaking it. One method is to rank all jobs in the company in terms of their "value". This ranking system is usually used in small to medium-sized companies, and the assessment is made by a panel of senior managers.

A second general method of job evaluation is the **factor comparison** method. According to this method, jobs are compared according to the demands they make on the employee with regard to factors such as knowledge, communication skills, level of responsibility and, especially, decision-making skill. Points are awarded to each factor (also known as **compensable factors**) and the total points indicate into which job grade a specific job falls. The information about the jobs can be obtained from the **job description**. Job descriptions therefore have a twofold purpose:

Example: A salary survey

The HR manager might find, for example, that the average salary of a factory manager is R20 000 per month, while in the HR manager's own company the salary is only R12 000 per month. There is, clearly, a risk here that the factory manager will not stay in the company very long. However, if he or she earns R30 000 per month, the company may be paying too much.

Critical thinking

One of the most significant tasks confronting HR managers is the design and implementation of compensation systems. The primary goal of these systems, which are designed to serve many purposes, is to provide fair and equitable remuneration for all employees. What approach should the HR manager follow to achieve success in this regard? In the excerpt below some answers to this question are provided.

Trends in remuneration philosophy

Examining the role of remuneration

Firms, like other economic organisations, serve to coordinate the actions of groups of people and to motivate them to carry out needed activities. The problem of motivating people in organisations comes from the fact that their own self-interest may not automatically lead them to act in ways that the organisation would want. This divergence of interest arises because the individual members of an organisation typically do not bear all of the costs and benefits of actions they take and the decisions they make within the organisation. Consequently, when they make decisions – about how to spend their time, how hard to work and on what, what risks to take – the choices that appear best from their personal point of view may not maximise the total value generated for the organisation. Even if they are cognisant of the larger interests, they may not automatically take these fully into account. Companies try to manage this through five primary mechanisms:

- *Developing and providing clear strategic direction*
- *Implementing good organisational design*
- *Creating a sense of shared purpose*
- *Effective performance management*
- *Appropriate remuneration and reward systems*

All of the five dimensions affect motivation. From an organisational design perspective, the motivation problem is to shape the organisation – the people, the architecture, the routines and processes and the culture – to bring a closer alignment of interests between the organisation and its members and thereby increase the efficiency of the choices they make. Motivation is not just a matter of monetary incentives. Organisations are increasingly trying to develop sets of coherent reward strategies that strike a balance between bureaucratic procedures and entrepreneurial freedom, fairness and effectiveness, good governance and meaningful incentives in order to manage the motivation problem, "best fit" with the organisation's strategies and "best practice" in the market place. There is no coherent view on what is the optimal choice.

Best fit approaches assume that one size does not fit all. The best practices approach assumes that there exists a universal, best way. What evolves is that while there are generally accepted best practice frameworks of broad principles, organisations should strive to be innovative and develop sensible best fits that are economically sound.

There is an overall design objective – that managing the pay strategy and structure creates the potential to support better organisational performance. If the structure does not motivate employees to help achieve the organisation's objectives, then it is a candidate for redesign. Further, if the cost of the remuneration approach exceeds the returns that it motivates, then it is a candidate for redesign. The challenge then is to be able to assess the economic value returned by the cost of employee motivation.

Many organisations follow an institutional model approach – that is, they interpret following the market norm as being best practice and ignore the question of strategy altogether. Recent examples include the moves to delayer pay bands, to emphasise teams, to de-emphasise individual contributions, to shift to a competency-based pay system and to follow these at great cost without assessing the real return. Most organisations today are trying to become more competitive by reducing their costs (amongst other strategies of course) – using fewer employees to do a wider variety of tasks without adjusting the fixed cost of pay. Employees need to be more flexibly matched to changes in work flow. Thus the importance of flexibility in behaviour is being made clear to employees. The challenge is how to reflect this dynamic in the design of the reward system.

A coherent total reward perspective

Much has been written about developing total reward strategies, but the reality is usually manifested in bureaucratic approaches to guaranteed pay, increasingly complex incentive schemes and evolving questions about the viability of share schemes. Changing

accounting regulations, requirements for disclosure and pressures for improved governance drive the increased questioning. So, too, does the recognition that the intangible assets of a business (such as the human capital, intellectual property and capability) increasingly represent the source of competitive advantage and the source of most costs of operation. Reviewing a company's approach to rewards and remuneration therefore must focus on improving the economic return on the investment in intangible assets. Remuneration can be defined as the return received in exchange for people's efforts and ideas given at the workplace. Exchange is the key part of the relationship.

Source: Adapted from Olivier, M., "Trends in remuneration philosophy", *People Dynamics*, Vol. 24, No. 9, 2006, pp. 47–48. Used with permission.

- Firstly, they form the basis for a **job specification**, with a view to recruitment, selection, and training.
- Secondly, they provide a basis for job comparison, with a view to job evaluation.

It is important to remember that in job evaluation, only the job is assessed, and not the job incumbent. The value of the job has nothing to do with how well or how badly the present incumbent carries it out.

Job evaluation in itself cannot indicate exactly how much a specific staff member ought to earn. The HR manager can only determine, in the light of the findings of the external comparison, what the broad salary range of an accountant, for instance, ought to be.

The decision as to what a specific employee ought to earn once he or she is employed will depend on years of experience, qualifications, what other employees on the same level earn, and other similar considerations. The question can be decided by the HR manager in conjunction with the line manager. However, the HR manager cannot decide on an individual

staff member's reward. That decision can be made only by the staff member's immediate superior. Nevertheless, the HR manager can make an important contribution by ensuring that line managers have suitable instruments for assessing their subordinates' performances, as mentioned earlier.

9.7 Summary

The primary function of the HR manager is to help other managers in the company to utilise their employees fully. How well the HR manager does this is not easily measurable. There are, furthermore, big differences in the views of HR managers regarding their task. One HR manager may regard his or her task mainly as HR administration. To such a person, as long as the HR records are kept up to date and salaries are paid regularly, the task is done. Another HR manager will concentrate on the full range of tasks discussed in this chapter. No matter how he or she regards the task, however, it is clear that the HR manager can make a unique and very important contribution to the efficiency and effectiveness of a company and therefore also to its overall profitability and competitiveness.

 Key terms

360°	Intensive assessment
Advertisement	Internal recruiting
Benefits	Job analysis
Compensation	Job description
Direct compensation	Job specification
Employment Equity Act 55 of 1998	Labour Relations Act 66 of 1995 (as amended)
External recruiting	Performance appraisal
Final selection	Preliminary screening
HR demand	Recruiting techniques
HR development (HRD)	Recruiting
HR forecasting	References
HR information system (HRIS)	Reward
HR plan	Salaries
HR planning	Selection
HR supply	Wages
Indirect compensation	

 Questions for discussion

Reread the case study at the beginning of the chapter and answer the following questions:

1. Will the HR manager (Barry) be able to supply a sufficient number of people to the HR department without proper HR planning?
2. Is it likely that the HR manager (Barry) will be able to obtain the services of enough people for the running of the HR department?
3. Is it possible for the HR manager (Barry) to make a correct decision when appointing a candidate for the HR department?
4. Why did Barry spend so much time on training the new staff he recruited for the HR department?

5. The case study indicated that the employees in the HR department received above average salaries. What does this mean and is it a good thing?

References

1. Pfeffer, J., *Competitive advantage through people*, Harvard Business School Press, Boston, Mass., 1994.
2. Williams, C., *Management*, South-Western College Publishing, Cincinnati, 2000, p. 546.
3. *Ibid.*, p. 546.
4. Bohlander, G., Snell, S. & Sherman, A., *Managing human resources*, 12th edition, South-Western College Publishing, Cincinnati, 2001, p. 28.
5. *Ibid.*, p. 28.
6. *Ibid.*, p. 28.
7. *Ibid.*, p. 30.
8. Jackson, S.E. & Schuler, R.S., *Managing human resources: A partnership perspective*, 7th edition, South-Western College Publishing, Cincinnati, 2000, p. 220.
9. Grobler, P.A., Wärnich, S., Carrell, M.R., Elbert, N.F. & Hatfield, R.D., *Human resource management in South Africa*, 3rd edition, Thomson Learning, London, 2006, p. 157.
10. Anthony, W.P., Kacmar, K.M. & Perrewé, P.L., *Human resource management: A strategic approach*, 4th edition, Harcourt College Publishers, Orlando, 2002, p. 221.
11. *Ibid.*, p. 221.
12. Grobler et al., *op. cit.*, p. 182.
13. Dessler, G., *Human resource management*, 8th edition, Prentice Hall, Upper Saddle River, N.J., 2000, p. 645.
14. Mello, J.A., *Strategic human resource management*, South-Western College Publishing, Cincinnati, 2002, pp. 242–245.
15. Williams, *op. cit.*, p. 565.
16. Grobler et al., *op. cit.*, p. 213.
17. Desimone, R.L., Werner, J.M. & Harris, D.M., *Human resource development*, 3rd edition, Harcourt College Publishers, Orlando, 2002, p. 10.
18. *Ibid.*, p. 3.
19. Jackson & Schuler, *op. cit.*, p. 367.
20. *Ibid.*, p. 371.

21. Livingston, S., Gerdel, T.W., Hill, M., Yerak, B., Melvin, C. & Lubinger, B., "Ohio's strongest companies all agree that training is vital to their success", *Plain Dealer*, Vol. 21, 1997, p. 305.
22. Bohlander et al., *op. cit.*, p. 318.
23. Mathis, R.L. & Jackson, J.H., *Human resource management: Essential perspectives*, 2nd edition, South-Western, Cincinnati, 2002, p. 93.
24. Williams, R.S., *Performance management: Perspectives on employee performance*, International Thomson Business Press, Filey, North Yorkshire, 1998, pp. 84–85.
25. Mathis & Jackson, *op. cit.*, p. 96.
26. Bohlander, et al., *op. cit.*, p. 320.
27. Williams, *op. cit.*, p. 152.
28. Milkovich, G.T. & Newman, J.M., *Compensation*, 7th edition, McGraw-Hill, New York, 2002, p. 7.
29. Dessler, *op. cit.*, p. 399.
30. Mathis & Jackson, *op. cit.*, p. 104.
31. Milkovich & Newman, *op. cit.*, p. 89.
32. Bohlander et al., *op. cit.*, p. 372.

MOTIVATING AND MANAGING HUMAN RESOURCES

<table>
<tr><td>

The purpose of this chapter

In this chapter theories on the motivation of human resources and aspects relating to managing human resources are discussed. In addition, the role of the human resources function, as well as human resources management and organisational effectiveness, are briefly explained. Theories relating to employee motivation constitute the bulk of the chapter, and are provided with the aim of exposing learners to the basic principles of various motivational theories.

</td><td>

Learning outcomes

The content of this chapter will enable learners to:
- Describe the role of the human resource function in organisations
- Explain the contribution human resource management can make to organisation effectiveness
- Provide an outline of who is responsible for human resource management
- List and explain the different content theories of motivation
- Discuss the process theories of motivation
- Evaluate the different motivation strategies

</td></tr>
</table>

10.1 Introduction

In today's society notions such as "people make up a business", "people are an organisation's greatest assets", "managing human resources is fundamental to organisational success", and "motivated employees make a difference" are in general use, and are crucial to organisational success. The emphasis has shifted from endeavouring to solve people-related problems in organisations in an ad hoc fashion, to a more professional approach where the overall organisational philosophy, culture and tone reflect this belief.

The case study on the next page provides an illustration of how theories of motivation are applied in the strategies of South African companies:

Case study

The most promising companies in South Africa: Their competitive advantage

The Corporate Research Foundation (CRF) profiles and publishes information about companies that are selected as South Africa's most promising companies. The following common features that gave the companies their competitive advantage were identified in the fourth edition of *South Africa's most promising companies:*[1]

- These companies are not only obtaining the right talent, but they are also nurturing that talent by means of skills development, transfer of knowledge, and the creation of an open and sharing environment. Flatter organisational structures are implemented, allowing for a more flexible working environment. Creativity and innovation are encouraged and lots of opportunities are provided for challenges, as long as the end result is added value to the clients and the business. These companies also give their employees more responsibility to the point were they feel they are part-owner of the firm.

- Major emphasis is placed on good working relationships with employees, clients, suppliers and other stakeholders. The employees get recognition for their loyalty, excellent client service and performance, by means of excellent remuneration, share options and other forms of incentive schemes.

- Other strategies employed by these companies include building and maintaining a strong brand in the market, an emphasis on excellent client service, and holding values such as honesty, integrity, open communication and transparency.

Some of the relevant strategies of four of these companies will be elaborated on later in this chapter.

Source: Brevis, T., "Most promising companies: What gives them a competitive advantage", *Management Today*, February 2005, pp. 8–12.

10.2 The role of human resource management in the organisation

Before continuing with a discussion on employee motivation as a crucial element in organisational success, we shall briefly discuss certain aspects of human resource management in organisations, such as the role of the human resource function, human resource management and organisational effectiveness. Finally, we shall look at the person who performs the human resource function in organisations.

10.2.1 The human resource function

Today, human resource management strategies should be integrated with organisational plans and be in line with the broad organisational strategy. The **human resource function** is concerned with much more than filing, routine administration actions, and record-keeping activities. Its main role should be that of **strategic partner**, and human resource strategies should clearly demonstrate the organisational strategy regarding people, profit and overall effectiveness. Various international competitive studies have indicated that

Links between HR strategies and profits: Research by PricewaterhouseCoopers (PWC)

PWC launched a global human capital survey in 2002–2003, and the survey's participants represented 1 056 organisations in 47 counties, with a combined workforce of more than 6 million employees. South Africa was represented by 25 organisations, 11 of which are from the financial services sector, and 9 of which are from the products sector. The results are briefly reported below.

Businesses with a documented HR strategy are more profitable, and typically benefit from 35% higher revenue per employee. This is one of the key findings to emerge from a global human capital survey by PWC.

Although the majority of South Africa's human resource leaders are members of their organisation's highest-ranking leadership team, they generally do not have an officially documented human resource strategy.

Furthermore, only around half of those with a strategy in place claim close integration of that strategy with the overall business strategy.

There is powerful evidence that good people management has a positive effect on a range of issues, from increased employee productivity and reduced absenteeism to improved profitability. To reap the benefits in terms of business performance, organisations need to address three important issues:

- An HR strategy that is documented and also integrated into the business strategy
- Effective people policies and practices that deliver the strategy across the business
- An HR function that can implement policy and strategy, and also influence the business

Highlights of the comparison of South African organisations with the global benchmarks include the following:

- The top business issue for South African organisations is revenue growth; global participants report cost reduction as their top issue, perhaps suggesting that the South African economy is in a growth phase. Leadership development is an important business issue, and it is the top HR issue in South Africa and globally.
- HR functions do not report on many of the business and HR issues they identify as most important to their organisation. Even the traditional measures of headcount, staff turnover and training are only reported by around 60% of organisations. Two-thirds of participants do not track absence from work, and yet the survey indicates that there is a clear link between reduced absenteeism and increased profit margins per employee.
- The ratio of full-time HR specialists to employees is lower in South Africa than in all other regions (50 employees per HR specialist against a global average of 62 employees).
- South Africa employs more females than most other countries, pointing to the likelihood that legislation has made a difference to gender diversity. Whereas regulatory compliance does not feature in the top five business issues globally, South African participants believe it is as important as leadership development, and nearly 50% of participants believe that regulatory compliance is an area where HR has clearly and measurably improved business performance.
- South African organisations provide an average of five days' training per employee per year, compared with the global average of three days – further evidence, perhaps, of the positive impact of skills development legislation. In the South African services sector this average was even higher – with seven days' training per employee per year.
- Among the minority of HR leaders who do have an officially documented HR strategy, only 62% (compared to a global result of 96%) report having an HR strategy that is closely integrated with the overall business strategy.

Source: PricewaterhouseCoopers, Global Human Capital Benchmarking Survey 2002/03, South African Survey Findings, Media Release, 5 February 2003.

labour productivity is one of the major factors that have to be addressed in South Africa in order to be competitive in a global market. In the South African context, a crucial role of the HR manager is to improve the skills base of employees and to contribute to the profitability of the organisation. The human resource function must be accountable for its actions and should operate as a "profit centre" (see box on the previous page).

The emphasis on accountability is even more important if one considers the legal environment in which human resource-related decisions have to be taken (see chapter 11) and the very negative consequences for the organisation if the right decisions are not made, for example if the correct procedures as prescribed by the Labour Relations Act 66 of 1995 are not followed in the event of a retrenchment.

Every manager in the organisation should realise the importance of recruiting, selecting, training, developing, rewarding, assisting and motivating employees (see section 10.2.3). However, to achieve organisational success both locally and internationally, the focus should be on integration and teamwork among employees.

10.2.2 Human resource management and organisational effectiveness

Among the things that organisations need in order to be effective are a mission and strategy, an organisational structure, and human resources. It is people in organisations who create the ideas and allow the organisations to prosper, and even in the most capital-intensive organisation, people are needed to run the organisation. A study done in Zimbabwe, for example, indicated that excellent, successful companies have the following human resource management attributes in common: a participative style of management, communication with all levels of employees, promotion from within, training of employees and rewarding of good work.[2] These findings are also in line with the profile of the most promising companies in South Africa. Human resources in organisations thus either limit or enhance the strength or weaknesses of organisations, and a problem that managers experience in organisations is how to put a monetary value to people in organisations. While it is easy on evaluate other resources, for example machines and equipment, in terms of their monetary value, putting a monetary value on people is very difficult. Various research projects, for example human resource accounting practices, have been launched to do this, but

---

Critical thinking

We often hear that, in attempts to create a leaner enterprise, companies start with downsizing in their HR departments. Could the reason be that the value of human resources is underestimated?

According to Dudu Msomi of the Institute of People Management, downsizing in the HR department may cut some costs initially, but in the long run this will prove to be a very shortsighted decision. She believes that a large part of most organisations' workforce is undervalued, undertrained and underutilised and it is the HR department's job to ensure that all employees are given the opportunity to realise their full potential. According to her, now, more than ever, organisations need to see the value of their HR professionals.

Source: "Don't underestimate the value of human resources", *Management Today*, February, 2005, pg. 12.

a conclusive methodology and process have not yet been established.

For organisations to be really effective, top managers should treat human resources as the key element of effectiveness. The contribution of human resources to organisational effectiveness includes the following:[3]

- Assisting everybody in the organisation to reach stated goals
- Employing the skills and abilities of the workforce efficiently
- Providing the organisation with well-trained and motivated employees
- Assisting in the attainment of the employees' job satisfaction and self-actualisation
- Developing a quality of work life that makes employment in the organisation desirable
- Assisting with the maintenance of ethical policies and socially responsible behaviour
- Managing change to the mutual advantage of individuals, groups, the organisation and the public
- Executing human resource functional activities in a professional manner

10.2.3 Who performs the human resource function?

As soon as a new person (employee) is recruited and appointed in an organisation, management's main concern must be to get that person to do his or her work as well as possible. In this process (see chapter 9) certain functions have to be performed by the **human resource specialist**, who would normally be situated in a human resource department, as well as by line managers and direct supervisors. Line managers are those people in other departments, such as operations, marketing and finances, who have the responsibility to utilise optimally all the resources at their disposal.

The human resource is a unique resource because if it is not properly managed, effectiveness can decline drastically. For this reason, it is essential to understand why

people work in organisations, and why some people want to perform better than other people. In South Africa, where there is high unemployment, having a job has become an important goal, and people compete fiercely for jobs. It is thus important for managers to take note of the complex issues motivating employees and to manage these. In most organisations – apart from capital-intensive organisations – the investment in people has more effect on organisational success than investment in other resources, for example materials, equipment or capital, does.

In large organisations the human resources function is mainly coordinated by the human resource department. In smaller organisations that do not have human resource departments, the main human resource functions – such as recruitment and selection, scheduling of work, performance management, compensation, training and development and labour relations (see chapter 11) – are performed by line managers over and above their normal duties. As the organisation grows and increases in size, the line manager's job is divided up, and some aspects, such as recruitment and selection, become more specialised. These duties are then dealt with by a human resource specialist.

Depending on the nature of the organisation, a human resource specialist is normally employed in organisations with approximately 50 to 150 employees. In South Africa, the ratio of full-time human resource specialists to employees is 50, while the global average is about 62 (see box about PricewaterhouseCoopers on page 229). A human resource department or section is typically created when the number of employees reaches a figure of between 200 and 500.

From the above discussion on the role of the human resource manager, it is clear that without well-trained and motivated workforces, organisations cannot be successful. Both human resource specialists and line managers are responsible for managing the people talent in organisations, and one aspect that can make a difference in achieving organisational success is the level of employee motivation, which is dealt with in the section below.

10.3 Employee motivation

The importance and uniqueness of the human resource in the effective functioning of organisations was discussed in section 10.2. Part of the responsibility of the human resource department and line managers is to turn the potential of the employees into performance.

10.3.1 Motivation in the workplace: A basic understanding

Employee performance in organisations is mainly determined by three things, namely a desire to do the job (motivation), the capability to do the job (ability), and the resources to do the job (work environment). If an employee cannot do the job, he or she can be trained or replaced (see chapter 11 on the requirements laid down by the Labour Relations Act) and if more resources are required, the manager can rectify the problem. The problem becomes more challenging if the employee is not motivated to do the job.[4] Because of the complex nature of human beings, managers may not fully understand the problems experienced by employees and the effect of these problems on individual performance. The level of **motivation** thus has a direct influence on performance, and it is important to understand how motivation takes place. However, motivation is not simply about performance – deviant behaviour such as sabotage and absenteeism are motivated behaviours as well!

Motivation refers to those forces within a person that effect his or her direction,

Applying the concept: Pick 'n Pay

Research has shown that customer service begins inside an organisation, with the way employees are treated, valued, respected, empowered and rewarded. For this reason, the emphasis on adding value and delivering good results is increasingly being linked to the way organisations manage and motivate their people. As Tom Peters explains in *In search of excellence*, "Business success today rests on quick action, service to customers, practical innovation, and the fact that you can't get any of these without virtually everyone's commitment."

No one knows this better than Pick 'n Pay CEO Sean Summers. He has been widely praised for *Vuselela*, a staff motivational campaign that involves extensive training, for example, trips for staff at all levels to courses at Disneyworld in the USA. In stark contrast to the knee-jerk antics of many panicky SA retailers, Summers is backing a long-term strategy aimed at creating a climate in which Pick 'n Pay employees are able to realise their own potential. He is reportedly a firm believer that motivated employees keep the tills ringing.

And the results speak for themselves. Pick 'n Pay came out tops in the retail sector of the *Financial Mail's* recent *Top Companies Survey*, and ranked 76th in the top 250. In a recent interview in the *IMM Journal of Marketing*, Summers cited dignity and respect as two commodities essential to growth. He also confirmed his belief that if you can't deliver a good experience for employees within the workplace, you are highly unlikely to deliver a positive experience for customers.

Yet, despite the clear need for staff motivation, there is very little of it to be found in the adult world of work. Why is it that the innovative spirit we are born with seems to get stamped out, and fear or passivity sets in?

Source: Burton, L., "Managing motivation", *People Dynamics*, 2001.

intensity and persistence of behaviour that is within the control of the person. A motivated employee is willing to exert a particular level of effort (intensity), for a certain amount of time (persistence), toward a particular goal (direction).[5] Whereas the emphasis in the past was on "effort" and subsequently on ways to energise employees, the concept of **direction** is currently emphasised. It is reasoned that all normal people will expend energy in one way or another. In a sense, employers are always competing with other forces for the time and effort of their employees. Work motivation must therefore always be looked at in the context of a rich and complex life of employees who often strive to find a work–life balance.[6]

Different approaches to motivation by different companies

The word "motivation" is not always used in companies to explain the critical role of motivation in the performance of their employees. What employers do to motivate their employees is, however, often implied by the strategies of the companies and can therefore only be deduced.

Four of the companies identified by the Corporate Research Foundation (CFR) as South Africa's most promising companies were eBucks, Fireworkx Internet, Sandvik Mining and Construction RSA, and MWeb. The following are some of the strategies that gave them this elevated position.

eBucks

eBucks is South Africa's leading multi-partner rewards programme and is driven by a hard-working creative team. The company has a flat structure, providing many employees with the opportunity to head a division. The company also believes in an open-door policy and employees take pride in teamwork, with a sense of cohesiveness. This creates an environment where people enjoy working together. The environment is, however, also challenging and develops employees. Employees are constantly seeking new ways of doing things better.

Fireworkx Internet

This small software company regards its very high level of staff expertise and a strong focus on product excellence as its competitive advantage. The company works on a project-by-project basis, with employees being largely responsible and independent and encouraged to be innovative. They are paid what they are worth and incentive bonuses and a staff share scheme are implemented.

Sandvik Mining and Construction RSA

This international company in the mining industry focuses its strategy on removing people from danger. Continuous training and skills transfer are regarded as essential to the success of the organisation. In addition, the health and safety of employees are critical and everything is done to protect them and their clients.

MWeb

MWeb's focus on human resources and customer relationships resulted in its being one of South Africa's leading Internet service providers. The company fosters an open and progressive environment with a relatively flat management structure. Human resources and strategies play a pivotal role, both in terms of business-focused development of human capital and general employee satisfaction and well-being. The employees function as a team that is results oriented and outcomes based. The company follows the principles of being open, straightforward, truthful and transparent, while delivering promises. Its primary values are to be customer focused, be innovative, have mutual respect, promote a culture of learning, perform and meet goals and participate. Internally there is a drive to be experimental in terms of new technology in order to remain ahead in the market.

Source: Brevis, T., "Most promising companies: What gives them a competitive advantage", *Management Today*, February 2005, pp. 8–12.

In order to distinguish between the different approaches to motivation, the theories can be classified in terms of **content approaches** versus **process approaches**:

- **Content approaches** try to determine those things that actually motivate people to do their jobs, or the "what" of motivation. These theories focus on the factors within a person that direct, energise, maintain or stop behaviour, and are therefore also known as **need theories**. Consequently, these theories try to identify employees' needs and the goals they want to attain in order to satisfy these needs.[7]

- **Process theories**, in contrast, try to explain the actual process, or the "how" of motivation. According to the process theories, employees have a cognitive decision-making role in selecting their goals and the means to achieve them. These approaches are therefore concerned with trying to establish how employee behaviour is energised, directed, maintained and stopped.[8]

10.3.2 Content approaches to motivation

The content approaches include **Maslow**'s hierarchy of needs, **Alderfer**'s ERG theory, **Herzberg**'s two factor theory and **McClelland**'s learned needs theory. While the first three theories are based on primary instinctive needs, according to McClelland needs are learned and reinforced. The different theories will now be discussed in more detail.

10.3.2.1 Maslow's hierarchy of needs

One of the best-known theories of motivation is Abraham Maslow's theory of a **hierarchy of needs.** The crux of Maslow's theory is that needs are arranged in a hierarchy where the lowest-level needs are physiological needs and the highest-level needs are self-actualisation needs.

At the bottom of the hierarchy are the **physiological needs**, which include food,

Figure 10.1: Maslow's hierarchy of needs

drink, sex and air – the basic ingredients for survival and for biological functioning. In an organisation these needs of employers are satisfied by the provision of things such as a salary, rest rooms, a cafeteria, heating and adequate lighting.

The next level in the hierarchy is **safety and security needs**, which include protection from physical and emotional harm. They also include the desire for clothing, job security, pension plans, structures in the organisation to deal with grievances, and employee assistance programmes. Affiliation needs include the need for friendships, love and affection, and the need to be accepted by peers. Family and, to some extent, office parties, for example, in the workplace, satisfy this level of need.

Esteem needs include the need for a positive self-image and self-respect, and the need for recognition from others. In organisations this need can be satisfied by means of compliments to employees, access to information, job titles, and challenging job assignments.

At the top of the hierarchy are **self-actualisation needs**, which involve realising one's potential through growth and development. In an organisational context the focus here is on providing development opportunities, challenging assignments, and decision-making opportunities. The focus on skills development, creativity, innovation and opportunities for challenges, for instance, are regarded as part of the strategies that give South Africa's most promising companies their competitive edge.

Maslow's theory assumes that a person attempts to satisfy the more basic needs before progressing to satisfying higher-level needs. A further assumption is that people strive to move up the hierarchy in terms of need satisfaction, and that a specific need ceases to motivate an employee once it has been satisfied. Unsatisfied needs cause stress, frustration and conflict within an individual and also between individuals. Management can help employees to satisfy needs at various levels by promoting a culture wherein, for example, self-esteem and self-actualisation needs can be satisfied. The opportunity of participation in decision making about work and the provision of learning opportunities are examples of self-actualisation opportunities.

Although a very popular and convenient theory to apply, Maslow's theory has many shortcomings for use in the workplace, as it oversimplifies matters. The idea that all needs originate intrinsically, for example, is questionable. Needs are often learned and develop because of social influences (see for instance McClelland's theory) and different life experiences. Esteem needs, for example, might be desirable because we see the positive effects esteem has on others. Research has shown that not all levels of needs as identified by Maslow are always present, and certain cultures may have different need categories and hierarchies. Some people, for example, are motivated mainly by money, while others mainly want to satisfy their social needs at work. See the example of Sandvik Mining and Construction RSA, where the safety needs of the employees are of the utmost importance. Furthermore, employees may also satisfy their needs outside the workplace, making it difficult for managers to determine the genuine levels

of motivation at work. Finally, it is also not the case that highly satisfied employees are always highly productive.[9]

10.3.2.2 Alderfer's ERG theory

Alderfer's theory represents a refinement of Maslow's five-level hierarchy in that, according to Alderfer, there are three core needs, namely "existence", "relatedness" and "growth" (ERG). These needs are summarised as follows:[10]

- **Existence needs.** These needs relate to a person's basic material, existence needs – the same as Maslow's physiological and safety needs.
- **Relatedness needs.** These needs relate to a person's desire for interpersonal relationships and interaction – similar to Maslow's affiliation/social needs and the external aspect of Maslow's esteem needs.
- **Growth needs.** These relate to the desire of an individual to make a creative or productive contribution – similar to Maslow's esteem and self-actualisation needs.

The ERG theory does not subscribe to a rigid hierarchy of needs, whereas Maslow maintained that a lower-level need must first be satisfied before a higher-level need will be entertained. According to the ERG theory, two or even all three need categories can influence behaviour simultaneously. The ERG theory also suggests that if a person is continually frustrated in his or her attempts to satisfy growth needs, relatedness needs re-emerge as a major motivating force, and this may force the person to redirect efforts towards satisfying a lower-order need category. The implication is that, for instance, employees' demands for higher pay or better benefits may occur because of a stifling work environment.

10.3.2.3 Herzberg's two-factor theory and job enrichment

Frederick Herzberg proposed a motivational

Critical thinking

Do you think that singing the song "Shosholoza" motivates employees? If so, which needs are probably satisfied by singing the song?

"*Shosholoza*": Does this song motivate?

Shosholoza is the song that black South Africans, especially long-term convicts engaged in hard labour, traditionally sang in conditions of hardship. *Shosholoza* is like a child with no parents, however. Nobody knows when or where it originated from, but what everyone does know is that when there is some kind of deep-rooted ache in the heart, the first sound to rise from the lips will be *Shosholoza*. It is a song with no beginning and no end, as old as misery itself.

Shosholoza	Shosholoza
Ku lezontaba	You are meandering on those mountains
Stimela si qhamuka e South Africa	The train is from South Africa
Wen u ya baleka	You accelerate
Wen u ya baleka	You accelerate
Ku lezontaba	On those mountains
Stimela si qhamuka South Africa	The train is from South Africa

Here are the lyrics as recorded by Ladysmith Black Mambazo:

Chorus

Shosholoza	Wena u ya baleka
Ku lezontaba	Wena u ya baleka
Stimela si qhamuka e South Africa	Ku lezontaba
Shosholoza	Stimela si qhamuka South Africa
Stimela si qhamuka e South Africa	

Verse 1	**Verse 2**
Shosholoza	Shosholoza
Work, work, working in the sun	Push, push, pushing on and on
We will work as one	There's much to be done
Shosholoza	Shosholoza
Work, work, working in the rain	Push, push, pushing in the sun
'Til there's sun again	We will push as one

Sithwele kanzima, sithwele kanzima (ooh, aah!)
Sithwele kanzima, sithwele kanzima (ooh, aah!)
Sithwele kanzima, sithwele kanzima (ooh, aah!)
Sithwele kanzima, sithwele kanzima (ooh, aah!)
Sithwele kanzima, sithwele kanzima (ooh, aah!)

Etshe!
Shosholoza
Repeat chorus
Repeat verse
Repeat chorus

Source: http://www.geocities.com/rembrandt/Lyrics/S/Shosholoza.html.

model called the **two-factor model**, which consists of maintenance and motivational factors:

- The **maintenance (hygiene) factors** do not act as motivational factors, but if they are absent in an organisation this could have a negative affect on employee morale. The maintenance factors are those aspects people consider essential to do any job, for example organisational policy and administration, equipment, supervision, interpersonal relationships with colleagues and supervisors, salary, status, working conditions, and work security.[11]
- **Motivational factors**, also called **growth factors**, are focused on the content of the job, and include aspects such as achievement (successful completion of tasks), recognition for what has been achieved, the job itself (meaningfulness and challenge), progress and growth, responsibility and feedback. Motivational factors are benefits over and above the normal job to be done, which tend to increase employee satisfaction because employees get more out of the normal job they do. When motivational factors are present these are likely to motivate

employees to achieve higher productivity, to be more committed to their jobs, and to find creative ways of accomplishing both personal and organisational goals.[12]

Herzberg's theory can be linked to Maslow's hierarchy of needs. The maintenance (hygiene) factors are similar to the lower-level needs in the hierarchy, while the motivators are the same as the higher-level needs.

Based on the theory of Herzberg, a distinction can be made between internal motivation (based on motivators) and external motivation (based on maintenance factors):

- **Internal motivation.** This motivation originates from the satisfaction that occurs when a task is executed or a duty is performed. For example, if a teacher enjoys teaching children, the activity is in itself rewarding, and the teacher will be self-motivated. The intrinsic rewards of the job motivate some people more than external influences such as money and trophies do. Herzberg's theory of motivation emphasises that jobs should be enriched to provide opportunities for growth and more responsibility. Compare the strategies of the most promising companies we have mentioned regarding the use of internal motivation.
- **External motivation.** In contrast to internal motivation, external motivation usually involves action taken by a third party. Here, a person is motivated because it is in anticipation that a reward of some kind – for example money, awards or feedback regarding performance – will be given. Incentives such as profit sharing, bonuses and awards are used by organisations to instil certain work habits that are beneficial both for the organisation and the individual. Unfortunately, external rewards are not enough to motivate people in the long term. Organisations should therefore focus on a combination of both internal and external rewards by allowing job satisfaction by means of challenging jobs and an appropriate number of external awards.

	Herzberg	**Maslow**
Motivational factors	• Recognition • Status • Advancement	• Esteem needs
	• Work itself • Responsibility	• Self-actualisation
Maintenance factors	• Social network • Supervision	• Social/belongingness
	• Policy/Administrative	• Safety/Security
	• Job security • Salary • Working conditions	• Physiological

Figure 10.2: Comparison of the theories of Herzberg and Maslow

Fireworkx Internet can be regarded as an example of an organisation in which both internal motivators (responsibility, independence and innovation) are encouraged and external factors (bonuses) are applied.

An important contribution of Herzberg's theory is his emphasis on the task itself as the source of job satisfaction. **Job enrichment** as a way to design jobs is therefore a valuable practical application of his theory. It entails incorporating, by means of vertical loading, the opportunity to experience achievement, recognition, stimulating work, responsibility and advancement in a job.

Most of the critiques of Herzberg's theory centre on the motivational role of lower-order needs, especially the role of money. Although money can be useful for facilitating acceptance of organisational change, research suggests that manual workers are more likely to be motivated by money than are more professional or managerial groups. More recent research however, indicates that lower-order factors such as pay and job security are not mentioned as either satisfying or dissatisfying by participants. The role of money is therefore still uncertain, though it may seem that the different needs for money by different employees or groups of employees are not taken into account by Herzberg's theory.[13] It is, however, interesting to note that although neither Maslow nor Herzberg cites money as a significant motivator, many organisations still use financial incentives as their primary motivational tool.

10.3.2.4 McClelland's theory of needs

Whereas the theories we have mentioned above focus on primary instinctive needs, according to McClelland's theory needs are learned and reinforced. This theory focuses on three needs that explain motivation, namely:[14]

- **Need for achievement (nAch)**. This is a need to excel, to be successful or to exceed a set standard.
- **Need for power (nPow)**. This is a need to be

influential, to control others, or to make others behave in a way they would not otherwise behave.
- **Need for affiliation (nAff)**. This is the need for warm and close interpersonal relationships, and to be liked and accepted by others.

Given the above needs of employees, managers have the challenge of determining the dominant need of their subordinates, and of offering opportunities whereby the individual needs can be met. This can be of value during the selection and placement process. For example, research has found that employees with a high need for power (nPow) and a low need for affiliation (nAff) make good managers, and that people with a high need for achievement (nAch) generally make successful entrepreneurs.

As needs can be learned, according to this theory, employees can also be trained to increase their achievement motivation. Managers should also create challenging goals or tasks because the need for achievement is positively correlated with goal attainment, which, in turn, influences performance.

EBucks is a good example of a company that makes provision for the affiliation, power, and achievement needs of its employees.

Critical thinking

If we compare the most prominent content-based approaches to motivation, it becomes clear that a distinction can be made between motivators and maintenance factors. In your view, what are the chances that employees will be motivated if managers take care of the maintenance factors only?

Although maintenance factors are not regarded as unimportant (see for instance Sandvik Mining and Construction RSA's emphasis on safety), a critical evaluation of the most promising companies will point in the direction of the importance of motivators such as providing recognition, challenges, opportunities for development and growth, and responsibility. Managers have to take care of maintenance factors, but if they really want motivated employees, they should create opportunities for their employees to experience internal motivation. Managers should thus be cautious that they do not rely too much on maintenance factors or external forms of motivation.

10.3.3 Summary: Implications of content-based approaches

The four content theories discussed above attempt to explain behaviour[15] based on the needs of employees. Firstly, these theories suggest that needs change. Different employees have different needs at different times. For example, a job with a high salary but without security might motivate a young person but be unacceptable to someone in his or her forties for whom job security is more important. Similarly, more vacation time may be desired near retirement age than earlier in life. The recommendation for management is to offer employees a choice of rewards in order to fulfil the different needs.

Secondly, managers need to balance the power need (competition) with the affiliation need (cooperation). Rewards that support both individual achievement and teamwork can be given, for example. Managers also need to support achievement needs by providing opportunities for growth, for instance by means of providing novel tasks or experiences. Lower-order needs should also be taken care of by minimising unnecessary threats to personal safety, well-being and social relationships.

Thirdly, needs may be unconscious. Most people are not fully aware of the inner needs and drives that influence their behaviour. The desire of an employee to win the "salesperson of the month" trophy, for example, may be due to an unconscious feeling of inadequacy, and this would be a way of proving him- or herself. Needs are therefore often inferred. However closely one may observe the behaviour

of a colleague, it is possible only to draw conclusions (infer) about what motives have actually caused the behaviour. It is sometimes very difficult to understand the real motives underlying certain behaviour. For this reason it is important that managers discuss with employees the things that motivate them so that suggestions can be made in order to meet the needs of employees more adequately.

Lastly, content-based approaches warn managers against relying too much on financial reward as a source of employee motivation.[16]

10.3.4 Process approaches to motivation

The difference between content and process theories has already been discussed. The process approaches are trying to identify the process by which factors influence motivation. The three most common process theories are discussed below, namely the expectancy theory, equity theory and goal-setting theory.

10.3.4.1 Expectancy theory

According to Vroom's **expectancy theory**, motivation depends on two aspects, namely how much we want something, and how likely we think we are to get it. There are four assumptions upon which the expectancy theory rests:

- Firstly, behaviour is a combination of forces controlled by the individual and the environment.
- Secondly, people make decisions about their own behaviour in organisations.
- Thirdly, different people have different needs, goals and desires.
- Fourthly, people will act in a certain way, and the tendency to act in a certain way depends on the strength of the expectation that the action will be followed by a given outcome, and the degree to which the person desires the outcome.

Three key concepts in the theory are expectancy, instrumentality and valance:

- **Expectancy** refers to a person's belief that a certain level of effort will lead to a particular level of performance (effort → performance expectancy). Factors such as a person's self-esteem, previous success, support from others, access to information and **self-efficacy** (see section 10.3.4.3) will influence his or her expectancy perceptions.
- **Instrumentality** refers to the strength of a person's belief that a certain performance will lead to a specific outcome (performance → outcome expectancy).
- **Valence** (desirability) refers to the attractiveness or anticipated satisfaction or dissatisfaction that the individual feels toward the outcome and is determined by the perceptions about how much the outcome will fulfil or interfere with the person's needs.

The process is discussed in the box below by means of an example.

Research indicates that the expectancy theory is able to predict employee motivation in different cultures.[17] Criticism of the theory, however, argues that, as a rational theory, it does not fully acknowledge the role of emotions in employee effort and behaviour.

Some of the most important implications of the expectancy theory for management are as follows:

- Managers are advised to enhance effort → performance expectancies by assisting employees to accomplish their personal goals, for instance by providing support, coaching, training and development, and also increasing their self-efficacy. **Self-efficacy** refers to a person's belief that he or she has the ability to complete a task successfully. Managers should focus on linking performance to rewards that are valued by employees.

Expectancy theory: An example

Imagine that we want to use the expectancy theory to determine if John, a sales representative, will be motivated to promote the products of the company.

- **Expectancy** refers to John's belief that a certain level of effort will lead to a particular level of performance (effort → performance expectancy). John may have the expectancy that if he works hard on promoting products, sales targets will be met (performance). If he has a zero expectancy that the effort will lead to performance (in terms of meeting the sales targets), he will most probably not promote the products. Factors such as John's self-esteem, previous success, support from others, access to information and self-efficacy will influence his expectancy perceptions. We assume John is of the opinion that his effort will most probably lead to performance.
- **Instrumentality** refers to the strength of John's belief that a certain performance will lead to a specific outcome (performance

→ outcome expectancy). This belief is probably based on learning from previous experiences, and the outcome refers to outcomes that are important at a specific time. John believes that meeting the sales target will lead to promotion to a managerial role. His belief is based on, among other things, the current practice in his company.

- **Valence** (desirability) refers to the attractiveness or anticipated satisfaction or dissatisfaction that John feels toward the outcome and is determined by his perceptions about how much the outcome will fulfil or interfere with his needs. John has strong power needs that can be fulfilled in a managerial role, making promotion to a managerial role very attractive.

Based on the above discussion, it seems clear that John will most probably put in a big effort to promote the products of the company, as this may fulfil his needs.

- Attempts should also be made to link personal goals to organisational goals. South Africa's most promising companies, for instance, encourage creativity and innovation and provide many opportunities for challenges, as long as the end result is added value to the clients and the business.

10.3.4.2 Equity theory and organisational justice

The crux of the **equity theory** advanced by Stacey Adams is that employees compare their efforts and rewards with those of other employees in similar situations. This motivational theory is based on the assumption that people are motivated by the desire to be equitably treated in the workplace. A state of equity exists when one employee's input–outcome ratio compared with that of another employee in a similar position is equal. In contrast, if input–outcome ratios are unequal, inequity is said to exist, with the result that the person will perceive the situation as unfair and therefore be motivated to do something else. Various means can be used to restore equity after equity tension has been experienced, including the following:[18]

- The employee may change inputs.
- The employee may change outputs.
- The employee may change his or her attitude.
- The employee may change the person he or she compares herself with.
- The employee may leave the job.

Despite the research that supports this theory, certain aspects remain unclear, for example how employees deal with conflicting equity signals, and how inputs and outputs are defined. Motivation is also not only influenced by relative monetary rewards, but by absolute monetary rewards as well. Another problem is that the theory incorrectly assumes that people are only rational, individualistic and selfish. Equity theory does, however, provide an important insight into employee motivation, and every manager should take note of its implications.

The role of the equity theory has been expanded to develop the concept of **organisational justice**. One of the lessons learned from the equity theory is that employers continually have to treat their employees fairly in the distribution of rewards.[19] Organisational justice reflects the extent to which employees perceive that they are treated fairly at work. It consists of three components, namely:

- **Distributive justice**, referring to the perceived fairness of how resources and rewards are distributed or allocated
- **Procedural justice**, defined as the perceived fairness of the process and procedures used to make allocation decisions
- **Interactional justice**, referring to the quality of the interpersonal treatment people receive when procedures are implemented[20]

The equity theory has at least the following practical implications for management:[21]

- Employees are motivated powerfully to correct the situation when their perception of fairness is offended. Accordingly, the best way to manage job behaviour is to understand underlying processes.
- The theory emphasises the need to pay attention to the perceptions of the employees of what is fair and equitable, and not to how fair management think its policies, procedures and reward systems are. Managers are thus encouraged to make hiring and promotion decisions on merit-based job-related information.
- Because justice perceptions are influenced by the extent to which management explains its decisions, it is important that management communicates the rationale behind decisions.
- Employees should participate in making decisions about important work outcomes. Research indicates that employees are more satisfied with their performance appraisals and resultant outcomes if they have a say.

- Employees believe that they are treated fairly if they have the opportunity to appeal against decisions that effect their welfare.
- Employees are more likely to accept and support change when they believe it is implemented fairly and when it produces equitable outcomes.
- Teamwork can be promoted by treating employees fairly.
- Employees denied justice are more likely to turn to litigation than employees who are given access to justice.
- Managers need to pay attention to their climate for justice. South Africa's most promising companies, for instance, pay attention to their climate for justice by having values such as honesty, integrity, open communication and transparency.

10.3.4.3 Goal-setting theory and feedback

Goal-setting theory is built on the assumption that, all things being equal, the performance of employees will improve if they strive towards a definite goal. MWeb is a good example of a company that focuses on the setting and meeting of goals. Goal-setting has motivational value because goals not only direct attention, but also regulate effort (motivate employees to act), increase persistence and foster the development and application of task strategies and action plans.[22]

The thrust of goal-setting theory is that the more difficult the goal, the higher the level of performance if employees are committed to the goals. Obviously, when goals are set, the person concerned must be capable of achieving those goals. Furthermore, research has shown that setting specific goals leads to higher performance for simple tasks than for complex tasks. This theory also presupposes that an employee will be committed to a goal if the goal has been negotiated between the employee and the organisation.

Another important factor is **feedback**. Providing feedback to employees most prob-

ably leads to the improvement of their performance. Goals inform employees about performance standards and expectations so that they can channel their energies accordingly. In turn, feedback provides information needed to adjust effort, direction and strategies for goal accomplishment. Management can give effective feedback by utilising the following principles:[23]

- Give feedback immediately.
- Evaluations should be descriptive by describing what was done well and why.
- The focus should be on behaviour and not on personality.
- Feedback should be specific and not general (components of performance and not performance as a whole).
- Feedback should be directed at behaviour that can be changed.
- Development activities should be agreed upon.

The concept of **self-efficacy** is also central to the goal-setting theory and refers to the belief in one's capability to perform a specific task to reach a specific goal. The concept is based on the work of Bandura, who proposed that motivated behaviour involves a cycle of setting challenging goals, monitoring success at meeting these goals, taking actions to reduce any discrepancies between the goal and the outcome, then setting new and more challenging goals, starting the cycle all over again. Self-efficacy can be increased by applying the following approaches:[24]

- Provide guidance and support to the employee, increasing the likelihood that he or she will experience success on a challenging task.
- Provide successful role models who have already mastered a similar task (mentors).
- Be a targeted "cheerleader" emphasising the employee's knowledge and ability.
- Reduce stress in the environment that is unrelated to the challenging task.

10.3.5 Summary: Implications of process-based approaches

Most modern approaches to work motivation are based on process theories. Process-based theories have some predominant themes that are important for our understanding of work motivation:

- Firstly, intention plays a key role in motivated behaviour, with a goal as the most common form of that intention (see for instance the example of MWeb). These goals are associated with anticipated happiness or unhappiness.
- Secondly, the concept of feedback is of critical importance.
- Thirdly, process-based theories all have a rational element, with employees critically gathering and analysing information.
- Fourthly, the theories also include some form of self-assessment. Employees tend to take stock of where they are, compared to where they want to be.
- Lastly, a non-rational component is also important in some of the most recent approaches. This element may be values, culture, or the feeling that arises from the self-efficacy belief.[25]

10.4 Employee motivational strategies

Employees need to be better motivated not only to improve organisational effectiveness, but also to provide a better quality of life for all employees. Possible broad motivational strategies to improve employee motivation are briefly discussed below. Whereas the implications for management of the different theories have already been discussed, most of the following strategies are applied on macro or organisational level:[26]

- **Job design.** Employees place a high value on jobs that provide satisfaction, are challenging, provide growth, and will allow adequate achievement opportunities.

Jobs can be redesigned to make them more challenging by using job rotation, job enlargement or job enrichment. **Job rotation** allows employees to move through a variety of jobs, functions or departments. Job enlargement focuses on expanding an

---

Critical thinking

A motivated employee has been described as someone who is willing to exert a particular level of effort (intensity), for a certain amount of time (persistence), toward a particular goal (direction). Now, reflect on a personal experience (or that of somebody known to you) that either positively or negatively impacted on your level of motivation (not a specific need that was satisfied or not). Try to remember the process that influenced your (or the person's) level of motivation. What happened? Who was involved? What were the outcomes? How did you/the person feel? How did the experience influence your/the person's behaviour?

The following questions may help you to reflect on the experience:

1. Was it related to effort you or the person put in, but which did or did not materialise in worthwhile results?
2. Was it an experience of fairness or unfair treatment in comparison with that of other employees/people?
3. Was the experience related to the setting of, and accomplishment of, very clear goals?

Now that you have reflected on the experience, identify the motivational theory most relevant to that experience.

All three questions represent different process approaches to motivation discussed in this section, namely the expectancy theory (1), the equity theory (2) and the goal-setting theory (3). They all are based on a specific process, or the "how" of motivation. The relevance of the different theories for different people under different circumstances is clear. Can you summarise the relevance of applying these theories in the workplace?

employee's duties and/or responsibilities, and **job enrichment** allows jobs to become more desirable and challenging by including new and more difficult tasks and granting an employee more accountability. Other aspects to consider are variable work schedules, flexible work schedules, job sharing and telecommuting.

- **Employee involvement programmes such as participative management and quality circles.** Employee involvement is a participative process that uses the entire capacity of employees to encourage commitment to the organisation's success. Employees are given autonomy and control in making decisions about their own work (see the influence of content theories, especially the theory of Herzberg, in section 10.3.2.3, and expectancy theory, in section 10.3.4.1 above). Quality circles are work groups that take over the responsibility from management for solving quality problems and they generate and evaluate their own feedback, while management retains final control regarding the implementation of recommendations.
- **Management by objectives (MBO) strategies.** MBO strategies are closely related to the goal-setting theory and comprise cascading of organisational objectives down to individual objectives. Goals and ways of measurement, as well as specific time frames for completion, are jointly determined, and feedback on performance is given.
- **Intrapreneurial incentives.** New ideas from employees can be developed within organisations with the financial support of the organisation. Such programmes are known as **intrapreneurship**, which encourages employees to come up with new suggestions and ideas (see the examples of MWeb, which allows for experimentation, and South Africa's most promising companies in general).
- **Training and education.** Learning opportunities can be a strong motivational force

since they are critical to individual growth and opportunity. Organisations that invest in the training and development of employees are generally more successful (see the examples of Pick 'n Pay and Sandvik Mining and Construction RSA). In South Africa, opportunities to invest in the training and development of employees have been created by means of the Skills Development Act 97 of 1998 and the Skills Development Levies Act 9 of 1999 (see chapter 11). Providing opportunities for skills development and transfer of knowledge, for example, is regarded as an important strategy that contributes to South Africa's most promising companies' competitive edge.

- **Employee recognition programmes.** Recognition for above-average work performance is widely used to drive results in organisations. Employee recognition programmes vary from cash, shares, profit sharing, overseas visits and bonuses, to trophies and certificates (see the examples of Pick 'n Pay and Fireworkx Internet).
- **Empowerment programmes.** Empowerment is an important method of enhancing employee motivation. Empowerment is the process of enabling employees to set their own goals, make decisions, and solve problems within their sphere of responsibility and authority.
- **Reward systems.** A basic management tool to motivate employees is the organisation's reward system. A reward system is directly related to the expectancy theory of motivation, and the effect of the reward system on attitudes and employee behaviour should be fully investigated (see the examples of South Africa's most promising companies, more specifically the example of Fireworkx Internet).
- **Career management.** Career management and development is the path that an employee identifies and follows in order to achieve his or her aspirations. Employees will be better motivated if they are personally involved in decision making about possible career options

open to them than if they are not involved. This personal involvement therefore leads to a better motivated workforce, and employees will have been empowered in being assisted by an organisational career management team to face challenges and make decisions that benefit both the individual and the organisation (see McClelland's theory of needs in 10.3.2.4).

10.5 Summary

This chapter has focused mainly on the importance of motivation in the workplace. It began, however, with a brief description of the role of human resource management in organisations, with particular emphasis on human resource management and organisational effectiveness, and the area of responsibility of the human resource function. It was clearly demonstrated that employee motivation is an important part of the task not only of human resource practitioners, but also of any manager in an organisation.

The section on motivation highlighted both the content theories of motivation and the process theories. Each approach endeavours to organise and explain the major variables associated with the relevant theory.

The implications of the different theories for management were also pointed out as part of the discussions. The bottom line is that managers need to be actively involved in the motivation of employees. In doing so, managers should be aware of subordinates' needs, intentions, preferences, comparisons and goals. Managers can also play a significant role in creating an atmosphere that supports improvement, in showing sensitivity towards employees' abilities and preferences, and in offering jobs that provide a challenge and are diverse.

Since the various theories have been only briefly discussed, we suggest that more specialised publications are consulted to obtain more detail about the theories.

 Key terms

Alderfer	Job enrichment
Content approaches	Management by objectives
Employee involvement	Maslow
Equity theory	McClelland
ERG theory	Motivation
Expectancy theory	Motivational strategies
Feedback	Organisational effectiveness
Goal setting	Organisational justice
Herzberg	Process approaches
Hierarchy of needs	Self-efficacy
Human resource function	Strategic partner
Human resources specialist	Two-factor theory
Job design	

? Questions for discussion

Use the information provided in this chapter to answer the following questions:

1. Do you think that justice is done to the role of the human resources function in South African organisations? Give reasons for your answer.
2. Which theories address content approaches to motivation? Describe them.
3. Why are the principles of the equity theory important for organisational success?
4. What are the differences between the content approach to motivation and the process approach to motivation?
5. Which different motivating principles or strategies have contributed to the successes of South Africa's most promising companies? Give reasons for your answer.

References

1. Brevis, T., "Most promising companies: What gives them a competitive advantage", *Management Today*, February 2005, pp. 8–12.

2. Khumalo, R., "The management of human resources in successful companies – An African context", *Journal of Industrial Psychology*, Vol. 25, No. 1, 1999, pp. 1–6.

3. Reece, B.L. & Brandt, R., *Effective human relations*, 6th edition, Houghton Mifflin Company, New York, 1996, p. 152.

4. Buelens, M., Van den Broeck, H., Vanderheyden, K., Kreitner, R. & Kinicki, A., *Organisational behaviour*, 3rd edition, McGraw-Hill, Berkshire, 2006, p. 172.

5. McShane, S. & Von Glinow, M.A., *Organizational behaviour*, 3rd edition, McGraw-Hill, Boston, IL, 2005, p. 140.

6. Landy, F.L. & Conte, J.M., *Work in the 21st century: An introduction to industrial and organizational psychology*, McGraw-Hill, Boston, IL, 2004, pp. 405–408.

7. Buelens et al., *op cit.*, p. 176.

8. *Ibid.*, p. 177.

9. Dick, P. & Ellis, S., *Introduction to organizational behaviour*, 3rd edition, McGraw-Hill, London, 2006, pp. 84–85.

10. Swanepoel, B., Erasmus, B., Van Wyk, M. & Schenk, H., *South African human resource management: Theory and practice*, 3rd edition, Oxford University Press, Cape Town, 2003, p. 357.

11. Nel, P.S., Gerber, P.D., Van Dyk, P.S., Haasbroek, G.D., Schultz, H.B., Seno, T. & Werner, A., *Human resource management*, 5th edition, 2001,Oxford University Press, Cape Town, p. 331.

12. Reece & Brandt, *op. cit.*, p. 162.

13. Dick & Ellis, *op. cit.*, pp. 86–87.

14. Robbins, S.P., *Organisational behaviour: Concepts, controversies, application*, 8th edition, Prentice Hall, Upper Saddle River, N.J., 1998, p. 134.

15. Kreitner, R. & Kinicki, A., *Organizational behaviour*, 7th edition, McGraw-Hill, Boston, 2007, pp. 253–254.

16. McShane & Von Glinow, *op. cit.*, p. 147.

17. *Ibid.*, p. 151.

18. Moorhead, G. & Griffin, R.W., *Organisational behaviour: Managing people and organisations*, 6th edition, Houghton Mifflin, Boston, 2000, p. 492.

19. McShane & Von Glinow, *op. cit.*, p. 163.

20. Kreitner & Kinicki, *op. cit.*, pp. 244–245.

21. *Ibid.*, pp. 252–253.

22. *Ibid.*, pp. 244–245.

23. Dick & Ellis, *op. cit.*, p. 95.

24. Landy & Conte, op. cit., p. 362.

25. *Ibid.*, p. 364.

26. Robbins, S.P., Odendaal, A. & Roodt, G., 2003, *Organisational behaviour: Global and Southern African perspectives*, Pearson Education, Cape Town, pp. 151–153.

11

THE LEGAL ENVIRONMENT AND HUMAN RESOURCES

The purpose of this chapter

This chapter contains a brief overview of the most important labour legislation that impacts on the workplace and that influences human resources in organisations.

The chapter commences with a discussion on the Constitution of South Africa, followed by a summary of the various labour-related legislation.

Learning outcomes

The content of this chapter will enable learners to:

- Understand the importance of the Constitution of South Africa
- Describe and analyse the impact of the following Acts on the management of human resources in organisations:
  - The Labour Relations Act 66 of 1995
  - The Basic Conditions of Employment Act 75 of 1997
  - The Skills Development Act 97 of 1998
  - The Skills Development Levies Act 9 of 1999
  - The Employment Equity Act 55 of 1998
  - The Occupational Health and Safety Act 85 of 1993
  - The Compensation for Occupational Injuries and Diseases Act 130 of 1993
  - The Unemployment Insurance Act 63 of 2001

11.1 Introduction

Several different environmental factors influence the way an organisation's human resources are managed. One such factor is the legal environment and, in particular, those laws that are applicable to people in organisations. Legal issues affect almost all aspects of human resource management, whether dismissal, retrenchment or retirement. The impact of legal rules is so complex that line managers and human resource professionals should have a good working knowledge and understanding of these laws. At times, legal expertise is required to solve workplace problems or to take legal aspects further, but in most cases, legal matters can be solved independently by line managers and/or human resources professionals. The management of human resources is a more complex matter than

Labour law issues in the workplace

Steelco (Pty) Ltd produces parts for motor vehicles and it has a large factory in Gauteng. More than 300 employees work in this factory. They work in three separate shifts because Steelco is a 24-hour operation. However, things have been going wrong in the workplace in the past few months. Three employees approached their trade union representative and claimed that their supervisor had made racist remarks to them. After these allegations were discussed at a meeting of all four trade union representatives in a regular meeting, the union representatives wrote a letter to the employer demanding that the racist manager be dismissed immediately and without a hearing.

But this is not the only problem in Steelco's operation, it seems. A large number of employees claim that they are regularly expected to work up to 18 hours overtime a week but that they receive only their normal hourly remuneration for these hours of overtime worked. The union and Steelco are preparing to negotiate about wages in three weeks' time and the Steelco managers are convinced that a collective agreement can be concluded between Steelco and the union. The union is not so sure about that, as it not only wants an 11% wage increase, but also an improvement of medical aid benefits and four extra days' sick leave during each leave cycle. The union also wants to hold monthly meetings, during a lunch break, with all union members working in the factory.

The union knows that management is facing a number of other problems as well. Three dismissal disputes have been referred to the **CCMA** and there are a number of allegations relating to **sexual harassment** made against one of the executive managers. This manager also tried to have his secretary dismissed when he discovered that she was **pregnant**.

Both the union and the employer hope, however, that this year's round of wage negotiations goes better than those they engaged in two years ago. Two years ago the negotiations between the parties broke down and the union called for a **strike**. The employer claimed that the strike was not protected and the employees were dismissed because of their participation in the unprotected strike. Some of these employees were eventually reinstated, but 14 of these were not reinstated after the strike had come to an end. The union has approached the **Labour Court**, claiming that the dismissal of these employees constituted an **automatically unfair dismissal**. Steelco's view on this point is that the dismissals were fair because the employees were engaged in an unprotected strike and because individual **disciplinary enquiries** had been held before the employees were dismissed – giving each employee an opportunity to say why he or she should not be dismissed.

the simple application of various laws (see chapter 9), but without a basic knowledge of the most important labour laws, organisations may find themselves with more people problems than anticipated.

The case study above provides an illustration of labour law issues in the workplace.

11.2 The Constitution of South Africa Act of 1996

The **Constitution** of 1996 is the single most important piece of legislation in South Africa. As its name implies, it sets out the structure of the state – it provides for national government, the legislature, the judiciary (the courts of law) and the executive arm of government. When it comes to the Courts, the Constitution provides that the Constitutional Court is the highest court in respect of constitutional matters (this means that the Constitutional Court is the highest court that can hear a matter relating to, for instance, an infringement of fundamental rights). But when it comes to human resource management, the most important part of the Constitution is the Bill of Rights (Chapter II of the Constitution). The Bill of Rights protects a number of important fundamental rights – section 23 of the Constitution relates specifically to labour rights. Everyone has the right to fair labour practices, for instance, and employers and trade unions have the right to organise and bargain collectively. Employees have the right to join a trade union of their choice (this is called freedom of association) and provision is made for a right to strike.

But it is not only these fundamental labour rights that have a direct impact on the workplace: other rights are as important. Section 9 of the Constitution provides that no one may be discriminated against unfairly and section 22 protects the right to freely choose a trade, occupation or profession.

The fundamental human rights contained in the Bill of Rights are formulated in a wide and general way. In most cases, specific pieces of legislation give further effect to these rights. In this way, the Labour Relations Act of 1995 gives effect to the fundamental labour rights contained in section 23 of the Constitution; the Employment Equity Act gives further effect to the right not to be unfairly discriminated against in the workplace.

The most important recent development relates to the right to fair administrative action, enshrined in section 33 of the Constitution. Again this fundamental right has its own specific piece of legislation: the Promotion of Administrative Justice Act 3 of 2000. One of the important questions that has arisen is whether employees in the public service (where the state is the employer) have additional rights and remedies in terms of the Promotion of Administrative Justice Act – and it seems that South Africa's Courts are now tending towards the view that workplace issues in the public service, especially dismissal of a public service employee, must also comply with the provisions of section 33 of the Constitution as given effect to by the Promotion of Administrative Justice Act.

Another important point in respect of fundamental rights is that none of these rights are absolutely unlimited. Section 23 of the Constitution provides for a right to strike, but the Labour Relations Act places certain limitations on this right. Employees engaged in essential services, for instance, may not strike. Furthermore, the Labour Relations Act also imposes a number of procedural requirements on strikes.

Constitutional rights

Section 23 of the Constitution provides that every employee has the right of freedom of association. This right is further given effect to in the Labour Relations Act. But this does not mean that an employee engaged in mining activities can choose to join a union representing workers in the chemical industry. The employee's right of freedom of association is limited by the union's constitution: the union's constitution will set out which employees are eligible to join that union.

11.3 Laws affecting business activity

Many laws affect business activities in South Africa – laws of this nature are found in most countries. These range from laws regulating the form and functioning of businesses (such as the Companies Act 61 of 1973 or the Close Corporations Act 69 of 1984). There are laws that provide for various forms of tax, ranging from value added tax and income tax to company tax. There are laws dealing with intellectual property (copyright, trademarks), laws dealing with insolvency, and even some laws dealing with specific forms of contracts. This means that the labour laws are just one set of laws a business will have to take into account – many other laws impose direct or indirect duties or obligations on a business.

But when it comes to the management of people in organisations, the most important pieces of legislation include the Labour Relations Act 66 of 1995 (usually simply referred to as the LRA) and the Basic Conditions of Employment Act 75 of 1997 (the BCEA). Other important laws include the Employment Equity Act 55 of 1998 and other laws relating to skills development and workplace health and safety. The following sections in this chapter look briefly at the most important of these laws.

In some cases, it may be necessary to look at the entire piece of legislation – most human resources managers have a copy of the LRA on their desks. Because the labour laws are changed (amended) from time to time, it is important to ensure that a manager refers to the correct version of the legislation. A number of important changes were made to the LRA in 2002 and some new provisions were included and a manager must therefore make sure that the version of the LRA he or she refers to contains all the amendments. The BCEA was also amended in 2002 – similar considerations therefore apply: a manager must ensure that the version of the legislation is up to date.

The Acts in this chapter are briefly discussed. If further information is required concerning these Acts, we suggest that the entire Act is studied. Copies may be obtained from the Government Printer.[1]

11.4 The Labour Relations Act 66 of 1995 (the LRA)

11.4.1 Background

Since the first democratic election in 1994 in South Africa the labour dispensation has

Important laws affecting business in South Africa

Insolvency Act 24 of 1936
Merchandise Marks Act 17 of 1941
Pension Funds Act 24 of 1956
Business Names Act 27 of 1960
Income Tax Act 58 of 1962 as amended
Capital Gains Tax (Section 26A of the Income Tax Act)
Sales and Service Matters Act 25 of 1964
Usury Act 73 of 1968
Companies Act 61 of 1973
Patents Act 57 of 1978
Copyright Act 98 of 1978
Protection of Business Act 99 of 1978
Credit Agreement Act 75 of 1980
Close Corporations Act 69 of 1984
Consumer Affairs (Unfair Business Practices) Act 71 of 1988
Banks Act 94 of 1990
Value Added Tax Act 89 of 1991
Aliens Control Act 96 of 1991
Trade Marks Act 194 of 1993
Designs Act 195 of 1993
National Road Traffic Act 93 of 1996
National Small Business Act 102 of 1996
Counterfeit Goods Act 37 of 1997
Non-profit Organisation Act 71 of 1997
Competition Act 89 of 1998
National Environmental Management Act 107 of 1998
Promotion of Access to Information Act 2 of 2000
Promotion of Equality and Prevention of Unfair Discrimination Act 4 of 2000
Protection Disclosures Act 26 of 2000 (Whistle-blowers)'
Electronic Communications and Transactions Act 25 of 2002

changed significantly and organised labour has played an important role in South Africa's transformation process. Not only do workers, through their trade unions, play a key role in the redistribution of wealth through collective bargaining over wages, but they are also instrumental in the broader socio-political process of transforming South African society. Consequently, the system of labour relations in South Africa has seen tremendous changes. For example, a new Labour Relations Act was introduced in 1995, and a new Basic Conditions of Employment Act and Employment Equity Act were introduced in 1997 and 1998, respectively. Before 1994, labour legislation was made and brought into effect by government alone. The process leading up to the passing of the LRA was therefore unique – for the first time, labour legislation represented basic consensus or agreement between organised labour, organised business and the state.

The implementation of sound labour relations in businesses not only ensures fair labour practices but also contributes to organisational success. **Labour relations**, from a business management point of view, may be described as a complex system of individual and collective actions as well as formal and informal relationships that exist between the state, employers, employees and related institutions concerning all aspects of the employment relationship.

Relationships in a business are considered to be a crucial element in labour relations, and in the next section more attention is given to the different parties in the labour relationship.

The parties involved in the labour re-lationship are the employer and employee as primary parties, and the state as a secondary role player. The state's role is to provide, by means of legislation, a framework within which the primary parties can conduct their

relationship. Figure 11.1 illustrates this tri-partite relationship. Basically, employees in managerial positions represent the interests of the owners of businesses in the workplace. In the private sector this essentially means safeguarding and improving the profitability of businesses. The state's primary role is, as stated, to provide the framework or infrastructure within which labour and management can conduct their relationship. A trade union is a permanent organisation created by workers to protect themselves at work, to improve their working conditions through collective bargaining, to better their quality of life and to provide a means of expressing their views on issues in society.

11.4.2 The contents of the LRA[2]

In day-to-day human resources management, the LRA is the single most important piece of legislation – especially because it contains the rules relating to dismissal of employees. But it is worth repeating that the LRA gives effect to all the fundamental rights contained in section 23 of the Constitution and it therefore deals with a large number of issues – it is wide in scope and this explains why the LRA is so long (there are 213 sections in the LRA and numerous schedules). The purpose of the LRA is set out in section 1, including giving effect to and regulating the fundamental rights contained in the Bill of Rights and providing a framework

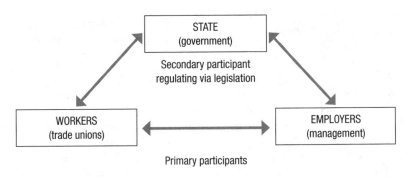

Figure 11.1: Participants in labour relations

within which employees, their trade unions, employers and employers' organisations can engage in collective bargaining and formulate industrial policy. The purposes of the LRA also include the promotion of orderly collective bargaining and the effective resolution of labour disputes.

The LRA applies to all employees and employers, but members of the South African National Defence Force, the National Intelligence Agency, the South African Secret Service, the South African National Academy of Intelligence and Comsec are excluded from the operation of the LRA. Comsec, or Electronic Communications Security (Pty) Ltd, was established by the Electronic Communications Security (Pty) Ltd Act 68 of 2002.

11.4.2.1 Freedom of association

Freedom of association means that employees have the right to form a trade union or to join a trade union of their choice. They also have the right to participate in the lawful activities of a trade union. The protection of freedom of association in the LRA must be seen within the context of the fundamental right of freedom of association contained in section 23 of the Constitution. Employers have a similar right: to form or to join an employers' organisation. These rights of association (the foundation of the notion of collectivism) are recognised in most modern labour relations systems and they are also enshrined in the international labour standards of the International Labour Organisation (ILO).

11.4.2.2 Organisational rights

Trade unions may apply for, and exercise, certain **organisational rights** in respect of the employer's premises or the employer's operations. Provision is made for the trade union to gain access to the employer's premises to recruit members, to communicate with members or to represent members' interests. Unions may hold meetings at the employer's premises after hours. This organisational right is not unlimited, of course: the union's right to gain access to the employer's premises may be subject to conditions regarding time and place that may be necessary "to safeguard life or property or to prevent the undue disruption of work". The right of access to the employer's premises is just one of a number of organisational rights provided for in the LRA. Other organisational rights include time off for trade union activities, the right of a trade union to have trade union dues or subscriptions deducted from employees' wages or salaries and the right of a trade union to information it needs when consulting or negotiating with the employer.

Organisational rights

An employer and a trade union are engaged in wage negotiations. In response to the union's demand for an 8% wage increase for all weekly-paid employees, the employer responds that it cannot afford an 8% increase because business has not been as good as it expected. The union challenges this statement by the employer, saying that there has been increased productivity and sales. The union then demands to see the employer's financial statements, but the employer responds by saying that this information is for the employer only. Section 16 of the Labour Relations Act provides that in this kind of situation a trade union representing the majority of employees in a workplace has the right of access to certain kinds of information that are relevant to the negotiations. The union may also demand to see details of the remuneration of senior executives, and the employer may then respond that this information is private and personal information (one of the exceptions to the union's right of access to information in terms of section 16 of the LRA).

11.4.2.3 Bargaining and statutory councils

Large parts of the LRA focus on collective bargaining. Bargaining councils are bargaining and dispute resolution structures introduced by the Act – centralised at sectoral level. One or more registered trade unions and one or more employers' organisations may form a bargaining council. The union and the employers' organisation agree to the council's constitution and the council is then registered.

The powers and functions of bargaining councils include the following:
- To conclude collective agreements
- To enforce collective agreements
- To prevent and resolve labour disputes
- To perform dispute functions set out in the Act
- To establish and administer a fund to be used for resolving disputes
- To promote and establish training and education schemes
- To establish and administer funds related to pension, provident, medical aid, sick pay, holiday, unemployment schemes, or other schemes or funds for the benefit of one or more of the parties to the bargaining council or their members
- To determine, by collective agreement, the matters which may not be an issue in dispute for the purpose of a strike or lock-out at the workplace
- To consider workplace forums or additional matters for consultation

A representative trade union (or more than one, combining forces), with members who constitute at least 30% of the employees in a sector, or one or more employers' organisations, may apply to the Registrar (Department of Labour) for the establishment of a statutory council in a sector or area in which no bargaining council is registered. The difference between a **bargaining council** and a **statutory council** lies in the fact that a bargaining council is established by agreement between unions and employers, while a statutory council is established by the state after receiving a request from either unions or employers.

11.4.2.4 The Commission for Conciliation, Mediation and Arbitration (the CCMA)

The CCMA is the best-known (and most important) labour dispute resolution institution established by the LRA. The CCMA deals with certain types of unfair dismissal disputes – these dismissal disputes constitute the bulk of the CCMA's workload. The CCMA has a director and commissioners who carry out its dispute resolution functions. It is independent of the state and of any political party or any other organisation. Its functions are to attempt to resolve, through conciliation, any dispute referred to it in terms of the LRA and then to arbitrate any dispute that remains unresolved by these means, if the LRA requires arbitration. Most labour disputes are referred to either a bargaining council (if there is a bargaining council registered for the sector and area in which the dispute arises) or the CCMA (if there is no council) for conciliation – this is where a commissioner tries to get the parties to agree to a settlement of the dispute. If conciliation fails, the LRA prescribes that certain disputes return to the council or the CCMA for arbitration (here a commissioner or arbitrator hears both parties to the dispute and then makes a final and binding ruling or award).

Other types of disputes are referred to the Labour Court if conciliation fails. The CCMA also has other functions: to assist in the establishment of workplace forums and to compile and publish statistics concerning its activities. The Commission may also:
- Advise a party to a dispute about the appropriate dispute resolution process
- Advise a party to a dispute to obtain legal advice
- Accredit councils or agencies to perform dispute resolution functions

- Oversee or scrutinise any election or ballot of a registered trade union or registered employers' organisation
- Issue guidelines in relation to any matter dealt with in the Act
- Publish research

Dispute resolution processes

In the course of one year, an employer has dismissed four employees for misconduct (allegations of fraud) and another two employees for poor work performance (the employees did not succeed in meeting their production targets). But the employer also retrenched more than 100 employees in the course of that year. In all cases the employees challenge their dismissals as being unfair. Different dispute resolution procedures apply in respect of these dismissal disputes in terms of the LRA. Dismissal disputes relating to misconduct or incapacity (poor work performance, for example) are referred to the CCMA (if there is no bargaining council with jurisdiction) for conciliation followed by arbitration if conciliation fails to settle the matter. Dismissal relating to the employer's operational requirements (such as a large-scale retrenchment) are referred to the CCMA for conciliation and, if conciliation fails, to the Labour Court.

11.4.2.5 The Labour Court and the Labour Appeal Court

The LRA establishes two courts of law to deal specifically with labour disputes. The Labour Court is similar to a provincial division of the High Court and it consists of a Judge President, a Deputy Judge President and as many judges as the President may consider necessary. The Court is constituted before a single judge and may sit in as many courts as the available judges may allow. The Court has various functions, which are stipulated in the Act. But unlike the High Court, the Labour Court's jurisdiction is limited – it can only hear and decide disputes as provided by the LRA. For some time now,

drawing the line between the jurisdiction of the Labour Court (in other words, the matters the Labour Court can or cannot decide) and other courts has become very difficult.

The Labour Appeal Court can hear and rule on all appeals against final judgments or final orders of the Labour Court and it may rule on any questions arising from proceedings in the Labour Court.

11.4.2.6 Strikes and lock-outs

The LRA defines a **strike** as "the partial or complete concerted refusal to work, or the retardation or obstruction of work, by persons who are or have been employed by the same employer or by different employers, for the purpose of remedying a grievance or resolving a dispute in respect of any matter of mutual interest between employer and employee, and every reference to 'work' in this definition includes overtime work, whether it is voluntary or compulsory". This definition is broad, in that it also covers any refusal to work overtime, irrespective of whether the overtime is compulsory or voluntary.

If a strike or lock-out does not comply with the provisions of the LRA, the Labour Court has exclusive jurisdiction to grant an interdict or order to restrain any person from participating in or furthering such action, and also to order the payment of just and equitable remuneration of any loss attributable to the strike or lock-out.

The LRA also makes provision for protest action, and includes stipulations regarding replacement labour during strikes, picketing, essential and maintenance services, and lock-outs.

11.4.2.7 Collective agreements

The aim of collective bargaining is to reach an agreement. The LRA provides mechanisms through which the parties can achieve this. Although disputes or industrial action may form part of the process of negotiation, the ultimate goal is to conclude collective agreements. The primary forum for collective bargaining is a bargaining council and the LRA contains a number of important provisions relating to bargaining council agreements. Other collective agreements concluded between a trade union and an employer outside a bargaining council are also provided for.

There are two types of collective agreements: **procedural agreements** and **substantive agreements**. Recognition agreements (procedural) regulate how the parties will conduct the relationship, and substantive agreements deal with the content of the relationship and conditions of service.

11.4.2.8 **Agency shop agreements and closed shop agreements**

A representative trade union whose members are in a majority in a workplace may conclude with the employer an agency shop agreement requiring the employer to deduct an agreed agency shop fee from the wages of its employees who are not members of the trade union and to whom the agreement applies.

Alternatively, a representative trade union whose members are a majority in a workplace may conclude with the employer a closed shop agreement requiring all employees in respect of whom the agreement applies to be members of the trade union.

11.4.2.9 **Workplace forums**

Workplace forums are designed to facilitate a shift at the workplace from an adversarial relationship between trade unions and employees to a joint problem-solving and participatory relationship on certain issues. These forums are also designed to foster cooperative relations through dialogue, information sharing, consultation and joint decision making, which is not possible through collective bargaining processes. The focus is on non-wage matters, such as restructuring, the

introduction of new technologies, changes in work scheduling, physical conditions of work, health and safety, and those issues that can best be resolved at workplace level.

The **functions** of a workplace forum are to promote the interests of all employees in the workplace, irrespective of whether or not they are union members, and to enhance efficiency in the workplace.

A workplace forum may be established in the workplace of any employer with more than 100 employees. Only representative trade unions may apply to the CCMA for the establishment of a workplace forum. Workplace forums employ a consultative approach and a joint decision-making approach.

11.4.2.10 **Unfair dismissals**

Section 185 of the LRA provides that every employee has the right not to be unfairly dismissed. This protection applies only in respect of employees (and not, for instance, independent contractors). The term "dismissal" is also defined in the LRA and specific provision is made for a special category of dismissals called **automatically unfair dismissals**. In the case of an automatically unfair dismissal, it is the reason for the dismissal that makes it automatically unfair. If an employee exercises a right conferred by the LRA (such as the right to freedom of association or the right to participate in a protected strike) and he or she is dismissed, the dismissal would be automatically unfair. If the dismissal relates to unfair discrimination (for instance if the employee is dismissed for reasons relating to his or her age, gender, language or political beliefs), the dismissal would be automatically unfair – the employee's right not to be unfairly discriminated against would be at stake. Other forms of automatically unfair dismissals include the following:

• Dismissal when the employee refuses to do the work of another employee who is participating in protected strike action, unless that work is necessary to prevent

actual danger to life, personal safety or health
- Dismissal in order to compel the employee to accept a demand in respect of any matter of mutual interest between the employer and employee
- Dismissal related to the employee's pregnancy
- Dismissal as a result of unfair discrimination, whether directly or indirectly, on any arbitrary ground

Even if a dismissal is not automatically unfair, it must still comply with certain requirements. A dismissal must be for a valid and fair reason (substantive fairness) and this reason must relate either to the employee's misconduct, incapacity or the employer's operational requirements. But a dismissal must also be done in a fair manner – Schedule 8 of the LRA sets out the procedural steps the employer must take in order to ensure that a dismissal is not only substantively fair but also procedurally fair. The essence of procedural fairness is that an employee must be given an opportunity to be heard: to respond to the charges or allegations made by the employer and to say why he or she should not be dismissed.

An employee who feels that he or she has been unfairly dismissed may refer an unfair dismissal dispute to either a bargaining council or the CCMA for conciliation. If the dismissal is for a reason relating to the employee's misconduct or incapacity, the dispute can then be referred to arbitration if conciliation fails. In the case of most dismissal disputes relating to the employer's operational requirements (including retrenchment), the dispute must be referred to the Labour Court for adjudication if conciliation has failed.

11.4.3 Communication: Grievances and disciplinary aspects

Communication has a tremendous influence on the quality of labour relations in any organisation. Structures, procedures and policies should be put in place to ensure constructive relations between management and workers. There are various ways of enhancing the quality of communication between the parties in the employment relationship, including one-on-one "chat sessions", performance appraisals, departmental meetings, safety and health committees, briefing sessions, workplace forums, and coaching sessions.

11.4.3.1 The grievance procedure

In the context of labour relations, a **grievance** is an employee's response to a real, perceived, or alleged breach of the terms of the employment

Unfair dismissal

An employee has had ten years' service with an employer, occupying a relatively senior position. The employee has been very active in the activities of the trade union to which he belongs – he is also a shop steward (a trade union representative). He has been involved in drawing up strategies for negotiations and he often represents other employees in disciplinary hearings and grievances. When the employer and the union were in dispute two years previously, the same employee was very involved in preparing various documents for the purposes of Labour Court proceedings.

The employer then dismissed the employee, stating that he had been insubordinate (refusing to comply with lawful and reasonable instructions) and that he had become "obstructive". The employee's response was that he had not been dismissed because of alleged misconduct, but because of his trade union activities. The Court found that the real reason for his dismissal was not the misconduct, as the employer alleged, but the employee's trade union role and activities. The dismissal was therefore automatically unfair. See *Kroukam v SA Airlink (Pty) Ltd* (2005) 26 ILJ 2153 (LAC).

contract, for example one-sided changes to the employee's conditions of employment, or being insulted by a supervisor. An effective grievance handling procedure has many advantages:

- It is a safety valve that will release the tension and dissipate the latent aggression inherent in all businesses
- It allows the raising and settlement of a grievance by a worker without fear of retribution or victimisation
- It makes for an open and honest relationship between manager and worker
- It allows managers to identify and remove legitimate causes of dissatisfaction or conflict

The LRA is silent on grievance procedures and what a grievance procedure should contain.

11.4.3.2 The disciplinary procedure

Discipline can be described as any action or behaviour on the part of authority (the employer) in a social system that is aimed at stopping member behaviour that threatens to disrupt the functioning of the system. It is therefore a normal and inherent part of any business's actions and responsibilities. Discipline should not be aimed at punishment for the transgression of rules, but rather at rectifying unacceptable behaviour. This is called a **corrective approach** to discipline.

The principles underlying the disciplinary procedure are:

- The employer's right to take disciplinary action against an employee who breaches a rule or standard governing conduct in the workplace (see box below)
- The employee's right to a fair procedure

Schedule 8 of the LRA (the Code of Good Practice: Dismissal) contains numerous provisions that are important in the context of workplace discipline. The Code of Good Practice confirms that discipline in the workplace must be corrective and it also provides that discipline must be progressive.

Progressive discipline means that dismissal is the last resort (except in the case of serious misconduct): counselling and warnings, in turn ranging from verbal warnings to final written warnings, may be more appropriate. Discipline should be applied consistently by the employer (similar cases should be treated similarly) and disciplinary standards must be communicated to employees. The most common way of communicating disciplinary standards is through the employer's disciplinary code and procedure (this code and procedure is often handed to an employee at the beginning of his or her employment).

Critical thinking

Dismissal for misconduct
Imagine two people, John and his supervisor, Peter. They have had some misunderstandings in the workplace about the way in which a certain piece of work is done. One Friday evening after work, both John and Peter are having a meal at a local restaurant. Words are exchanged and John attacks Peter physically outside the restaurant: Peter is not seriously injured. Would John's actions constitute a ground for dismissal?

11.5 The Basic Conditions of Employment Act (BCEA)

11.5.1 Introduction and application

The overall purpose the **Basic Conditions of Employment** Act 75 of 1997 (BCEA) is to advance economic development and social justice in South Africa. One of the objects of the BCEA is again to give effect to and regulate the right to fair labour practices conferred by section 23 of the Constitution. Other objects include establishing and enforcing basic conditions of employment and regulating the variation of basic conditions of employment. The BCEA applies to all employers and employees, except members of the National Intelligence Agency, the South African Secret Service, the South African National Academy of Intelligence and the directors and staff of Comsec.

Section 4 of the BCEA sets out the way the minimum standards contained in the BCEA interact with employment contracts. A minimum BCEA standard will, for instance, constitute a term of any employment contract unless the existing term in the contract is more favourable to the employee than the one contained in the BCEA. If the contract provides for more days' annual leave than the 21 days' annual leave provided for in the BCEA, the contract will apply.

The BCEA[3] covers a wide range of issues and only a few will be discussed below.

11.5.2 Working time

Chapter 2 of the BCEA, which regulates working hours, does not apply to senior managerial employees, to employees engaged as sales staff who travel to the premises of customers and who regulate their own hours of work or employees who work fewer than 24 hours a month for an employer. As a general rule, working hours must be arranged with due regard to the health and safety of employees and with reference to the Code of Good Practice on the Regulation of Working Time.

Ordinary hours of work are limited to a maximum of 45 hours in any week: 9 hours if the employee works 5 days a week or 8 hours if the employee works more than 5 days a week. **Overtime** may only be worked if the employee has agreed to work overtime and no more than ten hours' overtime may be worked in a week. Overtime is expensive: the employee must pay an employee one-and-a-half times the employee's normal wage. As an alternative to overtime pay, the employee may be granted time off.

The BCEA also provides for a **meal interval** (at least 60 minutes long after 5 hours of continuous work) which may be reduced to 30 minutes by agreement. An employee must have a daily rest period of at least twelve consecutive hours between ending work and commencing work the following day. Every employee must have a rest period of at least 36 consecutive hours each week. The rest period must include a Sunday, unless otherwise agreed. An employee may agree in writing to rather have a longer rest period of 60 consecutive hours every 2 weeks.

Night work is defined as work performed between 18h00 and 06h00. Employees must be compensated by the payment of an allowance or by a reduction of working hours. Transport must be available for employees who work at night. Employers must also inform employees who work between 23h00 and 06h00 of the health and safety hazards of night work, and, on request, provide employees with a free medical assessment. The limits on ordinary and overtime working hours, and the requirements for meal intervals and rest periods do not prevent the performance of emergency work.

The Minister of Labour may exclude or vary the provisions in respect of limits on hours of work and overtime to employees earning more than a certain amount.

11.5.3 Leave

Employees are entitled to 21 **consecutive** days fully paid **annual leave** after every twelve months of continuous employment. An employer may not pay an employee instead of granting annual leave. However, an employee whose employment is terminated must be paid out leave pay due for leave that he or she has not taken. An employee is entitled to 6 weeks' paid **sick leave** for every 36 months of continuous employment. However, during the first 6 months of employment an employee is entitled to only 1 day's paid sick leave for every 26 days worked. An employer may require a medical certificate for absence of more than two consecutive days from an employee who is regularly away from work, before paying the employee for sick leave. Sick leave may not run concurrently with annual leave or notice to terminate services.

A pregnant employee is entitled to four consecutive months' **maternity leave**. This leave may begin up to four weeks before the expected date of birth, unless otherwise agreed or if the employee is required to take the leave earlier for medical reasons. An employer may not require an employee to return to work for six weeks after the birth of a child. An employee may, however, elect to do so if a medical doctor or midwife certifies that she is fit to return to work. Maternity leave is unpaid leave, although an employee is entitled to claim maternity benefits in terms of the Unemployment Insurance Act. It is also possible that the employer may pay maternity leave. An employee who has worked for at least four months is entitled to three days paid **family responsibility leave** per leave cycle. This applies only to employees who work on four or more days in a week. The employee may take this leave in the event of the birth of a child, if the child is sick, or if a member of the employee's immediate family dies. An employer may require reasonable proof of the purpose for which this leave is taken before paying the employee. Unused days do not accrue.

11.5.4 Remuneration, deductions and notice of termination

An employer must pay an employee according to arrangements made between them. An employer may deduct money from an employee's pay only if permitted or required to do so by law, collective agreement, court order, or arbitration award. A deduction for loss or damage caused by the employee in the course of employment may be made only by agreement and after the employer has established by a fair procedure that the employee was at fault. An employee may agree in writing to an employer deducting a debt specified in the agreement.

During the first six months of employment, an employment contract may be terminated on one week's notice. The notice period during the remainder of the first year of employment is two weeks, while for employees with more than a year's service it is four weeks.

The notice period for a farm worker or domestic worker who has worked for more than four weeks is one month. The notice period may be altered (varied) by a collective agreement between the employer and a union. But even a collective agreement may not reduce a four-week notice period to less than two weeks.

Notice must be given in writing, and if the recipient cannot understand the notice, it must be explained to the employee in a language he

Leave

D has signed a written contract of employment with FGH CC in terms of which D works Monday to Friday, from 09h00 until 16h30. This contract also states that D is entitled to 20 working days' paid annual leave per year. After listening to a radio talk-show dealing with the issue of working hours, leave and the BCEA, D believes that his employer is contravening the Act by not giving him 21 days' leave. But D would be wrong in this case: the BCEA provides for 21 consecutive days' leave (in other words, 3 weeks). The BCEA refers to calendar days, not working days. If D is entitled to 20 working days, it means, in effect, that he is entitled to 4 weeks' leave. This in turn means that D's leave is more favourable to him than the provision in the BCEA and this contractually arranged leave benefit would apply, because nothing in the BCEA prevents an employer and an employee from agreeing to terms and conditions of employment that are more favourable to the employee.

or she can understand. An employer may pay the employee the remuneration for the notice period instead of giving notice. An employee who occupies accommodation situated on the employer's premises or supplied by the employer may elect to remain in the accommodation for the duration of the notice period.

Termination of employment by an employer on notice in terms of the BCEA does not prevent the employee from challenging the **fairness** of the dismissal in terms of the LRA.

On termination of employment an employee must be paid:

- For any paid time off that he or she is entitled to, which he or she has not taken, for example time off for overtime or Sunday work
- For any period of annual leave due and not taken
- In respect of annual leave entitlement during an incomplete annual leave cycle, either 1 day's remuneration in respect of every 17 days on which the employee worked or was entitled to be paid, or remuneration calculated on any other basis, whichever is the most favourable to the employee (this applies only if the employee has been in employment longer than 4 months).

When an employee's services are terminated because of the operational requirements of the employer (such as retrenchment), **severance pay** has to be paid – in addition to other payments due to the employee. The minimum amount of severance pay required by the BCEA is the equivalent of one week's remuneration for each completed year of continuous service. Employees who unreasonably refuse to accept an offer of alternative employment with the same or any other employer forfeit the entitlement to severance pay.

11.5.5 Administrative obligations

The employer must:

- Issue the employee with written particulars

of employment when the employee starts employment (these particulars include the employee's ordinary hours of work, the employee's wage, rate of pay for overtime work and leave)
- Retain these particulars of employment for three years after the end of the contract of employment
- Provide an employee with information concerning remuneration, deductions and time worked with regard to his or her pay
- Keep a record of the time worked by each employee, as well as of each employee's remuneration
- Display, at the workplace, a statement of employees' rights under the Act

Upon termination of employment, an employee is entitled to a certificate of service. Simplified provisions apply to employers who have less than five employees and to employers of domestic workers.

11.5.6 Prohibition of the employment of children and forced labour

No person may employ a child under fifteen years of age, and the Minister of Labour may make regulations prohibiting or placing conditions on the employment of children over fifteen years of age.

11.5.7 Variation of basic conditions of employment

Basic conditions of employment may be varied by bargaining council agreements, collective agreements concluded outside a bargaining council and individual agreements concluded by the employer and the employee. The Minister of Labour may also make determinations or issue sectoral determinations.

The Minister of Labour may make sectoral determinations establishing basic conditions of employment for employees in unorganised sectors. A number of important

Sectoral determination

Sectoral Determination 7 (15 August 2002, amended in November 2005) applies to the Domestic Worker Sector in the whole of South Africa. This sectoral determination contains provisions relating to wages, annual wage increases and the way wages are to be paid, to name just a few. Provision is also made for annual leave and sick leave. Item 8(b) of this sectoral determination, for instance, provides that an employer may deduct up to 10% of the employee's wage for a room or other accommodation but only if the room or accommodation is weatherproof and kept in a good condition, if it has at least one window and a door that can be locked and if it has a toilet and a bath or shower (if the domestic worker does not have access to any other bathroom).

determinations have been made, the best-known relating to domestic workers and to the farm workers. These sectoral determinations set out minimum wages and other conditions of employment. The BCEA prescribes the procedure that must be followed before a sectoral determination can be made. The Minister must direct a person in the public service to investigate conditions of employment in any sector or area in which it is proposed to make a sectoral determination. On completion of the investigation and after considering any representations made by members of the public, the Director General of the Department of Labour must prepare a report and the report must be submitted to the Employment Conditions Commission. Only once the Minister has considered the report and the recommendations made by the Commission may a sectoral determination for one or more sector and area be made.

Critical thinking

Basic Conditions of Employment
There are two fundamental aspects to the Basic Conditions of Employment Act. The first is to provide protection for employees in respect of minimum terms and conditions of employment. The second is to provide the employer with some degree of flexibility as to how to arrange work and when it is to be done. Which principle weighs the heaviest (and why)?

11.5.8 Employment Conditions Commission and inspectors

The Employment Conditions Commission was established to advise the Minister of Labour on the making of sectoral determinations, the effect of government policies on employment, and any matters arising out of the application of the Act.

The Minister of Labour may appoint labour inspectors who perform functions such as promoting, monitoring and enforcing compliance with employment laws. Labour inspectors must advise employees and employers on their rights and obligations in terms of employment laws. They may also conduct inspections, investigate complaints and secure compliance with an employment law.

11.6 The Employment Equity Act 55 of 1998 (EEA)[4]

11.6.1 Overview

The main aim of the EEA is to do away with all forms of discrimination in employment in South Africa by promoting equity and non-discrimination in the employment sector. The overall purpose of the Act is to achieve equity in the workplace, chiefly through the following two main elements:

- The prohibition of unfair discrimination, which applies to all employers

- Affirmative action measures, which apply only to "designated" employers

The most important provisions of the Act are as follows:
- Employers are required to take steps to end unfair discrimination in their employment policies and practices.
- Discrimination against employees or job applicants on the grounds of race, gender, sex, pregnancy, marital status, family responsibility, ethnic or social origin, colour, sexual orientation, age, disability, HIV status, religion, conscience, belief, political opinion, culture, language and birth is prohibited.
- Medical and psychometric testing of employees is prohibited unless properly justified.
- Employers must prepare and implement employment equity plans after conducting a workforce analysis and consulting with unions and employees.
- Equity plans must contain specific affirmative action measures to achieve the equitable representation of people from designated groups in all occupational categories and levels in the workforce.
- Employers must take measures to progressively reduce disproportionate income differentials.
- Employers must report to the Department of Labour on their implementation of employment equity.

- The EEA also establishes a Commission of Employment Equity.
- The labour inspectors and the Director-General of the Department of Labour are responsible for enforcing equity obligations.
- Any employer who intends to contract with the state must comply with its employment equity obligations.
- Employees are protected from victimisation for exercising rights conferred by the Act.

11.6.2 Scope of application of the EEA

Chapter 2 of the EEA, which deals with unfair discrimination, applies to all employees and employers. Chapter 3 of the EEA, which covers affirmative action, applies to "designated employers" and people from "designated groups" only.

A designated employer is:
- An employer who employs 50 or more employees
- An employer who employs fewer than 50 employees, but with a total annual turnover that is equal to or above the applicable annual turnover of a small business in terms of Schedule 4 of the Act
- A municipality
- An organ of state, but excluding local spheres of government, the National Defence Force, the National Intelligence Agency, and the South African Secret Service

Inherent requirements of a job

A professional couple employed a child minder. The employer (the husband) believed that the child minder should not have children of her own because this would have a negative impact on the attention she would devote to his children. The issue was raised during the initial interview when the child minder indicated that she was single and that she did not immediately plan on having her own children. Two years later, however, after having established sound working relationships, the child minder fell pregnant. The employer congratulated her and terminated her employment. One of the employer's arguments was that it was an inherent requirement of her job as child minder that she did not have children of her own, so that she could devote all her attention to her employer's children. The Labour Court concluded that it was not an inherent requirement of the job of a child minder that she not be pregnant or a parent. See *Wallace v Du Toit* (2006) 27 ILJ 1754 (LC).

- An employer that, in terms of a collective agreement, becomes a designated employer to the extent provided for in the collective agreement

Designated groups are:
- Black people (a general term meaning African people, coloured people and Indian people)
- Women
- People with disabilities

11.6.3 Prohibition and elimination of unfair discrimination

In chapter 2 of the EEA the emphasis is on the prohibition of unfair discrimination. Every employer (and not just designated employers) must take steps to promote equal opportunity in the workplace by eliminating unfair discrimination in any employment policy or practice. Section 6 provides that no person may unfairly discriminate (directly or indirectly) against an employee, in any employment policy or practice on one or more grounds, including race, gender, sex, pregnancy, marital states, ethnic or social origin, colour, sexual orientation, disability, HIV status or culture or birth. But it is not unfair discrimination to take affirmative action measures in terms of the EEA or to distinguish, exclude or prefer any person on the basis of an inherent requirement of a job. Sexual harassment constitutes a form of unfair discrimination.

Medical testing as part of the employment process is also prohibited, unless it is justifiable in the light of medical facts, employment conditions, fair distribution of employee benefits or the inherent requirements of the job.

11.6.4 Affirmative action

The EEA introduces a duty on designated employers to take **affirmative action** measures and to engage in a process of ensuring that, over time, progress is made towards employment equity. The main focus of the EEA is on getting employers to prepare plans to achieve progress towards employment equity and on the assessment of the plans by the Department of Labour. However, the eventual burden of the EEA on employers will, to a large extent, depend on how the Department of Labour applies the EEA, and its approach to the employment equity plans submitted by employers.

Unfair discrimination

Mr Video has opened up a new store and has placed an advertisement for shop assistants under the age of 25. S applied for the post even though she was 28 years of age. To justify its policy of employing only people under the age of 25, the employer said that the salary paid to shop assistants was not high, that there was a certain youthful approach and culture in the workplace in which an older person may not feel comfortable and that older people may be reluctant to take instructions from a younger person. The employer was also reluctant to appoint S because she was married and had children. The employee's argument was that this constituted unfair discrimination on the basis of her age. In subsequent arbitration proceedings, the CCMA commissioner stated that age should not be taken into consideration when determining whether a group of employees would be compatible and if a person was prepared to work for the salary offered and prepared to accept instructions from a younger person there was no reason why that person should not perform the work. The CCMA commissioner said the employer had unfairly discriminated against the employee not only on the basis of her age, but also on the basis of her marital status and family responsibilities. See Swart v Mr Video (Pty) Ltd (1998) 19 ILJ 1315 (CCMA).

In the context of affirmative action, a designated employer has the following obligations in terms of section 13 of the EEA:

- To consult with its employees
- To conduct an analysis
- To prepare an employment equity plan
- To report to the Director General on progress made in implementing the employment equity plan

The enforcement of the affirmative action provisions is part of a process that starts with a labour inspector and might end up in the Labour Court. The labour inspector may, for instance, issue a compliance order to an employer who refuses to give a written undertaking to comply with the Act, or an employer who fails to comply with such an undertaking.

If an employer fails to comply with the administrative duties in the Act, the Labour Court may impose a hefty fine, ranging from R500 000 for the first offence to R900 000 for four offences. Fines cannot be imposed for not achieving targets, although the Labour Court may make any appropriate order to ensure compliance with the Act if an employer makes no bona fide effort to achieve the targets. However, given South Africa's history, employers should be extremely sensitive as to how they manage employment relationships, particularly because there are so many possible discrimination traps that employers could fall into.

11.7 Skills Development Act 97 of 1998 (SDA)[5]

To improve the low skills base of people in South Africa, the government has promulgated three important pieces of legislation: the Skills Development Act (SDA), the Skills Development Levies Act and the South African Qualifications Authority Act. These Acts form part of the national skills development strategy, a new approach that aims, among other things, to link learning to the demands of the world of work, to develop the skills of existing workers, and to enable employers to become more productive and competitive.

It must be noted, however, that there is a clear link between the different pieces of training legislation and the Employment Equity Act. The principles of equity, access and redress underpin the transformation of the legislation. The links between the various pieces of legislation may be explained as follows: The South African Qualifications Authority Act (SAQA) creates the National Qualifications Framework (NQF), an integrated framework where all knowledge and skills outcomes can be registered as unit standards. The SDA introduces a strategic approach to skills development by creating 25 Sector Educational and Training Authorities (SETAs), learnerships and skills programmes that are to be assessed against NQF standards and qualifications. The Skills Development Levies Act imposes a skills development levy on employers, and the Employment Equity Act requires all employers to eliminate unfair discrimination and promote greater representation of black people (that is, African people, coloured people and Indian people), women and people with disabilities. The General and Further Education and Training Quality Assurance Act 58 of 2001 (not discussed in this chapter) transforms the governance and funding of technical colleges.

11.7.1 Objectives of the Skills Development Act

Section 2 of the SDA sets out the various purposes of the Act, namely:

- To develop the skills of the South African workforce
- To increase the levels of investment in education and training in the labour market and to improve the return on investment
- To use the workplace as an active learning environment, to provide employees with

the opportunities to acquire new skills, and to provide opportunities for new entrants to the labour market to gain work experience
- To employ persons who find it difficult to be employed
- To encourage workers to participate in learnership and other training programmes
- To improve the employment prospects of persons previously disadvantaged by unfair discrimination and to redress those disadvantages through training and education
- To ensure the quality of education and training in and for the workplace
- To assist work-seekers to find work, retrenched workers to re-enter the labour market, and employers to find qualified employees
- To provide and regulate employment services

The following institutions are established by the Act, namely:
- The National Skills Authority
- The National Skills Fund
- The skills development levy grant scheme as stipulated in the Skills Development Levies Act
- The SETAs
- Labour centres
- A Skills Development Planning Unit

11.7.2 National Skills Authority

The main functions of the National Skills Authority are as follows (Section 5 of the Act):
- To advise the Minister of Labour on a national skills development policy and strategy; guidelines on the implementation of the national skills development strategy; the allocation of subsidies from the National Skills Fund; and any regulations to be made
- To liaise with SETAs and the national skills development policy, and the national skills development strategy

- To report to the Minister on the progress made in the implementation of the national skills development strategy
- To conduct investigations on any matter arising out of the application of the SDA

11.7.3 Sector education and training authorities (SETAs)

The establishment of SETAs is described in Chapter 3 of the Act, and the Minister of Labour may establish a SETA with a constitution for any national economic sector.

The Minister of Labour must, however, take the following into account:
- The education and training needs of employers and employees
- The potential of the proposed sector for coherent occupational structures and career pathing
- The scope of any national strategies for economic growth and development
- The organisational structures of the trade unions, employer organisations and government in closely related sectors
- Any consensus there may be between organised labour, organised employers and relevant government departments as to the definition of any sector, and the financial and organisational ability of the proposed sector to support a SETA

SETAs have various functions, of which the most important are:
- To develop a sector skills plan within the framework of the national skills development strategy
- To implement its sector skills plan by establishing learnerships; approving workplace skills plans; allocating grants in the prescribed manner to employers, education and training providers and workers; and monitoring education and training in the sector
- To promote learnerships by identifying workplaces for practical work experience; supporting the development of learning

materials; improving the facilitation of learning; and assisting in the conclusion of learnership agreements
- To register learnership agreements
- Within a week from its establishment, to apply to the South African Qualifications Authority for accreditation as a body
- To collect and disburse the skills development levies in its sector

11.7.4 Learnerships

Learnerships are described in chapter 4 of the Act, and a SETA may establish a learnership if, firstly, the learnership consists of a structured learning component; secondly, if the learnership includes practical work experience of a specified nature and duration; thirdly, if the learnership leads to a qualification registered by SAQA and is related to an occupation; and, finally, if the intended learnership is registered with the Director General in the prescribed manner.

Learnership agreements are agreements entered into for a specified period between a learner, an employer or a group of employers, and a training provider. The employer has the responsibility to:
- Employ the learner for the period specified in the agreement
- Provide the learner with specified practical work experience
- Give the learner time to attend the education and training specified in the agreement

The learner has the responsibility to work for the employer and to attend the specified education and training. The training provider must provide the education and training specified in the agreement, as well as the learner support specified in the agreement.

The Act also makes provision (in chapter 6) for the establishment of the Skills Development Planning Unit. Labour centres are to provide employment services for workers, employers and training providers.

11.7.5 Financing skills development

The National Skills Fund (chapter 7 of the SDA) must be credited with, firstly, 20% of the skills development levies as stipulated in the Skills Development Levies Act; secondly, with the skills development levies collected and transferred to the Fund; thirdly, with money appropriated by parliament for the Fund; fourthly, with donations to the Fund; and lastly, with money received from any other source.

11.8 Skills Development Levies Act 9 of 1999[6]

The purpose of the Skills Development Levies Act 9 of 1999 is to provide for the imposition of a skills development levy. The most important aspects of the Act will be outlined below.

11.8.1 Levy to be paid

According to section 3 of the Act, every employer must pay a skills development levy, and the South African Revenue Services will be the national collection agency. Every employer must pay a levy at a rate of 1% of an employee's total remuneration. Pensions, superannuations or retiring allowances are, for example, excluded according to section 2(5) of the Act.

Employers who are liable to pay the levy must apply to the commissioner of the South African Revenue Services to be registered, and indicate the jurisdiction of the SETA within which they belong. The employer must also register with the relevant SETA.

11.8.2 Payment of levy to Commissioner and refund

An employer must pay the levy to the Commissioner of Inland Revenue Services not later than seven days after the end of each month. The National Skills Fund will receive 20% of the levy, and organisations will be able to claim for financing for up to 80% of the levy, less the set-up and running costs of the SETA.

11.9 South African Qualifications Authority Act 58 of 1995 (SAQA)[7]

11.9.1 Introduction to SAQA

After the publication in 1994 of the National Training Strategy Initiative document and the debate on it, the government's White Paper on Education and Training was published in 1995, and the South African Qualifications Authority Act 58 of 1995 (SAQA) was passed on 4 October 1995. The objective of SAQA is to provide for the development and implementation of the NQF and to establish the South African Qualifications Authority. The South African Qualifications Authority board has 29 members representing different sectors, for example education and training providers, non-governmental organisations, trade unions, and industry. It is responsible for establishing the National Qualifications Framework (NQF).

11.9.2 The South African National Qualifications Framework (NQF)

The **NQF** is based on a credit system for achieving learning outcomes. A **learning outcome** is, in essence, an ability developed by the learner that reflects an integration of knowledge and skill that can be transferred to different contexts. Qualifications can be obtained by means of full-time study, part-time study, distance education, work-based learning, or a combination of these, together with an assessment of previous learning experiences and general experience.

The NQF is a totally new approach to education and training in South Africa. Figure 11.2 on page 268 shows that the NQF consists of a framework with ten levels and three identified bands. The first or lowest band

is general education and training (GET), with two sub-sectors, namely formal schooling and adult basic education and training (ABET), culminating in level 1. This qualification represents 9 years of compulsory schooling and is equivalent to the present grade 9 at school.

The second band, further education and training (FET), comprises levels 2 to 4. Here a large number of sectors can provide education and training. Level 4 is equivalent to grade 12 (formerly standard 10) at school. The third band is higher education and training, and comprises levels 5 to 10. Moving from the ways of the past to those of the future requires a new mindset (or paradigm shift) among education and training providers. It also affects the way in which learners at schools and higher educational institutions, as well as employees in the workplace, learn and continue to learn. The concept of **lifelong learning** is introduced, in the sense that different forms of learning – for example part-time, full-time, in-company training, and also experience – are recognised, and credits are awarded and registered with the NQF. The NQF is the foundation for people wishing to achieve national qualifications through formal and informal learning, and in the process contributes to the government's aims of equality, quality, access to opportunities, and the redress of past inequalities.

11.10 Occupational Health and Safety Act 85 of 1993 (OHSA)[8]

11.10.1 Introduction to OHSA

The main purpose of this Act is the protection of employees by providing a healthy and safe work environment. The origin of the Act can be found in the late 1800s and early 1900s, when mining operations presented many dangers to workers, and poor working conditions led not only to various illnesses but also, at times, to death.

NQF Level	Band	Types of qualifications and certificates	Locations of learning for units and qualifications		
10	Higher Education and Training Band *	Doctoral degrees	Universities		
9		Master's degrees	Universities		
8		Honours/Post-graduate diplomas	Universities		
7		First degrees/ advanced diplomas	Universities		
6		Diploma/ higher certificates	Universities		
5		Occupational certificates	Universities		
Further Education and Training Certificates					
4	Further Education and Training Band	School/College/Training Certificates Mix and units from all	Formal high schools/ Private/ State schools	Technical/ Community/ Police/ Nursing/ Private colleges	RDP and labour market schemes/SETAs
3		School/College/Training Certificates Mix of units from all			Union/work place
2		School/College/Training Certificates Mix of units from all			
General Education and Training Certificates					
	General Education and Training Band	Senior Phase	ABET Level 4	Formal schools (Urban/ Rural/ Farm/ Special)	Occupation/ Work-based training/ RDP/Labour Market Schemes/ Upliftment programmes/ Community programmes	NGOs/churches/ Night schools/ ABET programmes/ Private providers/ Industry training Boards/Unions/ Workplace, etc
		Intermediate Phase	ABET Level 4			
		Foundation Phase	ABET Level 4			
		Pre-school	ABET Level 4			

Figure 11.2: Structure of the NQF
* At time of printing final approval for this has not been provided.
Source: Department of Education

The Act has a wide application and covers all workers, though there are the following exceptions:
- A mining area or any works as defined in the Minerals Act 50 of 1991, except insofar as the Act provides otherwise
- Vessels as defined in the Merchant Shipping Act 57 of 1957
- The Minister may grant exemptions from any or all of the provisions of the Act
- Labour brokers are not considered to be employers in terms of this Act

OHSA provides for an Advisory Council for Occupational Health and Safety, with certain functions as stipulated in the Act.

11.10.2 Duties of employers and employees

The general duties of employers to their employees are to:
- Provide and maintain a working environment that is safe and without risk to the health of employees
- Take whatever steps are necessary to eliminate any hazard or potential hazard to the safety or health of employees
- Provide any information, instructions, training and supervision as may be necessary to ensure the health and safety of all employees
- Take all necessary steps to ensure that the requirements of this Act are complied with
- Take any measures that may be necessary in the interests of health and safety
- Ensure that the work is performed and that this is done under the general supervision of a trained person
- Keep employees informed at all times

The general duties of employees at work are to:
- Take reasonable care for their own health and safety and also that of others
- Cooperate with their employer regarding this Act and its provisions
- Carry out lawful orders and obey health and safety rules and procedures
- Report any situation that is unsafe or unhealthy
- Report any accident they may have been involved in

11.10.3 Representatives and committees

Any employer with more than 20 employees must appoint one or more **safety representatives**, after consultation with the workers. Health and safety representatives

may perform certain functions and **must perform** other functions.

Health and safety representatives **may**:
- Review the effectiveness of health and safety measures
- Identify potential hazards
- Examine causes of incidents in collaboration with the employer
- Investigate complaints by employees
- Make representations to the employer and inspector
- Inspect the workplace
- Participate in consultations with inspectors
- Receive information from inspectors
- Attend meetings of the health and safety committee

Health and safety representatives **must** perform the following functions:
- Visit the site of an accident at all reasonable times and attend any inspection *in loco*
- Attend any investigation or formal inquiry in terms of this Act
- Inspect any document which the employer is required to keep
- Accompany an inspector on any inspection
- With the approval of the employer, be accompanied by a technical adviser
- Participate in any internal health and safety audit

The employer must provide such facilities, assistance and training as the representative may require. A health and safety representative shall not incur any civil liability by reason of the fact that he or she failed to do anything the representative was required to do in terms of this Act.

If two or more health and safety representatives have been designated in a workplace, the employer must establish one or more health and safety committees. The employer must also consult with the committee at each of its meetings to initiate, develop, promote, maintain and review measures to ensure the health and safety of employees at work.

Light in the workplace

OHSA imposes general duties on employers and employees, but the detailed regulations made in terms of OHSA contain numerous detailed duties. There are, for example, Environmental Regulations for Workplaces (October 1987, amended in 1989, 1994 and 2003) that contain details as to the lighting in the workplace, ventilation, noise, precautions against flooding, and fire precautions. The Facilities Regulations (August 2004, amended in September 2004) deal with issues such as changing rooms, dining rooms, drinking water and seating of employees.

Functions of health and safety committees include the following:

- Recommendations may be made to the employer or inspector.
- Any incident that has led to a person's death or illness must be discussed and a report may be sent to an inspector and the committee may report on the incident to an inspector in writing.
- The Minister appoints inspectors, and a certificate is issued as proof of their appointment. Their duties include general functions to ensure that the provisions of the Act are complied with – and here they have special powers relating to health and safety – and also functions with regard to incidents at the workplace.

11.11 Compensation for Occupational Injuries and Diseases Act 130 of 1993[9]

11.11.1 Introduction to the Compensation for Occupational Injuries and Diseases Act

In terms of the common law, an employee had no recourse if injured in the course of performing his or her duties. The only way to claim compensation was if intent or negligence on the side of his or her employer could be proved.

The first Act to give some form of protection to the employee was the Workmen's Compensation Act of 1941, which provided for payment of compensation even if intent or negligence on the side of an employer could not be proved. The basic principle has remained the same: compensation will be paid to an employee (or his or her dependants) if an injury has been caused by an accident "arising out of and in the course of the employee's employment". It is not necessary for the employee to prove negligence or fault on the part of the employer to qualify for compensation.

The following categories of persons are excluded from the operation of this Act:

- Persons performing military service or undergoing military training who are not Permanent Force members
- Members of the South African National Defence Force and South African Police Services while acting in defence of the country (note that members of the South African Police Service are covered by this Act while they are performing their normal duties)
- Domestic employees employed as such in a private household
- Persons who contract for the carrying out of work, and themselves engage other persons to perform the work (in other words, a contractor)

The Act provides for the establishment of a Compensation Board, whose main function is to advise the Minister on various matters concerning the application of this Act and its provisions.

11.11.2 Duties of an employer

An employer must register and furnish the Commissioner with details about his or her business. He or she must keep records of all employees, wages paid and time worked, for a period of four years. Such a record must be sent each year to the Commissioner. The Commissioner will then determine the amount of money that has to be paid by the employer to the Compensation Fund, and the employer must comply within 30 days. The state, parliament, provincial governments, exempted local authorities, and employers who have obtained an insurance policy for the extent of their potential liability, are exempted from giving the required details and paying the determined sum of money.

11.11.3 Procedure to claim compensation

The employee must, as soon as is reasonably possible, notify his or her employer of the accident, as well as his or her intention to instigate a claim. The employer will then notify the Commissioner within seven days. A claim for compensation must be lodged within 12 months of the date of the accident or the date of death.

There are, however, certain requirements that must be met before an employee qualifies for compensation:
- An employer–employee relationship must exist, and the employee must be an employee as defined in this Act.
- Injury or death must have been caused by an accident.
- The accident must have happened in the scope of the employee's employment; this would be if the accident happened in the nature of the employee's duties and in the course of his or her service.

11.12 The Unemployment Insurance Act 63 of 2001 (UIA)[10]

This Act provides for the payment of benefits for a limited period to people who are ready and willing to work, but are unable to get work for whatever reason. In terms of the UIA, some employees (those who qualify as contributors in terms of section 3 of the UIA) contribute monthly to the Unemployment Insurance Fund (UIF), which is administered by the Department of Labour. Employers also pay in a certain amount for every contributor (employee) that they employ. An employee who is out of work can claim benefits from the Fund. The UIA also provides for sickness benefits, benefits to dependants if an employee – referred to as a contributor – dies, and for maternity and adoption benefits.

The UIA should be read in conjunction with the regulations in terms of section 54 of the Act (*Government Gazette*, No. 23283, 28 March 2002) and the Unemployment Insurance Contributions Act 4 of 2002.

11.12.1 The scope of the Act

Most employees are covered by the Act. Section 3 of the UIA excludes the following categories of employees:
- Employees employed for fewer than 24 hours a month with a particular employer, and their employers
- Employees employed in terms of a learnership agreement registered in terms of the Skills Development Act 97 of 1998, and their employers
- Employees in the national and provincial spheres of government
- Persons in the Republic on a contract, apprenticeship or learnership, if the employer is required to repatriate the employee, or if the employee is required to leave the Republic at the end of the contract.

The Act provides for the institution of an Unemployment Insurance Board to assist the Minister of Labour.

11.12.2 Duties of employers

In terms of the Act, employers have certain duties. Every employer is obliged to do the following:

- As soon as commencing activities as an employer, the business must provide the following information regarding its employees to the Commissioner, irrespective of the earnings of such employees:
  - The street address of the business, and of its branches
  - The particulars of the authorised person who is required to carry out the duties of the employer in terms of this Act if the employer is not resident in the Republic, or is a body corporate not registered in the Republic
  - The names, identification numbers and monthly remuneration of each of its employees, stating the address at which the employee is employed
- Before the seventh day of each month, inform the Commissioner of any change during the previous month in any information furnished
- Pay into the Fund the required amount from the employer and every contributor in his or her employ. (Both the employer and the contributor must pay in an amount equivalent to 1% of the contributor's earnings – a total contribution of 2%. The employee's contribution can be deducted from his or her wages. Employers must make monthly payments into the Fund within seven days of the end of the month.)

11.12.3 Benefits and allowances

Contributors who lose their jobs are entitled (as are their dependants) to the following:
- **Unemployment benefits** for any period of unemployment lasting more than 14 days if the reason for the unemployment is the termination of a contract, dismissal, or insolvency; the contributor is registered as a work-seeker with a labour centre established under the Skills Development Act and is capable of and available for work
- **Illness benefits** if the contributor is unable to perform work on account of illness, and fulfils any prescribed requirements in

respect of any specified illness. The period of illness should be 14 days or more.
- **Maternity or adoption benefits.** The contributor will be paid the difference between any maternity or adoption benefit received in terms of any other law or any collective agreement or contract of employment, and the maximum benefit payable in terms of this Act.
- **Dependant's benefits** for a surviving spouse or life partner or dependent child, if an application is made within six months after the contributor's death.

In all instances, application should be made in accordance with the prescribed requirements.

> **Critical thinking**
>
> **A safe environment**
> Section 24(a) of the Constitution of 1996 provides that everyone has the right to an environment that is not harmful to their health or well-being. How does labour legislation seek to give effect to this right? Is it only the employer's responsibility to give effect to this right?

11.13 Summary

This chapter provided a brief overview of the legal environment that influences human resources managers in an organisation. The importance of the Constitution as the supreme law of South Africa was highlighted, followed by a brief overview of the most important labour laws that line managers and human resources practitioners should take note of in the workplace. The Labour Relations Act, which is the focal point of matters concerning labour relations in organisations, was explained. This was followed by a brief outline of the Basic Conditions of Employment Act (stipulating minimum employment conditions), the Skills Development Act, the Skills Development Levies Act, the South African Qualifications

Authority Act (which regulates, among other things, learnerships and the skills levy payable by employers), the Employment Equity Act (prohibiting unfair discrimination and regulating affirmative action, among other things), the Occupational Health and Safety Act (focusing on a safe and healthy work environment), the Compensation for Occupational Injuries and Diseases Act, and, finally, the Unemployment Insurance Act.

Key terms

Affirmative action	NQF
Basic Conditions of Employment	Occupational Health and Safety Act
Child labour (employment of children)	Organisational right
Constitution	Skills Development Levies Act
Employment Equity Act	Skills levy
Labour Relations Act	Strikes
Learnerships	Unemployment Insurance Act

Questions for discussion

1. The Labour Relations Act 66 of 1996 does not impose a duty to bargain on an employer. This means that there is no provision in the LRA that states that an employer must bargain or negotiate with a trade union. An employer may be reluctant to engage with a trade union, taking the view that it knows what is best for the employees. This is called a refusal to bargain. What can a trade union do to force an employer to the bargaining table? Hint: See section 64(2) of the LRA.
2. What is the role of the Constitution of South Africa in the labour environment of South Africa? Describe this role.
3. Which laws affect business activity in South Africa? List seven laws.
4. What are the main features of the LRA and BCEA? Describe them.

5. How is "affirmative action" part of an employer's responsibility? Explain.
6. What is the effectiveness of training legislation in South Africa?

References

1. While effort has been made to provide an accurate summary of the various Acts in this chapter, the editors, publishers and printers take no responsibility for any loss or damage suffered by any person as a result of reliance upon the information contained therein.
2. Based on the Labour Relations Act 66 of 1995, *Government Gazette*, Vol. 366, No. 17516, Government Printer, Pretoria.
3. Based on the Basic Conditions of Employment Act 75 of 1997, *Government Gazette*, Vol. 390, No. 18491, December, Government Printer, Pretoria.
4. Based on the Employment Equity Act 55 of 1998, *Government Gazette*, Vol. 400, No. 19370, Government Printer, Pretoria.
5. Based on the Skills Development Act 97 of 1998, *Government Gazette*, Vol. 401, No. 19420, November, Government Printer, Pretoria.
6. Based on the Skills Development Levies Act 9 of 1999, *Government Gazette*, Vol. 406, No. 19984, April, Government Printer, Pretoria.
7. Based on the South African Qualifications Act 58 of 1995, *Government Gazette*, Vol. 364, No. 1521 Government Printer, Pretoria.
8. Based on the Occupational Health and Safety Act 85 of 1993, *Government Gazette*, Vol. 337, No. 14918, July, Government Printer, Pretoria.
9. Based on the Compensation for Occupational Injuries and Diseases Act 130 of 1993, *Government Gazette*, Vol. 340, No. 15158, October, Government Printer, Pretoria.
10. Based on the Unemployment Insurance Act 63 of 2001, *Government Gazette*, Vol. 439, No. 23064, January, Government Printer, Pretoria.

Websites: www.acts.co.za
www.labour.gov.za
www.gov.za
www.ccma.org.za

CONTROLLING THE MANAGEMENT PROCESS

The purpose of this chapter

Control is the last of the four fundamental tasks of management. It is the final step in the management process, where the assessment of actual performance against planned performance initiates a new cycle of planning, organising, leading and control. This chapter deals with the nature of control and examines how the control process works. It also examines the areas of control that management should focus on, such as the control of physical resources, quality control, financial control, budgetary control, the control of information and the control of human resources. The characteristics of an effective control system are also briefly examined.

Learning outcomes

The content of this chapter will enable learners to:
- Give an overview of the importance of control
- Describe how a control process should function
- Explain the key areas of control in the organisation
- Discuss the characteristics of an effective control system
- Describe how the control process provides feedback for the revision of planning

12.1 Introduction

Organisations use control procedures to ensure that they are progressing towards their goals and that their resources are being used properly and productively. This chapter examines the final component of the management process, namely **control**. Although it is the final step in the management process, it forms the basis for a new cycle of management activities because it gives feedback to and influences the

first step in the management process, namely planning. Without any knowledge of how successfully the plans have been implemented or how effectively the goals have been achieved, managers would not be able to start the next management cycle of planning, organising, leading, and, ultimately, controlling.

Controlling is the final step in the management process and it is, as stated, an important part of the management cycle. Brilliant plans may be formulated, impressive organisational structures may be created, and good leadership may be applied, but none of these ensure that the activities will proceed according to plan or that the goals and carefully laid plans will in fact be realised.

An effective manager is therefore someone who follows up on planned activities, and sees to it that the things that need to be done are in fact carried out, and that the predetermined goals are reached. As we shall see in the IBM case study below, Louis Gerstner was responsible for the monumental task of turning IBM – the blue chip company that was in freefall – around.

Managers at all levels and in all departments should be involved in the process of control. Until the activities of individuals, departments or units are evaluated – that is,

Case study

Control in action: IBM

In 1993 Louis Gerstner undertook the monumental task of turning IBM around, the blue chip company that was in freefall. IBM had lost $17 billion and half their market share, the media was writing their obituary and competitors laughed at them. IBM dominated the industry for decades with mainframe systems used by virtually every corporation and government agency. In the late 1980s, competitors were offering mainframe alternatives at lower prices and the personal computer market, which IBM did not enter at that stage, exploded. Gerstner had only a few months to set IBM on the right track. The turnaround, Gerstner concedes, depended on actually focusing on controlling business fundamentals, such as consolidating the company's 266 bookkeeping systems, 128 chief information officers and 339 surveys for measuring customer satisfaction. He put an end to any talk of breaking IBM into several little blues – the prevailing wisdom on how to harness the company's valuable assets. Instead, Gerstner moved to transform the company into an "integrator" which would build, run and house systems for customers using its own components as well as those of competitors. Gerstner described the IBM of that era as suffering from "success

syndrome", a disorder afflicting companies that have been successful for decades. This locks them into repeating what made them successful in the past, even when the competitive environment changes and new control steps are required to remain relevant. He rebuilt company culture to focus on performance – employees returned to fundamentals like talking to customers and actually selling products rather than simply developing them. Gerstner also changed internal processes. For example, he revamped compensation, promotion and training programmes. All these efforts paid off. Between 1993 and 2001, IBM's annual net income rose to $7.7 billion from a loss of $8.1 billion; revenues rose to $85.9 billion from $62.7 billion, and the stock price rose to $120.96 per share from $14.12 per share. Gerstner says that "changing the attitude and behaviour of thousands of people is very, very hard to accomplish ... You cannot simply give a couple of speeches or write a new credo for the company and declare that a new culture has taken hold. You can't mandate it, can't engineer it. What you can do is create the conditions for transformation and provide incentives." Gerstner seems to have done that. After his retirement, he noted that IBM was rich with creative talent that only needed to be set loose.

Source: Brevis, T., "Lasting leadership: What you can learn from top business leaders", *Management Today*, Vol. 21, No. 4, 2005 18–23.

until actual performance is compared with the standard required – management will not know whether activities have been executed according to plan and will be unable to identify weaknesses in their plans. Controlling means narrowing the gap between what has been planned and the actual achievement of management, and ensuring that all activities are carried out as they should be. The management process takes place between planning and control, and successful management is often dependent on sound planning and effective control.

This chapter deals with the nature of control and examines how the control process works. It also examines the areas of control that management should focus on, such as the control of physical resources, quality control, financial control, budgetary control, the control of information, and the control of human resources. The characteristics of an effective control system are also briefly examined.

The IBM case study provides an illustration of the importance of effective control mechanisms in an organisation.

12.2 The importance of control

An organisation needs a control process because the best of plans may go wrong. In the case study above, we saw that IBM dominated the industry for decades with mainframe systems used by virtually every corporation and government agency. Gerstner described the IBM of that era as suffering from "success syndrome" – everything went according to plan, until the late 1980s, when competitors were offering mainframe alternatives at lower prices and the personal computer market, which IBM did not enter at that stage, exploded.

A control process is necessary for the following reasons:

- **The nature of the management process itself and, in particular, the task of planning.** Control is intimately linked with planning, organising and leading. Planning is the first step in control, and without control it is pointless. Again, control without planning is not possible.
- **The constantly increasing size of businesses.** As a business grows, more people are employed, new products are developed, new equipment is bought, new industries are entered, and branch offices are opened as the activities of the business expand into different geographical regions. Over time, the business becomes an extensive network of activities that include production, finance, administration, staff and marketing. Without an effective system of control it would be extremely difficult to spot weak points in a highly complicated network and rectify them timeously.
- **Managers and subordinates are capable of making poor decisions and committing errors.** An effective control system should detect such errors before they become critical.
- **The delegation of tasks to a subordinate does not mean that the job of management has been completed.** Management always has to check whether subordinates are doing their jobs properly. Without an adequate control system this task cannot be carried out.
- **Control enables management to cope with change and uncertainty.** If an organisation is to reach its goals according to plan, control is necessary. Because of the variables in the turbulent contemporary business environment, an organisation is seldom able to realise its goals strictly according to plan. Raw materials may not be delivered on time, labour unrest or defective machinery may delay the organisation's operations, unexpectedly high interest rates may affect the cost structure, and so on. Without control the impact of environmental change on the organisation will be difficult to detect.
- **Competition is a significant factor.** In chapter 1 we briefly discussed the disintegration of centrally directed economic systems

Critical thinking

At the end of this section on the importance of an effective control system in an organisation, we may ask ourselves the question "What could happen in an organisation without an effective control system?". The following excerpt provides a practical example of what could happen.

Saambou Bank

During the period of late 2001 to 2002, Saambou bank was exposed in the media to rumours indicating that the bank was facing insolvency. The rumours indicated that Saambou did not control the share dealing activities of its executives and that this weakened the proposed solvency of the bank. These rumours resulted in clients fleeing to the bank to withdraw deposits and funds. This hysterical reaction of clients had the result that, within a week, Saambou was no longer able to provide regular services and financial stability to clients. Saambou was placed under curatorship of KPMG, even though the bank was solvent. Today Saambou no longer exists, mainly due to poor governance and control and the negative reaction of clients to this possibility. Ineffective control, or limited control at all managerial levels, could have been a contributor to the downfall of one of South Africa's best-known financial institutions.

and showed how a market economy is better able to satisfy the needs of people. A successful market economy, however, also gives rise to more active competition. This in turn necessitates stricter cost and quality control if the organisation is to remain competitive. Globalisation is responsible for the fierce competition in international markets.

- **Control is applied to ensure that the organisation's resources are deployed in such a way that the organisation reaches its goals.** If there is no control, the organisation's resources could be wasted or misapplied.
- **Control usually results in better quality.**

12.3 The control process

An overview of the control process will further elucidate the importance of control. As we mentioned in the introduction, control is the process whereby management ensures that the organisation's goals are accomplished or that actual performance compares favourably with the predetermined standards. This process comprises four steps, which figure 12.1 on page 278 illustrates. The process includes setting standards against which actual performance can be measured, measuring actual performance, evaluating any deviations that might occur, and taking steps to rectify deviations. Each of these steps will now briefly be discussed.

12.3.1 Step 1: Establish standards

The first step in control is to establish performance standards at strategic points. Because of the close relationship between planning and control, it may be said that control in fact begins at the planning stage. It is often difficult to distinguish between these two tasks of management, because, in a sense, control means revised planning and the revised allocation of resources. The control system should therefore be a mirror image of planning, as the plans indicate the goals and setting of standards or norms necessary for control.

A performance or control **standard** is a planned target against which the actual performance will be compared. For example, a building project which has to be completed on a certain date will have control standards at strategic stages, such as completion of foundations by 31 March, completion of

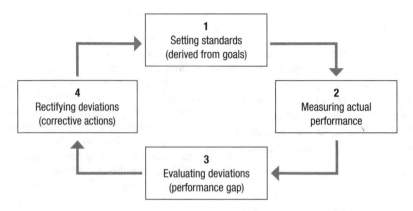

Figure 12.1: The control process

concrete structure by 30 June, completion of roof by 15 June, and so on.

To make the control process possible and worthwhile, the performance standard should be relevant, realistic, attainable and measurable, so that there can be no doubt about whether the actual performance meets the standard or not. Although it is difficult to make generalisations about suitable performance standards for different businesses, it should be possible in any particular business to convert strategy into comprehensive plans and goals. From these appropriate performance standards others can be developed, for example:

- **Profit standards** indicate how much profit the business expects to make over a given period.
- **Market share standards** indicate what share of the total market the business is aiming to conquer.
- **Productivity standards** are indicated by expressing inputs and outputs in relation to one another as ratios. Such ratios indicate the relative productivity with which tasks are performed.
- **Staff development standards** indicate the effectiveness of training programmes for staff.

In the case study at the start of this chapter, IBM would certainly have formulated performance standards related to profitability, market share, productivity and staff development.

Standards are a function of the goals that are set in the planning phase. Performance standards, of which the above examples are only a few, enable management to distinguish between acceptable and unacceptable performance. Performance standards also enable management to monitor strategies and goals. To be effective, these standards should be the responsibility of a particular individual at some strategic point.

12.3.2 Step 2: Measure actual performance

The collection of information and reporting on **actual performance** are continuous activities. As in the case of performance standards, it is also important for the activities to be **quantifiable** before any valid comparisons can be made. Another important requirement for the measurement of actual achievement is that the reports be **absolutely reliable**. Unless they are totally accurate, control will not be effective.

Moreover, observation and measurement must be carried out at the necessary strategic points and according to the standards determined by the control system.

Important considerations in the measurement and reporting of activities are **what information** and **how much** should be fed back, and **to whom**. In a small business or at the lower management levels of a fairly large business, operational management is more or less fully informed, and this is not of vital importance. But as a business increases in size, and information about activities has to be transmitted to higher levels, the issue of control becomes more important. It is at that point that the principle of **control by exception** is applied. This means that only important or exceptional disparities between real and planned achievement are reported to top management, and that less important deviations are dealt with by subordinates.

Management information is presented to indicate the disparities between performance standards and actual performance, and to enable management to concentrate on deviations or problem areas. For example, management might be highly satisfied with a report indicating that sales are 10% higher than in the previous year. However, management is likely to feel less complacent about the fact that sales of its market leader have shown a drop of 10%. The lapse of time between performance and measurement must be kept to the minimum so that deviations may be spotted as early as possible.

In the IBM case study, the company's actual performance measurement showed in 1993 a loss of $17 million and half the company's market share. Gerstner's task was to turn IBM around by concentrating on problem areas.

12.3.3 Step 3: Evaluate deviations

This step comprises the determination of the performance gap between the performance standard and actual performance. It is important to know why a standard has only been matched, and not exceeded, or even why performance has been much better than the standard. This could be the result of, for example, a new trend in the business environment, which might then be exploited more effectively. The nature and scope of the **deviations** responsible for the so-called performance gap may have various causes. In some cases the causes may be fairly obvious, while in others they may be so obscure that they become difficult to identify. It is therefore impossible to make generalisations about the causes of disparities between actual performance and standards.

Firstly, it is necessary to make sure that the disparities are genuine, that is, that both the performance standard and the actual performance have been objectively set and measured. If the standard is set too high, further examination of apparent deviations may be a waste of time.

Secondly, it must be determined whether the deviations are large enough to justify further investigation. Upper and lower limits should be set for each deviation, and only those that exceed the limits should be subjected to further examination.

Thirdly, all the reasons and activities responsible for the deviation should be identified.

At this point, decisions about corrective action, the last step in control, are needed.

12.3.4 Step 4: Take corrective action

The final step in the control process is to determine the need for **corrective action** and to ensure that deviations do not recur. If actual achievements match the standards, then of course no corrective action is needed, provided that standards have been objectively set. If actual achievements do not match the standards, management has a choice of three possible actions:

- Actual performance can be improved to reach the standards.
- Strategies can be revised to accomplish the standards.
- Performance standards can be lowered or raised to make them more realistic in the light of prevailing conditions.

In the IBM case study at the start of the chapter, Gerstner decided to focus on controlling business fundamentals, such as consolidating the company's 266 bookkeeping systems, 128 information officers and 339 surveys for measuring customer satisfaction. He rebuilt the company's culture to focus on performance. Internal processes were also changed.

This completes the cycle of the control process, and corrective action is, as stated, the point of departure of the next cycle in the management process. However, the term "control" has different meanings for different people. It often has a negative connotation for those who feel that their freedom and initiative are being restricted. It is therefore important to

---

Critical thinking

At the end of this section on the control process, we may ask ourselves the question "Are the steps in the control process also applicable in a crisis situation?" The following excerpt illustrates how the control process was applied in a crisis at Johnson & Johnson.

How the control process was applied in a crisis at Johnson & Johnson

James Burke's biggest career challenge came as chairman and CEO of Johnson & Johnson (J&J) in 1982, when seven people died in the Chicago area after taking cyanide-laced, extra-strength Tylenol capsules, a pain reliever sold by J&J subsidiary McNeil Consumer Products Co. The most prominent, and by now legendary, example of good crisis management remains J&J's handling of the Tylenol disaster. James Burke's actions in the weeks after the first death, which was reported on 30 September 1982, have been the subject of case studies in numerous business schools and management texts, not to mention the impetus for a new sub-speciality in public relations. Burke not only preserved the reputation of his highly respected consumer company, but he saved the Tylenol brand. At no point did he try to back off from the company's responsibility in the incident, even though it was later proven that the tampering had occurred at the retail level.

"When those people died," says Burke, "I realised there were some things we hadn't done right. Responsibility for that incident had to be, in part, ours. It wasn't easy to take

responsibility ... but it was clear to us, to me especially, that whether we could be blamed for the deaths or not, we certainly could have helped to prevent them. How? Through packaging. The fact is that the package was easily invaded. You could take the capsule out, open it up, put the poison in and then put the capsule back together. It was easy to do. I felt, and still feel, that it was our responsibility to fix it."

Burke's conviction, and his total commitment to the safety of the customer, led the company to spend $100 million on a recall of 31 million bottles of Tylenol, which before the tampering had been the country's best selling over-the-counter pain reliever. The recall decision was a highly controversial one because it was so expensive. There were plenty of people within the company who felt there was no possible way to save the brand, that it was the end of Tylenol. Many press reports said the same thing. But Burke had confidence in J&J and its reputation, and also confidence in the public to respond to what was right. It helped turned Tylenol into a billion dollar business. Within eight months of the recall, Tylenol had regained 85% of its original market share and a year later 100%. The person who tampered with the Tylenol was never found. In 1984, J&J replaced capsules with caplets and in 1988, the company introduced gel caps, which look like capsules but cannot be taken apart.

Source: Brevis, T., "Lasting leadership: What you can learn from top business leaders", *Management Today*, Vol. 21, No. 4, 2006, pp. 18–23.

maintain a balance between control measures and control of people. It should also be borne in mind that on consideration of costs alone, there are limits to the time and money that can be spent on control. Moreover, control should be continually adapted to changing circumstances.

12.4 **The focus of control**

In the preceding introductory discussion of control, the importance of control as a fundamental function of management was emphasised. But the question now is "What, in fact, is it that should be controlled?" The important point is that organisations control activities and processes in a number of different areas (areas of control), and at different levels (strategic points) in the organisation.

An organisation's activities should be controlled at strategic points. The issues surrounding the design of a control system may be complex and depend on a variety of factors, including the nature of the organisation, its activities, its size, and its structure. As a rule, management should identify the key areas to be controlled. These are the areas responsible for the effectiveness of the entire organisation.

For example, the production department of a manufacturing organisation is a key area, as is the purchasing department of a chain store. Generally, a small percentage of the activities, events or individuals in a given process is responsible for a large part of the process. Thus, 10% of a manufacturing organisation's products may be responsible for 60% of its sales, or 2% of an organisation's personnel may be responsible for 80% of its grievances. By concentrating on these strategic points, for example, the organisation's main activities are exposed to control.

In the IBM case study at the start of this chapter, Gerstner successfully identified the company's strategic points. He turned IBM around. Between 1993 and 2001, the annual net income rose to $7,7 billion from a loss of $8,1 billion, revenues rose to $62,7 billion and the stock prices rose to $120,96 per share from $14,12 per share.

Most organisations define areas of control in terms of the four basic types of resources they use. In chapter 5 we defined management as the process in which the organisation's human, financial, physical and information resources are deployed to accomplish specific goals, especially those revolving around profitability. The implication here is that control should focus on the effective management of these resources. Figure 12.2 illustrates the focal points or key areas of control, namely:

- **Physical resources.** Control of these resources entails factors such as inventory control, quality control and control of equipment.
- **Human resources.** Control of these resources involves orderly selection and placement, control over training and personnel development, performance appraisal and remuneration levels.
- **Information sources.** Control of these resources relates to accurate market forecasting, adequate environmental scanning, and economic forecasting.
- **Financial resources.** In figure 12.2 financial resources are situated at the centre of the other three resources not only because they are controlled in their own right (for example cash-flow or debtor control), but also because most control measures or techniques (such as budgets, sales, production costs, market share, and various magnitudes) are quantified in financial terms.

Figure 12.2: Key areas of control

Each of the focal points of control will now be discussed in greater detail.

12.4.1 The control of physical resources

An organisation's physical resources are its tangible assets, such as buildings, office equipment and furniture, vehicles, manu-facturing machinery and equipment, trading stock, raw materials, work in process, and finished products. Various control systems of an administrative nature can be established to **control physical resources** – in particular office furniture, equipment and vehicles – which normally appear on an asset register. Control systems for these resources involve usage procedures, periodic inspections and stocktaking, which often fall within the ambit of the internal audit. The control systems for inventories, raw materials and finished products are inventory control and quality control. Although inventory control falls within the field of purchasing and logistics management, we need to make a few remarks about it here.

12.4.1.1 Inventory

Inventory refers to the reserves of resources held in readiness to produce products and services, as well as to the end products that are kept in stock to satisfy consumers' and customers'

needs. As table 12.1 shows, inventory nor-mally refers to the four basic kinds of inventory, such as raw materials, work-in-process, pipeline, and finished products. However, inventory need not only have to do with manufacturing. For example, for an airline, a seat on an aircraft is inventory, and an unsold seat on a flight is a loss. By the same token, money in a safe in a bank is inventory that can be lent to clients at a certain interest rate.

Organisations keep inventories – and here the word is used in a wide sense – mainly for the following purposes:
- To satisfy the needs of customers and con-sumers
- In the case of raw materials and components, to keep uncertainties regarding delivery and availability to a minimum, so that the manufacturing process is not interrupted
- As a hedge during times of high inflation

There are a number of reasons[1] why organisations keep inventories, but, as the above discussion emphasises, there is one especially important reason, namely the cost of inventories and the need to control that cost.

It is estimated that it costs an organisation 20 to 25 cents per R1,00 of inventory per annum to keep inventories. These costs refer mainly to interest, space and risk factors. The most expensive cost is the price of money, or

Table 12.1: Types of inventory, purpose and sources of control

Type	Purpose	Source of control
Raw materials	Provide the materials needed to make the product	Purchasing models and systems
Work-in-process	Enables overall production to be divided into stages of a manageable size	Shop-floor control systems
Finished goods	Provide ready supply of products on customer demand, and enable long, efficient production runs	High-level production scheduling systems, in conjunction with marketing
In-transit (pipeline)	Distributes products to customers	Transportation and distribution control systems

Source: Griffin. R.W., *Management Today*, Houghton Mifflin Company, New York, 1999, pp. 663

interest, to finance inventories, followed by storage costs, insurance, and risk. Because of the high cost of inventories, it stands to reason that organisations, especially in times when interest rates are high, try to keep inventory levels as low as possible. Inventory control is introduced to keep inventory, and the costs involved, as low as possible without causing shortages that may delay the manufacturing process or other transactions. The following three control systems are relevant here:

- The concept of **economic ordering quantity** (EOQ), which has been in use since as early as 1915, is based on replenishing inventory levels by ordering the most economic quantity. The disadvantage of this control system is that inventory must be kept, regardless of the needs of the manufacturing department or customer, for particular raw materials, components or finished products. This means that items must be kept in stock for indefinite periods in spite of efforts to keep inventory costs as low as possible.
- The **material requirements planning** (MRP) system was developed in the 1960s to eliminate the shortcomings of the EOQ control system. With this system, an estimate is made of the demand for raw materials and the components necessary to produce a finished product. Inventories are ordered only when they are needed. The costs of maintaining inventory levels over extended periods are thus eliminated.

- The **just-in-time** (JIT) system is a refinement of the MRP system and originated in Japan, where it was developed by Toyota in the 1970s. The JIT philosophy is the same as MRP in the sense that organisations endeavour to manufacture products without incurring significant inventory costs. However, in contrast to MRP, where the need for raw materials and components is estimated and they are ordered according to demand, JIT is based on the premise that actual orders for finished products are converted into orders for raw materials and components, which arrive just in time for the manufacturing process. A manager applying the JIT principle orders materials and components more often in smaller quantities, thereby reducing risk and investment in both storage and actual inventory. The success of this complex inventory control system depends largely, however, on reliable deliveries of flawless components, stable relationships with outside suppliers, and a reliable labour force.

This discussion of inventory control systems has been extremely superficial, since the aim is merely to introduce the field of application and the complexity of control systems relating to physical resources.

We will now examine an element closely intertwined with inventory control, namely quality control.

Toyota and JIT: the origin of the JIT system

The JIT production method, although recent in origin, has become the backbone of Japanese manufacturing. JIT production was developed in the mid-1970s by the Toyota Motor Company in response to the energy crisis. Faced with increasing energy and production costs, Toyota had to find a way to make its products more competitive in the international market.

One way was to cut inventory costs. Rather than producing finished goods destined for storage as stock, Toyota decided to produce cars just in time to be sold. It fabricated parts just in time to be assembled into subcomponents and materials just in time for fabrication. By using the JIT programme system, Toyota was able to use all materials promptly, incurring no carrying or ordering costs.

Source: Chung, K.H., *Management: Critical success factors*, Allyn & Bacon, p. 607.

12.4.1.2 Quality control

Quality and productivity have become increasingly important issues in management, especially in the USA, where business organisations are continually searching for ways of countering the success of foreign competitors in American markets. The management approach, which emphasises the management of quality, is known as **total quality management** (TQM). Because of the importance of TQM, particularly in competitive international markets, we need to give a brief overview of quality control.

Japanese products were once regarded as cheap goods. Today, however, the quality of Japanese products is acknowledged globally. Because of the success of Japanese products, especially in the USA, contemporary managers are realising increasingly that access to international markets depends not only on mass production, but also on quality. Whereas quality control was formerly the responsibility of a single department or section, TQM means that quality is the responsibility of everyone in the organisation, from the chairman of the board of directors to clerks, purchasing managers, engineers and selling and manufacturing personnel. Figure 12.3 illustrates the major factors involved in improving quality.

A strategic commitment on the part of top management will ensure that quality is included in the mission statement of the organisation and transmitted to operational levels. The ultimate test of product quality is in the marketplace, where it becomes evident whether or not the product satisfies consumers' needs.

Quality control refers to the activities that management performs to ensure a level of quality that will satisfy the consumer, on the one hand, and have certain benefits for the organisation, on the other. Quality control usually comprises the following steps:

- **Step 1: The definition of quality goals or standards.** This entails setting standards as prescribed by purchasers, chosen by consumers and necessitated by competition. However, quality means different things to different people. Some might perceive it as value for money, and others simply as the durability of the product. In setting quality standards, management should focus on

Figure 12.3: Managing quality

Source: Griffin, R.W., *Fundamentals of management*, 4th edition, Houghton Mifflin Company, New York, 2006. p. 512.

both qualitative product characteristics such as reliability, durability, design, style and colour, and quantitative characteristics such as length, height and mass.

- **Step 2: Measuring quality.** This entails the use of the following: **benchmarking**, or the process of learning how other businesses do things exceptionally well; **statistical control methods** to analyse product data with a view to quality; **variation measurement**, that is, measuring variations in materials, processes, equipment and the final product; and the determination of whether or not **specification limits** have been met or exceeded.
- **Step 3: Rectifying deviations and solving quality problems in an effort to keep the cost of quality as low as possible.** This refers to the cost of control as well as the cost of failures, or the cost of poor quality. To be able to decide which products or product processes should be improved, management should conduct quality cost studies. These analyses indicate the cost–quality ratio of the organisation's products and services. Another technique that can be applied to improve quality is **quality circles**. These are forums of employees who get together to identify aspects of their jobs that impede, prevent or promote quality, and who endeavour, on the strength of their expertise, to find solutions. The influence of quality circles in improving quality is felt not so much in direct savings, but in the positive motivational effect that participative problem solving has on employees.

The discussion above of the control of the organisation's physical resources, though somewhat cursory, points not only to the complexity of controlling physical resources, but also to the importance of control for the success of the organisation. Aspects of control are expressed mainly in financial magnitudes. The control of the organisation's financial resources is the next topic of discussion.

12.4.2 The control of financial resources

An organisation's financial resources is the second group of resources that management must control. Financial resources and abilities are vital to the success of the organisation and are at the heart of the control process, as indicated in figure 12.2. While financial resources are a group of resources in their own right, the **control of financial resources** is central to the control of other resources of the organisation. Financial control is concerned with the following:

- Resources as they **flow into** the organisation (revenue returns on investments)
- Financial resources that are **held by** the organisation (working capital, cash)
- Financial resources **flowing out** of the organisation (salaries, expenses)

Each of these categories of financial resources is controlled so that revenues are sufficient to cover expenses and show a profit. Incoming funds – which normally represent revenue in the form of electronic transfers, cheques and cash – must be controlled rigorously because this is an area where fraud often happens. Funds that are held by the organisation, such as working capital, should not be tied up in areas such as outstanding debtors or slow-moving inventory. Of equal importance is the control of outgoing funds such as salaries and expenses, which are also areas where fraud and serious errors might be found.

Financial management principles that deal with cash flows, cash management, investment returns, and so on, can also be regarded as financial control measures, but it is beyond the scope of this chapter to deal with these in detail. However, since financial control is pivotal to the control process, we will examine two instruments of financial control, namely budgetary control and financial analysis.

12.4.2.1 The budget

As part of the planning process, management allocates financial resources to different departments of the organisation in order to enable them to accomplish certain goals, and by allocating funds to specific activities management can implement certain strategic plans. This allocation of financial resources is done by means of the **budget**. From the point of view of control, management wants to know how the financial resources are applied. The budget is therefore used as an instrument of control.

A budget is a formal plan, expressed in financial terms, that indicates how resources are to be allocated to different activities, departments or sub-departments of an organisation. At the same time, it forms the basis for controlling the financial resources, a process known as **budgetary control**. Budgets are usually expressed in financial magnitudes, but can also be expressed in other units such as sales volumes, units of production, or, even, time. It is precisely because of the quantitative nature of budgets that they provide the foundation for control systems – they provide benchmarks or standards for measuring performance and making comparisons between departments, levels and periods. More specifically, the contribution of a budget to financial control is as follows:

- It supports management in coordinating resources, departments and projects.
- It provides guidelines on the application of the organisation's resources.
- It defines or sets standards that are vital to the control process.
- It makes possible the evaluation of resource allocation, departments or units.

Various kinds of budgets, a few examples of which are provided in table 12.2, can be used to make financial control possible across the financial spectrum.

Budgets have traditionally been developed in a top-down fashion: top management would develop the budget and impose it on the rest of the organisation. However, the way budgets are set today, especially in larger organisations, is by involving all managers of operating units, from the bottom to the top, in the budget process. A great deal of interaction takes place between heads of operating units (supervisory management) dimensional heads (middle management) and top management. The budget is usually set by a budget committee consisting of top managers, and it is here that top management also implements its strategies, which it does by allocating financial resources to the areas or divisions that must lead the organisation's strategy.

Budgets have a number of strengths and weaknesses. The most important advantage of

Table 12.2: Types of budgets

Type of budget	Focus	Examples
Financial budgets	Focus on cash flow Focus on capital expenditure	• Cash-flow budget • Capital budget
Operational budgets	Revenue Focus on the operational aspects of the organisation	• Sales budgets, contract budgets • Sales budget • Income budget • Expenditure budget
Non-financial budgets	Focus on diverse aspects of the organisation not expressed in financial terms	• Production budgets in units • Sales volumes in units • Time projections of projects

a budget is that it facilitates effective control by placing a money value on operations, and in doing so it enables managers to pinpoint problems. Budgets also facilitate coordination between departments and maintain records of organisational performance. But on the negative side, budgets may sometimes limit flexibility.

Budgets are not the only instrument management uses to apply financial control, however. To complement the budget, management can use **financial analysis**, also known as **ratio analysis**, to apply financial control. This will be discussed in chapter 17.

12.4.3 The control of information resources

All the tasks of management, namely planning, organising, leading and controlling, are dependent on supporting information in order to function effectively. However, it is the relevant and timely information made available to management during the management process that is vital in monitoring how well the goals are accomplished. Only with accurate and timely information can management implement plans and determine on a continuous basis whether or not everything is proceeding according to plan, and whether or not adjustments need to be made. The faster managers receive feedback on what is going smoothly or badly in the course of the management process, the more effectively the organisation's control systems function.

12.4.4 The control of human resources

Although the control task of management focuses mainly on financial and physical resources, this does not mean that the performance of one of the organisation's main resources, namely people, is exempt from control. The management of people, that is, the **control of human resources**, also falls within the ambit of human resources management. A few remarks will be sufficient

to emphasise the scope of control of human resources throughout the organisation.

The main instrument used to control an organisation's human resources is performance measurement. This entails evaluating employees and managers in the performance of the organisation. More specifically, from a control point of view, the performance of individuals and groups is assessed and compared with predetermined standards. Tasks are subdivided into components, and the importance of each subtask is determined so that criteria and measuring instruments can be developed. Performance standards must then be developed, for example 40 production units per hour, an accuracy level of 98% in tuning machines, or a quality level of at least 93%. Actual performance can be measured against these standards for feedback to and action by management.

Other human resources control instruments include **specific ratio analyses** that can be applied in respect of labour turnover, absenteeism and the composition of the labour force.

The preceding discussion of the control of an organisation's resources mainly emphasises the formal control systems developed by management. As far as informal control systems are concerned, however, people in the organisation play a decisive role in social control mechanisms. This refers specifically to group behaviour. When a group of people work together on a regular basis, they develop norms that lay down guidelines for the behaviour of the group. These norms, which may include the quality of products, speed of production, and reliability, are usually not written down, and have nothing to do with the formal organisational structure. Nevertheless, they still have a profound influence on the behaviour of groups when it comes to control or social control. Members of the group subject themselves to the norms of the group because, if they do not, they may be punished by the group in ways that may range from light-hearted teasing to outright rejection. Compensation by the group for group cohesiveness and control consists of approval of action, emotional support, and the assignment of a leadership role to the leader of the group.

The above discussion of the areas of control provides an overview firstly of the control process as it applies to the organisation's different resources, and secondly of some of the instruments that enable management to control resources.

12.5 Characteristics of an effective control system

The following are characteristics of an effective control system:

- **Integration.** A control system is more effective when it is integrated with planning, and when it is flexible, accurate, objective, timely and not unnecessarily complex. The interface between control and planning is discussed in the introduction to this chapter. Control complements planning, because deviations highlight the need to review plans and, even, goals. In this way, control provides valuable inputs to planning. The closer the links between control and planning, the better

the eventual control system will be. This is why provision should be made at the planning stage to make control possible, for example by formulating goals so that they can be converted into or applied as control standards. This means setting quantifiable goals. Figure 12.4 shows how planning and control should be integrated.

- **Flexibility.** The second characteristic of an effective control system is flexibility. This means that it should be able to accommodate change. Timeous adjustments in objectives or plans should not be regarded as deviations, but as revised objectives or plans, and the control system should be able to adjust to such revisions, within limits, without management having to develop and implement an expensive new control system.

- **Accuracy.** A control system should be designed in such a way that it provides an objective and accurate picture of the situation. Errors or deviations should not be concealed in the data. A total amount expressed in rand certainly does not show a profit, nor does it indicate which products sell better than others. Similarly, production management can conceal indirect costs to make production performance look good. Inaccurate information leads to

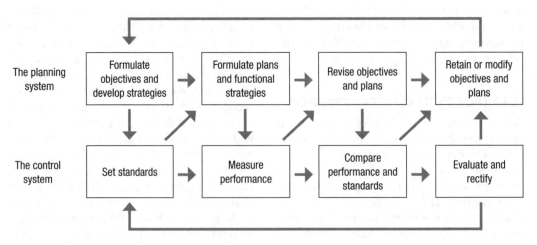

Figure 12.4: Integration of planning and control

incorrect modifications of new plans based on unreliable control data.

- **Timeliness.** Timely control data are not obtained by means of hasty, makeshift measurement; control data should be supplied regularly, as needed. A sensible approach is one based on the principle of timeliness.
- **Unnecessary complexity.** Unnecessarily complex control systems are often an obstacle because they can have a negative influence on the sound judgement of competent managers. If managers are hampered by red tape, they may leave the system to keep things going, and in so doing lose their personal involvement and motivation to see to it that things proceed according to plan. Unnecessary control is equally demotivating for personnel and leads to resistance to control systems. Too much information, especially if it is irrelevant, makes great demands on the time and attention of management, which means that the control process becomes too expensive. The unwritten rule of effective control is that control should not become so complex that the implementation of the control system becomes more expensive than the benefits derived from it. At the same time, a system should not be oversimplified to the extent that the essence of control is lost.

12.6 Conclusion

Control is one of the four fundamental management functions. It is the final step in the management process, and the starting point for planning and strategic development. The control process narrows the gap between planned performance and actual performance by setting performance standards in the right places, against which the performance of management, subordinates and resources can be measured, and deviations rectified, if necessary. Control focuses on virtually every activity or group of activities in the organisation, but normally aims at the control of physical, financial, information and human resources. Effective control systems are characterised by the extent to which planning and control are integrated, as well as the flexibility, accuracy and timeliness of the system. Management information plays an important role here.

However, too much information, especially irrelevant information, demands too much time and attention from management, which makes it too expensive. This ties in with the unwritten rule pertaining to control, namely that the application of the control system should not become so complex that it costs more than it saves. At the same time, the system should not be oversimplified to the point of losing its significance.

12.7 Summary

This discussion of control as the final fundamental element of management completes the examination of the management process and, with it, part 2 of this book. It should be clearly understood, however, that the general principles forming the subject of this section are also relevant in part 3, which deals with the specialised or functional areas of management. Less detail from this section is provided when discussing, say, financial planning or marketing control, where the emphasis in the treatment of different business functions falls mainly on the activities peculiar to a particular functional area.

 Key terms

Accuracy	Economic order quantity
Actual performance	Flexibility
Budget	Integration
Complexity	Inventory
Control	Just-in-time system
Control of financial resources	Material requirements planning

Control of human resources	Quality control
Control of physical resources	Standards
Corrective action	Timeliness
Deviation	

? Questions for discussion

Reread the case study at the beginning of the chapter and answer the following questions.

1. What steps did Louis Gerstner take to turn IBM around?

2. Identify the key areas of control in IBM.
3. How did the control process implemented by Louis Gerstner provide feedback for the revision of planning?
4. Explain the characteristics of an effective control system.

References

1. Griffin, R.W., *Management*, Houghton Mifflin, New York, 1999, p. 663.

PART 3

The functional
MANAGEMENT OF THE ORGANISATION

Chapter 1: The business world and business management Chapter 2: Entrepreneurship Chapter 3: The establishment of a business		Flows	
Chapter 24: Contemporary management issues		Products	
Chapter 4: The business environment		Services	
Chapter 5: Introduction to general management Chapter 6: The basic elements of planning	Chapter 13, 14, 15 and 16: Marketing and public relations management	Information	Customer satisfaction and value
	Chapter 17, 18, 19: Financial management	Financial	
Chapter 7: Organising Chapter 8: Leadership	Chapter 20 and 21: Operations management	Resource	
Chapter 9, 10, 11: Human resources management Chapter 12: Controlling the management process	Chapter 22 and 23: Purchasing and supply management	Demand	

Source: Adapted from: Mentzer, J. T. (ed.), *Supply Chain Management*, Sage, London, 2001 pp. 22–23.

THE MARKETING PROCESS

The purpose of this chapter

It is important to be aware of the role and the place of marketing in the business environment: marketing is a central part of any business's activities. This chapter will cover the marketing process. Initially we shall consider the evolution of marketing thought and the definition of marketing. Then the elements of the marketing process, and how these elements are linked, will be discussed. Marketing research forms part of the whole marketing process. The collection, analysis and interpretation of information are used to understand the behaviour of consumers and to segment the market, as well as to position an organisation's products.

Learning outcomes

The content of this chapter will enable learners to:
- Define marketing as a part of the management process
- Describe the establishment and evolution of marketing thought
- Describe the market offering
- Indicate how to use marketing research to know the environment
- Describe the behaviour patterns of consumers
- Explain how to segment the consumer market and how objectives are chosen in the market

13.1 Introduction

A business organisation can be described as an institution of the free-market system, which attempts to satisfy the needs and wants of the community while making a **profit**. A business can also be described as a system that converts inputs, for example raw material and labour, into outputs (**products** and **services**) for society. The marketing function is that aspect of the business involved in the **marketing process**, which is the transfer of products (or services) to the market.

The marketing process consists of the following:
- Environmental scanning (by means of **marketing research**) in order to collect information on which marketing management can base sound decisions
- The development of a market offering, which consists of tangible products and intangible services, offered at a specific price and convenient place, and about which the consumer has received adequate information

During this process, marketing management, which is also responsible for the marketing process, needs to monitor competitors and develop strategies to exploit opportunities in the business environment and to counter threats, bearing in mind the organisation's strengths and weaknesses. The basis for these activities is the primary objective of ensuring the maximisation of profit over the long term.

Marketing is central: it is the bridge between a business and its environment, bringing into contact the business and its market and consumers, providing an important input in the development of the organisation's mission and strategy, and helping to correlate the resources of the market with the demands of the market. The marketing instruments, also known as the four variables, are combined with the market offering, which help consumers to decide whether they want to purchase the product, or make use of the service delivered, to satisfy their needs and wants. The marketing function is the starting point for the organisation's management functions, because top management needs to determine what can be achieved in the market before making any decisions about production facilities, employing labour, purchasing raw materials, and financing all these activities.

In this chapter the evolution of marketing thought will be discussed, a description of marketing given, and the components of the marketing process examined.

The case study below provides an insight into the marketing process.

Case study

Calculating the risks in making investment decisions

Investment decisions involve weighing up the risk and the likely rewards of various options. It is often the riskiest alternatives that yield the highest possible gains while the least risky options may yield smaller rewards. Business decision makers therefore have to weigh up risk so as to provide the most suitable rewards for stakeholders including shareholders and customers.

The starting point is a company's overall aim which then filters down into a strategy, creating a balanced portfolio made up of numerous investments. This Case Study examines the processes involved in weighing up risks in order to create a balanced portfolio at BG Group, one of the leading energy businesses in the UK. The Case Study illustrates typical stages involved in deciding whether to bid for the right to explore for and develop new gas fields and, importantly, how much to bid.

Before weighing up the risks, ethics are an integral part of BG Group's considerations – i.e. making morally correct decisions, whether these be concerned with environmental issues, health and safety or any other decision involving the difference between "right and wrong" behaviour. In other words the "best" investment decision will balance economic, social and environmental considerations.

The gas industry is today in the private and public sector and there are a number of companies competing in the industry. Some of these companies are government owned. Others are owned by private shareholders who appoint directors to represent their interest. The directors appoint professional managers to run the business. Like electricity and telecommunications, gas is a "network industry". In the case of gas, consumers are linked to a central network of gas pipelines. BG Group is an integrated business in that it has activities across the whole range of gas operations, from the reservoir to the customer. BG Group's exploration and production (E&P) business finds and develops gas reserves.

The gas business has many characteristics that are particularly important in relation to investment decision making:

It is very capital intensive so that decisions may typically involve a spend of several hundred million pounds.

There are long lead times between the start of a project and the receipt of earnings from that project, typically over five years from first investment to first revenue.

The taxation and contract structure is unique to the energy industry and is complex. Gas is a finite resource for a nation. Its exploitation is of strategic importance to the host government for some time.

Governments own the rights to minerals found on land (onshore) and under water (offshore) in their countries. Governments divide the ground into exploration "blocks" and invite energy companies to bid for the right to explore for oil and gas in those blocks. To earn the right to explore a block, the energy company commits to a work programme, which describes the steps it will take in order to find oil/gas. The energy company's investment and expertise helps governments access the mineral wealth beneath the ground. BG Group makes important decisions as to whether or not to apply for the right to explore for new gas fields and how much to bid. The overriding goal of the company is to create shareholder value. In order to achieve the optimal growth for an acceptable level of risk the company invests on a portfolio basis. This means that it will invest in a number of different wells and at times share the costs and working interest with partners in order to improve the risk/reward balance and stay within a budget. Because the returns of these individual wells are likely to be uncorrelated or weakly correlated (e.g. failure in one exploration well is unlikely to affect the chance of success of another) the risk of the overall portfolio is lower than that of an individual well. This is especially important at the exploration stage due to the high risk of failure.

The gas market is an exciting one to be involved in. The world's demand for energy is growing rapidly and it is imperative that it is supplied with clean energy reserves by principled companies. BG Group is a major world player in this market and it constantly needs to make the right sorts of investment decisions which balance the needs of global consumers, its shareholders, the communities in which it operates, governments and other stakeholders.

Source: Adapted from "Calculating the risks in making investment decisions", MBA Publishing Ltd, 2005, http://www.thetimes100.co.uk/company_list.php.

13.2 Evolution of marketing thought

Over time, managers have realised the importance of marketing. Initially management believed that contact with consumers was unimportant. However, this approach changed over the years, mostly because of pressure from consumers and an increase in competition.

Before the Industrial Revolution, households were mainly self-sufficient. Many cottage industries produced goods that were made available for barter or sale. Trade had already developed to the extent that money was regarded as acceptable tender in exchange for products. The concept of the intermediary originated when the distances between producers and the market increased and intermediaries were needed to provide services to facilitate the bartering of products, which were then offered for sale. Hawkers were the link, since they bought and sold products, using mainly donkeys and camels as transport.

During the 17th and 18th centuries in South Africa, hawkers visited farms in donkey carts and traded their goods for the farmer's products. This whole process was market driven. What could not be sold was not produced.

The technical advances of the Industrial Revolution technology created machinery capable of mass manufacturing consumer products in a relatively short time. Large factories were built to house the new machine and these necessitated some form of management. Over the years, management approaches to the marketing function changed, with different aspects being emphasised.

We shall now discuss these approaches in more detail:

- **Operation-oriented management.** Initially, instead of focusing on the needs of the market, management focused on the capabilities of the organisation. Operation-oriented organisations tried to increase the number and variety of products they produced. According to this approach, management asked questions such as, "What can we do best?", "What can our engineers design?" and "What is easy to produce, given our equipment?" In the case of service organisations, management asked, "What services are most convenient for us to offer?" and "Where do our talents lie?" Organisations that engaged in this approach were organised around product lines. A major disadvantage of operation-oriented management was that management concentrated mainly on encouraging production in order to solve operation problems. The marketing of manufactured products did not cause many problems, because consumers were largely unsophisticated and not accustomed to the consumer products that factories and newly developed modern machinery produced in mass. Moreover, it was hardly necessary to encourage these unsophisticated consumers to buy the new products – they found them

extremely desirable. Thus, marketing as a management function was undervalued.
- **Sales-oriented management.** The situation gradually changed and top management succeeded in solving the most pressing operation problems. The new machinery worked steadily, and stocks began to accumulate, which became a problem. During the period 1930–1950, management became more sales oriented in an attempt to sell these mass-produced consumer products. Misleading advertisements and unethical sales methods were employed. The objective was to sell the products at any cost. Management had to get rid of over-produced stock and did not care if consumers were exploited in the process. This led to excessive promotion and hence high advertising and sales costs. Management was compelled, in the face of increasing competition, to look for more productive marketing methods. This gave rise to the idea that products needed to be marketed instead of merely sold.
- **Marketing-oriented management.** Marketing orientation means that not only the sales message and price of the product need to be considered, but also the quality of the product, the packaging, the choice of distribution channels and the methods of informing potential consumers about the market offering. After 1950 the use of advertising became increasingly important. Management realised that advertising was an effective way of transmitting information to a mass market. Top management focused its attention on the internal organisation of the marketing function. Management also realised that all functional departments of an organisation need to work closely together to ensure the successful marketing of the organisation's products.
- **Consumer-oriented management.** As increasingly competitive consumer products became available and the financial position of consumers improved, consumer demands also started changing.

Management began to understand the importance of the consumer demand and the marketing component. It became clear that consumers' needs, demands and preferences needed to be considered when decisions were made about the quality and packaging of a product, its brand name, the type of distribution channel used, price, and the marketing communication methods used to inform potential consumers. There is no sense in producing a product if there is no demand for it. An organisation which is market driven is also consumer oriented and applies a strategic approach to marketing.

- **The strategic approach to marketing.** This is a more recent development in marketing thought. Because of continual changes in the marketing environment and the need for survival and growth of the organisation, management concentrates on scanning the environment and on long-term issues. Scanning identifies environmental changes such as technological innovation, economic influences, political factors, changing consumer preferences, demographic aspects and increasing competition. It became clear that maintaining close relationships, both internally and externally, was of increasing importance in a changing environment. This led to relationship marketing.

- **Relationship marketing.** In order to survive in the changing environment, marketing management needed to establish long-term relationships with people and institutions in the environment in which the marketing task was to be performed. A long-term relationship with customers leads to loyalty and the repeated purchase of need-satisfying products. A long-term relationship with a supplier ensures the availability of the raw materials and the inventory. This is especially important in retailing, where out-of-stock situations can inconvenience customers. The primary objective of relationship marketing is to establish and maintain relationships with loyal, profitable clients. In order to achieve this goal, management needs to focus on the attraction, retention and enhancement of its customer relationships. Loyalty is of particular importance in clients that buy the products or services of the organisation most often. Loyal consumers are not only a basis for an organisation's existing operations, but are also important to the potential growth of the organisation. Although marketing management is not responsible for negotiations with suppliers, but in the light of the close relationship between **buyers** and **sellers**, marketing management should help to establish long-term relationships through mutual cooperation. Both buyers and seller need to strive towards the same objectives. These objectives can be achieved through understanding the needs of the consumer, treating consumers as partners, ensuring that employees satisfy the needs of consumers and providing consumers with the best quality relevant to their needs. The establishment of long-term relationships between producers and intermediaries such as retailers can ensure the availability of products in the right time and place. In order to establish a favourable corporate image, the goodwill of society towards the organisation and its products must be fostered. Here, marketing management can make a considerable contribution because of its close contact with the general public. Through internal marketing, all personnel (not only those in the marketing department) need to be involved in marketing objectives and plans. Everyone needs to realise that consumer satisfaction and marketing success will be reflected in their own career opportunities and remuneration. Relationship marketing is used to good effect by market-driven organisations.

This historical review of the evolution of marketing does not point to developments in the marketing thought only in the past. Even today, many organisations are still operation or sales oriented. They are not market driven at all, and cannot hope to achieve sustainable success.

The marketing task in a market-driven organisation needs to be performed according to an ethical code or philosophy. This is closely connected to the long-term objective of corporate management. The marketing process itself often provides many opportunities for exploitation, with one participant in a transaction being enriched by taking unfair advantage of another. Many such incidents occur daily. Salespeople often make promises they cannot keep, persuading naïve people to buy their products or to invest money in dubious schemes. Soon afterwards, these salespeople (or organisations) disappear with the money, without delivering the promised product. In such cases the marketing task is not performed according to an ethical code. In fact, these examples are not marketing at all, but rather fraud. A swindle has only a short-term objective, is mainly sales oriented and has no chance of long-term survival.

Because an ethical code according to which the marketing task ought to be performed is regarded as the basis of all marketing activities and decisions, it is necessary to describe it in more detail. The ethical code is known as the marketing concept, and will be discussed in chapter 15 as part of social responsibility and business ethics.

Against this background, we shall now provide a full definition of marketing.

13.3 Defining marketing

Many people, including managers, see marketing as sales or as advertising. However, these are only parts of marketing. **Marketing** consists of management tasks and decisions directed at successfully meeting opportunities and threats in a dynamic environment, by effectively developing and transferring a need-satisfying market offering to consumers in such as way that the objectives of the business, the consumer and society will be achieved.

Table 13.1 gives an explanation of the key concepts.

13.4 The components of the marketing process

In its simplest form, the marketing process entails the transfer of a product or service from one person to another, and is as old as humankind itself. Even in the earliest societies people performed marketing activities of one kind or another. One primitive marketing process involved bartering, where, for example, people would barter meat, of which they had a surplus, for grain that another person could spare. Initially, only useful products may have been bartered. It may sometimes have happened, however, that one participant in a bartering transaction would use force to compel the other to participate in the exchange process.

In business management, marketing entails the transfer of a product from a business to consumer. The fundamentals of the marketing process can be described as needs, and a transaction or exchange that leads to the satisfaction of these needs. Every time people attempt to satisfy their needs by means of an exchange, marketing is involved. However, in contrast to primitive bartering, where force was sometimes used to compel people to participate, nowadays, in a free-market society, consumers are free to decide which products or services will best satisfy their needs and also how much money they are willing to pay for them.

Although consumers, on the one hand, cannot be compelled to sacrifice money for a product offered by a marketer, and while they are free to decide for themselves, marketers, on the other hand, use marketing strategies to persuade consumers to accept their products. Hence, in its simplest form, the marketing

Table 13.1: Key words in the definition of marketing

Mangament tasks	Planning, organising, leading, control
Decisions	Product distribution, marketing communication methods and price
Opportunities	Favourable circumstances in the marketing environment which must be utilised by marketing management
Threats	Unfavourable conditions which marketing management must endeavour to change into opportunities
Dynamic environment	Continually changing environmental variables which necessitate appropriate reaction from marketing management
Development	Creating a need-satisfying product or service
Transferring	Effectively bridging the gap between the producer and consumer
Need-satisfying	Properties of a product based on what the consumer wants
Market offering	Product, price, distribution, marketing communication and service
Attainment of objectives • The enterprise • The consumer • Society	Maximisation of profitability in the long term Need satisfaction within the limits of the resources and capacities of the enterprise Ensuring the well-being of society in the longer term

process involves transaction between at least two separate parties, one being the marketer (or organisation) attempting to achieve a specific objective, and the other being a consumer who wants to satisfy his or her needs. Figure 13.1 on page 300 illustrates this process, the details of which we shall discuss in detail. Follow the discussion while referring to the figure.

In marketing management four variables are used for decision making:
- The product itself
- The place where it is offered for sale (distribution of the product)
- The marketing communication methods used to inform consumers about the product
- The price that reflects the product's value to consumers

These four variables, which are known as marketing instruments, combine to form the **market offering** which consumers purchase to satisfy their needs. Since the 1960s, these variables have been known as the 4 Ps of the

marketing mix (product, place, promotion and price). Decisions about the use of the four Ps result in the **marketing strategy**, which is directed at specific consumers in a specific environment.

The market offering to consumers comprises a basic product with need-satisfying attributes. The price of this product, its easy availability, and the information in the marketing communication message (advertisements) all contribute to the product's value or utility. A specific market offering is not supposed to satisfy the needs of one individual only, but rather a whole group of consumers or **market segment**.

The larger the market segment, the more the organisation will benefit. In the total consumer market, there are various different groups of people or market segments. The people in each market segment share common characteristics and preferences. They also have similar consumption patterns and make similar product choices. From all the different market segments, the marketer selects a **target market** or several

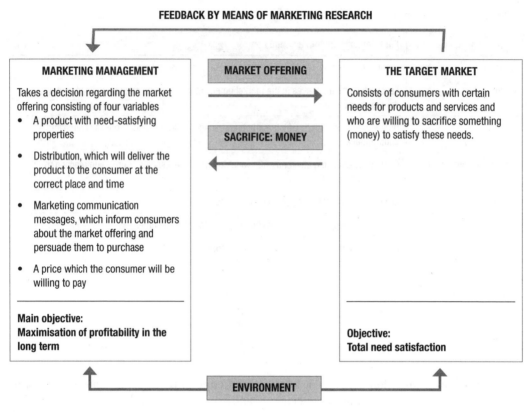

Figure 13.1: The marketing process

target markets. The market offering is often modified very slightly to meet the demands of the different target markets. It seldom happens that an organisation has only one target market.

The four decision-making variables will be discussed at length in chapter 14, while market segmentation and target market selection will be explained in this chapter.

As we stated in chapter 1, it is not possible for people to completely satisfy all their needs, because needs are unlimited (even though resources for satisfying them are not). This means that the marketer can never fully meet consumer needs, especially those that are unrealistic, such as demanding a Mercedes-Benz at the price of a Golf! The **behaviour patterns of the consumers** when attempting to satisfy unique needs, demands and preferences will be discussed in section 13.6.

Profit seeking has already been mentioned. Profit is the reason for the existence of any profit-seeking business. The marketing management of such an organisation therefore needs to strive towards this objective. This can be done by combining the four marketing instruments in an integrated marketing plan so as to maximise profits. Profitability should not only be achieved in the short term; profitability in the long term is necessary for the organisation to survive and to grow. Organisations which focus on short-term profit maximisation have a tendency to mislead or exploit consumers. To show any degree of long-term profitable growth, marketing management needs to maintain close contact with the market and to conduct market research regularly. Sometimes consumer preferences in the target market change or new competitors enter the market. Marketing management should be aware of every change that occurs, consider it carefully and then decide what to do about it.

In the business environment there are often opportunities that can be used to the organisation's benefit. There are also threats that have to be countered. By making timely changes in the four marketing instruments, marketing management can respond appropriately to opportunities and threats in the business environment. **Marketing research** (see section 13.5) is used to gain relevant information about the market, the competitors and other environmental changes. By means of marketing research, marketing management receives feedback on the market and the environment.

Look again at figure 13.1 and see the relationship between the various **components** of the marketing process. Note the direction of the arrows from the environment to marketing management and the target market. Both are influenced by environmental changes. In order to take effective decisions, marketing management needs feedback of the target market and the ever-changing environment.

The marketing process indicates a market-driven approach to marketing management, one that is a distinctive characteristic of a successful modern business. All the activities and decisions of marketing management are focused on the demands of the market. This is why marketing research is important.

Applying the concept: Marketing

If one looks at any international organisation, one can see the effect of marketing. For example, Apple will introduce the iPhone in Europe at the end of 2007. Soon after that, by means of marketing, the iPhone will arrive in South Africa, where it will be locally marketed. People in the various countries have similar needs, but there might be small differences between them, which require attention from marketing management.

13.5 Market research

13.5.1 The necessity of information

The components of the marketing environment were discussed in chapter 4, where it was shown that continuous scanning of the micro-environment, market environment and macro-environment is necessary to analyse effectively the internal strong and weak points, and the external opportunities and threats (the SWOT analysis), before managerial decisions can be taken. The following section describes how market research can be used to obtain internal and external information.

Marketing opportunities can be identified and evaluated only if the marketing environment is scanned or monitored continuously. Marketing management purposefully gather information about the external environmental variables and internal resources in the form of records and reports about, among other things, current prices, sales figures, market trends, technological changes, changes in market share, consumer preferences, new legislation, production schedules and internal financial problems. Information is then systematised and classified so that it is easily accessible to marketing management.

Note that all marketing decisions are based on information about the micro-environment, market environment and macro-environment. If a problem occurs, existing information sources are consulted. Sometimes, however, there are problems about which little or no information is available. In such cases marketing management has to search for information before decisions can be taken. This is done by means of marketing research, which reveals distinctive information that provides solutions for problems regarding marketing decisions. To ensure that managers make good decisions, the information needs to:
- Increase understanding of the relevant market segment and its consumers
- Be pertinent to planning and controlling

- Help in decision making, once alternative sources of information have been considered

Figure 13.2 indicates that marketing research includes two broad types of research, namely:
- Problem-identification research
- Problem-solving research

13.5.2 Marketing research methodology

In this section a method used to obtain primary marketing information will be discussed step by step. External ad hoc marketing research is undertaken to obtain marketing information about a specific problem in the external market environment, while internal ad hoc research is undertaken to obtain information about a problem in the internal (micro-) environment.

Marketing research can be defined as the systematic gathering, analysis and interpretation of information about all types of marketing problems by using recognised scientific methods for the accumulation of information to facilitate marketing management's decision making.

The definition of market research refers to the use of recognised scientific methods for obtaining market data. One of the most common recognised scientific methods is the **survey method**. There are other research methods that can be used, but only the survey method will be described here. This method is a good example of an ad hoc research project where the information collected concerns a specific problem in the external or internal environment.

In the survey method, a **questionnaire** is used and questions are put to respondents either by specially trained **field workers**, or telephonically or through the mail. The personal method of questioning is the most expensive and time-consuming method, because the field workers have to conduct a door-to-door survey, but it is still the best and reliable method. The results of the survey can be subjected to statistical analysis to enable the researcher to draw meaningful conclusions. If the research has been conducted in a scientific manner, then the research results may point to a solution of the marketing problem. We shall now discuss the steps in conducting a survey.
- **Step 1: Description of the problem to be investigated.** The research results will be useless unless the problem has been carefully defined.
- **Step 2: Formulation of probable explanations and causes for the defined problem.** The reasons provided are known as hypotheses. A hypothesis is a proposed explanation for the problem.

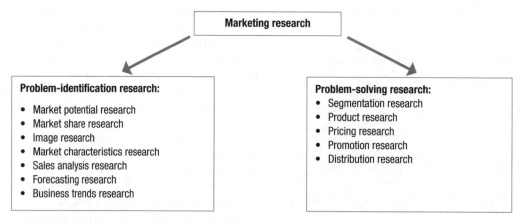

Figure 13.2: The two broad types of research in marketing research

Example

Assume that the sales for a specific product have suddenly declined. There might be various reasons for the decrease in sales figures (the problem), for example quality changes in the product itself, changes in consumer preferences, or the introduction of new and improved competitive product. These reasons (hypotheses) now need to be investigated to determine the real reason for the problem of decreasing sale figures.

- **Step 3: Investigate all the hypotheses in order to eliminate the less likely ones and to find a solution to the problem.** Secondary information sources need to be consulted, for example internal records and articles in trade journals, other marketing literature or on the Internet. The secondary data must be evaluated first in order to determine whether it can be used for the specific study. Investigation of existing secondary sources of information is known as desk research.
- **Step 4: Compilation of a questionnaire.** The compilation of a questionnaire requires skill. Each question has to be formulated carefully (involving the entire research department – often consultants and experts are called in to assist). Questions on gender,

age, origin and language of the respondent should be included. The design of the questionnaire follows these steps:
- Specify the information needed
- Specify the type of interviewing method
- Determine the content of individual questions
- Design the questions to overcome the respondent's inability and unwillingness to answer
- Decide on the structure of the questions
- Determine the wording of the questions
- Arrange the questions in order
- Identify the form and layout
- Reproduce the questionnaire
- Pretest the questionnaire
- **Step 5: Testing of the questionnaire.** The questions should be put to about ten respondents in order to determine whether the questions are clear and the answers obtained are meaningful. Errors can be eliminated and mistakes rectified if the answers are ambiguous or meaningless. All aspects of the questionnaire need to be tested, including the content of the questions, the wording, the sequence, the form and layout, and the degree of difficulty of the questions and the instructions. The respondents who participate in the testing need to be

Example

Suppose the secondary investigation (desk research) reveals that a drop in quality is probably the reason for the decline in sales. The problem can be resolved by asking the production section to maintain the quality standards that have been laid down. A primary investigation is therefore unnecessary. However, if the problem has not been solved, a survey may provide the answer.

Consider this example of the use of secondary data: Researchers need information about 13- to 18-year-old teenagers and the only information available is for the age groups 5–9, 10–14 and 15–19. The

researcher will have to convert the existing secondary data by taking two-fifths of the 10- to 14-year-old age group. Two-fifths are taken because the 13- and 14-year-old age groups form two-fifths of this category. Four-fifths of the 15- to 19-year-old age group is also used, as the 15-, 16-, 17- and 18-year-old age groups form four-fifths of the 15- to 19-year-old age group. Another instance in which secondary data can be converted is currencies: one country's currency can be converted into another country's currency. Sales figures and unit prices can also be used if numbers of units need to be determined.

Example

One of the possible hypotheses of the problem of declining sales is that consumer preferences have changed. This assumption now needs to be tested by means of relevant questions. Such questions would concern respondents' **perceptions** (do they know about the existence of the product?), **purchasing patterns** (have they ever purchased the product before?), **experiences** (were they satisfied with the product – if not, why not?), and **purchasing intentions** (do they intend to buy the product in the future?).

similar to those who will participate in the real study.

- **Step 6: Selection of the respondents to whom the questions will be put.** The selection of respondents is known as drawing a sample. It is an important step, because a biased sample leads to unreliable and invalid results. A representative sample should be selected so that every person in the target market has an equal chance of being included. For example, suppose homemakers are to be the respondents – then all the homemakers should have an equal chance of being selected. A list of all the names and addresses of the homemakers should be available to the marketer (researcher), who then randomly draws as many respondents as the size of the sample dictates. Only these homemakers are to be questioned, and the field worker has to obtain permission to substitute one name for another not included on the original list. If field workers are allowed to pick and choose, they may select only respondents who seem friendly, those who are about their own age or those whom they know personally. These answers given by such respondents will not be representative of all homemakers. As a rule, it is difficult and expensive to draw a representative sample, although this is the most reliable method. Usually a sample is

drawn according to the judgement of the researcher, decides how many respondents in each group need to be questioned. If is occurs that for some reason the answers given by such respondents are not representative, the error must be acknowledged and treated. This can be handled in three ways. Firstly, the population framework can be redesigned. Secondly, the respondents in the data set can be investigated. Thirdly, data can be adjusted by using the weighting method.

- **Step 7: Training of the field workers.** Field work is an exacting task requiring thorough training. Training ensures that all field workers understand the questionnaire in the same way. Training should cover making contact with the respondent and cover the whole process until termination of the interview. Field workers need to know how to react to possible respondents who do not want to participate in the study. Field workers should ask the questions exactly as formulated in the questionnaire, and should enter the responses correctly. Thus fieldworkers need to be reliable. If they are unreliable, they could succumb to the temptation of filling in the answers themselves, without asking real respondents. It is important to control the execution of the field work and the completed questionnaires. The head of the marketing research section can do this by contacting a few respondents to check whether the field workers have completed the questionnaires properly. Statistical techniques can be used to "catch" field workers when the analysed answers deviate from the answers on the field workers' questionnaires. Some field workers are paid more than R200 for each completed questionnaire. Very large samples increase the costs of a research project.

- **Step 8: Analysis and assimilation of information collected from the questionnaires.** A computer is usually used for this. Statistical methods can be used to facilitate the processing of information and the drawing of conclusions. Exploratory data analysis makes it possible for researchers to look at data to determine relationships and trends. Outliers and influenced observations are identified and a description and summary of the data set are given. Statistics cover the determination of population values which are based on the test values through the construction of confidence intervals and statistical hypothesis testing. Most of the research houses use more specialised programmes, such as SPSS, SAS or Statistica, for exploratory and inferential statistical analysis. These methods also include determining the mean, percentages, confidence intervals, regression and variance analysis.

- **Step 9: Interpretation of the information.** The researcher needs to decide which data to include in the research report. In the example we have been discussing, the information would show the reasons for the decline in sales. The initial hypothesis needs to be proved or disproved. The researcher interprets the reasons and draws meaningful conclusions.

- **Step 10: Writing of the research report and making of recommendations based on the conclusions.** The research report "tells the story" of the research project, gives the method used, and presents the collected information in tables, figures and graphs. It should not only be a summary of statistical results, but should be presented so that it can be used as direct information for management decisions. A conclusion and possible recommendations can be made from the information. Before writing the report, the researcher needs to discuss the important results, conclusions and recommendations with the decision makers. This will ensure that the final report satisfies the needs of the consumer. When the report is complete and has been presented to marketing management, the research team's task is complete.

Example

Suppose the research shows that 70% of the respondents drew negative comparison between the organisation's product and the product of a competitor. Further, 80% of the respondents' indicated that they did not intend to purchase the product. It is easy to draw the conclusion that there is something wrong with the product compared to its competitor. However, it is more difficult to make a recommendation. Should the product be withdrawn or should it be improved? If it is improved, who is to say that the improvement will be to consumers' liking? If the questionnaire has been properly compiled, the analysis will provide answers to these questions.

- **Step 11: Marketing management (and top management too, perhaps) studies the report and makes decisions.** Management must either accept or reject the recommendations.

Example

Suppose that marketing management has considered the research report and decided to accept the recommendation to improve the product. The purchasing and operation departments need to be informed about the proposed improvements (for example, if they require different raw materials or operation methods). Marketing management has to launch a campaign to inform consumers about the "new" product. Decisions need to be taken about the price, for example the announcement of a price discount for a period of one month after the announcement occurs. Old labels will not be used any more; new labels with information about the improvements need to be designed and printed.

- **Step 12: Implementation of management's decisions.** This is the final step which, it is hoped, will lead to the solution of the problem of declining sales.

After a period, a further research project will need to be undertaken to determine whether or not the decisions taken and implemented were indeed correct.

The examples we have discussed entailed a survey of consumer demands and preferences. Marketing research can be done in more or less the same way to investigate problems with dealers, competitors and suppliers. An internal survey can also be conducted to determine the opinions of the personnel of the organisation. Sale representatives, for example, could be chosen as respondents.

13.5.3 Market forecasting

When a marketing opportunity has been identified, its extent has to be measured in order to determine expected future profits. Measuring the size of the opportunity entails the forecasting of future sales (sales forecasting) and the forecasting of the contribution to profit.

13.5.3.1 Sales forecasting

The following types of forecasting are often used:
- Forecasting done by a panel of experts from within the organisation and from outside
- Forecasting based on market research results – the number of potential consumers who have indicated that they want to buy the product could serve as a basis for the sales forecast for the next period
- Forecasting based on the consumers' reactions in test marketing situations
- Forecasting based on historical data (the previous year's sales figures could serve as the starting point)
- Forecasting based on mathematical and statistical models (for example probability models)

A combination of sales forecasting methods is often employed in practice. It is difficult to make reliable sales forecasts because no one can see into the future. It is nevertheless the task of marketing management to forecast not only future sales but also how uncontrollable environmental variables will influence the sales figures. If reliable sales figures are available, financing, purchasing, operation and inventory decisions can be taken in good time. If this is not possible, the market share or profit position of the organisation may be harmed. There is even a danger that the organisation may not be able to survive.

13.5.3.2 Forecasting of the profit contribution

The forecasting of the profit contribution of a marketing opportunity is normally done for long-term periods: for the full payback period (the time taken to recoup capital expenses incurred in producing a product). During the payback period, the sum of money invested in utilising an opportunity has to be recovered through the earnings generated by sales. The payback amounts include the rate of return decided on at the outset by top management.

The financial aspects of forecasting the profit contribution are discussed in the chapters on financial management.

Because not all consumers are the same, and they are unpredictable, it is important to study **consumer behaviour**.

Applying the concept: Marketing research

Companies constantly engage in market research. Before deciding to invest vast sums of money in a new motor vehicle, a company such as BMW will do market research on every aspect of the proposed vehicle. The shape, engine size, features, styling and so on will all be researched in the market to ensure that it meets consumer demands. Various methods will be employed to obtain information, and various reference groups consulted.

Critical thinking

When they think of marketing research, most people think about face-to-face interviews, telephone interviews and surveys. Marketing research can be applied to any industry in order to improve service delivery, increase the level of customer satisfaction, understand the behaviour of consumers, and appreciate individual and group factors. Consider how the following excerpt shows the importance of marketing research.

The importance of excellent customer service

With a proven track record in supplying the highest quality accommodation, Portakabin hires and sells permanent and relocatable buildings. Clients include hospitals and schools, government ministries, universities and major business players such as Sony, Vodafone and Tesco. Its mission statement, as stated on its website, is:"To provide peace of mind for our customers across Europe through quality buildings and services". It is the leading brand in this market with 16% of the UK market.

The field in which Portakabin operates is highly competitive with strong players. Portakabin therefore has to work hard to stay market leader, and maintains its position by making sure it has quality products and customer service. It has built a premium brand, based on a good reputation of providing high quality products and excellent service levels. If a company wants to be a leader in its sector it must exceed the minimal requirements, to differentiate itself from its competitors. It has the expertise and resources to deliver modern, attractive buildings quickly, efficiently and exactly to the needs of the client.

This [critical thinking feature] focuses on how Portakabin keeps its competitive edge by making sure it provides not just good, but excellent, customer service.

The company's motto is "Quality – this time, next time, every time" and this is applied as much to its customer service levels as it is to the products it provides. A business cannot exist unless it has customers to buy the products it wants to sell. Customer service is the term used to describe what happens at the points at which the customer comes into contact with the business at Portakabin. Customer service is key during the process of buying or hiring a building, from a single office building to a complete school or medical centre. The importance of good customer service can be seen at all stages, beginning with the initial customer's enquiry, followed by a quotation and the drawing up of contracts.

It continues with the delivery of the product and the after-sales service. Portakabin has unique Customer Charters for its sales and hire customers. These set out, in detail, the high levels of service that customers can expect. These include:

- Completion of every project on time and to the agreed contract sum
- A service response within 24 hours from the customer services team
- Picking up the phone within four "rings" – and by a person, not an automated system
- A response or visit within 24 hours of a request
- To be included in the customer care programme

It is important for Portakabin to find out what inspires loyalty in its customers so it can encourage them to remain so. One way is to see how many are willing to come back for repeat purchases, but it is also vital to know why they return. This is the reason Portakabin carries out thorough market research.

Market research is the collection of data that can be used to see how well a business is doing in its chosen market. This can be collected through primary research or secondary research and can be either qualitative or quantitative.

Quantitative data was supplied when Portakabin surveyed its loyal customers to find out what factors distinguished the company. Most clients (53%) said the top factor was the experience.

This related to how the customer felt he or she was treated during the process of hiring or buying a Portakabin building. Value was the most important aspect to 34% of clients, while just 13% thought that product was vital – this is because they had come to expect top quality buildings from Portakabin as a given. They were therefore most impressed by the level of personal interaction with staff and with the overall level of support they received. Over the past four years, Portakabin has carried out a customer satisfaction interview with the vast majority of its clients. This asks questions on all aspects of customer service and records scores on a scale of 1–10 (where 1 is very poor and 10 is excellent).

Questions are asked in four categories:

- Customer experience with sales and administration – the company's response to an enquiry, the level of service received, the speed of a response and how clearly information was presented

- Delivery and installation – the service provided by the installation team and the haulier
- The building itself – whether it was clean and fault-free on delivery and if not, what steps were taken to put things right
- The client's overall impression of the service – the courtesy and technical knowledge of Portakabin staff, value for money and whether they received "peace of mind".

The scale of responses provides quantitative data, showing how well the company is doing in each area. Across all questions, it has improved in four years from an average score of 8.2 to 9. Portakabin uses the individual responses to spot extremely good service so staff can be appropriately praised. It also uses the results to quickly tackle problems should they arise.

Source: Adapted from "The importance of excellent customer service", 2005, http://www.thetimes100.co.uk/case_study.php?cID=35&csID=235&pID=5 (9 March 2007).

13.6 Consumer behaviour

Consumer behaviour refers to the behaviour patterns of decision-making units (individuals or families) directly involved in the purchase and use of products, including the decision-making processes preceding and determining these behaviour patterns. From this definition it is clear that consumer behaviour consists of **overt acts**, on the one hand, that is, acts that can be observed by people. A consumer can be seen buying a product, enjoy it, looking at, placing it back on the shelf or throwing it away unused. On the other hand, consumer behaviour also includes **covert processes**, which cannot been seen. A consumer cannot be seen considering his or her financial position, weighing the merits of different branded products, or doubting the promises made in advertising appeals. Marketers need to know why consumers behave as they do, because consumer behaviour can then be **explained, influenced** and **predicted.**

Knowledge of the factors that determine consumer behaviour forms the basis for consumer-oriented marketing strategies.

We shall now give attention to the determinants of consumer behaviour, that is, those factors that may explain consumer behaviour. We shall also look at the decision-making process and the continual changes in the behaviour patterns of consumers.

A consumer receives inputs (stimuli) from his or her environment. The outputs are what happen – the consumer's actions as observable results of the input stimuli. Between the inputs and outputs are the constructs: the processes though which the consumer goes to decide upon his or her actions.

Figure 13.3 illustrates a model that can be used to explain consumer behaviour. **Individual factors** and **group factors** influence consumer decision making, and may eventually lead to repeat purchasing of a specific market offering.

13.6.1 **Determinants of consumer behaviour**

Two main group of factors (determinants) determine consumer behaviour, namely:

- Individual factors peculiar to a particular person
- Group factors

Individual decision making is usually straight-forward. Decision making by a buying centre requires consideration of the different roles of members of the buying centre, differing interpretations of objectives, interpersonal influences, relative power, and the need for some resolution of possible conflicts among members of the buying group.

13.6.1.1 **Individual factors**

Needs, attitudes, perception, learning abilities and personal traits are individual factors that determine what a consumer will or will not buy. Needs (also called motives) are the driving force behind all behaviour patterns. Maslow's hierarchy of needs was discussed in chapter 10, where it was shown that people's behaviour patterns are directed at the satisfaction of basic survival, security, social and ego needs.

Consumers buy bread, for instance, to satisfy a basic **survival** need, namely hunger. They buy insurance to satisfy the need for **security**. They might buy flowers to fulfil their **social** need for love. They might buy expensive cars as a status symbol to provide some

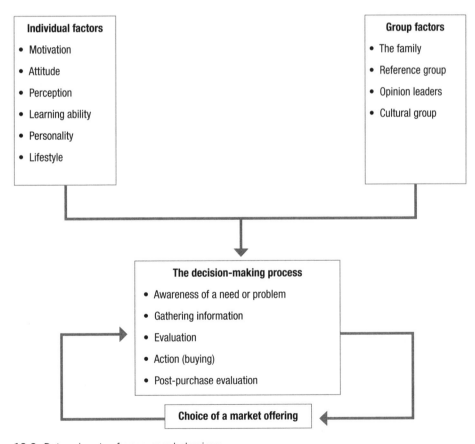

Figure 13.3: Determinants of consumer behaviour

measure of **ego** satisfaction. And they might focus on hobbies to satisfy the need for self-realisation. Maslow maintained that people attempt to satisfy their needs in a specific hierarchical sequence – the basic needs have to be satisfied before others can be attended to.

People's needs are unlimited, and they never reach a point where all their needs are met. This is why consumers keep buying, even if they already have more possessions than they can use. Advertisements attempt to draw people's attention to unsatisfied needs that can be met by buying a specific product. Although the needs are universal (that is, they apply to all people) need patterns differ from person to person. An asocial person does not have as many social needs as, for example, a very social person. People's needs determine what they decide to buy and what not to buy.

Attitudes also determine purchasing patterns. A consumer with a positive attitude towards a particular product can perhaps be persuaded to buy the product, whereas a person with a negative attitude will not buy the product. For example, a mother with a positive attitude towards healthy food might be persuaded to buy margarine with extra vitamins for her children. Conversely, a teetotaller has a negative attitude towards alcoholic beverages, and therefore he or she will not react positively towards advertisements for them. It follows that marketers need to make every effort to prevent the development of negative attitudes towards their market offerings. Once a consumer has decided to avoid a particular product because it was faulty, too expensive, of bad quality or had the wrong taste, the consumer's negative attitude will not change easily. Marketers can, however, try to reinforce existing positive attitudes or to turn neutral attitudes into positive attitudes through their marketing communication messages.

Consumers' **perceptions** determine what they pay attention to and what excites their interest. Consumers hear only those things that they want to hear and see only what captures their interest. This means that they subconsciously choose whether to pay attention to a marketing message or not. Furthermore, consumers' perceptions can cause them to attach their own interpretation to a message, which may not be quite what the marketer intended. Consumers seem able to defend or protect themselves against the content of communication in which they are not interested. For this reason marketers sometimes find it difficult to convey a message in such as way that the person receiving it understands. Marketers should bear this in mind when creating marketing messages. Thus an advertisement needs to be simple to ensure understanding of the message, it should have some impact to attract attention, and it must contain a promise of need satisfaction, or else consumers could distort the message or ignore it completely.

The **learning ability** of consumers determines whether they are able to learn the marketer's "lesson" about the benefits of a particular product that make it worth paying for. Further, the marketer should "teach" consumers the product's name in such as way that they remember it. Sometimes consumers forget the name of the product they intend to purchase, but they are still able to remember the characteristics of the packaging. This points to the importance of packaging. Reminder advertising, which shows only the name of the product in distinctive lettering, helps to remind consumers of what they have learned from the marketer.

Personality traits also influence consumers' purchasing patterns. People are described by means of these traits, for example, as cheerful, optimistic, or aggressive. It is difficult to relate personal characteristics to product choice. Usually people's traits, in conjunction with other characteristics, determine what they buy and use. As a rule, a combination of people's personality traits and other characteristics determine their **lifestyle**. Different groups have different lifestyles. The lifestyle of students, for example, differs from that of families, and the lifestyle of farmers differs from that of people in the city. Lifestyle classification can be used to segment the consumer market. We shall discuss market segmentation in section 13.7.

13.6.1.2 Group factors

Group factors refer to the influence of various groups on consumer purchasing patterns. These groups include the following:

(a) The family

Children learn their consumer function in their families. At seven, a child already understands that his or her needs can be satisfied by a process of purchase and consumption.

The family is also a decision-making unit whose members decide about purchasing products that will provide the greatest degree of need satisfaction for the family as a whole. Family members have certain roles. One member may be the buyer (perhaps the mother), another the decision maker (the father, possibly), while yet another (a child) may be the consumer. Marketers need to know the role structure of families in their target market, because the marketing message needs to be based on such knowledge. A marketer of breakfast cereal, for example, appeals to the child who could be the decision maker for this product. Children also play a role in family decision making by acting as initiators and making suggestions about products of which their parents may know little. For example, boys often know more than their parents about how to use a camera or video recorder, while teenage girls are knowledgeable about the cosmetics their parents might use.

(b) Reference groups

A **reference group** is any group against which people can evaluate their own behaviour (and purchasing patterns). Most people want to be part of some group or other and in order to gain acceptance maintain the habits and purchasing patterns of the group. A circle of friends, a social club and a work group are examples of reference groups. Often, people who do not conform to group norms are ignored, or held in contempt or ridiculed. For example, a teenage boy who does not own a motorbike cannot become a member of a biker group. A person who wants to become a member of a tennis club should not only be able to play tennis, but also needs to buy tennis outfits, a racquet, balls, socks and shoes.

Advertisements often portray group approval to attract the attention of those striving to gain acceptance and group membership. For example, an advertisement for a car could show friends and neighbours admiring the car, with a house in the background reflecting an upmarket neighbourhood. The implications of this is that the buyer of the car will automatically gain the acceptance in a wealthy neighbourhood. There are, however, also negative groups with which association is undesirable. Conservative, older and the highly educated people, for example, often see skinheads and bikers as negative groups, and therefore disapprove of everything they do or purchase. Choosing a particular reference group to portray in an advertisement is difficult, because what one person may regard as a positive group with which to be associated may well be regarded as negative by another.

There is a strong relationship between reference group influence and the choice of luxury products, but the relationship is rather weak in the case of necessities. However, if the product is visible, the relationship is stronger. A good example is detergent. As many advertisements suggest, a user of detergent can be easily influenced by the "expert" advice of other, more experienced users.

(c) Opinion leaders

They have an important function in the marketing communication process, acting as a go-between in what is known as the two-step flow of communication. Research has shown that information does not flow directly from the mass media to individual consumers in the target market, but is channelled through a person, the **opinion leader**. This person interprets and evaluates the information, and then relays acceptance or rejection of the message to other consumers in the market.

The role of the opinion leader is especially important in the purchasing of new products that have a high risk of financial loss. In the case of a new fashion, for example, a fashion opinion leader will accept the risk of ridicule or financial loss, which ordinary consumers are usually anxious to avoid. Ordinary consumers usually only become interested after the new fashion has been vetted and approved by the opinion leader. Sports stars often act as opinion leaders in advertisements for sports equipment, reducing the risk of poor decision making when an ordinary consumer makes the purchase.

Every consumer is a member of various reference groups and could be an opinion leader for a certain product while being a follower for another. It is a task of marketing management to identify the opinion leader and reference group which will ensure the accceptance of its advertising message in a specific target market.

(d) Culture group

The cultural group to which a person belongs has a strong influence on his or her purchasing and consumption patterns. Culture comprises a complex system of values, norms and symbols, which develop in a society over time and which are shared by the society's members. Cultural values, norms and symbols are created by people and transmitted from generation to generation to ensure survival and facilitate adaptation to circumstances. Schools, churches and other social institutions also play an important role (this process is referred to as socialisation).

Each cultural group comprises several subcultures, each with its own values, norms and symbols. There are four key subcultures, categorised according to nationality, religion, race and geographical area. Besides the four main groups, smaller subcultures can also develop, perhaps according to language, age, interests or occupation.

South African society consists of many cultural groups and subgroups. Although white people are not numerically dominant, their norms, values and symbols exert great influence on the economic environment. For this reason most advertisements reflect Western culture.

13.6.2 Consumer decision making

Every decision a consumer takes involves risks. The risks are often functional. If the products are deficient or do not work as the consumer expected them to, the consumer feels that he or she has wasted money. There are also social risks involved in decision making. If the reference group does not approve of the purchase, the consumer may be ridiculed. To reduce the risks inherence in decision making, consumers may wait a long time before taking a decision, thereby extending the decision-making process. During this time, and during all the phases of decision making, marketers attempt on more than one occasion to influence consumers to decide in favour of their market offering.

In any organisational buying decision there are four influences:

- The environment
- The organisation itself
- The buying group
- The individual buyer

Environmental influences include the techno-logical state of the buyer's industry, the state of the economy, government regulations, and legal and cultural factors. These factors influence the organisational climate. Group influences are broken down into task-related interactions and no-task interactions (personal motives). An individual's motives, perceptions, personality, and role within the organisation influence his or her interactions within a buying centre and thus influence the final decision process.

Applying the concept: Consumer decision making

When buying any product, consumers move through various steps in their decision making. People do not wake up one morning and suddenly decide to buy a new house. There must be a need or reason to do so. It may be that their house is too small or the neighbourhood has declined, for example.

Once the need has been identified, information must be gathered. This may be done by talking to friends, to estate agents from various estate agencies, and looking through newspapers. As soon as all the necessary information has been gathered, it is evaluated according to criteria that are important to the buyer. Price, area (location), distance from schools or shops, and so on, may be of importance.

The consumer may decide, for example on a security estate, as this offers more protection, and then proceed to buy such a property. It is possible that after the house has been bought, the buyer may wonder if it was the right thing to do (post-purchase evaluation). Marketers must be aware of the steps a buyer goes through, and address them in their marketing campaign.

When making a complex decision – regarding, for example high-priced products, complex products and specialty goods – consumers evaluate brands in a detailed and comprehensive way. More information is sought and more brands are evaluated than is the case in other types of decision-making situation. Marketing management needs to know how consumer decisions are reached, because consumer behaviour almost always entails a choice between alternatives. Marketers want to influence the decisions of the consumer. Consumer decisions are not made

suddenly – the process of decision making progresses systematically through various phases. Figure 13.3 (page 309), shows the five phases.

- **Phase 1: Awareness of an unsatisfied need or a problem.** A consumer experiences a difference between the current situation and the situation which he or she desires. This leads to the seeking of a solution to this problem. For example, an empty or broken container indicates a consumer need, and a leaking pen may indicate a need to buy a new one. marketers try, by means of advertising, to make consumers aware of problems and unsatisfied needs.
- **Phase 2: Gathering of information on how best to solve the problem.** Consumers recall information or collect relevant information from external sources. They consult friends, read advertisements or visit shops to obtain more information. Marketers must make sure that the necessary information is available.
- **Phase 3: Evaluation of the possible solutions.** This happens using criteria such as price, quality, performance standards, ethical characteristics, aesthetic qualities, as consumers gauge the contribution the product will make to need satisfaction and their lifestyle. Conflict is caused by conflicting or unsuitable criteria or criteria that cannot be easily compared. Advertisements therefore need to emphasise the benefits and utility of the product. For example, many pen advertisements reflect neatness, continuous writing, and style – all characteristics important for a consumer buying a pen. The provision of samples that can be used to test the product, a money-back guarantee, or a quality mark – such as the mark of the South African Bureau of Standards (SABS) – can help consumers resolve conflict.
- **Phase 4: Decision on a course of action or purchase.** Although consumers might indicate intent to buy a product, this does not mean that they will in fact do so.

Therefore advertisements encourage the consumer to act and purchase the product, for example by using an injunction such as "BUY NOW!". When consumers act and buy the product, this entails a sacrifice (money must be paid). The transaction should therefore be concluded as "painlessly" as possible. Consumers forced to queue to pay, or who come into contact with uninterested sales staff, can easily decide to reverse their decision to buy the product. When a consumer has made the decision to buy and is ready to pay, marketers should make a special effort to ensure their goodwill. Helpful sales staff, credit facilities and point of purchase promotions all help to encourage the purchasing action.

• **Phase 5: Post-purchase evaluation.** In this phase consumers evaluate purchases, by using them and testing whether or not they will satisfy their needs. Consumers might wonder whether they have made the right decision. If a product does not provide the satisfaction consumers expect, they may decide not to buy the product again and might influence friends to avoid it. Advertisements are often directed at people who have already purchased a product, in order to reassure them that they have indeed made the right decision.

In the case of expensive or important products (for example a house), decision making can sometimes be a long and arduous process. A person could take months to decide which type of washing machine to buy. however, in the case of impulse buying, the decision-making process, through all its phases, can be over in the wink of an eye. Habitual purchasing is the result of previous decisions. For consumers loyal to a particular brand, it may become a habit to purchase the product consistently without having to make the decision again every time. The conclusion to be drawn is that the theory of consumer behaviour, as it has been described briefly here, is **explanatory** to some extent. it provides guidelines for influencing consumers, for example through striking advertisements. However, because of many influencing factors, is it virtually impossible to predict the behaviour of consumers. Marketers nevertheless attempt to do so, because market forecasting depends largely on such prediction.

Marketing management will probably never satisfy all the needs, demands and preferences of the market. Therefore the market strategy should be directed only at those groups (market segments) that are profitable and accessible.

13.7 **Market segmentation**

No organisation can satisfy all the needs of all consumers (the market). It is therefore important that an organisation focuses on some groups or segments in order to satisfy their needs. The term "market" means different things to different people. In brief, the market consists of a relatively large number of people (or organisations) who:

• Have a need for a specific product
• Are able to buy it
• Are willing to spend money on it
• Are allowed to do so

All these requirements need to be met before the term "market" can be used. For example, teenagers under the age of 18 may perceive that they have a need for alcoholic beverages. They might even have enough money to buy these products, but because legislation forbids them to buy liquor, they are not allowed to buy these alcoholic beverages. Hence marketers cannot consider teenagers younger than 18 years old as a distinct "market" for alcoholic products.

The total market in a country can be subdivided into consumer, industrial, resale and government markets:

• The **consumer market** consists of individuals or households purchasing products for their own consumption.
• The **industrial market** consists of indivi-

duals, groups of people, or organisations purchasing materials and products to be used in the production process.

- The **resale market** includes individuals, groups or organisations purchasing products in order to sell the to final consumers, for example retailers.
- The **government market** consists of the state institutions and departments which purchase various products needed to supply services to the public.

In the discussion of the marketing function in this book, attention is focused mainly on the **consumer market**, although the principles of marketing are applicable to the other markets. In industrial marketing, though, personal selling is more important than advertising, which is the most effective way of communicating with the consumer market, but one that is seldom used in the government market.

The consumer market can be subdivided into many different types of market, such as a market for vehicles, a market for baby products, and a market for food. Consumers are, according to their needs, members of various markets. The family consisting of parents and children might not form part of the furniture market, because this family probably already has furniture and might prefer to spend its income on articles such as clothes, education, books, sporting equipment, musical instruments and DVDs. Young couples with toddlers and young school-going children are not usually part of the overseas tourist market, because, even if they have enough money to visit other countries, their family responsibilities could keep them at home. Each separate market for a specific product can further be subdivided into segments. Not all people want to purchase the same type of clothing, vehicles or books.

Effective market segmentation should follow five steps, namely:

- Identify the needs profile of the consumer population at the individual level
- Group the consumers into homogeneous subgroups or segments based on their needs profile
- Identify factors correlated with the needs-based subgroups or segments of the market
- Select target markets
- Position the product or service offering within the selected segment or segments

13.7.1 The total market approach (market aggregation)

According to this approach marketing management assumes that potential consumers have similar preferences and needs regarding the market offering, which may therefore be the same for all consumers. This uniform approach is followed in marketing staples such as salt, sugar and flour, because virtually everyone requires these products and wants them in more or less standard packaging.

Market aggregation is, however, more the exception than the rule – even in the case of staples it is not always applicable. Premier Milling, for example, markets different kinds of Snowflake flour in packs with different colours. Even though it would be cost effective to have one product, one type of packaging, one price, one distribution channel and one marketing message directed at the mass market, it is seldom possible to do so, because the market is not homogeneous. People are not the same and have different needs.

It is therefore to the advantage of the marketer to try to satisfy the divergent needs of the specific market segments rather than provide only some measure of satisfaction to everyone in the total market.

13.7.2 The market segmentation approach

Market segmentation, as was stated previously, refers to the process in which the total heterogeneous market is divided into smaller, more homogeneous groups with relatively uniform needs or characteristics. Attempts are made to satisfy the needs of different homogeneous groups by developing different market offerings. Marketing management can, on the one hand, follow a multisegment approach, whereby many different segments are served with some basic product or with small product modifications; it can also, on the other hand, select only one segment and concentrate its marketing effort on that.

Figure 13.4 illustrates the three approaches to market segmentation, namely:

- The total market approach (market aggregation)
- A single-segment approach
- A multisegment approach

Approach (1) in figure 13.4 shows that mar-

keting management concentrates on only one market offering aimed at the total market. Approach (2) shows that marketing management selects a specific target market and aims its market offering only at it, and pays no attention to other segments of the market. Approach (3) shows that three separate market offerings are made to three different target markets. One should bear in mind the fact that any changes, however small, in the product itself (for example, in packaging), price, distribution channel or marketing communication methods or messages, mean that a different market offering is being made.

The marketer of Johnson's baby products identified, in addition to people with babies, women and sportsmen as separate market segment. Even though the baby powder is sold

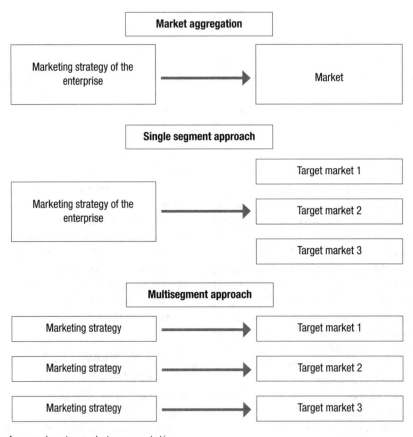

Figure 13.4: Approaches to market segmentation

in the same packaging and at the same price to all of three market segments, the marketing messages differ greatly. In reality this means that three different market offerings are being made to three separate market segments. If the product is intended for babies, the advertisement shows a mother lovingly caring for a baby. When it is intended for sportsmen or women, the advertisements show models with whom adults can identify. In these cases the models act as opinion leaders.

Even when marketing management has succeeded in identifying a promising segment of the market, it does not necessarily follow that a market offering will be developed for that segment. Certain requirements have to be satisfied before marketing management can claim a segment as a target market.

13.7.3 Requirements for meaningful market segmentation

To be useful, a segment must meet the following criteria:

- **Identifiability and measurability.** It must be possible to identify the segments and measure their size. Data about provinces, sex, age, etc. are readily available, but data on people who are prepared to test a new medical product are not.
- **Substantialness.** The segment should be large enough to make profitable exploitation possible. In South Africa, because of the fragmented population, various different small market segments can be distinguished. Some of these segments are, however, so small that it would not be profitable to develop separate market offerings for them all.
- **Approachability.** It should be possible for marketing management to reach its chosen segment. How can marketers reach such segments as black women in rural areas, who do not read magazines or listen to the radio, or older people with hearing and vision problems?
- **Responsiveness.** For a segment to be cultivated, it needs to be receptive to a

separate approach. If all the consumers are equally conscious of a product, there is no need offer high, medium and low prices to different segments.

When marketing management is satisfied that the above-mentioned requirements have been met with regard to a particular market segment, it can select this segment as a target market. A target market is a specific segment for which marketing management can develop and implement a marketing strategy. The question to be answered now is "How does marketing management isolate the factors or criteria according to which homogeneous groups in the total consumer market are to be distinguished?" Several of these criteria have already been mentioned – for example age and language.

13.7.4 Criteria for market segmentation

The total market can be **segmented** into different groups according to a variety of criteria, as shown in table 13.2 on page 318.

Segmenting the market according to demographic and geographic criteria usually gives a good indication of the potential of particular market segments, that is, the number of consumers in each segment. Segmentation according the psychographic and product usage criteria gives an indication of the reasons for consumers' choice and purchase of specific products. Each of these criteria merits further scrutiny.

13.7.4.1 Demographic criteria

Marketers often segment the market according to **demographic** criteria, as the information is easily obtainable. For example, it is easy to determine how many students are registered for this course, and therefore how large the potential market is for this book.

The other demographic variables mentioned in table 13.2 are self-explanatory and therefore will not be discussed separately.

Table 13.2: Criteria (bases) for segmenting consumer markets

Bases	Possible variables
1. Geographic	
Region	Gauteng, Durban-Pinetown, Cape Peninsula, KwaZulu-Natal, Northern Province
Size of city or town	Under 10 000, 10 000–20 000, 20 000–25 000, over 25 000 inhabitants
Density	Urban, suburban, rural
Climate	Summer rainfall, winter rainfall, very hot and humid, very hot and dry
2. Demographical	
Age	Under 7, 7–13, 14–19, 20–34, 35–49, 50–65, above 65 years
Gender	Male, female
Family size	1 and 2, 3 and 4, more than 4 members
Family life cycle	Young, married without children; young, married with children; older, married with children; married couples without children living at home; singles
Income	Under R20 000, R20 001–R50 000, R50 001–R80 000, R80 001–R110 000, R110 001–R140 000, R14 001–R170 000, over R170 000
Occupation	Professional and technical, managerial, clerical, sales and related services, farmers, students, housewives, unemployed, retired
Religion	Protestant, Catholic, Muslim, Hindu, Jewish
Race	White, black, coloured, Asian
Education	Gr. 10, matric, diploma, degree, postgraduate
3. Psychographic	
Lifestyle	Conservative, liberal
Personality	Gregarious, authoritarian, impulsive, ambitious
Social class	Upper class, middle class, lower class
4. Behavioural	
Purchase occasion	Regular use, special occasion
Benefits sought	Economy, convenience, prestige, speed, service
User status	Non-user, ex-user, potential user, regular user
Usage rate	Heavy user, medium user, light user
Loyality status	None, medium, strong, absolute
Readiness stage	Unaware, aware, informed, interested, desirous, intending to buy
Attitude to product	Enthusiastic, positive, indifferent, negative, hostile

Source: Strydom, J.W., Cant, M.C. and Jooste, C.J., conculting editor Van der Walt, A., *Marketing management*, 4th edition, Juta, Cape Town, 2000, p. 107.

13.7.4.2 **Geographic criteria**

Geographic criteria relate to place of residence. Geographic factors result in the development of different need patterns, thereby affording marketers opportunities they can use.

13.7.4.3 Psychographic criteria

Table 13.2 shows the main **psychographic** variables according to which markets can be segmented. The main variables in this group are personality factors and lifestyles.

Personality traits are difficult to quantify, but they nevertheless offer opportunities to marketing management for market segmentation.

Aggressiveness, conservatism, optimism, progressiveness and materialism are examples of personality traits of individuals. Marketers know that these traits are related to product and brand selection. Many advertisements aimed at men, for example, contain elements of aggressiveness to capture their attention, because they tend to be more aggressive than women. Lifestyle segmentation comprises a group of characteristics known as the AIO classification (activities, interests and opinions of the consumers).

13.7.4.4 Behavioural criteria

Table 13.2 shows the behavioural criteria according to which the consumer market can be segmented. **Product usage** refers to the way in which products are used by different consumers. Consumers can be light, medium or heavy users of a product, and they can be existing or potential consumers. Teetotallers are non-users of liquor, and all attempts by a marketer to persuade this group to become users will be to no avail. However, marketers often attempt to persuade light and medium consumers of a specific product to purchase more of the product. A good example is potato chips, which were initially seen as a snack for consumption at social events. However, consumers are now encouraged to eat them at any time of the day, even during ordinary meals.

Brand loyalty is a behavioural criterion that is encouraged by marketers, because when consumers are loyal to a particular brand, the competitive position of the marketer is strengthened. Brand-loyal consumers buy products that have provided need satisfaction previously, and they do not think twice about doing so. Black consumers tend to be more brand loyal than white consumers. The following brands enjoy considerable loyalty from many black consumers: Iwisa, Lion, Jordan shoes and Castle Lager. Brand loyalty develops only if a product provides such complete needs satisfaction that the consumer never even considers competing products.

Some consumers are extremely **price sensitive**, and can be persuaded to buy a product by means of small decreases in price. These consumers are always on the lookout for discount shops and like to bargain. Most wealthy consumers are not so price sensitive: they will usually purchase what they need and are averse to shopping around for bargains or sales.

Reverse price sensitivity means that consumers react negatively when a price is perceived to be too low. They immediately conclude that the cheap product lacks quality, and they therefore associate high prices with good quality and low prices with poor quality. If prices are reduced, these consumers buy less instead of more. Consumers can also be sensitive to service, quality and advertisements. The advertisement promising "You are Number 1" is directed at consumers sensitive to service quality, while the "Quest for Zero Defect" points to quality excellence for quality-sensitive buyers. Other consumers are sensitive to advertising, and respond immediately when an advertisement attracts their attention. They are ready to buy if they perceive the message as promising.

The total potential market for a product can also be subdivided in segments according to the benefits a product is thought to offer, as shown in the accompanying box on the next page.

Product benefits of a deodorant

The product benefits that a consumer expects from a deodorant might include:

- Fresh smell
- Long duration
- Social acceptance
- Dryness
- Safety (does not irritate the skin)
- Ease of use
- Effective

Applying the concept: Market segmentation

Volkswagen SA has segmented the market for its passenger vehicles into various categories. The CitiGolf is aimed at the small economy car segment, while the Playa is aimed at the medium-sized car market, as is the Jetta.

The Audi A3 is aimed at the exotic or sports car market. The larger Audi is aimed at the family or luxury car segment. Different strategies are required to market these cars.

The market for margarine is also segmented according to **product benefits**. Some people use margarine for a healthier life, others for its low cholesterol content, for its vitamins, as a slimmer, or as a substitute for butter. Some marketers follow a multisegment approach and promise all the benefits listed above. According to their advertisements, their margarine not only slims, but also prevents cholesterol and tastes pleasant.

Criteria are often combined to define a **segment profile**.

13.7.5 Segment profiles

Demographic, geographic and usage criteria together provide a profile of a specific segment, as shown in the example in the box below.

Profile of Rooibos tea consumer

The consumers of Rooibos tea can be divided into two groups, namely primary and secondary group. The primary group is black (all income groups) in the age groups between 16-34 years. The secondary group is white people in the age groups between 16-34 years. The reason for the grouping is because young adults have a high life time value and they will teach the younger people to drink tea.

Source: Cant, M.C. & Machado, R., *Marketing success stories*, 4th edition, Oxford University Press, Southern Africa, 2002, p. 169.

13.8 Target market selection and positioning

Once the heterogeneous total mass market has been subdivided into smaller homogeneous segments, a marketer has to identify a segment that looks promising as a target market. The objectives and resources of the business have to be carefully considered before as target market can be selected. When selecting target markets, the abilities and expertise of the business have to be linked to the characteristics of consumers in the different market segments. A market offering is developed for each target market chosen in this manner. It is clear that target-market selection does not necessarily involve only one target market – numerous individual target markets can be selected.

The fact that marketing management has analysed the market and decided to target a specific market does not mean that the organisation now owns that target market. On the contrary, a survey of the market would probably have indicated the presence of competitors. Marketing management has to consider the competitive situation in the market carefully, and decide if it wishes confront competitors directly or if it should rather seek and occupy a gap (or niche) in the market. A positioning guide is often used to show the competitive position confronting marketing management. This guide makes

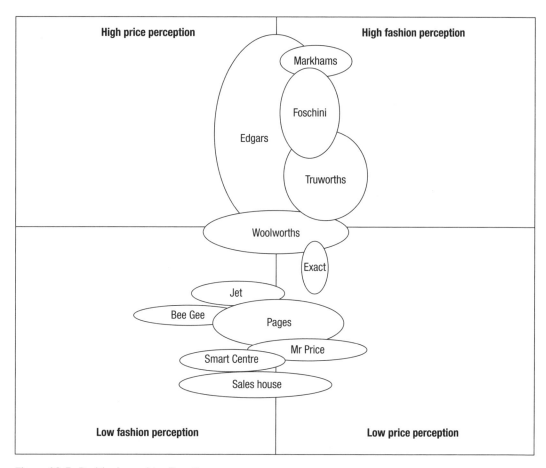

Figure 13.5: Positioning guide: Exact!

Source: Cant, M.C. & Machado, R., *Marketing success stories*, 4th edition, Oxford University Press, Southern Africa, 2002.

it easier to identify gaps in the market. Figure 13.5 is an example of such a guide.

13.9 Summary

This chapter focused on the marketing process, on the gradual change in management's approach to marketing, and on the definition of marketing.

It was shown that a market-driven organisation is essentially consumer oriented, takes strategic decisions based on pertinent information, and maintains close relationships, with a view to long-term profitability.

Marketing is a key function of an organisation, as is shown in the next two chapters, which deal with the four marketing instruments that are combined in a marketing strategy. Opportunities in the environment must be met and threats dealt with within the framework of an ethical code of conduct, the marketing concept.

To conclude, marketing is a paradox. While it is a simple process, it can, at the same time, be extremely complex. It is at once a philosophy and a dynamic function of a business. It is new, but it is also as old as humankind itself.

Key terms

Buyer	Marketing process
Consumer behaviour	Marketing strategy
Consumer orientation	Marketing thought
Demographics	Opinion leaders
Evaluating	Product
Field workers	Product orientation
Geographic	Profit
Group factors	Psychographic
Individual factors	Questionnaires
Manage	Reference group
Market forecasting	Relationship marketing
Market positioning	Research methodology
Marketing research	Sales forecasting
Market segment	Sales orientation
Marketing	Segment
Marketing components	Segment profile
Marketing mix	Seller
Marketing orientation	Service

? Questions for discussion

Reread the "Calculating the risks in making investment decisions" case study at the beginning of the chapter and answer the following questions:

1. How can market research help with the decisions about whether or not to bid for the right to explore and develop new gas fields and, importantly, how much to bid?

2. How do the determinants of consumer behaviour, individual factors and group factors affect the BG Group?

3. Do you think the way in which BG Group balanced its portfolio will ensure successful market segments?

4. Do you think that BG Group adapted to the environmental changes? Give reasons for your answer.

References

1. The following sources were used in the compilation of this chapter: I4U News, "Apple to show iPhone at CeBit 2007?", 2007, http://www.i4u.com/technology_news_1.html (26 February 2007); Assael, H., *Consumer behaviour and marketing action*, 3rd edition, PWS-KENT, California, 1987; "Calculating the risks in making investment decisions", 2005, http://www.thetimes100.co.uk/case_study.php?cID=51&csID=218&pID=1 (26 February 2007); Cant, M.C, Gerber-Nel, C., Nel, D. & Kotze, T., *Marketing research*, 2nd edition, New Africa Books, Claremont, 2005; Cravens, D.W., *Strategic marketing*, 5th edition, McGraw-Hill Companies, USA, 1997; Engel, J.F., Warshaw, M.R. & Kinnear, T.C., *Promotional strategy: Managing the marketing communications*, 8th edition, Richard D Irwin, Inc., USA, 1994; Malhotra, N.K., *Market research: An applied orientation*, Prentice-Hall, USA, 1993; Mercer, D., *Marketing*, Blackwell, Cambridge, 1992; and "The importance of excellent customer service", 2005, http://www.thetimes100.co.uk/case_study.php?cID=35&csID=235&pID=5 (9 March 2007).

THE MARKETING INSTRUMENTS

The purpose of this chapter

The marketing instruments consist of what are known as the four Ps, namely the product or service that the organisation sells, the price charged for the product or service, the promotion or marketing communication decisions needed to promote the product, and the place decision (distribution decision), which relates to the intermediaries used to distribute the product. This chapter deals with these four instruments and how they may be used to develop a unique marketing mix aimed at the target market. The process of identifying the target market and selecting the right marketing mix results in the development of the organisation's marketing strategy.

Learning outcomes

The content of this chapter will enable learners to:
- Understand the use of the marketing instruments as part of the development of a marketing strategy for the business
- Demonstrate how the product or service of the business is used in the development of the marketing strategy
- Show how the price decision is used by the enterprise in formulating the marketing strategy
- Conclude how distribution decisions are used by the business in the development of the marketing strategy
- Prove how the marketing communication instrument is used by the organisation in the formulation of the marketing strategy of the business

14.1 Introduction

The previous chapter provided a firm foundation for the development of a marketing strategy for a target market. The marketing strategy discussed in this chapter entails the following:
- An integration of the product decision which, as we shall see in the New Balance example

in the case study on page 324, includes providing a wide and deep product range
- Price decisions for the product or service (in the case of New Balance we shall see that the price is 10% cheaper than its major competitors)
- Decisions about distribution channels that will be used to get the product to the target market (New Balance, for example, is

focusing on grass roots level support for its product, ensuring that the product is freely available to the target market)

- Decisions about marketing communication to be directed to the chosen target market(s) (here New Balance is using an innovative approach of not following the traditional sales promotions strategy of getting endorsement by sports stars, but instead aiming at the ordinary consumer of its products to help market the brand)

The case study below provides an illustration of how the four marketing instruments are applied in a real-life situation in South Africa.

The **marketing strategy** is directly related to the market offering, and consists of the

Case study

New Balance: The new kid on the block

The Comrades Marathon is one of South Africa's premier sporting events and millions of South Africans watch this event every year. What is less well known about the Comrades event is the importance that marketers of running shoes attach to it to determine their success in South Africa. Participants enter their preferred brand of shoe in their application form, which is then forwarded to the marketers of running shoes in South Africa. For the last decade of the last millennium, the top brands were Asics, followed by Nike, Adidas and Reebok, with Saucony, Brooks and Mizuno being the laggards in this brand race. By 2000, a century old American sport shoe brand had entered the South African market: New Balance opened a head office in Cape Town and branches in Johannesburg, Durban and Port Elizabeth. It did not follow the traditional marketing communication approach, which is to get endorsement from high profile athletes. The family-owned business believes it has the best high-performance athletic shoes and it sees its target market as ordinary people – i.e. people with jobs and children and bonds and overdrafts – who are running, walking and playing. The company invests heavily in local events, club runners, and the youth, especially at schools. It believes that this bottom-up approach generates loyalty

that is sustainable over the long term. The product range is wide, with different lengths as well as different widths for running shoes – a factor appreciated by South Africans who have wider feet than the global average user of these shoes. New Balance's prices are about 10% cheaper than those of the established brand names such as Asics and Addidas. The company is happy being tagged "affordable" in the eyes of the customer. The company has good relationships with distributors and with final consumers, where consumer loyalty is quite high. In a recently released study from the USA, New Balance was rated the best, with a 60% customer loyalty rating. All also work in favour for New Balance in South Africa.

By 2005 New Balance was the third most popular brand in the Comrades (after Asics and Nike) with 11,37% runners using this brand. New Balance is now aiming to dominate the running shoe market as well as be number one in the walking and netball shoes segments and be one of the top three brands in trail running, tennis, training, athletic performance and children's sport shoes. In a market which has a year-on-year growth of 20% and an estimated rand-value turnover of R4,3 billion, New Balance is surely sending shock waves through the market with a fresh approach to the marketing instruments being used.

Source: *Business Day*, 12 June 2006, http://www.businessday.co.za/Printfriendly.aspx? (19 June 2006).

decisions that have to be made about the four marketing instruments. It is marketing management's task to combine the four marketing instruments (that is, product, price, distribution and marketing communication) correctly for a specific target market.

Marketing management constantly modifies decisions about the four instruments as circumstances change and consumers' acceptance of the product gradually increases. For instance, consumers first have to be educated to accept an innovation, that is, an original new product. At the same time, an existing product that is in a later phase of its life cycle should be actively promoted to prevent consumers from possibly buying a competing product.

In chapter 15 we will point out that the marketing strategy is, in fact, a key to unlocking marketing opportunities. This concept will now be briefly elucidated.

14.2 The key to the market

Figure 14.1 below is a symbolic representation of the marketing strategy in the form of a

key that has to unlock the target market in a specific environment.

In figure 14.1 the key is made up of all four marketing instruments, which are directed at the target market in a specific environment. To bring key and lock together, relevant marketing information, provided continually, is required, bearing in mind the business's objectives and resources. We shall now discuss the four marketing instruments, product decisions being the first.

14.3 Product decisions

14.3.1 The product offering

The **product offering** of a business may comprise a single product item or a number of **product items** and **product ranges**. This product offering changes according to the demands of time and the situation of the market.

Product decisions entail decision making about the product itself (for example the type of packaging and the brand), as well as about

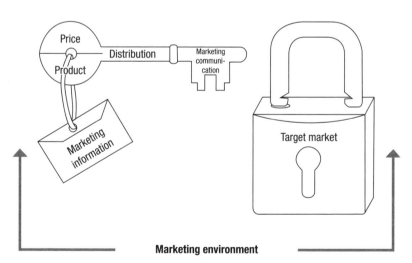

Figure 14.1: The key to the market

Source: Adapted from Murphy, P.E. & Enis, B.M., *Marketing. Series in Marketing*, Pearson Education Inc, 1985, p. 197.

the composition of the product offering. Before these decisions can be discussed, the concept "product" should be described in greater detail.

The differences between the concepts "product offering", "product range" and "product item"

A product offering consists of various product ranges. The product ranges of Toyota SA consist of following:

- Passenger cars
- Bakkies (also called light delivery vehicles)
- SUVs (also called sport utility vehicles)
- Heavy transport vehicles (also called lorries)

The product range consists of various product lines. The passenger car product range consists of four product lines:

- Tazz (until 2006) – the top selling car in South Africa for a number of years, now being replaced by the Yaris range of small cars
- Corolla – also exported to Australia
- Camry – fully imported from Australia
- Lexus – fully imported

In the Tazz product line, there were four product items, of which the Tazz 130 Sport was an example.

14.3.2 What is a product?

A **product** may be described as a composition of tangible and intangible need-satisfying utilities offered to consumers by a business, so that the consumers can take note of them, procure them, and use them. The need-satisfying utilities may include consumer products, **services** (for example those provided by a hairdresser), personalities (such as a film star), places (such as the local cinema), institutions (such as the SPCA) and ideas (such as the "Red Nose Day" campaign). As indicated in chapter 13, this book focuses on consumer products. Product decisions, however, also apply to the other types of "products" or utilities mentioned above.

A consumer product consists of:

- A **core product** that can be described in terms of technical and physical qualities (for example a crystal wine glass consisting of a round base, a long stem and a bell-shaped container, all made of glass)
- A **formal product** which, in addition to the core product, may also include specific features such as style, quality, brand and packaging (for example a wineglass with a Vitro trademark and packed in a red flannelled carton)
- A **need-satisfying product** comprising further need-satisfying utilities, such as guarantees, installation, repair services and free delivery (for example glasses guaranteed to have been manufactured by the best artisans)
- The **product image** that gives the product symbolic value by means of the type of marketing message, price and choice of distribution outlet (the Vitro glasses, for example, are sold only at exclusive shops and at a price 50% higher than ordinary wine glasses)
- The **total product** comprising all the above-mentioned components (that is, an expensive wine glass made by the best artisans which is sold only at exclusive shops)

When the concept of the total product is considered, it immediately becomes clear that there are large differences between different consumer products. Consumer products differ in respect of their particular features, their production and marketing methods, and their purposes. Marketing management consequently has to classify products in more or less homogeneous categories, according to their different qualities.

14.3.3 Classification of consumer products

Consumer products are intended for immediate use by households or consumers. A distinction can be drawn between durable and non-durable consumer products. **Durable**

consumer products, such as fridges, cars and furniture, are utilised over a longer period, whereas **non-durable consumer products**, such as cigarettes, chocolate and milk, have a relatively short lifespan. Consumer products can also be classified, on the basis of consumer buying habits, into convenience products, shopping products and speciality products.

- **Convenience products** are products such as sweets, cigarettes, milk, bread and newspapers, which should be within easy reach of the consumer. The qualities and prices of competing convenience products are reasonably homogeneous and the products do not require much explanation to be sold. Furthermore, the retailer does not receive much incentive to "push" one brand in favour of another.
- **Shopping products** are products – for example clothing and jewellery – in respect of which the consumer wants to compare suitability, quality, price and style before buying. He or she does not have sufficient knowledge of the range of shopping products available, and will "shop around" to acquire information. The consumer rarely has enough information and knowledge to visit just one store to buy the product, so he or she shops around to obtain enough information about the trademark before buying the product. New Balance shoes are examples of shopping products.
- **Speciality products** are products with unique characteristics for which consumers will make a special purchasing effort. A purchaser will often insist on a specific brand. Examples are cars (such as a BMW Z3 sports car), television sets (such as Panasonic) and hi-fi equipment (such as Marantz).

It is important to note that the above classification is based on the purchasing habits of consumers. As consumer purchasing habits differ, the same product (for example cigars) may be a convenience product for one consumer, a shopping product for another, and a speciality product for yet another.

The marketer has to make various product decisions based on the nature of the product to be marketed. One of the most important product decisions is the choice of brand. Almost all the consumer products classified into homogeneous groups have brands distinguishing them from competing products.

14.3.4 Brand decisions

14.3.4.1 The meaning of brands

The **brand** is a mark that is unique to the product items or ranges produced and marketed by a particular business and that is chosen to distinguish them from similar competing products. The brand of a product includes the brand name and a specially designed trademark. The **brand name** is a word, a letter or a group of words (for example Mercedes-Benz). Consumers use this name when they intend to buy the product. The concept of a brand name is therefore much narrower than the concept of a brand (in this case the three-point star within the circle which typifies the Mercedes-Benz trademark).

Brands can be registered under the Trademarks Act 194 of 1993, as amended. Such registration protects the exclusive right to use a particular brand for a period of ten years.

Figure 14.2 on page 328 shows a number of well-known brands. Some brands consist of only a brand name written in distinctive lettering. Pick 'n Pay is a good example. Some trademarks are so familiar that the names are almost unnecessary. The distinctive names and trademarks are often used in reminder advertising, such as that on the large billboards (usually positioned right in front of the television cameras) surrounding the field in a soccer stadium.

Figure 14.2 has the names of products in their characteristic lettering as well as their trademarks: in each case the reader knows what kind of product it is and, in most cases, what the marketing message is, although these are not mentioned.

Figure 14.2: Well-known South African brands

14.3.4.2 Advantages offered by the use of brands

Well-known brands offer the following advantages to **consumers**:

- They facilitate the identification of products when purchasing.
- They assure consumers of a quality standard they can count on.
- They offer a certain degree of protection to consumers, because branded products can be identified with a specific producer.
- They facilitate decision making, because consumers easily recognise the brands they usually buy.
- They serve as a warning against products that do not meet requirements set by consumers.

For the **marketer** the use of brands has the following advantages:

- Brands are the foundation stone of the marketing communication strategy, where the message indicates precisely which product should be purchased.
- Brands promote brand loyalty among consumers and make product substitution by the retailer or consumer more difficult. For example, the consumer insists on buying a Defy oven and perceives no other brand to be good enough.
- Brands make price comparison with competing products more difficult and, to a certain extent, protect the retailer against self-destructive price wars. If the consumer wants only a Bosch brand, for example, he or she will not easily buy a cheaper substitute. Price competition is therefore obviated.
- Brands are an inseparable part of the product image and offer the marketer the opportunity of creating the product image. Consider, for exmple, the connotation generated by the brand name Mercedes-Benz and the three-pointed star, in the mind of the ordinary consumer.
- Brands make product differentiation possible and enable the marketer to distinguish his or her product from competing products.
- Brands facilitate the expansion of existing product ranges, because consumers tend to accept new additions to an existing range more readily than an unknown product item that is not part of a range. A case in point is the success of Mercedes-Benz's smaller car (the A-series) in the market.

In fact, in a competitive market it is almost impossible to market a consumer product successfully if it has no brand identification. These days attempts are increasingly being made to brand products that traditionally have not had brand names, such as milk (Clover) and bread (Albany), to reap the benefits of brand identification.

Closely related to the advantages offered by the use of brands is the manifestation of brand loyalty.

14.3.4.3 Brand loyalty

The discussion of the New Balance range of shoes mentioned the brand loyalty of the consumers. **Brand loyalty** occurs when consumers show loyalty to certain brands. It the result of good product quality, proven usefulness, and repeated marketing communication. A brand not meeting consumer demands runs the risk of losing the battle against competing brands, and a brand not introduced properly will remain unknown and therefore unloved. The consumer gradually moves through three phases of loyalty, namely:

- **Brand recognition.** Consumers recognise the brand and know what it stands for.
- **Brand preference.** Consumers prefer the brand to other competing brands.
- **Brand insistence.** Consumers insist on the specific brand and refuse to accept a substitute.

Marketers naturally aim at achieving the third phase, because this gives the product speciality value in the eyes of consumers. The consumer will shop around until he or she finds the branded product. In such a situation a competitor will find it difficult to gain a foothold in the market. The marketer, however, still has to advertise the brand and bring it to the attention of consumers, even at this stage.

In chapter 15, the discussion of strategic marketing will refer to the need for maintaining long-term relationships with consumers and clients. Brand loyalty is the result of such a long-term relationship. Brand loyalty is possible only if the marketing concept is strictly adhered to. The box below shows the values of Avis in the execution of the marketing task. These values all point to the principles of the marketing concept and show that Avis strives to attain a long-term relationship with customers.

14.3.4.4 Manufacturer, dealer or generic brands

Producers usually give their own brands to the products they market, for instance Levi's

> **The values of Avis**
> - The customer is king
> - Service quality has to be consistent
> - Detail is important
> - Do it right the first time
> - Customer loyalty is not given, it is gained

jeans. Large **retailers** (or **dealers**) also often buy unmarked products from producers and give these products their own brands. For example Elements for small children, Free to B for teens and young adults (hip fashion wear), and Merien Hall for stately elder adults, which are used by Edgars for different ranges for different market segments. Then there are the **generic brands**, the so-called no-name brands. The branded products of manufacturers compete directly with dealer and generic brands in what is referred to as the "battle of the brands". It remains to be seen which type of brand will become the most popular. Table 14.1 on page 330 compares marketing strategies for the three brand types.

A **manufacturer** should decide whether it wants to market its products bearing its own brands or, instead, to market unbranded products directly to dealers. Sometimes large manufacturers have excess manufacturing capacity that they utilise to produce unmarked products for dealers. In such cases there should be clearly distinguishable market segments at which the market offering can be directed – otherwise the dealer brand will only aggravate the competitive situation by making inroads into the market share of the manufacturer.

> **SABMiller's range of brands**
> SABMiller is now one of the dominant players in the world beer market, with SAB having acquired the Miller group in the USA. Some of the brands of beer sold in South Africa are:
> - Castle Lager
> - Miller Lite
> - Carling Black Label
> - Hansa Pilsener

Table 14.1: Manufacturer, dealer and generic brands

Characteristic	Manufacfurer brand	Dealer brand	Generic brand
Target market	Quality conscious buyer, brand loyal	Price conscious, loyal	Price conscious, discriminating buyer, large family, accepts lower quality
Marketing mix			
• Product	Well-known product, strict quality control, clearly distinguishable brands, wide product ranges	Largely the same as for producer brands, but generally less known, limited number of product ranges	Poorer quality, less emphasis on packaging and labelling, few product items
• Price	High price, controlled by manufacturer	Price controlled by retailer	Lower price, controlled by retailer
• Distribution	Generally available at all large retail shops	Generally only available at branches of a specific retailer	The same as for dealer brands
• Marketing communication	Marketing communication campaigns launched by manufacturer	Campaigns launched by relevant retailer, most favourable shelf arrangement	Sales promotion at point of sales

Source: Griffin, R.W., *Management*, Houghton Mifflin Company, 1999, p. 663.

Compare the divergent characteristics of the three brands mentioned in table 14.1.

14.3.4.5 Individual/family brands

Marketing management also has to decide whether it is going to choose an **individual brand** for each product item (for example Carling Black Label and Hansa Pilsener Beer from SAB) or whether it is going to use a **family brand** (for example Kellogg's Rice Krispies, Kellogg's All Bran and Kellogg's Corn Flakes) for the whole range of products. Both decisions have advantages as well as disadvantages.

If a family brand is chosen, the costs of introducing a new product in the range into the market are lower. Spending on marketing communication usually decreases, because consumers are already familiar with the name of the products in the range. The new product can also benefit from the popularity of the others. The reverse is also true: if one product in such a range performs poorly, the reputation of the others bearing the same name is damaged.

Individual brands are expensive to market, because separate marketing communication attempts have to be made for each individual product. An individual brand requires another name, offering the opportunity for originality and aggressive marketing attempts aimed at specific target markets.

14.3.5 Packaging decisions

Packaging can be described as the group of activities concerned with the design, production and filling of a container or wrapper with the product item so that it can be effectively protected, stored, transported and identified, as well as successfully marketed.

Packaging should be designed so that the product can be handled without damaging the quality of the contents. It is even more important that packaging should promote product sales. The consumer should be able to identify the packaging standing on the shelf from packaging of competing products. The packaging therefore usually has a label bearing the characteristic brand and other important information. Bright colours and striking designs are used on packaging to attract the consumer's attention. The brand-loyal consumer, for instance, will recognise from a distance the characteristic packaging of the detergent he or she buys regularly.

New packaging did not stop the demise of old favourite Lion Lager

Beer aficionados were shocked when SABMiller decided to change the packaging of old favourite Lion Lager. Gone were the traditional old colours of cream and red and in their place was a more modern silver colour with blue lettering. The target market was also redefined to include the younger adults (18–24 years) and hip-generation of South Africa. The change in packaging and repositioning was not successful, however, and the Lion brand was discontinued in 2003.

14.3.5.1 Different kinds of packaging

Marketing management usually devotes a great deal of attention to choosing packaging and a packaging design that will show off the contents in the best possible way. The different kinds of packaging that can be chosen are the following:

- **Family packaging.** All the products in the range are more or less identically packed – the same packaging material is used, and the sizes of packaging are more or less the same. Family packaging is usually related to family brands. (There are, however, exceptions, as in the case of beer, where

each kind has an individual brand but all have more or less similar packaging.) All Koo jams are sold in identical packaging – obviously with different labels to indicate the contents. Family brands can facilitate consumer decision-making, because the packaging is easily recognisable. It can, however, also be a source of irritation – the consumer may purchase a product that he or she does not really want if the labels and colours resemble each other too closely.

- **Speciality packaging.** This gives an image of exclusivity to the product. Perfume, jewellery and expensive liquor (for example Chivas Regal whisky in its silver tin box) are often sold in speciality packaging. Such products are popular gifts.

- **Reusable packaging.** This creates the impression that the consumer receives a "free" container if he or she buys the product. The container can be reused for something else later. (An example is the metal container in which Bakers Tennis biscuits used to be sold. The container could be used to store cookies and future packets of Tennis biscuits.) Reusable packaging leads to repeat purchases because consumers tend to collect the containers. The danger is that consumers may stop buying when they have purchased enough containers or if they are reluctant to throw them away when the containers are empty.

14.3.5.2 Choice of packaging design

Regarding the choice of the packaging design, marketing management has to decide on the kind of packaging material, the shape and size of the packaging, and the graphic design on the label.

The packaging materials (for example glass bottles, cans, cardboard boxes, plastic tubs) best suited to the product itself are chosen. Glass bottles containing bottled fruit are more attractive than cans, for example, but they are impractical to transport and usually more expensive. Marketers often choose

Packaging: The silent salesperson

The average supermarket in South Africa stocks thousands of products. All these products compete for the attention of the consumer. One way to draw attention to a product is to use packaging to add value to the product. The use of striking colours and unique packaging helps the consumer to identify the product next to competitive products. Unique packaging such as the Toblerone chocolate package (triangular packaging) and Toilet Duck (spout in the form of an S to dispense the liquid beneath the toilet rim) are examples. Red is a colour that attracts attention and is especially used by national brand name products.

Using packaging to sell more wine

In an effort to enhance the consumption of wine in South Africa, Distell introduced a six-pack of 250 ml screwcap bottles to be sold in selected supermarkets in South Africa. The packaging is similar to that in which beer is sold in South Africa. The first brand was Two Oceans Sauvignon Blanc. The objective of this is to make wine more accessible to consumers. Consumers can now drink smaller amounts of wine more frequently without any form of waste. The screwcap makes it easy to reseal the wine for another occasion. The six-pack fits easily into any domestic fridge, is very portable and eliminates the need for a corkscrew. Wine producers are using different formats of packaging wine to promote accessibility. Some of the options being used are three-litre bag-in-boxes and wine in a can.

Source: Bizcommunity.com. "Six-pack wines piloting in SA", http://www.bizcommunity.com/Article.aspx?c=87&l=196&ai=10748 (4 July 2006).

different and better types of packaging material than their competitors in an attempt to differentiate their products from competitors' products. An example is the variety of packaging used for toothpaste. The traditional metal tubes have been replaced by plastic tubes, and there are now also stand-alone dispensers of toothpaste.

The shape of the packaging (or container) may have a specific functional value, such as reusable plastic tubs for margarine. The shape may also have a symbolic value, which may subconsciously influence buyers. A square shape is supposed to have male connotations, whereas female consumers prefer flowing and round shapes. These types of "male" and "female" shapes for packaging are especially noticeable in the case of toiletries.

Characteristic packaging helps consumers to recognise the product on the shelf – even from a distance. This explains why it is not desirabletochangepackagingwithoutinforming consumers properly. This does not mean that containers should never be modified. Changes are often made in the shapes of packaging and printed matter or labels either for the sake of improvements or for functional or aesthetic reasons. Just think how many times the word "new" is used in combination with a new kind of packaging. The product is then advertised in its new packaging to educate consumers about the new look of the packaging.

Packaging sizes are important in that marketing management has to retain the sizes traditionally used in the industry to save money, but in doing so has to forgo the competitive advantage of unusual sizes. Products packaged in unusual sizes draw the consumer's attention, but at the same time make price comparisons difficult.

The label differentiates the product from other similar products, especially if containers have been standardised. The label also serves as the carrier of the marketing message. The colours on the label and the graphic design (letter-types and illustration) help to attract and hold the consumer's attention.

14.3.6 Product differentiation

Marketing management also has to decide on the way in which the product should be differentiated from other competing products. **Product differentiation** means that a business distinguishes its product, physically and/or psychologically, from essentially identical competing products, so that the product is regarded as a different product by consumers in a specific target market. Physical and psychological differentiation can take place on the basis of design, quality, colour, taste, size, brand, packaging or any other distinguishing feature, such as price, the marketing communication message or the type of distribution outlet. One of the best examples of differentiation is found in the car market when a new model is added to the range to differentiate the product from competitors' products. Another example is New Balance's catering for South African feet by providing comfort for wider feet.

Different kinds of differentiation

- **Differentiation by means of packaging and brand.** The various types of margarine on the market are distinguished by the use of different types of packaging, such as plastic, foil or waxed paper, the brands, the designs on the labels, and the colours used.
- **Differentiation by advertising appeals.** Advertising appeals for one brand of detergent emphasise the "enzyme active ingredients", another the "stain removing power", and yet another the "clean fresh smell".
- **Differentiation on the basis of price.** There are big differences in the pricing of cosmetic products, for example Revlon products vs. Estee Lauder products. New Balance shoes are known as affordable, which is their point of differentiation.
- **Differentiation on the basis of distribution outlet.** Rolex watches are available only at the biggest and best-known jewellers.

14.3.7 Product obsolescence

An important product decision concerns **product obsolescence**. A product may intentionally, and in a planned way, be made technically and/or psychologically obsolete in order to compel the consumer to make repeat purchases. At the technical level, products can be designed to have a specific lifespan. An example is a light bulb. Psychological obsolescence points to the introduction of a new model or style resulting in the consumer rejecting the "old" product, which may still be completely effective technically. New car models and new fashions are well-known examples of planned psychological obsolescence.

The strategy of planned obsolescence is often criticised, because it leads to the waste of scarce resources and aggravates the pollution problem. However, the fact remains that new

Examples of product obsolescence in ordinary life

There was a time when mothers used only cotton nappies for their babies. On average 10 to 14 nappies were changed every day – only to be disinfected, washed and dried to be ready the next day for the next round of service to baby's bottom. Then suddenly a technological miracle happened! The disposable nappy made of paper and plastic was invented. Brand names such as Huggies and Pampers are now advertised and many affluent parents spend hundreds of rands a month on disposable nappies. The demand for cotton nappies has declined dramatically.

Long ago, a telegram delivered by a messenger from the Post Office was usually the bearer of important news – for example a new job, a family member's death, or someone coming to visit. A new technological innovation, the fax machine, replaced the telegram; even the Postal Service uses fax machines to send important documentation all over the world. Today, e-mail and cellphones are often used instead of telegrams and faxes.

models are usually technically better than the earlier ones, thereby contributing to greater consumer satisfaction. Planned obsolescence also contributes to economic progress and job creation. An interesting example of planned obsolescence is the Volkswagen Beetle, which made a dramatic comeback a few years ago. The new Beetle doesn't have a air-cooled engine at the back; instead it has a two-litre water-cooled engine in the front of the car. Not much of the old Beetle was incorporated in the new version.

14.3.8 Multiproduct decisions

Marketing management also has to make decisions on the composition of the product offering (see section 14.3.1). A business seldom manufactures and markets one specific product item only. The product offering usually consists of a product range or even a diversified variety of product items and ranges. The total product offering of a business changes continually. Profitable opportunities occurring in the market are utilised through the development of new products or by takeovers of existing businesses including, naturally, the product items and ranges marketed by those businesses.

Multiproduct items in the total product offering reduce the risk of failure and financial loss, because the success and profit of one product item can compensate for the poor performance of another.

Decisions on multiproduct items include **product range extensions, product diversification** and **product withdrawals**.

14.3.8.1 Product range extension

Product ranges can be **extended** by making additions to existing ranges of products marketed by the business. A product range is a group of products related to one another in one way or another – for example, a range of cosmetics for different skin types or a range of baby-care items such as baby oil,

soap and talcum powder. A range may also include complementary items such as razors and blades, cameras and films/image storage devices. Through new additions to a range, new market segments can be exploited, possibly offering more consumer satisfaction to specific consumers than a single item would offer. An example of this is the extension of the Vicks product line. The traditional Vicks blue bottle balsam was extended with the introduction of Vicks Medi-Nite, a medicine for the treatment of flu and colds.

14.3.8.2 Product diversification

Diversification points to the search for unknown products or markets, and usually leads to the expansion of the business into areas previously unknown to it. Diversification requires knowledge and expertise, and also processes that differ from those to which marketing management are accustomed. Therefore a great deal of risk is attached to the decision to diversify.

Diversification in the South African car market

The Colt bakkie, previously sold in South Africa by Chrysler of America, is now assembled by DaimlerChrysler South Africa (previously Daimler-Benz). Daimler-Benz had no light delivery vehicle of its own in South Africa and was losing out in sales to this very lucrative market of Southern Africa. The addition of the Colt bakkie to the product range therefore makes good sense.

14.3.8.3 Product withdrawal

Product items or ranges that do not meet requirements or are no longer profitable can be **withdrawn**. The decision to withdraw a product or range from the market is a very difficult one, because withdrawal implies failure. This may be negative for the image of a business and may cause employee problems (workers could be laid off because there are no more jobs available). Marketing management usually does everything in its power to prevent having to make the decision to withdraw.

The product offering changes continually as some products are withdrawn and new ones added.

14.3.9 New product decisions

Product decisions also have to be made about the development of new products. Each product starts its life as a mere idea, conjured up by someone. A sales representative, a dealer, a technician in the manufacturing division or a consumer may suddenly get an idea about a product which will meet specific consumer needs and which the business should be able to manufacture and market. Successful large businesses often have new product venture teams, consisting of various functional experts who actively and constantly seek new ideas for new products. In such businesses top management usually encourage staff to come forward with product ideas. The idea for a new product may be unique and original (an innovation). The product may also be "new" only in the sense that it is an improvement on or a modification of an existing product. The risk of failure and financial loss is usually greater with the marketing of an innovation – a unique, original product – but the possibility of releasing higher profits is also greater. Consider, for example, the introduction of the iPod and the price charged for this new innovative product.

New product development is planned and executed step by step, and the new product idea goes through various phases until the product is eventually introduced into the market. The phases of new product development are as follows:
- **Phase 1:** Development of product ideas
- **Phase 2:** Screening of product ideas according to financial criteria, for example sales projection and profitability analysis

- **Phase 3:** Elimination of product ideas that do not appear to be viable (profitable)
- **Phase 4:** Physical product development by the production division, during which a prototype is manufactured
- **Phase 5:** Development of the marketing strategy, which entails the following:
  - Positioning of the product in the market
  - Choice of brand
  - Design of packaging
  - Compilation of the marketing communication message
  - Decision on price
  - Choice of a distribution outlet
- **Phase 6:** Test marketing in a specific small segment of the market, for example in Cape Town only, to test the market's reaction
- **Phase 7:** Introduction into the market

Each of these phases is preceded by intensive research, and several factors can lead to the demise of the product idea. Nonetheless, the continual generation of product ideas remains a priority, for the survival and progress of a business are closely linked to the success achieved by the business in this field.

14.4 Price decisions

14.4.1 The meaning of price

Price may be regarded as the exchange value of a product or service, and it is closely linked to concepts such as benefit and value. The value of a product or service is determined by its benefit to the consumer and the sacrifice required in terms of money and effort to obtain the product.

Owing to the following factors, it is difficult to describe the concept of "price" and its meaning:
- The marketer and the consumer attach different meanings to the price concept. Marketing management regards price as one of the marketing instruments used to achieve a business's objective. For the consumer, the price he or she pays for a

Critical thinking

At the end of this section on product decision-making, we may ask "Why is the product decision so important and what could happen if we make the wrong decisions?" The following excerpt provides a practical example of what happened in such as case.

The implications of changing a product – the Lion Lager example

We noted earlier in this chapter that SABMiller saw the demise of its famous Lion Lager brand of beer in 2003. Some decisions made by SABMiller in the last few years of Lion Lager's product life cycle show the dilemma of the product manager of this venerable brand.

Lion Lager was a very strong brand in the product line of SABMiller, competing against its strongest brands, Castle and Carling Black Label. In the 1990s SABMiller was the main sponsor of the South African national rugby team and was responsible for some memorable slogans, such as "Down a Lion & Feel satisfied". It was, through the traditional link between beer and braais, also a key ingredient of another slogan which today is part of South Africa's folklore: "Braais, sunny skies and Chevrolet".

The following were some of the problems the product manager of Lion encountered:

- The brand came to the end of its life cycle due to changes in the target market and the growth of competing brands. With the growth of the mainstream brands such as Castle, cannibalisation occurred, which left Lion with an ever-decreasing market share. The Lion brand was also perceived to be old-fashioned by the target market.
- The Lion brand never occupied a well-defined niche in the consumers' minds.
- Trying to relaunch the product to a new target market wasn't successful; the target markets were too different. Eventually Lion targeted the macho, masculine and achievement-oriented market, but was then suddenly relaunched towards the young, black adult market. This was done to find a stopgap product for young adults who were targeted by the trendy spirit coolers such as Smirnoff Spin and Bacardi Breezer. The whole effort of relaunching a brand with new packaging and a slightly lower alcohol content just did not work. Subsequently, SABMiller introduced Miller Genuine Draft to this youth segment.

Source: "Down a Lion – it may be your last", *Sunday Times*, 20 July 2003. http://www.suntimes.co.za (5 July 2006).

product entails a sacrifice of disposable income. The final price usually represents a compromise between the seller (marketer), who wants to receive as much as possible, and the consumer, who wants to pay as little as possible.

- Because of the large number of products, the geographical distribution of consumers, and segmentation of the market, it is often not possible to specify a single price for a product.
- Price is but one of the four marketing instruments. Should any modification be made to any of the other marketing instruments, costs also change, necessitating a price adjustment. The product

price therefore cannot be fixed without considering the influence of the other marketing instruments.

The question now arises as to how the problems mentioned above can be solved, making it possible to determine the final price of a product in such a way that both the marketer and the consumer are satisfied. To find an answer we shall discuss the process of price determination.

14.4.2 The price determination process

The price determination process consists of the following four phases:

- **Determination of the cost price.** The first step in determining the price of a product is the responsibility of the cost accounting department, and not of the marketing management. The unit costs to produce and market the product are calculated. The product price cannot be lower than cost, because this would entail financial loss, which could ruin the business.
- **Determination of the market price.** The **market price** is the price the consumer is prepared to pay, or the current market price at which competing products are sold. It is marketing management's task to determine the market price. This can be done by launching a market-research project involving consumers or dealers. A survey of the prices of competitors' products can also be undertaken. If the cost price is much higher than the market price, a cost reduction adjustment has to be made – or else marketing management has to make a special attempt to convince consumers that the particular product warrants a higher price.
- **Determination of target price.** The **target price** is the price that will realise the target rate of return, taking into consideration the cost structure, the business's capital needs, and the potential sales volume of the product. One way of calculating the target price is the cost-plus method. This is done by adding the profit margin to the unit costs of the product. The accepted rate of return determines how large the profit margin will be.
- **Determination of the final price.** The **final price** is the price at which the product is offered to consumers. This price is determined through a reconciliation of the market price and the target price. The final price therefore lies somewhere between the market price and the target price. Should the market price for an article be, say, R5,00, and the target price R3,50, then the final price may be set at different levels between R3,50 and R5,00.

For various reasons, the final selling price cannot be still further adjusted.

Determining the price of a can of bottled mineral water

- Manufacturer's cost price to deliver a 500 ml bottle of mineral water = R2,00
- Manufacturer sells to Shoprite supermarket group at a 50% mark up = R3,00
- Shoprite is aware that the general market price for bottled mineral water is R6,00. Shoprite adds a 100% mark up on R3,00 to sell the product to the customer (target price). The selling price is also R6,00.

14.4.3 Adaptations of the final price

14.4.3.1 Skimming prices

If the product is an innovation, and therefore a unique new product, the final price may have a much higher profit margin. There are consumers who would be prepared to pay the high price, because such new inventions usually have prestige value. In fact, if the price is set too low, consumers could possibly doubt the new product's usefulness. For example, electric shavers were priced too low when they were first put on the market, and they started to sell only once the price had been almost doubled.

Yet another reason for an innovation to have a high initial price is that marketing management has to recover development costs before a profit can be made. It has already been pointed out that the development of a new invention is an expensive process with great attendant risks. As the product gains popularity, the high initial price can gradually be reduced. The more units produced and sold, the lower the costs will be, with the result that the price drops. Of course, competitors find high profits tempting, which means that marketing management cannot maintain a skimming price for a long time in the face of new competitive products.

14.4.3.2 Market penetration prices

Marketing management may decide against setting a high skimming price and rather set a market penetration price. Here the initial price of a new product is lower, and the marketer hopes to penetrate the market rapidly, discouraging competitors in the process. Competitors may decide that the small profit margin is not worth the effort of marketing a competing product themselves. New Balance followed this approach in pricing its shoes.

14.4.3.3 Market price level

This strategy is followed if there is keen competition and numerous similar products have to compete against one another. In such a situation marketers have to maintain the market price. If they set the price of their product higher than those of their competitors, consumers will tend to avoid it. If the price is lower than those of competing products, consumers will think there is something wrong with the product. Marketing management can escape the limitations of the market price strategy only if its product is successfully differentiated and is therefore regarded as unique. (Refer once again to section 14.3.6.)

14.4.3.4 Leader prices

Leader pricing concerns special offers widely used by retailers – the so-called specials. A very small profit is made on **leader price** products. These products are sold at a price lower than the current market price for a limited period only. The retailer uses this method to lure consumers to his shop. These purchasers purchase the low-priced "specials", as well as many other products with a higher profit margin. Manufacturers do not usually like leader pricing. Even though they can sell more products, the profit margin is inadequate and, later, when competitors' products are selected as a leader price item, sales figures drop. If manufacturers are not prepared to lower their profit margins so that their products can be sold as a special offer, the retailer refuses to give them shelf space, giving preference to competing products. The producer is in an unenviable position if the retailer is so large that, as channel captain, the retailer can enforce leader prices (the question of channel leadership is discussed in greater detail in section 14.5.3.2).

14.4.3.5 Odd prices

Odd prices indicate that the final prices of products have odd numbers. Even prices – for example R2, R4 and R10 – are avoided, and products are rather marked R1,99, R3,79 and R9,95, for example. It is thought that consumers are more likely to accept odd prices, and that an odd price looks smaller than an even price.

14.4.3.6 Bait prices

Bait prices are unethical and are therefore avoided by honest retailers. A bait price item has a particularly low price and is widely advertised. When coming to buy it, purchasers are encouraged to buy a far more expensive item. The retailer does not really intend to sell the bait price item – most of the time it is not even in stock or only one is available at the low price.

14.5 Distribution decisions

14.5.1 Description of distribution

In chapter 13 marketing was explained as being those activities that have to be carried out to direct the flow of products and services from the business to the consumer in such a way as to satisfy the primary objective of the business and meet the needs of the consumer. It is clear from this definition that a flow or transfer process takes place, and distribution plays an important role here. The transfer takes place along specific distribution

Critical thinking

There has been a long discussion in the popular press about how expensive South African cars are. The question that must be asked is "Are there reasons why South African cars are more expensive than their overseas counterparts?"

The pricing furore around South African cars

The South African Competition Commission did research on why South African cars were generally so expensive. On average, South African prices were 14% higher than those of the same cars in the United Kingdom and the European Union. According to the McCarthy Affordability Index, the average South African household needs to spend 164 weeks (that is, more than 3 years) of earnings to buy an average priced car. This compares poorly with the USA, where the average American needs only 26 weeks (6 months).

The following are some of the reasons for South African cars being more expensive:

- There is no flexibility on the wholesale prices at which manufacturers and importers sell to dealers. The dealer is not in a position to demand a lower price per car as the manufacturer/importer is the channel captain.
- There is no discount flexibility for the dealer. The dealer was forced in the past to adhere to minimum resale prices to consumers, ensuring that all the dealers' prices were the same (that is, dealer collusion). Furthermore, the franchise deals signed by the dealers inhibit or stifle any form of price competition.
- There are structural flaws in the pricing policy followed by motor companies. For example, in order to curb price rises in the past, the motor company reduced dealer margins – resulting in less discount flexibility in the hands of the dealer.
- Some motor companies allocate certain regions to a single dealer group. For example, DaimlerChrysler has assigned single dealerships to some of the main cities of South Africa. In a city, the Imperial group, for example, will be the sole dealer of DaimlerChrysler products or DaimlerChrysler's own dealership – Sandown Motors. This is an example of forward vertical integration which results in price control from the manufacturer.

The Competition Commission fined the eight South African car manufacturers a total of R52 million after finding evidence of price fixing and anticompetitive behaviour.

Sources: "Why cars can cost more than a house", *Financial Mail*, 16 December 2005, http://free.financialmail.co.za/cgi-bin/pp-print (28 June 2006) and "SA cars cost too much – Brand Pretorius", *Business Day*, 20 March 2006, http//:www.businessday.co.za/printfriendly.aspx? ID=BD 4A172785 (28 June 2006).

channels, which consist of intermediaries (wholesalers and retailers) who are involved in the transfer of products from the manufacturer to the consumer. It is the task of marketing management to link the manufacturer and the various intermediaries in such a way that the product is made available to the consumer in the right place and at the right time.

Distribution entails decision making about the type of distribution channel. It also entails decisions about the performance of certain activities, for example physical distribution (also called logistical activities) such as transport scheduling and stock keeping.

Distribution as a marketing instrument is represented as the shaft of the key to the market in figure 14.1 (see page 325).

Later in this chapter we shall pay attention to the various types of distribution channels, to the question of channel leadership, and to the various types of market coverage. The channel leader or captain is the channel member who may decide which type of channel should be used to achieve the most effective transfer of the product. Distribution decisions also demand that a choice be made regarding the degree of market coverage required.

14.5.2 The choice of the distribution channel

The first decision to be made in respect of distribution strategy entails the choice of intermediaries. Five different **distribution channels** are distinguished, namely:

- **Producer → consumer.** Direct distribution takes place through this channel. Although the intermediary is eliminated, physical distribution activities involved in the transfer of products still have to be performed, in this case by the producer – for example a vegetable farmer who sells them at a farm stall. Manufacturers usually sell industrial products directly to other businesses such as factories, which use the products in their manufacturing processes. Door-to-door sales, for example selling vacuum cleaners, are also an example of direct distribution.
- **Producer → retailer → consumer.** This indirect distribution channel is found especially in large retail businesses that buy from manufacturers. Pick 'n Pay, for example, is a large retailer that buys directly from manufacturers.
- **Producer → wholesaler → consumer.** This indirect distribution channel is often found nowadays. **Wholesalers** may sell directly to the final consumer, provided these sales constitute less than 50% of their total sales. Examples include Makro and Metro wholesalers.
- **Producer → wholesaler → retailer → consumer.** This is the classic indirect distribution channel that is still regarded as the most effective by a large number of manufacturers. For example, wholesalers supply stock to the informal retailing sector, such as the spaza shops in disadvantaged areas.
- **Producer → wholesaler → wholesaler → retailer → consumer.** In this case, the first wholesaler is usually a speciality

wholesaler, which obtains a specific product from numerous producers and then sells it to the second wholesaler, which sells it to the retail trade, which in turn sells it to the consumer. For example, the first wholesaler is located in a foreign country and buys products from the manufacturer in that country and delivers them to a wholesaler in South Africa. This wholesaler delivers these products to a retailer.

The type of product, the type of market, and the existing distribution structure determine which of the channels will offer the greatest advantages. If the product is perishable and the market localised, direct distribution is the ideal method. A stall next to the road, where a farmer sells fresh garden vegetables and milk, is an example of a situation in which advantages offered by a direct distribution channel (producer → consumer) are utilised. If the product has to be handled and transported in bulk, and the market is such that consumers are widespread, the manufacturer probably has to depend on the specialised knowledge and facilities of intermediaries (such as the wholesaler and retailer) to make the product(s) available to consumers. The indirect channel is the ideal choice in such a case.

14.5.3 Channel leadership

Traditionally, the marketing division of a manufacturer or consumer products makes distribution channel decisions and consequently decides which retail outlets should market the business's products. More recently, however, it is frequently the retailer – for example Pick 'n Pay – that makes the decisions and therefore controls/dominates the channel. The business that controls/dominates the channel is known as the **channel captain**.

14.5.3.1 The manufacturer as channel captain

If the manufacturer or producer is the channel captain, specific intermediaries often have

South African retailers

There are various types of retailers in South Africa. Below are some examples:

- **General dealers** are one of the oldest forms of retailers in South Africa. They offer a wide range of products and operate mostly in rural areas. They sell items from coal stoves to bicycles to clothing to groceries.
- **Department stores** are large stores that sell products in departments, for example women's clothing, haberdashery, children's clothing, etc. This retailing format is on the decline in South Africa mainly because of the introduction of category killer stores (that is, a retailer, for example Mr Price, that wants to achieve merchandise dominance by creating narrowly focussed, jumbo-sized stores).
- **Speciality stores** have a narrow but deep product range, for example jewellery stores.
- **Chain stores** are similar shops that are centrally controlled by a head office. Woolworths is an example of a chain store group.
- **Supermarkets** operate on a self-service basis and sell mostly fast-moving consumer goods (FMCG). An example is Shoprite.
- **Convenience stores** are found all over South Africa. Typical examples are corner cafés, which sell typical convenience products such as bread, milk, newspapers and cigarettes. They are open for extended periods, providing a service to the customer. Another form of convenience store is the forecourt store at petrol filling stations.
- **Discount stores** have a high stock turnover and low prices. South African examples include Dion and Game.
- **Hypermarkets** are larger in size than supermarkets, and, in addition to FMCGs, they sell more durable products such as lawnmowers, furniture, etc. They attract people from a large geographical area. South African examples include Pick 'n Pay hypermarkets.
- **Shopping centres** are usually found on the periphery of large cities or in suburbs outside the central city. Shopping centres are large buildings that house independent retailers as well as some anchor stores that draw people to the shopping centre. Anchor stores include a supermarket, discount store and/or department store. South African examples are the Menlyn Retail Park centre in Pretoria's eastern suburbs, Cavendish Square to the south of Cape Town's city centre, and East Gate in Johannesburg.
- **Mail order stores** such as Leading Concepts market by means of catalogues. People order by mail.
- A number of **informal retailers** also operate in South Africa. One of the most well-known is the spaza shop. The spaza shop is a form of a convenience store found in townships. The shop typically forms part of the home of the entrepreneur. Basic commodities such as bread, milk, cooldrinks and cigarettes are sold through these stores.

to be persuaded to distribute the product. The producer may persuade the intermediaries to create a demand for the product by directing intensive marketing communication messages at consumers. This is known as "pull" because the product is "pulled" through the channel by means of consumer demand (the intermediary is obliged to stock the product, because the consumer demands it). An example of this was Shell Helix oil, which was launched by advertisements aimed directly at the consumer. The consumer asked the retailer to stock the product.

Intermediaries may also be persuaded to "push" a product by actively encouraging sales of products in a store.

They may be persuaded to do this by, for example, offering a high profit margin on sales. Demonstration material, shop competitions and special display shelves may also be supplied by the channel captain to encourage the push strategy. Most consumer products such as soft drinks and coffee are marketed this way. In the marketing of groceries, where competition between different producers is particularly keen, there is often a battle for shelf space. A combination of push and pull is used by the manufacturer as channel captain to persuade the retailer to find shelf space for a particular item between other competing products. It is especially difficult to obtain shelf space for a new competing product. In this case the manufacturer should create a demand for the new item (pull) by thoroughly informing the consumer about it through advertising. The retailer should then be expected to apply the required push strategy.

14.5.3.2 The retailer as channel captain

If the retailer has a network of branches, enjoys store loyalty, and has adequate financial resources, it can take over the channel leadership and lay down its conditions to the producer. An example of this is the Pick 'n Pay store group, which can be seen as a channel leader. In such cases, the retailer can pull as well as push the product. The retailer advertises the producer's products, actively promoting its sales by granting a price discount to consumers or by means of special exhibits to attract consumers' attention. Special shelf space is also allocated to such products. It is understandable that manufacturers are not very happy with this state of affairs and would rather retain the leadership themselves. If the manufacturer succeeds in obtaining brand loyalty for its products, it is not easy for a retailer to take over the channel leadership. Consumers then look for the specific brand of products and tend to avoid stores that do not stock them. This means that a retailer can be the channel captain for only some of the products in its store.

14.5.4 Market coverage

The number of intermediaries in the channel is directly linked to the type of **market coverage** being aimed at. Types of market coverage include intensive, exclusive and selective market coverage.

- **Intensive market coverage** indicates a situation where as many suitable and available intermediaries as possible are utilised, especially by convenience product producers. An example is Coca-Cola, whose products are distributed through cafés, liquor stores, supermarkets, spaza shops and petrol station forecourts.
- **Exclusive market coverage** results when a manufacturer purposely limits the number of people handling its product. Only a few intermediaries obtain exclusive rights to sell the product in a specific geographical area. The intermediaries undertake not to stock other competing products. This type of market coverage is found particularly in shopping and speciality products such as men's evening clothing and cars.
- **Selective market coverage** refers to the selection of only those intermediaries that will distribute the product efficiently. Selective market coverage lies somewhere between intensive and exclusive market coverage and can be used by manufacturers of convenience, shopping and speciality products. Medicine, for example, is distributed by pharmacies (chemists), because chemists are the ideal shops to do this efficiently. New Balance follows this market coverage strategy for its sport shoes.

14.5.5 Physical distribution

A further aspect of the distribution strategy is decision making about the **physical distribution** activities that have to take place to make a product available to the final consumer. These activities, in order of their relative importance from a cost point of view, include:

- Transportation
- Storage
- Inventory holding
- Receipt and despatch
- Packaging
- Administration
- Ordering

The purpose of the physical distribution function is to maintain a specific satisfactory level of service to clients at the lowest possible distribution costs. The optimal service level is that level above which an increase in costs incurred in respect of physical distribution activities will not result in a corresponding increase in sales.

Physical distribution is becoming increasingly important. In earlier times management was under the impression that physical distribution consisted of transport scheduling only. However, more attention was paid to this function after managers realised that the effective performance of the physical distribution activities could mean large cost savings for the business and, in addition, could ensure that the product was in the right place at the right time for the convenience of consumers. The three main components of physical distribution are:

- Selecting warehouses
- Selecting the most suitable mode of transport
- Selecting optimal inventory holding levels

A compromise between cost and service must be reached in all three components. The most effective performance of physical distribution activities ensures:

- The timeous and reliable delivery of orders
- Adequate inventory so that shortages do not occur

Critical thinking

Why would an organization use different channels of distribution? And furthermore, why can organizations selling the same type of product be successful using different distribution channels? The excerpt below provides some of the reasons for this:

Dell and Acer: Using different distribution channels

It is important to understand that there is more than one distribution option which could be successful in the marketplace. The following example refers to two global manufacturers of personal computers and shows how they use different distribution channels. Both Dell and Acer sell their range of computers in South Africa as well as in various other countries. Acer was founded in 1976 and is today rated as one of the top five computer sellers in the world. Acer South Africa started in 1996 and is focusing on the small and medium business sector. Its distribution system is a channel-leveraged model, which means setting up a traditional distribution channel in which Acer works closely with its partners, distributors, dealers and resellers. Acer's distribution partners are Tarsus Technologies, which is the distribution partner for the full range of notebook, desktop and server products in South Africa. There is also Aziz, which is a focused IT infrastructure distributor for in-campus computing, which sells servers, desktops, mobiles, printers, networking, storage, memory, peripherals, components and consumables. Jet Distribution is a specialist distributor selling Acer's whole product range throughout Africa, excluding South Africa.

Michael Dell started his Dell company in 1984 using the principle of selling computer systems directly to customers, that is, a direct sales model using advertisements and the Internet and telephone network. Dell has a negative cash conversion model whereby customers pay upfront for the ordered computer before Dell has to pay for the material to build the computer. In 1990 Dell tried using alternative distribution channels such as wholesalers and retailers but without any success. It refocused on the direct to consumer sales model. By 1999 Dell was the largest seller of personal computers in the USA. In 2004 Dell had a 17,9% share worldwide of personal computers. Recently Dell became the lowest-priced computer manufacturer in the USA.

Source: http://www.acer.co.za/acereuro/page7.do?sp=page5&UserCtxParam=0&GroupCtxParamÉ (1 July 2006).

- Careful handling of stocks to eliminate damage, perishing and breakage, as far as possible.

Physical distribution activities are discussed in greater detail in the chapters dealing with purchasing management. As far as marketing is concerned, close liaison between the marketing manager and the purchasing manager is required, and the marketing manager has to be involved in planning and decision-making. If this is not the case, the flow of products from manufacturer to final consumer could be seriously hampered.

14.6 Marketing communication decisions

14.6.1 The nature of marketing communication

The consumer is removed from the manufacturer, intermediaries or point of sale in time and space. Obviously, it is the task of the marketing management to communicate with consumers, inform them and make them aware of the variety of products offered on the market. Consumers should also be persuaded by the marketing message to select and buy the producer's product time and again.

Marketing communication can be regarded as the process of informing, persuading and reminding the consumer. Marketing communication comprises five elements that can be used in a specific combination to communicate with consumers. These five elements are:

- Advertising
- Personal selling
- Direct marketing
- Sales promotion
- Publicity

Figure 14.3 shows the elements of marketing communication. All five elements have to work together to convey the marketing message to the target audience.

Marketing management has to decide on the best combination of the five elements. A marketing communication budget allocates funds to each of the five marketing communication elements. Within the restrictions of this budget, consumers have to be made aware of the business's market offering. They should be persuaded to select and buy

Figure 14.3: Elements of marketing communication

product(s) and reminded constantly to buy the product(s) again. A discussion of the five marketing communication elements follows.

14.6.2 Advertising

Advertising is a controlled and paid-for non-personal marketing communication related to a need-satisfying product and directed by a marketer at a specific target audience.

14.6.2.1 Advertising media

The advertisements shown on television or in the movies, broadcast on the radio, or placed in magazines and newspapers are examples of advertising. A single placement of such an advertisement is very expensive – hence the need to pay careful attention to both the choice of the media used and to the marketing communication message. Marketing managers should be very sure that their messages will reach the target market (or target audience in this case), and that this audience will notice the message, understand it, accept it, and react to it by repeatedly buying the same product.

Outdoor advertising on billboards, posters, bus stops and public transport vehicles reaches consumers at a time when they are busy with other activities. This is also a good way of reaching a target market that does not read regularly or does not have access to television and the movies. An advertising budget, as part of the marketing communication budget, is prepared to indicate the percentages of the budgeted amount that should be allocated to the various media. Obviously, market research is done to establish the way in which the target market can be reached most effectively.

14.6.2.2 The advertising message

The formulation of the marketing message in advertisements in the different media requires careful consideration. An advertisement in the print media generally consists of three main components, namely the heading, the

illustration and the copy. The heading is supposed to attract the consumer's attention and to deliver the main or most important appeal or the reason why the product should be bought. The most important message is often repeated at the bottom of the copy. The headline and subheadline are printed in big bold letters to attract attention. The illustration may be a drawing or a photograph, in black and white or colour. The illustration stimulates interest and invites the reader actually to read the copy, which contains information about the product and the need satisfaction that it can provide. Rational reasons (for example petrol consumption of 10 kilometres per litre in city traffic for the Honda Ballade car) and emotional reasons (such as a claim that a certain toothpaste will have the effect of all the girls swooning over you) for purchasing the product are given.

The product itself and the package and label should also appear in the illustration. All the components of the illustration itself are chosen to transmit a symbolic message. Models are carefully selected to play a specific role. A homemaker might be chosen to transmit a message about the excellence of a new detergent, while Miss South Africa might be portrayed as a successful user of cosmetics. The intended target audience must be able to relate to or identify with the model in the illustration. (For example, it would be ineffective to use a male as a role model for buying washing powder.) It is important, also, to achieve coherence in all three components. The headline, illustration and copy should not tell conflicting stories.

In radio advertisements, only words and sounds can be used to transmit the advertising message. Music is often used to reinforce the message or to create a specific mood. Jingles and slogans are especially effective in teaching the brand name to potential consumers.

Television advertisements are effective because the spoken and written word can be used to spell out the message clearly. Pictorial material, music, jingles and other sounds can be used to reinforce the message. For this reason, television commercials are very expensive and every second counts. Advertisers cannot afford to waste time on irrelevant material. Sometimes television advertisers get so caught up in the entertaining story line of the television advertisement that they forget what the most important message is – namely the brand name.

The success of the Red Bull advertising campaign

Red Bull is an energy drink that was launched in South Africa in 1997. The marketing mix used is based on the following:

- The product as an energy drink was new to the market, and it worked.
- The packaging was eye-catching.
- The distribution channel was good, that is, the product was at the right place at the right time.
- The pricing strategy used was effective (a price-skimming premium strategy, implying that if it is expensive it must be working).
- The marketing communications strategy was highly visible – for example, cartoon characters on TV with silly voices were used, providing humour and entertainment value with the slogan "Red Bull – gives you wings!"

14.6.3 Personal selling

Personal selling is a verbal presentation of a product, service or idea to one or more potential purchasers in order to conclude a transaction. Sales representatives are used to inform buyers about a business's product(s) and to persuade buyers, through face-to-face communication, to buy the business's products time and again.

Sales representatives of manufacturers visit other businesses and dealers, communicating the marketing message directly. This is the method followed by New Balance to promote sales of its range of shoes. In the same way, wholesalers' sales representatives can be used to visit retailers to try to sell the variety of products handled by the wholesaler. Personal selling between sales representatives and final consumers also takes place: this is known as door-to-door selling (for example, the selling of Tupperware utility plastic containers and the selling of cosmetics from Avroy Shlain). Sales by shop assistants over the counter may also be regarded as personal selling, but normally the retailer does not see it in this light – merely regarding the shop assistant as someone who helps with the physical distribution of the product, that is, a person who does not have to be trained in the art of selling.

Example

Cosmetic products are often sold on a door-to-door basis. Avroy Shlain, for example, succeeded in building his extremely successful business by training (and motivating) his sales representatives to sell his cosmetic products, bearing his own brand name, by means of personal communication.

14.6.4 Direct marketing

Direct marketing uses advertising media (for example radio and television) to communicate information of a product or service to customers, who can then respond by purchasing them via mail, the telephone or the Internet. The benefit of direct marketing is that customers can do the buying from the comfort of their homes, resulting in greater shopping convenience. This ties in with the notion of cocooning. Cocooning implies that more and more customers create a cocoon in their home and as part of their lifestyle and, because of various factors – of which crime is one – are prepared to spend more time at home. A recent study found that most Internet shoppers are mostly doing recreational buying and that they see this kind of shopping as a pleasurable experience.

The benefits of direct marketing are that a long-term relationship can be developed with the customer, that the message can be directed at a specific customer, that a customer database can be developed, and that the results of a direct marketing campaign can be directly measured.

A number of direct marketing methods can be used. One example is telemarketing, which uses the telephone to call the customer at home to offer a product or service. Other examples are direct mail that solicits the customer to order a product, catalogues that are sent to potential customers, and direct-action/response advertising done on TV and in the newspapers, to which customers can respond by phoning and ordering products on a toll-free number. Verimark and Glomail are two South African companies that use direct marketing.

14.6.5 Sales promotion

Sales promotion consists of those marketing communication methods that are not normally classified as advertising, personal selling, direct marketing or publicity, but that complement the other elements in trying to influence consumer behaviour. Examples of such methods are diaries, calendars and T-shirts displaying the brand name and a short sales message. Competitions, demonstrations, and the handing out of samples (for example a small bottle of Handy Andy Micro floor cleaning liquid) are also examples of sales promotions. Sales promotion has also been used by New Balance in the marketing of its range of shoes.

Sales promotions often have short-term objectives only, for example to introduce a new product to the market. However, they are valuable methods, because they reinforce the effects of the other marketing communication elements. For example, if a consumer has seen a supermarket demonstration of a new pan that browns meat delectably without oil being added (sales promotion), he or she would possibly understand the television advertisement (advertising) better and find it easier to accept the message, especially if he or she has also read an article in a newspapera column (publicity) in which the columnist explained the new cooking method.

14.6.6 Publicity

Publicity is the non-personal stimulation of the demand for a product or service of a business by making its actual current news value available to the mass media to obtain a favourable and "free" media review of the business and its product.

Publicity also interfaces with the business's public relations function, discussed in chapter 16. Should the business or its product receive favourable coverage in the press or on the radio or television, the publicity (created by the activities of the public relations division) has a specific marketing communication value for the business.

The distinguishing feature of publicity is that the message to be conveyed should have a certain degree of news value for the audience. Consider, for example, the write-up New Balance received just before the Comrades Marathon in 2006. This is an example of a massive publicity boost to a relative newcomer in this market. Publicity is also more credible than advertising, because the audience is more receptive to the message. A further feature of publicity is that marketing management has no direct say in formulating the message, because the editors of publications, for example, decide what they want to publish. It is therefore clear that publicity can have a negative effect (imagine the negative publicity a motor journalist would give a test car that broke down on a rural road).

Publicity is not always "free", as is suggested in the definition. A business often has to spend large sums of money on favourable mentions in the press or on radio or television. Businesses often sponsor sports events or donate large amounts to charity. By doing this, a business effectively shows its responsibility towards the community and, in addition, gets free mentions of its name or product in

Critical thinking

Advertising is the most visible part of the marketing communications campaign and most students think advertising is the only way that an organisation can succeed in the mass market. The question is "How can you use the elements of marketing communication to promote the product and is there any form of control over the use of marketing communication messages?" The excerpt below shows how Glomail sells slimming products and the control that is exerted over the communication messages to the target market.

Certain products and services need to be sold by making use of heavy investment in marketing communications. Some of these products are basic commodities such as washing powder and fabric softeners. There are also other categories of products which make heavy use of marketing communications. Below are examples of such products.

It is a well-known fact that if someone has a perceived physical flaw, he or she will be more inclined to fall for too-good-to-be-true advertising claims. These claims prey on the insecurities of customers about such things as baldness in males and body weight and size in females. Advertising claims that promise miracle weight loss are made by companies that sell slimming products such as fat burners, fat blockers, craving curbers and metabolism boosters. The Advertising Standards Authority (ASA) is the watchdog on spurious claims made in the mass media and has the authority to instruct an advertiser to pull an advertisement. Over the years it has been instrumental in getting advertisers to adapt or completely drop their advertising claims.

Glomail, a mail order store group that also sells its product range through retail outlets, holds the record for complaints lodged and upheld by the ASA. One of the most famous products sold by Glomail is Bioslim, which has been advertised in the mass media with the message "Eat what you like and still lose weight". This claim was modified after complaints from a few medical crusaders in South Africa. Each time the ASA instructed Glomail to change the advertising message to make it clear that the product would be effective only when used in conjunction with a kilojoule-controlled, balanced diet. Glomail said it adhered to this ruling by adding "in conjunction with a kilojoule-restricted diet" to its advertisement. The ASA was not happy because this warning was added only in the fine print of the advertisement, and it asked Glomail to make this message more legible.

Over the years some weird advertising messages have been used to convince women that only thin people are beautiful and the silver-bullet solution lies in slimming products. Some of the more memorable ones are:

- 1969: "Still dieting the hard way? And losing hope? Indulge, and lose weight instead … with Choc-o-Slim!" – a chocolate bar with a bulk ingredient that tricks your stomach into thinking it is full
- 1975: "Are you ready for the String (Bikini)? To look good in the String you can't afford even a hint of fat" – Redupon appetite suppressant
- 1991: "Why Shape is the last diet you'll ever try" – Shape two-meal-per-day replacement
- 1994: "The fun only begins when you are slim" – Hawkins Home Slimming System
- 2003: "Decrease your desire. Increase your desirability' – Eatless tablets

No wonder several women's magazines decided no longer to accept advertising that promised miracle weight loss or contained messages that played on women's insecurities regarding their body size!

Sources: "TV ad for diet pill banned as misleading", *Sunday Times*, 24 August 2003, http://www.suntimes.co.za/2003/08/24/news/news10.asp (30 June 2006) and "Slim chancers", Women 24, http://www.women24com/Women24/Life/BodySoul/Article/0,7173, 1-2-4-64_7750,00.htÉ (2 July 2006).

the media. Consumers who notice the hidden message are then more inclined to accept the marketing messages of such a "good" business.

Marketing management should decide which sponsorships or donations could be of benefit to the product(s) to be marketed. Top management sometimes decides on sponsorships that are of interest to the top managers personally, notwithstanding the nature of the product or market. In this way, funds are often wasted on matters that do not have sufficient positive marketing communication value and hence will not succeed in demonstrating social responsibility. Specific marketing communication objectives should also be set in respect of sponsorships.

14.7 Summary

In this chapter, the marketing strategy was represented as a key and the target market as a lock. All four parts of the key have to work together to open the lock. The various product decisions – including the product range, the brand, the packaging, the method used to differentiate the product from other products and new product development – were discussed. Product decisions consist of decisions regarding price, distribution and marketing communication or promotion. Distribution decisions entail considering the various distribution channels and the market coverage. It has been shown that a channel captain is able to dominate an entire channel and that large retailers, rather than producers, can act as channel captains. Price decisions are important, because too low a price may lead to financial loss, perhaps giving the impression that the product is of inferior quality. Prices should be determined in such a way that they stimulate a demand for products. The marketer communicates with consumers through advertising, personal selling, direct marketing, sales promotion and publicity, endeavouring to inform them and persuade them to buy a specific brand repeatedly. Large sums of money are spent on effective messages to reach consumers.

 Key terms

Advertising	Marketing communication
Bait prices	Marketing strategy
Brand	New product decisions
Brand decisions	Odd prices
Brand insistence	Packaging
Brand loyalty	Personal selling
Brand name	Physical distribution
Brand preference	Price
Brand recognition	Product decisions
Channel captain	Product differentiation
Channel leadership	Product diversification
Consumer products	Product items
Cost price	Product lines
Dealer	Product obsolescence
Distribution	Product offering
Distribution channels	Product range extensions
Exclusive market coverage	Product ranges
Family packaging	Product withdrawals
Final price	Publicity
Generic brands	Retailer
Individual/family brands	Reusable packaging
Intensive market coverage	Sales promotion
Leader prices	Selective market coverage
Manufacturer	Services
Market coverage	Skimming prices
Market penetration prices	Speciality packaging
Market price	Target price
Market price level	Wholesalers

? Questions for discussion

Reread the "Marketing instruments in action" case study at the beginning of the chapter and answer the following questions:

1. Do you think that the specific use of the marketing instruments by New Balance can be replicated in other industry sectors? Give reasons for your answer.

2. Do you think that the use of the Internet to promote products and services in South Africa is a viable proposition? Explain.

3. Does a provider of a product always have to offer the lowest price to attract customers to buy from it?

4. Would you personally buy running shoes by means of the Internet? Give reasons for your answer.

5. Which communication media would you personally prefer to use to advertise running shoes in South Africa?

THE INTEGRATED MARKETING STRATEGY

The purpose of this chapter

The integrated marketing strategy shows how all the marketing activities discussed in the previous two chapters are integrated. It provides an overall picture of the decision-making process required of the marketing manager. It commences by looking at the marketing concept, which is the philosophy upon which marketing is based, and indicates how the marketing objectives tie in with the organisational objectives. It also shows how the marketing strategy must adapt over the product life cycle. In addition, it examines the marketing planning and control process that is followed by the marketing manager.

Learning outcomes

The content of this chapter will enable learners to:
- Explain the role of the marketing concept and marketing objectives in the running of the business
- Demonstrate how changes in the product life cycle will influence the marketing strategy formulation of the business
- Show how marketing planning and control are exercised in the business

15.1 Introduction

In the previous chapter the four marketing instruments were discussed. As has already been explained, decisions pertaining to the four marketing instruments that are under the direct control of marketing management must be combined in an integrated marketing strategy that is aimed at a specific target market.

One of the dangers of being involved in a study of marketing is that one becomes so immersed in the details of marketing research, segmentation and the marketing instruments that the overall picture becomes blurred. The focus of an integrated marketing strategy is therefore to put all the pieces together so that a marketing strategy can be developed – one that can best satisfy the needs of the target market. In this process, the marketing concept guides the enterprise. Changes in the life cycle and marketing strategy also form part of an integrated marketing strategy formulation.

In this chapter, the integrated marketing strategy is discussed in terms of the marketing concept, decision making during the different phases of the life cycle, and the marketing warfare that occurs. Finally, the question of the role of marketing planning and control is also addressed.

The case study below provides an illustration of how the four principles of the marketing concept, on which the integrated marketing strategy is based, are applied in a real-life situation in South Africa.

15.2 The marketing concept

Four principles are contained in the marketing concept, which is the ethical code according to which the marketing task (as described in this book) is performed. All four principles are equally important, and each one invariably influences the application of the others. The marketing concept directs all marketing decisions about products, distribution methods, marketing communication and price determination. In chapter 13 we pointed out that the evolution in marketing thought has led to the development of the following four principles of an ethical code known as the marketing concept, namely:

- Profitability
- Consumer orientation
- Social responsibility
- Organisational integration

Case study: The marketing concept in action

Pick 'n Pay: A retail giant

Pick 'n Pay is the largest grocery retail chain in South Africa. It has stores throughout the country, from hypermarkets to supermarkets to clothing stores to family stores and minimarkets. Its annual report highlighted the opening of 49 new stores in 2006, with 59 confirmed for 2007. All these stores must be managed continually as an integrated whole.

Pick 'n Pay's headline earnings at R705,6 million increased by 15,2% for the year and as a result of the concentration effect of share repurchases mainly towards the end of the year, headline earnings per share at 153,02 cents were up 17,1%. It had an increase in trading profit of 16,9%, with trading margin increasing from 2,8% to 3%.

Pick 'n Pay's founder and chairman, Raymond Ackerman, is known to be the homemaker's friend and his motto of "The customer is queen" is well known throughout the country. Pick 'n Pay's quick reaction to matters that affect the consumer shows its consumer orientation. Its reaction to increases in the bread price has positioned it as a fighter for the interests of the consumer. Raymond Ackerman is also known for his fight against the high petrol price in South Africa. He is agitated by the continued system of regulation in the industry, which he says is designed to protect the oil companies at the expense of the consumers.

Pick 'n Pay demonstrates its responsibility towards society by sponsoring various educational and charitable events. It is very visible in athletics, sponsoring the Comrades Marathon as well as cycling, for example the Pick 'n Pay Cycle Challenge and the Argus Pick 'n Pay Cycle Tour. Its ongoing focus is work in promoting black economic empowerment (BEE) and the group is active in supporting the development of small entrepreneurial BEE suppliers and Family Store Franchises. It also gave R8,72 million to the Kids in the Park programme through the sale of green bags.

Source: "Pick 'n Pay to roll out 59 new stores", *Business Report*, 7 June 2006, http://wwwbusrep.co.za/index.php?fSectionID=563&fArticleId=3281045 (7 November 2006).

15.2.1 The principle of profitability

The first principle of the marketing concept, in a profit-seeking business, is the long-term maximisation of profitability. This is the primary objective of the business in a free-market system and is therefore also the main objective of marketing management. The principle of profitability is fundamental to the marketing concept and emphasises profitability instead of sales, which do not necessarily maximise profits.

15.2.2 The principle of consumer orientation

The satisfaction of consumer needs, demands and preferences constitutes a consumer-oriented approach to marketing where emphasis is placed on what the consumer needs. Marketing decision making is based on what the consumer wants, but even though the consumer is regarded as "the king or queen", complete need satisfaction can never be achieved.

Satisfaction can only be given within the constraints of the profit objective and the resources of a business. If the consumer is neglected and his or her wishes are ignored, this can have serious financial implications for the enterprise. Competitors are especially keen to note and turn such opportunities to their own advantage. Consumer orientation also means that the consumer has to be supplied with adequate and correct information about the business's market offering. This information is usually incorporated into marketing communication messages. Pick 'n Pay's commitment to the consumer is illustrated in the case study on page 352.

15.2.3 The principle of social responsibility

Besides its responsibility towards the consumers of its products, marketing management also has a responsibility towards the community in which the marketing task is performed. Business often discharges this responsibility by spending money on projects such as housing, education, job creation and health. The objective of these projects is to create a stable economic, social and political environment in which future profits can be optimised. Responsibility in this regard enhances the corporate image in the eyes of employees, consumers and the general public. It has long-term dimensions that might well have a positive influence on the profit position in future. Sporting events and educational institutions such as schools are also often sponsored by large businesses. The Pick 'n Pay case study on page 352 illustrates Pick 'n Pay's involvement in sport.

The other dimension of social responsibility hinges on the authority (legislation) under which the business operates. Should the business act irresponsibly or fail to abide by the laws of the land, reaction in terms of punitive legislation or, even, prosecution could result, as in the case of Leisurenet.

If a business was to disregard the norms of society, consumer resistance could result, thereby harming the primary objective of the business. Nothing should be done to violate the current norms or general moral and ethical standards of the community.

A sponsorship or a social responsibility project must have a certain marketing benefit for the sponsor. Usually top management must decide on the merits of alternative projects, but it is the responsibility of marketing management to initiate projects, because of management's close relationship with the public and its ability to evaluate projects in terms of marketing benefits. A sponsorship must be supported by marketing communication to ensure a large audience. A sponsored event must also be well organised and managed, which usually requires the help of the public relations department. An imaginative and successful social responsibility project may mean publicity value for the business enterprise. Because such projects are newsworthy, coverage in the mass media (newspapers, radio, television) is ensured. In sporting events, players usually display the name of the sponsor on equipment and clothing, while the sporting event itself offers opportunities to display brand names and marketing messages on billboards, flags, etc.

Marketing management should ensure that nothing is done that could be detrimental to the community. A case in point is the trouble taken to ensure that containers of harmful substances cannot easily be opened by children (tamper-free packaging). Also, an advertisement that mocks religion, for example, offends the prevalent moral or ethical values of the community. This may provoke consumer resistance. Consumers may decide to avoid the product in future.

15.2.4 The principle of organisational integration

This principle expresses the need for close cooperation between all the functions of the business. All the functional decision-making activities should be coordinated in a way that will eventually lead to the successful marketing of the products of the business. Organisational integration entails close cooperation between the marketing, operational, purchasing, and all other functions of the business in pursuit of the business's mission and objectives. Organisational integration is a prerequisite for success – the primary objective can never be achieved without it.

15.2.5 Merits of the marketing concept

The criticism often levelled at marketing – that it purposely exploits consumers, "robbing" them of hard-earned money to be wasted on useless articles – is refuted by the principles of the marketing concept. The true marketer is proud of his or her product and of the way it satisfies the needs of consumers. The marketer jealously guards the product's

CineMark's responsibility to society

It is estimated that one in five South African children is either overweight or obese and whilst this is related to unhealthy eating habits, it is also linked to the fact that children are less active today than in the past.

CineMark has donated free screen time for the Let's Play initiative's cinema advertising campaign, a social responsibility initiative from SuperSport to encourage children to participate in sport. Let's Play highlights the problems associated with inactivity and aims to generate enthusiasm for participation in sport by young South Africans.

Source: www.bizcommunity.com/Article. aspx?c=97&1=196&ai=9126 (9 November 2006).

name, paying meticulous attention to complaints and criticism, even though his or her main purpose is continually to improve the profit position.

According to the first principle of the marketing concept, long-term maximisation of profitability is the primary objective of the business and also that of marketing management. The business is entitled to this profit to offset the risks involved in developing products for the market. It is necessary to discuss this primary objective in more detail because it is the guideline for activities and the criterion for success. The other secondary objectives of marketing management are also discussed in the following section.

Figure 15.1 on page 355 illustrates the four principles of the marketing concept, the philosophy according to which all marketing tasks are performed.

15.3 Marketing strategy during the product life cycle

The management of an integrated marketing strategy also requires that attention be focused on the specific phase in which the

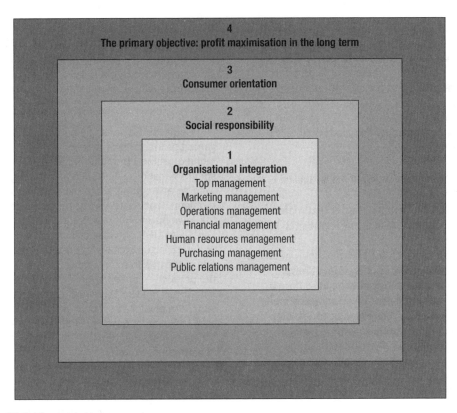

Figure 15.1: The marketing concept

business's products are at a specific moment in time. There is a close relationship between the management of the four marketing instruments (as discussed in chapter 14) and the management of the product range during its life cycle. Marketing warfare, which uses the four marketing instruments as weapons in the attack on competitors, ties in with this. Aspects of the adaptation of the marketing strategy during the product life cycle and marketing warfare will now be discussed.

15.3.1 The four marketing instruments as an integrated whole

It has often been stressed that the four marketing instruments have to work together as an integrated whole – they cannot function in isolation. It is marketing management's responsibility to achieve this unity because of the numerous variables, and because the marketing instruments not only complement each other, but are also mutually interchangeable. In the following discussion it will be shown how the four marketing instruments can be combined in an **integrated marketing strategy** during the product's life cycle.

Chapter 14 (section 14.3.9) showed how a new product is developed, and which phases can be distinguished in new product development. During the product's life cycle (as indicated in figure 15.2) the further development of the product can be sketched, from its introduction to the market until it eventually becomes obsolete and is withdrawn from the market.

Critical thinking

When it comes to social responsibility, most people think only in terms of large retail organisations and their contributions to society. But can it also be applied in service industries? The following excerpt shows how social responsibility can also apply to the banking sector.

The social responsibility principle applied in the banking sector

The global investment banks that roared on to the local investment scene in the mid-1990s garnered a reputation as ruthless, profit-focused firms – firms that took their pound of flesh from staff but offered great rewards.

But these conglomerates also have a softer side – a corporate social investment conscience. On a recent visit to SA, high-ranking Citigroup management handed a donation of R1,42m to the Save the Children programme, which helps provide comprehensive care for orphans and vulnerable children affected by HIV/AIDS and poverty.

Citigroup also partners with Operation Hunger on the Hippo Water Roller Project, which gives poor rural communities a way to transport water. The Habitat for Humanity programme is the company's contribution to the dire housing shortage in this country. The global giant also provides university scholarships and converted shipping containers that serve as classrooms.

The local division contributes at least R7m–R8m a year to social investment. It focuses on education and projects for vulnerable children. It is a key sponsor of Nurturing Orphans of AIDS for Humanity. The bank encourages a philosophy of giving and philanthropy among staff, allowing them two extra days leave a year to get involved with special projects. The personnel, for instance, helped to build eight houses in the Ivory Park area.

Deutsche Bank has helped design a game used in schools to teach entrepreneurial techniques, and the Sparrow School it sponsors teaches skills such as catering, welding and computers to those with learning problems. Their Little Artist project auctions the artworks of Hillbrow street children.

Swiss UBS provides calculators to underprivileged schools in Eastern Cape, and takes this to a more advanced level with the production of senior-phase mathematics kits. It has made a three-year commitment to support a cluster of schools in the Diepsloot area in Gauteng, developing a best-practice school management module for heads of departments.

UBS also has a partnership agreement with the National Institute for Communicable Diseases in Johannesburg. Through the partnership UBS explores the biological control of malaria mosquitoes using fungi.

JPMorgan is specifically involved in the Gauteng area, helping to build classrooms and libraries, paying school fees for orphans, and supporting various old age homes and places of safety for foster and street kids. It contributed a portion of the funds required by the Vuleka School to purchase a property and helps fund the annual running costs. Vuleka is a type of preparatory school for children about to enter grade one. It teaches the children English and other skills needed for "real school".

Who said investment bankers don't have any heart?

Source: "Cold world of commerce shows its human side", *Business Day*, 22 August 2006, http://www.businessday.co.za/articles/economy.aspx?ID=BD4A254366 (10 September 2006).

15.3.2 **The nature of the product's life cycle**

The **product's life cycle**, as shown in figure 15.2, is indicated as a curve in respect of which sales/profits are indicated on the vertical axis and time duration on the horizontal axis. Four phases are indicated, namely:

- The introductory phase
- The growth phase
- The maturity phase
- The declining phase

Figure 15.2 also illustrates the sales and profit curves during the four phases of the product's life cycle. The sales curve ascends during the introductory and growth phases, reaching a peak in the maturity phase and levelling off (stagnating) and descending during the declining phase. The profit curve looks similar, but starts rising only later in the development phase. The reason is the high costs related to new product development. Costs first have to

be recovered before any profit can be made.

The profit curve starts to decline earlier than the sales curve. This is because the product meets keen competition in the maturity phase, causing a price cut (thereby lowering profits).

The marketing communication costs normally rise in this phase, since competition necessitates stimulation of demand. The increased costs naturally affect profits. Marketing management's objective is to sustain the profitable phase of the life cycle for as long as possible. This can be done by constantly modifying the integrated marketing strategy. The declining phase should, at all costs, be avoided.

The curve in figure 15.2 illustrates the traditional life cycle of a product. Obviously, not all products have identical life cycles. Where an enterprise, for example, markets a whole range of products, each product has its own life cycle. Figure 15.3 illustrates the different life cycles. Although the seven cycles differ, each one reflects a rise, a peak, a stagnation

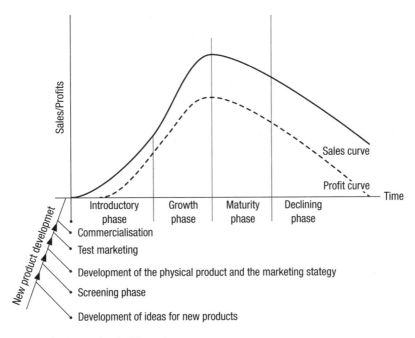

Figure 15.2: Phases in the product's life cycle

and, in most cases, inevitably a decline. In each of the life cycle phases the decisions regarding the price, product, distribution and marketing communication are adjusted.

15.3.3 Integrated marketing strategy in the introductory phase

The integrated marketing strategy entails the following:

- **Objective.** The objective is to create a demand. A demand for the product has to be created in the first place, because at this stage consumers are not aware of such a new product (for example the demand for DVD systems).
- **Target market.** The target market consists of consumers who are adventurous and prepared to try out new things and run risks, for it is possible that the new product may be a great failure.

- **Product decisions.** The product decisions that are taken during product development are implemented (for example dimensions and colour of the product, etc.).
- **Distribution decisions.** These involve exclusive or selective market coverage. Only a few shops will be prepared to allocate shelf space to the new product (see chapter 14, section 14.5.2).
- **Price decisions.** A high initial price (skimming price) is fixed, since a new product (innovation) usually has a certain degree of prestige value.
- **Marketing communication decisions.** Initially, the business relies heavily on personal selling to dealers. Full-page colour advertisements appear in the more prestigious speciality periodicals. The sales message may contain highly technical information. Publicity is obtained fairly easily, because the product usually has news value. Sales

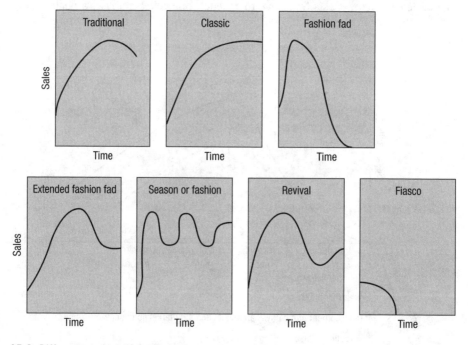

Figure 15.3: Different product life cycle patterns

Source: Strydom, J.W., Cant, M.C., Jooste, C.J., consulting editor Van der Walt, A., *Marketing management*, Juta, Cape Town, 2000, chapter 15.

promotion techniques can be used to attract attention to the product.

15.3.4 Integrated marketing strategy in the growth phase

This entails the following:

- **Objective.** The objective here is to develop a demand. The demand for the specific brand has to be created. At this stage there are several competing products on the market and the target market is no longer unfamiliar with the product.
- **Target market.** The target market consists of consumers who are less receptive to new things and new ideas. They first want to establish whether the innovators approve of the product.
- **Product decisions.** Minor product modifications are made. The brand is emphasised.
- **Distribution decisions.** This involves selective market coverage.
- **Price decisions.** The price declines because of competition.
- **Marketing communication decisions.** Advertising occurs through the mass media, such as newspapers, radio and television. Sales promotion methods are utilised. All of this is done to promote the specific product and the brand name.

15.3.5 Integrated marketing strategy in the maturity phase

This entails the following:

- **Objective.** The objective is to counteract competition and prolong the life cycle of the product.
- **Target market.** New target markets are sought and exploited because marketing management is aiming at a large market share. Most consumers are aware of the product and its benefits.
- **Product decisions.** Modifications or improvements have to be introduced to differentiate the product from numerous

similar products on the market. (Product differentiation is discussed in chapter 14, section 14.3.6.) All four marketing instruments should help to achieve product differentiation. If this is successful, the product will be perceived as unique by a specific target market. In such a favourable situation little direct competition will be encountered, even though the product is in the maturity phase. Other product decisions that should receive attention in this phase are the development of new products, extending the product range, and product obsolescence. A new product or model starts its life cycle again in the introductory phase.

- **Distribution decisions.** There is intensive market coverage. All suitable dealers with the required facilities are allowed to stock and sell products.
- **Price decisions.** The current market price or market price level should be adhered to, unless marketing management has succeeded in differentiating the product successfully. The product is then accepted as unique. Marketing management has price discretion, because the consumer perceives the product as unique and does not mind paying more for it.
- **Marketing communication decisions.** There is persuasive advertising through the mass media. The sales message is less technical and more emotional than during the introductory phase. In a television advertisement, for example, children might be depicted as expressing love for their parents because they have bought them a specific brand of DVD player. This type of emotional appeal is often the most important way of differentiating a product from competing products in a highly competitive market.

15.3.6 Integrated marketing strategy in the declining phase

This entails the following:

- **Objective.** The objective is either to maintain the market share or to withdraw the product.

- **Target market.** The target market consists of an older, more conservative group of consumers who resist change and avoid innovation.
- **Product decisions.** No modification of the product is considered. Attention is paid to the development of substitute new products or models. The obsolete product is eventually withdrawn from the market.
- **Distribution decisions.** There is limited market coverage, and this only in areas where the product is still in demand.

- **Price decisions.** Prices are reduced and the product is offered on sales.
- **Marketing communication decisions.** There is personal selling and advertising only in areas where the product is still in demand.

15.4 Marketing warfare during the product life cycle

The different phases in the product life cycle were discussed above. During the progression

Critical thinking

Is it possible for a motor vehicle to have a life cycle? The following excerpt provides a practical example of the lives of two well-known motor vehicles in the South African market.

The product life cycle of two South African cars
Toyota South Africa responded to the explosion in demand for entry-level vehicles in August 1996 with the introduction of the Tazz as a single budget model within the long-running Conquest hatchback range. Anticipating demand far ahead of industry observers' forecasts, Toyota entered the market with high stock levels and an aggressive marketing campaign and soon began getting Tazz orders of close to 2 000 units per month.

An important reason for Toyota's move to enter the entry-level segment of the South African market was the government's Small Vehicle Incentive (SVI), which kicked off in 1995 with a rebate of 3% for cars costing less than R40 000. This allowed Toyota to introduce the Tazz at a price of R35 905 in August 1996. The price of the base model Tazz 130 in 2006 was more than double, at R74 706, but the car was still one of the least expensive cars on the local market.

After its introduction it was not only a dominant player in the entry-level segment, but on occasion it rose to the position of South

Africa's most popular passenger car. In 2001 and 2002 the Tazz was the overall top selling passenger car in the country, averaging 2 000 sales per month over the two-year period.

Total Tazz sales amounted to more than 200 000 units for an average of 1 700 vehicles a month sold since its launch. Despite its success, Toyota decided to discontinue the Tazz and the last Tazz was manufactured near Durban on 5 July 2006.

The Tazz has been extremely popular as a family car, a rental car, a "pool" car, a security company response car and a student's car. The company has no direct replacement for the Tazz, but will offer a selection of vehicles for less than R100 000, among them the one-litre Aygo hatchback.

Another car that had an exceptional life cycle was the Volkswagen Beetle. It was first manufactured in Germany in the late 1940s and had a life cycle that ended in 1981 in South Africa. During this time various changes were made to the car, including a larger engine, sporty colours and trimmings, etc., all of which illustrate how the marketing strategy changed over the intervening years. The old Beetle was eventually discontinued in Mexico in 2003, showing how long the life cycle of a car can be. The new Beetle was introduced and is continuing its life cycle.

Source: "Tata Ma Tazz", *Toyota News*, 2006.

of the product through its life cycle, adaptations must be made to the marketing strategy to obtain the optimum sales of the product and to keep the competition off balance.

15.4.1 Marketing warfare over the product life cycle

In all the phases of the product life cycle, marketing management is constantly involved in a struggle against direct and potential competitors. In this struggle the marketing strategy is implemented and the four marketing instruments are used as "weapons". The word "strategy" has a military connotation: "The art of war or the art of planning and directing large military movements" (*Oxford English Dictionary*). Emery says: "Marketing is merely a civilized form of warfare in which most battles are won with words, ideas and disciplined thinking."[1]

In the introductory phase, the product's future success in the battle must be carefully considered. While there are few direct competitors during this phase, the danger of future competition lurks if the product should prove successful in the market.[2] In this phase it is important for the business to identify a lucrative niche in the market, a position that can be defended at all costs. This is obtained by making it difficult for potential entrants to enter the market. The following are examples of how entry can be made more difficult: by registering patent rights on new products, by obtaining the source of raw material and thus ensuring that nobody else can obtain this resource, and by delivering such excellent after-sales service that potential competitors will find it difficult to compete profitably in this market.

In the growth and maturity phases, when competition intensifies, the business must launch attacks against competitors and defend its position against counterattacks.

15.4.2 Attack alternatives

There are four main forms of attack:

- In a **frontal attack**, a competitor is threatened on all fronts, and especially on its strong points. Products are matched against products, prices against prices, and advertisements against advertisements. The strongest opponent in terms of resources and skills wins this attack.
- A **flanking attack** is a surprise attack on the opponent's weak points. A good example is an attack launched by Japanese and German automobile manufacturers, which succeeded with small economical cars in the traditional, luxury automobile market in America. The American manufacturers were not even aware that a gap existed in their market.
- In **encirclement**, attacks are launched on many different fronts. Similar products are launched in the same target markets using the same distribution outlets and "me-too" marketing messages. The opponent must defend on all these fronts. The worldwide success of Seiko (a Japanese watch manufacturer) can be ascribed to encirclement. Seiko used all possible distributor outlets and overwhelmed competitors (especially Swiss watch manufacturers – at the time the world's leading watch manufacturers) and consumers with an enormous variety of models (about 2 300) that were constantly changed according to fashion and consumer preferences.[3]
- A **guerrilla attack** is used to launch surprise attacks at the opponent's weak points while a frontal attack is being planned. One example is a retailer cutting the price of a well-known range of products for a limited time and advertising it for a while, and then returning to the normal price. All this is done before the large competitor can react to the price decrease. This is usually a tactic used by a small business in its fight against a larger business.

15.4.3 Defence alternatives

A business that has been attacked should carefully select an appropriate defence method:

- It can launch a **counter-attack** by concentrating mainly on the weaknesses of the attack that is launched against it.
- In **offensive defence** the business can pre-empt the attack if it discovers the plans of the attackers (market intelligence).[4] For example, a business may decide to pre-empt a decrease in the price by a competitor. It can cut the price of the same product – before the announcement by the competitor – by a few cents more, thus creating confusion in the mind of the competitor.
- In **mobile defence** the business can move away from current markets and products

by focusing on other expansion methods. However, research is essential here. Shell Oil's mission, for example, states that it wants to satisfy the energy needs of customers worldwide.[5] Shell succeeded in moving away from providing only petrol.

- In **strategic withdrawal** the business vacates the war zone until a later date when winning the war may be easier. For example, the Apple computer group of the USA withdrew from South Africa in the early 1980s because of political pressure. After the introduction of a freely elected democratic government, Apple returned, however, to win back the lost market share and to engage with IBM in a fight for market leadership. In the decline phase of the product life cycle, the enterprise

---

Critical thinking

At the end of this section on marketing warfare, we might ask ourselves "How can marketing strategies be compared to war tactics?" The following excerpt demonstrates how companies can "attack" in a "war" situation.

Counter-attack: War in the air

Kulula.com first introduced low-fare air travel into South Africa. (This was after Sun Air unsuccessfully tried for a few years to enter the market.) This strategy was soon followed by South Africa's second budget airline, 1time. In a deliberate attempt to undercut the fares by its more established competitors, national carrier SAA launched its low-cost airline, called Mango, which is based on successful low-cost carriers such as Europe's Ryanair or America's Southwest Airlines (the only difference is that Mango is part of SAA, which is financed by the government).

Mango fired the first salvo by offering 40 000 one-way tickets for R169 (including

taxes) between Johannesburg and Durban and Johannesburg and Cape Town. It also promised to offer air fares that were 20% less than any other tickets offered in the market. By mid-morning of the first day of sale, more than 11 000 tickets had already been reserved; 15 000 requests were received within the first ten minutes of launching the website. Due to the unprecedented demand, the website crashed on the first day.

Mango's competitors then fought back, with kulula offering 40 000 tickets for R168 a trip on the same route that Mango served. Not to be outdone, 1time also slashed prices of 5 000 tickets to R165 a journey on the same routes.

Mango keeps its operating costs down by using four fuel-efficient Boeing 737-800s leased from SAA. These aircraft consume 10% less fuel than other available models on the market. Most of the ticket sales are done online or by telephone, which eliminates expensive intermediaries.

Sources: Adapted from "Can Mango give low-cost rivals the pip?", *Business Day*, 3 November 2006, http://www.businessday.co.za/articles/companies.aspx?ID=BD4A308933 (6 November 2006) and "Mango likely to fuel air-travel price war." *Business Day*, 6 November 2006, http://www.businessday.co.za/articles/topstories.aspx?ID=BD4A306192 (8 November 2006).

is often compelled to decide on strategic withdrawal.

15.5 Marketing planning and control[6]

Marketing planning firstly entails the analysis of the marketing environment in order to identify and evaluate certain marketing opportunities and threats so that realistic objectives can be set. The task of marketing management includes the implementation and control of all the activities that form part of the integrated marketing strategy.

15.5.1 Planning

15.5.1.1 Strategic market planning

The business must firstly develop strategic plans that are generated at top management level. The input of marketing management at this level centres on two basic decisions, namely the competitive decision and the investment decision. The **competitive decision** answers the question of how the business is going to compete in the market. There are three basic options, namely:

- **Differentiation.** The business competes in the market in such a way that consumers perceive its range of products as different. As section 15.3 indicated, Toyota decided to introduce an entry-model car that could compete at the cheap end of the car market. This market segment showed sharp growth with the Fiat Mia, Daewoo Matiz, Volkswagen CitiGolf and Mazda Sting as the main competitors. Toyota's answer was to add more value to its Tazz. The cheapest car in the Toyota range in 2006 was the Toyota Tazz at R74 706.
- **Focus (or niche) strategy.** The business tries to attain a small section of the large market by focusing solely on this section. This is probably the best strategy for a small business. The small business does not want

to compete against a large competitor, but rather to concentrate on a geographic area in which a large competitor is not well represented.
- **Low cost strategy.** The business tries to obtain savings by mass manufacturing products, thereby attaining economies of scale. Thus lower prices are asked for its products.

The **investment decision** (or **growth decision**) centres on the following four options that exist for the business:
- Growth of the business unit and its products
- Maintaining the present position (status quo)
- Harvesting
- Divesting

If the enterprise decides on growth, it has the following options:
- Growth in existing markets (for example, by increasing market share)
- Growth by means of product development (such as adding new products to the existing product range)
- Growth by means of market development (such as by entering new geographic areas and by selling the existing product in markets where the consumers have not previously bought the product)
- Growth by means of diversification (such as adding totally new products to the existing product range)

The **status quo strategy** implies that funds are allocated so that the current position can be maintained. The current market share is maintained and no further growth is sought.

Harvesting implies that no further money is spent in the business unit or on the specific product. The cash that would have been invested is reallocated to other business units or products where there is a better chance of attaining future profits.

Divesting occurs when the business unit

Vodacom's product development

Vodacom added two totally new products to its existing product range. Firstly, it introduced a free e-mail service for users, accessible from their cell phones. With this service, customers pay only for the amount of data downloaded via cell phones or a Vodafone Mobile Connect Card to their PCs.

Secondly, it entered the credit-card market by introducing its own branded card. This card is available to its qualifying contract and top-up customers. It carries no annual card fee, but customers pay a monthly members' fee in return for discounts, special offers and benefits linked to its rewards programme.

Sources: "Vodacom enters tough market in credit cards", *Business Day*, 6 November 2006, http://www.businessday.co.za/articles/article.aspx?ID=BD4A291805 (6 November 2006) and "Vodacom goes for a slice of the online market", *Business Report*, 13 September 2006, http://wwwbusrep.co.za/index.php?fSectionId=164&fArticleId=3436526 (7 November 2006).

or products show losses. All activities are then shelved.

15.5.1.2 Functional marketing planning

After strategic marketing planning, the marketing plans must be formulated so that the activities for every business unit or product can be planned to attain the stated marketing objectives. This is known as the formulation of a marketing strategy at functional level. A detailed marketing plan must be developed for every product or brand name. The first part of the marketing plan forms part of the planning process. This is followed by the development of the action programme and the preparation of the budget, which both form part of the implementation phase. Control is the third leg

of the management task. Figure 15.4 depicts the marketing plan.

The marketing plan entails the following:
- A management summary providing the highlights of the marketing plan
- A discussion of market conditions
- An outline of the opportunities and threats that exist

The next step is the formulation of the marketing objectives. As mentioned previously, the marketing objective relates directly to the primary objective of the business. The primary objective of the business is long-term profit maximisation within the constraints imposed by the environment.

The marketing department, more than the

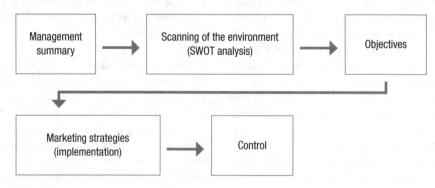

Figure 15.4: Components of a marketing plan

Source: Adapted from Kotler, P. & Armstrong, G., *Marketing: an introduction*, Pearson Education Inc, 1993, p. 3.

other departments in the business, is closely involved in the achievement of profit, for by selling the business's products, it generates income. It can further contribute to profits by attempting to reduce marketing costs.

Attaining marketing objectives may contribute to the achievement of the primary objective either by effecting cost savings or by generating income. The following are the most important of these objectives:

- **Consumer orientation.** This marketing objective has been discussed as the second principle of the marketing concept. Thus far, we have emphasised repeatedly that the marketing strategy must be based on consumer needs, demands and preferences – for if not, the primary objective cannot be attained.
- **Survival and growth.** This marketing objective is, by implication, part of the long-term dimension of the primary objective. Marketing management must continually strive to survive, even in difficult circumstances, and should encourage growth by timeously adapting to the ever-changing environment. Environmental scanning and realistic projections of sales may contribute to the attainment of the primary objective.
- **Increase in sales.** An increase in sales is often regarded as a relevant marketing objective because it is easy to monitor changes in sales figures. However, a high sales volume does not necessarily lead to high profits, because the cost of maintaining a high sales volume may be exorbitant, thus eroding profits. Consider, for example, the high costs of intensive distribution, aggressive marketing communication, and the maintenance of low prices.
- **The highest possible market share.** A large market share relative to that of competitors ensures a high sales volume as well as lower unit costs with regard to production and marketing – thereby contributing to profits. Marketers therefore continually strive to increase their market share.

- **Efficiency motive.** Non-profit-seeking businesses strive to maximise efficiency, instead of maximising profitability. However, this motive also applies to profit-seeking businesses, especially in times of economic decline. The efficiency motive has a beneficial effect on the profit position on account of cost savings.
- **Marketing instrument objectives.** Depending on environmental circumstances, other marketing instrument objectives can be set for different target markets, for example:
  – Introducing a new product to consumers
  – Promoting cooperation in the distribution channel
  – Launching a new advertising campaign
  – Creating an image for the product
  – Discouraging competitors from entering the market

It is important to realise that all marketing objectives eventually have to contribute to profit, even if only indirectly.

The next step in the marketing plan entails the formulation of the marketing strategy aimed at an identified target market (discussed in chapter 13), which entails combining the four marketing instruments (product, price, marketing communication and distribution).

15.5.2 Control

A changing environment demands that the implementation of the marketing strategy be controlled on a continuous basis, to ensure that the formulated objectives are attained and, if necessary, to effect changes in the objectives and the marketing strategy. The marketing control process is shown in figure 15.5.

Figure 15.5 shows that there is in fact a difference between the set objective (increase sales by R1 million) and what is actually happening in the market (turnover decreased by R500 000). This means that the enterprise

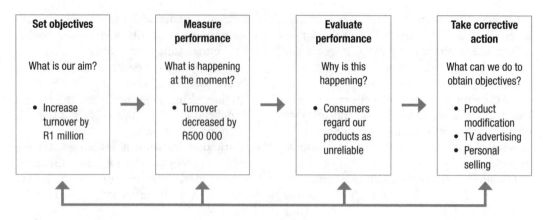

Figure 15.5: The marketing control process

Source: Adapted from Kotler, P. & Armstrong, G., *Marketing: an introduction*, Pearson Education Inc, 1993, p. 52.

is R1,5 million below expected turnover. By conducting marketing research, it is found that the main reason for the sales decline is because of a consumer perception that the product is unreliable. Corrective action implies that minor product modifications are necessary, and that a marketing communication campaign should be implemented to bring the "new improved" product to the attention of consumers.

15.6 Summary

This chapter focused on the integrated

Critical thinking

Growth is but one of the strategies that a company can apply. But what can a company do to grow continually? The excerpt below illustrates how Pick 'n Pay is following a growth strategy.

The growth strategy: Pick 'n Pay

As mentioned at the beginning of the chapter, Pick 'n Pay is the largest retail grocery chain in South Africa, and it is still following a growth strategy. It has increased its market share in existing markets and its half-year net profit to August 2006 increased by 18,5% to R295 million compared with the same period in 2005.

Pick 'n Pay intends to introduce new-format hypermarkets, where it intends to invigorate its fresh produce and ready-prepared meals sections, and spruce up departments such as toys and baby goods. The first two stores will be introduced at the end of 2006, and two more will be added in 2008. It will also revamp the 14 existing stores which it views as "tired". Pick 'n Pay will also open six corporate stores, seven Family-franchise stores, as well as five Score Supermarkets and five Boxer Superstores, which are positioned for the lower segments of the market.

In order to grow still further, Pick 'n Pay also entered a new market segment when it bought the Franklins stores in Australia. In addition to all of this, it also diversified by opening its HealthPharm stores (a franchised pharmacy).

Source: "Pick 'n Pay hypermarkets to take on Woolies", *Business Report*, 18 October 2006, http://wwwbusrep.co.za/index.php?fSectionID=563&fArticleId=3491317 (7 November 2006).

marketing strategy and the management task of marketing. The primary task of marketing management is to plan and carry out the marketing activities and then control them. A specific philosophy underscores the marketing task. Marketing management should adhere to the principles of this philosophy, namely profit maximisation, the satisfaction of consumer needs and preferences, social responsibility and integration. This, rather than misusing the consumer in the short term, should be seen as the long-term objective of marketing management. Marketing management is also closely involved in the process of strategic decision making during the different life cycle phases of the product.

 Key terms

Competitive decision	Investment (or growth) decision
Counter-attack	Low cost strategy
Declining phase	Marketing communication decisions
Differentiation	Marketing planning
Distribution decisions	Marketing warfare
Divesting	Maturity phase
Encirclement	Mobile defence
Flanking attack	Objective
Focus (or niche) strategy	Offensive defence
Frontal attack	Price decisions
Growth phase	Product decisions
Guerrilla attack	Product's life cycle
Harvesting	Status quo strategy
Integrated marketing strategy	Strategic withdrawal
Introductory phase	Target market

? Questions for discussion

Reread "The marketing concept in action" case study at the beginning of the chapter and "The growth strategy: Pick 'n Pay" critical thinking feature on page 366. Then answer the following questions:

1. To how many of the principles of the marketing concept do you think Pick 'n Pay adheres? Explain.
2. Do you think Pick 'n Pay adequately follows the principles of the marketing concept? Give reasons for your answer.
3. Do you think Pick 'n Pay experiences any advantages by following the principles of the marketing concept?
4. What type of customer service would you personally like to experience in a Pick 'n Pay store?
5. Which growth strategy options would you say Pick 'n Pay is following? Give reasons for your answer.

References

1. Kotler, P. & Singh, R, "Marketing warfare in the 1980s", *Journal of Business Strategy*, Vol. 8, No. 3, 1981, p. 30.
2. Durö, R. & Sandström, B., *The basic principles of marketing warfare*, Wiley, Chichester, 1987, p. 143.
3. "Seiko's smash", *Business Week*, 5 June 1978, p. 89.
4. Thompson, A.A., & Strickland, A. J., *Strategy formulation and implementation*, 5th edition, Irwin, Homewood, Illinois, 1992, p. 116.
5. Busch, P.S. & Houston, M.J., *Marketing strategic foundations*, Irwin, Homewood, Illinois, 1985, p. 47.
6. Based on Kotler, P. & Armstrong, G., *Principles of marketing*, 9th edition, Prentice Hall, Englewood Cliffs, New Jersey, 2001, p. 73.

PUBLIC RELATIONS

The purpose of this chapter	Learning outcomes
This chapter explains the role and functions, and the importance of public relations in a business.	The content of this chapter will enable learners to: • Explain the nature of the functional management area of public relations • Describe the management process in public relations • Explain the communications task of public relations • Identify and describe the issues pertaining to social responsibility and business ethics

16.1 Introduction

In chapter 4 the interaction between a business and the environment in which it operates was discussed, including the numerous relations between the business and such variables in the environment as consumers, competitors, suppliers, the government, and the community. These variables and their relation to the business are examined and analysed to identify potential **opportunities and threats** that could affect the profitability of the business. Although Nike sought to gain an advantage by purchasing products produced in countries where the costs were lower, the decision led to a threat to the success of the Nike brand in terms of the damage to its corporate image.

A business is described as an open system that influences the environment, on the one hand, and is influenced by it, on the other. As an open system in a specific environment, a business maintains close relationships with consumers, shareholders, suppliers, government institutions, several other target audiences (publics), as well as its own employees. The relationship between the business and its publics must be managed so that a favourable **corporate image** is created. To do this, purposeful communication is essential, and therefore a large part of this chapter is devoted to the **communication process**, that is, how a business communicates with its employees and its external publics. The impact of the publics on Nike is evident, as

The box below provides an example of how public relations (PR) can be important in the success of any business organisation.

Public relations in action – Nike

Many of us recognise the success of Nike Corporation, which has become a well-recognised global brand and a leader around the world in marketing sports apparel. Nike has built up strong brand equity and its brand associations are some of the strongest in the world, such as its successful sponsorships and associations with sports stars like Tiger Woods and its "Just Do It" slogan. In the recent past, however, some unfavourable associations were linked to the Nike brand. Critics of the firm have highlighted some of its corporate policies and marketing strategies that led Nike to purchase products from countries where the products were produced in less-than-acceptable conditions. This has been termed "sweatshops", where the workers who produced these products do not have working conditions or pay scales comparable with those that have become acceptable

to developed parts of the world. In the late 1990s Nike was one of many large companies that contracted with companies in many less-developed countries in the East to produce sports apparel. Some of the issues around the allegations of using sweatshop labour revolved around overtime, child labour, holiday and vacation, and working conditions.

In order to counter the damage to its corporate image Nike conducted a public relations campaign using speeches and press releases, and even hired an independent consulting company chaired by the former American ambassador to the United states to monitor environmental and labour conditions at its producers around the world. In spite of the concerted effort by Nike, there still remains doubt in many consumers' minds as to whether Nike products are made in sweatshop conditions.

its consumers asked questions as to the ethics of Nike, the financial analysts were worried about the possibility of legal action against Nike, and the governmental agencies in the United States and around the world were urging Nike to comply with generally accepted standards of behaviour regarding its producer companies.

In managing public relations, **social responsibility and business ethics** are of considerable importance. All the functional areas of management are involved in maintaining an ethical code of conduct. The public relations section is closely involved in formulating such a code of conduct, in which practices that are good and correct and others that are wrong and dishonest are spelled out. The way in which the code of conduct is maintained is reflected in the corporate image. Nike has taken action to ensure that it voluntarily follows an ethical approach,

yet the damage to its image will take time to correct and overcome.

16.2 The nature of public relations

16.2.1 The approach to public relations

One of the tasks of public relations is to create and maintain a favourable public opinion of the business (or a positive image of it). Bringing about good relations requires the performance of numerous activities. There is no agreement in the literature or in practice as to what these activities are or should be. Some experts hold that the management of public relations is a matter of communicating with the external environment and getting publicity; it deals with the manipulation of perception, and with the influencing of opinion inside as well as outside the business. Others say that public relations is a form of propaganda, that it is an attempt to obtain media coverage, or even that public relations operates in the same area as marketing communication. These different approaches to public relations management account for the many and divergent definitions in the literature.

To explain the nature of public relations against the background of these different approaches, one must understand that everything revolves around creating a positive image of the business. To do this, public relations management must help to create a favourable corporate culture, that is, one in which a code of business ethics plays a role. Only then can the public relations practitioner communicate: with consumers to reinforce customer loyalty; with suppliers to clear up misunderstandings; or with the public to counter negative perceptions. Employees must also be motivated to demonstrate loyalty as well as enthusiasm for their work. Links with the media are important because the media (newspapers, radio, television) relay communication messages to the various publics. This is especially true today with global access to the Internet and the many sites, such as YouTube, where consumers and other publics can express their opinions about a company and its brands. Recently in YouTube the global coffee-house brand Starbucks had employees posting video clips of unacceptable working conditions in some of its outlets, and this is available for the global community to access!

Public relations management is therefore an interface between a business and its environment: it interprets the mission, programmes and operations of management to its publics; it monitors trends in the business environment and the public perception of the business for management; it gives support to the marketing and other functions of the business; it helps management in its endeavour to satisfy the need for social responsibility.

A favourable corporate image has many advantages, which ultimately influence the profitability, survival and growth of the business. These include the following:

- Consumers more readily support a friendly or responsible business that shows some respect for the interests of its community. Even though Eskom has been criticised lately for lack of performance as to provision of power, its strong community involvement meant that it was still highly rated in the 2007 Sunday Times Top Brands Survey.
- Suppliers more readily give credit for longer periods to reliable businesses.
- Banks more readily lend money to "businesses that don't need it", that is, to reliable borrowers.
- Investors more readily invest in a "good" or "safe" business. The recent concern about mine safety in South Africa has led to the closure of some platinum mines until the safety issues are resolved, and this has had a negative effect on the share price of these mining companies.
- Governments are more likely to give favourable consideration to requests from "responsible" businesses. For example, Gold Reef City casino emphasises that its customers should gamble sensibly, while SABMiller encourages all its consumers to drink responsibly and especially not to drink and drive. This behaviour helps to promote the idea that these companies are voluntarily trying to act responsibly and to encourage their customers to also do so.
- People like to work for such a business. Companies such as SABMiller and ABSA have been identified as great companies to work for in recent results of the Sunday Times Top employer surveys, and the manner in which they conduct their business is one of the factors contributing to their success.

16.2.2 Defining public relations

Public relations entails decision making to help an organisation's ability to listen to, appreciate and respond appropriately to those persons and groups whose mutually beneficial relationships the organisation needs to foster as it strives to achieve its mission and vision.

In the light of the discussion on the nature of public relations, the definition[1] below explains the main elements of the function.

> Public Relations is the management function that establishes and maintains mutually beneficial relationships between an organisation and its publics. It is a deliberate, planned and sustained process of communication between a business and its publics for the purpose of obtaining, maintaining or improving good strategic relations and mutual understanding between the organisation and its various publics – both internal and external.

The most important elements of this definition of public relations are the following:

- It is a **deliberate activity**. An analysis of the above definition shows that public relations is a conscious, purposeful activity of business management. Every programme is geared to realising clearly formulated objectives. Nike set clear goals to establish that its operations were not based on sweatshops and to communicate that to all its stakeholders.
- It is a **planned activity**. It is not an incidental process, but an operation that anticipates events, and is prepared for problems and contingencies. It includes a conscious evaluation of all business activities and their influence on the business's image. The management of public relations should act proactively – it should be oriented to the future and always ready for any difficulty or emergency. Although the Nike action in launching a public relations campaign to counteract the negative publicity was reactive, it has actively been communicating its actions in developing countries to ensure that its brand is not tarnished again.
- It is a **sustained activity**. It takes account of the fact that the public is in a constant

process of change, that people have short memories, and that amid all the numerous matters competing for their attention, consumers easily forget a business unless they are continually kept informed about it. It therefore has a long-term dimension. Nike's founder, Phil Knight, actively communicates with analysts and stakeholders to ensure that all are aware of Nike's stance regarding ethical production practices in Third World countries. This has become a consistent message from the Nike top management team.

- It is a **communication process**. The term public relations presupposes communication between individuals and businesses. Establishing communication channels, especially through the mass media, is therefore a responsibility of public relations. Public relations management needs to have the necessary communication skills to convey information to the various publics of the business so that the members will grasp and accept the message and ultimately respond as management wishes them to. This means that public relations management should include communications experts who, in addition to their knowledge of the principles of communication, should also be familiar with the policy and activities of all the functional areas of the business. Public relations should therefore be part of top management. As highlighted above, the top management team of Nike, including the founder, all communicate the policies and approach of Nike to ethical practices. This is evident even in its website which emphasises it procurement policies.
- It **deals with publics – both internal and external**. A public is any group that influences the organisation or its operations. Internal publics exist within the organisation, such as employees and management. External publics exist outside the organisation. Examples of external stakeholders include unions, the media,

the community, government, financial institutions, and the general public. There have been many examples where the messages to the internal and external publics differed, with dire consequences for the companies. Enron boasted to external publics about its performance and results-driven culture, but the internal messages were that anything goes. When the bubble burst and the Enron debacle took its course it was clear that there were two different messages given by Enron top management to the general public and to its top management team. This resulted in prison sentences for Enron top management in the United states for purposefully deceiving the public and the business community.

Public relations is pre-eminently – but not exclusively – concerned with the external environment. Of course, all business functions interact with the external environment. The difference between public relations and, for example, marketing, human resources management, finance, and purchasing is that their interaction is confined to a particular segment of the external environment. For example, marketing management concentrates on the consumer market, human resources management on the labour market, financial management on the money market, and purchasing management on the materials market. No restrictions apply to the public relations function, and, in principle, it interacts with the total internal and external environment. In other business functions, the nature of their interaction is based on their separate fundamental objectives. The same is true of the public relations function.

Public relations entails creating and maintaining goodwill towards a business. It is clear from the definition that goodwill is the decisive factor. Ill will is something that everyone prefers to avoid, and this applies in business too. The matter of goodwill and ill will occurs in all environmental markets: consumer, labour and financial. Public relations management concentrates on obtaining goodwill and avoiding ill will in all these markets. It is also important to maintain and improve goodwill once it has been obtained. Sasol has had very good growth lately and has been a good performer in financial terms, yet the numerous accidents that have occurred at its plants have led the analysts and governmental safety agencies to be less than enthusiastic about the performance of the company at times.

Mutual understanding has to be created, fostered and extended. This means that a business needs to understand change in its external environment and constantly endeavour to keep abreast of current opinions, demands, preferences and dislikes in it, so that it can adjust its activities in accordance with them. The converse is also true: a business should try to promote understanding of its actions (and problems). Hence public relations is concerned with obtaining, maintaining and extending mutual understanding. Stormhoek wine estate has managed to crack the difficult overseas export market through its creative and innovative use of alternative media such as its blog site to influence the external environment and its external publics – visit

Public Relations websites
Visit the Public Relations Institute of South Africa's (PRISA) website. Here are some other websites that might be of interest if you want to get further information on Public Relations.

www.prisa.co.za	Public Relations Institute of South Africa
www.instituteforpr.com	Institute for Public Relations
www.prsa.org	Public Relations Society of America
www.ipra.org	International Public Relations Association

their site at www.stormhoek.co.za and see for yourself!

Profitable growth and survival should be the ultimate objective for all businesses. The overall objective of a business is to maximise profits in the long term. It is clear that public relations is closely involved in this endeavour because it strives to maintain and reinforce public goodwill toward the business.

From another perspective, public relations is defined according to its managerial functions. Public relations evaluates public opinion and identifies the procedures for the planning and implementation of a programme of action directed at achieving goodwill. The Public Relations Institute of South Africa has a very clear code of conduct to ensure that public relations practitioners attempt to attain their objectives in a moral and ethical manner.

16.2.3 The development of public relations as a functional management area

16.2.3.1 The phases in the development process

Public relations, like other business functions, has progressed through a series of developmental phases to the point where it can now be regarded as a fully fledged functional management area. Three such phases can be distinguished, namely:

- The manipulation phase
- The information phase
- The mutual influence phase

During the first phase, public relations was concerned mainly with **manipulation**. It was a typical technique used by press agents in the 18th century to launch and direct political campaigns. In order to drum up political support for candidates, supporters were not always over-fastidious about telling the truth – something that has caused, and still causes, much damage to the reputation of public relations. Many politicians are still accused of hiring so-called spin doctors, whose role is to manipulate the media to get a favourable result for their candidate.

The public became antagonistic, and, in response to its resistance to such methods, public relations management changed tactics, and adopted a policy of providing **information** about the business. This change began at about the beginning of this century. By 1910 it had become apparent that businesses did not communicate with the public merely by means of words in newspapers, but also through their policies and actions. Many of the initial websites for companies, for example, merely told those who visited the site about the company and posted links to other published material such as the annual report and the social responsibility reports.

This led to the third phase, that of **mutual influence**, in which an endeavour was made to win the approval of the public for the actions of the business. It is interesting to note that public relations developed in essentially negative conditions, for example, in a threatening situation or when public support was needed. A good example is the situation in which the image of a business has been harmed among consumers and a specific public relations campaign is launched to improve this image. The campaign by Nike to counter the perceptions in the publics about the use of sweatshop labour is an example of this. An excellent example of managing harmful aspects of the business is the British American Tobacco (BATSA) website which has a link to the BATSA's social reporting attempts (go to www.batsa.co.za). Since tobacco is highly regulated and has very serious health implications it is a good example of a company taking a proactive approach to its social responsibility.

In South Africa today, many businesses have a fully fledged public relations function, with a manager or director at the helm who is a member of top management. SABMiller, for example, has a Public Affairs Manager who becomes the "voice" of the organisation in communicating to the public. This is the angle from which public relations is approached in this book.

In other cases where an appreciation of the importance of public relations has filtered through, the managing director or general manager will often be responsible for the function. A general manager is familiar with the activities of all functional departments, and by virtue of his or her position, comes into direct contact with opinion formers among the external publics and business community. He or she is therefore able to project and establish a favourable image of the business. The question then arises whether he or she has the time to do the job properly.

In a situation where the general manager is responsible for the public relations function, there is usually a special section that assists with image-creation activities. The general manager decides what should be done and acts as the appointed spokesperson to the media. Where a separate public relations manager has senior status, he or she is a member of the top management team and shares in decision making. This manager is then responsible for liaison with the media. In virtually all businesses, media interviews with ordinary employees are frowned upon and often even

PR in non-profit organisations

Increasingly, companies and organisations – right up to the top levels of government – are having to explain the value of what they do, the products, services and jobs they provide, and their contribution to society. Even the President has a spokesperson whose job it is to explain the aim of legislation and presidential actions in areas such as the situation in Zimbabwe and the government's approach to the Aids crisis, as well as liaise with media representatives. Many of the different levels of government, from regional to municipal, are finding that good relations with stakeholders are critical to the performance of their tasks.

prohibited. The Springbok rugby team and Bafana Bafana, for example, appoint a senior manager to handle liaison with the media.

Many non-profit organisations and even government organisations have realised that the public demands **accountability** for what they do. Think of the situation in terms of the Department of Health, or the difficulties experienced by the head of the Wet-Nose organisation – who had some legal trouble and had to make sure her animal rescue organisation did not suffer negatively from the situation. Many of these organisations have a public relations department. A spokesperson will often participate in high-level talks on television and release statements on public affairs. The emphasis is usually on transparency and honesty. Non-profit organisations such as the SPCA and the Red Cross have senior representatives of management who appear in the media on a regular basis.

With increasing emphasis on the necessity for **strategic planning** in a changing and turbulent environment, maintaining close cooperation between the public relations department and the marketing department is imperative. Kotler refers to this cooperation as megamarketing.[2] Advertising agencies that previously handled only clients' advertising campaigns now also offer PR services in a total package. They are thus involved in the total communication campaigns of clients, including media advertising, displays, publicity and sponsorships. In this way, synergy between communication media is obtained, reinforcing the message while avoiding conflicting communication contents. Effective public relations contributes to the marketing effort by maintaining a hospitable social and political environment. Likewise, successful marketing and satisfied customers make good relations with others easier to build and maintain. In the early 2000s it was estimated that brand-related public relations was the fastest growing segment in the public relations industry in the United States. The estimate was that up to 70% of the revenue of public relations firms comes from marketing-related business. In fact, thirteen of the fifteen largest public relations firms in the United States were acquired by advertising agency conglomerates.[3]

Writers refer to this development as the MPR function. In addition, the most recent development in marketing thought emphasises the need for close relations between management and the internal and external groups with which it should communicate (Nike made sure that the ethical behaviour of the organisation in terms of its procurement was communicated to all of its stakeholders through the speeches and interviews by its top management team with the external media and with internal media in Nike itself).

16.2.3.2 Reasons for the development of public relations

Some reasons have already been touched on in the previous section. The following changes have, to a greater or lesser extent, influenced the rate of development:

- The development of **trade unionism** all over the world, as well as increasing labour disputes and strikes, show the need to forge links with labour markets. The 2007 strike by government employees, which affected the education of schoolchildren, highlights this need.
- The **image of consumerism** in the West, and also pressure from consumer groups, demonstrate the need for establishing links with consumer markets. Standard Bank had to take action when its decision to charge customers a fee for unused parts of their overdraft facilities led to a customer outcry as to the way this was implemented without warning to the customers.
- Increasing **competition** has emphasised the benefits of a positive corporate image.
- There has been increasing hostility, particularly among young people, towards large businesses, the profit motive, and indeed the whole free-market system. This demands a new **frankness** about the

activities of profit-seeking businesses. The sweatshop accusations against Nike were a contributing factor to the No-Brand movement of the late 90s and early 2000s, where consumers were encouraged to shun the established brands in many categories as a protest against the actions of the multi-national corporations.

- There is a continued awareness of the **social responsibilities** of businesses (in contrast to the effort to make a profit at all costs). This has led to acceptance that a business should make some contribution to the well-being of the community in which it makes its profits. Coca-Cola topped the 2006 and 2007 Sunday Times Top Brands Survey as both the top brand and the brand that had contributed the most to community upliftment in the eyes of the survey respondents.
- A theory of public relations has been developed, and textbooks by acknowledged authorities have appeared, focusing the attention of management on the public relations function and what it can achieve.
- The development of communication media such as newspapers, magazines, radio stations and television channels has emphasised the need for **competence in communications**, and at the same time created opportunities for more and better communications with the world at large. The Internet has revolutionised the way a business communicates with its public. It is generally accepted that about 60% of the content on the Internet is generated by the Internet users, and since there is no control of access this means that companies not only have to use the Internet to communicate but also have to monitor what is said about it and its brands. Many of the leading companies in South Africa have dedicated staff to monitor the "hellopeter" website to handle possible damaging incidents and to respond quickly to customer issues that are posted on this site. (Visit the site at www.hellopeter.com.)
- There have been negative developments

Applying the concept: Public relations

Thomas Madibane is the proprietor of a small business that provides a tour service to tourists who want to visit the Pilanesberg Game Reserve. He is talking to his friend, Valusela, about his business. Valusela asks, "Thomas, do you use public relations in your business at all? I hear it can be effective in helping you create a good image." "Oh yes," replies Thomas, "I use it a lot. I always answer the tourist's questions when they ask me things. Of course, this only happens when I'm on tour with them." "Is that all you do?" asks Valusela. "Don't you do other things to communicate with those who might be interested?" "No," replies Thomas, "Besides, I'm too busy to go around doing too many other things. If there are any requests for information I let my clerk, Thandi, answer the query."

Is Thomas really practising public relations in his business? Refer to the definition of public relations (see section 16.2.2) in answering this question.

Let us now consider the above in relation to the following key elements of public relations:

- A **deliberate activity**. Public relations is a purposeful activity, with every action geared towards achieving clearly formulated objectives. Thomas is not adhering to this, as he only responds to requests.
- A **planned activity**. The public relations process means that managers have prepared and are acting proactively. The approach of Thomas is ad hoc and purely responsive.
- A **sustained activity**. A business must continually interact and inform its publics, as public relations is a long-term process. Thomas only responds to questions when he is "on tour", which means very little happens when he is not on tour. This is clearly not a sustained activity, but something that happens only once in a while.
- A **communication process**. This implies that communication channels have been established and that the staff responsible for public relations activities have the necessary communication skills. It is highly unlikely that Thandi has been properly trained in public relations and communication skills. In fact, it appears that Thomas himself is sadly lacking in the necessary skills and knowledge to use effective public relations correctly in his business!

at international level regarding many multinational corporations, and these have shown how essential it is to promote **goodwill** and a favourable image. The Nike and Enron examples mentioned in this chapter are good examples of this.
- The need for **economic growth** and the **creation of new** jobs means businesses must be more sensitive to public disapproval.

16.2.3.3 What public relations is not

One should always consider what falls outside the scope of public relations:
- Public relations is not part of marketing communication, although the tasks of the two departments sometimes overlap in the areas of advertising and publicity.

- The public relations department is not a charitable organisation, even if charity often contributes to an image of involvement and responsibility.
- Public relations is not part of the human resources department, although the labour relations and human resources department and the public relations department are both interested in conditions in the labour market.
- Public relations does not necessarily mean currying favour through entertainment and parties, although these are often necessary to show goodwill toward certain groups.
- Public relations is not intended to put up a false front behind which the defects of a business can be hidden. The Fidentia scandal in South Africa shows that

---

Critical thinking

The Royal Canin Case

At the end of this section we can ask ourselves the question: "Why is public relations important to a company in ensuring its long-term success?" The following short case study shows us what a company can do to recover from a very bad situation and to re-establish the trust of the public in the company.

In early 2007 the Royal Canin company was in a crisis when it was discovered that its dog food brand Vet's Choice had used contaminated ingredients that resulted in the deaths of dogs in South Africa. The company had issued warnings to the public and to veterinarians about the problem and had withdrawn its product off all the shelves in South Africa until tests confirmed that the food was responsible for the dog's deaths. It

encouraged all customers who had purchased the product to not feed it to their dogs until the true situation could be established. The head of the company was often on television and in the media explaining the steps the company was taking and what consumers of the brand should do. Once the product was corrected, it was re-launched to the public with health notices about the contents being tested positive for safety. It also undertook actions such as sponsorship to rebuild the goodwill that had been damaged. For example, the company sponsored the water points for dogs in the 702 Big Walk event, and provided ribbons and certificates for all dogs who finished the event. It provided free specially designed water bottles for dog-owners, and gave free pictures mounted in a key chain of the dog and its owners for all finishers.

---

even though Fidentia was active with sponsorships and community work it did not keep it from going bankrupt when the financial shenanigans were uncovered.

- Public relations does not mean employing attractive young men or women to put guests in a good mood, although attractive and agreeable people are always an asset when dealing with important people.
- Public relations is not there to think up foolish and expensive ways of wasting money.
- Public relations is not there exclusively to put out fires and save a business from difficult situations, although it may sometimes be called upon to do so.

16.3 Public relations management

16.3.1 The management task

Against the above background regarding the nature and development of the public relations

function, it is clear that the management of public relations is indeed important for the profitable survival and growth of a business and therefore needs careful consideration. Planning, organising, leading and controlling public relations activities are discussed separately in the following sections, keeping in mind, however, that the management of public relations is a continuous process. Control over public relations activities provides, for example, new inputs to further planning, as indicated in figure 16.1.

Every project or action programme undertaken by the public relations department should be managed. When a special event (for example, a reception) is planned, information must be gathered, objectives set, responsible people appointed to perform specific tasks, and a budget established. Control is also important to ensure that nothing happens during the reception to harm the image of the business.

Figure 16.1 shows the steps in managing public relations activities. The arrow shows that control methods lead to a new planning phase. The steps in figure 16.1 are discussed in

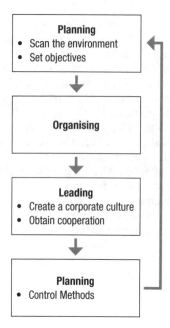

Figure 16.1: Steps in public relations management

the following sections. As you go through the steps think of an organisation such as the 2010 Soccer World Cup organising committee to see if you can apply the steps to that situation.

16.3.2 Planning public relations activities

16.3.2.1 Scanning the environment

Information on environmental variables is crucial for planning. Scanning involves secondary and primary information, as well as internal and external research.

Secondary information that may be used in planning can be obtained from government and professional publications, libraries, newspapers, trade periodicals, the Internet and reports. There is, however, also internal information available, such as sales reports and the annual financial report. Information files can also be useful in preparing speeches, reports and brochures, and, prior to embarking on advertising campaigns, exhibitions and special projects. The public

relations practitioner should also be aware of new products launched by the business, any planned big expansions, and threatened strikes by employees. It often happens in practice that questions that cannot be answered by other departments are referred to the public relations division. Editors of newspapers and compilers of radio and TV programmes make use of the public relations information service as a source. The public relations department should therefore be up to date not only with changing external environmental variables, but also with internal developments.

The 2010 committee has to monitor the effects of the economy and the labour

The Foundation For Human Rights campaign

Research conducted during 1999 on behalf of the Foundation for Human Rights showed that at grass roots level at least half of all South Africans did not know their rights under the new Constitution. They were aware of the Bill of Rights, but had a poor understanding of its contents and implications. Awareness of institutions to help citizens, such as the Public Protector, was non-existent, and there was also low awareness of issues such as disability, immigrants, and rights of people living with HIV/Aids.

On the basis of this, emphasis was placed on informing the target publics on three aspects: the role of the Foundation, the basic rights of every South African, and the rights to redress where human rights abuses are suffered. Media liaison was critical in drawing attention to and coverage of human rights days, and the publication of features on human rights. The corporate identity of the Foundation was redesigned and emphasis was placed on human rights events of the Foundation and also non-governmental organisations (NGOs).

Source: Adapted from Rensburg, R. & Cant, M., *Public relations: South African perspectives*, Heinemann, Johannesburg, 2002, pp. 87–96.

market on the targets for completion of the stadium and infrastructure projects, as well as monitor any internal developments in terms of secondments and job responsibilities for ensuring everything runs smoothly in the run-up to the World Cup.

Ad hoc research is conducted internally to obtain primary information on employees' opinions on specific issues, or externally to determine public opinion and the perception of the image of the business. All information thus gathered must be systematised and processed, and be readily available to assist management in decision making.

Intensive **analysis of publics**, both external and internal, will indicate the special characteristics of various publics as well as their opinion makers. This information is necessary for the correct formulation of the message to be addressed to a particular public. The question to be answered is: Who are the people most important to our organisation? From this may follow a wide-ranging classification, such as employees, shareholders, dealers, suppliers, educational institutions, government, consumers, competitors, communications media, financial institutions, welfare organisations, and business and professional associations. The 2010 committee had to establish contact and liaison with the municipal governments and mayors of the metropolitan areas where the construction of stadiums is taking place – as these are critical in meeting the time and budget deadlines.

Figure 16.2 on page 380 shows key publics for a multinational corporation such as Anglo American Corporation, Coca-Cola or SABMiller.

The public relations function is aimed at specific publics, and the complexity of external groups points to the necessity for deliberate and planned research. Each group has a certain relationship with the business, and has an interest in it. For example, employees want employment and wages; shareholders, dividends; consumers, good products and services; the government, taxes; distributors and dealers, profits; suppliers, orders; educators and the community, financial support. The diverse interests of external groups must be identified.

Every business has to decide which of the publics is important to it. Few businesses have enough time or resources to keep in touch with all the possible publics. Nor is it always necessary for the public relations department to do so. For example, information about consumers can be obtained from the marketing department, about suppliers from the purchasing department, and about financial institutions from the finance department. Public relations should cooperate with all functional departments, taking care not to trespass on specialised areas. The 2010 committee will have to make sure all the different objectives of stakeholders are managed in a balanced manner – the construction companies, the munincipal government, the national government, the media representatives, the players, the South African public, and FIFA. It will have to work with the hospitality industry, transport industry, and the safety and security industry to make sure all events run smoothly and safely and that all visitors to South Africa have pleasant experiences here.

16.3.2.2 Setting objectives for public relations

The objectives of public relations have already been partly explained in the definition and include the following:

- Demonstrating the social involvement of the business in an effective way
- Promoting a positive image of the business
- Bringing about mutual esteem and understanding between the business and external groups through effective communication
- Ensuring that the goodwill of external groups is obtained and preserved
- Preventing the image of the business from being harmed, and its operations from being impaired by dissatisfaction

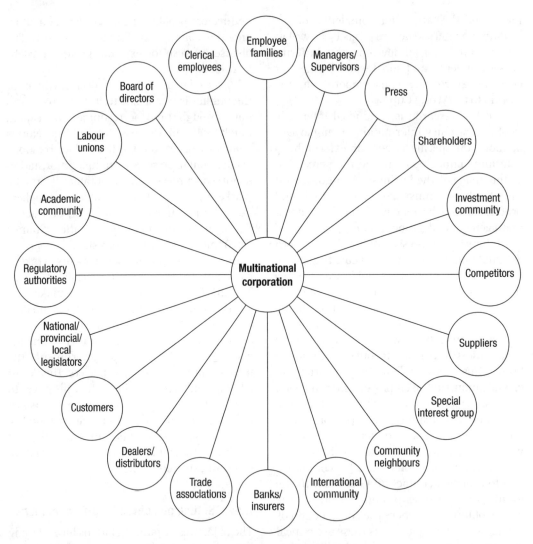

Figure 16.2: Twenty key publics of a typical multinational corporation

Source: Adapted from Seitel, F.P., *The practice of public relations*, Prentice-Hall, Upper Saddle River, 2001, p. 12.

The public relations activities by Nike were an attempt to prevent Nike's image as an ethical company from being damaged and to prevent the goodwill of customers to the Nike brand from being damaged.

Specific communication objectives are determined by whatever public relations programme is being launched as well as by the situation. Such objectives might be:

- To bring new ventures of the business to the attention of the publics. Automobile companies such as Toyota use events such as a launch to introduce new models to the customers and the automotive media.
- To correct negative publicity. Sasol had to re-establish its credentials as a strategically well-managed company with strong growth prospects after the accidents at its plants

damaged its reputation with financial analysts.

- To get "free" publicity for the business through press releases about newsworthy events. Airports Company South Africa (ACSA) announced the commissioning and completion of its infrastructure projects such as the parking arcades at the major airports because it is very topical in terms of the run-up to a successful 2010 Soccer World Cup.
- To try to gain the goodwill of a certain public by means of sponsorship. Vodacom has become one of the largest sponsors of sporting teams and events in South Africa to ensure it gets the goodwill of the sports-minded public.
- To counteract public resentment of certain actions taken by the business by showing willingness to listen to accusations and complaints. The Social Report by BATSA shows how British American Tobacco met face to face with many of its critics and the steps that it tried to take to address the issues that they may have had with the firm.
- To promote the image of the business in the eyes of potential employees. Netcare has promoted its community involvement in terms of health care and paramedic training and facilities to try to ensure that it is at the forefront of the minds of potential health care professionals. In this way it can try to ensure it gets the best of a decreasing talent pool in terms of South African health care staff.

16.3.3 Organising

16.3.3.1 Public relations as part of top management

The approach in this book is that public relations is a fully fledged functional management area and that the public relations manager is on an equal footing with top managers, such as in marketing, purchasing and human resources departments. Top management takes the strategic decisions that must be implemented at functional level. Where public relations is regarded as a fully fledged functional management area, it follows that an organisational structure must be designed for it, with the various public relations activities grouped together under the leadership of a public relations manager. Precisely how the department is organised differs from one business to the next, and is influenced by factors such as the number of people, the clients or external groups to be served, and geographical position. Figure 16.3 shows a typical organisation chart for public relations.

There are various advantages in a well-designed public relations department that functions at top management level. Here the public relations manager has personal and participative relations with other managers and subordinates; is familiar with the relationships between various departments and between employer and employees; is familiar with the undercurrents and knows key staff; knows the conservatives and the liberals, as well as those whose personal ambitions or convenience matter more to them than the welfare of the business. Because of his or her position in the business and commitment to it, the public relations officer is constantly available, and can carry out all manner of

Figure 16.3: The organisational structure in a typical public relations department

public relations duties. If something unexpected and potentially disastrous should happen, he or she is within easy reach for consultation with top management, will have established reliability and credibility with the press, and can save top management the embarrassment of communicating with the media by means of a consultant called in from outside.

The main disadvantage of a public relations department is the danger that the manager may simply come to agree with all the activities of the business, and whose objectivity may be suspect because of loyalty to the products, the people and, most of all, the top management of the business.

The public relations department of Enron did little to help establish the true situation at Enron, and in fact was seen as simply the mouthpiece of top management that helped to hide the malpractices that led to Enron's demise.

16.3.3.2 Public relations as a staff function

Public relations may also operate as a staff function. In this case the head of public relations is usually responsible only to the general manager, is not a member of the top management team, and has no line responsibility. All decisions are channelled through the general manager, and such a situation can make coordination between the various heads of departments difficult.

16.3.3.3 Public relations consultants from outside

Instead of a public relations department in the business, management sometimes prefers to use independent outside consultants. Consultants provide the necessary services to smaller businesses that do not have the expertise or resources. External consultants can act on the same level as top management and are more objective.

There are several public relations consulting firms in South Africa, mostly with their head offices in the big cities. Most consultants are members of the Public Relations Institute of South Africa (PRISA). One of the Institute's aims is the maintenance and improvement of professional standards and practices of external public relations consultants.

The reasons why the services of independent public relations consultants are used include the following:

- A business may lack the necessary knowledge and experience.
- The head office may be so far removed from communication and financial centres as to make liaison difficult.
- Public relations consultants usually have a wide range of useful contacts in the business sector and the mass media.
- Public relations consultants often offer the services of experienced specialists who earn salaries that a small business could not afford to pay.
- A business may have its own public relations department, but may occasionally need highly specialised advice.
- Critical matters concerning the general image of the business often require the independent, objective judgement of an outsider.
- An emergency situation can compel a business to call in public relations consultants from outside to help solve the problem.

Large consultancies are able to employ highly specialised staff, such as writers of "spots", editors of trade magazines, and compilers of radio and TV programmes. They also often employ trained researchers, education experts, legal advisers, sociologists, fund-raisers, economists, photographers and artists. The latest development is that advertising agencies provide this service. The result is that the marketing communication programme and the public relations programme are integrated and presented to the client as a package. An integrated programme has obvious advantages and virtually no disadvantages.

16.3.4 Leading the public relations activities

Public relations managers should play a leading role in all management decisions concerned with creating an image. They also have to make recommendations to top management concerning ways in which a positive image can be conveyed. They play an important role in establishing a positive corporate culture in which everyone will enthusiastically cooperate to achieve their objectives.

Nike would have consulted with its own internal department as well as the consulting company co-chaired by Andrew Young, the former American ambassador to the United Nations, for advice on how to proceed with the sweatshop issue and to get an unbiased outsider's viewpoint on how to protect its hard-earned image.

The 2010 Soccer World Cup committee will arrange periodic activities, such as press conferences, official tours, press releases, site visits to stadiums, and publications to ensure all stakeholders remain positive about the progress to the Cup and its success.

By making use of internal channels of communication such as a house journal, information concerning policy directives, management decisions, business decisions and other related messages can be conveyed to the functional departments.

Corporate culture is the sum total of the values, symbols and traditions of the business, as well as the ways in which it is led, people are motivated, communication takes place and conflict is handled. This is obviously not the responsibility of the public relations department only, but of the whole management team. It is, however, an area that requires much input from the public relations department. All the activities indicated in figure 16.4 on page 384 are aimed at creating and maintaining a positive corporate climate.

16.3.5 Evaluation and control of the public relations programme

Although public relations managers, like all other managers, must exercise control over the activities of their personnel, their real task is to evaluate public relations programmes. One of the problem areas of public relations management is the absence of criteria by which to measure the total success or failure of a programme. The following are some methods that could measure the impact of a public relations programme:

- The sheer amount of publicity accepted by the media in itself gives some indication of the exposure obtained (for example, two 20-line exposures in newspapers, coverage in the main news on TV and radio, and an article with photographs in a financial journal, on the beginning of the construction of the 2010 World Cup stadiums). Exposure does not, however, necessarily mean that all of the target audience has in fact been reached and has understood the message.
- Readability tests can be carried out to ascertain whether the reports were sufficiently readable and therefore intelligible. However, this does not necessarily mean that any of the publics have accepted the message.
- Listener research gives some indication of the number of people who watched or heard a particular radio or TV programme. Respondents can be asked to keep a daily record of their listening and watching times, or the times can be noted electronically.
- Attitudes can be gauged by surveys, using questionnaires, and rating scales, to determine people's responses to reports or programmes. Nike would have to monitor public opinion as to its success in ensuring the sweatshop accusations are negated, and this could be reflected in the brand standings and the brand equity figures.

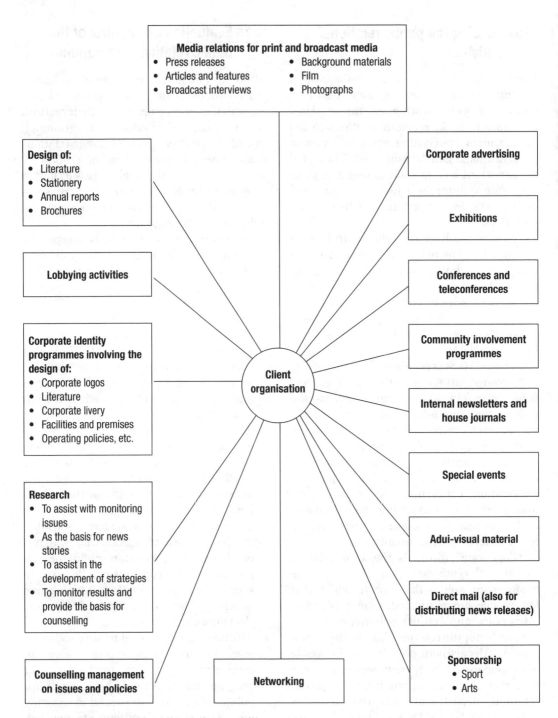

Figure 16.4: Examples of public relations activities

Source: Adapted from Skinner, J.C. & Von Essen, L.M., *The handbook of public relations*, International Thomson Publishing, Johannesburg, 1999, p. 12.

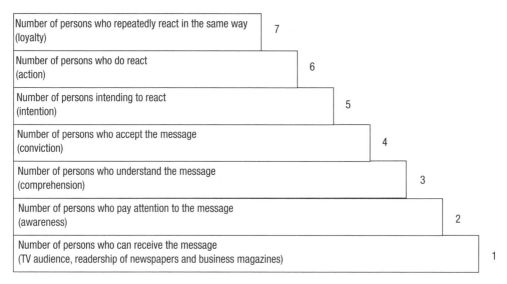

Figure 16.5: Systematic evaluation of a communication message

Source: Adapted from Cutlip, S.M.Center, A.H. & Broom G.M., *Effective public relations*, 9th edition, Prentice-Hall, Upper Saddle River, N.J., 2006, p. 368.

Applying the concept: publics and objectives to achieve

Assume you have been given a project to identify all the possible publics that a large retail chain-store group (such as Shoprite or Pick 'n Pay) should interact with. What would the important publics be, and what would you try to achieve with each of them? In order to answer these questions, we have to begin by identifying the important publics (see section 16.3.2.1). Some of the important publics are: employees, customers, the financial community, suppliers, government authorities, local communities, and the media.

What would be a good objective to achieve with each of these publics? We have to establish objectives that would improve the image of the group with each of these important publics. Possible objectives to consider include:

- **Employees**. Establish good internal communication channels, generate awareness of, and commitment to, being consumer oriented.

- **Customers**. Make sure they are aware of the efforts of the business to provide after-sales service, an environmentally friendly product range, as well as efforts to look after customers' interests.
- **The financial community**. Communicate the new growth and investment strategy and make them aware of the financial performance of the businesss.
- **Suppliers**. Communicate that cooperation is required to meet the need for environmentally friendly products at a cost-effective price.
- **Government authorities**. Try to influence legislation on recyclable packaging and the use of products bearing environmentally friendly logos or trademarks.
- **Local communities**. Communicate an anti-pollution strategy and the efforts of the business to provide environmentally friendly products. Emphasise extent of local community involvement.
- **Media**. Communicate overall group strategy and performance objectives to establish the group as financially sound.

All these methods of evaluation are difficult, expensive and time-consuming, and the researchers need specialised knowledge, not only to carry out the research but also to interpret the results. The public relations manager should have a reasonable knowledge of research methods, and should apply them regularly, or else employ an agency, so that there is control over public relations activities.

A budget is used to plan and control the

Critical thinking

At the end of this section on the PR activities, we could ask ourselves what kind of activities we could undertake if we were Group five company and we were trying to manage our relationships with our current stakeholders. Here is a copy of an exhibit from the 2007 Group Five Annual Report (2007:p. 163) that shows the activities the company undertakes with some of its stakeholders. Note the range and extent of the activities and communication efforts!

Main Audiences

Audience	Method of engagement
Shareholders, investors analysts	• Results presentation • SENS announcements • Site visits • One-on-one meetings • Media releases • Roadshows • Management days • Annual report • Annual general meetings • Group Five website • Annual reviews with providers of debt finance • Feedback forum – feedback@g5.co.za
Media	• Results presentation • Site visits • Media releases • One-on-one meetings • Annual report • Feedback forum – feedback@g5.co.za
Employees	• International communication developments in the group – InTouch • Magazine communicating contracts awarded – InSite • Newsflashes • Performance appraisals • Management presentations • Informal events, such as employee gatherings • Roadshows • Intranet • Internal results presentations • Internal operating committees, including OPSCO, MANCO, FINCO, shared services joint management forum • Anonymous tip-off line
Government	• Continuous interaction and at least one annual meeting with SARS and all significant over-border tax authorities

activities of the public relations department. The objective-and-task method is often used in budget allocations. A budget should be set for each separate programme of action. Deviations from these allocations must be investigated and corrected regularly.

Large businesses tend not to reconsider budget allocations, but use the same budget each year, perhaps because it is easier to do so. Budget allocations should, however, be reconsidered for each new venture. The so-called zero-based budget is recommended, as it provides for the planning and launching of new programmes and campaigns called for by recent developments and problems.

Evaluation of a communication message is done systematically, as indicated in figure 16.5 on page 385. The figure shows that even if the message succeeds in reaching many people, its impact decreases until only a few people respond in the way the message intended.

Consider, for example, a communication message aimed at improving the image of business X, which received bad publicity because of fraud. The communication message is contained in a press release as well as a television advertisement in which someone from top management is the spokesperson. Although the message will reach many people, not all of them are likely to believe the message, and still fewer will demonstrate their loyalty by continuing to patronise business X.

Control therefore involves a great deal more than a mere survey or an audit – it is a continuous process that should enable managers of public relations to take corrective steps wherever necessary, and to bring about, maintain and improve relations between the business and its environment.

16.4 The communication programme

16.4.1 The nature of communication

The principles of communication are universal and applicable to all levels of life. Humans communicate by means of sounds and gestures. The most common communications methods in the business world are spoken and written words. The Internet, however, may change this. Non-verbal communication methods can also be used to convey certain messages. The purpose of communication is to convey a message in such a way that the receiver responds as the sender intended.

Communication involves the transmission of ideas, attitudes and thoughts from one person to another. People can communicate through visible behaviour without uttering a word (non-verbal communication), for example, expressing anger or irritation by a shrug of their shoulders, the tap of heels as they walk away, the waving of arms, and so on. Other forms of non-verbal communication are pictures, graphs and statistical equations.

Communication is a process whereby one person – the communicator (or encoder) – conveys a particular message to another – the receiver (or decoder). Of course, the communicator has to formulate the message so that the receiver clearly understands its content and purpose. Furthermore, practically all communication is intended to produce a response in the receivers. It is not enough for them to grasp the content correctly – they must also perform the appropriate action. If a mother says to her child "Tidy up your room", it is not enough for the child to grasp the meaning – he or she also has to respond physically and actually begin to tidy up. It is the task of the public relations department to act as a transmitter of messages aimed at many kinds of receivers. The public relations department tries to induce a particular group to respond in a specific way when a message is addressed to it.

Communication also involves feedback. The child communicates with his or her mother with a vigorous shake of the head. She interprets the signal as meaning that the child is unwilling to tidy up, and in turn makes an appropriate response.

The public relations department has to ensure that the audience correctly receives and interprets messages or signals sent to it, and that the proper response is made. Effective mutual communication is possible only if both parties – that is, sender and receiver – in turn correctly formulate and interpret messages. All the activities of the public relations department should be tested in accordance with the operation of the communication process.

16.4.2 The communication model

Figure 16.6 below shows the components of the communication model from the aspect of public relations management. Each of the components will now be discussed in greater detail (refer also to figure 16.6). We will use the example of Nike trying to communicate to its customers about the sweatshop situation as an example throughout.

16.4.2.1 Communicator

Humans have a natural need to exchange ideas and opinions and, when they do so,

they try to convey a message to someone who can understand it. Normally this means the structuring of an idea in the mind, and its transmission in the form of speech to somebody else. Speech, however, constitutes only a small proportion of communication. People also communicate by the manner in which they speak, by how they sound, by their appearance, or by whatever actions or gestures accompany their words. Conveying a message therefore includes both conscious and unconscious elements. Conscious transmission means the deliberate attempt to convey an idea, while unconscious transmission means the unintentional conveying of information. In our example the communicator would be Nike, and it would be even better if a specifc person at Nike, such as the founder Phil Knight, were specifically identified as the communicator.

The sender has to be a credible communicator – in other words, the receiver needs to have confidence in the sender and respect for his or her competence with regard to the subject matter. **Interpersonal skills,**

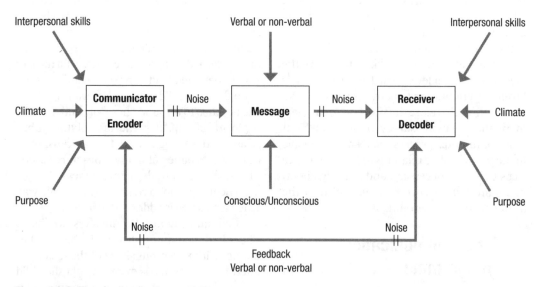

Figure 16.6: The communication model

Source: Adapted from Newsom, D., Turk, J.V. & Kruckeberg, D. 2007. *This is PR: The realities of public relations*, Thomson Wadsworth, California, p. 121.

as shown in figure 16.6, are particular skills that the communicator has to possess in interpersonal communication. We often say, "Unable to work with people", of someone who lacks interpersonal skills. Environmental factors (social climate) also influence the communication process (aggressive workers do not listen to the explanations of even a popular manager).

16.4.2.2 Receiver

Communication occurs only if there is a receiver for the message transmitted. Messages are received not only through the sense of hearing, but also through the senses of sight, smell and touch. In the course of their daily routine, people continually receive both intentional and unintentional signals from all manner of sources about them. As with the communicator, the receiver's interpersonal skills and circumstances affect the process of communication. Messages should be composed to take all this into account.

Note that "noise" gets in the way of receiving the message. Noise is anything that interferes with the reception of the message. It may be something that distracts attention, or competitive actions (such as advertising) by other businesses.

The receiver is usually not a single person, and in the business world mainly comprises a group of people referred to as a **target audience**. The target audience can be employees, a specific group of consumers, shareholders, or the public at large. The target audience in our Nike example would be the customers, but any of the stakeholders could obviously be a target audience.

16.4.2.3 Message

The message is the idea or information being transmitted. There are two kinds of messages: verbal (spoken or written) and non-verbal (that is, all other forms by which information can be conveyed, such as symbols). Figure 16.7 provides examples of these.

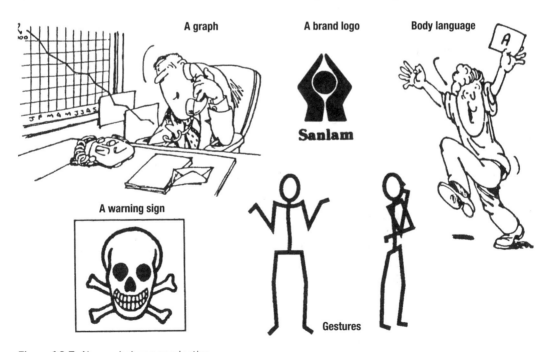

A graph

A brand logo

Sanlam

Body language

A warning sign

Gestures

Figure 16.7: Non-verbal communication

The message has to make sense to the receiver, and must have reference to his or her situation and system of values. It must be simply composed, and carry the same meaning for both communicator and receiver. The message must be sent via suitable channels (for example, radio, television, the Internet or newspapers). The most effective channel for transmitting a message is face-to-face communication. Both words and gestures can be combined in the message. The receiver is virtually compelled to pay attention. This is why it would be important, for example, for Mr Knight of Nike to appear personally on television to make a statement about the bad publicity received as a result of the sweatshop accusations and what would be done to ensure they are unfounded.

The message should be formulated in such a way that it engages the receivers' attention, arouses their interest and persuades them to respond. The composition of a message with persuasive impact is a task that requires specialised knowledge.

16.4.2.4 Feedback

For both participants to be fully involved in communication, the communicator of the message needs to know what effect it has on the receiver, or target audience. Feedback is the response of the receiver to the information that he or she has received, and may be verbal or non-verbal. Feedback ensures that the cycle of communication is completed by linking the communicator and the receiver, thereby keeping the process dynamic. In face-to-face communication feedback is received immediately. The communicator can see the effect of the message and can then reformulate it if necessary. For example, Mr Knight of Nike would have to find out what the reaction of the audience is. Did they hear the message? Understand it? Believe it? These questions can only be answered after evaluation research has been conducted. Television viewers have

to be questioned on their reactions, for only then can the message be reformulated.

It is interesting to test the activities of the public relations department through the operation of the communication model. What does the business propose to say to whom at a reception it is planning, in a news report sent out for publication, or when it sponsors a sporting event? What feedback is expected?

16.4.3 The communications media

Communications media are the channels used to convey the communication message. The spoken word, the printed word, sight and sound symbols, the electronic word, images on the Internet, and special events are examples of the communications media used by the public relations department to transmit messages. Nike could use all of these media to ensure all customers hear Mr Knight's message. Nike could tape the television message and distribute it to customers through the Internet site, it could make the radio available to radio stations, it could publish excepts from the speech in printed material by buying space and placing it in the space, and it could repeat the taped message at a nationwide roadshow of its new apparel lines.

16.4.3.1 The spoken word

The spoken word is used in face-to-face communication and is probably the most important method of communication in any business. Both communicator and receiver must speak the "same language" for the one to understand the other. In South Africa effective communication is difficult with so many languages, but even without a language problem, misunderstandings frequently occur because people interpret communication messages differently.

The public relations department also uses the spoken word to communicate with external publics. This is usually done by means of news conferences, panel discussions, and interviews, often on radio and television. In all these cases communicators must have the ability and fluency to deliver the message, even under pressure. They must give the right answers in arguments, and when confronted by difficult questions. In a news conference, a carefully prepared statement is read to reporters to ensure that the message is correctly conveyed. In question-and-answer sessions following the statement, the public relations officer must be diplomatic and able to talk "off the cuff". This makes it clear why the choice of a suitable spokesperson is so important, and why ordinary employees cannot be allowed to communicate freely with the media. Mr Knight of Nike could appear at all the business shows in the major media in a question-and-answer session to get the Nike message and actions across.

16.4.3.2 The printed media

Newspapers, magazines and company publications are important printed media for the written word. Receivers can read (and try to understand) the message, while carefully selected pictures (illustrations) are used to support and reinforce a non-verbal message.

- **Newspapers**. There are many morning, evening and Sunday papers available in urban and most rural areas. They appear in different languages and are read by a diverse audience. News reports are rigorously selected, and it is by no means easy for the public relations department to get its press releases accepted. Favourable mention of a business or its activities will be obtained only if the items are really newsworthy. Good relations with the press have to be cultivated, as it is the opinion of journalists and editors that will determine the placing of news items. The distribution of newspapers is well organised, and they are available in virtually every city and village on the day of publication.

  Besides numerous urban and national

papers such as *The Star*, the *Sunday Times* and *Business* Day, there are also regional or local papers, for example, the *Pretoria News* and the *Sowetan*. Their purpose is to provide news about events and conditions in their immediate locality, and they are therefore generally very popular. Such publications are excellent media for public relations because they are usually willing to publish news items about the activities of local business entrepreneurs or notable personalities.

- **Magazines**. There are also a great number and variety of magazines. The following types normally appear weekly, fortnightly or monthly, and are aimed at particular readers:
  - General magazines with articles on a variety of topics of general interest and a wide public readership
  - Magazines aimed at a particular section of the public – men (*Men's Health*) or women (*Bona, Fair Lady, True Love*)
  - Specialised publications for those interested in particular sports, or with specific interests (health-conscious people like to read *Longevity*; outdoor-oriented people read *Getaway*)
  - Professional journals read by academics, doctors, lawyers, farmers, engineers, and so on (business people, for example, read *Financial Mail*).

- **Company publications**. A wide range of publications are used: handbills, brochures, annual reports, news sheets, books, road maps, guides, directories, recipe books, posters, wall charts, photographs, pictures, pocketbooks, desk diaries and, in some cases, personal newsletters or circulars. Annual reports and newsletters constitute particularly effective means of conveying news about a business and its activities. It is the job of the public relations department to issue such publications, with the requisite input from other departments. The purpose of these publications is to obtain goodwill or to create a favourable corporate image.

The publication of **annual financial statements** is prescribed by law for public companies, and this has given rise to a highly competitive aspect of public relations, as companies vie with one another to bring out the most comprehensive and attractive report. Besides information about the year's activities, such a report contains photographs, diagrams and graphics, as well as information about notable achievements, difficulties, expectations, forecasts, expansions and developments. Its main purpose is to influence shareholders and investors positively.

The purpose of **newsletters** is to provide information about a business, its employees and its activities to various publics. Some newsletters are intended chiefly to promote a sense of solidarity among employees, and are therefore directed entirely at them. Such newsletters contain news about the employees themselves, their interests and achievements, and employees also learn about the business and its activities. Newsletters can also be used to reach other target audiences.

Nike could publish a **Code of Ethics** that could be placed in both external and internal printed media, and could print the code on plastic cards to distribute to each and every Nike employee around the world.

16.4.3.3 Sight and sound

The most effective method of conveying a message combines sight and sound, because receivers can see what is happening while sounds (like words and their sound effects) support and reinforce the message.

- **Radio and television**. Just as the public press is the most important medium for the written word, radio and television are the most important media for sound and picture communications. Today practically everybody owns a radio, and most households have a TV set too. The influence of these media is therefore as great as or even greater than that of printed media. The impact of TV is felt nationwide, while

that of radio is both national and regional. The advent of television may have reduced the impact of radio to some extent, but it would be a mistake to underestimate its importance. Some people even prefer radio to TV, while others might be unable to watch TV because they are working or travelling.

The public relations department can use radio and TV as communication media in three ways to transmit messages:
- It can present prestige advertisements, designed to build the image of a business and to make its brands known to the public.
- It can provide news reports, for example, when there are notable achievements, or newsworthy events take place.
- A public relations officer might appear on news reviews or participate in discussion programmes in which newsworthy topics are discussed at length.

- **Films and videos**. Another way of bringing the activities of a business to the attention of the general public is to sponsor documentary films or videos, usually shown on TV, or in cinemas as a supporting feature. Sponsorship of films is not intended as direct sales promotion, but rather to create a positive and favourable attitude towards the business.

Nike could release a viral campaign of the code of ethics on the Internet which could include video clips of the inspection of its production plants around the world. A viral campaign is when the clip is sent by customers who access it to each other, or even place it on a media vehicle such as YouTube to let anyone access it. It could even sponsor the making of a documentary to highlight the problem of sweatshops in developing countries, and what it is trying to do to end this practice.

16.4.3.4 Special events

Visits, receptions, exhibitions and sponsorships are special occasions that present opportunities for communicating messages. The arrangements for such events are the responsibility of the public relations department. Crises that occur regularly and unexpectedly are also special events that make substantial demands on the expertise and communication skills of public relations practitioners. Special events include the following:

- **Press conferences**. Press conferences, which are usually organised and managed by the public relations department, are special events that afford the business an opportunity to communicate with the public through the mass media. Both the spoken and written word are used at these events. News reporters usually receive a copy of a specially formulated statement made by the spokesperson, after which questions are allowed. This is normally followed by a news report in the mass media. The public relations officer responsible for the organisation of the conference must show diplomacy in fielding difficult questions and an ability to encourage further questions by offering positive answers. A press conference on television often causes amusement when an inept spokesperson has to answer embarrassing questions.

- **Visits to the business**. Visits are usually encouraged because they create opportunities for the business to give out information that will foster goodwill. Of course, this is only done if there is nothing unfavourable to hide. There are usually set visiting times, when employees and members of the public are conducted through the premises by somebody with sufficient knowledge of the business to be able to answer any questions. Visitors or employees have an opportunity to see for themselves how products are manufactured, what working conditions are like, the facilities and amenities provided for employees, what safety regulations are taken, and how quality control methods are implemented. They are usually given pamphlets or brochures with additional information about the business. It is also common practice to treat visitors to refreshments at the end of the tour, which presents yet another opportunity of passing on more information. Nike could encourage independent worker rights organisations to visit any of its plants for themselves to see the true situation there.

- **Receptions**. Businesses often take advantage of a particular occasion to entertain a select group of people at a luncheon or cocktail party. This is usually accompanied by a speech informing those present about particular achievements or developments, and provides an opportunity for hosts and guests to meet and mix informally. Again, the primary objective is to further the image of the business rather than to promote sales, although increased sales may in many cases result from a favourable image.

- **Exhibitions**. Most large businesses have places in their own buildings suitable for holding exhibitions. They may demonstrate the process that a product undergoes through to its completion, or what equipment or apparatus is used, or may provide information, accompanied by photographs, of performances achieved. Practical demonstrations can also be given. In 3M's head office in Minneapolis, for example, there is a Hall of Fame in which the products of the business, made over the years, are exhibited.

- **Crisis management**. Crises (and other unforeseen events) constitute threats to the continued survival of a business. The public relations department must have a crisis plan ready to manage these unfortunate events. A crisis can be caused by a strike, a fire, a big accident on the factory floor, fraud and theft, defective products which threaten danger and even loss of life to consumers, and a whole range of unexpected and unwelcome events. The purpose of a crisis plan is to limit as far as possible the physical and financial damage caused by the event, and to protect the corporate image.

A specially appointed crisis coordinator must also be responsible for the following, which relate to internal and external communications:

- Compiling a list of persons to be informed about the nature of the crisis
- Training of telephone operators to answer enquiries in the correct way
- Appointing a spokesperson
- Informing and training employees to act correctly in emergencies. An emergency number should be readily available
- Formulating a message to prevent further possible damage caused by negative rumours

After the crisis has passed, the public should be reassured that everything is back to normal. In handling a crisis, transparency and honesty should prevail. The Royal Canine product recall, the Sasol plant accidents, and the recent product recall by Mattel toys of some of its toys are recent examples of companies that had to manage a crisis.

16.4.3.5 The Internet

There is no doubt that the interactive workplace (cyberspace, the Internet, the World Wide Web) has affected the way many businesses operate. One of the most important developments is the use of public relations tools on these channels. Examples of this are the use of podcasts, blogging, Web sales, intranet operations and using the Web to communicate with target publics. These electronic channels will become an increasingly powerful communications tool for public relations practitioners. Seitel[4] identifies three reasons for this:

- **An increasing consumer demand to be educated as opposed to merely being sold things.** Many consumers and target publics are better educated and know when someone is trying to oversell them. Communications programmes should respond by using more education-based information rather than blatant promotion. The Internet is a good example of the use of such information.
- **Time is of the essence.** The need to move quickly is well known in business, but there is an even greater pressure to operate in a real-time mode. The world has become a global village where immediate communication is possible. The Internet and the instantaneous access it provides can be used by public relations practitioners to respond instantly to any emerging issues or market changes.
- **An increasing need for customisation.** There are more and more choices available to consumers. Think of the number of television channels there used to be in South Africa and compare this with the

Promoting the "Blair Witch Project" on the Internet

The 1999 film "The Blair Witch Project" was filmed on a budget of $35 000, but was one of the most successful films that year and helped to introduce Hollywood to the power of the Internet. A year before the release of the film the filmmakers launched a very realistic website and continued to add information to it over time. To build anticipation, the site reported a number of "events" surrounding the disappearance of the three students around which the plot of the movie revolved. Visitors to the site began to discuss the movie in chat rooms, and hypertext links were set up between the various chat sites, funnelling thousands of interested visitors to the site through the Blair Witch experience.

The production company kept placing new information on the site, and the updated site was tied to a number of promotions from books and TV specials to university campus events. The filmmakers even produced a soundtrack CD, which was unusual since the film did not have any music.

Source: Adapted from Seitel, F.P., *The practice of public relations*, Prentice Hall, Upper Saddle River, 2001, pp. 320–321.

current situation (satellite television has exponentially increased the number of possible channels available to consumers).

This increase in choice means that consumers today have increased expectations. They expect a more focused approach, catering to their specific needs and offering one-to-one communication. Businesses will have to focus on ever-narrower target segments or audiences, and the Internet offers the vehicle to do this.

In businesses, electronic mail or e-mail is an increasingly important channel for communication with internal publics or other employees. It has become the preferred choice over traditional print media or fax technology. The advantages of e-mail are that it is more immediate and more interactive. Employees can provide feedback immediately to what they read or hear, and businesses can respond quickly to this feedback.

16.4.4 Publicity

16.4.4.1 The nature of publicity

Obtaining publicity is one of the most important communication tasks of the public relations department. Publicity is the free (hopefully positive) mention of the business, its products and activities in the mass media. The public relations department coordinates all efforts to gain positive publicity. This is no easy task and other departments should assist in the quest for publicity. In chapter 14 it was pointed out that the marketing department, which has direct contact with the market, also uses publicity to promote product sales.

All departments should be involved in the avoidance of harmful publicity, but the public relations department has the greatest responsibility in this regard. Firstly, it must help to establish an ethical climate in which transparency and honesty prevail. Secondly, everybody should be made to realise that

confidential information should not leak out, and that only the official spokesperson may talk to the media. And thirdly, the public relations department has the responsibility to reduce, as far as possible, the harmful effects of negative publicity. This can only be done if the corporate climate is positive and the spokesperson very diplomatic.

Negative publicity can lead to boycotts, ill-will and even legislation. The business consequently loses the goodwill of its employees and external publics, which could threaten its survival. If something unforeseen happens it is regarded as newsworthy by the media. Negative publicity is the result. If this happens, it serves no purpose to try to reduce its harmful effect by being dishonest. An acknowledgement and corrective action usually have positive results, especially as these actions also have news value. Sometimes even negative publicity can have positive results. There is a rather cynical view that says it is always a good thing to get one's name mentioned, no matter what is being said! We have identified the case of Vet's Choice brand of dog food, where the parent company Royal Canine was fairly unknown in South Africa until the product recall was extensively covered in the media – an example of unwanted publicity if ever there was one.

16.4.4.2 Methods of obtaining publicity

There are four important methods that can be used in the quest for publicity, namely unique special events, unique communication messages, press releases and sponsorships. Red Bull has been one of the most innovative companies using publicity and we will use examples related to them to illustrate the concepts.

- **Unique special events**. The more usual events are discussed in section 16.4.3.4, but to be really certain of publicity, the event must be unique and newsworthy. Media reporters are usually invited to special events, but only those that capture their interest are reported on. An ordinary event may merit a news item on the society page, but reports on a unique event reach the front page or the day's main news broadcast. The launch of a new model luxury motorcar is often a unique event where no expense is spared in treating reporters. Publicity is therefore not really free, but sometimes very expensive to obtain. Red Bull devised its own event where participants tried to "fly" their creations off a ramp over water to see who could go the furthest. They filmed this event and used it to produce their own TV show around it. They are also active in producing special events for some extreme sports which they sponsor, such as skiing, snowboarding, skateboarding and motorcycle jumping.

- **Unique communication messages**. The media often report on imaginative advertisements, unusual billboards or other communication methods. The value of such positive publicity to an innovative business cannot readily be determined. Innovation in any area usually merits positive mention in the mass media. A recent newspaper article reported the ten most downloaded Internet advertisements, and identified both the products and the site address where they could be accessed. Red Bull has stuck to its "Red Bull gives you wings" message but updated it with different executions of it in the media to keep it fresh.
- **News releases**. The public relations department is responsible for carefully formulated news releases, which should be supplied on a regular basis to the media. This is done according to a prescribed method and is cleared by management beforehand. These news releases contain information regarded as newsworthy by the business, for example, information about new products, markets, appointments and promotions. The decision to give coverage to these releases depends on what the editor of the news medium regards as important. For newsworthy items, reporters are

sent out to gather more information, for example, by visiting the business. An ordinary news release is perhaps given coverage in the business section of the newspaper, while something that is more newsworthy may merit placement on the front page.

Media such as radio and television are informed in the same way as the print media. Many of their reports follow on original reports in the press, which can then be subjected to closer scrutiny. Press releases during and after a crisis situation are especially important. The news about the crisis should be handled diplomatically, and one should bear in mind that reporters will not be satisfied until they are absolutely convinced that they know all the details. The Vet's Choice situation in South Africa was handled by none other than the CEO, who gave the press conferences himself and which made the news releases available to the media as to the revolving situation in terms of finding out the cause of the dog's deaths.

- **Sponsorships**. Sponsorships are possibly the most popular method used by businesses in the current quest for publicity. A sponsorship entails financial assistance to a deserving cause, with a view to obtaining goodwill, and to demonstrate social responsibility. Such projects are not launched simply because they have captured the interest of management. There should be definite reasons for some projects being undertaken and others rejected, and the main reason should be that the business will be likely to benefit. Hence, public relations management should have a specific policy on this, as well as a method of evaluation to differentiate between projects that will benefit the business and those that lack any advantages. Social responsibility does not consist of mere "bleeding-heart" charity – the business definitely expects something (goodwill) in return for what it gives. Red Bull in 2007 signed as a sponsor for a

Formula One car – some would consider that the ultimate sponsorship!

Businesses are usually reluctant to publish details about the contributions they make to different sponsorships because there are always people who will object to them, and this fosters ill-feeling. People who abhor boxing and wrestling, for example, will disapprove of a business that devotes large sums to such sponsorship, but of course the fans will feel differently. Shareholders are also apt to take exception to what they consider "a waste of money" – they naturally prefer a bigger dividend. Therefore, a budget for the control of contributions is necessary. A contributions committee usually assesses various proposals and requests. The public relations department is involved in the management of large sponsorships, on which thousands of rands are sometimes spent. Try to think of the sponsorships of a company such as Vodacom in terms of sports teams and events – it obviously runs into millions of rands. Vodacom would have to show how that spend benefited the company in terms of communication with its stakeholders and/or building better brand equity.

A sponsorship must also be well marketed. The good deeds of the business should not go unnoticed. The sponsorship itself also offers the opportunity for marketing communication messages on T-shirts, stickers, flags, billboards, etc. Receptions, demonstrations and exhibitions are used extensively in sport sponsorships such as cricket, and also in cultural sponsorships, such as a music concert. The following types of sponsorship are popular:

- **Employee benefits**, for example, the funding of educational, cultural and scientific and social institutions serving the employees' community. Assistance with housing and education assistance for the children of employees, are usually also forthcoming, thus providing opportunities to attract and keep good workers.
- Community development programmes, for example, in education, health and charity
- Nature conservation programmes
- Sports or cultural events

An excellent sponsorship, or one that is successfully managed, is rewarded with broad, favourable publicity. That's real *news*!

16.4.5 The communication campaign

All the different messages in all the different media should be combined in one communication campaign. The message in one medium must support another in another medium. The messages are designed to have the greatest possible effect, and the various communication media are therefore carefully considered. The media serve as channels through which the message reaches the target audience. The choice of media is often limited by the budget, however. Usually a business simply does not have enough money for all the available channels that might be used to get all its messages to all its possible target audiences. Obviously, "free" channels must be utilised as far as possible.

Unfortunately, publicity is not easily obtainable if a business is reluctant to advertise. A newspaper or magazine will obviously not be disposed to give free

---

Planning a sponsorship

Sponsorship involves more than just financial support. The entire affair must be well planned, professionally executed and expertly marketed. A poorly planned sponsorship can damage the company's image.

SABMiller sponsors mainly sport because there is a high correlation between sports participants and beer drinkers. However, it only sponsors events where there is a clear link between their products and the sponsored event. For this reason, SABMiller would not consider motor sport and other high-risk activities, where the use of alcohol is inappropriate, for sponsorship.

publicity to a business that does not return the favour by purchasing advertising space. Through careful planning, public relations management has to devise a programme of action that will produce the greatest effect and convey its message to the greatest number of target audiences at the least possible expense. Unfortunately, there is no method of selecting an optimum programme. The choice of an optimum combination of advertisements, TV programmes, press handouts, entertainment, sponsorships, and so on, depends not only on a specialised knowledge of the activities of the business, the nature of the target audiences, and the principles of good communication, but also on experience and a good sense of interpersonal relations.

Cooperation between public relations and marketing is essential in formulating a communications campaign. The ultimate objective of both departments is to stimulate the sales or services of the business to ensure survival and growth in a complex environment.

A business committed to the well-being of society will have an ethical **code of conduct** pertaining to all its activities, and directed at benefits to its own employees and the general public. The code of conduct will stipulate that legislation should be obeyed and that community welfare be emphasised in the pursuit of profit.

It is difficult to lay down universal rules on ethical and unethical conduct, because of

---

Applying the concept: Publics and communication methods

Below are two lists: one identifying possible publics and the other identifying communication methods. Match the public (a–g) with the best communication method to effectively reach it (1–7).

PUBLICS	METHODS
a Employees	1 Publicity
b Shareholders	2 Press releases about the business
c Local community	3 Annual financial reports
d Customers	4 Participation in presentation to parliamentary committee
e Government authorities	5 Internal company newsletter
f Suppliers	6 Visits to manufacturing plants
g Media	7 Sponsorship of local school plays

What are the possible matches?

a = 5   Businesses can communicate with their employees through the use of internal company newsletters.

b = 3   Annual financial reports are used to communicate the performance of a business to its financial publics such as shareholders.

c = 7   Many businesses support the local community by sponsoring or making donations to local schools.

d = 1   Effective publicity is a good way of helping to create a good image for the business with its customers.

e = 4   The use of lobby groups and participating and supporting activities aimed at legislation is a good method of keeping communication channels open with government authorities.

f = 6   One way of communicating with suppliers is to go and visit their plants, to see how they produce their goods and services.

g = 2   A good method of supplying the media with newsworthy items is through the use of effective press releases.

individual differences and the varying norms and values of subcultures and communities. However, it is desirable for a business to have its own code of conduct, for such a code is directly reflected in the prevailing corporate culture and has an impact on the image of the business.

16.5 Social responsibility and business ethics

In the present era, the spotlight in many quarters is on the social responsibility of business and the ethics of people in business. This trend is also evident in the news media and in the most recent literature on business management.

It is not possible to deal with social responsibility and business ethics in depth in this section, but the following are nevertheless dealt with, though briefly:
• A definition of the concepts of business ethics and social responsibility
• The areas in which issues pertaining to the social responsibility of business and business ethics are especially relevant

16.5.1 Definition of concepts

16.5.1.1 Business ethics

The term "ethics" refers to views or convictions about what is right and wrong, and good and bad. Therefore, ethical conduct is conduct or action that observes generally accepted social norms or values, while unethical conduct indicates action that is in conflict with generally accepted social norms and values. It follows that business ethics indicates generally accepted views on right and wrong behaviour in the business context. Ethical business behaviour is individual behaviour that corresponds with what is generally regarded as right (correct) business conduct, while unethical business practices refer to conduct that is in conflict with what

is generally seen as right or correct business conduct.

It is clear from the above definition that what is regarded as ethical or unethical conduct is dependent on:
• The norms or values of a particular community or subculture
• The views of individuals in that community or subculture regarding what is right and wrong in certain circumstances

Within the general standards of a particular community or subculture, individuals develop their judgement of right and wrong behaviour. Their judgement stems from a variety of influences, such as parental upbringing, circles of friends, education, religious conviction, community involvement, and the work environment.

It is clear from the above discussion that it is impossible to have a universal set of rules on ethical and unethical conduct – different subcultures and communities, for example, have different social norms and values. Therefore, in a country such as South Africa, with its diverse ethnic and cultural groupings, it is out of the question to speak of generally accepted social norms and values.

• Some people feel that it is wrong to take a packet of sweets from the local café, but think nothing of taking home stationery from their office for their children's use.
• Some people do not think it wrong to evade tax and inflate their insurance claims.
• Some people think nothing of taking sick leave, even though they are in good health.
• Some people who consider themselves law-abiding citizens do not feel it is wrong to use radar-detection devices to evade speed traps.

Because many businesses in South Africa employ people with divergent views on ethical and unethical conduct, it is imperative to draw up a code of conduct for employees if the business is to survive in the long term. Such a code should contain rules for employees on what is regarded as ethical or unethical business behaviour. In compiling such a code, the following points pertaining to ethical conduct should be taken into consideration:

- The general social norms and values of the community in which the business operates should provide the basis of the code of conduct.
- Vague generalisations about ethical conduct are meaningless. A code of ethics should be as specific as possible and contain details about ethical issues that employees might be confronted with, as well as their desired reaction to them.
- In the same way that management exercises control over the functional areas of a business, it should also ensure that employees adhere to the code of conduct at all times.
- Employees should be held accountable for their behaviour. Compliance with the code of conduct should be one of the

Organisations that engage in dialogue with their publics, and that evaluate organisational performance on ethical standards developed in dialogue with publics, should gain in positive reputations with their publics. As we move further into the century, the role of public relations will need to change from that of merely wielding self-serving influence, crafting communications and researching publics. Ethical practice for the field of public relations will require practitioners to be facilitators of dialogue and listeners, as well as speakers. Strong leadership will be needed from high-profile organisations that exemplify best practices in opening their own practices and decision making to public criticism.

Source: Adapted from Dougherty, E.L., Public relations and social responsibility, in Heath, R.L., *Handbook of public relations*, Sage, Thousand Oaks, 2001, p. 409.

conditions of service, and employees who transgress the code should be subjected to disciplinary action.

- When employees are remunerated according to the profitability of the business only, there is a tendency to ignore ethical questions. Remuneration should also be based on upholding ethical standards.
- Employees may be unsure of what represents ethical behaviour in a particular situation, especially if they are suddenly confronted with it, for example, a supplier inviting one of the buyers of the business to lunch at an upmarket restaurant. Employees should be encouraged to discuss such situations with management and co-workers so that consensus can be reached about suitable action.

16.5.1.2 Social responsibility

While business ethics is concerned with the behaviour of individuals (employees) at work, social responsibility has to do with the behaviour of a business towards **stakeholders** such as consumers, suppliers, competitors, employees, owners or shareholders, and the community at large. Being socially responsible essentially means that a business tries to reconcile the interests of its different stakeholders with each other. For example, profit maximisation is the primary concern of the owners or shareholders, while consumers are mainly interested in quality products at affordable prices. There is, clearly, a conflict of interests. In this case, one often finds that businesses act "irresponsibly" towards consumers in an effort to best serve the interests of their owners.

What are the factors that influence a business's approach to social responsibility? Firstly, businesses are dependent on the business ethics of their employees, and especially of top management. Secondly, social responsibility is often forced on businesses by the government (through legislation), and by consumer action (for example, boycotts). Thirdly, the approaches of competitors to this issue also influence the approach of a particular business.

16.5.2 Areas of social responsibility and business ethics

Issues concerning the social responsibility of businesses and business ethics are mainly prevalent in interactions with the following groups:

- Customers or clients (consumers)
- Suppliers
- Competitors
- Employees
- Owners and shareholders
- The community

Some of the issues that businesses are confronted with in these areas will now be examined.

16.5.2.1 Consumers

There are numerous ethical and social responsibility issues that confront businesses in their dealings with consumers, but these revolve mainly around marketing actions (product, price and marketing communication). Most countries have introduced legislation to protect consumers from exploitation and deceit in these areas, while many professional and industrial associations (pharmacists, attorneys, dentists, medical practitioners, builders and the motor trade) have codes of ethical conduct. Besides these, businesses and business people have wide powers of discretion when it comes to considering whether the following, as examples, are ethical and socially responsible:

- The placing of tobacco, cigarette and alcohol advertisements
- Advertisements aimed at children
- The use of sex-oriented advertisements in media to which all people have access

- Keeping quiet about defects in products when selling them
- The extending of excessive credit to buyers
- A bank not informing a client about the interest rates charged on an overdrawn account
- Increasing interest rates without prior notice
- Basing price discrimination on gender and age
- Providing poor after-sales service or none at all
- Refusing to give customers credit for products they are dissatisfied with, or "forcing" them to buy other products in their place.

The recent passing of the National Credit Act is an attempt to ensure that businesses do not encourage their customers to get into heavy debt situations where the customer may not be able to repay the debt payments. The life insurance industry has come in for much criticism lately in terms of the heavy punishment meted out to policyholders who change terms of a policy – the fees charged for this are substantial. The industry is also challenging the decisions made against it by the insurance adjudicator, with the hopes of overturning the decisions in the higher courts so as not to have to pay out the customer. Is this really reflective of a customer-centric approach?

16.5.2.2 Suppliers

In the interaction between a business and its suppliers, there are numerous cases of questionable ethics, for example:

- Where a supplier is in a strong position relative to that of a client, it is not unusual for the former to enforce unreasonably high prices or order quantities. This happens, for example, when the supplier is the sole source of a particular product or raw material. Mittal has recently been charged with passing exorbitant price increases on steel prices in South Africa, but the Mittal management is unrepentant as to the strategy and defended the increases.

- It is not unusual for a strong customer to compel suppliers to accept unreasonably low prices for their products or raw materials. Market gardeners, for example, often complain that retail groups (Shoprite, Pick 'n Pay, etc.) exploit them when they sign contracts to deliver vegetables. Nike was challenged in court about its responses to the charges of using sweatshop-made products, as some felt that its statements were deliberately misleading. To this day Nike has to deal with the results of the damage to its image, with many consumers wanting to know exactly where Nike has its products made and how.
- It is common knowledge that suppliers often invite purchasing personnel to luncheons, offer them trips abroad, and give them expensive Christmas gifts. Is this fair to competing suppliers who are not in a position – or simply do not wish – to make such offers?

16.5.2.3 Competitors

The following are examples of questionable actions in the interaction between a business and its competitors:

- Circulating rumours about the financial stability, product quality, service quality and business ethics of competitors
- Luring away a competitor's core personnel
- Attempting, in any conceivable way, to obtain confidential information about a competitor
- Waging price wars to eliminate competitors. British Air was recently fined a large amount of money by the American courts because it conspired with Virgin Airlines to keep prices on flights to the United States high. Virgin avoided prosecution by reporting British Air to the authorities.

16.5.2.4 Employees

The following are examples of issues that businesses have to cope with in their interaction with employees:

- A proper and fair general code of conduct for employees in their interaction with the other stakeholders of a business, and the monitoring of such a code, are necessary.
- A policy on sexual harassment, smoking, drinking, drugs, and dress in the workplace is required.

  Toyota recently settled a sexual harassment suit brought against its North American CEO. The employee who complained had brought the charges to the attention of senior management, but no action had been taken. As part of the settlement policy changes have been made that allegations of misconduct against an executive must be investigated immediately and if it is the CEO then a report must be submitted immediately to the board of directors.
- A language policy is important.
- There should be equity without discrimination on the basis of creed, race, gender, skin colour, age, and so forth. An American court awarded two Lebanese employees of FedEx US$12,4 million because a manager constantly harassed them with racial slurs for two years. The men had complained to senior managers, but the company had ignored their claims.
- A safe and healthy working environment must be provided. The new CEO of Anglo-American has gotten the resignation of a few senior managers because there has not been enough action on the worker safety issues in the mines.
- Employees must have the right to privacy both inside and outside the workplace.
- The replacement of permanent staff who enjoy pension and medical benefits with temporary, part-time staff who do not enjoy such benefits is not considered ethical.
- Health and child care must be provided in the workplace.

16.5.2.5 Owners and shareholders

Issues of ethics and social responsibility that businesses have to deal with in their interaction with owners and shareholders include the following:

- Choosing between short-term and long-term benefits. The decision making of top management, boards of directors, and even shareholders of many businesses appears to revolve around the financial benefits (stemming from the business) that they can realise for themselves in the short term. In the process, the healthy continued existence of the business becomes a long-term, less important concern. This may happen, for example, if exceptionally high salaries are paid to top management, or profit is paid out in the form of dividends, rather than reserving it to create a healthy capital structure.
- The tendency to make things seem rosier than they are to attract new investments. Good profits, for example, are shown by writing off inadequate depreciation on fixed assets. For the same reason, there is often a tendency to make unrealistic sales or profit forecasts.

- The investment of business capital in other businesses or projects. This can include, for example, the manufacture of cigarettes and alcohol, pornographic magazines, the production of weapons, and projects that are a threat to nature and wildlife.

16.5.2.6 The community

In its interaction with the community, the social responsibility of a business involves its views and actions on matters such as the following:

- Conservation of the physical environment. This is concerned with issues such as air, water and soil pollution, as well as nature conservation, wildlife conservation, and damage to the ozone layer.
- Utilisation of scarce resources. This is achieved through soil and water conservation and the recycling of waste matter and water.
- Socio-economic issues. These include community capacity development, health programmes (HIV/Aids, TB, etc.), crime prevention, education and training (bursaries, training facilities, etc.).

Opposing views on social responsibility

- **Proponents' view of social responsibility**. This view holds that corporations should contribute to worthy causes addressing social concerns. Corporations are viewed not only as economic institutions but also as social institutions, which, as such, have responsibilities to society. Thus, corporations have an obligation to solve some of society's most pressing social problems and to devote some of their resources to the solution of these societal problems.

- **Opponents' view of social responsibility**. Milton Friedman, a Nobel Prize-winning economist, believes that corporations have no responsibility to society besides adhering to the law and maximising profits for shareholders. Opponents of social responsibility say business makes its biggest contribution to society by producing useful products, providing jobs, and generating the wealth that makes a better standard of living possible. They caution that efforts to deal with social problems must not interfere with business's ability to perform its primary economic function.

Source: Adapted from Daugherty, E.I., Public relations and social responsibility, in Heath, R.L., *Handbook of public relations*, Sage, Thousand Oaks, 2001, p. 392.

Critical thinking

Think about the groups that need to be considered when thinking of business ethics and social responsibility that we identified above. Can you identify any recent cases where South African individuals or organisations transgressed in terms of these? Chances are, unfortunately, that it is not so hard to think of specific South African examples. The media is often full of these negative examples. Here are some related to overseas situations:

- Royal Dutch Shell was fined US$137 million for asphalt price-fixing from 1996–2004 along with seven other suppliers and six road builders. The highest fines were given to Shell as it was a repeat offender and played a leading role in the cartel.
- Constellation Brands in the UK was accused on trying to improperly influence a trial by a pub group of a few wines to see which one would become the house wine at is 650 outlets. Constellation management wrote e-mails to employees urging them to go to the pubs and buy a certain bottle of Constellation wine and expense it back to the company. Staff were asked to redouble their efforts with two weeks left to go in the trial. When the e-mail was leaked to the public the company denied it had been trying to distort sales but claimed it was a mystery shopper exercise.
- Virgin illegally downloaded Madonna's single "Hung Up" to resell on its own site. The site ignored an exclusive deal reached with competitive sites to sell the new song. It had to pay $350 000 in penalties, as it downloaded the song, cracking protection measures and then selling it on its own website.
- SAP and IBM were found guilty with a Hungarian software provider of collusion and sentenced to pay fines worth a total of 5,5 million euros.
- In recent years Wal-Mart has had to pay fines in millions of dollars to Tommy Hilfilger Fendi, and Nike over charges that it was selling counterfeit version of products.

Corporate social responsibility used to be thought of as not something for hardnosed business people, but now it is not an option. The reason is that customers are demanding it. Early in 2007 McKinsey and company did research on more than 4 000 global CEOs and other executives, and found that it was clear that ethical leadership and emphasis on corporate social responsibility can be a strong driver for enhancing profits.[5]

16.6 Summary

The management of public relations entails the planning of a programme of action aimed at specific target audiences, the organisation of public relations activities, leading these activities, and controlling all programmes. The main objectives of public relations are to create a positive image of the business and to obtain the goodwill of specific target audiences. The public relations department is responsible for the communication campaign, where the spoken and written word, sight and sound media, and special events, exhibitions and sponsorships may be used to communicate with different publics. All the communication methods and media must be combined to have maximum impact and to obtain the required reaction. A budget must be prepared to give direction to all the different activities. Budget allocations are made for a variety of projects aimed at image building, obtaining goodwill and demonstrating social responsibility.

The manager of the public relations department should preferably be a member of the top management team and should have a say in the formulation of policy, the planning of strategy, and the taking of decisions. He or she must also be a communications expert and know how to direct messages to external groups; have insight into human behaviour; a gift for maintaining interpersonal relationships; and an ability to cooperate with managers of other functional departments so that the business is always presented in a positive light. Creating goodwill and avoiding antagonism are of prime importance to the survival and growth of a business. Even a great company like Nike has had to focus on continuously managing its relations with all its publics so as to protect the image of the company and ensure the long-term success of the Nike brand.

🔑 Key terms

ad hoc research	non-verbal message
blogging	norms
business ethics	open system
code of conduct	PR activities
communication	PR consultants
communication programme	PR department
communications campaign	PR evaluation
communications media	PR management
communications model	PR objectives
communicator	PRISA
conscious transmission	propaganda
corporate culture	public opinion
corporate image	public relations
crisis management	publicity
environmental scanning	publics
ethical conduct	receiver
feedback	social involvement
goodwill	social responsibility
manipulation	special events
media	sponsorships
megamarketing	stakeholders
message	unconscious transmission
MPR function	unethical conduct
mutual influence	verbal message
noise	

❓ Questions for discussion

Please re-read the Nike case study at the beginning of the chapter and answer the following questions:

1. Do you think that Nike should have the public relations function as a self-standing concept or should it fit under another business function?
2. Is Nike fighting a losing battle trying to run its operations ethically?
3. Why is it important for Nike to perform the public relations task?
4. If Nike again got accused of using sweat labour overseas, how would it best approach the regaining of its brand reputation?
5. What type of activities would you recommend Nike follow to counteract any other competitive activities?
3. How could Nike ensure that it follows more socially responsible agenda?

References

1. This definition was adapted from Cutlip, S.M., Center, A.H. & Broom, G.M. 2006. *Effective public relations*, Pearson: Upper Saddle River, p. 5 and Rensburg, R. & Cant, M., *Public relations: South African perspectives*, Heinemann, Johannesburg, 2002, p. 34.
2. Kotler, P. & Keller, K.L. 2006, *Marketing management*, 12th edition, Prentice-Hall, Upper Saddle River, p. 265.
3. Adapted from Duncan,T., 2002, *IMC: Using advertising and promotions to build brands*, McGraw-Hill, New York, p. 544.
4. Seitel, F.P., *The practice of public relations*, Prentice-Hall, Upper Saddle River, 2001, p. 304.
5. Leffel, R. & Sweeney, V. "Doing the right thing", *Ethisphere*, Quarter 01//2007, p. 019.

THE FINANCIAL FUNCTION AND FINANCIAL MANAGEMENT

The purpose of this chapter

This chapter explains financial analysis, planning and control as key elements of the financial function of a business organisation.

Learning outcomes

The content of this chapter will enable learners to:
- Describe and apply the fundamental principles of financial management

- Determine the break-even point of a business organisation
- Calculate the present and future value of amounts
- Analyse and interpret the financial statements of a business organisation
- Understand the financial planning process

17.1 Introduction

In the introductory chapters of this book, the financial function was identified as one of the functional management areas in a business. In this chapter, the nature and meaning of the financial function and its management, that is, financial management, will be analysed. Thereafter, the relationship between financial management, the other functional management areas, related subject disciplines, and the environment will be shown. An introduction to a few basic concepts and techniques used by financial management will then follow. The goal and fundamental principles of financial management will also be explained. In conclusion, we will discuss one of the tasks of financial management, namely financial analysis, planning and control.

17.2 The financial function and financial management

A business must have the necessary assets such as land, buildings, machinery, vehicles, equipment, raw materials and trade inventories at its disposal if it is to function efficiently. In addition, business organisations need further resources such as management acumen and

Case study

The case study below provides an illustration of how financial management is applied in a real-life situation.

Financial management in action

Imagine that you own 20 000 shares of a retail firm listed on the JSE. You bought these shares at R5,20 each two years ago, but the price has subsequently declined to R1,90 each. Other firms in the same sector have seen increases in their profitability and share prices.

The annual general meeting (AGM) is scheduled to take place in six weeks' time. From the firm's financial statements you have determined the following in Table 17.1.

The economic outlook is positive, interest rates are expected to decline, consumer spending is on the increase and inflation is below 3%. However, the top management seems to be divided about the issues facing the firm.

a What can management do to improve the firm's profitability?
b What can the investors (shareholders) do to improve matters?

a The actions management could consider for improving the firm's profitability are summarised in table 17.2.
b An ordinary shareholder of a public company is entitled to vote at the annual general meeting of the company. The shareholder can improve matters by attending the AGM and by nominating and voting for new members of the board of directors. If the shareholder cannot attend the meeting him- or herself, he or she can complete a proxy form and nominate someone who will be attending the meeting to vote in a particular manner on behalf of the shareholder. Selling your shares will cause a loss of at least R3,30 per share, or R66 000 (R3,30 × 20 000 shares) before any transaction costs are taken into account. It might be worth engaging management and exerting pressure to implement a turnaround strategy, which includes the actions described in table 17.2.

Table 17.1: Information determined from the firm's financial statements

Ratio	This financial year	Average of the previous five years
Gross profit margin	40%	55%
Net profit margin	15%	30%
Return on assets	10%	21%
Return on equity	9%	24%
Earnings per share	45 cents	480 cents
Debt ratio	2%	10%
Current ratio	2,6:1	2:1
Quick ratio	0,8:1	1:1

Table 17.2: Actions management could consider for improving a firm's profitability

Ratio	Suggestions
Gross profit margin	1. Increase sales by means of more effective marketing and/or by relaxing the credit standards (increasing credit sales) 2. Reduce the cost of goods sold by either buying goods at a lower cost from another supplier, stocking goods with a faster turnover rate, and/or reconsidering products with slow turnover rates
Net profit margin	1. Increase sales by means of more effective marketing and/or relaxing the credit standards (increasing credit sales) 2. Reduce the operating expenses and/or improving productivity by means of, among other things, performance management systems, training and more effective use of technology
Return on assets	1. Increase sales by means of more effective marketing and/or relaxing the credit standards (increasing credit sales) whilst decreasing expenses or using existing capacity more effectively 2. Review assets (disinvest non-core business units, use outsourcing and/or improve productivity)
Return on equity	1. Increase sales by means of more effective marketing and/or relaxing the credit standards (increase credit sales) and reduce the cost of goods sold, as well as operating expenses; improve productivity 2. Reduce equity (buy back shares and cancel them), borrow to do so (increase the debt ratio)
Earnings per share	1. Improve profitability (as indicated above) by increasing sales and reducing expenses 2. Reduce the number of shares (buy back shares and cancel them or consolidate shares) and replace this financing with debt financing

labour, as well as services such as a power supply and communication facilities.

A business needs funds, also called **capital**, to obtain the required assets, resources and services. The people or institutions (including the owners) who make funds available to the business lose the right to use those funds in the short or long term, and they also run the risk of losing those funds, or a portion thereof, should the business fail. As a result, suppliers of funds expect compensation for the funds they make available to the business (and also a repayment of funds lent to the business) when the business starts to generate funds through the sale of the products or services it produces. Hence, there is a continual flow of funds to and from the business.

The **financial function** is concerned with this flow of funds, and in particular with the acquisition of funds (which is known as **financing**), the application of funds for the acquisition of assets (which is known as **investment**), as well as the administration of, and reporting on, financial matters.

Financial management is responsible for the efficient management of all facets of the financial function and, within the broad framework of the strategies and plans of the business, has as its objective making the highest possible contribution to the objectives through the performance of the following tasks:

- Financial analysis, reporting, planning and control
- Management of the application of funds,

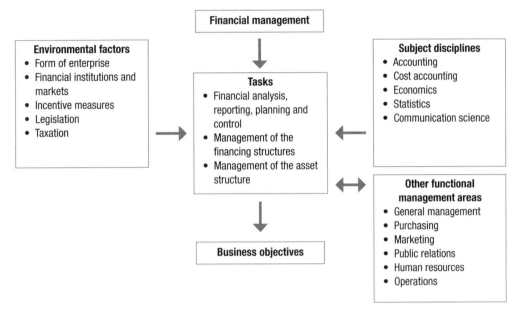

Figure 17.1: The relationship between financial management, other functional management areas, related disciplines and the environment

also known as the management of the asset structure
- Management of the acquisition of funds, also known as the management of the financing or capital structure

(See section 17.3.1 for a further explanation of the concepts of "financing" or "capital structure" and "asset structure", and chapters 18 and 19 for an exposition of the management of the asset and capital structures of a business.)

Financial management cannot function in isolation. Besides the interdependence between the functional management areas (without production and marketing, for example, no funds will be generated, and vice versa), financial management should also depend on other related subject disciplines such as accounting and economics, if it wants to be efficient. As a subsystem of the business, the financial function, and therefore its management, is also influenced by environmental factors. The relationship between financial management, the other

functional management areas, related subject disciplines, and the environment is illustrated in figure 17.1.

17.3 Concepts in financial management

As in any field of study, it is necessary to describe certain concepts in financial management to present the subject in a meaningful manner.

17.3.1 The balance sheet, asset and financing structure

The **balance sheet** is an "instant photo" of the financial position of a business and may be diagrammatically represented as in figure 17.2.

The information in figure 17.2 is largely self-explanatory – hence a few comments will suffice. The **asset side** reflects all the possessions of the business, together with their respective values as at the balance sheet date, and therefore shows the mutual coherence between these

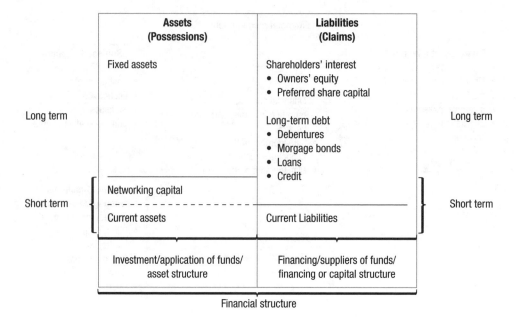

Figure 17.2: A diagrammatic representation of the balance sheet

possessions. These assets represent the asset structure of the business. Assets are normally divided into two broad categories in the balance sheet, namely:

- **Fixed assets** (also called non-current assets) such as land, buildings, machinery, vehicles and other equipment
- **Current assets** such as cash in the bank, as well as other possessions of the business that will be converted into cash within one year during the normal course of business, such as marketable securities, debtors and all inventories

The values at which the assets are recorded in the balance sheet differ according to the objectives for drawing up the balance sheet. For this reason it is essential that the balance sheet should provide an indication of the values at which the assets have been recorded, for example cost, cost less depreciation or cost plus appreciation.

The **liability** or claims **side** of the balance sheet reflects the nature and extent of the interests in the assets – in other words, the mutual coherence of the claims of the persons or institutions that provided funds (capital) for the "purchase" of the assets. Therefore the liability side of the balance sheet shows the **financing** or **capital structure** of the business as at the balance sheet date.

The liability side of the balance sheet is usually subdivided on the basis of two criteria, namely:

- The term for which the funds have been made available
- The source from which the funds have been obtained

Therefore, the liability side of a company's balance sheet will contain the following details:

- **Long-term funds.** This is also known as non-current liabilities and comprises shareholders' interest and long-term debt.
- **Shareholders' interest** is further subdivided into owners' equity (made up of ordinary share capital, reserves, and undistributed

profits, that is, retained profits) and in some instances preference share capital. **Long-term debt** is usually made up of debentures, mortgage bonds, secured loans, and long-term credit.

- **Short-term funds.** These are also referred to as current liabilities, and represent all debts or credit that are normally repayable within one year. Examples of these funds are bank overdrafts and trade creditors. The favourable difference between the current assets and the current liabilities represents the net working capital or that portion of the current assets that has been financed from long-term funds.

The shareholders' interest on the liability side of the balance sheet of businesses – for example sole proprietorships, partnerships and close corporations – that do not have ordinary or preference shareholders is replaced by a capital account that reflects the owners' interest in the business.

17.3.2 Capital

Capital can be described as the accrued power of disposal over the goods and services used by a business to generate a monetary return

or **profit**. Stated differently, the capital of a business may briefly be described as the monetary value of the assets of the business at a specific time. The finance provided is shown on the liability side of a balance sheet, as explained in section 17.3.1.

A business needs capital for investment in fixed assets – referred to as the **need for fixed capital** – and capital for investment in current assets – referred to as the **need for working capital**.

In a business of a given size, the need for fixed capital is permanent in that the business cannot carry on its current level of activities without such capital. For the same reason, a business has a permanent need for a certain minimum portion of working capital. The remaining need for working capital will vary according to factors such as seasonal influences and contingencies that result in an increase or decrease in production activities.

The capital requirements of a business can therefore be depicted as in figure 17.3.[1]

17.3.3 Income

The **income** of a business consists primarily of receipts resulting from the sale of its products

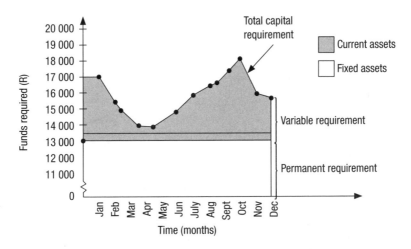

Figure 17.3: The capital requirements of a business

Source: Adapted from Keown, A.J., Martin, J.D., Petty, J.W. & Scott, D.F. *Foundations of finance*, 5th edition, Pearson, NJ, 2006, p. 474.

and/or services. The extent of these receipts for a given period will depend on the quantity of goods and/or services sold within that period, and the unit price for which they were sold.

Income = units sold × price per unit

The income of the business can also be obtained from other sources, such as interest earned on investments. However, this income will not be taken into account in the discussions that follow.

17.3.4 Costs

Costs can be regarded as the monetary value sacrificed in the production of goods and/or services produced for the purpose of resale.

Example

In a manufacturing firm cost will consist of used material, rent for premises and building, depreciation of equipment, wages and salaries for all employees, payment for electricity and communication services, etc.

Costs are further subdivided according to certain criteria, and hence the business has direct costs, indirect costs, overhead expenses, fixed costs and variable costs.

The subdivision of total costs into fixed costs and variable costs is of particular importance for decision-making purposes. Hence, the remainder of this section will be devoted to this aspect. A further subdivision will be introduced in the discussion of the income statement in section 17.3.6.

Fixed cost is that portion of total cost that remains unchanged – within the boundaries of a fixed production capacity – regardless of an increase or decrease in the quantity of goods and/or services produced.

By way of illustration, we will now consider an accountancy practice with production capacity (that is, office space, equipment and permanent staff) to offer accounting services

to 100 people. Office rent, depreciation on equipment, and staff salaries will not change as long as the clientele does not exceed 100. An increase in the number of clients will necessitate an increase in the staff required. The increase in staff will have an effect on office space and furniture requirements. In this way, a new production capacity is created, which gives rise to a new fixed cost component.

Total fixed costs as part of total costs for a particular period and capacity can be represented graphically as in figure 17.4.

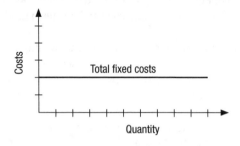

Figure 17.4: A graphical representation of total fixed costs

Total fixed costs are constant, irrespective of the volume produced. Therefore the fixed costs per unit produced will decrease with an increase in the quantity produced, as illustrated in figure 17.5.

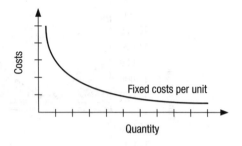

Figure 17.5: A graphical representation of fixed costs per unit produced

Variable cost is that portion of the total costs that changes according to a change in the volume produced. Some variable cost items, such as manufacturing material costs, can be regarded as pure variable costs because they change in direct proportion to a change in the volume produced. Other variable cost items contain a fixed cost component, such as the fixed telephone rental. In this instance, there is not a pure linear relationship between these variable cost items and the volume produced. Therefore, these costs are referred to as **semi-variable costs**. Since these semi-variable costs do not have any substantial effect on the principle of fixed and variable costs, a pure linear relationship can, for illustration purposes, be assumed between total variable costs and volume produced, as represented in figure 17.6.

Figure 17.6: A graphical representation of total variable costs

The **variable costs per unit** produced remain more or less constant, irrespective of the quantity produced. This point is illustrated in figure 17.7.

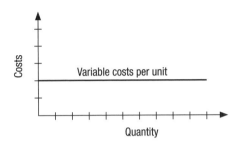

Figure 17.7: A graphical representation of variable costs per unit

The **total costs** involved in the production of a specific number of products produced in a particular period consist of the total fixed costs and the total variable costs incurred in the production of those products. Figure 17.8 graphically illustrates how total costs are arrived at.

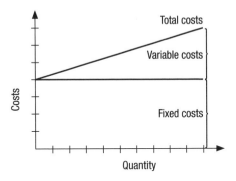

Figure 17.8: A graphical representation of total costs

To summarise, it may be stated that the total costs of the business comprise a fixed and a variable component, each of which has a specific relationship with the volume of production. These relationships have a specific influence on the profit made by businesses – as discussed in more detail in section 17.5.

17.3.5 Profit

Profit is regarded as the favourable difference between the income earned during a specific period and the cost incurred to earn that income. A loss results when the cost exceeds the income.

Profit or loss = Income − cost

or

Profit or loss = (Price × units sold) − cost

Although the above comparison applies in general, various profit concepts in the different stages of the profit-determining process may be identified in the income statement.

17.3.6 The income statement

The **income statement**, one of the annual financial statements of a business, furnishes details about the manner in which the profit or loss for a particular period was arrived at, and how it has been distributed.

Figure 17.9 represents, in diagram form, the income statement of a manufacturing business in company form. A numerical ex-

ample of an income statement of such a business appears in section 17.7.1.1, while certain profit concepts are also further highlighted in figure 17.15 (see page 430). Note that the income statement of a sole proprietorship, a partnership, and a close corporation will in essence differ solely in the division of the net profit.

The information in figure 17.9 is largely self-explanatory.

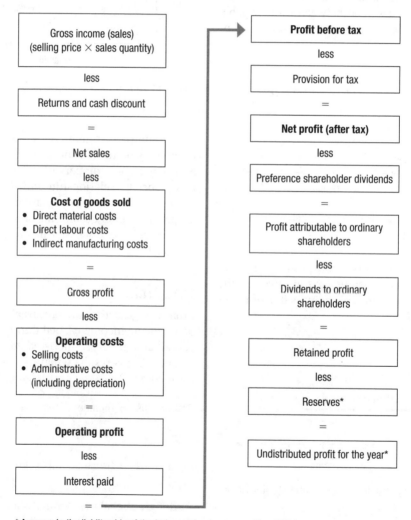

* Appears in the liablity side of the balance sheet – see section 17.3.1

Figure 17.9: A diagrammatic representation of an income statement

Note that accountants sometimes use certain terms associated with income statements interchangeably, for example:
- Sales *and* Turnover
- Operating profit *and* Earnings before interest and tax (EBIT)
- Profit *and* Earnings

17.4 Objective and fundamental principles of financial management[2]

The long-term objective should be to increase the value of the business. This may be accomplished by:
- Investing in assets that will add value to the business (as will be explained in chapter 18)
- Keeping the cost of capital of the business as low as possible (as will be explained in chapter 19)

The short-term financial objective should be to ensure the profitability, liquidity and solvency of the business. Profitability is the ability of the business to generate income that will exceed cost. In order to maximise profit a firm will have to maximise revenue from sales whilst limiting expenses to the essential.

Liquidity is the ability of the business to satisfy its short-term obligations as they become due – in other words, to be able to pay the trade creditors by the due dates. Liquidity can be improved by accelerating cash inflows (collecting accounts receivable as fast as possible or making cash sales only) and paying creditors as late as possible.

Solvency is the extent to which the assets of the business exceed its liabilities. Solvency differs from liquidity in that liquidity pertains to the settlement of short-term liabilities, while solvency pertains to long-term liabilities such as debentures and mortgage loans.

Financial management is based on three principles, namely the **risk–return** principle, the **cost-benefit principle** and the **time value of money** principle.

17.4.1 The risk–return principle
Risk is the probability that the actual result of a decision may deviate from the planned end result, with an associated financial loss or waste of funds. Risk differs from uncertainty in that in the case of uncertainty there is no probability or measure of the chances that an event will take place, whereas risk is measurable by means of statistical techniques.

Similar to the cost–benefit principle, the risk–return principle is a trade-off between risk and return. The greater the risk is, the greater the required rate of return will be.

17.4.2 The cost–benefit principle
Decision making, which is based on the cost of resources only, will not necessarily lead to the most economic utilisation of resources. Sound financial decision-making requires making an analysis of the total cost and the total benefits, and ensuring that the benefits always exceed the cost. One application of the cost–benefit principle will be illustrated in section 17.5 when the cost–volume–profit relationship will be explained.

17.4.3 The time value of money principle
The time value of money principle means a person could increase the value of any amount of money by earning interest. If, however, the amount is invested in inventory, equipment, vehicles, etc., then the amount cannot earn interest. This ties up with the previous two principles. From a cost–benefit point of view, the investor will have to earn a greater return on the investment in inventory, equipment and vehicles than on the best alternative type of investment. Equally, from a risk–return point of view, the return must compensate

adequately for any risk incurred. The time value of money principle will be illustrated in section 17.6.

17.5 Cost–volume–profit relationships

In section 17.3 the concepts of costs, fixed costs, variable costs, income, and profits, among other things, were explained. In essence, the profitability of a business is determined by the unit selling price of its product, the costs (fixed and variable) of the product, and the level of the activity of the business (the volume of production and sales). A change in any one of these three components will result in a change in the total profit made by the business. The components therefore have to be viewed in conjunction with one another, and not in isolation. The underlying connection can be explained by means of a simplified numerical example in which only the volumes of production and sales change.

The calculation in the example is referred to as **break-even analysis**, where the break-even point is reached when total costs are equal to total income. At the break-even point no profit or loss is realised.

The break-even point in a specific case can be calculated by using the following formula:

$$N = \frac{F}{(SP - V)}$$

N in the formula is the number of units

(volume) where no profit or loss is made. The term $(SP - V)$ is referred to as the marginal income or variable profit.

Example

Sales price (SP): R12 per unit
Variable cost (V): R8 per unit
Total fixed cost (FC): R100 000 per annum

Number of units manufactured and sold:
- N: 30 000 (case 1)
- N: 40 000 (case 2)

Profit: P
From
P = Income − cost

It follows that
$P = (N \times SP) - [(N \times V) + F]$

Where
N = 30 000
P = (30 000 × 12) −
    [(30 000 × 8) + R100 000]
  = R360 000 − R340 000
  = R20 000

Where
N = 40 000
P = (40 000 × 12) −
    [(40 000 × 8) + R100 000]
  = R480 000 − R420 000
  = R60 000

The break-even analysis can also be done with the aid of a graph, as in figure 17.10 on page 417.

The break-even point is reached when the total income and total cost curves intersect – that is, at a sales and production volume of OY where the total costs and total income equal OX.

In the event of any change in the income as a result of a change in the selling price or a change in variable costs and/or fixed costs, the slope and point of intersection of the curves will change. The new break-even point is then obtained accordingly. The profit or loss at any sales volume can also be obtained. These values are the vertical differences between the total cost and the total income curves.

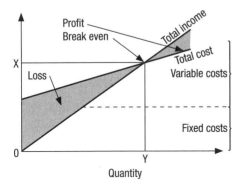

Figure 17.10: A graphical representation of a break-even analysis

Example

$$N = \frac{R100\ 000}{(R12 - 8)} = \frac{R100\ 000}{4} = 25\ 000$$

Substitute 25 000 for the value of N in the previous example:

$$P = (25\ 000 \times R12) -$$
$$[(25\ 000 \times 8) + R100\ 000]$$
$$= 300\ 000 - R300\ 000$$
$$= R0$$

From the foregoing examples it is apparent that the production and sales volumes, the unit selling price and the fixed and variable costs together have an important effect on the profitability of a business. In practice, this type of analysis is carried out especially in the determination of the minimum size at establishment of a business manufacturing and marketing only one product, and also where the feasibility of potential expansion is concerned. A firm that provides more than one product will have to make use of a budgeted income statement in order to determine its break-even point.

17.6 The time value of money

17.6.1 Introduction to the time value of money

In section 17.2 it was stated that all businesses require capital. As will be evident from the following discussion, the payment or remuneration for the use of money or capital is fundamental to the financial structure of any free market society. In the investment and financing decisions of a business, it should be kept in mind that interest has to be paid for the use of capital. Also, funds or capital are normally required and used for either shorter or longer periods, and the use of capital therefore has a time implication.

Consequently, the purpose of this discussion is to explain the concept of the **time value of money** – the combined effect of both interest and time – in the context of financial decision making.

In principle, the time value of money bears a direct relation to the opportunity of

Critical thinking

What would you choose if you were faced by the choice of receiving a gift of R100 cash today or a year from now? Obviously the R100 today. Why?

- The R100 received today can be invested to earn interest, resulting in a larger amount after one year – purely because of time value of money.

- The person who wishes to donate the money may not be able or willing to donate the amount a year from now. To wait causes risk and uncertainty.
- In times of inflation the real purchasing power of R100 will decline as time goes by.

earning interest on an investment. This is the opportunity rate of return on an investment. The opportunity to earn interest in the interim period is foregone if an amount is expected some time in future rather than received immediately.

The time value of money can be approached from two different perspectives. On the one hand, the calculation of the **future value** of some given present value or amount is possible. On the other hand, the calculation of the **present value** of some expected future amount is also possible.

The processes for the calculation of future values (compounding) and for the calculation of present values (discounting) proceed in opposite directions, as indicated in figure 17.11.

17.6.2 **The approach to future value and present value**

For the purpose of the following discussions on future values and present values, a number of assumptions and principles underlying these concepts are mentioned briefly below:

- **The assumption of certainty.** It is assumed that all receipts and payments occur in the absence of risk and uncertainty.
- **The assumption of discrete periods.** It is assumed that the time periods over which future values or present values are calculated have been divided into discrete time periods

– normally periods of one year.
- **The assumption concerning receipts and payments at the end of periods.** Unless stated otherwise, all payments and receipts are assumed to occur at the end of the specific time periods concerned. The initial investment, however, is normally assumed to occur at time t_0, the beginning of the investment period.
- **The assumption concerning inflation.** The effect of inflation is ignored, notwithstanding the direct though complex relationship between interest rates and inflation.
- **The assumption concerning taxation.** The effects of taxation are ignored.
- **The principle of the zero point in time.** The zero point in time refers to that specific point in time, in relation to a given time frame, where amounts (in terms of either future value or present value) are comparable. As will be explained in section 17.6.5, the zero point in time could be the beginning or the end of the investment period.

17.6.3 **The future value of a single amount**

The future value of an initial investment or principal is determined by means of **compounding**, which means that the amount of interest earned in each successive period is added to the amount of the investment at the

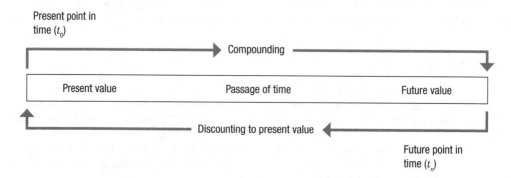

Figure 17.11: The relationship between present value and future value

end of the preceding period. Interest in the period immediately following is consequently calculated on a larger amount consisting of capital and interest. Interest is therefore earned on capital and interest in each successive period.

The formula for calculating the future value of an original investment is

$$FV_n = PV (1 + i)^n$$

Where
- PV is the original investment or present value of the investment
- FV_n is the future value of the investment after n periods
- i is the interest rate per period expressed as a decimal number
- n is the number of discrete periods over which the investment extends

In fact these symbols also appear on financial calculators.

The factor $(1 + i)^n$ in the formula is known as the **future value factor** (FVF) or **compound interest factor** of a single amount.

The process for future value calculation is illustrated in figure 17.12 on page 420.

The future value of an original investment can also be calculated by using tables. An extract from these tables are in Table 17.5 on page 420.

The example below for a three-year investment at an interest rate of 5% per annum is calculated as follows with the aid of the table on page 420:

$$FV_3 = R100(1,1576)$$
$$= R115,76$$

The result is identical to the one obtained by using the formula.

Bear in mind that the future value factor

Example

- What is the future value of R100 invested for one year at an interest rate of 5% per annum?

$$FV_1 = R100(1 + 0,05)^1 = R100(1,05)^1$$
$$= R105$$

By means of a financial calculator the calculation can be done as shown in table 17.3:

Table 17.3: Calculating future value with a financial calculator (example 1)

Key in	Press	Calculator display	Press
100	±	−100	PV
1	n	1	
5	i	5	
	FV	105	

- And if the investment term is three years?

$$FV_3 = R100(1 + 0,05)^3$$
$$= R100 (1,1576)$$
$$= R115,76$$

By means of a financial calculator the calculation can be done as shown in table 17.4:

Table 17.4: Calculating future value with a financial calculator (example 2)

Key in	Press	Calculator display	Press
100	±	−100	PV
3	n	3	
5	i	5	
	FV	115,76	

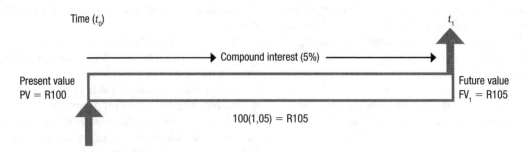

Time (t_0)

Compound interest (5%)

t_1

Present value
PV = R100

Future value
FV_1 = R105

$100(1,05) = R105$

Figure 17.12: Process for future value calculation

Table 17.5: Extract from a table used to calculate future value of an original investment

Periods (n)	Future value factors $(1 - i)^n$		
	5%	10%	15%
1	1,0500	1,1000	1,1500
2	1,1025	1,2100	1,3225
3	1,1576	1,3310	1,5209
4	1,2155	1,4641	1,7490
5	1,2763	1,6105	2,0114
6	1,3401	1,7716	2,3131
7	1,4071	1,9487	2,6600
8	1,4775	2,1436	3,0590
9	1,5513	2,3579	3,5179
10	1,6289	2,5937	4,0456

$(1 + i)^n$ is an exponential function, which means that the initial amount will grow exponentially over time.

The higher the interest rate, the faster the future value will grow for any given investment period as a result of the compounding effect and, consequently, interest is earned on interest in each successive period. The concept of the compound interest rate as a growth rate is of vital importance in financial management.

The values of any of the four variables in the equation for the calculation of the future value can be determined if the values of the remaining three are known, as shown below.

Example

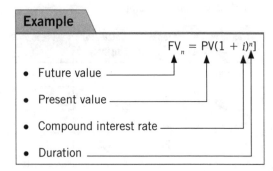

$FV_n = PV(1 + i)^n]$

- Future value
- Present value
- Compound interest rate
- Duration

17.6.4 Present value

17.6.4.1 The present value of a single amount

The present value is also based on the principle that the value of money is, among other things, affected by the timing of receipts or disbursements, as in the case of the future value.

If it is accepted that a rand today is worth more than a rand expected at some future date, what would the present value be now of an amount expected in future? The answer to this question revolves around the following:

- Investment opportunities available to the investor or recipient
- The future point in time at which the money is expected

An amount of R105 which is expected one year from now will have a present value of R100, provided the opportunity exists to invest the R100 today (time t_0) at an interest rate of 5% per annum.

The interest rate, which is used for discounting the future value of R105 one year from now to a present value of R100, reflects the time value of money and is the key to the present value approach. This interest rate or opportunity rate of return is the rate of interest that could be earned on alternative investments with similar risks if the money had been available for investment now. Stated differently, it is the rate of return that would

be foregone by not utilising the investment opportunity. The process of discounting is explained by means of the time line in figure 17.13.

The **discounting process** is the reciprocal of the compounding process.

Consequently, the formula for the calculation of the present value of a future single amount is:

$$PV = FV_n \left(\frac{1}{(1 + i)} \right)^n$$

The factor $\left(\frac{1}{(1 + i)} \right)^n$ is known as the **present value factor** or **discounting factor** for a future single amount.

Tables have also been compiled for the calculation of present values. Table 17.8 on page 422 shows an extract from these tables.

In the example above, the present value of R115,76 expected three years from now is calculated as follows, with the aid of table 17.8, at an opportunity rate of return or discounting rate of 5%.

$$
\begin{aligned}
PV &= R115{,}76(PVF5\%,_3) \\
&= R115{,}76\ (0{,}8638) \\
&= R100
\end{aligned}
$$

The present value of a single amount is, accordingly, defined as follows:

> The **present value (PV)** of a future FV_n is the monetary amount which can be invested today at a given interest rate i per period in order to grow to the same future amount after n periods.

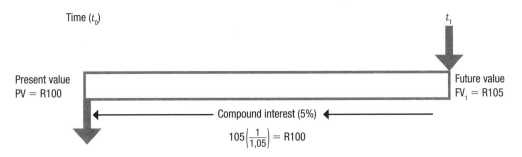

Time (t_0) t_1

Present value
PV = R100

Future value
FV_1 = R105

Compound interest (5%)

$$105 \left(\frac{1}{1{,}05} \right) = R100$$

Figure 17.13: Process for calculating the present value of a single amount

Example

- What is the present value of R105 expected one year from now if the investor's opportunity cost (discount rate) is 5% per annum?

$$PV = FV_1\left(\frac{1}{(1 + 0,05)}\right)^1$$

$$= R105\left(\frac{1}{(1,05)}\right)^1$$

$$= R100$$

By means of a financial calculator the calculation can be done as shown in Table 17.6:

Table 17.6

Key in	Press	Calculator display	Press
105		105	FV
1	n	1	
5	i	5	
	PV	−100	

(The minus sign in front of the R100 can be ignored here. It is displayed purely as a result of the convention of financial calculators in order to distinguish between cash inflows and cash outflows, where negative figures normally indicate cash outflows.)

- What is the present value of R115,76 invested under the same circumstances and expected in three years' time?

$$PV = FV_1\left(\frac{1}{(1 + 0,05)}\right)^3$$

$$= R105\left(\frac{1}{(1,05)}\right)^3$$

$$= R100$$

By means of a financial calculator the calculation can be done as shown in Table 17.7:

Table 17.7

Key in	Press	Calculator display	Press
115,76		115,76	FV
3	n	3	
5	i	5	
	PV	−100	

Table 17.8: Extract from a table used to calculate present values

Periods (n)	Discouting factors $\frac{1}{(1 + i)^n}$		
	5%	**10%**	**15%**
1	0,9524	0,9091	0,8696
2	0,9070	0,8264	0,7561
3	0,8638	0,7513	0,6575
4	0,8227	0,6830	0,5718
5	0,7835	0,6209	0,4972
6	0,7462	0,5645	0,4323
7	0,7107	0,5132	0,3759
8	0,6768	0,4665	0,3269
9	0,6446	0,4241	0,2843
10	0,6139	0,3855	0,2472

As illustrated in the example on page 421, as long as the opportunity for investment at 5% per annum exists, the investor should be indifferent to a choice between R100 today or R115,76 in three years' time.

Closer investigation of the preceding discounting factors reveals that the values of these factors decrease progressively as i, or n, or both, increase. The exceptionally high decrease in the discounting factor with relatively high interest rates and long time periods means that:

- The higher the interest rate is, the smaller the present value of a given future amount will be
- The further in the future an amount is expected, the smaller its present value at a given interest rate will be

Interestingly, the present value factor $\text{PVF}_{10,10} = 0{,}3855$ implies that the present value of R1,00 expected in ten years is only 38,55 cents today, if the R1,00 could have been invested today at 10% for ten years. If an investment opportunity at 15% should exist – which is not unrealistic – the present value of R1,00 expected ten years from now is only 24,72 cents ($\text{PVF}_{15,10} = 0{,}2472$). Put differently, this also means that the value or purchasing power of R1,00 will decline to 24,72 cents over the next ten years if the average annual inflation rate is to be 15% a year over this period.

The present value factors and the future value factors (as well as the tables for these factors) are based on the assumption that any funds generated in any period over the total duration of the investment or project (such as annual interest receipts) are reinvested at the same interest rate for the remainder of the total investment period.

The values of any one of the four variables in the equation for the calculation of the future value can be determined, provided that the values of the three remaining variables are known.

Example

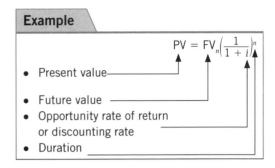

$$PV = FV_n\left(\frac{1}{1+i}\right)^n$$

- Present value
- Future value
- Opportunity rate of return or discounting rate
- Duration

17.6.4.2 The present value of an uneven cash flow stream

One approaches the determination of the present value of a series of unequal cash flow amounts in the same way as one would approach a single amount, irrespective of the total duration or the number of time periods involved. As in all applications of the time value of money, the timing of the cash receipts or disbursements is of crucial importance. This is evident from the following example of the calculation of the present value of an uneven cash flow stream at an interest rate or discounting rate of 10%.

The appropriate discounting factors are found in the table on page 422.

$$
\begin{aligned}
PV &= R1\,000\,(0{,}9091) + R500\,(0{,}8264) + \\
&\quad 0 + R4\,500\,(0{,}6830) + R6\,000 \\
&\quad (0{,}6209) \\
&= R909{,}10 + R413{,}20 + 0 + R3\,073{,}50 \\
&\quad + R3\,725{,}40 \\
&= R8\,121{,}20
\end{aligned}
$$

Example

Year (t)	Annual cash inflow (CF$_t$)
1	R1 000
2	R500
3	R0
4	R4 500
5	R6 000
Total	R12 000

By means of a financial calculator the calculation can be done as shown in Table 17.9:

Table 17.9

Key in	Press	Calculator display
0	Cf	0
1000	Cf	1000
500	Cf	500
0	Cf	0
4500	Cf	4500
6000	Cf	6000
10	i	10
	NPV	8121,40

Notes:
1. Financial calculators assume the first cash flow (Cf) for this type of calculation occurs in time period 0. The figures in table 17.9 indicate that the first cash inflow of R1 000 only occurred in period 1. Thus the cash inflow of R0 for time period 0, followed by the R1 000 of time period 1 and the subsequent cash inflows.
2. The NPV procedure by means of a financial calculator does not require that the number of periods (n) be keyed in.
3. Financial calculators use up to ten digits in order to perform calculations. Financial tables normally indicate only three or four digits. This leads to different answers when time value of money calculations are performed. In the above example the financial calculator produced an answer of R8121,40 compared to R8121,20 by means of financial tables.Note that no cash flow occurs at the end of the third period, and no contribution to the total present value at time t_0 therefore originates from that period. The cash flow amounts at the end of the first, second, fourth and fifth years respectively are multiplied by the respective discounting factors $PVF_{10,1}$, $PVF_{10,2}$, $PVF_{10,4}$ and $PVF_{10,5}$. The present values of the individual cash amounts are eventually added to obtain the total present value for the above uneven cash flow stream at time t_0. Capital investment decisions in particular require the calculation of the present value of uneven cash flow streams.

This brief overview of the present value approach is deemed sufficient for the purposes of this discussion. However, in practice, interest on savings accounts and deposits are often calculated biannually, quarterly, monthly, weekly and, even, daily. This could apply to both future value and present value applications and is known as intra-year compounding and discounting.

17.6.5 The principles of equivalence and comparability

The **equivalence** of two different amounts at two given points in time is solely dependent on the investment opportunities available to the individual or business. If an amount of R100 today is invested for three years at a compound interest rate of 5% a year, this amount will grow to R115,76, as we have shown. The present value of R100 and the future value of R115,76 in three years is equivalent, if there are investment opportunities at 5%. The fact that these two amounts, at the specific points in time, reflect a time-adjusted equivalence only at an interest rate of 5% confirms the critical importance of the interest rate.

The comparison of the financial merits of two or more investment opportunities with different cash flow streams is meaningful only if the individual cash flow amounts for each investment alternative are adjusted to present values at a common point in time, normally t_0, using an appropriate discounting rate. However, the specific point in time selected for the comparison of alternative investments is not critical, as long as

- The alternatives are compared at the same point in time
- The same interest rate or discounting rate is applied in the evaluation of all alternatives

The principles of equivalence and comparability are explained with reference to the three investment alternatives A, B and C, in table 17.10 , each requiring the same initial investment.

Table 17.10: Timing and the principles of equivalence and comparability

Timing of receipts (t)	Annual cash receipts		
	A	B	C
t_1	R100	R350	R 50
t_2	200	200	150
t_3	300	50	450
Total	R600	R600	R650

The total receipts for both investments A and B amount to R600. The only difference between A and B is found in the time patterns of their cash flow streams. Based on the time value of money, it is obvious that, as an investment, B is preferable to A, owing to B's larger cash flows in earlier years.

But is investment B also preferable to C? Although investment B has higher cash receipts in previous years than investment C, C has a larger total cash inflow than B. Hence, any choice merely on qualitative considerations on the basis of the time value of money, as in the case of A and B, is no longer straightforward. Investments B and C will now be compared with reference to the principle of comparability. All cash receipts for B and C are discounted to present values at time t_0 by means of an opportunity investment rate or discounting rate of 10% using the discounting factors $PVF_{i,n}$. The results are presented in table 17.11.

The present value of investment B at time t_0 (R521,04) is equivalent to the cash receipts of R350, R200 and R50 at times t_1, t_2 and t_3 respectively, provided that investment opportunities at an interest rate of 10% exist. Likewise, the present value of investment C at time t_0 (R507,51) is equivalent to the cash receipts of R50, R150 and R450 at times t_1, t_2 and t_3 respectively, provided that investment opportunities at an interest rate of 10% exist.

Table 17.11: Calculation of the present values for investments B and C

Year	Timing	Investment B			Investment C		
		Receipts (1)	PVF (10%) (2)	Present value (1) × (2)	Receipts (1)	PVF (10%) (2)	Present value (1) × (2)
1	t_1	R350	0,9091	R318,19	R50	0,9091	R45,46
2	t_2	R200	0,8264	R165,28	R150	0,8264	R123,96
3	t_3	R50	0,7513	R37,57	R450	0,7513	R338,09
	Total present value (t_0)			R521,04			R507,51

Note: Because the present values for B and C are required at t_0, each individual cash receipt at the end of years 1, 2 and 3 has to be discounted to present values at t_0.

It has already been pointed out that the point in time at which investment alternatives are compared is not critical. This is illustrated in table 17.12, where it is shown that the end of the investment period at time t_3 could serve equally well for purposes of comparison, and that investment B is also preferable on the basis of future value.

Where cash flows differ with regard to the size of the cash flow amounts and the timing or occurrence of the cash flows, either the present value or the future value approach could be used for evaluation purposes in accordance with the principle of equivalence. This important relationship between present value and future value is illustrated in figure 17.14 with reference to investment B.

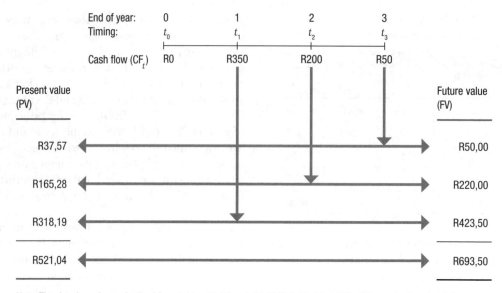

Note: The data have been obtained from tables 17.11 and 17.12. Note that the R50 at time t_3 is already a future value and requires no further adjustments.

Figure 17.14: The equivalence of present and future values (10%)

The time-adjusted present value for investment B exceeds that for investment C, and investment B is, consequently, preferred. Despite the differences in the size as well as the timing of the individual annual receipts for investments B and C, their present values are, however, comparable at time t_0, provided that the same interest or discounting rate were used in evaluating both investments.

It is evident from figure 17.14 that the

Table 17.12: Calculation of the future values for investments B and C

Year	Timing	Investment B			Investment C		
		Receipts (1)	PVF (10%) (2)	Present value (1) × (2)	Receipts (1)	PVF (10%) (2)	Present value (1) × (2)
1	t_1	R350	1,2100	R423,50	R50	1,2100	R60,50
2	t_2	R200	1,1000	R220,00	R150	1,1000	R165,00
3	t_3	R50	1,0000	R50,00	R450	1,0000	R450,00
	Total present value (t_3)			R693,50			R675,50

Note: To determine the future values of B and C, each receipt has to be adjusted to a future value at time t_3, from the time of the receipt for the remainder of the investment period, by multiplying each individual cash receipt by the appropriate compound interest or future value factor, $FVFt_{i,n}$. Receipts at the end of the third year already constitute future values and do not require any further adjustment.

cash flows of R350, R200 and R50 at times t_1, t_2 and t_3 respectively are equivalent to the present value of R521,04 at time t_0 and also to the future value of R693,50 at time t_3 at an interest rate of 10%.

The following should be kept in mind with regard to the principle of equivalence and comparability:

- The "equivalence" of amounts at different points in time holds only for the same rate of interest.
- Comparison of alternative investments at any point in time – even earlier than t_0 or later than t_n – is acceptable, although t_0 and t_n are usually convenient points in time for comparison purposes.

The critical assumption that all interest or amounts generated by an investment are reinvested at the same rate for the remainder of the investment period applies to both present value and future value. All future value factors and present value factors in the respective tables have been developed on the basis of this assumption.

17.6.6 Conclusion to the time value of money

The principles and application of compounding and the time value of money as a basis for the determination of present values as well as future values have been explained in this section. The present value approach is an indispensable aid in financial management, particularly for a large business and listed company, where the majority of investment and financing decisions are taken in accordance with the goal of the maximisation of the value of the business. Even for small business organisations, a basic knowledge of compound interest methodology and unsophisticated discounted cash flow applications could be invaluable for capital investment decisions.

The most important implications of time value of money are as follows:

- Inflow must be accelerated (encourage debtors to pay their accounts as soon as possible)
- Outflow should be delayed without damaging the firm's credit record (pay creditors as late as possible)
- Manage inventory as optimally as possible because it represents capital which does not earn a return before it is sold

17.7 Financial analysis, planning and control[3]

In section 17.2, effective financial analysis, planning and control were identified as tasks of financial management. In this section, a short review of these related tasks is given.

17.7.1 Financial analysis

Financial analysis is necessary to monitor the general financial position of a business and, in the process, to limit the risk of financial failure of the business as far as possible. Financial analyses will reveal certain trends and also the financial strengths and weaknesses of the business so that corrective measures, if necessary, can be taken in time. To help them with financial analyses, financial managers have the following important aids at their disposal: the income statement, the balance sheet, the funds flow statement, and financial ratios. The following sections will focus on the various statements and the calculation of certain financial ratios.

17.7.1.1 The income statement

The income statement has already been described in section 17.3.6, and diagrammatically represented in figure 17.9 (on page 414). Consequently, a numerical example of a manufacturing company's abridged income statement (see table 17.13 on page 428) will suffice for the purposes of this section.

Table 17.13: An example of an abridged income statement (rand values)

Abridged income statement of ABC Limited for the year ended 28 February 2007		
Net sales (net income)		R3 000 000
Less cost of sales (cost of goods sold)		2 250 000
• Direct labour costs	1 000 000	
• Direct material costs	900 000	
• Indirect manufacturing costs	350 000	
Gross profit		750 000
Less operating costs		400 000
• Selling expenses	150 000	
• Depreciation	80 000	
• Administrative costs	170 000	
Operating profit		350 000
Less interest paid		30 000
Profit before tax		320 000
Tax (29%)		92 800
Net profit after tax		227 200
Less dividends to preference shareholders		5 000
Profit attributable to ordinary shareholders		222 200
Less dividends to ordinary shareholders		75 000
Retained profit (earnings)		147 200
Less reserves		–
Undistributed profit for the year		147 200

Table 17.14: An example of a company balance sheet (rand values)

Balance sheet of ABC Limited at 28 February 2007

Assets (Employment of capital)			Equity and liabilities (capital employed)		
		R			**R**
Fixed assets		800 000	**Shareholders' capital**		
Land and buildings (cost price)		200 000	Authorised and issued – Ordinary shares (200 000 at R1 each)		200 000
Plant and equipment (cost price)	1 200 000				
Less			**Distributable reserves**		
Accumulated depreciation	600 000	600 000	Capital reserves	300 000	
			Undistributed profit	350 000	650 000
Other assets			*Owners' equity*		850 000
Investments		–	Preference share capital		50 000
Total long-term assets		800 000	*Shareholders' interest*		900 000
Current assets		550 000	**Long-term debt**		
Cash	60 000		Debentures		200 000
Marketable securities	30 000		*Total long-term liabilities*		1 100 000
Debtors (net)	220 000				
Inventory	200 000		**Current liabilities**		250 000
Pre-paid expenses	40 000		Trade creditors	100 000	
			Bank overdraft	100 000	
			Arrear expenses	50 000	
		1 350 000			1 350 000

17.7.1.2 The balance sheet

The balance sheet of a **company**, as well as the most important balance sheet items, have already been discussed in section 17.3.1, and diagrammatically represented in figure 17.2 (see page 410). Thus, a numerical example of a company's balance sheet will suffice for the purposes of this section (table 17.14).

17.7.1.3 The flow of funds in a business

A business has to make optimum use of its limited funds to achieve its objectives. It is therefore necessary to conduct an analysis of how the capital of the business is employed and supplied. This analysis involves the flow of funds in the business.

The flow of funds of a firm is a continuous process and, following on the previous explanations of the balance sheet and income statement, can be represented as in figure 17.15.

The following are apparent from figure 17.15:
- The business obtains funds in the financial market and utilises these funds at a cost to produce goods and/or services.
- The business sells these goods and/or services at a price higher than the production costs and therefore shows an operating profit.

- Interest is paid to the suppliers of loan capital from the operating profit. This means an outflow of funds from the business.
- The profit remaining after the interest has been paid is taxable. This means a further outflow of funds from the business.
- The profit remaining after tax can be applied to preference and ordinary shareholders' dividends (outflow of funds), reserves and undistributed profits, resulting in a reinvestment in the production process.

It is clear from the above that there is a continuous flow of funds to and from the business. If the sales value of the goods and/or services produced by the business exceeds the costs incurred in the production of those goods and/or services, including the depreciation on equipment, the business will show a profit. A portion of the profit, after payment of interest and tax, is normally distributed among the preference and ordinary shareholders in the

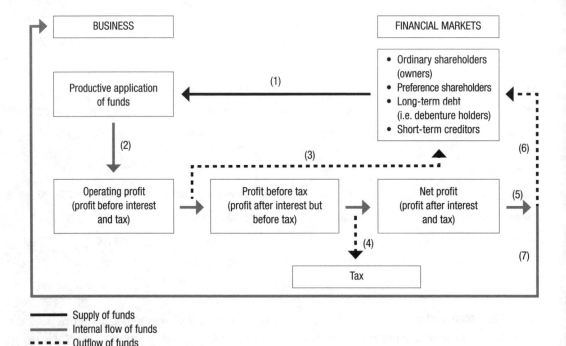

Figure 17.15: A simplified diagrammatical representation of the flow of funds of a business

form of dividends. The remaining profit is reinvested in the business. The reinvestment leads to an increase in the available funds of the business.

17.7.1.4 The funds flow statement

The funds flow statement helps with the analysis of the changes in the financial position of the business between two consecutive balance sheet dates and, in the process, reflects the net effect of all transactions for a specific period on the financial position of the business. With this in mind, the balance sheets at the beginning and end of the period under review, as well as the income statement for the same period, are used.

The funds flow statement is based on the self-explanatory point of departure that the employment of funds depends on the availability of funds. In other words, before funds can be applied, they have to be obtained from some source.

There are two particular approaches to drawing up a funds flow statement, namely:
- According to changes in the net working capital
- According to changes in the cash position, including the current bank account

Both approaches have their merits. However, the remainder of the discussion of the funds flow statement will be based on the second approach, simply because funds flow statements drawn up according to this method contain more information than those drawn up using the first approach.[4]

The funds flow statement that is drawn up on a cash basis contains a summary of the sources from which cash has been generated between two consecutive balance sheet dates, as well as a summary of the purposes for which cash has been used during the same period. If more cash has been generated than employed during the period under review, the cash available to the business will increase, and vice versa.

Funds flow statements drawn up according to this approach can be presented in various forms. Table 17.15 represents one of the forms that can be adopted.

An analysis of the funds flow statement offers many advantages, including the following:
- It gives an indication of whether the cash dividends are justified in terms of the cash generated by the business activities (profit).
- It gives an indication of how the growth in fixed assets has been financed.
- It gives an indication of possible imbalances in the application of funds.
- It helps financial management to analyse and evaluate the financing methods of the business.

17.7.1.5 Financial ratios

As mentioned earlier, **financial ratios** are aids that financial management can employ in the process of effective financial analysis and control.

A financial ratio gives the relationship between two items (or groups of items) in the financial statements (especially the income statement and the balance sheet) and serves as a performance criterion to point out potential strengths and weaknesses of the business.

However, we must emphasise that financial ratios do not identify the reasons for the strengths and weaknesses – they indicate only symptoms that need to be further diagnosed by financial management.

The financial ratios of a business are used by various interested parties, namely:
- **Financial management**, with a view to internal control, planning and decision making
- The **suppliers of borrowed capital**, to evaluate the ability of the business to pay its debt and interest
- **Investment analysts**, to evaluate the business as an investment opportunity
- **Labour unions**, with a view to salary negotiations

Table 17.15: A framework for a funds flow statement on cash use

Funds flow statement for the period 1 March 2006 to 28 February 2007

Source of funds	R	R	Application of funds	R	R
Profit before tax		....	*Loss*		....
			Depreciation in share and preference share capital		....
			Income tax paid		....
Depreciation[1]		....			
Increase in share and preference share capital		....	*Cash dividends*		....
Increase in debt (excluding bank overdraft and provisions)			*Decrease in debt* (excluding bank overdraft and provisions)		
• Trade creditors	....		• Trade creditors	....	
• Arrear expenses	....		• Arrear expenses	....	
• Long-term loans	....	....	• Long-term loans	....	....
Decrease in assets (excluding cash in bank and on hand)			*Increase in assets* (excluding cash in bank and on hand)		
• Debtors	....		• Debtors	....	
• Stocks	....		• Stocks	....	
• Prepaid expenses	....		• Prepaid expenses	....	
• Sales of fixed assets[2]	....	....	• Sales of fixed assets[3]	....	....
Subtotal			Subtotal		
Balance (decrease in cash)[4]		(X)	Balance (increase in cash)[4]		(X)
		XXX			XXX

Notes:
1. Depreciation is deducted as a cost in order to caluculate the profit (loss) before tax. Because it actually represents a non-cash cost, depreciation has to be added back to reflect the actual cash position.
2. Shown at net selling price.
3. At cost.
4. If the total source of funds exceeds the total applicliation of funds, the difference will mean an increase in cash, and vice versa. The balances have to tally with the difference in cash between the opening and closing balance sheets.

Financial ratios as such have little, if any, usage value, and must be viewed against certain significant standards or norms to give them usage value. Three types of comparisons are significant in this regard:

- A comparison of the current financial ratios of the business with the corresponding ratios of the past and/or expected future ratios, with a view to revealing a tendency
- A comparison of the financial ratios of the business with those of other similar businesses
- A comparison of the financial ratios of the business with the norms for the particular industry as a whole

There is a large variety of financial ratios as well as various classification methods. In this section only a few are mentioned, without paying attention to their respective merits. The calculations of the various ratios are explained by using the information given in the previous income statement and balance sheet.

(a) Liquidity ratios

Liquidity ratios provide an indication of the ability of a business to meet its short-term obligations as they become due, without curtailing or ceasing its normal activities. Providers of loan capital are interested in liquidity ratios because these ratios give an indication of the degree to which a business can meet its debt obligations fully and punctually in the normal course of events.

Two liquidity ratios are of importance, namely the current ratio and acid-test ratio. The **current ratio** reflects the relationship between the value of the current assets and the extent of the current liabilities of a business.

$$\text{Current ratio} = \frac{\text{Current assets}}{\text{Current liabilities}}$$

Using the figures of ABC Limited contained in table 17.14 (page 429) results in a current ratio of 2,2:1, calculated as follows:

$$\text{Current ratio} = \frac{\text{Current assets}}{\text{Current liabilities}}$$

$$= \frac{550\ 000}{250\ 000}$$

$$= 2,2:1$$

This means that the business had R2,20 of current assets available for each R1 of its current liabilities (short-term obligations). A larger ratio reflects a more favourable liquidity position than a smaller ratio does. The smaller the ratio is, the greater is the possibility that the business will not be able to meet its debt obligations fully and punctually, without curtailing or ceasing its normal activities. Traditionally a current ratio of 2:1 is recommended.

Since inventory cannot always be readily converted into cash in the short term, it may be misleading to evaluate the liquidity position of a business simply on the basis of the current ratio. The **acid test ratio** should therefore be used in combination with the current ratio as a criterion for evaluating liquidity.

$$\text{Acid test ratio} = \frac{\text{Current assets} - \text{inventory}}{\text{Current liabilities}}$$

Using the figures of ABC Limited contained in table 17.14 results in an acid test ratio of 1,4:1, calculated as follows:

$$\text{Acid test ratio} = \frac{\text{Current assets} - \text{inventory}}{\text{Current liabilities}}$$

$$= \frac{550\ 000 - 200\ 000}{250\ 000}$$

$$= \frac{350\ 000}{250\ 000}$$

$$= 1,40:1$$

This shows that for each rand's worth of current liabilities, the business had R1,40 of current assets, excluding inventory. As in the case of the current ratio, a larger ratio reflects a healthier liquidity position than a smaller ratio represents. Normally, a minimum acid test ratio of 1:1 is recommended.

Liquidity ratios should be evaluated with

caution. The nature and condition of the current assets, and the "correctness" of the values at which they were recorded in the balance sheet, can cause the actual liquidity position to differ radically from that which is reflected by the liquidity ratios.

Although it is important for a business to be liquid, it is also possible to be excessively liquid. A current ratio of, for example, 5:1 could be an indication that the firm is carrying too much inventory, or selling too much on credit, or collecting accounts receivable too slowly and/or has too much cash on hand. An acid-test ratio of, for example, 3:1 could be an indication that the firm is selling too much on credit, collecting accounts receivable too slowly, and/or has too much cash on hand. In such a case funds are not being used optimally but are confined to unproductive use in current assets. It is therefore important to realise that one should not strive unrestrictedly towards an improvement in the liquidity ratios.

(b) Solvency ratios

Solvency ratios indicate the ability of a business to repay its debts from the sale of the assets on cessation of its activities. Capital lenders usually show strong interest in solvency ratios because these indicate the risk level of an investment in the business. Seen from another angle, a solvency ratio gives the business an indication of the extent to which it will have access to additional loan capital, and the extent of its risk in its current financing.

There are two particularly important solvency ratios, namely the debt ratio and the gearing ratio.

The **debt ratio** may be calculated using the following equation:

$$\text{Debt ratio} = \frac{\text{Debt}}{\text{Assets}} \times \frac{100}{1}$$

Using the figures of ABC Limited contained in table 17.14 results in a debt ratio of 37%, calculated as follows:

$$\text{Debt ratio} = \frac{\text{Debt}}{\text{Assets}} \times \frac{100}{1}$$

$$= \frac{500\ 000}{1\ 350\ 000} \times \frac{100}{1}$$

$$= 37\%$$

This means that 37% of the assets were financed by debt (including preference shares if they are callable). A lower percentage reflects a more favourable position than a higher percentage, and a maximum debt ratio of 50% is normally required.

The **gearing ratio** may be calculated using the following equation:

$$\text{Gearing ratio} = \frac{\text{Owners' equity}}{\text{Debt}}$$

Using the figures of ABC Limited contained in table 17.14 results in a gearing ratio of 1,7:1, calculated as follows:

$$\text{Gearing ratio} = \frac{\text{Owners' equity}}{\text{Debt}}$$

$$= \frac{850\ 000}{500\ 000}$$

$$= 1,7:1$$

This indicates that for each R1 of debt (including preference shares), the business had R1,70 of owners' equity. (The value of preference shares in the balance sheet should be regarded as debt if the preference shares are callable). A larger ratio once again reflects a more favourable situation than a smaller ratio, and a minimum gearing ratio of 1:1 is normally required.

The following aspects concerning solvency ratios need to be emphasised:
• The three solvency ratios illustrate the same situation as seen from different angles. To evaluate the solvency situation of a business it is therefore necessary to use only one of these ratios.
• Solvency ratios should not simply be accepted at face value. What constitutes a safe ratio for a particular business depends on various factors such as the risks to which it is subject, the nature of the assets and

the degree to which creditors will be accommodating in emergency situations.

(c) Profitability, rate of return or yield ratios
Firms strive to achieve the greatest possible profitability. They therefore also wish to achieve the greatest profitability ratios. To achieve this, they must maximise their income and limit cost (expenses) to the essential. Sound profitability not only enables the firm to survive financially, but it also enables the firm to obtain financing relatively more easily. The share prices of listed companies normally increase in reaction to announcements of good profitability figures.

• Gross profit margin
The gross profit margin may be found by:

$$\frac{\text{Gross profit}}{\text{sales}} \times \frac{100}{1}$$

The gross profit margin indicates how profitable sales have been. The gross profit also gives an indication of the mark-up percentage used by a firm. A firm with a gross profit margin of 50% uses (on average) a mark-up of 100%, as will be illustrated here. Assume sales equal R200 and the cost of goods sold equals R100. This yields a gross profit of R100 and a gross profit margin of 50%:

$$\text{Gross profit margin} = \frac{\text{R200} - \text{R100}}{\text{R200}} \times \frac{100}{1}$$

$$= 50\%$$

Using the figures of ABC Limited contained in tables 17.13 and 17.14 results in a gross profit margin of 25%:

Gross profit margin

$$= \frac{3\,000\,000 - 2\,250\,000}{3\,000\,000} \times \frac{100}{1}$$

$$= 25\%$$

Firms prefer to achieve the greatest possible gross profit margin. In the case of ABC Ltd the 25% gross profit margin indicates that the firm

uses a mark-up percentage of approximately 33%, in other words goods manufactured or bought at for example R100 are sold at R133:

$$\text{Gross profit margin} = \frac{133 - 100}{133} \times \frac{100}{1}$$

$$= 25\%$$

A firm aiming to improve its gross profit margin will have to improve its marketing efforts in order to increase sales, whilst reducing the cost of goods sold simultaneously. The firm could, for example, reconsider aspects of the marketing instruments (product, price, promotion, and distribution) and make suitable adjustments. These adjustments would, in turn, require adjustments to the manufacturing process (if it is a manufacturing firm) and/or procurement. Firms intent on reducing cost should, however, do so with care in order not to sacrifice quality and alienate clients in the process. In this respect firms normally prefer to improve product features (including quality) in order to justify a price increase.

• Net profit margin
The net profit margin gives an indication of the overall profitability of the firm and management's ability to control revenue and expenses.
Net profit margin may be found by:

$$\frac{\text{Net income}}{\text{sales}} \times \frac{100}{1}$$

Using the figures of ABC Limited contained in table 17.13 results in a net profit margin of 7,57%:

$$\text{Net profit margin} = \frac{227\,200}{3\,000\,000} \times \frac{100}{1}$$

$$= 7,57\%$$

In order to improve profitability, management needs not only to consider the same measures as those suggested for improving the gross profit margin, but it also has to focus on reducing operating expenses. Productivity will have to be evaluated and, if necessary, improved.

Firms could calculate annually or quarterly the percentage of sales each operating expense (for example salaries) constitutes. Management can compare these figures with those of previous years in order to identify deviations.

- Return on total capital

This ratio may be computed as follows:

$$\text{Return on total capital} = \frac{\text{NOPAT}}{\text{total capital}} \times \frac{100}{1}$$

Where NOPAT = operating profit − tax

Using the figures of ABC Limited contained in tables 17.13 and 17.14 results in a return on total capital (after tax) of 19,1%, calculated as follows:

Return on total capital

$$= \frac{350\ 000 - 92\ 800}{1\ 350\ 000} \times \frac{100}{1}$$

$$= 19,1\%$$

A firm wishing to improve its return on total capital needs to consider the same measures as those proposed in respect of the gross profit margin and net profit margin. Since the total capital (capital employed) is equal to the total assets (employment of capital) the firm needs to investigate whether it could function with less capital and/or improve the productivity (if possible) of its assets. A firm can reduce its capital by paying off long-term loans more quickly (especially during periods of rising interest rates), by paying greater dividends (if the profitability and cash flow permit it) repurchasing and cancelling a portion of the firm's shares. The firm also needs to review its core business. Parts of the firm which cannot be regarded as core business can be sold (for example company houses which are let to employees).

- Return on shareholders' interest

The return on shareholders' interest may be calculated using the following equation:

$$\frac{\text{Net profit after tax}}{\text{Shareholders' interest}} \times \frac{100}{1}$$

Using the figures of ABC Limited contained in tables 17.13 and 17.14 results in a return on shareholders' interest of 25,2%, calculated as follows:

Return on shareholders' interest

$$= \frac{227\ 200}{900\ 000} \times \frac{100}{1}$$

$$= 25,2\%$$

A firm wishing to improve its return on shareholders' funds should consider the same measures as those proposed for the profitability ratios discussed so far.

- Return on owners' equity (ROE)

The return on owners' equity may be calculated using the following equation:

$$\text{ROE} = \frac{\text{Net income}}{\text{Sales}} \times \frac{\text{Sales}}{\text{Total assets}} \times \frac{\text{Total assets}}{\text{Owners' equity}}$$

A firm's return on equity (ROE) therefore depends on the firm's net profit margin, asset turnover and financial leverage. Alternatively

$$\text{ROE} = \frac{\text{Net income}}{\text{Owners' equity}} \times \frac{100}{1}$$

Using the figures of ABC Limited contained in tables 17.13 and 17.14 results in a ROE of 26,7%, calculated as follows:

$$\text{ROE} = \frac{227\ 200}{850\ 000} \times \frac{100}{1}$$

$$= 26,7\%$$

An increase in ROE can be achieved by means of an increase in the net profit margin, asset turnover and financial leverage. Financial leverage can be attained by using more long-term borrowed funds and less ordinary share capital. A firm could, for example, borrow money in order to buy back its own ordinary shares and cancel the shares which have been bought back. Such an approach can be applied relatively safely during periods of declining interest rates but is risky during periods of rising interest rates.

The ROE, in turn, has an important influence on the sustainable growth rate (g) of a firm. The sustainable growth rate is found by:

ROE × retention ratio

where retention ratio = $\dfrac{\text{retained earnings}}{\text{net income}}$

> **Example**
>
> ABC Ltd achieved a ROE of 26,7% and R75 000 of the net income was paid out as dividends. The retained earnings equal R222 200 − R75 000 = R147 200, representing a pay-out ratio of 33,8% or a retention ratio of 66,2%.
>
> Retention rate
> $$= \frac{\text{R147 200}}{\text{R222 200}} \times \frac{100}{1} = 66{,}2\%$$
>
> Given a ROE and a retention rate of 66,2%, the firm's sustainable growth rate is equal to:
> $$= 26{,}7\% \times 0{,}662 = 17{,}68\%$$

So far liquidity, solvency and profitability ratios have been described. As was described earlier, normally an increase in the profitability of a listed company leads to an increase in the share price of such a firm. Since the long-term goal of the firm is to increase the value of the firm, management should also focus on measures of economic value.

(d) Measures of economic value[5]
Measures of economic value are the economic value added (EVA) and market value added (MVA). These measures can best be applied to public companies, in other words companies listed on a securities exchange such as the Johannesburg Securities Exchange (JSE), the London Stock Exchange (LSE) and the New York Stock Exchange (NYSE).

EVA is defined as:

EVA = EBIT(1 − T) − Cost of capital expressed in rand

Where
EBIT = earnings before interest and tax
T = tax rate

> **Example**
>
> Assume a firm has achieved an EBIT of R2 400 000 and is subject to a tax rate of 29%. The firm's balance sheet shows owners' equity at R8 000 000 and debt at R2 000 000. The firm's weighted average cost of capital (WACC) is 16%.
>
> EVA = R2 400 000(1 − 0,29) − 0,16(R800 000 + R200 000)
> = R2 400 000(0,71) − 0,16(R1 000 000)
> = R1 704 000 − R160 000
> = R1 544 000

A positive EVA is an additional contribution to shareholders' wealth made during the year. The market value of a public company's equity is simply the number of shares which have been issued times the price of the share. If this market value is greater than the book value of the shares, then the value added is called market value added (MVA).[6]

17.7.1.6 Concluding remarks on the financial analysis task

The preceding explanation offered a brief survey of the financial analysis task of financial management. From the explanation it is apparent that the income statement, balance sheet, funds flow statement, and financial

> **Example**
>
> Assume the ordinary shares of Telkom Ltd were issued at R10 each (the par value). A year later these shares trade at R79,15 each. The R69,15 difference is regarded as the MVA of the share.

ratios are important aids in the performance of this task.

In the following section the focus is on financial planning and control on the basis of this planning.

17.7.2 Financial planning and control

Financial planning forms an integral part of the strategic planning of a firm. Top management has to formulate the vision and mission for the firm, analyse the strengths and weaknesses of the firm, and identify opportunities and threats in the external environment. The probability of successfully implementing the strategy that top management has decided on depends on the extent to which the firm has suitable human and financial resources at its disposal, or can attract such resources.

Financial planning and control are done in most business organisations by means of budgets.

A **budget** can be seen as a formal written plan of future action, expressed in monetary terms and sometimes also in physical terms, to implement the strategy of the business and to achieve the goals with limited resources. As such, budgets are also used for control purposes. Control is done by comparing the actual results with the planned (budgeted) results periodically or on a continuous basis. In this way deviations are identified and corrective action can be taken in time.

This section provides a brief overview of the following:
- The focal points of budgets in the control system of a manufacturing business
- An integrated budgeting system for a manufacturing business
- Zero-base budgeting
- The balanced scorecard (BSC) approach

17.7.2.1 The focal points of budgets in a control system

Control systems are devised to ensure that a specified strategic business function or activity (for example manufacturing or sales) is carried out properly. Consequently, control systems should focus on, and budgets be devised for, various responsibility centres in a business. A responsibility centre can be described as any organisational or functional unit in a business that is headed by a manager responsible for the activities of that unit. All responsibility centres use resources (inputs or costs) to produce something (outputs or income). Typically, responsibility is assigned to income, cost (expense), profit and/or investment centres.

- In the case of an **income centre**, outputs are measured in monetary terms, though the size of these outputs is not directly compared with the input costs. The sales department of a business is an example of such an income centre. The effectiveness of the centre is not measured in terms of how much the income (units sold × selling prices) exceeds the cost of the centre (for example salaries and rent). Instead, budgets in the form of sales quotas are prepared, and the budgeted figures are compared with actual sales. This provides a useful picture of the effectiveness of individual sales personnel or of the centre itself.

- In a **cost centre**, inputs are measured in monetary terms, though outputs are not. The reason for this is that the primary purpose of such a centre is not the generation of income. Good examples of cost centres are the maintenance, research and administrative departments of a business. Consequently, budgets should be developed only for the input portion of these centres' operations.
- In a **profit centre**, performance is measured by the monetary difference between income (outputs) and costs (inputs). A profit centre is created whenever an organisational unit is given the responsibility of earning a profit. In this case budgets should be developed in such a way that provision is made for the planning and control of inputs and outputs.
- In an **investment centre** the monetary value of inputs and outputs is again measured, but the profit is also assessed in terms of the assets (investment) employed to produce this profit.

It should be clear that any profit centre can also be considered as an investment centre because its activities require some form of capital investment. However, if the capital investment is relatively small or if its manager(s) have no control over the capital investment, it is more appropriate from a planning and control – and thus from a budgeting – point of view to treat it as a profit centre.

17.7.2.2 An integrated budgeting system for a manufacturing business

In essence, an integrated budgeting system for a manufacturing business consists of two main types of budgets, namely:
- Operating budgets
- Financial budgets

Figure 17.16 diagrammatically shows the operating and financial components of an integrated budgeting system of a manufacturing business.

Operating budgets parallel three of the responsibility centres discussed earlier, namely cost, income and profit:
- **Cost budgets.** There are two types of cost budgets, namely manufacturing cost budgets and discretionary cost budgets. Manufacturing cost budgets are used where outputs can be accurately measured. These budgets usually describe the material and labour costs involved in each production item, as well as the estimated overhead costs. These budgets are designed to measure efficiency, and if the budget is exceeded it means that manufacturing costs were higher than they should have been. Discretionary cost budgets are used for cost centres in which output cannot be measured accurately (for example administration and research). Discretionary cost budgets are not used to assess efficiency because performance standards for discretionary expenses are difficult to devise.
- **Income budgets.** These budgets are developed to measure marketing and sales effectiveness. They consist of the expected sales quantity multiplied by the expected unit selling price of each product. The income budget is the most critical part of a profit budget, yet it is also one of the most uncertain because it is based on projected future sales.
- **Profit plan** or **profit budget.** This budget combines cost and income budgets and is used by managers who have responsibility for both the expenses and income of their units. Such managers frequently head an entire division or business.

Financial budgets, which are used by financial management for the execution of the financial planning and control task, consist of capital expenditure, cash, financing and balance sheet budgets. These budgets,

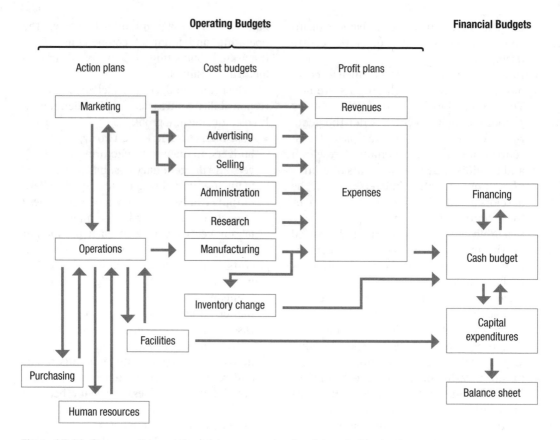

Figure 17.16: The operating and financial components of an integrated budgeting system

prepared from information contained in the operating budgets, integrate the financial planning of the business with its operational planning. Financial budgets serve three major purposes:

- They verify the viability of the operational planning (operating budgets).
- They reveal the financial actions that the business must take to make the execution of its operating budgets possible.
- They indicate how the operating plans of the business will affect its future financial actions and condition.

If these future actions and conditions are undesirable (for example over-borrowing to finance additional facilities), appropriate changes in the operating plans may be required.

The **capital expenditure budget** indicates the expected (budgeted) future capital investment in physical facilities (buildings, equipment, etc.) to maintain its present or expand the future productive capacity.

The **cash budget** indicates:

- The extent, time and sources of expected cash inflows
- The extent, time and purposes of expected cash outflows
- The expected availability of cash in comparison with the expected need for it

The **financing budget** is developed to assure the business of the availability of funds to meet the budgeted shortfalls of receipts (income) relative to payments (expenses) in the short term, and to schedule medium-term and long-term borrowing or financing. The financing budget is therefore developed in conjunction with the cash budget to provide the business with the funds it needs at the times it needs them.

The **balance sheet budget** brings together all the other budgets to project how the financial position of the business will look at the end of the budget period if actual results conform to planned results. An analysis of the balance sheet budget may suggest problems (for example a poor solvency situation due to over-borrowing) or opportunities (for example excessive liquidity, creating the opportunity to expand) that will require alterations to the other budgets.

17.7.2.3 Traditional budgeting

Traditional budgeting involves using the actual income and expenditure of the previous year as a basis and making adjustments for expected changes in circumstances. The projected sales serve as the point of departure for the budgeting process. Information must be gathered in order to determine which factors will lead to an increase or decline in sales, as well as factors that will influence cost.

Applying the concept

Retail firms (for example Edgars) can expect that during times of inflation, accompanied by increases in interest rates, the firm's sales could decline, bad debts increase, the collection of debt slow down and/or the cost of collecting outstanding debt increase (as a result of follow-up work). At the same time, the firm has to pay more interest on its loans, pay increased rent on hired retail space and face wage demands. The opposite can be expected during times of declining inflation and interest rates.

Examples of these are inflation, interest rates, exchange rates, wage demands, the actions of competitors and changes to tax legislation.

The firm's plans and budgets are usually negotiated and finalised during a time-consuming process. A lack of insight into and commitment to the firm's strategy can cause managers to pursue the interests of their own departments only during this phase, instead of thinking enterprise-wide. Such behaviour leads to suboptimum budgets.

One of the disadvantages of the traditional budgeting approach is that some managers continue the same activities year after year without critically re-evaluating priorities and possible changes in the external and internal environments. Two possible ways of handling this managerial challenge is the use of either zero-base budgeting or the balanced scorecard approach.

17.7.2.4 Zero-base budgeting

In contrast to traditional budgeting, **zero-base budgeting** enables the business to look at its activities and priorities afresh on an annual basis. In this case, historical results are not taken as a basis for the next budgeting period. Instead, each manager has to justify anew his or her entire budget request.

In theory, zero-base budgeting leads to a better prioritisation of resource allocations, and to more efficient businesses. In practice, however, it may generate undue amounts of paperwork and demoralise managers and other employees who are expected to justify their activities, expenses and, in essence, therefore, their existence, on an annual basis.

17.7.2.5 The balanced scorecard approach[7]

The **balanced scorecard (BSC) approach** was introduced by Kaplan & Norton (1996). The balanced scorecard approach enables managers to align their departments' budgets with the firm's vision and mission.

This approach suggests that strategy be implemented from four perspectives (each with its own goals, measures, targets and initiatives):

- **Financial.** What do investors expect from the firm in order to be financially successful?
- **Customers.** What do customers expect from the firm in order to reach the vision?
- **Internal processes.** Which processes must be excellent in order to satisfy customers and shareholders?
- **Learning and growth.** How will the ability of the firm to change and improve be maintained in order for the firm to reach its vision?

The BSC approach improves the budgeting process. It makes it essential for management to identify and focus on relevant information in order to budget effectively. From a planning point of view it exposes the internal and external challenges that confront management. Managers therefore must consider measures to best deal with these challenges. The allocation of resources is linked to specific measures of the scorecard. This approach offers a uniform way according to which departments can achieve their goals in respect of finances, customers, processes and growth perspectives.[8]

This approach requires that managers review the scorecard on a monthly or quarterly basis. In contrast with other approaches to budgeting, BSC enables managers to make adjustments to their budgets during a financial year to enable them to achieve their goals.

17.8 Summary

In this chapter we firstly examined the nature of the financial function and the tasks of financial management, as well as the relationship between financial management, the other functional management areas, related subject disciplines, and the environment. Thereafter, various concepts generally used in financial management, as well as certain techniques employed by financial management, were explained. The goal and fundamental principles of financial management were also explained. Finally, one of the tasks of financial management, namely financial analysis, planning and control, was outlined. The remaining tasks of financial management, amongst other things, are dealt with in chapters 18 and 19.

Critical thinking

Is it better for a manager at the middle management level to exceed his/her cost budget at the end of a financial year, or is it better to have funds to spare?

Both are problematic. Exceeding a cost budget could be interpreted as a lack of planning and control on the part of the manager (although there might be valid reasons for exceeding the budget, for example an increase in activity). Funds to spare are sometimes regarded by middle management as proof to the top management of how

sparingly it has used the firm's resources under its control. However, this may be indicating that the manager intentionally overestimated costs to create the impression that his or her budget is managed well. It may, however, be an indication that the manager did not achieve all the objectives that had been set at the beginning of the year. Unspent funds at the end of a financial year may also result in a reduction of the manager's budget for the following year.

Key terms

Balance sheet	Future value
Balanced scorecard approach	Income
Break-even analysis	Income statement
Budgeting	Present value
Capital	Profit
Cash flow	Risk–return
Cost	Time value of money
Cost–benefit	Zero-base budgeting
Financial ratios	

? Questions for discussion

1. How would you respond if you were the owner and manager of a business and the quarterly financial reports started showing your firm was making a loss?
2. Looking at the financial statements of your firm, you notice the net profit is not equal to your bank balance on 28 February. How do you explain this?
3. How would you determine whether it is financially viable to start your own business?
4. A group of managers discuss financial planning. "Compiling a budget is a waste of time. The business environment is simply too unpredictable," says one. Another responds, "One must work according to a plan. Yes, your results will not match the budgeted figures 100%, but failing to plan is planning to fail". What is your view?
5. One of your fellow students remarks that you can be a good financial manager only if you are a chartered accountant (CA). Would you agree or disagree? Why?

References

1. Keown, A.J., Martin, J.D., Petty, J.W. & Scott, D.F., *Foundations of finance*, 5th edition, Pearson, NJ, 2006.
2. Marx, J., De Swardt, C.J., Beaumont-Smith, M., Naicker, K.S. & Erasmus, P, *Financial management in Southern Africa*, 2nd edition, Pearson, Cape Town, 2003.
3. Partially based on Gitman, L.J., *Principles of managerial finance*, 11th edition, Pearson, Boston, Mass., 2006.
4. For example Gitman, *op. cit.*
5. www.eva.com (17 November 2006).
6. Marx, J., Mpofu, R.T. & Van de Venter, T.W.G., *Investment management*, 2nd edition, Van Schaik, Pretoria, 2004.
7. Kaplan, R. & Norton, D., *The balanced scorecard: Translating strategy into action*, Harvard, Boston, Mass, 1996.
8. Frye, C.D. "Improve budgeting using balanced scorecards", http://office.microsoft.com (23 November 2006).

ASSET MANAGEMENT:
THE INVESTMENT DECISION

The purpose of this chapter

It is important that managers or investors manage or understand the management of assets of a business by focusing on the management of the asset structure of a business, namely short-term investment decisions and long-term capital investment decisions. Rational and purposeful decisions in these areas will, to a large extent, ensure that the goals of the business are pursued as effectively as possible. Some important guidelines and techniques for both types of investment decision will be presented in this chapter, with the understanding that current and fixed asset management is totally integrated in practice.[1]

Learning outcomes

The content of this chapter will enable learners to:

- Manage the current assets of a business by:
  - Identifying and describing the current asset categories
  - Describing the principles involved in managing each category
  - Applying the elementary techniques to manage each category of current assets
- Manage the fixed assets of a business to create wealth for stakeholders by:
  - Describing and justifying the principles of capital budgeting and applying capital budgeting techniques such as the net present value (NPV) method
  - Illustrating the ability to incorporate risk into the capital budgeting decision
  - Explaining and applying the elementary techniques of capital budgeting

18.1 Introduction

In chapter 17 management of the asset structure is identified as one of the main tasks of financial management. To pursue the main objective successfully, management of the asset structure requires that decisions regarding investment in current and fixed **assets** be taken effectively. These decisions have a direct influence on the scope of the investment in current assets and the acquisition of fixed assets that will maximise the wealth of stakeholders. The example in the case study below illustrates this.

Case study

Table 18.1 shows an extract of the **balance sheet** of ABC Limited, and indicates how proper management of **current assets** and non-current assets can translate into good business management and lead to an increase in shareholder value.

Table 18.1: Extract of ABC Limited Balance Sheet as at 31 December 2006

Assets	Value	Link to value creation
Current assets		

Stock or inventories	950 500	Inventories normally form the core of the day-to-day trade of the business. For a clothing retailer such as Edgars, examples are shoes, clothes and bedding. Inventories are purchased from a supplier at a particular price and the merchant then adds a mark-up to cover the cost of running the business, as well as provide for a profit margin. This is usually referred to as the mark-up. For example:
		    Purchase price for 1 pair of shoes: R45,00 per pair
		    Mark-up of 50% (50% x R45): R22,50 per pair
		    Selling price per pair: R67,50 per pair

Debtors or receivables	450 250	Edgars sells most of its inventories on credit to its customers. These are then referred to as debtors. A customer who buys on credit would be expected to pay the company over 30 days or more. This presents a problem to Edgars since it does not receive cash immediately and yet has had to pay for the inventories from its supplier. If the customer pays on due date, then Edgars can manage and plan for cash-flow movement. If the customer defaults on payments, this can present a cash-flow squeeze, which can lead to reduced profits and/or possibly a loss for the company. This loss is normally deducted from the shareholders funds.
Cash and cash equivalents	250 950	That cash and cash equivalents need to be managed as cash is the key in managing the business on a day-to-day basis. Cash is used to settle creditors and for purchasing inventories, as well as settling overheads. While it is important to have adequate cash resources, managers should remember that holding too much cash can lead to low returns – or low shareholder value.
Total current assets	**1 651 700**	
Non-current assets		
Land and buildings	450 000	These are long-term assets that provide the basis for production and for long-term value of the business. It is a well-documented fact that land and buildings generally appreciate over time, meaning that their value always increases. Managers should, however, be conscious not to invest too much in unnecessary land and buildings, since cash is then tied up in non-core business. For Edgars, it might be a better strategy to lease or rent its properties (this also has a tax advantage as lease/rental payments qualify for tax deduction, which leads to increased tax savings).

Assets	Value	Link to value creation
Equipment and machinery	250 000	These form part of the productive capacity of the business. Machinery that is underutilised is very costly to the business. Not only does it cost the company in terms of maintenance, but it also loses value by depreciation on an annual basis. An example is a folk-lift truck used in stacking up inventories in a warehouse. This equipment is vital for the business but having too many fork-lifts does not add value to the business.
Vehicles	455 000	Most vehicles are used for deliveries and for collections of inventories. Issues regarding machinery also apply to vehicles, but are even more important here since vehicles generally lose their value (depreciate) within a period of three to five years.
Equity investments	450 000	These are investments by a company in other businesses. The company would therefore receive a return on its investment via a dividend payout. The choice of an equity investment is important since it should always be compared to the returns the company receives from its own operations. For example, if Edgars receives 25% return from R1 invested in Edgars operations, it should ensure that it receives at least the same return or more from outside equity investments. There are exceptions, for example when the equity investment is made for strategic reasons. For Edgars, this could be an investment in a company that supplies it with scarce raw material for the production of clothes (silk production could be a good example).
Goodwill	356 250	Goodwill is an intangible asset that a company receives when it acquires another business. For example, if Edgars were to acquire Truworths assets valued at R7 million, but pay a price of R12 million, the difference of R5 million represents an asset called goodwill. This arises from a number of sources, for example favourable location, strong management talent, skilled workers, a stable brand name on the market, and so forth. This asset can be used by Edgars as a tax deduction on an annual basis. For example, after a profit of R712 500, Edgars could write off the goodwill of R356 250 as an expense called amortisation. This would reduce the taxable profit by half, leading to lower taxes paid, and thereby leading to more cash flow being available to Edgars.
Non-current assets	**1 861 250**	
TOTAL ASSETS	**3 612 950**	

Anglo American says, "Our corporation exists to create wealth and generate rewards for its key stakeholders – its shareholders and employees who, together with their dependants, account for 1,5 million South Africans. That is its first responsibility, to the community at large as much as to its stakeholders, for if it fails in that aim it will lack the means of discharging any broader social responsibilities."

Source: Relly, G., in Supplement to *Financial Mail*, 28 September 1989, p. 41.

As can be seen from the graph in figure 18.1, companies differ in their holdings of current assets as a percentage of total assets. Some differences are due to the type of industry. For example, it is evident that Sasol has a very low percentage of current assets compared to Edcon. Sasol is in the petroleum and related industries, while Edcon is mostly in clothing retail, with companies such as Edgars, Jet and CNA. Pick 'n Pay and Shoprite are predominantly supermarket retailers and have a slightly lower holding of current assets than Edcon. Pick 'n Pay also differs from Shoprite in its holdings since it has a lower holding of current assets. This can be attributed to its broader diversification of businesses that have more non-current assets than Shoprite.

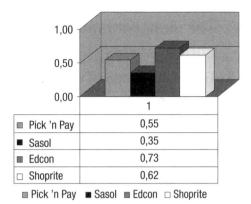

	1
▨ Pick 'n Pay	0,55
▪ Sasol	0,35
▪ Edcon	0,73
▫ Shoprite	0,62

▨ Pick 'n Pay ▪ Sasol ▪ Edcon ▫ Shoprite

Figure 18.1: The ratio of current to total assets for selected South African companies (2006)

Source: Compiled from data from 2006 annual reports of various companies

---

Critical thinking

Using information from the extracted balance sheet of ABC Limited (table 18.1 in the case study on page 445), discuss the following questions:

- A mark-up of 50% on cost implies that the price of a product will be calculated as follows: Cost Price multiplied by (1 + 50%). This means that ABC Limited will make a net profit margin of 50%. Is this true? Discuss.
- The following financial statements represent a firm's actual position as of December 31, 2006.

a. In this situation, what will the ending current liabilities account for 2007 be?
b. Assuming no new common stock is issued, what will be the change in the common equity account in rands?

Balance sheet	2006	2007
Cash	250 950	
Receivables	450 250	
Net fixed assets	1 861 250	
Current liabilities		
Common equity	R1m	
Income statement		
Sales	R1m	
Gross profit	R600 000	
Operating profit	R200 000	
Net income (after tax)	R120 000	

Assumptions:
A. Sales are expected to increase by 20% in 2007.
B. Gross profit, operating profit, net income, current assets, and current liabilities will be the same percentage of sales in 2007 as they were in 2006.
C. Depreciation in 2007 will be R25 000.
D. Dividends will be R50 000.
E. Gross fixed assets will remain constant.

18.2 The management of current assets

18.2.1 The cost and risk of investing in current assets

In chapter 17 you will have seen that current assets include items such as cash, marketable securities, debtors and inventory. These items are needed to ensure the continuous and smooth functioning of the business. **Cash**, for example, is needed to pay bills that are not perfectly matched by current cash inflows, while an adequate supply of **raw materials** is required to sustain the manufacturing process. Sales may be influenced by the **credit** the business is prepared to allow.

Current assets are therefore a necessary and significant component of the total assets of the business. Figure 18.1 on page 447 shows that the ratio of current to total assets may vary from company to company. A retailer such as Pick 'n Pay has a large ratio of current to total assets compared to, say, Sasol, which is listed under the JSE Oil and Gas Exploration and Production sector and produces fuels and chemicals for the chemical industry. Pick 'n Pay's large ratio of current to total assets occurs because most of the assets of retail stores are in the form of inventory (current assets). Its main business is trading in inventory, not manufacturing. The chemical industry, in contrast, has large investments in plant and other fixed assets.

In managing current assets, management should always keep in mind the consequences of having too much or too little invested in them. Two factors play a role, namely **cost** and **risk**.

An **over-investment** in current assets means a low degree of risk, in that more than adequate amounts of cash are available to pay bills when they fall due, or sales are amply supported by more than sufficient levels of inventory. However, over-investment causes profits to be less than the maximum, firstly because of the cost associated with the **capital** invested in additional current assets, and secondly because of income foregone which could have been earned elsewhere – the so-called **opportunity cost** of capital. The funds invested in excess inventory could, for example, have been invested in a short-term deposit earning interest at the prevailing interest **rate**.

An **under-investment** in current assets, however, increases the risk of cash and inventory shortages and the costs associated with these shortages, but it also decreases the opportunity cost. For example, a business short of cash may have to pay high interest rates to obtain funds on short notice, while a shortage of inventory may result in a loss of sales, or even mean that the business has to buy inventory from competitors at high prices to keep customers satisfied. The optimal level of investment in current assets is a trade-off between the costs and the risks involved.

Having made these general introductory remarks on investment in current assets, we shall now discuss the management of the following current assets in more detail:

- Cash and marketable securities
- Debtors
- Inventory

18.2.2 The management of cash and marketable securities

Cash is the money (currency and coin) the business has on hand in petty cash drawers, in cash registers, and in current and savings accounts with financial institutions.

The costs of holding cash are:

- **Loss of interest.** Cash in the form of notes and coins, and, even, money in a current account at a bank, earns no interest.
- **Loss of purchasing power.** During a period of inflation there is an erosion in the value of money, and this becomes even more serious if no interest is earned on that money.

Applying the concept: Risks and costs of investing in current assets

The example below illustrates that cost and risk are of prime importance in the management of current assets.

Table 18.2: Balance sheets and operating profit (after tax)

	Business	
	A	B
Cash	R1 000	R1 000
Marketable securities		R10 000
Debtors	19 000	19 000
Inventory	30 000	30 000
Current assets	100 000	100 000
Fixed assets	R50 000	R60 000
Total	R150 000	R160 000
Current liabilities	20 000	20 000
Debt (long-term)	30 000	30 000
Shareholders' funds	100 000	110 000
Total	R150 000	R160 000
Operating income (after tax)	**15 000**	**15 300***

* B earns 6% on an investment of R10 000 in marketable securities. At a tax rate of 50% the income after tax is R300.

$$\text{Current ratio} = \frac{\text{Cusrrent assets}}{\text{Current liability}}$$

Business A	Business B
$\frac{50\ 000}{20\ 000} = 2{,}5{:}1$	$\frac{60\ 000}{20\ 000} = 3{:}1$

$$\text{Rate of return (after tax)} = \frac{\text{Operating income (after tax)}}{\text{Total capital}}$$

$\frac{15\ 000}{150\ 000} = 10\%$	$\frac{15\ 300}{160\ 000} = 9{,}6\%$

B is more liquid than A (current ratio of 3:1 compared to a ratio of 2,5:1 for A) and therefore also less risky than A. The rate of return of B, however, is less than that of A (a rate of return of 9,6% compared to that of 1 of 10%). See section 17.7.1.5 for a discussion and a definition of the current ratios and rate of return (after tax).

The costs of little or no cash are:

- **Loss of goodwill.** Failure to meet financial obligations on time due to cash shortages will seriously affect the relationship between the company and its employees, creditors, and suppliers of raw materials and services.
- **Loss of opportunities.** Cash shortages will make it impossible to react quickly to a lucrative business opportunity.
- **Inability to claim discounts.** Discounts for prompt and early payment are very advantageous in percentage terms. Cash shortages may preclude the claiming of such discounts.
- **Cost of borrowing.** Shortages of cash may force a business to raise money at short notice at expensive rates.

Marketable securities are investment instruments on which a business earns a fixed interest income. They can easily be converted into cash and are therefore also referred to as near-cash assets. An example of a marketable security is a short-term treasury bill issued by the government.

There are three reasons for a business having a certain amount of cash available:

- **The transaction motive.** The transaction motive exists primarily because receipts and disbursements are not fully synchronised. Expenses must often be paid before any cash income has been received. The business needs to have sufficient cash available to meet normal current expenditures such as the payment of wages, salaries, rent and creditors.
- **The precautionary motive.** The precautionary motive entails the keeping of cash, in addition to that prompted by the transaction motive, for contingencies. Contingencies are unexpected events such as a large debtor **default**ing on its account, or employees making an unexpected wage demand that may strain the financial position of the business. These funds are usually held in the form of marketable securities that can easily be converted into cash.
- **The speculative motive.** The speculative motive implies that the business must be able to capitalise on good opportunities such as unexpected bargains and bulk purchases. Additional funds for this purpose are usually also held in the form of marketable securities. A competitor may, for example, be declared insolvent and its inventory sold at bargain prices. The business can capitalise on this opportunity only if it has extra cash available to take advantage of this opportunity.

Cash management is essential to obtain the optimal trade-off between the liquidity risk and the cost of being too liquid. This is achieved by focusing on the **cash budget** and the **cash cycle**. These two aspects of cash management will now be considered in more detail.

18.2.2.1 The cash budget

Determining the cash needs of a business is an important aspect of cash management. Unutilised cash surpluses or cash shortages result in the cost and risk of the cash investment increasing unnecessarily. Cash-flow problems were advanced as the primary cause of the demise of several large real estate development companies, such as Corlett Drive Estates, in the early 1970s.

> **Quote the banker, "Watch cash flow."**
> Though my bottom line is black, I am flat upon my back,
>
> My cash flows out and customers pay slow.
>
> The growth of my receivables is almost unbelievable;
>
> The result is certain unremitting woe!
>
> And I hear the banker utter an ominous low mutter,
>
> "Watch cash flow."

Source: Bailey, S.H., "Quote the banker: Watch cash flow", *Publishers Weekly*, 13 January 1975.

The cash budget facilitates the planning and control of cash. Its purpose is to identify future cash shortages and cash surpluses. The cash budget is therefore a detailed plan of future **cash flow**s for a specific period and is composed of the following three elements:

- **Cash receipts.** These originate from cash sales, collections from credit sales, and other sources such as cash injections in the form of, say, bank **loan**s.
- **Cash disbursements.** These are broadly categorised as cash paid for purchases of merchandise, raw materials, and operating expenses.
- **Net changes in cash.** These represent the difference between cash receipts and cash disbursements.

The cash budget serves as a basis for determining the cash needs of a business and

Applying the concept: the cash budget

For Save Retailers there is a 30-day collection period on debtors, which means that there is a lag of 30 days between a credit sale and the receipt of cash. Consequently, cash collections in any month equal the credit sales one month prior. Purchases on credit must also be paid within 30 days.

Table 18.3: Save Retailers

	March	April	May	June
1. CASH ON HAND (A)	0	20	(32)	(13)
2. CASH RECEIPTS				
(a) Cash sales	25	23	30	50
(b) Collections from debtors	225	200	270	450
TOTAL CASH RECEIPTS (B)	250	223	300	500
3. CASH DISBURSEMENTS				
(a) Creditors	144	144	144	144
(b) Wages	60	60	66	66
(c) Overheads	26	26	26	26
(d) Owners' withdrawal	0	45	45	43
TOTAL CASH DISBURSEMENTS (C)	230	275	281	277
4. NET CASH POSITIONS (A + B − C)	20	(32)	(10)	210

indicates when bridging finance will be required. The following example shows how the cash budget is used to determine cash needs.

It is clear that the cash budget can be used to identify temporary cash shortages, and that this information can be used to arrange bridging finance timeously. It also indicates excess liquidity, and this information can again be used to plan temporary investments in marketable securities.

The cash budget for Save Retailers in the box above shows, for example, that bridging finance will have to be arranged for April and May, and that arrangements will have to be made to invest the cash surplus that will arise during June.

Although one assumes that profit equals an amount held in cash, this is almost never

the case. The difference between profit and cash flow is illustrated in the example on page 452. This example shows that a profitable business may not be able to continue its operations due to a cash shortage. The shortage arises despite growing sales and the accumulation of profits.

18.2.2.2 The cash cycle

The cash cycle in a manufacturing business, as illustrated in figure 18.2 on page 454, indicates the time it takes to complete the following cycle:
• Investing cash in raw materials
• Converting the raw materials to finished products
• Selling the finished products on credit

Example: Profits and cash flow

Suppose we have a product that costs R75 to manufacture and is sold for R100. Payment is received within 30 days of sale. Production is based on the expected sales of the following month. Sales for the next three months, January to March, are expected to increase. Production costs are paid during the month in which production takes place. From December to April, the course of events is as follows:

December   1 500 units were sold on credit. Debtors on 1 January amount to R150 000, and 1 500 units were in stock.

January

1 January:	Cash	R 75 000
	Inventory (1 500 @ R75)	R112 500
	Debtors (1 500 @ R100)	R150 000

During January, 2 000 units are sold and 2 500 are manufactured to keep one month's sales (1 500 − 2 500 − 2 000 = 2 000) in stock.

Profit for January: 2 000 units × (R100 − 75)
    = 2 000 × R25
    = R50 000

February

1 February: CASH

Opening balance	R 75 000
Plus: Received from debtors	R150 000
Minus: Production costs (2 500 × R75)	R187 500
Closing cash balance	R37 500

Inventory (2 000 units @ R75)   R150 000

Opening balance	1 500
Plus: Manufactured	2 500
Minus: Sales	2 000

Debtors (2 000 @ R100)   R200 000

During February, sales increase to 2 500 units, and in preparation for sales expected in March, 3 000 units are produced.

Profit for February: 2 500 units × (R100 × 75)
    = 2 500 × R25
    = R62 500

Cumulative Profit   = R50 000 + R62 500
    = R112 500

March

1 March: CASH

Opening balance	R37 500
Plus: Received from debtors	R200 000
Minus: Production costs (2 500 × R75)	R225 000
Closing balance	R12 500

Inventory (2 500 units @ R100) =   R187 500

Opening balance	2 000
Plus: Manufactured	3 000
Minus: Sales	2 500

During March, sales increase to 3 000 units, and in preparation for sales expected in April, 3 500 units are produced.

Profit for March: 3 000 units × (R100 − 75)

= 3 000 × R25

= R75 000

Cumulative Profit: R50 000 + R62 500 + R75 000

= R187 500

April

CASH:

Opening balance:	R12 500
Plus: Received from debtors	R250 000
Minus: Production costs (3 000 × R75)	R262 500
Closing cash balance	R0

Inventory (30 units @ R75) =   R225 000

Opening balance	2 500
Plus: Manufactured	3 500
Minus: Sales	3 000

Debtors: (3 000 @ R100) =   R300 000

Notwithstanding a total net profit of R187 500 after 3 months (on April 1) the business is without cash and production cannot be continued.

Figure 18.2: The cash cycle in a business

- Ending the cycle by collecting cash

Wholesalers and retailers are not involved in the second step, but are rather concerned with directly converting cash into inventory. Businesses that offer no credit have no conversion from debtors to cash. As a rule, cash is available only after money has been collected from debtors.

The cash cycle is a continuous process, and it should be clear that the demand for cash can be greatly reduced if the cycle is speeded up. This is achieved by rapid cash collections and by proper management of debtors and stock (inventory).

18.2.3 The management of debtors

Debtors arise when a business **sells on credit** to its clients. Debtors have to settle their accounts in a given period (usually within 30 or 60 days after date of purchase). Credit may be extended to either an individual or a business. Credit granted to an individual is referred to as **consumer credit**. Credit extended to a business is known as **trade credit**. Debtor accounts represent a considerable portion of the investment in current assets in most businesses and obviously demand efficient management.

Credit sales increase total sales and income. As pointed out in the management of cash, debtor accounts have to be recovered as soon as feasible to keep the cash requirements of the business as low as possible. Once again, an optimal balance has to be struck between the amount of credit sales (the higher the credit sales, the higher the income and, it is hoped, the profitability) and the size of debtor accounts (the greater the size of debtor accounts and the longer the **collection period**, the higher the investment and **cash needs** of the business will be, and the

lower the profitability).

In any business, the three most important facets of the management of debtor accounts are the following:
- The credit policy
- The credit terms
- The collection policy

The **credit policy** contains directives according to which it is decided whether credit should be granted to clients and, if so, how much. Essentially, this involves an evaluation of the creditworthiness of debtors, based on realistic credit standards. Realistic credit standards revolve around the "four Cs of credit":
- **Character** – the customer's willingness to pay
- **Capacity** – the customer's ability to pay
- **Capital** – the customer's financial resources
- **Conditions** – current economic or business conditions

These four general characteristics are assessed from sources such as financial statements, the customer's bank, and credit agencies. Credit agencies specialise in providing credit ratings and credit reports on individual businesses.

Credit terms define the credit period and any discount offered for early payment. They are usually stated as "net t" or "$d/t1$, n/t". The first (t) denotes that payment is due within t days from when the goods are received. The second ($d/t1$, n/t) allows a discount of d% if payment is made within $t1$ days; otherwise the full amount is due within t days. For example, "3/10, $n/30$" means that a 3% discount can be taken from the invoice amount if payment is made within 10 days; otherwise, full payment is due within 30 days.

The **collection policy** concerns the guidelines for the collection of debtor accounts that have not been paid by due dates. The collection policy may be applied rigorously or less rigorously, depending on circumstances. The level of **bad debt**s is often regarded as a criterion of the effectiveness of credit and collection policies.

The costs of granting credit include the following:

- **Loss of interest.** Granting credit is similar to granting interest free loans. This means that interest is lost on the amount of credit advanced to trade debtors.
- **Costs associated with determining the customer's creditworthiness.** The procedure to determine the creditworthiness of a customer costs money, but fortunately needs to be incurred only once. After the initial screening procedure, the company reassesses the customer on its own experience of the customer's track record of payment.
- **Administration and record-keeping costs.** Most companies that grant credit find it necessary to employ people to administer and collect trade debts.
- **Bad debts.** Unless a company adopts an extremely cautious credit granting policy, it is almost inevitable that some trade debts will not be paid. Although this risk can be insured against, it still remains a cost to the company.

The costs mentioned above must be considered against the loss of goodwill if credit is denied in a competitive market where customers may obtain the same products on credit terms.

> Saying "no" to a customer may be an easy answer, but your competitors may gain a profitable sale. This is not the way to increase turnover and profit.

Source: Posner, M., *Successful credit control*, BSP Professional Books, New York, 1990, p. 1.

18.2.4 The management of stock (inventory)

The concept "inventory stock" includes raw and auxiliary materials, work in progress, semi-finished products, trading stock, and so forth and, like debtors, represents a considerable portion of the investment in **working capital**. In inventory management there is once again a conflict between the **profit objective** (to keep the lowest possible supply of stock, and to keep stock turnover as high as possible, in order to minimise the investment in stock, as well as attendant cash needs) and the **operating objective** (to keep as much stock as possible to ensure that the business is never without, and to ensure that production interruptions and therefore loss of sales never occur).

It is once again the task of financial management to combine optimally the relevant variables in the framework of a sound purchasing and inventory policy, in order to increase profitability without subjecting the business to unnecessary risks.

The costs of holding inventory stock are:

- **Lost interest.** This refers to the interest that could have been earned on the money that is tied up in holding inventory stock.
- **Storage cost.** This cost includes the rent of space occupied by the inventory stock and the cost of employing people to guard and manage the stock
- **Insurance costs.** Holding inventory stock exposes the business to risk of fire and theft of the stock. Insurance will provide cover against these losses but this will involve an additional cost in the form of premiums that have to be paid to the insurance company.
- **Obsolescence.** Stocks can become obsolete, for example because they go out of fashion. Thus, apparently perfectly good inventory stock may be of little more value than scrap.

The cost of holding little or no inventory stocks are:

- **The loss of customer goodwill.** Failure to be

able to supply a customer due to insufficient stock may mean the loss of not only that particular order but of other orders as well.

- **Production interruption dislocation.** Running out of stock for certain types of companies can be very costly. For example, a motor manufacturer running out of a major body section has no choice but to stop production.
- **Loss of flexibility.** Additional stock holding creates a safety margin whereby mishaps of various descriptions can be accommodated without major and costly repercussions. Without these buffer inventory levels, the company loses this flexibility.
- **Re-order costs.** A company existing on little or no stock will be forced to place a large number of small orders with short intervals between each order. Each order gives rise to costs, including the cost of placing the order and the cost of physically receiving the goods.

18.2.5 Final comments on the asset side of the balance sheet

In our discussion of the asset side of the balance sheet, we have given only a brief overview of the management of current assets and discussed only a few fundamental financial implications to show how complex the management of current assets is.

18.3 Long-term investment decisions and capital budgeting

18.3.1 The nature of capital investments

Capital investment involves the use of funds of a business to acquire fixed assets such as land, buildings and equipment, the benefits of which accrue over periods longer than one year.

Long-term investment decisions determine the type, size, and composition of a business's fixed assets, as well as the amount of permanent working capital required for the implementation and continued operation of capital investment projects.

The importance of capital investments and the capital investment decision-making process cannot be over-emphasised.

Critical thinking

A company collects R1 million per month in October, November and December. The company's cash payments represented 85% of October's receipts, 120% of November's receipts, and 95% of December's receipts. On 1 October, the company had a cash balance of R100 000, which also represented its minimum operating needs.

1. Which of the following methods would be used to forecast this company's cash position?
   A. Distribution
   B. Percentage of sales
   C. Time series
   D. Receipts and disbursements
2. Which of the following represents the company's ending cash position for November?
   A. (R200 000)
   B. (R50 000)
   C. R50 000
   D. R100 000
3. In addition to short-term investments, which of the following provides liquidity reserve?
   I. Long-term investments
   II. Unused short-term borrowing
   III. Unused long-term borrowing
   A. I only
   B. II only
   C. II and III only
   D. I, II, and III

Table 18.4: Three major capital expenditure projects

Project	Company	Value (R billion)	Estimated completion date
Coal Power Generation Project	Eskom	150	2012
Power Supply Infrastructure	Eskom	150	2012
Airports Upgrade	Airports Company SA	20	2010

Table 18.4 gives the three major capital expenditure projects in South Africa with estimated completion dates after 2005.

The success of large businesses ultimately depends on their ability to identify capital investment opportunities that will maximise stakeholders' wealth. Conversely, examples abound of business failures because businesses failed to identify such opportunities, or invested in unprofitable projects.

The importance of capital-investment projects is reflected by the following three factors:

- **The relative magnitude of the amounts involved.** The amounts involved in capital investment are much larger than those relating to, say, decisions about the amount of credit to be extended, or purchasing inventory.
- **The long-term nature of capital investment decisions.** The benefits from capital investment projects may accrue in periods varying from two or three years to as much as 30 or 40 years.

Example

Despite a massive effort by Eskom, involving more than R150bn of capital expenditure over the next five years, electricity supply security will remain inadequate and reserve margins will be paper thin. Eskom is probably doing all it can to restore supply security. Its current installed net generation capacity of about 37 000MW will be boosted by the return to service of about 3 500MW of old coal-fired stations, about 2 000MW of new open-cycle gas turbines, a small 100MW wind farm and a massive new coal plant of about 4 200MW (the so-called Alpha and Charlie projects).
Source: "Faults in plan for supply security", *Business Day Internet Edition*, http://www.businessday.co.za/articles/topstories.aspx?ID=BD4A419095 (29 March 2007).

Eskom will bump up its capital expenditure to generate additional capacity to a massive R150bn over the next five years, which could see the cost of generating and distributing electricity rise as much as 34%. This is an increase of 55% on the R97bn projected five-year expenditure to upgrade SA's power supply infrastructure announced only last year. The latest figure emerged from a briefing note to Eskom executives on the plan, which has already been approved by Eskom's board. The material increase in capital expenditure, half of which will be funded by Eskom and the balance through internationally raised debt.
Source: "Eskom growth 'ends cheap power'", *Business Day Internet Edition*, http://www.businessday.co.za/articles/topstories.aspx?ID=BD4A412810 (29 March 2007).

The decision of the Ford Motor Company during the 1950s to manufacture and market the Ford Edsel required an investment of US R250 million. With losses amounting to US R200 million in the first two-and-a-half years of the project, it was "... in all, a R450m mistake".
Source: "The Edsel dies and Ford regroups survivors", *Business Week*, 28 November 1959, p. 27.

Example

Three of Eskom's power stations were closed down in 1988. Together they had given 153 years of service. They had burnt 144 million tons of coal and produced 140 000 million kilowatt hours of electricity.

Source: "Three oldest power stations closed down", *Eskom Annual Report*, 1988, p. 29.

- **The strategic nature of capital investment projects.** Investment decisions of a strategic nature, such as the development of an entirely new product, the application of a new technology, or the decision to diversify internationally or to embark on rendering a strategic service could have a profound effect on the future development of a business. For example, Honda's decision to branch out from motorcycles to passenger vehicles entirely changed the strategic direction of the company.

Example

Airports Company SA (Acsa) has ramped up its capital expenditure to R19,3bn to meet expected growth in passenger traffic beyond 2010, says Transport Minister Jeff Radebe. Addressing the annual conference of the Board of Airline Representatives of SA in Hermanus on Friday, Radebe said Acsa expected to handle 31-million passengers at its nine airports by 2010 when SA hosts the Soccer World Cup. Acsa's previous capital expenditure figure mentioned last month was R5,2bn. Later in the month, the company announced it would go to the bond market to raise R12bn for investment in airport capacity. It completed its first, oversubscribed bond issue of R2bn earlier this month with another planned for later this year.

Source: "Airports get R20bn facelift for 2010", *Business Day Internet Edition*, http://www.businessday.co.za/articles/topstories.aspx?ID=BD4A421007 (29 March 2007).

18.3.2 **The evaluation of investment projects**

The basic principle underlying the evaluation of investment decision making is cost–benefit analysis, in which the cost of each project is compared to its benefits (see figure 18.3). Projects in which benefits exceed the costs add value to the business and increase stakeholders' wealth.

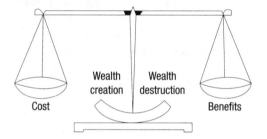

Figure 18.3: A cost–benefit representation of investment decision making

Source: Adapted from Kolb, B.A., *Principles of financial management*, Business Publications, Plano, Texas, 1983, p. 323.

Two additional factors require further consideration when comparing benefits and costs. Firstly, benefits and costs occur at different times. Any comparison of benefits and costs should therefore take the time value of money into account. The time value of money is discussed in chapter 17.

Secondly, "cost" and "benefits" (income) are accounting concepts that do not necessarily reflect the timing and amounts of payments to the business. The concept "cash flow" is therefore used instead, which minimises accounting ambiguities associated with concepts relating to income and costs.

18.3.2.1 **Cash-flow concepts**

Cash flow represents cash transactions. The net effect of cash revenues (sources of cash) and cash expenses (uses of cash) is the net cash flow.

Net cash flow = cash revenues − cash expenses

Table 18.5 provides examples of transactions that result in cash inflows (sources of cash) and cash outflows (uses of cash).

Table 18.5: Examples of the sources and uses of cash

Sources of cash	Uses of cash
A decrease in assets	An increase in assets
An increase in liabilities	A decrease in liabilities
Cash sales	
Investment income	Dividend payments to shareholders

Cash flow differs from profit shown on the income statement in that the latter also includes non-cash costs such as depreciation.

Example

Assume that a printing business, ABC Litho Printing, buys a printing machine that will last for ten years. The business spends a large sum of money to acquire the machine but will not spend any significant amounts until the end of the tenth year, when the machine has to be replaced.

It does not make sense to assume that the business makes profits during years one to nine and then incurs a large loss in year ten when it has to replace the machine. The machine will be used for the entire period, and not only in year ten.

The net profit of the business is adjusted for the use of the machine in years one to nine by deducting depreciation from income. The amount of depreciation is determined by depreciation rules laid down by the tax authorities, as tax is levied on profits after depreciation has been deducted.

However, the cash-flow amount the business has available for reinvestment is equal to the profit after tax plus the depreciation. This amount is the net cash flow into the business.

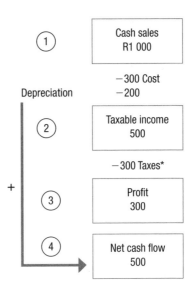

Figure 18.4: Profit and cash flow for ABC Litho Printers

As shown in the representation of the cash flow for ABC Litho in figure 18.4, the net cash flow is the difference between cash income and cash expenditures. If the net cash flow is positive, it means an inflow of cash and is referred to as a net cash inflow. However, cash expenditures can also exceed cash income. This results in a negative cash flow and is then referred to as net cash outflow.

The following three cash-flow components are distinguished for capital budgeting purposes:

- **The initial investment.** This is the money paid at the beginning of a project for the acquisition of equipment or the purchase of a production plant. The net cash flow during this phase is negative and represents a net cash outflow.
- **The expected annual cash flows over the life of the project.** The annual net cash flow can be positive or negative. The net cash flow is positive when cash income exceeds cash disbursements, and this represents a cash inflow for the business. The opposite is true when cash disbursements exceed income. This may happen, for example, when expensive refurbishing is required

after a number of years of operation, and cash income is insufficient to cover these cash expenses.

- **The expected terminal cash flow, related to the termination of the project.** This terminal net cash flow is usually positive. The plant is sold and cash income exceeds cash expenses. It may happen, however, that the cost of cleaning up a site is so high that the terminal net cash flow is negative. Think, for example, of a nuclear power plant where the terminal value of the plant is low, because of its limited use, but where the cost of disposing of the enriched uranium is very high.

The **magnitude of the expected net cash flows** of a project, and the **timing of these cash flows**, are crucial in the evaluation of investment proposals on the basis of the present value or discounted cash-flow approach, where the **net cash flow (the cash inflow minus cash outflow) can occur during a specific period or at a specific time.**

For evaluation purposes it is therefore imperative to approach potential projects in a future-oriented time framework and to present the expected cash-flow stream of a potential project on a time line, as illustrated in figure 18.5 (on page 462).

The **annual net cash flows** are normally calculated as the profit after interest and tax, plus any non-cash cost items such as depreciation minus the cash outflows for the particular year.

- The **initial investment** (C_0) is the net cash outflow at the commencement of the project at time t_o, usually for the acquisition of fixed assets and required current assets.
- The **annual net cash flows** (operating cash flows) (CF_t) are the net cash flows after tax which occur at any point during the life of the project minus cash outflow for the year. A positive net cash flow means that the cash inflow exceeds the cash outflow. A negative net cash flow implies the opposite.

- The **life of the project** (n periods or years), also referred to as the economic life of the project, is determined by the effects of physical, technological and economic factors.
- The **terminal cash flow** (TCF) is the expected **net cash flow after tax**, which is related to the termination of the project, such as the sale of its assets and the recovery of the working capital that was initially required. Depending on circumstances, the terminal net cash flow can again be positive or negative, if it occurs only at the end of the final year of the life of the project life. This is indicated by TCF_n.

18.3.2.2 The net present value method (NPV)

Decision criteria that take the time value of money into account and are based on cash flow are called **discounted cash-flow** (DCF) methods. They involve discounting estimated future cash flows to their present values, and take the magnitude and timing of cash flows into account.

This discussion is limited to the **net present value** (NPV) method. The NPV is the difference between the present value of all net cash inflows (after tax) and the present value of all cash outflows (usually the initial investment) directly related to the project.

The formula for the calculation of NPV is as follows:

NPV = Present value of net cash inflows − initial investment

The application of NPV involves the following:

- Forecasting the three components of project cash flows (the initial investment, the annual net cash flows, and the terminal cash flow) as accurately as possible
- Deciding on an appropriate discounting rate
- Calculating the present values of the above three project cash flow components for a

Table 18.6: Information regarding potential projects X and Y

Relevant information: initial investment (C₀)		Project X	Project Y
		R10 000	R10 000
Year	Time	Net cash flow (CF_t)	Net cash flow (CF_t)
1	$t = 1$	R2 800	R6 500
2	$t = 2$	R2 800	R3 500
3	$t = 3$	R2 800	R3 000
4	$t = 4$	R2 800	R1 000
5	$t = 5$	R2 800	R1 000

Notes:
1. The initial investmant C_0 at time t^0 is the same for both projects, namely R10 000.
2. In this example it is assumed that the net cash flow at the end of year 5 in both cases comprises only onnual cash flows and not terminal cash flow.

project determining the NPV of the project (the difference between the present value of the net cash inflows and that of the net cash outflow), where the NPV may be positive or negative

- Accepting all projects with a positive NPV and rejecting all those with a negative NPV, in accordance with NPV decision criteria

We shall explain the NPV method by means of a practical example and compare it to investment proposals X and Y (the information regarding these projects appears in table 18.6).

Assuming that the business's cost of capital is given as 15%, determining the NPV for project Y, for example, involves discounting the estimated net cash inflows at a discounting rate of 15% and subtracting the net cash outflow of R10 000 from the sum of the present value of the inflows.

To form a better idea of the cash flow at each point in time (year-end) over the entire project life, the total cash flows for project Y can be presented on a time line, as illustrated in figure 18.5 on page 462.

In addition to a **time line**, NPV_x and NPV_y can also be determined by using a tabular format as illustrated in table 18.8 on page 462 at a discount rate of 15%. (See table 18.7 for the discounting factors.)

At a discount rate of 15%, NPV_x is negative and NPV_y is positive.

The **decision criteria** for the NPV are as follows:

- **Accept** projects with a positive NPV (NPV > 0).
- **Reject** projects with a negative NPV (NPV < 0).
- Projects with NPV = 0 make **no contribution** to value and are usually **rejected**.

The following questions might now be asked: "How should the NPV as a criterion for decisions on investment possibilities be interpreted?" and "In short, what does NPV mean in this context?"

Table 18.7: Discounting factors

Period (n)	Discount rate	
	10%	15%
1	0,9091	0,8696
2	0,8264	0,7561
3	0,7513	0,6575
4	0,6830	0,5718
5	0,6209	0,4972

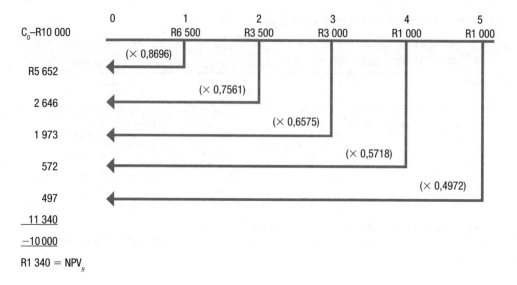

Figure 18.5: A time-line for project Y

Table 18.8: Calculation of the NPV for projects X and Y

Year (t)	Project X			Projects Y		
	Net cash inflow (CF_t) (1)	15% discounting factor (PVT_{15,t}) (2)	Present value (PV) (1) × (2)	Net cash inflow (CF_t) (1)	15% discounting factor (PVT_{15,t}) (2)	Present value (PV) (1) × (2)
1	R2 800	0,8696	R2 435	R6 500	0,8696	R5 652
2	2 800	0,7561	2 117	3 500	0,7561	2 646
3	2 800	0,6575	1 841	3 000	0,6575	1 973
4	2 800	0,5718	1 601	1 000	0,5718	572
5	2 800	0,4972	1 392	1 000	0,4972	497
		Total present value	9 386			11 340
		Minus: investment (C0)	−10 000			−10 000
		NPV_x =	**− 614**		**NPV_y =**	**1 340**

Notes:
- Since the initial investment C_0 occurs at time t_0, it represents a present value and requires no discounting.
- The NPVs for projects X and Y are: **NPV_x** = −R614; **NPV_y** = R1 340.]

Applying the concept: The net present value method

Cola Company considers buying a new bottling machine at a cost of R45 000 that will increase bottling speed and save costs. The use of this machine will result in the following net cash flows:

- Year 1: R15 000
- Year 2: R20 000
- Year 3: R25 000

The cost of the capital to be used to purchase the machine is 10%. It will have to be replaced after three years and will have no resale (terminal) value. (See table 18.7 for the discounting factors.)

Should the machine be purchased?
The present values of the net cash inflows are:

Net cash inflow (R)	Discounting factor (10%)	Present value (R)
15 000	0,9091	= 13 636
20 000	0,8264	= 16 529
25 000	0,7513	= 18 783

Total present value of all net cash inflows	= R48 948
Minus: present value of the net cash outflow	= R45 000
Net present value	= R3 948

The net present value is positive. This means that Cola Company should purchase the machine – it will add value to the business.

- **NPV = 0.** For a project with NPV = 0, the given project net cash flow, discounted at the business's cost of capital, is just sufficient to repay both the financing costs of the project and the total amount of financing.
- **NPV > 0.** A positive NPV means that both the initial investment amount and all financing costs, as well as an addition to the value of the business – equal to the amount of the positive NPV – are sustained by the net cash flow of the project. In the case of project Y in table 18.8, an investment of R10 000 will increase in value to R11 340 in present value terms.
- **NPV < 0.** The negative NPV of project X means that the project net cash flow at a discount rate of 15% is insufficient to redeem the initial investment amount and the related financing costs. Such a project would consequently have an adverse effect on the value of the business, because additional funds (cash) would have to be found elsewhere to meet the shortfall. In the case of project X in table 18.8, an investment of R10 000 will decrease to R9 386 in present-day terms.

18.3.2.3 Risk and uncertainty

The limitation of the above analysis of new investments is that it does not take risk into account.

Risk is defined as any deviation from the expected outcome. Such deviations may or may not occur. Managers are therefore not sure that they will occur, but the managers are able to identify the size of the deviations and even the likelihood that they will occur.

Example

Throwing the dice is an example of something involving risk. The person throwing knows that the outcome must be a number from 1 to 6. He or she also knows that each number has the same chance of occurrence (1 in 6), but does not know which number will come up in any particular throw.

Uncertainty, in contrast to risk, describes a situation where the managers are simply unable to identify the various deviations and, also, are unable to assess the likelihood of their occurrence. Most business decisions have an element of uncertainty, but since there is no formal way of dealing with uncertainty, managers focus only on taking risk into account when making capital investment decisions.

Example

Assume that Khumbali Resources is considering the investment in a mineral extraction process. The demand for the product is 5 000 tons for 5 years. The following data relates to this decision:
- The plant is expected to cost R500 000 and it has no resale value.
- The investment in the plant has to be paid immediately.
- The selling price is R100 per ton.
- The cost of producing 1 ton of the product is R70.
- The cost of capital for Khumbali Resources is 10%.
- Tax is ignored.

Requirements:
- An assessment of the project by using the NPV method
- A sensitivity analysis of the project

Solution:
The cash flow of the project will be as follows:
Year 0   (500 000)
Year 1   5 000 × (100 − 70) = R150 000
Year 2   5 000 × (100 − 70) = R150 000
Year 3   5 000 × (100 − 70) = R150 000
Year 4   5 000 × (100 − 70) = R150 000
Year 5   5 000 × (100 − 70) = R150 000

The NPV is equal to
$-500\ 000 + (150\ 000 \times PVIF_{10,1}) + (150\ 000 \times PVIF_{10,2}) + (150\ 000 \times PVIF_{10,3}) + (150\ 000 \times PVIF_{10,4}) + (150\ 000 \times PVIF_{10,5})$

$= -500\ 000 - (150\ 000 \times 0,909) + (150\ 000 \times 0,826) + (150\ 000 \times 0,751) + \cdot (150\ 000 \times 0,683) + (150\ 000 \times 0.621)$

$= -500\ 000 + 136\ 350 + 123\ 900 + 112\ 650 + 102\ 450 + 93\ 150$

$= 68\ 500$

* PVIF = Present value interest factor

The project should therefore be accepted on the NPV. The NPV is positive.

Sensitivity analysis requires that a determination of how sensitive the project is to deviations in each of the cash flows. Our discussion of sensitivity analysis is limited to the sensitivity of the following factors whose estimates were used in calculating the NPV:
- Original investment (−I)
- Annual demand (V)
- Net cash flow per ton (C)

In terms of the above, the NPV of the project is given by:
$(-I) + (V \times C \times PV_{r,1}) + (V \times C \times PV_{3,2}) + (V \times C \times PV_{r,3}) + (V \times C \times PV_{10,4}) + (V \times C \times PV_{10,5})$

$= (-I) + (5\ 000 \times 30 \times PV_{10,1}) + (5\ 000 \times 30 \times PV_{10,2}) + (5\ 000 \times 30 \times PV_{10,3}) + (5\ 000 \times 30 \times PV_{10,4}) + (5\ 000 \times 30 \times PV_{10,5})$

- **The original investment.** The present value of the cash inflows amounts to R568 500. This means that the original investment could increase by R68 500 before the project might become marginal.
- **Annual demand (V).** For the NPV to equal zero the annual demand has to decrease to:

$(-I) + (V \times 30 \times 0,909) + (V \times 30 \times 0,826) + (V \times 30 \times 0,751) + (V \times 30 \times 0,683) + (V \times 30 \times 0,621) = 0$

That is:
$0 = -500\ 000 + 27,27V + 24,78V + 22,53V + 20,49V + 18,63V$

$113,7V = 500\ 000$
$V = 4\ 397,53$

This means that demand can decrease to 4 397 tons before the project becomes marginal.
- Net cash flow per ton. For the NPV to equal zero, the net cash flow has to decrease to:

$(-I) + (5\ 000 \times C \times 0{,}909) + (5\ 000 \times C \times 0{,}826) + (5\ 000 \times C \times 0{,}751) + (5\ 000 \times C \times 0{,}683) + (5\ 000 \times C \times 0{,}621) = 0$

That is:

$0 = -500\ 000 + 4545C + 4\ 130C$
$\qquad + 3\ 755C + 3\ 415C + 3\ 105C$
$189\ 50C = 500\ 000$
$\qquad C = 26{,}38$

The net cash flow can therefore decrease from R30 to R26,38 before the project becomes marginal.

The results can be tabulated as in table 18.9.

The results in table 18.9 show at a glance how sensitive the NPV is on the basis of the original estimates to changes in the variables used in the decision. This gives some indication of the riskiness of the project.

Table 18.9: The sensitivity analysis of the Khumbali Resources project

Factor	Original estimate (R)	Value to give NPV of zero (R)	Difference as percentage of original estimate (%)
Original investment (I)	500 000	568 500	13,7
Annual demand (V)	5 000	4 397	12,1
Net cash flow (C)	30	26,38	12,1

By referring to a practical example, we will now discuss **sensitivity analysis** as one method for taking risk into account in capital investment decisions. Other methods will be discussed in later chapters on finance.

As was indicated earlier, investment decisions based on the NPV criterion are made on the basis of "best" predictions of the various cash flows. Sensitivity analysis takes each cash flow and determines by how much the estimate of that factor could be incorrect before it would affect the decision.

18.3.2.4 Final comments on the evaluation of investment projects

In this section we have discussed the important facets of fixed asset management, namely the evaluation of potential capital investment projects, and decisions on the desirability of such projects. After briefly referring to the importance of capital investments, we described the net present value method (NPV) for the evaluation of capital investment proposals and the riskiness of projects.

The NPV is a discounted cash-flow method that takes the timing and the magnitude of cash flows into account. Investment decision making based on the NPV therefore maximises stakeholders' wealth.

Sensitivity analysis can be used to assess the riskiness of the factors that are used to determine the NPV.

18.4 Summary

In this chapter we explained the management of the asset structure of a business, namely short-term investment decisions as well as long-term capital investment decisions. Rational and purposeful decisions in these areas will to a large extent ensure that the goals of the business are pursued as effectively as possible. Some important guidelines and techniques for both types of investment decisions were presented in this chapter, bearing in mind that current and fixed asset management is totally integrated in practice.

Critical thinking

1. A company is considering the purchase of land and the construction of a new factory. The land, which would be bought immediately, has a cost of R200 000 and the building, which would be erected at the end of the year, would cost R1 000 000. It is estimated that the firm's after-tax cash flow would be increased by R200 000, beginning at the end of the second year and this incremental flow would increase at a 10% rate annually over the next 10 years. What would be the payback period correct to the nearest number of years?

2. a. Discuss the importance of managing working capital in a retail business. Use an example to illustrate your answer.
   b. What do you understand by the concept "time value of money"?
   c. What is the difference between the net present value and the internal rate of return?

 Key terms

Assets	Default
Bad debt	Equity
Balance sheet	Loan
Capital	Opportunity cost
Cash flow financing	Rate
Current asset	Receivables
Current liability	Term
Current ratio	Working capital
Debt	Write off
Debt	

? Questions for discussion

1. If the net present value (NPV) of a project is greater than zero, which of the following statements is true about the project's internal rate of return (IRR)?
   a. It is less than the company's opportunity cost
   b. It is equal to the company's after-tax cost of debt
   c. It is equal to the company's opportunity cost
   d. It is greater than the company's opportunity cost

2. Generally, a cash manager is responsible for which of the following?
   I. Managing bank relationships
   II. Forecasting cash flows
   III. Preparing financial statements
   IV. Preparing corporate tax returns
   a. I and II only
   b. II and III only
   c. I, II, and IV only
   d. I, III, and IV only

3. Which of the following are sources of funds in a statement of cash flows?
   I. Proceeds from long-term debt issuance
   II. Increases in liabilities
   III. Decreases in assets
   IV. Increases in assets
   a. I and IV only
   b. II and IV only
   c. I, II, and III only
   d. I, III, and IV only

4. In an organisation's financial management team, who is normally responsible for monitoring accounts receivable?
   a. Cash manager
   b. Internal auditor
   c. Controller
   d. Credit manager

5. Which of the following best describes the cash flow time line?
   a. A diagram that shows the sequence of cash management and other production and accounting events
   b. A diagram that shows the flow of cash through a company's banking systems
   c. A procedure for making timely cash disbursements

d. *A procedure that transfers a firm's excess bank balances into money market funds*

6. A company's receivable balance pattern is as follows:
    - 95% sales from current month
    - 70% sales from 1 month prior
    - 10% sales from 2 months prior
    - 0% sales from 3 months prior

    Sales are as follows:
    February R430, March R500, April R750, May R600, June R400
    What is the accounts receivable balance at the end of May?
    a. *R1 850*
    b. *R1 145*
    c. *R1 060*
    d. *R600*

7. Use again the information given at the beginning of question 6. What is June's estimated cash inflow?
    a. *R400*
    b. *R561*
    c. *R670*
    d. *R875*

8. A company has R100 000 per year in purchases from a vendor offering terms of 2/10, net 30. Currently, the company pays all invoices on day 30 without the discount and considers its cost of funds to be 12% per year. How much would the company save per year if it paid the vendor on day 10 with a discount?
    a. *R1 014*
    b. *R1 347*
    c. *R1 945*
    d. *R2 000*

9. Use again the information given at the beginning of question 8. If the vendor assessed a 1,0% per month penalty for payments made after day 30, the company should pay on which of the following days?
    a. *Day 10*
    b. *Day 30*
    c. *Day 60*
    d. *No difference between days 10 and 60*

10. Which of the following objectives is most crucial to a company's cash management?
    a. *Optimally structuring the balance sheet*
    b. *Providing optimal money market investments*
    c. *Providing enough liquidity to pay obligations when they are due*
    d. *Monitoring bank balances*

References

1. The following sources were used in the compilation of this chapter:

Eberhard, A., "Faults in plan for supply security", *Business Day Internet Edition*, 29 March 2007, http://www.businessday.co.za/articles/topstories.aspx?ID=BD4A419095 (29 March 2007).

Bailey, S.H., "Quote the Banker: Watch cash flow", *Publishers Weekly*, 13 January 1975.

Brigham, E.F. & Capenski, L.C., *Financial management: Theory and practice*, 9th edition, Dryden, New York, 1999.

Damoran, A., *Corporate finance*, Wiley, New York, 1997.

Danech dropped the ball", *Financial Mail*, 6 January 1998, p. 43.

Du Toit, G.S., Oost, E. & Neuland, E.W., *Investment decisions: Principles and applications*, University of South Africa, Pretoria, 1997.

Edcon, *Annual report 2006*, http://www.edcon.co.za/OnlineResults/Current/Annual%20Report/2006/balance_sheets.htm (29 March 2007).

Eskom, *Annual report 1988*, p. 29.

"FM Top 100 companies – Capital expenditure", http://secure.financialmail.co.za/topco99/zktab1.htm (29 March 2007).

Kolb, B.A., *Principles of financial management*, Business Publications, Plano, Texas, 1983, p. 323.

Ensor, L. "Airports get R20bn facelift for 2010", *Business Day* Internet Edition, 29 March 2007, http://www.businessday.co.za/articles/topstories.aspx?ID=BD4A421007 (29 March 2007).

Le Roux, M., "Eskom growth 'ends cheap power'", *Business Day Internet Edition*, 29 March 2007, http://www.

businessday.co.za/articles/topstories.
aspx?ID=BD4A412810 (29 March 2007).

McLaney, M., "Business finance for decision
makers", Pitman Publishing, London,
1991.

Pick 'n Pay, *Annual report 2006*,
http://www.picknpay.co.za/investor/
annualreport2006/holdings_balance_
sheet.htm (29 March 2007).

Posner, M., *Successful credit control*, BSP
Professional Books, New York, 1990, p. 1.

Relly, G., in Supplement to *Financial Mail*,
28 September 1989, p. 41.

Sasol, *Annual report 2006*, http://www.sasol.
com/sasol_internet/downloads/sasol_ar_
2006_full_web_1162366248241.pdf (29
March 2007).

Shoprite, *Annual report 2006*, http://www.
shoprite.co.za/files/19204235/Investor_
Centre_Files/Annual%20Report%202006/
Complete_Shoprite_Eng.pdf (29 March
2007).

"The Edsel dies and Ford regroups survivors",
Business Week, 28 November 1959, p. 27.

FINANCING DECISIONS

<table>
<tr><td>

The purpose of this chapter

This chapter introduces the financing structure of companies, which entails making decisions about the forms of financing (types of finance) and the sources of finance (the suppliers of finance) in order to minimise the cost and risk to the business. Financial markets and the sources and forms of short-term finance are examined. This is followed by a discussion of the sources and forms of long-term finance, the cost of long-term capital, and the establishment of an optimal capital structure. Finally, the role of financial markets in the pooling and efficient distribution of financing of businesses is examined.

</td><td>

Learning outcomes

The content of this chapter will enable learners to:

- Describe the money and capital markets as providers of finance
- Explain the types of short-term financing and the short-term financing decision (the financing of current assets)
- Describe the forms and sources of long-term financing
- Describe the forms and sources of finance for small businesses
- Explain the cost of capital
- Explain the long-term financing decision and the establishment of an optimal capital structure

</td></tr>
</table>

19.1 Introduction

In chapter 17 we indicated that the management of the financing structure is one of the tasks of the financial manager. This entails making decisions about the forms of financing (types of finance) and the sources of finance (the suppliers of finance) to minimise the cost and risk to the business.

In this chapter we will first examine financial markets and the sources and forms of short-term finance. This will be followed by a discussion of the sources and forms of long-term finance, the cost of long-term capital and the establishment of an optimal capital structure.

19.2 Financial markets

Financial markets and financial institutions play an important role in the financing of businesses. The following section explains their role.

At a given point in time an economic system consists of individuals and institutions with surplus funds (the savers) and those with a shortage of funds. Growing businesses require funds for new investments or to expand their existing production capacity. These businesses have a shortage of funds, and to grow they must have access to the funds of individuals and institutions that do not have an immediate need for them.

- Financial markets are the channels through which holders of surplus funds (the savers) make their funds available to those who require additional finance.
- Financial institutions play an important role in this regard. They act as intermediaries on financial markets between the savers and those with a shortage of funds. This financial service is referred to as **financial intermediation**.
- Financial intermediation[1] is the process through which financial institutions pool funds from savers and make these funds available to those (for example, businesses) requiring finance.

Through financial intermediation the individual saver with relatively small savings is given the opportunity to invest in a large capital-intensive business, such as a chemical plant. The saver who invests in a business is referred to as a **financier**. The business rewards the financier for the use of the funds, so that the financier shares in the wealth created by the business.

The financier receives an asset in the form of a **financial claim** in exchange for his or her money. Financial claims have different names and characteristics, and include savings and cheque (call) accounts, fixed deposits, debentures and ordinary and preferred shares. In everyday usage, these financial claims are referred to as securities or financial instruments.

19.2.1 Primary and secondary markets

As indicated above, a saver receives an asset in the form of a financial claim against the institution to which money was made available. These claims are also referred to as **securities**. New issues of financial claims are referred to as **issues on the primary market**.

Some types of financial claims are negotiable and can be traded on financial markets. Trading in these securities after they have been issued takes place in the secondary market. This means that a saver who needs money can trade the claim on the secondary market to obtain cash. The Johannesburg Securities Exchange (JSE) is an example of a market where savers can virtually immediately convert their investments to cash. The tradability of securities ensures that savers with surplus funds continue to invest. Once issued, they can be traded on the market, and the holder may again obtain cash.

Company shares and debentures are examples of negotiable financial instruments, and savings and call accounts are non-negotiable claims.

19.2.2 Money and capital markets

The money market is the market for financial instruments with a short-term maturity. Funds are borrowed and lent in the money market for periods of one day (that is, overnight) or for months. The periods of the transactions depend on the particular needs of savers and institutions with a shortage of funds. The money market has no central physical location, and transactions are conducted from the premises of the various participants, for example, banks using telephones or on-line computer terminals.

Funds required for long-term investment are raised and traded by investors on the capital market. In South Africa, much of this trading takes place on the Johannesburg Securities Exchange. However, long-term investment transactions are also done privately. An investor may, for example, sell shares held in a private company directly to another investor, without channeling the transaction through a stock exchange.

19.2.3 Types of institutions

As indicated previously, financial institutions interpose themselves as intermediaries between savers and institutions with a shortage of funds by rendering a service to both. Financial institutions are divided into two broad categories, namely deposit-taking institutions and non-deposit-taking institutions.

19.2.3.1 Deposit-taking institutions

- The South African Reserve Bank is the country's central bank. It acts as a banker to the central government, keeps the banking accounts of government departments, and advances loans to the state. It also regulates private banks so that government monetary policy is adhered to, and has the sole right to issue bank notes. Its most important liability is the bank notes and coins in circulation. For example, a R50 note in circulation means that the Reserve Bank owes the holder an amount of R50.
- The Land and Agricultural Bank (Land Bank) grants loans to farmers and agricultural cooperatives.
- The Corporation for Public Deposits (CPD) accepts surplus funds from departments, institutions and organisations in the public sector, and is owned by the Reserve Bank. It accepts short-term deposits, pays interest on them and repays the deposits on demand.
- Private sector banks, as a group, are the single largest type of financial intermediary in the financial system. Banks take deposits from individuals and organisations with surplus funds and lend them to others with a shortage of funds. In addition to this function they provide financial services such as insurance broking and administering estates. They also facilitate foreign trade.
- The Post Office Savings Bank accepts deposits from the public but does not grant credit or offer cheque facilities. The government is ultimately responsible for its solvency. In contrast to other banks, the Post Office Savings Bank is therefore not regulated by the Banks Act 94 of 1990.

19.2.3.2 Non-deposit-taking institutions

Non-deposit-taking institutions are considered in three categories: public sector, private sector and other.

- **Public sector institutions**
  - **Public Investment Commissioners (PIC).** The PIC operates as an investment intermediary for long-term public funds. It administers and invests the public sector's retirement and provident schemes and social security funds, for example, the Workmen's Compensation Fund. The funds it administers amount to approximately one-third of the total administered by all private insurers and retirement funds.
- **Private sector institutions**
  - **Life assurers, pension and provident funds.** The main purpose of life assurers, pension and provident funds is the payment of lump sums to beneficiaries at death, on retirement or the attainment of a certain age. They provide people with income after retirement until death. To fulfil this function, life assurers collect premiums from policyholders, and pension and provident funds receive monthly contributions from employers and employees. The premiums and contributions received are made available to institutions until required by the insurance company or pension fund.
  - **Short-term insurers.** Short-term insurers provide cover against accidental losses caused by fire, theft, storms, etc. The premiums received are sufficient to cover the risk for a particular year. These premiums are also made available to borrowers by investing them on the money market.

– **Unit trusts**. Unit trusts provide small investors with the opportunity to invest their surplus funds in large companies. The administrators of unit trusts invest funds received in, for example, a number of companies listed on the JSE. The fund is divided into small affordable units and each investor receives an allocation of units according to his or her investment. The funds are managed by professional investment managers.

- **Other institutions**
  – **Industrial Development Corporation (IDC)**. The main purpose of the IDC is to promote industrial development by assisting the private sector in financing new businesses and expanding existing ones. It extends credit, takes up shares and facilitates the financing of expansion of industrial businesses. For example, it helped to finance a business such as Sasol.
  – **Khula Enterprise Finance Limited (Khula)**. Khula was established to provide wholesale finance for new small businesses and for the expansion of existing ones. For example, a person wishing to start a panel-beating business may approach Khula through its retail financial intermediaries (RFIs) for funds.
  – **Ntsika Enterprise Promotion Agency (Ntsika)**. Ntsika's role is to render an efficient and effective promotion and support service to small, medium and micro-enterprises (SMMEs) in order to contribute towards equitable economic growth in South Africa. Ntsika provides wholesale non-financial support services for SMME promotion and development. It also provides funding to organisations providing approved services.
  – **Development Bank of South Africa (DBSA)**. The purpose of the DBSA is to promote development in areas not served by the private sector. It provides finance for projects such as roads, dams and telecommunications.

19.3 Short-term financing

The short-term financing decision requires finding the optimal combination of long-term and short-term financing to finance current assets.

As in the management of current assets, risks and costs must be weighed against each other when making this decision. This section introduces different forms of short-term financing, and this is followed by a discussion of the implications of a combination of long-term and short-term financing for the financing of current assets.

The following are the most common forms of short-term financing:

- Trade credit
- Accruals
- Bank overdrafts
- Factoring

Each of these forms of financing will now be discussed.

19.3.1 Trade credit

Trade credit is an important form of finance for businesses, and is mainly in the form of suppliers' credit. This means that a supplier does not take payment from the business when goods or services are purchased. The business is expected to pay only after 30, 60 or 90 days, depending on the credit terms.

When Pick 'n Pay, for example, purchases cereal on credit from Tiger Oats (the supplier) it implies that Tiger Oats finances the purchase for Pick 'n Pay for the period for which the supplier's credit is granted, namely 30, 60 or 90 days.

As shown in Figure 19.1 on page 473, wholesalers and retailers such as Pick 'n Pay make extensive use of trade credit as a form of finance because of the nature of their business. Smaller businesses also rely on trade credit, because they find it more difficult to obtain funds on money and capital markets. As a rule, trade credit can be obtained quite readily by any business with a reasonable financial record.

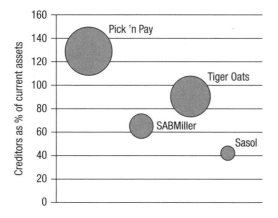

Figure 19.1 The use of trade credit as a form of finance – selected listed companies

Example

Simeka Retailers purchases an average of R5 000 a day on terms of "net 30" from Mega Wholesalers, that is, the goods must be paid for within 30 days of the invoice date. This means Mega Wholesalers provides R5 000 × 30 = R150 000 in short-term financing to Simeka. Now assume that Simeka's sales – and therefore purchases – double. The trade credit that Mega extends to Simeka also doubles to R300 000, and Simeka obtains this additional amount of financing virtually automatically, that is, it is obtained spontaneously.

To ensure prompt payment, the supplier often offers a cash rebate for early payment. This rebate applies only if the buyer pays before a stated date, which precedes the due date of the account.

How do we calculate the advantage of the cash rebate? The following formula can be used:

Cost of not accepting the rebate

$$= \frac{(\% \text{ rebate})}{100\% - \% \text{ rebate}} \times$$

$$\frac{365}{\text{(additional number of days after rebate period for which funds are available)}}$$

Management may also decide to delay payment within certain limits. Funds are consequently available to the business for a longer period, which decreases its additional cash needs. This is risky, as the consequence of such a decision could be that the creditworthiness of the business is jeopardised and suppliers may refuse to supply it in future.

Trade credit offers the following advantages as a source of short-term funds:[2]

- It is readily available to businesses that pay their suppliers regularly and is also a source of spontaneous financing, which is explained in the following example:
- It is informal. If a business currently pays its

bills within the discount period, additional credit can simply be obtained by delaying payment until the end of the net period at the cost of foregoing the discount.

- Trade credit is more flexible than other forms of short-term financing, because the business does not have to negotiate a loan agreement, provide security, or adhere to a rigid repayment schedule.

19.3.2 Accruals

As with trade credit, **accruals** are also a source of spontaneous finance. The most common expenses accrued are wages and taxes.

Accrued wages represent money that a business owes its employees. Employees provide part of the short-term financing for the business by waiting a month or a week to be paid, rather than being paid every day.

Accrued tax is also a form of financing. The level of financing from accrued taxes is determined by the amount of tax payable and the frequency with which it is paid.

Accruals have no associated cost. They are therefore a valuable source of finance because they are cost-free substitutes for otherwise costly short-term credit.

19.3.3 Bank overdrafts

An overdraft facility is an arrangement with a bank that allows a business to make payments from a cheque account in excess of the balance in the account. The purpose of an overdraft is to bridge the gap between cash income and cash expenses. An overdraft usually increases through to the month-end, when the clients of the business pay their accounts.

An overdraft arrangement is reviewed annually, usually when the annual financial statements become available, so that the bank can evaluate the current financial position of the business. The interest charged on an overdraft is negotiable and relates to the risk profile of the borrower.

Interest is charged daily on the outstanding balance. This means that the borrower only pays interest on that part of the overdraft that is being used. In contrast to other forms of financing, a bank overdraft is repayable on demand. This means that the bank may cancel the facility at any time.

An overdraft is a flexible form of short-term financing. It is cost-effective if used correctly.

19.3.4 Debtor finance

Debtor finance consists of factoring and invoice discounting. In contrast to a bank overdraft, debtor finance is, strictly speaking, not borrowing. It is not a loan secured by the book debts of the business. Instead, it involves the sale of debtors to a debtor financing company.

Invoice discounting is the sale of existing debtors and future credit sales to a debtor financing company. It then converts credit sales to cash sales and provides the business with a cash injection by releasing funds tied up in working capital. Invoice discounting is usually confidential, that is, debtors are not advised of the arrangement between the business and the finance company.

Factoring is similar to invoice discounting,

but goes one step further. With factoring, the financier also undertakes to administer and control the collection of debt. In contrast to invoice discounting, debtors are aware of the agreement between the business and the financier.

The financier to whom the debtors are sold is known as the **factor**. The factor buys approved debtors from the business after carefully examining each account individually. The factor receives commission and interest on amounts paid to the business before the expiry date of the debt. The factor usually pays the business 70% to 80% of the amount outstanding from debtors immediately, and the remainder when the debtor pays.

Two common types of factoring practice are:

- **Non-recourse factoring**. The factor buys the debtors outright and bears the risk of bad debts. The factor accepts responsibility for credit control, debt collection and sales records. Customers pay the factor direct.
- **Recourse factoring**. In recourse factoring, the factor provides the same services as

Case study

Factoring a new financing alternative for small companies

Factoring, where companies sell their book of debtors to a bank or a factoring company to obtain cash immediately, has traditionally only been available to large companies. Small to medium-sized enterprises (SMEs) find it difficult to obtain working capital from banks. But a South African company developed a world first by allowing small to medium-sized enterprises the opportunity to factor their Invoices. This will provide them with an entirely new form of financing which they could not access previously.

Source: Fin Week, 23 August 2007, p. 4.

in non-recourse factoring, but the seller guarantees that debts are recoverable. The factor recovers any bad debt from the seller.

Factoring of debtor accounts has the following advantages:
- The cost of debtor administration is transferred to the factor.
- The turnover of current assets is increased and less capital is required to finance debtors.
- Liquidity ratios improve.
- More cash is available for other purposes.

The cost of factoring fluctuates according to the conditions laid down by the factor. In considering factoring, the cost should be compared to the savings achieved through not having the administrative liability of debt collection.

19.3.5 The short-term financing decision

The cost of short-term funds is generally lower than that of long-term funds. One reason is that trade credit does not really involve a cost. From a cost or profit point of view, it is advantageous for a business to make use of short-term funds for the financing of its current assets, but too heavy a dependence on them increases the risk of finance not being available when required.

Consider, for example, a financial manager who relies on having short-term debt rescheduled. There is an unforeseen economic downturn, the financial position of the business deteriorates, and the bank manager refuses to renew its overdraft. It is clear that the financial manager is faced with a liquidity crisis, and a plan will have to be devised to meet the crisis.

The more frequently a business has to refinance its debt, the greater the risk of becoming illiquid. This risk therefore increases as the period for which the debt is granted decreases.

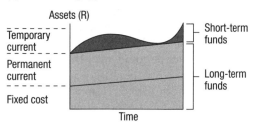

(a) The matching approach

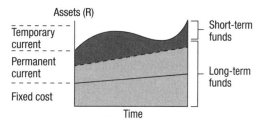

(b) The aggressive approach

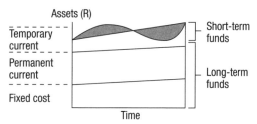

(b) The conservative approach

Figure 19.2: Short-term financing plans

The use of long-term funds to satisfy working capital requirements has exactly the opposite implications for a business. From a cost point of view it is disadvantageous, because long-term funds are generally more expensive than short-term funds. They will also be underutilised because of the variable nature of portions of working capital requirements. On the other hand, by using more long-term funds there is less risk of funds not being available if and when required.

Figure 19.2 illustrates the following three approaches to the short-term financing problem:

- The **matching approach** (also referred to as the hedging approach) involves matching the period for which finance is obtained with the expected life of the asset. Financing arranged for periods longer than the life of an asset is costly because it is not utilised for the entire period. However, if finance is arranged for a period shorter than the life of the asset, there will be additional transactional costs to repeatedly arrange for new short-term finance.

  According to this approach, fixed assets and permanent current assets are financed with long-term financing, and temporary current assets with short-term funds.
- In the **aggressive approach** the financial manager uses more short-term financing than is needed with the matching approach. Permanent current assets are partially financed with short-term funds, instead of using only long-term funds as in the case of the matching approach.
- In the **conservative approach**, the financial manager uses more long-term funds than is needed with the matching approach. The temporary current asset requirement is financed with long-term funds. This plan is conservative because it involves the use of a relatively large proportion of long-term funds, which is less risky.

19.3.6 **Concluding remarks**

The choice of a financing plan for a business's current assets entails a trade-off between risk and return. From a cost point of view, it is preferable to finance current assets needs with

---

Critical thinking
- -
Thabeng Enterprises is running into cash flow problems. It is a privately owned company. Thabeng can finance its working capital by extending its bank loan or by factoring debtors. Taking risk considerations into account, which would be the most appropriate form of financing for Thabeng?

---

short-term funds, while risk considerations demand the use of long-term funds.

19.4 **Long-term financing**

In this section, we focus on the characteristics of the various forms of long-term financing and the implications of the various sources of financing for the business.

This is followed by a discussion of the cost of capital (section 19.4.5) and the establishment of an optimal capital structure (section 19.5), with specific reference to financial gearing.

19.4.1 **Shareholders' interest**

Shareholders' interest in a company is subdivided into owner's equity and preference shareholders' capital.

19.4.1.1 **Owner's equity**

Owner's equity consists of the funds made directly available by the legal owners (ordinary shareholders) in the form of share capital, as well as indirect contributions in the form of profit retention as reserves and undistributed profits.

- **The ordinary share**. Ordinary shareholders are the true owners of a business. An ordinary share therefore gives right of ownership (right of possession). Shareholders receive share certificates in exchange for the money they make available to the business.
- There are two types of ordinary shares, namely **par value shares** and **non-par value shares**. Par value shares all have the same value, while that of non-par value shares differs. A business can only issue one of the two types of shares, not both.
- A co-owner of the business, the ordinary shareholder, has a claim to profits. The portion of profit paid to ordinary shareholders is known as a **dividend** and is paid out in proportion to the shareholding of each ordinary shareholder. The following

Table 19.1: Sources and forms of long-term financing for a business in the form of a company

	Source	Balance sheet classification	Form
1	Owners or ordinary shareholders	Owner's equity or own capital	• Ordinary shares • Reserves • Undistributed profit • Preference shares
2	Preference shareholders	Preference shareholders' capital	
1 + 2	Share capital	Shareholders' interest	Total of the above
3	Suppliers of debt capital/Credit suppliers	Long-term or borrowed capital over a long-term period	• Debentures • Bonds • Registered term loans • Financial leases
1 + 2 + 3		Total long-term capital	

Notes:
The sources and forms of long-term financing for other forms of businesses differ only in some respects to those for a company:

1. Other forms of business do not have any preference shareholders and therefore there are no preference shares and no preference shareholders' capital.
2. The own capital or owner's equity comprises funds that the owner(s) contribute to the business, as well as profits that are not withdrawn by the owners. The owners' equity is included in a capital account in the balance sheet.
3. Other forms of business do not make use of debentures.

are important characteristics of the ordinary share:

- The liability of ordinary shareholders is limited to the amount of share capital they contributed to the business. This means that if the business is liquidated, shareholders may lose this money, but may otherwise not be held liable for its debts. That is why we add the word "Limited" to the name of a public or private company.
- Shareholders have no certainty that the money paid for the shares will be recouped, for this depends on the success of the business.
- Ordinary shares in a listed company (that is, a public company traded on the stock exchange) are tradable on a stock exchange.
- Ordinary shareholders are the owners of the business and usually have full control of it, in that they can vote at general meetings to appoint directors

of the company, and on such matters as the amount of dividends to be paid to shareholders. Voting rights are usually in proportion to shareholdings.

- In contrast to interest payable on borrowed capital, a business has no legal obligation to reward ordinary shareholders in the form of dividends for their investment in shares.
- Share capital is available to the business for an unlimited period. Ordinary share capital does not have to be repaid. Shareholders may, however, convert their investments into cash by selling their shares to another investor. Currently, South African businesses are not allowed to buy back their own shares. This differs from the situation in other countries and this legislation may change in the near future.
- The issue of additional ordinary shares by an existing company may have the following disadvantages:

- The earnings per share (profit attributable to ordinary shareholders divided by the number of issued shares) of existing shareholders may decrease, because the profit attributable to ordinary shareholders does not immediately increase in relation to the increase in the number of issued shares. This phenomenon is known as the dilution of existing shareholders' earnings.
- Existing shareholders may lose control, because voting rights are linked to shareholdings, and people other than existing shareholders may take up new shares and become majority shareholders. This danger applies not only to the issue of new shares, but generally also to a business whose shares are listed on a stock exchange and can therefore easily be obtained by others, including competitors.
- The cost of issuing new ordinary shares and the riskiness of an investment in ordinary shares may result in the cost of ordinary share capital being higher than that of other forms of financing.
- Ordinary shares, however, hold some advantages for a business, the following being the most important:
  - There is no risk involved for the business, because payment of dividends and redemption of capital are not compulsory.
  - Additional ordinary shares serve as security for attracting additional borrowed capital, which provides greater flexibility for capital structure decisions. The base of shareholders' capital gives the financial manager the additional flexibility to use a combination of share capital and debt to finance the business.
- Retained profit consists of reserves and un-distributed profit, and represents amounts that would otherwise have been paid out to shareholders as dividends. Retained profit is also referred to as self-financing or internal financing, and as a form of financing holds various advantages for a business:

- Because no issue costs are involved, it is cheaper than the issuing of additional ordinary shares.
- Capital is immediately available for use.
- It lends flexibility to the capital structure, because it serves as security for attracting additional borrowed capital.
- In contrast to the issue of new shares, there are no control implications for existing shareholders.
- It serves as an alternative form of financing, if conditions are unfavourable in the capital market as a result of, for example, high interest rates.
- It entails no interest or redemption obligations.

Internal financing is consequently an easy and inexpensive form of financing for a business. However, from the point of view of the owners (ordinary shareholders) it has a serious short-term disadvantage, because the retention of profit means the forfeiting of dividends.

19.4.1.2 Preference shareholders' capital

Preference shares fall somewhere between debentures (discussed later) and ordinary shares in terms of risk. They have some characteristics of both debentures and ordinary shares. If a business is doing poorly, it will first pay debenture holders their required interest and then pay dividends to preference shareholders. Anything left goes to ordinary shareholders.

Two forms of preference shares are distinguished, namely the ordinary preference share and the cumulative preference share. In the case of the ordinary preference share, shareholders forfeit a dividend if the directors decide not to declare one in a particular year. Cumulative preference shareholders retain the right to receive an arrear dividend in the following year.

A preference share has the following characteristics:

- It has a preferential claim over an ordinary

share on profit after tax. In contrast to the dividend on an ordinary share, however, a preference share dividend is limited to a certain maximum. For example, the holders of a 10% preference share will never receive more than a 10% return on their investment, but could in bad times receive no dividend, or one of less than 10%.

- It has a preferential claim over ordinary shares on the assets of the business in the case of liquidation.
- The term of availability is unlimited.
- Authority can vary between full voting rights and no voting rights at all, but usually an ordinary preference share provides no voting rights.

From the viewpoint of the business, preference shares have an advantage over ordinary shares, in that their cost is usually lower. For the shareholder, ordinary shares are more risky, because preference shareholders have a priority claim on net profit after tax and on assets in the case of liquidation.

19.4.2 Long-term debt

Long-term debt generally refers to debt that will mature (has to be repaid) in a year or more, and can usually be obtained in two ways, namely:

- Through a loan
- Through credit

A loan is a contract in which the receiver of funds (the borrower) undertakes to make interest payments at specified times to the supplier of funds (the lender) and to redeem the total principal sum in payments over an agreed period or on a specific due date.

With credit, the supplier of credit (the supplier of capital) provides the business (receiver of capital) with power of disposal over an asset and receives extended payments in return, consisting of a principal sum and an interest component. Financial leasing, discussed later, is an example of credit financing.

Some debt instruments (such as debentures, which are discussed later) bear a fixed rate of interest for the period of the debt. In other cases, for example, mortgage bonds, the interest rate is not fixed but fluctuates with market forces. This is known as variable interest.

Debt that is secured on one or more assets of the business is known as secured debt. In the event of liquidation of the business, the proceeds from the secured assets would be used first to satisfy the claim of the secured supplier of credit. For example, the holder of a mortgage bond that is secured on any property must be repaid on liquidation before the proceeds from the sale of the property may be used to satisfy the claims of other creditors.

In the case of unsecured debt, a creditor does not have any preferential claim on the assets of a business.

In practice, there are various forms of long-term debt, and we now briefly discuss the most important ones.

19.4.2.1 Loans

The following types of loans are of special importance:

- **Debentures** are the most common form of long-term debt in the case of companies. The business (the borrower) issues a certificate to the lender showing the conditions of the loan. This certificate is negotiable, and means that it can be traded on financial markets. Payment of the loan, consisting of a principal sum plus interest, is made to the presenter of the certificate. A debenture has a fixed-interest charge, and the loan is available to the business over a specified term.
- **Bonds** are secured loans and are issued with fixed assets such as fixed property as security (mortgage bonds). The amount that can be raised depends primarily on the value of the property. Typically a mortgage bond will not exceed 75% of the value of the property.

- **Registered term loans** are unsecured loans and, in contrast to debentures, are not freely negotiable. The name of the lender and the credit conditions are recorded in the books of the lender (business).

For a business, loans have the following advantages:
- Costs are limited in that they are determined by the loan interest rate.
- Interest payments are deductible for tax purposes.
- The control of the owners is usually not influenced by the issue of more loans.
- Loans do not dilute the earnings of ordinary shares.

A disadvantage is that the fixed interest obligations and the priority claims of loans in the case of liquidation increase the risks, inherent in the business, to its owners.

19.4.2.2 Financial leasing

A financial lease is a contract that provides the right to the use of an asset, legally owned by the lessor, in exchange for a specified rental paid by the lessee. The lessor is the party that promises to make the asset available for use by the lessee.

A financial lease is a form of credit financing that should not be confused with an operating lease. In contrast to an operating lease, financial leasing gives the lessee the opportunity of owning the asset at the end of the lease. An operating lease can be terminated by giving the required notice, but a financial lease is a non-terminative agreement between the lessee and the lessor. Hence it is a financing agreement (lease) and not an operating lease agreement.

Two basic forms of financial leasing are the following:[3]
- **Direct financial leasing** of operating equipment such as motor vehicles and computers. In direct leasing, the lease amount, which is repayable in regular instalments, is determined in such a way

that the value of the asset, plus an interest charge, is paid back by the end of the term of the lease, which is usually related to the lifespan of the asset. Maintenance and insurance of the asset are normally the responsibility of the lessee. Financial leases are used to finance motor vehicles, equipment and plant.
- **Leaseback agreements**, in which more permanent assets are involved. In leaseback agreements, certain assets that the business owns are sold to the credit supplier and at the same time leased back by the business according to a long-term agreement. Leaseback agreements are usually entered into by businesses that need to raise funds. The assets are generally of a highly specialised nature and through leaseback arrangement the business obtains cash without losing the use of this equipment. For example, a dentist may decide to obtain additional funds by financing his or her equipment on a leaseback arrangement.

The lease payments of a financial lease are deductible for tax purposes. When the advantages of financial leasing are weighed against ownership through purchase with loan capital, the after-tax costs have to be compared. One should therefore bear in mind that in the case of ownership through the use of loan capital, depreciation, investment rebates and interest payments contribute to tax savings.

19.4.3 Sources of financing for small businesses

It is always sad to see a new business with great profit potential fall by the wayside only because it was not properly financed from the beginning. And this happens too often among the thousands of new small businesses started in this country every year. The error comes from either not knowing the total financial needs of the business or failing to provide for those needs in the planning stage.

No business should ever be started without a clear and positive understanding of where its total capital needs are coming from. As we have seen in previous chapters, a very important phase of the entire planning process is to determine what assets will be needed and how they are to be provided. When the amount of the net ownership capital needed has been determined, the proprietors turn to the problem of making sure that the entire amount is available. The total sum should preferably be deposited in the company's bank account before any commitments are made by the new owners.

When several sources of capital are available, the planners must still bear in mind that all sources may not be equally desirable. Borrowed capital is shown on the balance sheet as a liability. It must be paid back at specific periods. These repayments of principal amounts are not operating expenses, which are deducted on the income statement before planned profits are produced. They are payments for the provision of investment capital, and are to be paid out of the profits shown on the income statement. Many researchers have found that failure to recognise this basic fact is the commonest cause of financial strain among small businesses. It is important, therefore, to consider the repayment schedules when choosing among sources of financing.

The various types of financing available to small businesses usually have a similar classification to those of a company, with a few differences and additions. We will discuss a few of these forms of financing a small business in the sections that follow.

Two things should be recognised when one is faced with the problem of obtaining outside capital assistance:

- An established business with a good record of operations usually has better access to available sources of capital than a new business.
- Some personal capital available for investment in the business by the owner is

almost always essential to obtaining any type of outside assistance.

Against this background, we will now investigate the possibilities of each of the sources of funds listed.

19.4.3.1 Personal funds

Whenever potential creditors, partners, or shareholders are invited to invest in, or lend financial assistance to, a business, their first question is, "How much does the owner have invested?" Every business contains an element of risk, and outsiders who invest in a new business wish to be sure that such risk is shared by the owner. Trading on "too thin an equity base" means that the owner's investment is too small relative to the investment of outsiders. A financing plan that indicates that the business is starting out on this basis does not usually invite confidence from creditors. As we saw in the previous section on capital structure, this does not always mean that the new owners must have 50% of the total capital needs to invest, but it does mean that they should look to other ownership capital rather than only to creditor capital in their financial plan. In any event, it is important that the owners have assets of their own to invest in the business. The closer to 50% of the total capital needs that can be provided, the greater will be their independence and share of net profits.

19.4.3.2 Loans from relatives and friends

Although this type of borrowing to provide original investment capital is generally frowned upon by experienced business operators, it remains a prominent device used in the financial planning of small businesses. Many owners are encouraged in their enterprise by parents, relatives, or friends who offer to supply loans to the business to get it started. Quite often, no other sources are available after normal trade credit and supplier contracts have been utilised.

It is unfortunate, however, that many otherwise successful businesses have been beset by troubles because relatives or friends interfered with the operations. Mixing family or social relationships with business can be dangerous. Many such situations might have been averted if the terms of the loans had been more clearly specified, including the rights of the lenders to insist upon making operational policy. The best way to avoid subsequent problems is to make sure that loans are made on a businesslike basis. They should be viewed as business dealings. The right of the owner to make decisions should be respected by all parties involved. Arrangements for retiring such loans, including any options for early payment, and the procedure if loans become delinquent, should be clearly understood and set forth in writing. The owner should be sure such loans are properly presented on the balance sheet – payments due in one year are current liabilities; the others are fixed liabilities.

19.4.3.3 Trade credit

Trade credit is the financial assistance available from other businesses with whom the business has dealings. Most prominent are the suppliers of an inventory that is constantly being replaced. We have previously noted that wholesalers who desire a retailer business, for example, will offer generous terms for payment of invoices. Manufacturers will do the same for wholesalers whose business they desire. Financing the opening inventory usually represents one of the larger investments in a typical small business. If a R20 000 inventory can be purchased for a R10 000 down payment and the balance in 30 days, the wholesaler has virtually provided R10 000 of the required capital to open the business. The owner then has an opportunity to sell that inventory at a profit and thus to have the funds to pay off the original balance. As a record for successful operation is established, even more attractive terms may be offered on subsequent

purchases. A grocer may have several such suppliers. Other businesses may have only one or two major suppliers. The inducement of a sales discount for prompt payment of invoices should always tempt the owner to pay within the maximum discount period.

19.4.3.4 Loans or credit from equipment sellers

This type of financial aid is often considered another form of trade credit. It does, however, have distinct characteristics. The small business may need counters, shelves, display cases, delivery trucks, and other equipment such as air conditioning, refrigeration units, and food counters. These, too, are a large investment for the new small business and are recognised as such by the major suppliers of items like these. The purchases, it is hoped, are not made on a regular basis, but represent a large part of the capital needed to get started. The suppliers usually offer good credit terms with a modest down payment and a contract for the balance spread over one, two, or three years.

This type of credit, when financing charges are reasonable, can be most helpful to the planner. The caution is in its overuse – remembering, again, that the principal payments must be paid out of profits anticipated. Any principal repayments of this type, too, are for the provision of capital and are not operating expenses. Too much of this type of financing can distort the current and quick ratios, and upset the business's financial liquidity. Many cases are on record where the monthly payments on such fixed assets exceed the profits earned from sales in the month.

19.4.3.5 Mortgage loans

If the small business owners own a commercial building, they can normally secure a mortgage on it with payments over as many as 20 years. This may, for example, be the building in which the new business will operate. In that case, the planners will be making mortgage payments instead of rental payments to a landlord. They may wish to risk a mortgage on their homes. Even second mortgages are sometimes used, although not recommended. When profits are uncertain, caution is advised in committing any assets to mortgage claims. As a clear profit pattern becomes more infinitely established, the use of mortgage credit becomes less risky.

19.4.3.6 Commercial bank loans

Historically, a line of credit at a chartered bank was designed to enable a merchant to purchase an inventory of merchandise. When the merchandise was sold at a profit, the bank was paid its loan. This situation is still followed by many banks. This use of bank credit is still the best way to establish credit with a commercial bank. Since the relaxation of bank restrictions in recent years, however, many other types of loans and financing are now available to qualified applicants. In fact, we now have banks that advertise: "If you are planning to go into business, come see us." The cold, hard facts of economic reality will be faced in such a visit, but the prospective business owner with an otherwise sound financing plan, a reputation for integrity, and a business deemed likely to succeed, may still establish some bank credit in the planning stage. Long-term loans are less generally available than short-term loans. Short-term loans are usually considered those for not more than one year. If adequate collateral is available, longer-term loans may usually be obtained. Getting influential or wealthy friends to co-sign notes also may be helpful.

The policies of several of the chartered banks should always be checked in the planning stage. Many small business owners with experience have long described banks as "a place where you can borrow money when you prove that you don't need it". Some banks are earnestly trying to remove that image today. In keeping with our previously noted axiom that rewards must be commensurate with cost and risk, however, interest rates

charged by banks to small businesses are significantly higher than the rates charged to large businesses.

Although commercial banks still dominate small business lending, credit unions and some trust companies are beginning to offer commercial loans to small business, and it is expected that in the 1980s these financial institutions will move very forcefully to compete for customers.

19.4.3.7 Small business loans

The proprietor of a small business enterprise, or one who is about to establish a new business, may borrow funds under this programme for the acquisition of fixed assets, modernisation of premises (leasehold improvements), or the purchase of land or buildings necessary for the operation of the business. The loans are usually provided and administered by the chartered banks and other designated lending institutions such as Khula Enterprise Finance Limited. The loans have fixed terms of repayments of the principal, typically five years, and the interest charged on these loans is fluctuating (floating), with the commercial bank's prime lending rate with an additional one or more per cent above the prime rate.

19.4.3.8 Taking in partners

Despite all the necessary precautions, raising capital often necessitates taking one or more partners into the business. If more than one manager is not needed, the new partners may not be employed in the business, but may hold full partner status as a result of their investment in the business. The partnership agreement is important here. Inducements can be offered to such a finance partner, but the duties, responsibilities, and authority of each partner must be clearly understood. At this point we are looking at the partnership only from the standpoint of providing a source of investment funds.

19.4.3.9 Selling capital shares

Aside from the technical, legal, and operational advantages of the corporate form of legal organisation, its advantages are greater that the disadvantages as a device for raising capital. Many small business owners seem to believe that the corporate form was designed only for very large businesses. This is false, however. It is true that this legal form has not been as widely used as it might be, but this is believed to be due to lack of knowledge of its advantages.

Let us consider the new business planner who needs R100 000 in ownership capital, but has only R30 000 to invest. Would it not be desirable to go to a local investment dealer as a corporation and request the sale of R50 000 of 7% preference shares and R50 000 of common shares? The owner takes title to R30 000 of the voting common shares. The owner can hold the unsold shares in the business for possible future financing for expansion. The preference share is given a priority of dividends and may not have voting privilege. Usually only the common share has voting power. The owner still owns a majority of the common shares outstanding, and has no problem of control. The investment dealer sells the shares to customers who are probably unknown. A detailed study of the plans of the business is contained in a prospectus, which the investment dealers will prepare. The business planner does not have to pursue relatives or to plead with friends for financial "favours", does not have to take in undesired partners to raise capital, has assured a financial plan for expansion, and has all the protections of the corporate form of organisation. The investment dealer will charge for this service. The charge will be higher if the dealer guarantees the sale of the full amount, and less if the shares are sold on a "best efforts" basis. The investment dealer's fee is chargeable to organisation expense and can be amortised over the succeeding five to ten years. This procedure is followed by the most informed new business planners who desire growth. It should be investigated for appropriateness by many more.

The raising of funds described above is called "private placement" of limited share distribution. When stock market conditions are depressed, this financing route can be an important alternative to the public distribution of the company's shares – that is, "going public".

19.4.3.10 Venture capital funding

Small businesses may sometimes (albeit not too often) qualify for investment funds from venture capital businesses. These companies provide equity and loan capital to potentially high-growth small companies. Examples of these are Khula Equity Scheme, whereby Khula has set up regional venture capital companies to invest a minimum of R1 million in small businesses needing significant equity investment.

When applying to a venture capital business, it is absolutely essential to provide it with a comprehensive business plan. If it passes the first screening, the venture capitalist will investigate further and examine "with due diligence" the product, the technology, potential market share, competitive situation, financial requirements and projections, and, most importantly, the competence of management. After the venture capitalist decides to make an investment, it will usually do so in return for part ownership in the business (common or preference shares) and/or by the provision of direct loan with share purchase options. Typically, a venture capital business will not seek controlling interest in the business. However, it will try to protect its investment by being able to assume control if the small business gets into financial trouble.

19.4.4 Concluding remarks

In the discussion above, the forms and sources of long-term financing available to a business were briefly analysed. The question that now arises is how the financial management of a business can combine the various forms of financing in the most efficient way. This consideration will now receive attention.

19.4.5 The cost of capital

Profitable and growing businesses continually need capital to finance expansion and new investment. Because of the costs involved in using capital, namely dividends to shareholders and interest paid to credit suppliers, financial management must ensure that only the necessary amount of capital is obtained, and that the cost and risk are kept to a minimum.

In attracting capital – one of the main tasks of financial management – the various forms of financing must be combined in a mix that results in the lowest possible cost and lowest risk for the business. We will now briefly discuss the concept cost of capital.

The cost of capital is of crucial importance in both capital investment decisions and financing decisions:

- In capital investment decisions, the cost of capital serves as a measure of profitability for investment proposals. In the discussions in chapter 18, the cost of capital was assumed as given, in the calculation of the net present value (NPV).
- In financing decisions, the various types of capital earmarked for financing the investments of a business should be combined so that the cost of capital to the business is kept to a minimum.

It is clear from the above that investment and financing decisions should be considered simultaneously because, in practice, they cannot really be separated.

Capital structure refers to the combination of forms of long-term financing, namely ordinary and preference shares and debt, to finance the business.

The weighted average cost of capital, k_a, is determined by weighting the component cost of each type of long-term capital in the capital structure by its proportion to the total. This involves the following three steps:

- Calculate the after-tax cost of each individual form of capital (for example, ordinary shares, preference shares and long-term debt).
- Calculate the proportion or weight of each form of capital in the total capital structure.
- Combine the costs of the individual forms of capital and the corresponding weights of each of these forms to determine the weighted average cost of capital.

For privately owned businesses, as well as small businesses, it is extremely difficult to arrive at a reliable cost of capital figure, primarily because of a lack of information. The inherent uncertainty in small businesses has resulted in relatively high rates of return being required by those investing in such businesses.

19.4.6 Risk

For an investor, risk consists of two components, namely:

- The possible loss of the principal sum (the original amount invested)
- The possibility that no compensation will be paid for the use of the capital (no interest or dividend payments)

Any action that increases the possibility that the principal sum might be forfeited (as in the case of liquidation) or that compensation (in the form of dividends) will not be paid, increases the risk for the supplier of capital. The use of borrowed capital such as debentures increases the possibility that dividends might not be paid, and therefore increases the risk to ordinary shareholders.

With the cost of capital and risk in mind, capital structure will now be discussed.

19.5 The optimal capital structure

One of the chief facets of the management of the capital structure is effectively satisfying the planned capital requirements of a business by ensuring that funds are acquired at the lowest possible cost and on the most favourable conditions.

Financing decisions: the pecking order

Managers generally prefer using sources (of finance); when they must turn to external, debt is the first choice because it is the cheapest. Managers also usually prefer short-term debt if interest rates are high, to avoid locking in long-term rates at higher level. As a last resort, managers would elect to issue new equity (share capital). Thus, company leverage tends to increase over time.

For the purposes of this discussion, let us assume that the capital structure consists of the following two components:
- Owners' equity
- Long-term debt

Decision making regarding the capital structure entails deciding on the ratio of debt to equity.

Long-term financing decisions

The purpose of the long-term financing decision is to combine owners' equity and long-term debt so that the risk and the cost of capital to the business will be at a minimum.

19.5.1 Capital structure and risk

As we have seen, there are good arguments for taking up as much debt as possible. However, this is impractical in the real world. As the level of debt increases, so does the risk of bankruptcy. The effect of debt is explained by

referring to the functioning of the financial leverage.

Financial risk and financial leverage come into being the moment a business introduces fixed interest-bearing capital, such as debentures, into its capital structure. The presence, as well as the extent of financial risk, is a direct result of the financing policy of the business. For example, the decision to finance the business equally with owners' equity and debt will result in a capital structure comprising 50% shareholders' funds and 50% loan capital. The presence of debt in the capital structure gives rise to financial risk and financial leverage.

The reason why debt results in financial risk is that variable financing costs (dividends payable out of after-tax profits) are in part

Table 19.2: The effect of financial leverage at a 15% interest rate

Company	A	B	C
Number of issued shares	100	60	30
Owners' equity	R1 000	R600	R300
Long-term debt	–	R400	R700
Total assets	R1 000	R1 000	R1 000
Debt ratio (leverage factor)	0%	40%	70%
Operating profit (20% rate of return on total assets before tax)	R200	R200	R200
Minus: interest (15%)	–	R60	R105
Profit after interest before tax	R200	R140	R95
Minus: tax (40%)	R80	R56	R38
Net profit after tax	R120	R84	R57
Earnings per share (EPS)	R1,20	R1,40	R1,90
Rate of return on equity (ROE)	12%	14%	19%

replaced by fixed financing costs (fixed-interest payments out of profit before tax).

The example (see p. 473) shows that long-term debt affects profit after interest and tax, and earnings per share, through the functioning of the financial lever. Table 19.2 illustrates that the positive effect of the financial lever for a given level of operating profit increases with an increase in the debt ratio or the leverage factor.

The positive effect of the lever is because funds are obtained at an interest rate of 15% and then used by the business to earn 20% before tax. The excess return of 5% goes to shareholders. This increases the rate of return on equity (ROE) for a given level of operating profit.

The financial lever may, however, also have a negative effect. This will happen when interest rates in this example increase above 20%. Let us see what happens if interest rates rise to 25% (see table 19.3).

From this table we see that the rate of return on owners' equity now decreases with an increasing debt ratio, and it may even become negative.

This illustrates the financial risk lever that the inclusion of debt in the capital structure causes.

19.5.2 Capital structure and the cost of capital

In the previous section we indicated that the capital structure results in financial risk. The level of risk is reflected by the cost of capital. This means that investors expect a higher return on their investment as risk increases.

The financial manager has to take this into account when evaluating different financing proposals. The purpose is to identify the alternative with the lowest weighted average cost of capital. The alternative with the optimal ratio of debt to shareholders' equity will make the largest contribution to the wealth of shareholders.

The factors to be considered in deciding on the most suitable form of finance and the mix between debt and equity are summarised in table 19.4 on page 488.

Table 19.3: The effect of financial leverage at a 25% interest rate

Company	A	B	C
Number of issued shares	100	60	30
Owners' equity	R1 000	R600	R300
Long-term debt	–	R400	R700
Total assets	R1 000	R1 000	R1 000
Debt ratio (leverage factor)	0%	40%	70%
Operating profit (20% rate of return on total assets before tax)	R200	R200	R200
Minus: interest (25%)	–	R100	R175
Profit after interest before tax	R200	R100	R25
Minus: tax (40%)	R80	R40	R10
Net profit after tax	R120	R60	R15
Earnings per share (EPS)	R1,20	R1,00	R0,50
Rate of return on equity (ROE)	12%	10%	5%

19.5.3 Concluding remarks

The effects of financial risk and financial leverage on the total risk of the business were discussed in this section.

Knowledge of financial risk is valuable in planning the optimal capital structure for a business.

Businesses in industrial sectors characterised by a stable demand for products, and therefore subject to little variability or fluctuation in sales, as well as low fixed cost ratios, could accept a relatively high degree of debt financing. For example, the demand for

Table 19.4: Summary of considerations in deciding on a form of finance

Cosideration	Debt	Owners' equity
Return/cost	• Interest is tax deductable • Debt increases return on equity by leveraging profits	• Dividends not tax deductable
Risk	• As the level of debt increases, so does the risk of financial distress • Repayment of debt represents a fixed obligation that must be met	• Higher levels of equity reduce the risk of financial distress • No fixed obligations
Control	• Debt does not represent an ownership stake in the business • Owner retains full control	• Control may be diluted if the business issues new shares

electricity is relatively stable. Eskom therefore uses a large percentage of debt capital to finance its operations and has a high degree of financial leverage.

In contrast, businesses in predominantly capital-intensive sectors, characterised by a high fixed cost ratio and widely fluctuating sales, are obviously exposed to a high degree of risk. Because of the possibility of the negative effects of financial leverage, a financing policy requiring a minimal amount, or at most a moderate amount, of debt capital, based on accurate forecasting and sound financial planning, will probably be more acceptable. For example, a manufacturer of fashion goods, whose sales may fluctuate because of changing demand, will be well advised to restrict the amount of debt capital in the capital structure in order to limit the financial risk.

An optimal capital structure should also ensure that the business's cost of capital is kept to a minimum, and thus the profitability of the business is maximised for its owners.

19.6 **Summary**

In this chapter we described the various forms of short-term finance and indicated that the short-term financing decision is a trade-off between risk and return.

The nature and characteristics of the various forms of long-term capital were also discussed. This was followed by a discussion of the factors involved in establishing the cost of capital and determining the weighted average cost of capital. We then explained the long-term financing decision based both on the various forms of long-term capital and also on the risk involved.

The brief overview of financial management in chapters 17, 18 and 19 aimed to put into perspective not only the interesting and important facets, but also the challenges and complexities, of this functional area of management. Bear in mind, however, that the various aspects of financial management are all interrelated and integrated in the course of business operations, and that the function of financial management should be performed with full awareness and in the context of all other functions of the business.

 Key terms

Accruals	Financial markets
Bank overdrafts	Long-term debt
Cost of capital	Optimal capital structure
Factoring	Owner's equity
Financial gearing	Preference shares
Financial institutions	Shareholders' interest
Financial intermediation	Trade credit
Financial lease	Trade credit

? Questions for discussion

1. What factors affect the level of gearing at which your organisation operates?
2. Explain what you understand the term "cost of capital" to mean.
3. Determine the cost of capital for your own organisation.
4. What would you take into consideration when choosing between preference and ordinary shares when choosing financing for your company?
5. Explain the meaning of financial intermediation briefly.

References

1. Kohn, M., *Financial institutions and markets*, McGraw-Hill, New York, 1994.
2. Damadoran, A., *Corporate finance: Theory and practice*, Wiley, New York, 1997.
3. ABSA Bank, *Principles of finance and your business*, ABSA, Johannesburg, 1996, p. 23.

Websites: www.finforum.co.za/markets
www.BFA.co.za
www.24.com
www.khula.org.za

20

THE OPERATIONS MANAGEMENT FUNCTION

The purpose of this chapter	Learning outcomes
This chapter defines and examines the nature of operations management. It also depicts an operations management model and its components. Finally, the classification of different operational processes for manufacturers and service providers is discussed.	The content of this chapter will enable learners to: • Explain why operations management is important for a business • Define what operations management encompasses • Identify and explain the components of the operations management model put forward • Explain how systems for classifying operational processes may assist operations managers in understanding how best to manage them

20.1 Introduction

Countries of the international community are frequently classified as **developed** or **developing** on the basis of different criteria. One of the criteria used is the extent and growth of a particular country's **gross domestic product** (GDP). The GDP represents the total value of all the final goods (referred to hereafter as **products**) and **services** produced in a country within a specific period of time (usually a year). The GDP per capita (or per person) is therefore a good indication of a particular country's economic wealth.

Developed countries – for example the USA, Japan, Germany, the United Kingdom and France – will therefore have a higher GDP per capita than developing countries such as Argentina, Brazil, Malaysia and South Africa (see table 20.1 on page 491).

Table 20.1: Gross domestic product by country (2006)

Country	GDP US$ per capita
USA	44 000
Japan	33 100
Germany	31 900
UK	31 800
France	31 100
Argentina	15 200
Brazil	8 800
Malaysia	12 900
South Africa	13 300

Source: SA 2005–2006, *South Africa at a glance*, Editors, Inc., Greenside, p. 149.

Note: South Africa's GDP per capita (US$) of 13 300 (based on the 2006 mid-year estimate of total GDP of US$254,9 billion and population of 46,6 million) is higher than the GDPs of Brazil and Malaysia, Nigeria, Russia and Turkey, on a par with those of Mexico and Poland, but way below those of Australia, Spain and the other developed countries mentioned above.

In simple terms, the businesses of a developed country will jointly produce **more products and services** than those of a developing country. To increase the economic wealth of a country, businesses in that country must therefore provide more (and preferably better) products and services. Bearing in mind that the operations function is that function in a business directly responsible for manufacturing products and/or rendering services, its importance cannot be adequately emphasised – not only for the business concerned but also for the country in which it operates (see table 20.2).

This chapter first looks at the nature and definitions of operations management and then puts forward an operations management model. This model comprises operations management strategies and objectives, a basic transformation model, and a management component. The management strategies and

Table 20.2: Percentage contribution to GDP by sector, 2004

South Africa	Contribution to GDP
Agriculture	2,6%
Industry	30,3%
Services	67,1%

Source: SA 2005–2006, *South Africa at a glance*, Editors, Inc., Greenside, p. 149.

Note: The largest percentage contribution to South Africa's GDP by sector comprises the services sector, followed in descending order by manufacturing activities with agriculture contributing the least.

objectives of operations management and the basic transformation model are discussed in this chapter, as is a classification system for different operational processes of both manufacturers and service providers. In chapter 21, the management component – which includes the principal activities and tasks of operations management, namely operations design, operations planning and control, and operations improvement – is examined more closely.

The case study on pages 492–493 provides an illustration of a South African business's operations system and its transformation processes and performance objectives. The case study illustrates how important effective operations processes are and how high-quality products can fail without sufficient operational support.

20.2 The nature and definition of operations management

In chapter 1 we indicated that a business transforms **inputs** from the environment into **outputs** to the environment. The operations function is that function of the business aimed at executing the transformation process. The operations function and the management

Case study: Variphone

Background

More workers in the USA are exposed to potentially dangerous noise levels than to similar levels of any other noxious agent. Factories and mining operations are noisy, and environmentalists and governments are seriously seeking solutions for noise pollution and resulted noise-induced hearing loss (NIHL). In Sweden, 70% of construction workers do not have normal hearing and 70% of Germany's population are noise disturbed. In the Netherlands, a million people's proximity to Schiphol Airport causes suffering from excessive noise. Noise has contributed significantly to the fact that heart disease and the use of sleeping pills have increased. NIHL compensation statistics are so alarming as to be unbelievable. Noise per se may not cause death, which is the only reason why it is not the current number one health pandemic addressed by the World Health Organisation (WHO). In October 2005, the Hearing Academy (Gent University, Belgium) hosted its first international conference on Hearing at Work. The harmful effects of noise on the public, organisations, soldiers, musicians and industrial workers need to be addressed on a national and international level. New models for hearing conservation, different types of hearing protectors and methods for predicting hearing loss (by means of oto-acoustic emissions referred to as OAEs) are on the agenda to address this public and industrial health problem. Some mining groups (for example Harmony Gold) are moving towards introducing best practice hearing protection devices within a professional hearing conservation programme. Noise affects tasks requiring accuracy rather than speed and noise detrimentally affects demanding tasks, especially those requiring attention to multiple signal sources. The value of quality hearing conservation goes beyond hearing protection.

Variphone

Variphone is a patent/product for hearing protection. It is manufactured in Peer, Belgium. It has also made inroads into the South African market (with a laboratory in South Africa) with a very sophisticated custom-made hearing protection device (HPD) with special features (designed for the European market). Variphone is more than a product – it is a concept that is integrated with a professional service and maintenance plan. Buyers are actually forced to buy the service contract if they purchase the Variphone HPD (to re-check attenuation and the seal). The Variphone is tailor fitted, custom made and physically very similar to a hearing aid, although functionally the opposite of one. The difference is in its function – a hearing aid amplifies sound and the Variphone attenuates sound. The Variphone is therefore a high-quality, personally made hearing protector for each worker; it is produced for purposes of noise control and to eliminate NIHL.

Features of the unconventional Variphone HPDs are very different from the "ear-muff", or the one-size-fits-all basic earplug. Conventional ear dampers do not look good, are not user-friendly, are not durable (cost-effective), do not cultivate pride and cannot be regarded as truly "personal". If an HPD is not comfortable, its application will be compromised. The ideal is a durable, comfortable (custom-made) HPD that allows certain sounds, such as speech frequencies, through. The Variphone has these sophisticated features – it is durable (made of acrylic material), has an adjustable filter (to adjust or calibrate the attenuation according to noise levels), and also offers ventilation, communication ability and localisation. The Variphone is cost-effective over the long term since workers do not replace or replenish it every day and can use it for a few years. User-friendliness, high ownership (maintainability) and a perfect fit confirmed by a seal test (after the fitment procedure) are other quality dimensions. It is clear that this product needs an effective and efficient operation system because operators (audiometrists) have to visit workers at the plants to do impressions (take moulds), manufacture to specification and revisit the plant for personal fitments of Variphone HPDs. This basically describes the transformation process in terms of a labour-intensive professional service (make appointments, do work station set-up, do basic training, do impressions, do fitments etc.) and the manufacturing transformation process in the laboratory where silicon imprints are transformed into a complete, packed acrylic unit with assembled cords and filters.

The Variphone competitor

Pretoria-based Noise Clipper (Pty) Ltd also manufactures a custom-made HPD similar to Variphone, but it has an operations management function embracing principles such as creativity, innovation, additional value creation, elimination of waste, quality and the timeous completion of things (elements of the JIT philosophy). Noise Clipper is in direct competition with Variphone and realised the need in the market not only to improve on Variphone's weaknesses (for example long lead times, high cost, implied service contract, etc.), but to have a productive operations system to counter the typical challenges of the make-to-order business it is in. Its HPD product and service demand an intermittent operation with flexibility for an agile market. Noise Clipper's strategy (among others) is to shorten lead times, offer a "go the extra

mile" service and enforce its engineering competences in terms of innovation and modern operations management.

The idea was to design and patent a HPD for African conditions. It would be "less sophisticated" and more cost-effective than the Variphone, without compromising product effectiveness. It was also decided to offer the Noise Clipper HPD in different colours with each user's name imbedded in the product, with the filter in a fixed factory setting and made tamperproof (not adjustable, as this demands re-calibration and additional servicing costs). This filter was also not calibrated at the premises (and in the time) of the client. An engineer, Chris Botha from the CSIR, was contracted to finalise the R&D and the patent and also to design and innovate two important machines for the Noise Clipper process. These machines are the "Sealometer" (to do seal tests) and the "Calometer" (to calibrate filters). These process technologies were successfully designed and developed. Noise Clipper's production process was initially designed to be a batch operation to produce small quantities per day. The operation is labour intensive because of the custom-made process, and the capacity could be adjusted fairly easily to meet demand. Noise Clipper anticipated rapid growth after large mines adopted the concept. Noise Clipper had to adapt: if the scope of the job demanded it to manage a contract as a project, then it had to be flexible and run the operation as a resource-to-order business. Noise Clipper's primary marketing strategy was to do marketing through effective operations. It received the AHI business of the Year award (2004) due to this operations strategy. Noise Clipper has partnerships with the CSIR and obtained the SABS mark of approval in 2007.

Source: Personal interview with the General Manager, Mr T. Pienaar, Persequor Park, Pretoria, 2007.

thereof (operations management) are therefore directly concerned with creating products and providing services in order to realise the objectives of the business.

20.2.1 The importance of operations management

Generally considered, an effective and efficient operation can give a business four types of advantages:[1]

- **It can reduce the costs of making the products or offering the services.** If we keep in mind that profit = revenue − costs, reducing the costs of production by being more efficient and having less waste, rework, scrap, spillage, etc. will directly contribute towards the profitability of production.

- **It can increase the revenue the business receives for offering its products and services to its customers/clients.** Again, according to the profit equation given above, increasing sales through superior quality products and service excellence, or offering just plain "good value for money", again directly contributes towards the profitability of a business.

- **It can reduce the amount of investment (capital employed) needed to manufacture the type and quantity of products or offer the service required.** Increasing the effective capacity of the operation by better use of facilities, machines or equipment and seeking new ways and procedures to optimise the functioning of the operation may decrease the amount of capital required for investment in the acquisition and running of the production/operations capacity.

- **It can provide the impetus for new innovation by using its solid base of operational skills and knowledge to develop new products and services.** This can involve the production/operations capability in manufacturing or the offering of new products and services in accordance with international best standards and practices.

Other reasons for operations management being considered important to a business include the following:

- **It can improve productivity.** Productivity, measured as the ratio of output to input, is a yardstick for the efficacy with which operations management transforms (or converts) the resources of a business into products and/or services. If a business – for example Addis, which manufactures plastic products – produces more error- or defect-free outputs, for example plastic buckets, with less wastage of material inputs, or puts its manufacturing staff to better use, its overall productivity will improve. Higher productivity, in turn, is directly related to increased profitability for businesses, which benefits the country in which the business operates.[2]

- **It can help a business to satisfy the needs of its customers/clients more effectively.** The customer/client is an important focal point in operations management, and the operations manager should see to it that quality products or services are provided for the consumer at a reasonable price. Satisfied customers/clients are of crucial importance to any business since its long-term survival or existence is dependent on them. Businesses will endeavour, by means of their particular operations skills, to satisfy the needs of their customers/clients more effectively than their competitors do.

- **It can be decisive for the general reputation of the business.** Some businesses have, through their particular operations skills, built up outstanding reputations as far as high-quality products or services, low costs, or plain and simple "good value for money" are concerned. The operations skills of a business make (and also break) such reputations. Businesses such as Woolworths and Panasonic have, over the years, built up exceptionally good reputations for high quality. For such businesses, quality is a competitive weapon (or competitive advantage) that can be used to protect and further expand their market position.

In the remaining part of this section, concepts generally used in operations management are defined.

Critical thinking

How important is operations and operations management? Is it more important than marketing, finance and other management functions? Generally considered, an effective and efficient operation can give a business several types of advantages (as discussed above) but is it really particularly important?

Some people argue that nothing is possible without a good idea and others say that without money nothing is possible. Some see operations management as a dynamic and creative discipline: if human beings are seen as the rulers of creation, then operations management brings humans as close as they can be to the act of creation and creating value. Business life is primarily concerned with creating goods and services, putting operations management at the heart of its existence. All managers directly and indirectly create products and/or services, be they through micro or macro processes, for internal and external customers. In this sense, all managers can be viewed as operations managers. Every manufactured thing people see around them, sit on, eat, read, wear, buy and enjoy comes to them courtesy of operations managers who planned and controlled the production system involved.

20.2.2 Definitions

There are many definitions of operations management in the literature. A common characteristic of all these definitions is that operations management is concerned with the management of the **transformation process** (also referred to as the **operations process**) whereby products are manufactured and/or services rendered.

To clarify further what is meant by operations management, the following concepts are defined:[3]

- The **operations function** is that function in the business primarily aimed at the utilisation of resources to manufacture products and/or render services.
- **Operations managers** are the personnel in the business who are directly responsible for managing the operations function.
- **Operations management** (also referred to as **the operations management function**) involves operations managers' activities, decisions and responsibilities that tie in with the execution of the operations function. The operations management process includes operations planning, operations organising, operations scheduling and operations control.

20.3 An operations management model

An operations management model that can be used for the management of the operations function is depicted in figure 20.1 on page 496 and provides the basis of the discussion in this chapter and chapter 21.

Three points stand out clearly in this operations management model, namely that operations management strategies and objectives, as well as management activities (see chapter 21), influence the transformation process to produce outputs.

20.3.1 Operations management strategies and objectives

All businesses formulate business objectives, and if a business intends surviving in the long term, consumers who are satisfied with the business's products or services should be a top priority objective. The operations management function should take cognisance of customers'/clients' needs and continually formulate its management **strategies** and

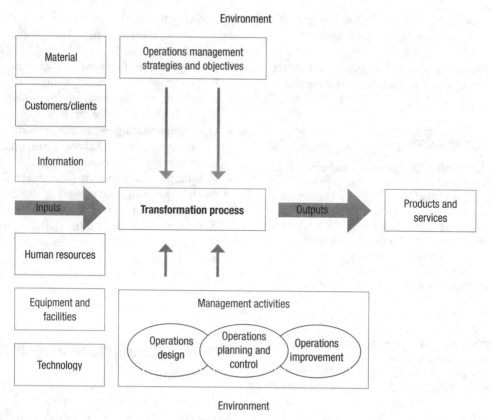

Figure 20.1 A general model of operations management

Source: Adapted from Slack, N., Chambers, S. & Johnston, R., *Operations management*, 4th edition, Harlow: Financial Times Prentice Hall, 2003, p.5.

objectives in such a way that the competitive position and customer/client base not only remain intact, but, where necessary, are also strengthened and expanded.

Although customer/client needs are numerous, they can be reduced to six main elements, namely:[4]

- Higher quality
- Lower costs
- Shorter lead time (quicker manufacturing or provision of services)
- Greater adaptability (flexibility)
- Lower variability with regard to specifications (reliability)
- High level of service (better overall service)

With these six customer/client requirements as a basis, operations management objectives can be formulated which give the business an "operations-based advantage"[5] over other businesses. Managing operations for competitive advantage or as a "competitive weapon" is an imperative for the modern businesses in the face of increased global competition, rapid technological change and the higher visibility and importance of ethical business practices, workforce diversity issues and environmental protection concerns.[6] Operations management objectives must therefore indicate the specific areas within the domain of the operations function which will be emphasised when products and/or services are produced or provided. The operations management objectives are formulated in such a way that they are applicable to both manufacturers and service providers. To acquire operations-based advantages, the following general guidelines (which incorporate the above-mentioned customer/client needs) can be followed:

- **Do things right the first time.** This means that the operations function should not make mistakes. By providing error-free products and services that are ready and suitable for consumption by customers/clients, the business will gain a **quality advantage**. Higher quality not only means increased error-free outputs resulting in lower costs, but also an improved competitive position, which could lead to higher prices and a greater market share. Think again of Woolworths food products in this regard. This business is certainly one of the best-known for providing top quality food products for which some consumers are prepared to pay higher prices.

- **Do things cost effectively.** It is imperative that products and services be produced or provided at a cost that will enable the business to place them on the market at a price that will ensure an acceptable profit for the business. This also applies to non-profit organisations because taxpayers and funders insist on good value, which they will receive only if institutions function cost effectively. Hence, when the operations management function operates cost effectively, it can provide the business with a **cost advantage**. However, when this does not happen, for example in the case of a gold mine where the cost per metric ton of mined gold-bearing ore is too high to run the mine profitably, drastic cost-saving measures, such as the large-scale retrenchment of miners, are necessary. In the case of Mossgas, for example, where the high procurement cost of the gas and oil made the project uneconomical, the state had to subsidise the project continuously at the expense of the taxpayer.

- **Do things fast.** This means that the period of time that elapses between the demand for a product or service and the delivery thereof should be as short as possible – or, put differently, the **lead time** should be shortened. This will increase the availability of the products and services and will give the business a **speed advantage**. Businesses that do not place their goods and services on the market quickly enough will not only initially have to accept lost sales, but will later on also have to overcome strong competition from established brands. Think, for example, of a paving construction business that promises to have a new driveway paved in three weeks, but then takes seven weeks to complete the job. Would you recommend this business to your friends? Businesses such as Boss Paving, which is reputed to complete paving faster than its competitors, acquire a speed advantage from which they will later build up a sound reputation in the market.

- **Change things quickly.** The operations management function should be able to adapt or change activities if unforeseen circumstances make it necessary to do so. This applies, for example, when more customers/clients demand a product or service, or if a customer/client requires the delivery of a wider variety of products or services within the agreed time. If the operations management function can change activities in this way to satisfy customer/client demands both quickly and adequately, the business will have an **adaptability advantage**. During the 2002 World Summit on Sustainable Development in Johannesburg, South African businesses reacted quickly to the sharp increase in overseas visitors, and car rental companies such as Avis, for example, were able to cope with the sudden increased demand for rental cars. Businesses such as Toyota, in turn, are known for their ability to adapt their product line quickly to changing customer needs for cheaper, less luxurious motor vehicles such as the Toyota Tazz.

- **Do things right every time.** Error-free products and services that satisfy set specifications should regularly and continuously be provided to customers/clients. This gives the business a **high reliability or low variability advantage.** This guideline ties in with the customer/client requirement of high quality. However, it emphasises the ability of the business to meet specifications continuously in the long term. This is of particular importance to businesses that produce or provide products or services on a continuous (or mass) basis. Take the example of McDonald's Big Mac hamburgers. McDonald's is an international business that claims that a Big Mac hamburger will taste the same in any place in the world where business is conducted. Thus, when people buy their second Big Mac, they will know exactly what they are getting! Big Mac hamburgers are so international by nature that a so-called Big Mac index has been calculated (see the example below). South African Airways (SAA) also strives for low variability in respect of times of scheduled departures to various destinations. If SAA's flights over a period of a year, for example, depart on schedule and reach their destinations 90% of the time, one could say that the airline renders a reliable service.

- **Do things better.** With due regard to all the preceding operations management guidelines, a business will also endeavour to provide a better total product or service package, compared to that of its competitors. This gives the business a service advantage. Think of businesses such as M-Net and BMW, which have gained reputations because they stand out above their rivals as far as service is concerned. This guideline is closely intertwined with the concept of total quality management (TQM), which is today the focal point of many top businesses internationally. TQM's point of departure is that quality products or services cannot be produced or provided unless the whole business (all the different functional management areas) work together to achieve this goal. TQM will be discussed in more detail in chapter 21.

Applying the concept: Consistency of a product

McDonald's Big Mac Hamburgers

The so-called Big Mac index shows the price (in US$) per Big Mac hamburger in various countries, for price comparison purposes (see page 499). The average number of minutes that a person needs to work in order to buy a Big Mac hamburger in various countries is calculated, which gives an idea of relative remuneration, productivity and prosperity levels.

The Hamburger Standard (based on February, 2007 BigMac Prices)

Country	BigMac Price		Actual Exchange Rate 1 USD =	Over(+) / Under(-) Valuation against the dollar, %	Purchasing Power Price
	in Local Currency	in US dollars			
United States	$3.22	3.22	1.00	—	—
Argentina	Peso 8.25	2.6041	3.1681	−19.1945	2.56
Australia	A$3.45	2.8407	1.2145	−11.8979	1.07
Brazil	Real 6.40	3.2645	1.9605	1.5047	1.99
Britain	£1.99	4.0072	2.0137 ‡	24.302	0.6173
Canada	C$3.63	3.4509	1.0519	7.4247	1.13
Chile	Peso 1670	3.1905	523.427	−0.8458	519
China	Yuan 11.0	1.4548	7.561	−54.7679	3.42
Columbia	Peso 6900	3.1517	2189.26	−2.113	2.143
Costa Rica	Colones 1130	2.1386	528.377	−33.5702	351
Czech Republic	Koruna 52.1	2.5704	20.269	−20.075	16.2
Denmark	DKr27.75	5.0871	5.455	58.0202	8.62
Egypt	Pound 9.09	1.5953	5.698	−50.509	2.82
Estonia	Kroon 30	2.6096	11.496	−18.9283	9.32
Euro area	€2.94	4.0022	0.7346	23.7532	0.9091
Hong Kong	HK$12.00	1.5396	7.794	−52.1427	3.73
Hungary	Forint 590	3.1382	188.003	−2.6611	183
Iceland	Kronur 509	7.8607	64.7524	144.0064	158
Indonesia	Rupiah 15.900	1.6901	9407.5	−47.51	4.938
Japan	¥280	2.4181	115.793	−24.8659	87
Latvia	Lats 1.35	2.627	0.5139	−18.272	0.42
Lithuania	Litas 6.50	2.5628	2.5363	−20.3564	2.02
Malaysia	M$5.50	1.5666	3.5108	−51.2932	1.71
Mexico	Peso 29.0	2.6238	11.0525	−18.48	9.01
New Zealand	NZ$4.60	3.1856	1.444	−0.9695	1.43
Norway	Kroner 41.5	7.1473	5.8064	122.1686	12.9
Pakistan	Rupee 140	2.3088	60.6368	−28.2614	43.5
Paraguay	Guarani 10.000	1.9292	5183.41	−40.0781	3.106
Peru	New Sol 9.50	2.965	3.204	−7.9276	2.95
Philippines	Peso 85.0	1.8178	46.7593	−43.5406	26.4
Poland	Zloty 6.90	2.4633	2.8011	−23.6014	2.14
Russia	Rouble 49.00	1.9085	25.6746	−40.7975	15.2
Saudi Arabia	Riyal 9.00	2.3993	3.7511	−25.3552	2.80
Singapore	S$3.60	2.3577	1.5269	−26.6488	1.12
Slovakia	Crown 57.98	2.3334	24.8476	−27.5584	18.0
South Africa	Rand 15.5	2.1404	7.2418	−33.58	4.81
South Korea	Won 2.900	3.0862	939.68	−4.1163	901
Sri Lanka	Rupee 190	1.6759	113.369	−47.9576	59.0
Sweden	SKr 32.0	4.6522	6.8784	44.5104	9.94
Switzerland	SFr 6.30	5.2075	1.2098	62.0102	1.96
Taiwan	NT$75.00	2.2693	33.0504	−29.5016	23.3
Thailand	Baht 62.0	1.885	32.8907	−41.3208	19.3
Turkey	Lire 4.55	3.4745	1.3096	7.6665	1.41
UAE	Dirhams 10.0	2.7223	3.6733	−15.335	3.11
Ukraine	Hryvnia 9.00	1.7632	5.1044	−45.1454	2.80
Uraguay	Peso 55.0	2.3059	23.8515	−28.3064	17.1
Venezuela	Bolivar 6.800	3.1648	2148.62	−1.7043	2.112

‡ Dollars per pound

Source: The Economist. 2007. *The hamburger standard.* [Online] Available from: http://www.oanda.com/products/bigmac/bigmac.shtml [Accessed: 2007-09-06].

Critical thinking

Is it possible for a business to achieve all operations performance objectives such as quality, costs, short lead time (quicker manufacturing or provision of services), adaptability (flexibility), variability with regard to specifications (reliability) and level of service (better overall service)? Many believe there is always a trade-off. Is it true that quality is always compromised if costs are cut? Consider BMW, for instance. How would that company rate, according to you?

Applying the concept: The priority of operations management objectives may vary

Some operations management objectives (also referred to as performance objectives) may become more or less important under different circumstances. One influence that is of particular importance to businesses in determining the relative priority that they will place on a specific objective is the actions of competitors.

Krüger[7] anticipated that this influence would be of special significance for South African manufacturers just after the historic 1994 democratic elections, when it was expected that most international sanctions against South Africa would be lifted. He empirically determined that the majority (more than 80% of those sampled) of so-called large South African manufacturers (that is, those employing more than 500 people in businesses located in any of the geographical regions in South Africa, and who undertook any kind of manufacturing activity in all of the standard industry code [SIC] categories) acknowledged that manufacturing-based strategies enhanced the competitive capabilities and advantages of their businesses, and that this contributed to long-term, superior business performance and success.

Furthermore, an even larger majority of the manufacturers (98% of those sampled) recog¬nised that superior manufacturing capabilities would become a prerequisite for improving their national and international competitive positions in the future. In this regard, Krüger[8] later reported further findings showing that if South African manufacturers were to better their positions against national competitors, the relative priority that had to be observed for the five selected performance objectives should be (1) low cost, (2) high quality, (3) high dependability (high reliability or low variability), (4) high speed (shorter lead times), and (5) high flexibility (greater adaptability). (Note: the terminology used for the equivalent operations management objectives used in this book are indicated in brackets. Also, this rank order is derived in a purely mathematical way, and is not necessarily statistically significant. With regard to better competitive positions against international competitors, a positional movement occurred between the relative priority of low cost and high quality, but this is not of statistical significance.

Finally, when the relative priority for the five operations management objectives for better competitive positions against both national and international competitors were considered together, it was found (this was confirmed statistically significant at a 0,05 level or with a 95% probability) that high quality, low cost and high dependability should all rank as priority number (1), high speed as priority number (2) and high flexibility as priority number (3).

Plans were afoot to replicate this study in 2007 in order to determine whether there were any significant changes in the ranking of the relative priorities by South African manufacturers (10 years later) in terms of bettering their positions against both international and national competitors.

Operations management guideline		Positive result
Doing things right the first time	can lead to	Higher quality
Doing things cost effectively	can lead to	Lower cost
Doing things fast	can lead to	Shorter lead time
Changing things quickly	can lead to	Greater adaptability
Doing things right every time	can lead to	Lower variability
Doing things better	can lead to	Better service

Figure 20.2: Positive results obtained by the application of operations management guidelines

Source: Adapted from Slack, N., Chambers, S., Harland, C., Harrison, A. & Johnson, R., *Operations management*, Pearson Education (UK), 1995, p. 54.

Figure 20.2 illustrates the positive results that can be obtained by each of the above-mentioned operations management guidelines.

20.3.2 The transformation model

The operations function is primarily concerned with the application of resources (inputs) by means of a transformation process to provide outputs. A basic transformation model (also referred to as an input–transformation–output model) is depicted in Figure 20.3 on page 502.

This model could apply to both manufacturers and service providers.

The transformation model comprises three main components: inputs, the transformation process itself, and outputs. Each of these will now be discussed in more detail.

20.3.2.1 Inputs

Inputs used in the transformation process comprise both the resources that are to be processed, changed or converted (jointly known as **transformation**) and the resources required to make the transformation possible. The resources to be transformed (input transformed resources) include the following:

• **Material.** A wide variety of material (both processed and unprocessed) can be used as inputs in the transformation process. For example, a motor manufacturer will use mainly processed material such as steel, glass and plastic, while a gold mine will use primarily unprocessed material (gold ore). For a service provider such as a hairdresser, different hair products, for example shampoo and tinting agents, represent the material inputs.

• **Customers/clients.** Clients can serve as the inputs in the transformation process when the client himself or herself is the subject who is "transformed or processed". For example, in a dentist's rooms or hairdressing salon, the client who receives dental treatment or undergoes a change in his or her appearance is the primary input in the transformation process. The same applies to recreational facilities (for example cinemas or gymnasiums) and recreational events (for example symphony or rock concerts) because the client is the most important input who is "transformed" or entertained.

• **Information.** Information can either be the primary input that is processed or converted (for example the information processed into news for a newspaper) or it can be used as the secondary input in a transformation

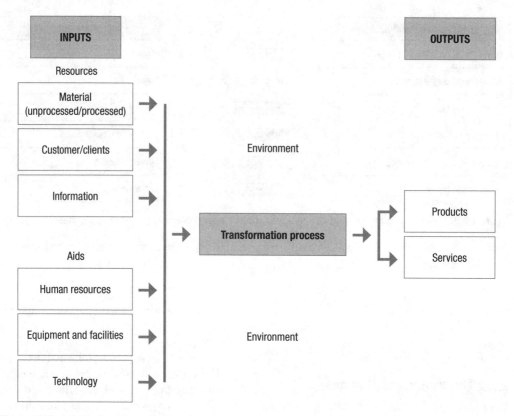

Figure 20.3: A basic transformation model

Source: Adapted from Schonberger, R.J. & Knod, E.M., *Operation management: Improving customer service*, 4th edition, Homewood, IL: Irwin, 1991.

process, for example information about consumer preferences in respect of a particular product, such as a motor vehicle (colour, size and shape).

The resources required to make transformation possible (input transforming resources) include the following:

- **Human resources.** In most transformation processes some or other form of human involvement is necessary. This includes workers who are physically involved in the transformation process and the people involved in a supervisory capacity. Some manufacturing processes are more labour intensive than others. A gold mine, for

example, is more labour intensive than a motor vehicle manufacturing plant, where many of the processes have been automated. Service providers such as hotels are normally also labour intensive and the service sector is therefore seen as the sector with the most potential for job creation.

- **Equipment and facilities.** Equipment and facilities can assume many different forms. A few examples of specific facilities are the following:
  - A manufacturer uses factories, machinery and equipment.
  - Hospitals use wards, examination rooms and operating theatres.

- Banks, attorneys and auditing firms use offices, computers and telephones.
- Restaurants use eating areas, tables and chairs, gridirons, serving tables and take-away counters.
- Universities use lecture halls, laboratories, theatres and sports fields.
- Supermarkets and other retailers use shopping areas, storage rooms, display areas, shelves, aisles and cash registers.
- **Technology.** The role of technology as an input in the transformation process is becoming increasingly important. Technology is generally used to enable the transformation process to function more efficiently. Thus, new knowledge and techniques (automation) can help a manufacturer to manufacture better products of higher quality more quickly. Service providers can also apply technology (for example satellite communication) to render better services more quickly.

20.3.2.2 The transformation process

The inputs are converted to outputs in the transformation process. The nature of the process is determined by the type of input that is predominantly processed in the process itself. Three main types of resource inputs,[9] namely the transformation of materials, information and customers/clients, will now be discussed.

- **Transformation of materials.** The transformation process is primarily geared to processing materials by changing their physical characteristics (shape or composition). Most manufacturers, such as motor vehicle or furniture manufacturers, employ such transformation processes. Service providers that also fall into this category include those which involve the material changing location (a delivery business), changing of ownership (wholesalers and retailers), or primarily being stored (warehouses).
- **Transformation of information.** Information is the primary input processed in this

transformation process, which includes processes whereby information changes in composition or shape (for example an auditor's report), changes ownership (for example a market research publication), is disseminated and changes location (for example telecommunication), or is merely stored (for example a library).

- **Transformation of customers/clients.** Transformation processes that primarily process "clients" may also occur in a variety of ways. Some change the physical characteristics of clients (for example hairdressing), while others change their physiological condition (for example medical treatment at hospitals) or emotional condition (for example entertainment at cinemas). The location of clients can also be changed (for example by airlines) or merely be "stored" or accommodated (for example in hotels).

20.3.2.3 Outputs

The ultimate goal of any transformation process is to convert or process inputs into **outputs**. Outputs assume the form of products (goods) or services. Manufacturers normally produce some or other product (for example motor vehicles or furniture), while service providers render certain services (for example hairdressers or airlines). However, the characteristics of products manufactured and services provided differ. It is important to note these differences because they have specific implications for the management of the various operations processes. Important differences between products and services are represented in table 20.3 on page 504.

These differences represent two extreme positions on a continuum between pure product manufacturers and pure service providers. In practice, however, businesses are, to a greater or lesser degree, involved in both the manufacture of products and the provision of services.

The example in the box below illustrates such differences between the characteristics of products and services.

Table 20.3: Characteristics of products and services

Products (product manufacturer)	Services (service provider)
Physically tangible and durable	Intangible and perishable
Output kept in stock	Output not kept in stock
Low customer contact	High client contact
Manufactured before use	Provision and consumption simultaneous
Long response time	Short response time
Local and international markets	Mainly local markets
Large production facilities	Small service provision facility
Capital intensive	Labour intensive
Quality easily measurable	Quality difficult to measure

Source: Krajewski, L.J. & Ritzman, L.P., *Operations management*, 3rd edition, Pearson Education Inc., 1993, p. 5.

The transformation process – which comprises three main components of inputs, the transformation process, and outputs – has been explained. Table 20.4 on page 505 provides examples of the inputs, the nature of the transformation process, and outputs of a variety of businesses.

20.3.2.4 Operational processes have different characteristics

While the basic nature of all operational processes is similar in that the processes transform input resources into outputs, these processes may fundamentally differ in a number of ways, viewed from the perspective of the following four distinctive characteristics[10] (the so-called four Vs):

- **Volume of output.** This refers to the number of items produced by the operation over a given period of time. The more (or greater volume of items) of one type of product made, the greater the benefit that may be obtained through standardisation and repeatability of the tasks and procedures. The most important implication of this characteristic with regard

Applying the concept: A manufacturer of products (goods) versus a service provider chain

A product manufacturer. Toyota and Nissan manufacture motor vehicles. The product is physically tangible (the vehicle itself), durable (is not used up in one period) and can be kept in stock (where more vehicles are manufactured than the number in immediate demand). There is no customer contact while the vehicle is being manufactred and unless there are already a few vehicles in stock, it may take a while to deliver the vehicle to the customer. Motor vehicle manufacturers usually have large production facilities and expensive equipment, which make this a capital-intensive industry. Because of the tangible nature of vehicles, it is possible to set, monitor and ensure objective standards as far as quality is concerned.

A service provider. A dentist renders a professional service. The service itself is intangible (it cannot be held or touched) and can also not be kept in stock if it is not used immediately. The presence of the user of the service (the patient) is necessary while the service is being rendered, and the response time is usually short. Provision of the service takes place in a small service facility (a dental surgery), the service itself is labour intensive (the dentist is involved), and because the service is intangible, it is more difficult to set and maintain objective standards.

Table 20.4: Inputs, transformation processes and outputs of various businesses

Type of business	Inputs	Transformation process	Outputs
Rail transport	Locomotives Passenger coaches and trucks Locomotive drivers and personnel Railway tracks and sleepers Passengers and freight	Changes location of passengers and freight	Passengers and rail freight at new destinations
Banks	Bank tellers and financial advisers Safes and computers Bank notes and coins Clients	Receipt and payment of money (cash) Recordkeeping of accounts Safekeeping of valuable articles	Clients with financial peace of mind Accurate bank statements Financial earnings (interest)
Hairdressing salon	Hairdresser and assistants Combs, brushes and scissors Treatment agents Clients	Shampooing, tinting, treating, drying and cutting of hair	Clients with neat appearances
Gold mine	Gold-bearing ore Pneumatic drills and explosives Lifts and conveyor belts Miners and engineers	Mined gold-bearing ore and transport to processing plant Process ore and melt gold concentrates	Gold bars
Furniture manufacturer	Wood, steel and material Saw and planing equipment Factory workers	Design furniture Make furniture Sell furniture to wholesalers	Completed furniture such as lounge and dining-room suites
Printing works	Printing and binding machines Paper, cardboard and ink Design and printing personnel	Design, print and bind books, periodicals and reports	Designed and printed material
Construction firm	Sand, cement and other building material Construction equipment Construction workers Building plans	Plan and construct buildings according to plans	Office accommodation
Missile manufacturer	Electronic components Rocket launchers Engineers and technicians Computers	Design, assemble and test missiles	Air-to-air or ground-to-ground missiles

to the operational process is its influence over the cost of making a product or delivering a service – lower production cost per unit is possible as fixed costs are spread over a larger number of units. Volume of output may range from high (for example 220 motor vehicles per day) to low (for example 20 aeroplanes per year).

- **Variety of output.** This refers to the range of different items produced by the operation over a given period of time. The more (or greater variety of items) types of products made by the same operation, the greater is the flexibility and ability to provide non-standardised products or services – though these will inevitably come at the price of a higher cost per unit of manufacture or delivery. The most important implication of this characteristic with regard to the operational process is its capability of matching its products and services with the exact needs of customers/clients. Variety of output may range from high (for example a taxi service to and from any location in and around Johannesburg) to limited (for example a fixed route and time schedule for a metropolitan bus service).
- **Variation of output.** This refers to the particular demand pattern for the output of the operation, which may be highly irregular, non-routine and unpredictable or the converse, that is, fairly constant. The most important implication of this characteristic with regard to the operational process is the possibility of a sudden and dramatic change in the operations capacity required to supply products and services in order to meet the needs of customers/clients. Operations likely to experience seasonal variations (for example hotel resorts in coastal locations) must be able to deal with marked variation in demand levels, from full occupancy during peak season to under-utilisation for the remainder. Other hotels located in city centres may have constant patronage from business guests during most of the week and utilise special tariffs over weekends to level the demand. It should be apparent that the unit costs in this latter case will be lower than those of a comparable hotel with a highly variable demand pattern.
- **Visibility of output.** This refers to how much of the operation's activities the customers/clients experience themselves or are exposed to. In high-visibility operations, the customers/clients experience most of the value-adding

---

Example

An example of such extreme operational processes is found in the tertiary education sector in South Africa. Firstly, there is the University of Pretoria (UP), which is the largest contact, residential university with approximately 38 500 residential students, versus Unisa (University of South Africa), the largest distance, non-residential university, with approximately 250 000 students. The tuition cost and fees per student for UP will be markedly higher than in the case of Unisa because of on-campus class attendance with lecturers for all courses/modules, multiple group sessions limiting class sizes, and other more customised learning assistance found in laboratories and practical class sessions, for example. Unisa is not limited to a fixed geographic region because of compulsory on-campus classes, it accepts students from across South Africa country and even worldwide, it offers distance education with hard copy study materials with no or minimal lecturer contact. Unisa can therefore offer a quality tertiary education package to students far afield at much lower tuition fees per student. UP is good at what it does through its particular tuition model. Unisa, similarly, has been exceptionally good for over 130 years at non-contact, distance education and should not try to emulate residential universities in offering high-cost, customised tuition activities, since, inherently, its operational processes are not designed for these and cannot be modified superficially for such a different tuition model.

activities firsthand or directly (for example a designer's wedding dress shop). This type of operation must be able to deal with short waiting tolerance compared to low- or zero-visibility operations, with which the customer/client does not have much contact (for example a larger departmental clothes store) or no contact at all (for example catalogue clothing retailer).

The implications of these four Vs of operations can be quite significant in terms of the cost of creating the products and services. On the one hand, high volume, low variety, low variation and low customer/client contact operational processes keep processing costs down. On the other hand, low volume, high variety, high variation and high customer/client contact operational processes generally have a "cost penalty". See the example in the Example box.

20.4 The classification of operational processes for manufacturers and service providers

In section 20.3 an operations management model applicable to both the manufacture of products and the provision of services was depicted. However, the nature of the transformation processes (operational processes) differs because of the different types of products and/or services manufactured and/or provided. Such differences are of special importance when the management of a particular operational process is considered, because certain management techniques and methods are suitable for application only in certain types of operations processes.

In the following two sections, a classification system of the operational

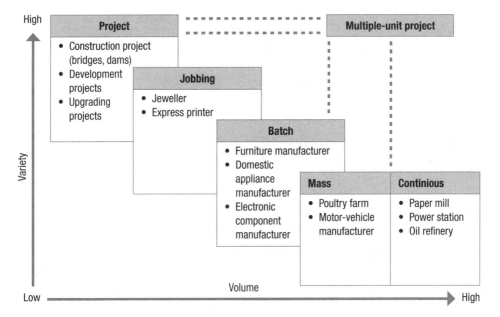

Figure 20.4: Classification of operational processes: Manufacturers

Source: Adapted from Slack, N., Chambers, S., Harland, C., Harrison, A. & Johnston, R., *Operations management*, Pearson Education (UK), 1995, p. 141.

processes for both manufacturers and service providers is depicted.

20.4.1 Classification of operational processes for manufacturers

In manufacturing, the most common classification system classifies different operational processes according to scope (volume of output) and variety of products. Thus, a business that produces a product in large volumes with little variety (for example a manufacturer of bricks) will be placed in a different category from a business that manufactures small volumes of a large variety of products (for example a clothing manufacturer). According to such a classification system (see figure 20.4 on page 507), five main categories are identified. Each is discussed with the aid of practical examples.[11]

- **Project processes.** Projects represent operational processes that are highly individual and unique, but which are normally tackled on a large scale. It can take a project team months or even years to complete such projects. Examples are construction projects (such as the building or upgrading of an airport, bridge, highway or office and shopping complex), a development programme for a new car or the upgrading of an assembly line. Each project produces an output volume of one (the volume is therefore low), but a wide variety of types of projects can be undertaken (variety is therefore high). Two such large projects currently being planned in South Africa are the hosting the 2010 FIFA World Cup™ for soccer and the construction of the Gautrain (a high-speed commuter railway line between Johannesburg, Midrand and Pretoria).
- **Jobbing processes.** Jobbing normally represents operational processes conducted on a small scale with a low volume output. The nature of the work is the same throughout, but the specific requirements differ from one task to the next. Examples

are the process whereby a goldsmith manufactures jewellery (each piece of jewellery is usually unique and takes the unique design preferences of the client into consideration) and the printing of wedding invitations at a printing works (two wedding invitations for two different couples are usually not exactly the same in all respects). Thus, an important feature of these types of processes is the great or wide variety, though small volumes, of products supplied by the business.

- **Batch processes** (also referred to as **job lot** or **lot** production). Batch production appears to be nearly the same as jobbing but it does not have the same degree of variety. A limited range of products is thus manufactured by the business and production occurs in lots or batches. Examples here are the manufacture of domestic appliances such as toasters, grills, irons, and fridges (by Defy); TV, video, DVD and sound equipment (by Samsung); or clothing or garments (by Jeep).
- **Mass processes**. Mass production is a well-known term for the production of products in high volumes but with relatively low (or narrow) variety. While there may be some variants of the product itself (for instance the colour, engine size, optional equipment offered by motor vehicle manufacturers BMW, Mercedes-Benz, VW, or Toyota), the basic process of production is the same, repetitive in nature, largely predictable and easier to manage than both jobbing and batch processes.
- **Continuous processes.** Continuous production is a further step beyond mass production because the volumes are even greater but there is very little variety in the type of product. Such processes provide the same product on a continuous basis without a break other than the occasional need for maintenance or plant upgrading. Examples are a wheat mill (Sasko), an electricity generation utility (Eskom), a cement manufacturer (PPS cement), a

petrochemical refinery (Sasol) and a paper manufacturer (Sappi).

20.4.2 Classification of operational processes for service providers

The same classification system as that depicted for manufacturers can be used for service providers (one based on output volume and output variety).[12] Three main categories are identified, according to such a classification system (see figure 20.5).

Each will be further explained on the basis of practical examples.

- **Professional services.** Professional services represent operational processes provided on a high client-contact basis, where the client himself or herself is usually present within the service process for a considerable period of time. The nature of the service provided takes the specific needs of clients into consideration and is therefore more people oriented than equipment oriented. Because of the client-focused nature of these

services, the extent (volume) of presentation is low, while the variety of services that can be provided is high. Examples of professional services (referred to as such because of the formal academic qualifications and registration that such professional practitioners need to obtain) include the services of dentists, attorneys, auditors, doctors and management consultants.

- **Service shops.** Service shops represent operational processes where the characteristics of service provision fall between those of professional services and those of mass services. Hence, there is a fair amount of client contact and services are standardised to a certain extent, but the services are also adapted to accommodate the unique needs of clients (there is more variety than there is in mass services). The number of clients served is also greater (the volume is more than, primarily, the one-to-one basis of professional services). Examples of service shops are banks, hotels, beauty salons and retail stores.

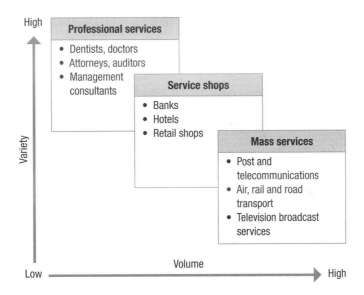

Figure 20.5: Classification of operational processes: Service providers

Source: Adapted from Slack, N., Chambers, S., Harland, C., Harrison, A. & Johnston, R., *Operations management*, Pearson Education (UK), 1995, p. 143.

- **Mass services.** Mass services represent operational processes in which many client transactions take place with limited client contact, and in which the nature of the services provided is largely standardised (variety is therefore low). These services are usually equipment oriented and are provided on a larger scale (volume is therefore high). Examples of mass services include post and telecommunication services, air and rail transport services, and television broadcast services.

In the above discussion, a classification system based on the scope (or volume) and variety of products and/or services for both manufacturers and service providers was depicted. Sometimes, in practice, it is difficult to place a specific operations process encountered in one category, or even to make a clear distinction between manufacturing and service provision. The example in the box below illustrates such a case.

Applying the concept: Classification of a restaurant

Pachalla is a restaurant serving à la carte meals. Is it a manufacturer or a service provider? Obviously, food is prepared, but clients are also served. The nature of the activities that have to be undertaken (for example the labour intensity thereof and the need for the client to be present) corresponds to that of a service provider (see the differences between the characteristics of products and services, as listed in table 20.3. On the strength of this, the restaurant is classified as a service provider. However, since there is a certain amount of standardisation (a fixed menu is normally used), it can also be placed in the category of a service shop.

20.5 Summary

The aim of this chapter was to introduce operations management. The nature and definitions of operations management were first examined, followed by the presentation of an operations management model. This model comprises three components, namely the operations management strategies and objectives and the management activities that influence the transformation process to produce outputs.

In conclusion, classification systems for the operations processes for both manufacturers and service providers were presented. These systems are based on a classification of the operations processes on the basis of scope (volume) and the variety of products or services manufactured or provided. The classification system for manufacturers has five main categories (project, jobbing, batch, mass and continuous systems), while the classification system for service providers contains three main categories (professional services, service shops and mass services).

 Key terms

Batch operation/process	Operations objectives
Continuous operation/ process	Operations strategy
Flexibility	Outputs
Gross domestic product	Productivity
Inputs	Project operation/process
Jobbing operation/process	Quality
Lead time	Transformation
Mass operation/process	

? Questions for discussion

Reread the case study about Variphone at the beginning of this chapter and answer the questions below.

1. Do you agree with the argument that a high-quality and "very sophisticated product" will be dependent on a similar "sophisticated" operation?

2. The case study about Variphone should make it clear that a quality product may not necessarily guarantee success. What are the weaknesses of Variphone? What mistakes did Variphone make?

3. Variphone pursued several performance objectives. Its product has a long list of special features and its operation seems to offer a few as well. Many of the features (fitment, seal test and calibration) are dependent on a service. The product may mean nothing without these. Do you agree that Variphone's business is primarily offering a service rather than a product?

4. With reference to the transformation process or model of operations management, it is clear that Variphone has two primary processes – the professional service of impression-taking and fitments and the manufacture of the HPD (physical transformation of the soft silicon material into the acrylic HPD). Distinguish between transformed resources and transforming resources for both transformation processes.

5. What are the main operational differences between Variphone and Noise Clipper?

6. How important are effective operations for business reputation?

References

1. Slack, N., Chambers, S. & Johnston, R., *Operations management*, 4th edition, Pitman Publishing, London, 2004, p. 7.

2. Krüger, L.P., The changing role of production and operations management: Moving towards the ultimate in robotic manufacturing and service provision, University of South Africa, Pretoria, Unpublished inaugural lecture, 2000, p. 6.

3. Slack, N., et al., *op cit.*, p. 6.

4. Schonberger, R.J. & Knod, E.M. (Jr), *Meeting customers' demands*, 7th edition, McGraw-Hill, New York, 2001, pp. 17–18.

5. Slack, N., et al., *op cit.*, p. 51.

6. Krajewski, L.J. & Ritzman, L.P., *Operations management: Processes and value chains*, 7th edition, Pearson, Upper Saddle River, NJ, 2005, p. 15–18.

7. Krüger, L.P., *Strategic manufacturing priorities for South African manufacturers*, Centre for Business Management, University of South Africa, Pretoria, Published research report, 1996, pp. 1–117.

8. Krüger, L.P., "Strategic manufacturing priorities for South African manufacturers: The need to shift emphasis and improve on current performance levels", *South African Journal of Business Management*, Vol. 28, No. 4, 1997, pp. 138–146.

9. Slack, N., et al., *op cit.*, pp. 13–14.

10. *Ibid.*, pp. 20–25.

11. *Ibid.*, pp. 111–116.

12. *Ibid.*, pp. 116–119.

CHAPTER

21

OPERATIONS MANAGEMENT: ACTIVITIES, TECHNIQUES AND METHODS

The purpose of this chapter

This chapter deals with the three main activities of operations management, namely operations design, operations planning and control, and operations improvement. Selected tools, techniques and methods that can be used with these operational activities are also introduced.

Learning outcomes

The content of this chapter will enable learners to:
- Identify the aspects involved in operations design
- Explain how these aspects need to be

managed in order to develop an effective design for products and services, including the operational processes for their manufacture or delivery
- Identify the aspects involved in operations planning and control
- Explain how these aspects need to be managed to manufacture or deliver products and services efficiently that the business will supply to the market
- Identify the aspects involved in operations improvement
- Explain how these aspects need to be managed in order to provide a more effective and efficient operation for the manufacture of products and delivery of services for competitive advantage

21.1 Introduction

In chapter 20 an operations management model was introduced. This model among others comprises the operations management strategies and objectives, the inputs (resources and aids) as well as the operations management activities that influence the transformation process in order to provide outputs. The

operations management activities (referred to hereafter only as activities) are the direct responsibility of operations managers.

This chapter deals specifically with the three activities of operations managers, namely operations design, operations planning and control, and operations improvement. Certain tools, techniques and methods that operations managers can use to perform these activities "better" will also be discussed. In this context, "better" means with **greater efficiency** and **greater effectiveness**.

The case study below provides an illustration of how a local company (with its parent company in Germany) can design, plan and control, and improve its operational processes so that it can compete against some of the best car manufacturing plants in the world.

Case study

BMW (South Africa) (Pty) Ltd: A world-class operation found at the BMW World Plant Rosslyn, Pretoria

BMW (South Africa) was established in 1973 when it acquired Praetor Monteerders, which at the time assembled BMWs at its factory in Rosslyn, Pretoria. It was then the first BMW plant to be established outside Germany away from the parent company, BMW AG, Munich. Over the past thirty-plus years, BMW (South Africa) has moved from operating a limited vehicle production plant merely assembling vehicles with few customisation possibilities for the local market to a world class plant capable of producing highly customised cars for customers across the globe. BMW's billion rand investment in the Rosslyn plant during the mid-1990s paved the way for the upgrade of the production facility into one of the most modern in the world and brought the particular plant itself in line with other BMW plants across the world. This earned the local plant the "right" to be known, since 1996, as "BMW World Plant Rosslyn". BMW World Plant Rosslyn is capable of producing up to 60 000 units per annum, a large percentage, up to 80%, directly destined for the export market – going to such countries as the USA, Japan, Australia, New Zealand, the United Kingdom, Taiwan, Singapore, China (Hong Kong) and Iran.

BMW process technology

The production of BMWs takes a car through different "shops" where specific technology is applied to ensure a quality car is delivered to a customer. The process starts at "Body-in-White Shop", where different body parts are assembled into a body shell. From here it moves to the "Paint Shop", where it is painted according to the customer's order. Finally, the painted body goes to the "Assembly Shop" where parts are fitted as per specification requested by the customer.

BMW quality

The aim is to deliver world-class quality products to customers across the globe. All production operations are managed for delivering uncompromising, optimum quality. Each and every process involved in manufacturing the car must be checked for process capability and inspections are implemented where required. Parts fitted into the car are assessed every step of the way from supplier to plant and the supplier's production facilities are audited against process conformity at pre-determined intervals. In 1994 BMW (South Africa) was the only local motor manufacturer to achieve ISO 9002 certification. This certification proves the company is capable of producing cars and components within a quality management system that meets the highest international standards. In recognition of its commitment to quality, BMW World Plant Rosslyn has won numerous awards including the coveted and prestigious J.D. Power and Associates's European Gold Plant Award for best car from a European plant (the BMW World Plant Rosslyn is included in this section for evaluation purposes), in June 2002* and the J.D. Power award for Best South African Manufacturing Plant, in 2004 and 2005.

BMW staff and employees

BMW (South Africa) invests up to 10% of the company's total annual payroll in various training and development initiatives encompassing technical, managerial and specialist training, as well as providing assistance for "higher education". Following the decision to manufacture the BMW 3 Series at BMW World Plant Rosslyn, the intensity of the training provided both locally and abroad contributed to the acquisition of the necessary skills required to build a quality product. The J.D. Power Gold Award of 2002 referred to above is testimony of the commitment to quality by all members of staff and employees at BMW (South Africa).* The demand for higher skills in the future will increase as the manufacturing processes of BMW products become more and more complex. Training interventions must thus continually increase in order to play an even greater role in meeting these demands for higher and more sophisticated skills. BMW (South Africa) was one of the first companies in South Africa to receive accreditation as an "Investor in People" which is an International Standard for a level of good practice for training and development. BMW (South Africa) actively supports, encourages and commits to the so-called People Brand Philosophy. which adopts the human resources vision and central theme that "The best people drive our business". Its people strategies are therefore geared towards the promotion of an enabling environment which seeks to foster a culture and promote processes that value the individual, reward performance, provide clear opportunities for growth and recognise potential in order to attract, develop and retain dynamic people.

BMW's environment and sustainability commitment

In BMW (South Africa)'s SHE Status Report of 2004/5, the safety, health and environmental practices of the company are communicated to the public. Briefly, the company believes it must act responsible in the use of technology, which encompasses questions with regard to the use of raw materials, the sources of energy, the entire question of mobility as relevant to a car manufacturer, including the demands for the protection of the environment, safety and health. The company feels it should be possible for humankind to enjoy mobility, expand knowledge by providing new insights on underlying considerations, and safeguard and improve health with a better quality of life without damaging or impairing the planet. Taking into consideration that the cars being designed in the development departments will be on the market in three or four years time and continue to be manufactured for a further seven or eight years, and also that the vehicles produced today will continue to be used for a further eleven to twelve years, decisions made today have an effect over almost 25 years and this does not even consider the long-term repercussions of irresponsible waste disposal.

BMW World Plant Rosslyn virtual tour

A "virtual tour" of the plant can be taken. The tour contains panoramic views by web camera (from the website referred to below) of the following production processes and specific sections at the BMW World Plant Rosslyn: assembly overhead, door assembly, final line, trimming, pre-trim: C-hangers, painted body bank, body shop, manual welding station, sealer line, and polishing line.

*The authors of the two chapters on operations management in this book were actively involved with quality training (by lecturing on the Unisa, Centre for Business Management [CBM] six-month course in Basics of Total Quality Management) at the BMW World Plant Rosslyn at the time the J.D. Power Gold Award was bestowed. Remembering this momentous event – a local car manufacturing plant being ranked first above European plants for quality, including beating its parent company in Munich, Germany, which was placed second with the silver award – the authors felt that the following stood out:

- The commitment of BMW's management to quality training
- Dedicated individuals at the plant who encouraged all to be part of the quality drive
- The emergence of a quality culture through the combined efforts of management and staff
- The eventual enthusiasm of the employees on the assembly lines to learn more about quality management in general and apply it in their specific work practices.

Source: BMW (South Africa) (Pty) Ltd website: http://www.bmw.co.za. Material and information used from website by kind permission from BMW (South Africa) (Pty) Ltd March 2007.

21.2 Operations design

21.2.1 The nature of operations design

The design of a product, for example a motor vehicle, entails far more than merely determining its physical appearance in terms of shape, colour and finish. It also includes the design of the operational processes for manufacturing the different components of the motor vehicle itself, such as the body assembly, paintwork and composition of the chassis and engine. In the design of a service, too, for example a 24-hour security monitoring and reaction service, the processes (or systems) should be designed to execute the particular service according to promise (or specification). This may include an alarm system, control room, security personnel, and reaction vehicles.

As was stated above, operations design entails two interdependent aspects, namely:
- The design of products and services (also referred to as **product or service design**)
- The design of operational processes to manufacture or provide these products or services (also referred to as **process design**)

It stands to reason that operations management, as well as other functional managers, are actively involved in the design of the business's products and/or services. The design process will be briefly explained as a whole, followed by a more in-depth discussion of the operations manager's role.

Figure 21.1 on page 516 provides a broad framework of the different activities involved in operations design.

The primary aim of **operations design** is to provide products and/or services and the corresponding **operational processes**, so that the needs of customers/clients can always be satisfied in the best possible way.

Obviously, design, as an operations activity, helps to achieve the operations management objectives with regard to quality, cost, lead time, adaptability, variability and service (see section 20.3.1). The designers of a product such as a fridge, for example, will endeavour to design an aesthetically acceptable product that will satisfy customers' expectations in that it should function well, be reliable during its lifetime, and be quick and easy to manufacture. The design should also be such that errors in the manufacturing process are kept to a minimum so that manufacturing costs can be kept at

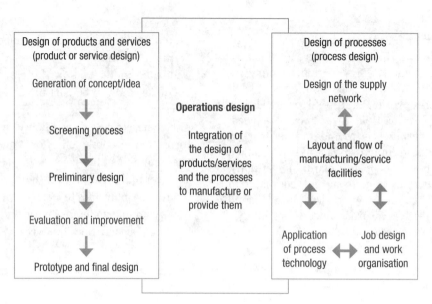

Figure 21.1: The nature of operations design

Source: Slack, N., Chambers, S., Harland, C. & Johnston, R., *Operations management*, 4th edition, Pearson Education (UK), 2004, p. 95.

a reasonable level. Designers of services (for example a telephone service) are also expected to construct the service in such a way that clients' expectations are met and the service can be rendered within the operational ability of the business and be affordable.

Most, if not all, products or services encountered in the market today first have their origin as a vague idea or concept put forward as a suitable solution to a perceived need of a customer/client. The idea or concept is refined over a period of time and, in the process, more and more detailed information is attached to the idea or concept. Ultimately, there is sufficient information to put together a specification for the product or service, and the process for the manufacture or provision thereof.

21.2.2 The design of products and services

Although the operations manager is usually not solely (and directly) responsible for the design of a product or service, he or she is, however, indirectly responsible for providing the information and advice on which the ultimate success of the development and manufacture or provision of the product or service depends.

21.2.2.1 The competitive advantage of good design

The **design of a product or service** begins and ends with the **customer/client**. Initially, products and services are designed with a view to satisfying the needs of the customer/client in the best possible way. If products and services are well designed, produced and provided, so that the expectations of customers/clients are realised or even exceeded, the business's competitive position will be reinforced through increased sales of these products and services. For example, the design and production of the well-known Venter trailers is a good example of how a competitive advantage can be gained in the market. Other manufacturers have also entered the market, but Venter is still the market leader.

21.2.2.2 The composition (or components) of products and services

A **product** or **service** is broadly defined as anything that can be offered to a customer/client in order to satisfy his or her needs. More specifically, however, all products or services consist of three interdependent components,[1] namely an idea or concept, a package, and a process. Each of these will now briefly be discussed.

(a) Idea or concept

In chapter 14, brief mention was made of the fact that when customers/clients buy a product or service, they do not buy only the physical product or intangible service – they in fact also buy a set of expected benefits which they deem will satisfy their needs. Hence, the product or service should meet all their expectations. For example, when someone buys a product such as a new car, not only the car itself is bought but also all the expected benefits that go with it, such as safety, outstanding road-holding ability, good reliability, and a possible high value at resale. The same applies when a service, for example medical treatment at a hospital, is purchased. The patient expects a set of benefits such as good medical care, the timeous receipt of prescribed medication, and a secure and peaceful environment so that he or she can recover from the illness. In both cases the set of expected benefits is referred to as the **product or service concept**. Thus, when the product or service is designed, the operations manager should understand exactly what the customer/client expects from the business. This knowledge and insight is of vital importance to ensure that the transformation process provides the "right" product or service concept.

(b) Package composition of products and services

Concepts involve a package of products or services. The concept of product usually refers to a tangible physical object like a car, dishwasher or article of clothing, while the concept of service indicates an intangible object such as a visit to the theatre, a hairdressing salon or a night club. However, as was mentioned in chapter 20, it is often difficult to make a clear distinction between these two concepts. Take, for example, a new car. The physical vehicle is clearly a tangible object, but the other benefits – such as a guarantee and the regular repairs at scheduled times – are an intangible service. A meal in a restaurant comprises physical products such as food and drink, but also service in that food is prepared and served at the tables, and even the atmosphere in the restaurant plays a role here. Thus, regardless of whether a product or service is designed, the package comprises a combination or "bundle" of products and services. It is this package that the customer/client in fact purchases.

Two further aspects should be kept in mind in the composition of a service package:

- Services cannot be inventoried. While goods or products can be kept in inventory until needed, services cannot be so kept. Services are, rather, "acts that are performed at a specific point in time". An example is an aeroplane ticket for a specific flight to a particular destination on a particular day and time (for example Flight SA 260 from Johannesburg to Frankfurt on 8 December 2007 at 20h20). If not used then – the ticket "lapses" and is wasted.
- Services usually involve direct interaction between the customer/client and the process.[2] Services require the customer/client to be present in the performance of the act of the service at a specific point (place and time). While the degree of customer/client contact may vary for different services, at some point the client must be present to receive the "act of service" – for example having a haircut at a hair salon (high contact) or posting a letter at the post office (low contact).

(c) Process for creating the package

A process is necessary to create the products and services. As was stated earlier in section 21.2.1, the design of the products and/or services takes place in conjunction with the design of the processes required to manufacture or provide them. The design of processes needed to manufacture products and/or provide services will be discussed in section 21.2.3. At this stage of the discussion, however, it is necessary to bear in mind that it is this operational process that creates the products and/or services, combines them into a product or service concept, and makes them available to customers/clients in order to satisfy their needs.

Critical thinking

New products and/or services are essential for both the emergence of new businesses and for the continued existence of many others. Consider, for example, the relatively new product now known as a cellphone (or mobile, as it is referred to in some other countries). Some new businesses (for example Nokia) came into being as manufacturers of cellphones, but other existing businesses (for example Sony, Motorola and Samsung) merely expanded their product ranges. In South Africa, no service providers were initially in business at the time when cellphones first made their appearance, some new businesses (for example Vodacom, MTN, and later Cell C) were started.

Not only can new products and/or services be seen as catalysts for the emergence of new businesses, but they can also be considered as vital for continued success of others. Some countries (such as the USA and Germany) are better known for regularly offering new product/service ideas or new technologies and innovations, while others (such as Japan and China) are said to prefer, in the main, to copy others or apply technology already discovered. Some innovative new products/services are accredited to South Africans. Do you know which?

The following new product/service ideas received recognition from the MTN ScienCentre in Cape Town as the top ten inventions/discoveries by South Africans:

1. **Dolosse.** These concrete blocks, shaped like a sangoma's bones, are used on breakwaters to withstand wave action. First used in East London and later around the world, they were invented by harbour engineer Eric Merrifield and his team.

2. **Kreepy Krauly.** This automatic pool cleaning device was originally a South African invention but is now owned by an American company. Other pool cleaning devices which originated from South African include brand names like Aquanaut, Baracuda and Pool Ranger.

3. **Tellurometer.** This pioneering distance measuring device was invented by Trevor Wadley.

4. **Pratley's putty.** This is a two part clay-like mixture which bonds into a very hard and strong compound. It is the only South African invention to have gone to the moon. It was invented by K.G.M. Pratley.

5. **Lunar stick.** The oldest mathematical artefact in the world (35 000 years old), this was found in a cave in northern Zululand.

6. **Scheffel bogey.** This revolutionary train carriage wheel assembly is used in Austria and South Africa.

7. **Disa telephone.** This was the first push button telephone in the world. It was invented by Telkom technicians.

8. **Appletiser and Grapetiser.** These use a pure fruit juice recipe in sparkling gas format.

9. **Computicket.** This was the first computerised ticket-sales system in the world.

10. **Vibol fuel-saving exhaust system.** This is found all over the world.

Source: SA 2005–2006, *South Africa at a glance*, Greenside: Editors, Inc., p. 268–269.

21.2.2.3 The stages in the design of products and services

The ultimate result of the design of products and services is a full detailed specification of the product or service. To compile this specification, detailed information must be obtained about the above-mentioned three components of any product or service, namely information on the idea or concept (the form, function, aim and benefits of the design), the package (the composition of products and services required to support the idea or concept), and the process of creating the package (which determines the way in which the individual products and services of the package will be manufactured or provided).

To obtain this full detailed specification, it is necessary to first follow certain consecutive steps. Figure 21.1 on page 516 illustrates the stages in the design of a product and/or service from the stage where the idea or concept is generated to the stage where the final specification for the product or service is compiled. These stages briefly entail the following (note that not all businesses necessarily follow exactly all the stages indicated below and these may further also differ within a particular industry and between industries):

- **Idea or concept generation.** The first step in designing a product or service starts when different ideas for new products or service concepts are generated. New ideas for products or services come from within the business itself (for example the ideas of personnel or those from formal research and development programmes) or from outside the business (for example the ideas of customers/clients or competitors).
- **The screening process.** Not all ideas or concepts that are generated will necessarily develop into new products and services. Ideas or concepts are evaluated by means of a screening process based on certain design criteria such as feasibility (how difficult is it and what investment is needed?), acceptability (how worthwhile is it and what

return is possible?) and vulnerability (what could go wrong and what risks are there?). Each of the stages that follow progressively refine the original idea or concept up to the point where there is sufficient information and clarity for it to be turned into an actual product/service with an operational process to produce or deliver it. Such progressive reduction of the multitude of design options for a new product and service occurs through a process of elimination referred to as the "design funnel".[3] Overall, the purpose is to determine whether the new idea or concept will make a significant contribution to the product and/or service range of the business. Several functional management areas – such as marketing, operations and finance – are involved in the screening process of new ideas and concepts, and each may use different criteria in this process. The operations manager is responsible for operations-focused screening to determine whether the business has both the ability (people, skills and technology) and the capacity to produce or provide the ideas and/ or concepts.

- **Preliminary design.** Once the ideas and/ or the concepts generated by the particular functional management areas in the business are reduced to one or two potentially acceptable products or service concepts, the next step is the preliminary design of the product or service. The preliminary design is the first attempt to specify the composition of the components of the product or service to be included in the package and to identify the processes that will be necessary to produce or provide the product or service package.
- **Evaluation and improvement.** The aim of this step is to evaluate the preliminary design with a view to improving it and making the process of manufacture and/or provision less expensive and easier. Various techniques and methods can be used as aids in this step. Two of these techniques and methods will be described in section 21.2.2.4.

- **Prototype and final design.** The last step in the design of products and services is the development of a prototype of the product, or simulation of the service, in order to test it in the market. If the prototype, which is based on the improved preliminary design, is favourably received in the market, the final design and specifications of the product or service can be compiled.

21.2.2.4 Techniques and methods used during the product or service design

Various techniques and methods can be used during the design of products and services to execute this design activity in a better way.

While some techniques and methods – such as process flow diagrams, quality function deployment (QFD), value engineering, and Taguchi methods – are regarded as advanced subjects and are therefore not included in this book, we shall consider two relatively simple methods or techniques:

- **Basic product structures and bills of materials.** Basic product structures are used to determine precisely which components or parts are required for a specific product. A **bill of materials** reflects the quantity of each component or part (also known as item). The example below illustrates a product structure and bill of materials for a basic office chair.

Applying the concept: A product structure and bill of materials for a basic office chair

Basic product structure

Level 0	Office chair			
Level 1	Seat	Backrest	Armrest	Leg unit
Level 2	Base	Base		
	Upholstery	Upholstery		

Bill of material

Level 0	Level 1	Level 2	Quantity
Office chair			1
	Seat		1
		Base	0,25 m²: 0,50 × 0,50; 10 mm thick
		Upholstery	0,90 m²; 2/0,5 × 0,50 m + 4/0,50 × 0,20 m
	Back		1
		Base	0,25 m²: 0,50 × 0,50; 10 mm thick
		Upholstery	0,70 m²; 2/0,50 × 0,50 m + 4/0,50 × 0,10 m
	Armrest		2 (pre-moulded)
	Leg unit		1 (pre-manufactured)
			4 spoke with coaster wheels, centre strut and 2 adjustment levers
	Fastening	Screw	6 × 5 mm diameter × 50 mm long
		Liquid glue	20 ml

Applying the concept:
A simple flow chart for the manufacture of a basic office chair

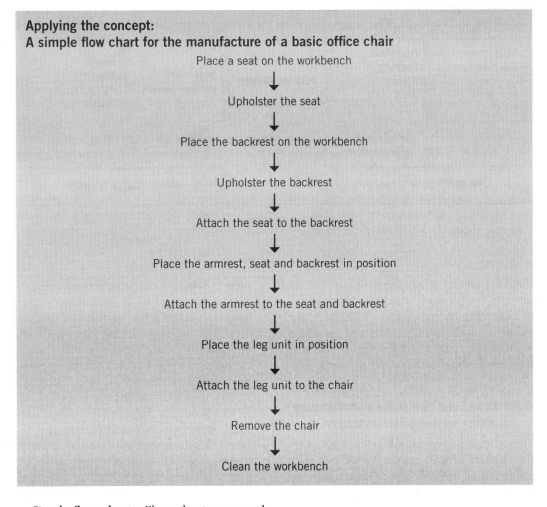

Place a seat on the workbench

↓

Upholster the seat

↓

Place the backrest on the workbench

↓

Upholster the backrest

↓

Attach the seat to the backrest

↓

Place the armrest, seat and backrest in position

↓

Attach the armrest to the seat and backrest

↓

Place the leg unit in position

↓

Attach the leg unit to the chair

↓

Remove the chair

↓

Clean the workbench

- **Simple flow charts.** Flow charts are used to identify the main elements of a specific process. The example below illustrates a simple flow chart for the manufacture of a basic office chair.

21.2.3 The design of operational processes

The design of operational processes to manufacture products or provide services is just as important as the design of the products or services themselves. Without both good product and service design and a good process design it is impossible to develop, manufacture or provide a successful product or service.

21.2.3.1 The design of the supply network

No operational process exists in isolation – it is part of a greater, integrated supply network.[4] Besides the specific operational process itself, the supply network also includes the suppliers of materials or services, as well as intermediaries and final customers/clients. The example in the accompanying box illustrates a supply network for a poultry farmer.

In the design of a particular operational process, it is important for the entire supply network to be taken into consideration. This enables the operations manager to determine precisely what the inputs for the specific operational process are, as well as the

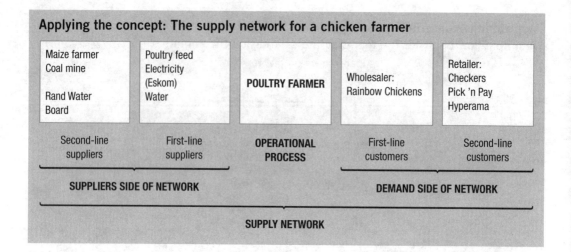

Applying the concept: The supply network for a chicken farmer

Maize farmer Coal mine Rand Water Board	Poultry feed Electricity (Eskom) Water	POULTRY FARMER	Wholesaler: Rainbow Chickens	Retailer: Checkers Pick 'n Pay Hyperama
Second-line suppliers	First-line suppliers	OPERATIONAL PROCESS	First-line customers	Second-line customers

SUPPLIERS SIDE OF NETWORK   DEMAND SIDE OF NETWORK

SUPPLY NETWORK

customer/client needs that have to be satisfied. Such a study also helps the business to determine its competitive position in the supply network, identify significant interfaces in the supply network, and reflect on its long-term involvement in the supply network.

21.2.3.2 Layout and flow of the manufacturing and/or service provision facility

The layout of the operations facility determines the physical arrangement of resources such as machines, equipment and personnel used in a particular transformation process. The layout of a manufacturing or service provision facility is usually the first characteristic of an operational process to be observed because it determines the physical form and appearance of the facility. At the same time, the layout determines the way in which resources such as materials, information and customers/clients flow through the transformation process. Both the **layout and flow** of an operations facility are of particular importance since small changes in the placement of machines and the flow of material and people can greatly influence the operational process in terms of cost and efficiency.

The layout of a manufacturing/service facility entails the following three steps:

- **Step 1: Selecting the process type.** The first step in the layout of an operations facility involves selecting the appropriate process type. The different process types for both manufacturers and service providers were identified in section 20.4. The process types in manufacturers are project, jobbing, batch, mass and continuous processes. In service providers they are professional services, mass services and service shops.
- **Step 2: Selecting the basic layout type.** Once the appropriate process type has been selected, the next step involves selecting a basic layout type. Four basic layout types,[5] which depict the general form and arrangement of operations facilities, can be identified. The box on the next page illustrates the four basic layout types. These entail:
  - The **fixed position layout**, in which the product cannot be shifted on account of its size, shape or location. The resources for transformation (equipment, machinery and people) are taken to the receiver of the processing, which is static, for example a construction site (such as a soccer stadium) or a shipyard.
  - The **process layout** (also termed **flexible-flow layout**), in which similar processes (or operations) are grouped together into

Applying the concept: Four basic layout types

Fixed position layout

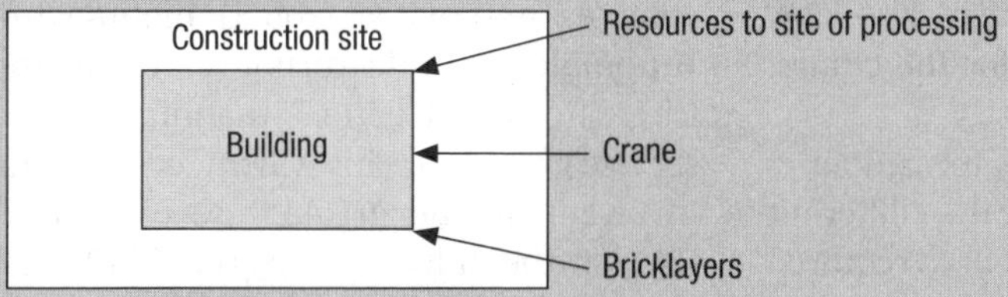

Construction site

Building

Resources to site of processing

Crane

Bricklayers

Product layout or Line-flow layout

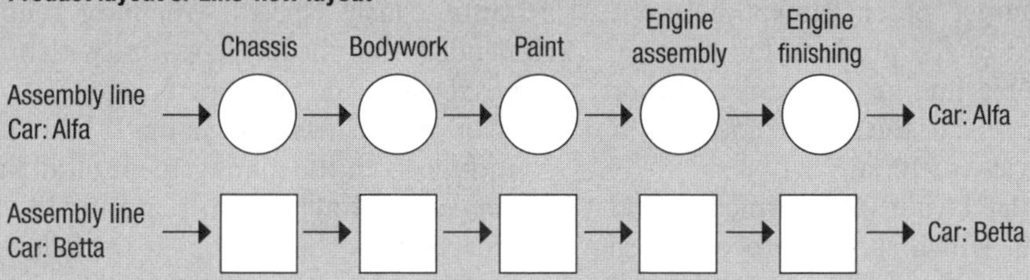

Chassis   Bodywork   Paint   Engine assembly   Engine finishing

Assembly line
Car: Alfa → ○ → ○ → ○ → ○ → ○ → Car: Alfa

Assembly line
Car: Betta → □ → □ → □ → □ → □ → Car: Betta

Process layout or Flexible-flow layout

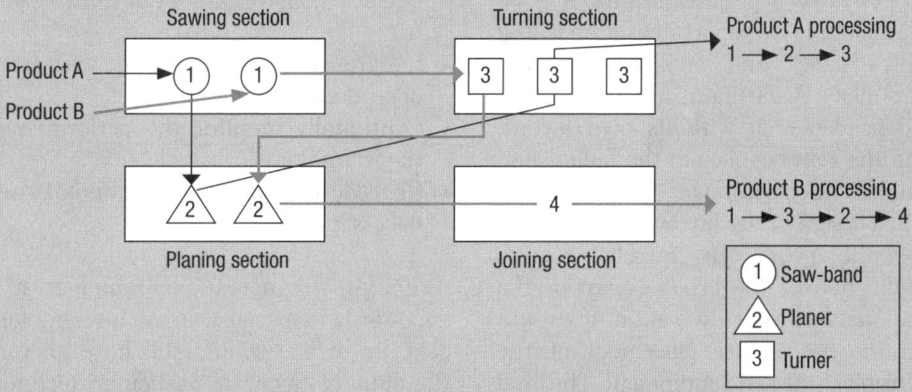

Sawing section

Turning section

Product A processing
1 → 2 → 3

Product A → ① ①

3 3 3

Product B →

Planing section

△2 △2

Joining section

4

Product B processing
1 → 3 → 2 → 4

① Saw-band

△2 Planer

3 Turner

Cellular layout or Hybrid layout

Department store floor plan

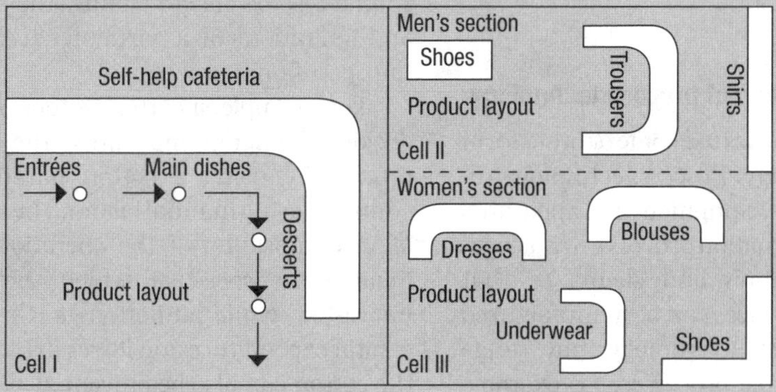

Self-help cafeteria

Entrées → ○   Main dishes → ○

Product layout

Cell I

Desserts

Men's section
Shoes
Product layout
Cell II

Trousers

Shirts

Women's section
Dresses   Blouses
Product layout
Underwear   Shoes
Cell III

sections. If a business manufactures not only basic office chairs, but also tables and desks, for example, such sections can be grouped together for the tasks – saw, plane, turn and attach – for the chairs, tables and desks.

- The **product layout** (also termed **line-flow layout**), in which the different processes or operations are required to manufacture or provide a specific product or service and are arranged in consecutive order. Thus the layout is adapted to the product, for example an assembly line for motor vehicles or television sets, or the service counters in a self-service cafeteria.

- The **cellular layout** (also termed **hybrid layout**), in which specific processes are placed in a cell, and the particular cell itself is then arranged according to either a process or a product layout. A good example here is a department store selling men's, ladies' and children's clothing. The men's department functions as an independent cell with its own layout, and the same applies to the ladies' and children's departments.

• **Detailed design of the layout.** The selection of a basic layout type merely provides an indication of the broad layout of the operations facility. However, it does not determine the precise placement of the various machines and equipment. The final step in the layout of a manufacturing or service facility therefore entails the detailed design of the layout.

21.2.3.3 The application of process technology

All operations processes use some or other form of **process technology**. Process technology refers to the machines, equipment and apparatus used in the transformation process to transform materials, information and clients so that products and/or services can be manufactured or provided. Process technology may range from relatively simple processes, for example

a basic extraction process such as digging a hole for a new pipeline with a machine, to highly complex and sophisticated systems, such as automated (robot) manufacturing. Automated manufacturing represents the future of "overall better" manufacturing and service provision. This will involve less human involvement and greater use of robotics to develop the "ultimate machine" that will be able to deliver extraordinary high levels of error-free goods and services (quality), nearly instantaneously (speed), whenever required (dependability), cheaply (cost) and with much-reduced waste and greater efficiency.[6]

The operations manager has to be involved continuously in the management of all facets of process technology. To perform this task effectively, he or she needs to do the following:

• Foresee how technology can improve a specific operational process
• Decide which technology or technologies to use
• Integrate the new technology with existing operations activities
• Continually monitor the performance of the technology
• Upgrade or replace the technology when necessary

Although the operations manager is not necessarily a specialist in each technological field, he or she should still have an understanding of what a particular technology essentially entails, and how the technology performs the particular function. He or she should also be able to identify the advantages and limitations of a particular technology in the operational process.

For example, a cotton farmer will have to decide whether to mechanise the harvesting process by using a cotton harvester or to continue using manual labour. The advantages of mechanisation of the operational process include the speed at which the cotton is harvested, while limitations such as greater capital expenditure and losses in the quality of the cotton can also be prevented.

21.2.3.4 Job design and work organisation

Operations management focuses not only on the technologies, systems, procedures and facilities in a business (the so-called non-human component), but also on people's involvement in the operations activity itself. The way in which human resources are managed in a business has a fundamental effect on the effectiveness of the operations function.

Since most people who are appointed in a business are usually active in the operations function, this places a huge responsibility on the shoulders of the operations manager as far as leadership in the business and development of employees are concerned. The design of jobs (or **job design**) is of vital importance in operations management because it determines how workers perform their various daily tasks.

Work study is a scientific approach that can be used to great effect in job design and work organisation. It refers to the application of different techniques to study systematically all the factors influencing the people in the work environment in order to improve the execution of tasks, in terms both of efficiency and effectiveness. Two work study techniques often encountered in the literature are method study and work measurement.[7] **Method study** entails the systematic recording and critical investigation of present and proposed work methods, with a view to the development and application of easier and more effective methods in an effort to reduce costs. **Work measurement** entails the application of techniques designed to determine how long it takes a trained and qualified worker to do a specific job at a fixed level of performance. The components of work study are illustrated diagrammatically in figure 21.2.

21.2.3.5 Techniques and methods used in process design

Various techniques and methods can be applied in the design of processes to perform the design activity better. The basic weighted-scoring method for alternative location decisions, the centre-of-gravity method for alternative location decisions, break-even analysis, production flow analysis (PFA) and line-balancing techniques are examples of such techniques and methods, but are regarded as advanced subjects and are therefore not included in this book.

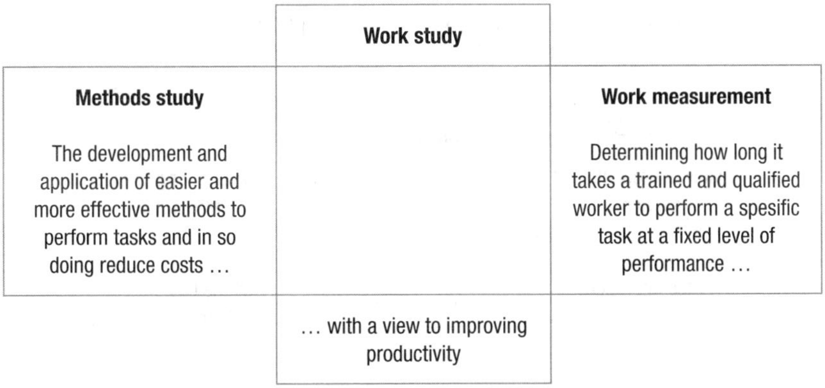

Work study		
Methods study		**Work measurement**
The development and application of easier and more effective methods to perform tasks and in so doing reduce costs ...		Determining how long it takes a trained and qualified worker to perform a spesific task at a fixed level of performance ...
	... with a view to improving productivity	

Figure 21.2: Components of work study

Source: Slack, N., Chambers, S., Harland, C. & Johnston, R., *Operations management*, 4th edition, Pearson Education (UK), 2004, p. 294.

21.3 Operations planning and control

21.3.1 The nature of operations planning and control process

In section 21.2 design was examined as one of the activities of operations management. It should be clear that this design activity determines the physical form and structure of the operations process. Within the limits imposed by the design of the operations process, however, this process now has to be put into operation or be activated. This is done by means of operations planning and control. **Operations planning and control** focuses on all the activities required to put the operational process into action efficiently on a continuous basis so that products can be manufactured and/or services provided to meet the needs of customers/clients.

In contrast to operations design, which may be regarded as a "passive" activity primarily aimed at determining the broad limits of the operational process, operations planning and control is an activating activity to start "physically" the operational process so that products can be manufactured and/or services rendered. In the activation of the operational process, the operations manager is responsible for ensuring that the operations

management objectives of quality, cost, lead time, adaptability, variability and service (see chapter 20, section 20.3.1) are pursued and achieved.

Operations planning and control broadly endeavours to reconcile two entities. Firstly, on the supply side, there are the products and/or services manufactured or provided in the operational process, and secondly, on the demand side, there are the specific needs of actual and potential customers/clients for products and/or services. Planning and control activities are aimed at reconciling the provision ability of the operations facility with the demand for specific products and/or services. Figure 21.3 illustrates the nature of operations planning and control in this process of reconciliation.

Reconciling the supply of products and/or services with the demand for them by means of planning and control activities occurs in terms of three dimensions, namely:

- Volume (or quantity)
- Timing
- Quality

The dimensions of volume (quantity of products and/or services) and timing (when the products and/or services have to be manufactured or provided) will be briefly explained. The quality dimension will be discussed later in section 21.3.4.

Figure 21.3: The nature of operations planning and control

Source: Adapted from Slack, N., Chambers, S., Harland, C. & Johnston, R., *Operations management*, 4th edition, Pearson Education (UK), 2004, p. 323.

To reconcile the volume and timing dimensions with each other, three different but integrated activities are performed. They entail the following:

- **Loading of tasks.** This refers to the volume or quantity of work allocated to a particular work centre. The available capacity of the operations process needs to be taken into consideration in the loading of work centres. For example, a medical practitioner will examine only one patient at a time in his or her consulting rooms, while the other patients wait in the waiting room.
- **Sequencing of tasks.** This refers to the sequence in which the tasks are performed. The sequence in which tasks are performed can be determined beforehand by the use of certain priority rules such as earliest deadline first, or first in first out. A commercial bank, for example, will serve the client who is in front of the queue first.
- **Scheduling of tasks.** This refers to the use of a detailed roster which indicates when a specific task should start and when it should be completed. Gantt charts are especially popular for planning and scheduling projects, and also give an indication of which tasks are late and which are at a more advanced stage than anticipated.

In this section, operations planning and control have been viewed from a general perspective. The operations manager, however, is responsible for the planning and control of specific operations activities, such as capacity and quality.

21.3.2 Capacity planning and control

Capacity planning and control focus on the provision of manufacturing and/or service capacity of a particular operations process. When a suitable balance is found between the available capacity and expected demand, it is possible that the business will have both satisfied customers/clients and acceptable profits. However, if the balance is "wrong" – that is, too much capacity with too little demand, or too little capacity with too much demand – the business is faced with a potentially disastrous situation. Businesses in this position may either sit with costly surplus capacity or possible lost sales opportunities. Because of the far-reaching impact capacity decisions may have on the business as a whole, capacity planning and control are of vital importance in operations management.

21.3.2.1 Definition of capacity

The term "capacity", as it is used in everyday parlance, usually refers to the fixed volume of, say, a fuel tank (50 litres) or the space in a parking garage (parking bays for, say, 500 vehicles). From an operations point of view, these scale or size dimensions are not sufficient, since capacity also has a time dimension. The example in the box illustrates this point.

Capacity in an operations process is defined as "the maximum level of value-added activity over a period of time that the process can achieve under normal operating circumstances".[8]

Applying the concept: Calculation of the total capacity of a parking garage

If there are 500 parking bays in a parking garage at a supermarket, 500 vehicles can park there at a given time. However, this is not the total capacity. If the parking garage and supermarket are open ten hours a day, and customers take on average an hour to do their shopping, the total capacity of the parking garage is actually 5 000 motor vehicles (number of parking bays × number of hours the parking garage is open ÷ average time one car is parked).

21.3.2.2 The nature of capacity planning and control

While long-term capacity is already determined during the design of the operations process (see section 21.2.3) in the medium and short terms, there is the possibility of adapting (or varying) the capacity of the operations process in accordance with changes in the demand for particular products and/or services. Thus, particular machinery or equipment can be used for longer periods each day, or workers can be asked to work overtime during peak periods.

Operations managers generally have to work with a demand forecast which is by no means completely accurate and, moreover, is sometimes subject to regular fluctuation. Quantitative data on the expected demand, and the required capacity to satisfy it, must be obtained by applying the following three steps:

- **Step 1: Determine the total demand and required capacity.** As a rule, the marketing function is responsible for determining the total demand by means of demand forecasting. Since this forecasting is an important input in determining the required capacity, the operations manager must at least have a knowledge of the basis of and rationale behind the demand forecasts. The way in which the required capacity will be determined depends on the nature of the products or services manufactured or provided. In standardised and repetitive products and services (high volume with little variety), capacity will be measured in terms of output – for example the number of television sets to be produced per week or the number of flights to be provided (flown) to Cape Town each day. In the case of less standardised and repetitive products and/or services (lower volume and more variety), capacity will instead be measured in terms of input. Examples here are the number of working hours per week of a goldsmith making items of jewellery or the number of beds available in a hospital per day.

- **Step 2: Identify alternative capacity plans.** The operations manager is expected to have alternative capacity plans in order to accommodate possible changes in demand. Three options are available[9] (in practice, operations managers usually use a mixture of the three alternatives, although one of them may be more dominant than the others):
  - A **level capacity plan** in which the capacity levels are kept constant and demand fluctuations are ignored
  - A **chase-demand plan** in which capacity levels are adjusted according to fluctuations in demand
  - A **demand-management plan** in which demand as such is adjusted to tie in with available capacity

- **Step 3: Choice of a particular capacity planning and control approach.** The final step entails choosing the most suitable capacity planning and control approach. Here an endeavour is made to choose an approach that will best reflect the business's specific circumstances. For example, a fruit packing plant will employ more temporary workers during the harvesting season to help with the packing of the fruit; supermarkets will also staff more checkout points at the end of the month when more customers tend to visit supermarkets.

21.3.2.3 Techniques and methods used during capacity planning and control

Various techniques and methods can be applied during capacity planning and control to execute this planning and control activity better. Two of these methods will be examined here: the moving average demand forecasting technique and the cumulative representations of demand and capacity. Other techniques and methods, such as exponential levelling, demand forecasting accuracy measures, and the application of the queuing theory are regarded as advanced topics and are therefore not included in this text.

Applying the concept:
Three-month moving average demand forecast for washing machines

Month	Demand (actual)	Demand (forecast)	Three-month moving average (calculation)
December 2007	480		
January 2008	530		
February 2008	520		
March 2008	540	510	480 + 530 + 520 = 1 530 ÷ 3 = 510
April 2008	590	530	530 + 520 + 540 = 1 590 ÷ 3 = 530
May 2008	–	550	520 + 540 + 590 = 1 650 ÷ 3 = 550

Based on a three-month moving average, the demand forecast for May 2008 is therefore 550 units of washing machines

- **Moving average demand forecasting technique.** Based on the availability of actual demand data over preceding periods, this technique can be used to forecast the demand for the following period. This technique is especially suitable for application to the demand for products or services that manifest a stable demand pattern over the short term. The example in the accompanying box shows the application of the technique in forecasting the demand for washing machines for May 2007. The disadvantage of this approach is that if the demand continues to grow, the predicted demand is always going to be too low. In the example in the box, the actual demand may be 610 but, according to the moving average, only 550 washing machines will be manufactured and there will therefore be a shortage.
- **Cumulative representations of demand and capacity.** This method can be used to evaluate graphically the effect of different capacity plans. The example below shows the application of the method for evaluating a capacity plan for a coal mine. It would appear from the example that the production of coal during the months January to April was greater than the demand for it, and that there was a

"surplus" production during this period. From April to July (autumn and winter) the demand for coal was greater than production – hence there was a period of "underproduction".

21.3.3 Inventory and supply chain planning and control

These days, **inventory and supply chain planning and control** are regarded as activities executed by a separate functional management area, namely purchasing management. However, since the inventory of materials and the purchase thereof have significant implications for the smooth functioning of the transformation process, for which the operations manager is mainly responsible, inventory is usually defined (from an operations management perspective) as all stored resources (material, information or clients) required for the smooth functioning of the operations process. The operations manager should therefore liaise closely with the purchasing manager in order to manage inventory levels optimally.

Since inventory and purchasing planning and control are discussed in chapters 22 and 23, it is not necessary to continue the discussion here.

Applying the concept:
Cumulative representation of demand and capacity for a coal mine

	Jan	Feb	March	April	May	June	July	Aug
Demand ('000 m³ coal)	50	75	75	200	200	100	100	100
Cumulative demand	50	125	200	400	600	700	800	900
Production ('000 m³ coal)	100	100	100	100	100	100	200	200
Cumulative production	100	200	300	400	500	600	800	1 000
Production surplus/(shortfall)	50	75	100	0	(100)	(100)	0	100

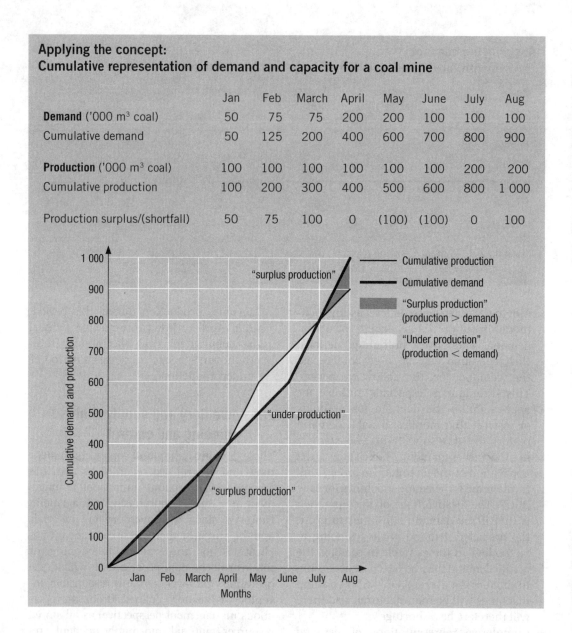

21.3.4 Quality planning and control

Nowadays, quality is regarded as being so important in many businesses that responsibility for it is not confined to the operations management function only. The basic premise of concepts such as **total quality management (TQM)** is that quality products and/or services can be manufactured only if the entire or total business contributes to the achievement of such an objective.

Quality is one of the main methods of adding value to products and/or services, and thereby obtaining a long-term competitive advantage. Better quality influences both factors that contribute to the business's profitability, namely income and cost. Income can be increased by more sales and greater market share, while costs can be reduced by lower repair and inspection costs and reduced wastage, inventory and processing time.

21.3.4.1 Definition of quality

Different definitions of quality are often advanced. Each of them stems from a different approach to or view of quality. Thus, quality has been defined as "the absolute best", "something flawless", "suitable for the purpose for which it was designed", "meeting a set of measurable characteristics" or "good value for money". From an operations management perspective, quality is defined as "consistent conformance to customers'/ clients' expectations".[10]

Operations management therefore defines quality in terms of what a customer/client expects of a particular product or service, while the customer/client sees quality in terms of his or her own perception of the product or service. This difference between expected quality (operations management) and per-

ceived quality (customer/client) is known as the **quality gap**. Operations management, in conjunction with the other functional management areas, should endeavour to eliminate any quality gaps.

21.3.4.2 The nature of quality planning and control

The aim of **quality planning and control** is to ensure that the products and/or services that are manufactured or provided should conform to or satisfy design specifications. The discussion of the design of the products and/or services (see section 21.2.2) stated that the ultimate goal of this activity is to establish specifications for products and/or services that will satisfy the needs of customers/clients. Hence, what exists here is a customer/client–marketing–design– operations cycle. This design cycle (see figure 21.4) can be further extended to include quality planning and control activities to ensure that products and/or services do in fact meet the design specifications.

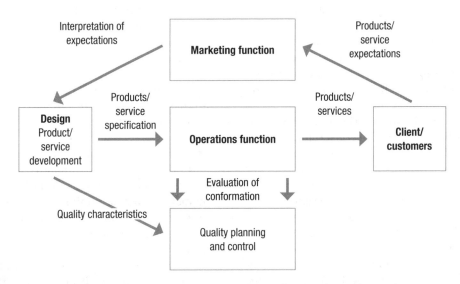

Figure 21.4: Extending the product/service design cycle for quality planning and control

Source: Slack, N., Chambers, S., Harland, C., & Johnston, R., *Operations management*, 4th edition, Pearson Education (UK), 2004, p. 601.

21.3.4.3 The steps in quality planning and control

Quality planning and control can be divided into six steps:

- **Step 1: Defining the quality characteristics of the product or service.** The design speci-fications for products/services are deter-mined in the design activity. The design speci-fications as such are not monitored by quality planning and control, but rather by the operations process that manufactures and/or provides the products or services, to ensure that the specifications are met. For the purposes of quality planning and control, it is necessary to define certain quality characteristics that relate directly to the design specifications for products or services. Quality characteristics that are often used include:
    - Functionality (performance ability)
    - Appearance (aesthetic attractiveness)
    - Reliability (continuous performance ca-pability)
    - Durability (total life expectancy)
    - Serviceability (reparability)
    - Contact (convenience of interaction)
    Thus, for example, a customer will expect an expensive video recorder to record and replay TV programmes clearly, to be aesthetically pleasing, and to have a long and reliable lifespan and problem-free maintenance and repair.
- **Step 2: Measuring the quality charac-teristics of the product or service.** For each individual product or service, the quality characteristics should be defined in such a way that they can in fact be measured and controlled. The different quality characteristics should thus be further broken down to make such measurement possible. For example, if the quality charac-teristic "functionality" of a motor-vehicle is measured, it can be broken down into the measurable dimensions of speed, acceleration, fuel consumption and road-holding ability. However, it is sometimes difficult to measure specific quality charac-teristics, such as the "friendliness" of the cabin crew of an airline. Here, an effort will instead be made to gauge passengers' perceptions of the friendliness of staff, in order to measure this. Indeed, every few months, SAA conducts such a survey among its regular passengers (SAA Voyager members).

- **Step 3: Setting standards for each quality characteristic of the product or service.** Once the operations manager has ascer-tained which quality characteristics are going to be measured, and how, the next step is to set specific quality standards against which the achievement of, and conformance with, the quality characteristic can be measured. Although most businesses strive for "absolutely per-fect" standards (for example "the quest for zero defect"), it is generally too expensive or unrealistic to expect a motor vehicle, for example, to last forever. Instead, realistic achievable standards are set, for example, that the motor vehicle will have an effective lifespan of ten years.

- **Step 4: Controlling quality against the set standards.** Once realistic standards for measuring the output of the operations process have been laid down, the next step is to determine whether or not the product or service does in fact measure up to them. Three questions in particular are of importance to the operations manager here:

    Where in the operations process should one check to see if the standards have been satisfied? There are three possible positions, namely at the beginning of the process (preventive control), during the process (in-time control), or after the process (reactive control).

    - Should each individual product or ser-vice provided be checked to determine whether the standards have been met? It is not always possible or desirable to inspect fully all products and/or services, and managers could instead use samples to determine whether the products and/or services do in fact meet the standards.

– How should the inspection be conducted? In practice, most businesses use sampling to ascertain whether their products and/or services measure up to standards. Two methods used here are statistical process control (SPC), whereby the inspection of a quality characteristic takes place during the process of manufacturing and/or service rendering, or acceptance sampling (AS), whereby inspection occurs after the process of manufacture and/or service rendering.

- **Step 5: Identifying and rectifying the causes of poor quality.** An important goal in quality planning and control is to identify and rectify the presence of poor quality and the reasons for it. This step will be discussed further in section 21.4.

- **Step 6: Continuously improving quality.** As was mentioned earlier, quality is one of the most important ways of adding value

---

Critical thinking

Much attention is paid in the business world to the concept of a "good quality products and/or services". However, for some businesses "quality" is viewed as important but not necessarily critical for business success. Others stake their reputations and are known for providing their customers/clients with the best possible quality of products and services. Think of Woolworths foods and Avis car rentals in this regard. The question which thus arises is this: "Is quality really so important?"

To answer this question, we may begin with a counter question: "Who wants a product which is broken from the outset or does not perform as it was expected to and, similarly, who wants to pay for non-service or poor service delivery?" Undoubtedly the answer to this is, "No one".

Thus if we accept that good quality products and services are considered important for customers and clients alike, it logically follows that businesses that want to be successful over the long term should pay attention to these requirements.

We may thus further argue that better quality products/services have definite advantages for a business. On the one hand, better quality products/services improve the competitive position of the business in two ways, both of which lead to increased revenue for the business through market-route benefits and, in the end, increased profitability:

- Enabling it to sell its products/services at a premium or higher price in the market place
- Creating the possibility of increasing the business's market share

On the other hand, better quality products/services increase the defect-free output of the business in two ways, both of which lead, again, to increased revenue for the business through, this time, cost-route benefits and, in the end, increased profitability:

- Lowering the costs of operations (reduced waste, rework, scrap, etc.)
- Increasing the level of overall productivity

Clearly, better quality products/services through the market and cost routes have the possibility of not only increasing the revenue of the business but, more importantly, improving its long-term profitability.

To conclude: good or better quality products and/or services are important for customers/clients and businesses can only profit from improving their total quality initiatives.

Source: Based on an illustration of the benefits of TQM as contained in Schonberger, R.J. & Knod, E.M. (Jr), *Operations management: Improving customer service*, 4th edition, Irwin, Homewood, Ill, 1991, p. 139.

to products and/or services in order to obtain a long-term competitive advantage – hence the importance of improving quality on a continuous basis. This aspect will be further discussed in section 21.4.

21.4 Operations improvement

21.4.1 The nature of operations improvement

In sections 21.2 and 21.3, the design of and planning and control of the operational process were examined. Even if both of these activities are successfully executed, the task of the operations manager is still not complete, however. Any operational process, regardless of how well it is initially designed, or how well it is planned and controlled, can certainly be improved. Nowadays, the improvement of the operational process of a business is seen as a further (and probably even more important) activity of the operations manager.

Figure 21.5 provides a broad framework of the various activities that are pertinent in operations improvement.

Before any operational process can be improved, it is necessary to determine what its current performance is. Performance measurement is therefore a prerequisite for any improvement. In measuring performance, managers ascertain the extent to which

the present operations process satisfies the formulated operations management objectives as far as quality, service, adaptability, lead time, cost, and variability are concerned.

21.4.1.1 Different types of performance standards

Once managers have determined by means of performance measurement the extent to which the present operations process satisfies the set operations management objectives, the overall performance of the process should be evaluated. This is done by comparing the present performance level with certain standards. Four kinds of **performance standards** are generally used:

- **Historical standards**, whereby present performance is compared to the particular business's own performance in previous years
- **Target performance standards**, whereby present performance is compared to predetermined standards, which indicate an acceptable or reasonable level of performance
- **Competitors' performance standards**, whereby present performance is compared to that of one or more similar competitors (nowadays, benchmarking is a popular approach that businesses follow in evaluating their own operations function by comparing their product and/or service package with that of their competitors)

Figure 21.5: The nature of operations improvement

Source: Adapted from Slack, N., Chambers, S., Harland, C. & Johnston, R., *Operations management*, 4th edition, Pearson Education (UK), 2004, p. 639.

- **Absolute performance standards**, whereby current performance is compared to the theoretical maximum achievable performance standards

21.4.1.2 Priorities for improvement

Once the performance of the present operations process has been measured and compared with one or more of the performance standards, the areas that need improvement should be clear. However, not all areas earmarked for improvement are equally important. **Priorities for improvement** therefore need to be determined. This is done by taking into consideration the needs and preferences of customers/clients and the performance and activities of competitors.

The needs of customers/clients provide an indication of those performance area(s) of particular importance to them. Operations management objectives should reflect such preferences as high quality or low costs for the internal operation or functioning of a specific operations process.

However, the roles of the performance and activities of competitors in establishing priorities for improvement are somewhat different. Of concern here is the performance of the business's operations process in relation to the performance of competitors. This comparison enables the business to identify its operations-based advantages as compared with those of its competitors.

21.4.1.3 Approaches to improvement

Once the priority areas for improvement have been determined, a specific approach or strategy for improvement must be decided upon. Two divergent **approaches to improvement** can be followed, namely:
- **Breakthrough improvement.** In breakthrough improvement there is less regular, but large-scale, dramatic change, which occurs in leaps and bounds in the functioning of an operations process. The

major changes in respect of products and/or services, **process technology**, or methods of work will, it is hoped, lead to improved performance. Business process re-engineering (BPR) is an example of a radical, breakthrough improvement approach that is today encountered in practice.
- **Continuous improvement.** In continuous improvement, also known as Kaizen improvement, more regular, but smaller, incremental changes take place in the functioning of the operations process. The aim is to improve the process on a continuous basis. The plan–do–check–act (PDCA) cycle is an example of a continuous improvement approach that is used in practice. South African motor manufacturers make frequent use of this approach. Their staff are, accordingly, strongly encouraged to suggest continuous small changes in the work process.

21.4.2 Failure prevention and recovery

Regardless of how well a particular operations process is designed, and thereafter put into operation by means of planning and control, there is always the chance of failures or breakdowns occurring. No operations process is ever (or always) perfect. Acceptance of the fact that failures will occur, however, does not mean that such events should be ignored. Some failures may have less serious consequences than others, while others may be critical for the functioning of the operations process itself. Hence, a continuous endeavour should be made to limit the occurrence of failures. Operations managers have a particular responsibility to improve the reliability of the operations processes that manufacture or provide products or services on a continuous basis.

21.4.2.1 Types of failures

Failures in operations processes may occur for one or more of the following reasons:

- **Design failures.** These occur when the design of the process is found to be wrong or inadequate. For example, all Pentium personal computers were withdrawn after it was established that there was a design error in the processors.
- **Facility failures.** These happen when one or more components of the facility itself, such as machines or equipment, breaks and causes parts of, or the whole facility, to grind to a halt – for example if lightning strikes out all the computers of a service provider.
- **Staff failures.** These happen when mistakes are made, or set procedures are not followed, for example when workers are not properly trained or where job performance comes to a standstill because of strikes.
- **Supplier failures.** These happen when suppliers do not provide products or services according to the agreement, for example when supermarkets place advertisements for special offers and the suppliers do not deliver the order on time.
- **Customer/client failures.** These occur when customers/clients use a product or service incorrectly or do not use it for the purpose for which it was designed. An example of this failure is the failure resulting from a customer using a 1 300 cc car to tow a caravan that requires a car engine of at least 3 000 cc for towing.

21.4.2.2 Failure detection and analysis

If one accepts that failures will occur, operations managers should have mechanisms in place to detect such failures, and then be able to put procedures into operation to determine the causes of the failures. Mechanisms to detect failures include process monitoring, complaints, and feedback questionnaires from customers/clients. In failure analysis, techniques such as cause–effect diagrams and analysis of customer/client complaints are used. Feedback questionnaires from clients are especially important to detect shortcomings in the rendering of services. This is one of the principal reasons for hotels asking their guests to fill in forms on the quality of service.

21.4.2.3 Systems reliability improvement

When there is clarity about the causes and consequences of failures, operations managers should endeavour to prevent them in the first place. This will increase the **reliability** of the entire operations process. This can be done by redesigning the products and/or services or processes that manufacture or provide them, using additional back-up systems or components in the case of a failure, or implementing regular maintenance and repairs. It may also be necessary to launch a training or motivation programme for the staff.

21.4.2.4 Recovery of failures

Operations managers attempt to reduce the occurrence of failures and the results thereof by means of failure detection and analysis and systems reliability improvement. However, when failures still occur, recovery procedures and contingency plans should already have been devised and put in place to minimise the potential detrimental effects on customers/clients.

21.4.3 Total quality management (TQM)

Mention was made in section 21.3.4 (in the discussion of the quality planning and control activities of operations management) of the concept of total quality management (TQM). It was also stated that the quality of products or services today is not regarded as the responsibility of the operations manager alone. The concept of TQM is far wider – hence, the entire business is responsible.

21.4.3.1 Definition of TQM

TQM as a concept did not develop overnight. Many so-called quality gurus, such as Feigenbaum, Deming, Juran, Ishikawa, Taguchi and Crosby, contributed to what has today become known as TQM. TQM is a management philosophy, a method of "thinking and doing" with the primary aim of satisfying the needs and expectations of customers/clients by means of high-quality products or services. It endeavours to shift the responsibility for quality from merely the operations management function to the entire business (that is, all other functional management areas and the employees therein). TQM is further primarily aimed at:[11]

- Meeting the needs and expectations of customers/clients
- Covering all parts of the business regardless of how small or seemingly insignificant they are
- Making each and every employee (every person) in the business quality conscious and holding him or her responsible for his or her contribution to the achievement of TQM
- Identifying and accounting for all costs of quality (both prevention and failure costs)
- Doing things right the first time (proactive rather than reactive action)

- Developing and implementing systems and procedures for quality and the improvement thereof
- Establishing a continuous process for improvement

According to Oakland's (2000) TQM model (see figure 21.6), the focal point of total quality is the underlying processes that occur at each customer/client and supplier interface. To this should be added specific human or so-called soft management components (commitment, communication and culture) and hard management components (of quality systems, techniques and/or methods, and teams).

21.4.3.2 The ISO 9000 quality standard for quality systems

Improving quality within a business requires a great deal more than good intentions. It demands concrete action. One such action should be the development of a quality system. Such a system includes the organisational structure, the responsibilities, procedures, processes, and resources for implementing quality.

A quality standard used throughout the

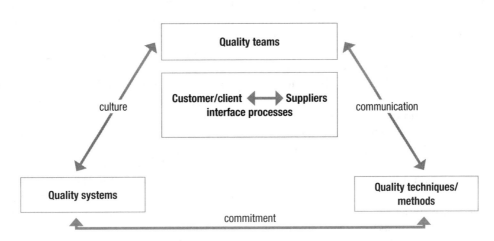

Figure 21.6: Total quality management model

Source: Oakland, J.S., *Total quality management*, 3rd edition, Butterworth-Heinemannn, Oxford, 2003, p. 21.

world to lay down the requirements for the specific quality systems of businesses is the ISO 9000 series. This series provides comprehensive recommendations as to how a quality system should be compiled for a particular type of business. The ISO 9001:2000 document[12] – under five major headings of documentation requirements, management responsibility, resource management, product realisation, measurement, and analysis and improvement – includes guidelines on the following aspects:

- Defining documentation requirements for the establishment, implementation and maintenance of the quality management system (QMS), compilation of the quality manual, and setting procedures for the control of quality documents and records
- Demonstrating management commitment to the QMS; dedicated customer focus for understanding the needs and requirements; use of the quality policy for leading the organisation in its quality endeavours; planning aspects for setting quality objectives and the QMS itself; management responsibility, authority and communication of quality matters, and conducting management review of the whole QMS
- Providing resources for implementation of QMS; developing and improving human resources; satisfying infrastructure requirements; and creating a working environment to enhance performance
- Planning the operation and supporting processes for the realisation of the required outputs; defining the customer-related processes for communication; designing and developing the organisation's products and services; setting purchasing procedures and supplier evaluation; controlling the production and service provision; and controlling the monitoring and measuring devices to inspire confidence in the QMS
- Establishing methods for the improvement of the QMS; monitoring and measuring through customer satisfaction, internal audit and process achievement; controlling

non-conforming products; analysing data, including use of statistical techniques; and creating a continuous improvement culture and environment with corrective and preventive action

21.4.3.3 The implementation of TQM

The way in which TQM is implemented in a business determines the ultimate success of the application thereof. Factors that should be taken into account are listed below.[13] (Note that the corresponding "hard" and "soft" management components of Oakland's (2000)[14] TQM model (see figure 21.6 on page 537) are also given for each factor):

- Integration of TQM in the overall business strategy (systems)
- Top management's and employees' support and involvement (commitment)
- Teamwork in the improvement initiatives (teams)
- Feedback on quality successes that have in fact been achieved (communication)
- Creation of a quality awareness (culture)
- Training of employees in quality techniques and methods (techniques/ methods)

In the "new" revised model for TQM, Oakland (2003)[15] referred to the 4Ps (hard components) and 3Cs (soft components) of TQM. While the "soft" components of the earlier model remain the same, the new "hard" components are **processes** (systems), **people** (teamwork) and **planning** (techniques/methods), which are all linked to **performance**.

21.5 Summary

This chapter examined in more detail three of the activities of operations managers, namely design, planning and control, and improvement.

Operations design is concerned with the design of products and/or services that will satisfy the needs of customers/clients.

and the design of the operational processes to manufacture or provide them. Specific responsibilities with regard to the design of the operational processes include the design of the supply network, the layout and flow of the operations facility, the application of process technology, and job design and work organisation.

Once the design activities have been completed, the operations process must be put into action by means of operations planning and control. Specific responsibilities in this regard include:

- Capacity planning and control, in which manufacturing or service provision ability should be reconciled with the demand for the business's products or services
- Inventory and purchasing planning and control, in which adequate inventory resources should be obtained and made available to enable the operations process to function smoothly (if this is not the responsibility of the purchasing manager)
- Quality planning and control, in which conformity with the design specifications of products or services should be ensured

However, once the foregoing activities have been executed, the task of the operations manager is still not over. Any operational process, regardless of how well it is initially designed and how well it has been planned and controlled, can still be improved. Operations improvement as an identifiable activity of operations management endeavours in two ways. Firstly, it tries to improve the reliability of the entire operations process on a continuous basis by failure prevention and recovery. Secondly, in applying the concept of TQM, it attempts to improve the operation of the entire or total business so that quality products or services can be manufactured or provided to satisfy the needs of customers/clients optimally.

 Key terms

Approaches to improvement	Operational processes
Capacity planning and control	Operations design
Competitive advantage of good design	Operations improvement
Composition of products and services	Operations planning and control
Customers/clients	Performance standards
Design of products/services	Priorities for Improvement
Design of supply network	Process technology
Failure prevention and recovery	Quality planning and control
Inventory and supply chain planning and control	Reliability
ISO 9000 quality standard for quality systems	Stages of product and service design
Job design and work organisation	Total quality management (TQM)
Layout and flow	

 Questions for discussion

Reread the case study about The BMW World Plant Rosslyn, Pretoria at the beginning of this chapter. Then visit the BMW (South Africa) (Pty) Ltd and BMW AG websites if you have access to the Internet, and conduct your own further research and investigation of aspects you are not familiar with. Then answer the following questions.

1. Do you agree with the argument that BMW (South Africa) (Pty) Ltd winning of the J.D. Power and Associates Gold Award in 2002, is testimony to the fact its operational process was well designed, planned and controlled and improved on a continuous basis? Give reasons for your answer by explaining why you agree or disagree.

2. In 1999 BMW (South Africa) (Pty) Ltd was the first motor vehicle manufacturer

in the world to achieve certification for its integrated SHEQ Management System (Safety, Health, Environmental and Quality) ISO 9001:2000, ISO 14001 and BS 8800 certifications. What is the importance of such certifications for the company and its customers?

3. BMW (South Africa) (Pty) Ltd was the first BMW plant to be located outside the country of its parent company, BMW AG Munich, Germany, in 1973. Even today it is one of only three complete BMW manufacturing plants where cars are produced to end items. The other such plants are the Spartenburg plant in the USA and the original BMW plant in Germany. Why is this significant for South Africa and its people?

4. At the end of the 1970s, BMW (South Africa) (Pty) Ltd was the only South African car manufacturer to export cars on a regular basis and in significant numbers. The export drive has steadily continued over the years with the full integration into BMW's worldwide supply network and the production of both left-hand and right-hand drive vehicles for the South African and overseas markets. Why are such continued exports so important for South Africa and what positive effects could one expect for the South African economy at large?

5. To ensure optimum customer satisfaction, the "build quality" of the vehicles produced at BMW World Plant Rosslyn is measured through a process of complete product audit. What does this audit entail? When are such audits performed? Are similar or different standards applied at the various BMW plants to make provision for local circumstances?

References

1. Slack, N., Chambers, S. & Johnston, R., *Operations management*, 4th edition, Pitman Publishing, London, 2004, p. 131.
2. Davis, M.M. & Heineke, J., *Operations management: Integrating manufacturing and services*, 5th edition, McGraw-Hill, New York, 2005, p. 11.
3. Slack, N. et al., *op. cit.*, pp. 133–135.
4. *Ibid.*, p. 161.
5. Krajewski, L.J. & Ritzman, L.P., *Operations management: Processes and value chains*, 7th edition, Pearson, Upper Saddle River, N.J., 2005, pp. 302–303.
6. Krüger, L.P., *The changing role of production and operations management: Moving towards the ultimate in robotic manufacturing and service provision*. University of South Africa, Pretoria, Unpublished inaugural lecture, 2000, p. 21.
7. Slack, N. et al., *op. cit.*, p. 294.
8. Slack, N. et al., *op. cit.*, p. 359.
9. Knod, E.M. (Jr) & Schonberger, R.J., *Operations management: Meeting customers' demands*, 7th edition, McGraw-Hill, New York, 2001, pp. 138–140.
10. Slack, N. et al., *op. cit.*, p. 595.
11. Slack, N. et al., *op. cit.*, pp. 722–723.
12. *SABS ISO 9001, South African Standard, Code of practice, Quality management systems – requirements*, SABS, Pretoria, 2000.
13. Slack, N. et al., *op. cit.*, pp. 734–737.
14. Oakland, J.S., *Total quality management: Text with cases*, 2nd edition, Butterworth-Heinemann, Oxford, 2000, pp. 81–91.
15. Oakland, J.S., *Total quality management: Text with cases*, 3rd edition, Butterworth-Heinemann, Oxford, 2003, pp. 26–27.

PURCHASING AND SUPPLY MANAGEMENT[1]

The purpose of this chapter

The purpose of the chapter is to place the purchasing or sourcing function and its role into perspective, to elucidate new concepts, and to explain the management of the function.

Learning outcomes

The content of this chapter will enable learners to:

- Place the purchasing and supply function

and the nature of purchasing and supply activities in perspective

- Elucidate new concepts or approaches to the provision of materials to a business
- Emphasise the role and importance of the purchasing and supply function in the success and efficiency of a business
- Explain the application of the management tasks of planning, organising and control in the purchasing and supply function
- Point out certain management aids at the disposal of the purchasing and supply manager

22.1 Introduction

Just as consumers need to make purchases almost on a daily basis to satisfy their normal needs, and large purchases, such as buying a motorcar, to satisfy their long-term needs, a business also has to make purchases to meet its daily and long-term needs. Because people make purchases almost every day, the value of the **purchasing and supply function** in business is often underestimated. There is a perception that anyone is capable of making purchases for a business.

However, purchasing and supply in a business entails far more than merely com-

paring the prices of two or more competitive bids and then buying material from the supplier that offers the best prices and service. Buyers in a manufacturing business buy a great variety of materials: from stationery, cleaning agents, cafeteria services and globes to bulk fuel, strategic material (which is sometimes difficult to obtain) for production processes, and equipment for office and production processes. They are also involved in the purchase of capital goods, for example robot-controlled processing equipment and complicated computer systems.

Buyers are expected to keep abreast of better substitute materials, new developments

Applying the concept: Purchases by different organisations

- Eskom purchases coal, water, copper cable, poles, materials, parts and services (for example civil and electrical engineering, cleaning and security services) for the construction and maintenance of power plants and office buildings, motor vehicles, computer systems, office equipment, stationery, legal services, training services and transport services, consumables such as toilet paper, cleaning materials and refreshments.

- Woolworths purchases merchandising and materials handling equipment (for example shelves, trolleys, baskets and refrigerators); products for selling in the retail shops, for example perishable products (fruit, meat and dairy products), groceries, clothing products, home products (crockery, cutlery, curtains and bedding), computer systems, office equipment, stationery, legal services, training services and transport services, consumables such as toilet paper, cleaning materials and refreshments.

and technology in the market. A buyer's expertise can improve the progressiveness, productivity and profitability of a business. Buyers often have to make trips abroad or develop local **suppliers** because of the lack of existing sources. They also have to ensure that materials purchased meet laid-down quality requirements, because this has a decisive effect on the quality of the business's final product (in the case of a manufacturer) and the quality of products resold (in a retail business). Buyers need to be aware of market trends, fashion, seasons and the state of the market. They should, for example, know how many suppliers and how many buyers are present in a particular market, as this has a crucial effect on the purchase price of materials, the way in which suppliers should be approached and the type of relationship required.

The **purpose** of the purchasing and supply function is not only to provide the right materials, services and equipment, but also to ensure that they are purchased at a reasonable price, satisfy quality requirements, and are received at the right place and time, in the correct quantities. The activities of the purchasing and supply function are derived from this. The purchasing and supply function should:

- Select suppliers
- Purchase and arrange for the transport of materials to the business

- Decide what prices to accept
- Determine the quantity and quality of materials or services
- Expedite and receive materials
- Control warehousing and the inventory holding
- Determine the timing of purchases

To perform these activities optimally, the purchasing and supply function needs to be managed, that is, planned, organised and controlled.

Purchasing and supply management

Purchasing and supply management entails the planning, organising, leading and controlling of all activities relating to the purchase of materials and services from an external source, and is aimed at maintaining and increasing the business's profitability and efficiency of customer service.

To manage the purchasing and supply function optimally, purchasing and supply managers use certain management aids to facilitate their task, for example benchmarking, purchasing budgets, and a **purchasing and supply policy**. To execute purchasing and supply activities optimally, a buyer or purchasing and supply manager applies certain purchasing and supply techniques such as negotiation, purchasing and supply research, price analysis, and learning curves. This chapter deals with the **management** of the purchasing and supply function, and management aids. The principal purchasing and supply **activities** and techniques are covered in chapter 23.

The case study below provides insight into the scope of the purchasing (or procurement) and supply function. All the points covered in the case will be explained in this chapter and chapter 23.

22.2 Broadening the provision function

Often one hears of concepts such as "**materials management**", "**logistics management**", and "**supply chain management**" in relation to the supply of materials to organisations. These concepts or approaches (which are what they really are) mean a broadening of the traditional purchasing function.

Case study

Procurement at South African Breweries (SAB)

Procurement at SAB is centralised in Johannesburg and operates across the supply chain. This includes packaging materials (glass bottles, cans, labels and glue, crowns, foils, crates, cartons and pallets), brewing raw materials (a particularly specialised field that purchases malt, barley and hops from predominantly local, but also foreign, sources), freight and logistics (a critical link between suppliers, transporters and SAB depots and breweries) and non-production spend (including air travel, cell phone charges, information systems and merchandising material).

The company has a dedicated preferential procurement executive to ensure that SAB Ltd's commitment to transformation and black economic empowerment extends fully into its supplier base.

During the 2004 financial year, the company spent over R730-million with empowerment suppliers, constituting approximately 14% of the company's local procurement spend. The goal for the 2005 financial year was R895-million, which was exceeded to reach R938-million, or 17,3% of total procurement.

Apart form negotiating the procurement of raw materials, goods and services, SAB's commercial (procurement and supply) function also analyses key commodity industries to understand how they operate and their impact on SAB.

An important part of the success of procurement is managing the supplier relationship which also involves ensuring the right quantities of the right supplier's product are delivered to SAB at the right time.

Keeping the price of beer in South Africa well below the world average is part of the task, and detailed total cost exercises are done to ensure all raw materials, goods and services supplied to SAB are of the best quality and at the best price.

The commercial (procurement and supply) function will play a key role in the execution of SAB's recently announced 5-year R5-billion capital project strategy. The commercial expertise in negotiation, contract drafting and sourcing of required capital equipment will be key skills required to ensure SAB obtains the best possible return on investment.

Being part of a global entity means that interaction with other worldwide subsidiaries in the SABMiller group results in an understanding of global industry trends and the ability to leverage buying power between the different companies in the group.

Source: SAB, http://www.sabreweries.com/SABLtd/Primary/CorporateResponsibility/Bee/Commercial (11 January 2007)

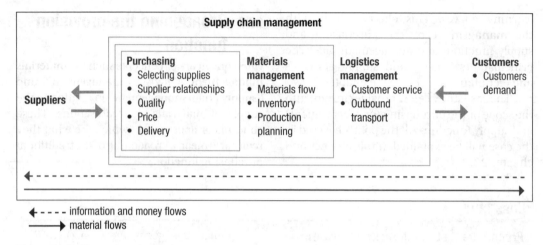

Figure 22.1: The scope of materials supply approaches and activities

Materials management, logistics management and supply chain management approaches are often found in manufacturing, assembly industries, and large retail and service organisations. Even in government procurement there is a movement towards these approaches. Figure 22.1 provides an exposition of the extent of the various concepts.

Materials management is an overarching organisational concept embracing purchasing, warehousing, and certain operations functions such as the movement of materials through the transformation (production) process. It is an effort to combine all materials provision activities under one head, that is, the materials manager. The aim is to eliminate the often conflicting objectives of different materials provision activities by combining them under a materials manager. Materials management integrates all the provision activities up to final product stage. Figure 22.1 shows the activities included in the materials management approach.

Logistics management entails integrating all movements (transport) and warehousing activities, from the point where the materials are purchased, through the transformation process, to the final consumer. Some activities of purchasing, operations and materials managers are therefore integrated under the logistics manager, together with the physical distribution of final products, which traditionally fell under the control of the marketing manager. The movement of materials and products, and the flow of information, are vital to the provision of ef-

Example

The different sub-functions involved in the provision of materials often have conflicting objectives. A buyer's aim, for example, is to purchase at the lowest possible price per unit. With this goal in mind, in the negotiation process the buyer may be persuaded by suppliers to purchase larger quantities in order to obtain lower unit prices. However, this is in direct conflict with the goal of inventory management, which strives to keep inventory levels as low as possible. If a materials management approach is adopted in a business, all materials provision activities are integrated under one head, and the goal is the pursuit of lowest total costs and optimal service provision in the whole materials provision chain, rather than a focus on individual activities.

ficient and satisfactory customer service. The aim of logistics management is to provide the best customer service at the lowest possible logistics cost.

Supply chain management is an extension of the systems approach. According to the systems approach, the internal functions of the business (marketing, finance, purchasing and supply, production, human resources, etc.) are managed as an integrated whole. In the supply chain management approach, the integration extends beyond the individual business. The "system" in supply chain management consists of managing, in an integrated fashion, the flow of materials in all the linked organisations, from the raw material stage, through all the stages of transformation, to delivery of the final product to the end user (consumer). The intention is that businesses in the supply chain cooperate in networks with mutual long-term agreements to deliver the end product to the final consumer in the most effective way and at the lowest cost. This is achieved by sharing information and know-how (and even facilities), and by eliminating waste between the various stages of the transformation process. Figure 22.2 shows a simplified supply chain – the supply chain of a milk processing plant.

In conclusion, supply chains are a series of linked suppliers and customers. Each customer is in turn a supplier to another business lower down the supply chain, until the finished product reaches the end-user.

All businesses are part of one or more

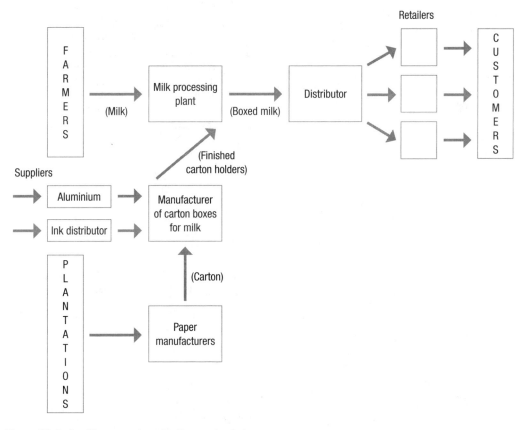

Figure 22.2: A milk processing plant's supply chain

supply chains. The emphasis in supply chain management is to manage processes in the entire supply chain (instead of concentrating on internal functions and direct suppliers and direct customers). Naturally, this is a complex task, and strategic alliances, long-term contracts and shared information networks form important components of supply chain management.

As seen in figure 22.2 and the example in the box below, a supply chain represents a network of organisational relationships that tie firms together and may tie their success to the supply chain as a whole. A supply chain as a whole may have its own identity, and function like an independent firm. The network of organisation is a loose and flexible coalition, guided and managed from a hub (the strongest partner in the supply chain, such as the milk processing plant in figure 22.2 – for example, Bonnita or Clover; Volkswagen SA in an example in the motor industry). This hub organisation takes the lead in managing the supply chain, and its key functions and activities include the following:

- The development and management of the alliances with other organisations/firms in the supply chain
- Coordination of financial resources and technology in the supply chain
- The definition and management of core competencies (the most important activities of each party) and strategies in the supply chain

Applying the concept: The supply chain of a vehicle assembler

A vehicle assembler such as Volkswagen SA has a supply chain consisting of three main sections:

- Suppliers
- Assembly plant
- Car dealers

The supplier network consists of numerous businesses providing a wide range of parts or items to be assembled into a motor vehicle. These include engines, panels, chassis, lights, bulbs, seats, exhausts, windscreens, etc. All these parts at one time consisted of raw materials, and had to be converted (in the transformation process) by suppliers to render them useful so that Volkswagen SA can assemble them to create a vehicle. The vehicle is then supplied to the final consumer through the dealer network. The accompanying graphic shows the sections in the supply chain of a motor vehicle.

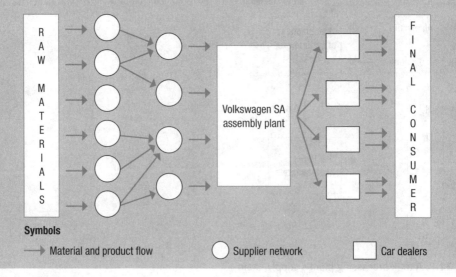

Symbols

→ Material and product flow   ○ Supplier network   ▢ Car dealers

- The development of relationships with customers and suppliers
- The management of information systems that bind the network

---

Critical thinking

Recall the SAB case study at the beginning of the chapter. Which purchasing approach does SAB follow? Can you provide more than two reasons for this?

The current trend of broadening the supply function does not mean that the purchasing function is less important. On the contrary, at the core of all these concepts is the purchasing function, which has a direct influence on the profitability of the business, as is shown in the next section.

22.3 The importance of the purchasing and supply function to the business

The importance of the purchasing and supply function differs from one business to the next, but in most, purchasing has a profound influence on profit and in the aspects discussed below.

22.3.1 Greatest expenditure for the business

It is a worldwide phenomenon that purchasing costs are a business's biggest expense, especially in businesses where final products are purchased and no actual value is added to the product. In retailing businesses such as Spar or Edgars, up to 90% of each available rand may be spent on purchases, and as much as 60%

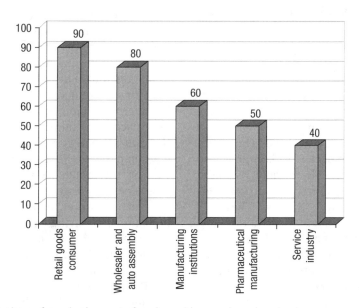

Figure 22.3: The share of purchasing cost of each rand income in various businesses

Source: Compiled from Leenders, M.R., Fearon, H.E., Flynn, A.E. & Johnson, P.F., *Purchasing and supply management,* 12th edition, McGraw-Hill, New York, 2002, p. 13 and Hugo, W.M.J., Badenhorst-Weiss, J.A. & Van Biljon, E.H.B., *Purchasing and supply management,* 5th edition, Van Schaik, Pretoria, 2006, p. 11.

in manufacturing businesses such as Sappi or Unilever, and 80% in car assembly businesses such as Toyota or Ford. It therefore stands to reason that purchasing costs is an area where cost savings can make a vital contribution to the business's profits, if one accepts that profit is the favourable difference between income and expenditure. Figure 22.3 on page 547 illustrates the share of purchasing in the spending of each available rand in various businesses.

Applying the concept: The scope of purchasing costs

- **Honda motor vehicle.** Purchasing costs contribute to more than 80% of a Honda motorcar's final price. The cost of steel, tyres, glass, paint, fabric, aluminium, copper and electronic components represents more than 60% of the final price of the motor vehicle.
- **Coca-Cola soft drink.** Purchasing costs contribute 65% of the price of a bottle of Coca-Cola. These include the cost of bottles, caps, cans, packaging materials and transportation.

22.3.2 Inventory holding

Stock is held to prevent disruptions in the transformation process (production or operational) when there is an interruption in the flow of materials to a business. The aim of **inventory management** is to keep inventory levels as low as possible, without risking an interruption in the operational process (as a result of an out-of-stock situation). The reason for this is that large sums of operating capital are tied up in inventory, and these could be applied elsewhere to earn revenue. If too much capital is tied up in inventory, a business could encounter cash-flow problems (discussed in the chapters on financial management). Besides cash-flow problems, warehousing costs are a big cost element, usually ranging from 10% to 25% of total investment in inventory.[2]

Warehousing costs include the costs of

financing (interest) warehousing, warehouse staff, insurance and obsolescence. Effective purchasing and supply management can reduce inventory holding by ensuring an uninterrupted flow of materials of the right quality, at the time when they are needed, to the production process. The more reliable the provision or purchase of materials is, the smaller the amount of inventory that needs to be stored.

22.3.3 Profit-leverage

The **profit-leverage effect** can be deduced from the preceding two sections on the contribution to profit of effective purchasing and supply. The profit-leverage effect means that if purchasing costs constitute a major portion of the total cost of a business, a saving in purchasing costs has greater profit potential than a similar increase in sales. For example, a 4% reduction in purchasing costs can make the same contribution to profitability as an increase of 20% in sales would make.

The contribution of the purchasing and supply function to profitability differs from business to business, and from sector to sector. Effective purchasing normally has a greater profit potential in a commercial organisation than in a manufacturing business, as can be inferred from section 22.3.1. In the pharmaceutical industry, for example, where the value of patent medicine content is very low compared to the research and marketing costs of the product, saving on purchasing costs does not have such a profound effect on profit. However, in the motor assembly industry, any saving on purchasing costs, where material costs are very high, has a decisive effect on the business's profitability, as illustrated in the Honda example.

Purchasing as a factor in profitability is also more critical when a business frequently changes its suppliers, if the price of materials fluctuates continually, where fashion is concerned, and where markets for the final product are highly competitive, for example in the case of everyday consumer articles. The contribution of purchasing to profitability is less critical but still important where prices and suppliers are relatively stable, and where the industry is not characterised by innovation.[3]

22.3.4 Contributions to the marketing of products

By purchasing materials of the right quality and price at the right time, a manufacturer can make final products available in the right quantities at a competitive price at the right time to its customers (for example retailers or the final consumer). A retail buyer has a greater and more direct influence on the marketing of merchandise (for example clothing) where the availability of the right product (type, quality, style and brand) at the right time in the right quantities is an important consideration in successful marketing. Effective purchasing can therefore facilitate the marketing of a business's products, and indirectly contributes to profit through the marketing function.

22.4 The management task of the purchasing and supply manager

In part 2 of this book, you were introduced to the general management principles of planning, organising and control. As was mentioned earlier, purchasing and supply, like all other functional areas (marketing, finance, operations, etc.), must be managed to ensure that the purchasing and supply function operates effectively and makes the best possible contribution to the profit of the business and efficient client service. In the following sections, without discussing the principles in detail, we shall look at the application of the main management elements of the purchasing and supply function: planning, organising and control.

22.4.1 Purchasing and supply planning

Essentially, the planning of the purchasing and supply function means "managing the purchasing and supply function for the future". Purchasing and supply planning entails formulating objectives, which the purchasing and supply function should strive to reach by a particular future period (purchasing and supply objectives), and the drawing up of plans to achieve the objectives (purchasing and supply plans), including the optimal application of resources (people, physical facilities and funds) to achieve the objectives.

Purchasing and supply is a service function in a business, and purchasing and supply planning is therefore subject to business planning; purchasing and supply objectives are similarly subordinate to business objectives. In other words, purchasing and supply planning should support business planning and purchasing and supply objectives should help to realise the business's objectives which, in a profit-seeking business, are usually minimum costs, maximum efficiency, profitability, and customer value in the long term. Purchasing and supply planning should also be conducted in consultation with other functional management areas, because the plans of marketing, operational and financial functions affect the purchasing and supply function.

The planning of the purchasing and supply function, like planning in the business itself and other functional management areas, takes place at the following levels (see chapter 6):

- **Strategic level.** At this level, planning entails the purchasing and supply manager providing input to business planning. The elements of strategic purchasing and supply planning differ from one business to the next. Where the purchasing and supply function is deemed to be less important and merely involves a clerical function, the purchasing and supply function is not involved in strategic planning. When a business has accepted the supply chain management approach, purchasing and supply will be involved in strategic planning. Planning at strategic level is normally of a long-term nature and is aimed at safeguarding materials provision, developing supplier sources, and maintaining the competitive position of the business. Typical strategic planning elements are supplier alliances, supplier development, supply chain process integration, availability forecasting, and purchasing and supply policy.

- **Tactical or middle-management level.** This type of planning may cover the medium-term needs of the business, budgeting, the purchasing and supply system and organisation, purchasing and supply methods, negotiation, development of human resources, interface development with other functions and suppliers (by means of **cross-functional teams**), contracting, and employing cost-reduction techniques.
- **Operations level.** At the lowest operations level, plans are formulated to allow the daily functioning of the purchasing and supply function to proceed as smoothly as possible, to the benefit of the business as a whole and other functions serviced by the purchasing and supply function. Planning at this level

is short-term, and includes planning the tasks of expediting, keeping records, and maintaining the purchasing and supply system, invoice clearance, handling of requisitions, enquiries and quotations, and pricing decisions.[4]

The levels of purchasing and supply planning are depicted in figure 22.4.

The formulation of objectives is one of the most important planning tasks. As mentioned earlier, purchasing and supply objectives can be derived from the business's objectives. Table 22.1 on page 551 provides an indication of the purchasing and supply objectives that can be derived from the business's objectives.

The purchasing and supply function should also formulate specific objectives on how to realise the general objectives. Specific objectives should be formulated, if possible, in quantitative terms, for instance in periods of time and figures. A specific objective for cost reduction (the last objective in table 22.1) would be to standardise inventory items such as drills, screwdrivers, pliers, lubricants and batteries within a month, and to enter into a contract with only one supplier of the items,

Strategic level

Supplier alliances

Supplier development

Supply chain integration

Long-term planning

Availability forecasting

Policy formulation

In/outsourcing decisions

Tactical management level

Systems integration

Negotiation

Interface development

Human resources development

Total quality management

Contracting

Cost-reduction techniques

Operational level

Communication with suppliers' operational staff

Expediting

File and system maintenance

Enquiries and quotations

Pricing

Returns and recycling

Figure 22.4: Levels of purchasing and supply planning

Source: Baillie, P., Farmer, D., Jessop, D. & Jones, D., *Purchasing principles and management*, 9th edition, Prentice Hall (Pearson Education), Essex, England, 2005, p. 531.

Table 22.1: Purchasing and supply objectives derived from the business's objectives

Business objectives	Purchasing and supply objectives
• To retain the market share • To move from the speciality market to the general market	• To search for more unique products in the supplier market • To seek new and larger suppliers and develop a new materials flow system to handle larger quantities and a greater variety of items while keeping total inventory volume as low as possible
• To develop specific new products and services • To develop an overall production capacity plan, including an overall make-or-buy policy	• To seek or develop new suppliers • To develop systems that integrate capacity planning and purchasing and supply planning, together with a policy of make-or-buy
• To initiate a cost-reduction plan	• To standardise materials and reduce suppliers

for delivery as and when they are needed. Thus, inventory holding is kept to a minimum and better prices can be negotiated because the total value of purchases per supplier is higher over a specific period.

Purchasing and supply budgets are also a significant element of purchasing and supply planning. (Refer to section 22.5.2.)

22.4.2 Organising the purchasing and supply function

While chapter 7 has an in-depth discussion of organising as an element of management, the focus in this section is merely on the application of organising in the purchasing and supply function.

Purchasing and supply organisation

Purchasing and supply organisation involves the creation of a structure of responsibility and authority for the purchasing and supply function, and the organisation of purchasing and supply activities to realise purchasing and business ojectives.

There are four main issues that need to be addressed in organising the purchasing and supply function:
• The place of the purchasing and supply function in the organisational structure
• The internal organisation of the purchasing and supply function

• Coordination with other functional management areas
• Cross-functional teams (organising the purchasing and supply function according to the supply chain management approach)

22.4.2.1 The place of the purchasing and supply function in the organisational structure

The place of the purchasing and supply function in the business is affected by three elements: **centralisation** or **decentralisation**; the hierarchical level of the purchasing and supply function in the organisational structure of the business; and the approach to the integration of purchasing and materials flow activities under the materials management, logistics management or supply chain management approach (discussed earlier).

(a) Centralisation or decentralisation

In a business with a centralised purchasing and supply function, the purchasing and supply manager and his or her personnel have the authority and are responsible for the purchasing and supply function. In an organisation with a single business unit, this is the obvious organisational structure, but if an organisation has a head office with different business units, branches, or plants, there are various options:
• One option is for a centralised purchasing

and supply function, situated at head office, to be responsible for purchasing.

- Another option is for each plant or branch to do its own purchasing, which means that the purchasing and supply function is organised on a decentralised basis.
- The final option is a combination of centralised and decentralised functions, where some materials and services are bought on a centralised basis and others on a decentralised basis.

A **centralised purchasing and supply structure** has certain advantages, one of them being that the standardisation of (i) purchasing and supply procedures and (ii) materials or services purchased is possible. Standardisation has

great cost-saving advantages, for example a greater volume of materials of one kind being purchased from a supplier, resulting in lower inventory levels and lower prices because of better discounts for volume orders. Because of volumes, purchasing and supply personnel can concentrate on buying a specific commodity (material or service), which makes specialisation possible. A centralised purchasing and supply organisation is especially suitable if the needs of different business units, plants or branches are much the same, for example all Pick 'n Pay hypermarkets. If the greatest proportion of a business's purchases is made from a single supplier or a few suppliers, and if the material is of strategic importance to the continuation of the business's activities,

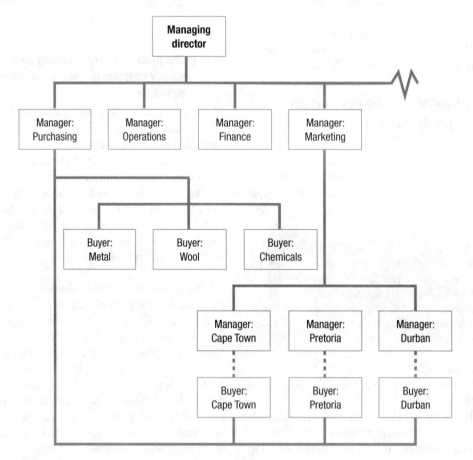

Figure 22.5: Business with a centralised purchasing and supply structure

it is preferable to purchase on a centralised basis. Figure 22.5 on page 552 illustrates a centralised purchasing and supply structure for a multiplant business.

A **decentralised purchasing and supply structure** is particularly suited to a business comprising geographically dispersed plants whose purchases are made from a number of their local suppliers. Also, if the plants perform divergent activities and therefore have unique needs in terms of purchases, decentralisation is the obvious choice. Where the different decentralised plants are regarded as profit centres, it is necessary for each plant to have autonomy over its own expenditure, hence, in this case, decentralisation of purchasing and supply is the right option. A decentralised purchasing and supply structure has the advantage that buyers have closer contact with users (users of the purchased goods and services in the business) and local suppliers, and reaction times to the requests of users are quicker. Figure 22.6 depicts a decentralised purchasing and supply structure in a business with various plants.

A **combination of centralisation and de-centralisation** is a useful middle course. In this application the centralised purchasing office purchases collective requirements, enters into long-term contracts on behalf of the whole business, purchases capital equipment, formulates purchasing and supply policy and strategies, trains buyers, and evaluates decentralised purchasing and supply per-

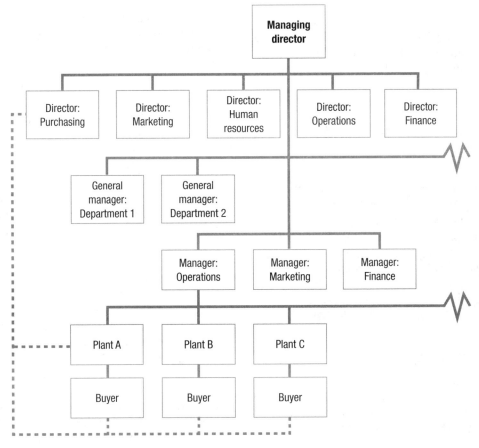

Figure 22.6: Business with a decentralised purchasing and supply structure

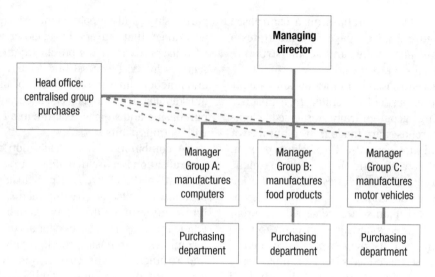

Figure 22.7: Business with a centralised/decentralised purchasing and supply structure

formance. Decentralised purchasing and supply provides for the specialised needs and small purchases of the plant, and the buyers report directly to the head of the plant, but operate within the parameters of policy laid down by the centralised purchasing and supply authority. Figure 22.7 shows a centralised/decentralised purchasing and supply structure.

Applying the concept: A combination of centralised and decentralised purchasing and supply

At Telkom, the head office negotiates large contracts with suppliers of copper cable, optic fibre, and microwave dishes. Decentralised regional offices buy non-strategic items such as tools, maintenance materials and services from local suppliers.

Critical thinking

Recall the case study about SAB at the beginning of this chapter. How does SAB organise its purchases? Why would it choose to organise its purchases in such a way?

(b) The hierarchical level of the purchasing and supply function in the organisational structure

The hierarchical level of the purchasing and supply function is primarily determined by the importance of the purchasing and supply function to the business. The importance of the function is determined by the following factors, among others:

- **The value of the purchased materials in relation to the total expenditure of the business.** The greater purchasing's share of total expenditure, the more important the purchasing and supply function is. If solely this factor is taken into consideration, one could say that purchasing and supply is more important in a retail organisation than in a manufacturing business. However, it is not the only factor that determines the importance of purchasing and supply.
- **The situation in the supplier market.** If the supply market is a monopoly (only one supplier) or an oligopoly (only a few suppliers), as is the case in certain markets in South Africa, negotiation should take place at a high level to negotiate the best value for the business. Purchasing and supply is important here, and the head

of the purchasing and supply function should put forward proposals and operate at a high level in the business.

- **The size of the business.** In larger businesses, the purchasing and supply manager is usually placed on the same level as other functional managers, such as the marketing manager, the financial manager, and the operations manager. In smaller businesses, the purchasing and supply function often falls under the financial manager or the marketing manager.
- **The nature of the materials purchased and the specialised knowledge and skills of buyers.** This determines the status of buyers and the purchasing and supply manager in the business. For example, in the purchase of technologically advanced custom-made materials, the buyer needs in-depth technical knowledge and also negotiating and commercial skills. However, when it comes to purchasing cleaning agents and stationery, no special knowledge or skills are required.
- **Top management's perception.** The top management's perception of the importance of the purchasing and supply function will determine its status in the organisation.

The approach to the integration of activities. In a materials management or logistics management approach, the purchasing and supply manager falls under the materials or logistics manager, and may be seen to have lower status than other functional managers. In the supply chain management approach hierarchical levels are reduced (disappear to some extent). The business is operated and managed by process or cross-functional teams. Purchasing staff play an important role in cross-functional teams who are responsible for supply chain processes. (See section 22.4.2.4.)

22.4.2.2 Internal organisation of the purchasing and supply function

The purchasing and supply function can be organised internally in a variety of ways. The organisation may consist of an **informal structure** in which buyers purchase any material or service and processing whatever requisitions or enquiries are placed on their desks. In such a case, the buyer is responsible for the whole spectrum of activities, from asking for quotations or calling for tenders to the expediting and receipt of the product. Conversely, the function can be divided into **specialist groups** in which each person takes responsibility for buying a specific material or service, or in a larger business, split so that a buyer is responsible for all the purchases from a specific supplier, especially in the case of strategic materials.

In the case of the purchase of a specific commodity or material, the buyers concerned may develop into specialists who come to know the product and supplier market extremely well, thus bringing large-scale cost benefits for the business. A buyer who is responsible for purchasing from a specific supplier can build up a long-term relationship with that supplier, with an open and personal relationship developing over time, which is especially important when procuring scarce or strategic materials.

The organisational structure can also be subdivided internally into activity groups in which specific people assume responsibility for executing specific activities such as:

- Purchasing and negotiation
- Follow-up and expediting
- Administration
- Purchasing and supply research
- Inventory holding
- Maintaining long-term relationships with suppliers

The disadvantage of this approach is that certain staff members have to do stereotyped work and do not have the opportunity for further development.

22.4.2.3 Coordination with other functional management areas

Traditionally coordination was regarded as a management task. However, this book follows the latest trends and sees coordination as part of organising. Therefore, little mention is made here of coordination.

However, because the purchasing and supply function has a support role and function, coordination with other functions in the business and with suppliers is important. The purchasing and supply function cannot make an optimal contribution to the objectives of the business and the supply chain in isolation. Coordination of the purchasing and supply function occurs at three levels:

- Various purchasing and supply activities must be coordinated internally in the purchasing and supply function.
- The purchasing environment (suppliers) must be coordinated with purchasing and supply activities.
- The purchasing and supply function must be coordinated with other functional management areas such as finance, marketing and production and eventually the needs of the final consumer.

Purchasing and supply coordination

Purchasing and supply coordination may be regarded as the conscious effort to harmonise the activities of the purchasing and supply function, the activities of other functional areas, and those of suppliers in ways to ensure full cooperation in the pursuit of purchasing and supply objectives.

Open communication, conscious motivation, standardisation of specifications, procedures and documentation are aids to improve coordination internally in the purchasing and supply function, in the business itself, and externally with suppliers. Strategic alliances with suppliers and integrated systems are important aids for coordination. The just-in-time (JIT), materials requirements planning (MRP), and other systems plan and control not only the inventory and materials flow process, as is generally accepted, but are also important coordinating instruments within the purchasing and supply function and the business, and with suppliers.

22.4.2.4 Cross-functional sourcing teams

Cross-functional sourcing teams

A cross-functional sourcing team consists of personnel from at least three functions brought together to execute a purchasing related (materials or services) assignment or solve a purchasing related problem.

The use of cross-functional sourcing or purchasing teams is an important practice in the supply chain management approach. The purchaser cooperates on a team with colleagues in other functional management areas to perform numerous tasks, which include supplier selection, negotiating corporate wide purchasing agreements, developing cost reduction strategies, developing sourcing strategies, developing suppliers and the evaluation of suppliers' performance. Purchasers are also involved in other teams tasked with specific tasks such as value analysis and the development of new products.

The objective is to obtain a wide perspective on problems, stimulate innovative thinking and obtain the best value for the organisations and the customers. The teams may be permanent, or else exist only for a specific period or until a specific task has been completed. Suppliers can be included in a functional team for certain tasks, such as new product development or the establishment of quality standards. Personnel of various firms in the supply chain may also be included in a purchasing and supply (sourcing) team.

To be a member of a cross-functional team, a buyer must have the ability to work with groups and display leadership qualities.

22.4.3 Control in the purchasing and supply function

Purchasing and supply control, like control in other functional management areas of a business, is the measure adopted to ensure that purchasing and supply objectives are pursued within acceptable and accepted standards or norms and guidelines according to a specific policy established during purchasing and supply planning. Purchasing and supply planning, and, more specifically, the formulation of objectives, is therefore the first step in the control process. The steps comprise setting objectives, setting criteria and norms, measuring actual performance, comparing actual performance with the norms, studying deviations, and taking corrective measures (if necessary). The steps in the control process are discussed in detail and illustrated in chapter 12. Areas of control in the purchasing and supply situation, however, require further investigation. The management task in the purchasing and supply function, and the performance of purchasing and supply activities, need to be evaluated (controlled).

22.4.3.1 The assessment of purchasing and supply management

The **management** performance of the purchasing and supply function should be evaluated just like other activities of the purchasing and supply function, because management can influence the overall job performance and achievement of the purchasing and supply function and, ultimately, the performance of the business. Management is intangible, and difficult to measure quantitatively. Therefore, there is a certain amount of subjectivity in measuring management:

An evaluation sheet or questionnaire can be used to assess management performance in purchasing.[5] This may include aspects such as:

- The leadership shown in the introduction of new ideas, systems, approaches or strategies
- The number or percentage of purchasing contracts established
- The knowledge and skills to lead the purchasing and supply function in an increasingly complex purchasing environment
- The relationships established with strategic suppliers
- The adequacy of performance appraisal and control systems in the purchasing and supply function
- The contribution to cross-functional teams
- The role in the establishment and management of supply chains
- The effectiveness of the use of the total purchasing leverage of the firm
- The scope and demarcation of authority of purchasing and supply activities at the level of supply chain, business, function and plant
- The appropriateness of purchasing and supply policies, procedures and practices

22.4.3.2 Assessment of purchasing and supply activities

As was mentioned earlier, the aim of the purchasing and supply function is to supply the business in the most effective way with the right materials, of the desired quality, at the right place and time, in the right quantities, at the right price. To realise this objective, the purchasing and supply function has to perform certain activities. Control is necessary to ascertain whether these activities are being performed **effectively**. The following control points or criteria can be used to gauge the effectiveness of purchasing and supply activities:[6]

- **Price proficiency**, by, for example, comparing actual prices with planned or market prices, the number and value of discounts negotiated for a specific period, and determining which part of every rand turnover constitutes purchasing costs
- **Supplier performance**, by, for example,

noting rejected orders, orders received late, and the number of times it was necessary to expedite
- **Timeliness**, by, for example, noting the number of orders indicated as urgent and the number of operations interruptions or operations rescheduling as a result of shortages
- **Cost saving**, by, for example comparing costs with those of previous periods
- **Workload**, by, for example, looking at the number of orders and requisitions
- **Purchasing costs**, by expressing administrative purchasing costs as a percentage of the monetary value of purchases
- **Inventory holding**, by calculating inventory turnover and making further enquiries into inventory losses and obsolescence of stock
- **Relationship performance with suppliers**, by means of a survey or scrutiny of supplier turnover, or number of alliances formed
- **Relationship with other functional management areas**, by monitoring the diligent execution of requests to the purchasing and supply function, and the contribution purchasers make in cross-functional teams

Once these measurement criteria have been laid down, the actual results can be measured and compared with a standard or norm, for example past performance or that of similar businesses. A report on performance and problem areas should be compiled and submitted to top management with the necessary recommendations. (See again the elements of or steps in the control process in chapter 12.)

22.4.3.3 Concluding remarks about control

A brief overview of the important management task of control in the purchasing and supply function has been given. Only a few criteria have been mentioned for the assessment of performance. However, every business should develop as many criteria for control as possible and cooperate with other businesses to develop **benchmarks**.

Critical thinking

Recall the case study about SAB at the beginning of this chapter. What in the scenario gives an indication that the management has a high regard for the purchasing function and that management is satisfied with the performance of the function?

22.5 Tools available to purchasing and supply management

Purchasing and supply managers have certain aids at their disposal to facilitate the execution of the management tasks of planning, organising and control. Each of these aids will now be briefly discussed.

22.5.1 Benchmarks

A tool in laying down standards for setting objectives and measuring the performance of the purchasing and supply function is to obtain benchmarks in the industry or other industries. One way of doing this is to obtain a benchmarking partner in a similar industry and then for both to compare the performance of various aspects of their two businesses, for example prices, purchasing costs, inventory turnover and supplier turnover. Thus, for example, Eskom, Transnet and Telkom could be benchmarking partners, because all three operate in the same environment, have the same background, and purchase a large quantity of materials – for example copper wire, wooden poles and fuel – in the same markets. Such a partnership can help iron out problem areas, especially in respect of purchasing and supply processes and practices.

Benchmarks are also frequently compiled by outside organisations such as the Centre for Advanced Purchasing Studies in the USA and by consultants who develop benchmarks to "sell" or use during consultations for businesses. Some organisations use benchmarks more liberally than is explained above. They will, for example, use benchmarks from other industries and also international benchmarks.

Critical thinking

Recall the case study about SAB at the beginning of this chapter. What would you say is the most logical way in which SAB should do their benchmarking?

22.5.2 Purchasing and supply budgets

The chapters on financial management (chapters 17 and 18) deal with budgets. Clearly, a budget is, in essence, the financial plan for the allocation of the business's resources for a specific period. A purchasing and supply budget, like other budgets, is a planning aid as well as a financial standard for control. Besides planning and control, the purchasing and supply budget also has a role in coordinating the activities of the purchasing and supply function with the activities of other functional management areas in the business. In fact, it would be impossible to prepare the purchasing and supply budget without inputs from marketing, operations and financial budgets. The purchasing and supply budget mainly comprises two components, the materials and the administrative budget:

- **The administrative budget.** This consists of budgeted cost components such as salaries for the purchasing and supply function, stationery, telephone costs, travelling and hotel costs, and the cost of renting offices and warehouse equipment. This budget is not as important as the materials budget, but still plays a major role in the control of costs in the purchasing and supply function.
- **The materials budget.** The materials budget is especially important because of the broad use of the money involved and because it is an instrument for planning purchasing and supply quantities and inventory levels, timing of purchases, and purchase prices. The materials budget is closely related to the operations and marketing budget. The marketing budget forms the foundation of the operations budget, which, in turn, underpins the materials budget (see figure 22.8 on page 560). The materials budget is therefore also an important instrument in the coordination of the purchasing and supply function with other functional management areas in the business.

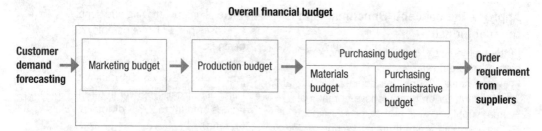

Figure 22.8: The relationship of the purchasing and supply budgets with other budgets

22.5.3 Purchasing and supply policy

The purchasing and supply policy is a written directive from top management (usually supported by the head of the purchasing and supply function) to the purchasing and supply function to act in a prescribed manner in handling specific purchasing and supply issues. The purchasing and supply policy is subordinate to the policy of the business, and in practice should support it. If the policy of the business is, for example, to make affirmative action a priority, purchasing and supply policy should make provision for this, not only in respect of appointing and developing personnel of designated groups within the purchasing and supply function, but also with regard to purchasing from designated suppliers. The purchasing and supply policy gives direction and can be regarded as a framework within which buyers act. It reduces the need to refer too many matters back to higher authority. It also eliminates misunderstandings and concentrates purchasing efforts on the achievement of the agreed objectives.

The purchasing and supply policy comprises sub-policies, of which the following are the most important:

- **Policy in respect of ethical purchasing practices.** This policy usually contains guidelines on the actions of buyers in terms of loyalty and the protection of the interests of the employer in the purchasing situation; avoidance of conflict of interest; acceptance of gifts and samples; purchases by employees; selling to employees; and adherence to the law during buying transactions.
- **Policy in respect of internal purchasing and supply matters.** This policy usually contains guidelines on matters such as the organisation of the purchasing and supply function (for example the extent of centralisation or decentralisation) and guidelines on the authority and responsibility of each of those subject to the policy; guidelines on the use or non-use of contracts; purchases by employees in other functions; administrative and operational guidelines that find expression in the purchasing and supply procedure manual. (Refer to section 23.2 for purchasing and supply procedures.)
- **Supplier policy.** This policy contains guidelines on supplier related issues: one or more suppliers per item; the use of local or foreign suppliers or suppliers in far-off places; the selection of suppliers; evaluation of suppliers' performance; reciprocal purchasing and supply. The policy on purchasing from previously disadvantaged suppliers and small businesses is often included in this policy. However, the issue of disadvantaged purchasing and supply is sometimes regarded as too important, and a separate policy is therefore formulated in this regard.

Critical thinking

Recall again the case study about SAB. How important do you think the empowerment of disadvantaged suppliers is for SAB? Based on your conclusion, do you think SAB has a separate policy document for purchasing from disadvantaged suppliers?

22.6 Summary

The purchasing and supply function is an important one because:

- It has a significant influence on the profitability of the business.
- It is often the greatest spender of business revenue.
- This function makes it possible for the business to sell its final products at competitive prices.

The purchasing and supply function, like all other functions in the business, should be planned, organised and controlled to ensure that it helps achieve the objectives of the business. This chapter has provided some insight into the management of the purchasing and supply function. The main sourcing activities (activities of the purchasing and supply function) will be discussed in chapter 23.

Key terms

Benchmarks	Profit-leverage effect
Centralisation	Purchasing and supply budgets
Cross-functional sourcing teams	Purchasing and supply function
Decentralisation	Purchasing and supply policy
Ethical purchasing practices	Supplier policy
Inventory management	Suppliers
Logistics management	Supply chain management
Materials management	

? Questions for discussion

1. What is the nature of purchasing and supply activities? Discuss this in the context of the purchasing and supply function.
2. What are the new concepts or approaches to the provision of materials to a business? Identify and explain them.
3. What is the role and importance of the purchasing and supply function in the success and efficiency of a business?
4. How are the management tasks of planning, organising and control applied in the purchasing and supply function?
5. What management aids are at the disposal of the purchasing and supply manager? identify and explain them.

References

1. "Purchasing" is also known as "procurement". "Supply" is added because purchasing or procurement is no longer seen as a reactive, service function of organisations. In modern firms it is acknowledged that purchasing makes a strategic contribution. Purchasing management is involved in processes, both in the firm and at suppliers, to ensure the efficient flow of materials and services in the right quantity and of right quality at the right time to the organisation and through the supply chain as a whole at the lowest possible total cost. For example, the purchasing function studies the supply market of strategic commodities and develops supply strategies accordingly. When the purchasing or procurement function is on such a level that it makes a strategic impact (when "supply" is added) companies (for example Mittal Steel and SABMiller) often call the function the "commercial function". (Refer to the case study "Procurement at South African Breweries" at the beginning of this chapter.)
2. Baillie, P., Farmer, D., Jessop, D. & Jones, D., *Purchasing principles and management*, 9th edition, Prentice Hall (Pearson Education), Essex, England, 2005, p. 138.

3. Lysons, K. & Farrington, B., *Purchasing and supply chain management*, 7th edition, Prentice Hall (Pearson Education), Essex, England, 2006, p, 20.

4. Hugo, W.M.J., Badenhorst-Weiss, J.A. & Van Biljon, E.H.B., *Purchasing and supply management*, 5th edition, Van Schaik, Pretoria, 2006, pp. 27–32.

5. *Ibid.*, p. 45.

6. Baillie et al., *op. cit.*, p. 397.

SOURCING ACTIVITIES

The purpose of this chapter

The purpose of this chapter is to explain the purchasing or sourcing process in organisations, and to provide an overview of the most important activities involved in the process.

Learning outcomes

The content of this chapter will enable learners to:

- Illustrate and explain the logical steps to be followed in a purchasing and supply transaction

- Indicate the role of the purchasing and supply function in quality decisions
- Emphasise the role of quantity decisions in the purchasing and supply process
- Give an overview of the selection and management of suppliers
- Pinpoint certain aspects of pricing as purchasing and supply activity
- Place the right time for purchasing and supply in perspective
- Briefly explain the outsourcing strategy
- Give an overview of purchasing and supply research as an aid for decision making
- Briefly explain negotiation as an aid in concluding purchasing transactions

23.1 **Introduction**

Purchasing and supply activities are mentioned in chapter 22, section 22.1. The main activity groups of the purchasing and supply function emerge from the traditional definition of the purchasing function: the purchase and supply of a product of the **right quality**, at the **right price**, in the **right quantities**, at the **right time**, and from the **right supplier**.

Each purchasing and supply activity is discussed separately in this chapter, but this does not mean that purchasing and supply activities exist, and are performed, in isolation. In fact, purchasing and supply activities are often executed simultaneously and are interdependent. Price and quality, price and time, price and choice of suppliers, and time and quantity are inseparably intertwined. The practical execution of purchasing and supply activities is clear from the discussion of the stages in the purchasing and supply process or cycle.

The case study on page 564 provides insight into how a purchasing and supply related problem can have a negative effect on many participants in a supply chain.

Case study

Cooldrinks lose their fizz

While the world worries about an oversupply of carbon dioxide, caused by increasing emissions, in South Africa, we've almost run out of carbon dioxide (CO_2) to put into soft drinks.

The national CO_2 shortage has in the past four weeks affected normal production of Coca-Cola brands, and it is likely to persist right into the new year.

Sasol and PetroSA, the primary suppliers of CO_2, closed their plants for routine maintenance earlier this year. Consequently, they were not able to meet commitments to Afrox, which supplies Amalgamated Beverage Industries (ABI) with gas. ABI bottles Coca-Cola in South Africa. Since the shortage, ABI has only been able to meet at least 60% to 75% of the normal demand. But in November and December, demand is 150% higher than usual, resulting in a significant shortfall.

Retailers, general dealers and neighbourhood supermarkets throughout the country are affected. The company has more than 43 000 customers who supply soft drinks to consumers. ABI is planning to import about 20 million soft drink cans during November and December, said company spokesperson Michael Farr, but the usual variety of brands and sizes will not be available.

"We are expecting our first shipment from (the United Kingdom) and Singapore (this week)," he confirmed. He said ABI would focus on Coca-Cola core brands, which include Coca-Cola, Sprite and Fanta. These soft drinks make up about 80% of what is currently consumed in the market. However, lower volume brands such as the Fanta Pine and Grape, Sprite Zero and Tab will remain in short supply for the next four months.

ABI says it hopes the shortage will be under control by January 2007, but it could ease in a matter of days. Farr said the company is expecting a full supply of food grade CO_2 from Afrox next week. "We are working flat out to normalise supplies as soon as we can and, in the short term, we are doing our best to ensure that all our customers receive the maximum stock that we are able to provide," said Farr. He added that fair supply to customers is currently done on the basis of how much the customers need and that ABI has an obligation to meet this need. But at least we still have alcohol. Contrary to earlier reports, SABMiller has confirmed that beer production won't be affected, as its breweries are self-reliant as far as CO_2 is concerned.

PetroSA spokesperson Butana Nkosi said it would be able to supply CO_2 by next Friday. Sasol spokesperson Marina Bidoli said the company's Sasolburg plant had been shut down last month, resulting in a 12-day CO_2 shortage. However the plant has been operating at full production since October 27.

Shoprite spokesperson Brian Weyers said the shortage was unpredictable and that all areas would not be affected in the same way. "Should a shortage of carbonated soft drinks arise, it is expected that consumers will switch to alternative products in the beverage category, such as cordials, nectars and fruit juices."

But spaza-shop owner Tshepo Tshikane of Mogale City felt betrayed by ABI for failing to communicate the CO_2 shortage to informal business sector players. He explained that carbonated drinks make up half of his income in summer and that limited stock could damage his business. "Why can't these people come up with alternatives, such as importing carbon dioxide?" he asked.

Source: Dibetle, M., "Cooldrinks lose their fizz", *Mail & Guardian online*, http://www.mg.co.za/articlePage.aspx?articleid=290233&area=insight/insight_econ (21 November 2006).

23.2 The purchasing and supply cycle

The discussion of the **purchasing and supply cycle** or process in this section provides a clear picture of the steps in the purchasing and supply transaction, how the steps follow each other logically, who in the business is involved in each step, and the documentation involved in each step. Not all the steps are necessarily taken in each purchasing and supply transaction, and some steps often take place simultaneously.

A large number of businesses in South Africa have computerised their purchasing and supply process. Computerised systems are also based on the purchasing and supply cycle discussed here. Computerisation expedites the process considerably and usually reduces the documentation involved. The steps in the purchasing and supply cycle can be divided into three main phases:

- **The notification phase**, when the purchasing and supply function is informed of the need
- **The order phase**, during which the purchasing and supply function checks the documentation, assesses the newness of the purchase, contacts suppliers, orders, receives and inspects the materials, and acknowledges their receipt
- **The post-order phase**, which primarily entails sorting out discrepancies, processing and handling documentation, paying suppliers, and keeping sound relations with suppliers

Figure 23.1 on page 566 reflects the basic steps in the purchasing and supply cycle, the functional management areas involved, and the documentation.

These steps are now explained in more detail:
- **The development and description of a need.** Because of the activities of other functional management areas (also called "users" or "consumers"), there is a need

for materials and services. The need is conveyed by means of a requisition, order card, or materials and specification list to the purchasing and supply function. To ensure that the desired materials or services are purchased, the buyer must take careful note of the specification, which is actually a description of the need. The specification not only describes the material, but also the quality. The buyer should also look closely at the quantities specified and the date on which the materials or service are required. In a manufacturing business, the greatest need is for materials and services in the production or operational function, and in a retail organisation, in the marketing function (merchandise). (Note that operational and marketing functions are included as "Consumers" in figure 23.1.)

Critical thinking

What will happen if the consumer or functional departments do not describe their needs for materials or service clearly on a requisition? What will happen if a purchaser does not analyse the requisition carefully?

- **Choice of suppliers.** The choice of the right supplier is the principal activity of the purchasing and supply function, and is discussed in more detail later. The complexity of this decision will depend on various factors, for example whether it is a new purchase or a repurchase, whether a contract needs to be entered into or already exists, or whether standard or specialised materials are required. Depending on the factors, the buyer will use documents such as the register of suppliers, order forms, contracts, price lists, **quotations**, or **tenders**. In a new buying situation, especially where a contract has to be drawn up, determining the present and future availability of the materials or services is a vital consideration in the choice of suppliers. Determining the future availability of materials or services

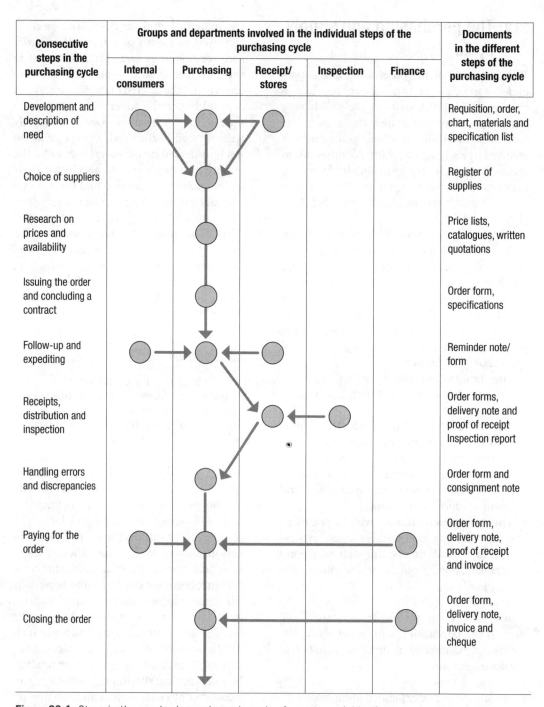

Consecutive steps in the purchasing cycle	Groups and departments involved in the individual steps of the purchasing cycle					Documents in the different steps of the purchasing cycle
	Internal consumers	Purchasing	Receipt/ stores	Inspection	Finance	
Development and description of need						Requisition, order, chart, materials and specification list
Choice of suppliers						Register of supplies
Research on prices and availability						Price lists, catalogues, written quotations
Issuing the order and concluding a contract						Order form, specifications
Follow-up and expediting						Reminder note/ form
Receipts, distribution and inspection						Order forms, delivery note and proof of receipt Inspection report
Handling errors and discrepancies						Order form and consignment note
Paying for the order						Order form, delivery note, proof of receipt and invoice
Closing the order						Order form, delivery note, invoice and cheque

Figure 23.1: Steps in the purchasing and supply cycle of a commercial business

Source: Adapted from Hugo, W.M.J., Badenhorst-Weiss, J.A. & Van Biljon, E.H.B., *Purchasing and supply management*, 5th edition, Van Schaik, Pretoria, 2006, p.16.

is no easy task. A study of the technical, managerial and financial abilities of suppliers, their progressiveness, idle capacity and past performance (if used in the past) is necessary. This is done by analysing the financial statements of suppliers, making personal visits and conducting interviews with their staff and management, and obtaining credit bureau reports. It is important to note that user functions (for example marketing or production) may make recommendations about a particular supplier, but the final choice rests with the purchasing and supply function.

Critical thinking

How will the decision process on suppliers differ if a construction firm purchases maintenance materials, iron rods, cement and consulting engineering services?

- **Determining prices.** This is actually part of the previous step. The prices of standard materials or services and materials or services with a low monetary value are determined with the aid of price lists and telephonic, verbal or written quotations. Because standard materials or services are available everywhere, prices are in fact determined by competition. The prices of non-standard or specialised materials or custom-made items are often determined by tender or quotation in conjunction with **negotiations**.
- **Placing an order or concluding a contract.** The order and the contract are important documents because they spell out unequivocally to the supplier the needs of the business and the conditions of the purchasing transaction, and because they constitute a legally valid contract to which both parties are bound by law. The order or contract should contain specific conditions for the transaction in respect of quantities, quality, prices, discounts, delivery dates, customs clearances, and exchange rate clearances.

- **Expediting and follow-up.** The purchasing and supply function's task is completed only when materials or services of the right quality have been received, in the right quantities, at the right place, and, most importantly, at the right time. One of the administrative tasks in the purchasing and supply function is to determine whether materials are received or services performed in good time. If not, or if they are overdue, the supplier should be reminded by letter, facsimile, telephone, or electronically if a computer system links the business and its suppliers, that it has not adhered to the clauses of the contract and that it should concentrate on the speedy delivery of required materials. The importance of this task is often underestimated. If a supplier is late with deliveries, this can interrupt the production or operational process in a manufacturing business, or leave a retailer with empty shelves. This can also have serious implications for supplier relations and the continued use of a specific supplier.
- **Receipt, inspection and distribution.** As mentioned previously, stores reception (as a sub-function of purchasing and supply) is responsible for checking the quantities and conditions of materials when they are received. The delivery note of the supplier is signed and is proof that the materials were received. Inspection (a sub-function of purchasing and supply) checks the quality of the materials and compiles an inspection report. The materials are sent to the users (that is, the functions that requested the products) with a copy of the order, or they are taken up as inventory in the stores. In the case of services the specific users who requested the services need to compile a report on the performance of the service provider.
- **Handling errors and discrepancies.** Communication and keeping good relations with suppliers are important tasks of the purchasing and supply function. If defective

materials are received or services performed poorly, the purchasing and supply function should communicate with the suppliers concerning these in a way that will prevent future defective consignments, but still ensure good relations.

Critical thinking

How will the handling of errors differ when a furniture maker receives an unacceptable consignment of wood, on the one hand, and screws, on the other hand?

- **Paying for the order.** It is the task of purchasing and supply to prepare authorisation for payment of the supplier. The purchasing and supply function checks the delivery note, the inspection report, the invoice, and the order, to confirm that the quantities, quality, price, and discounts are correct, and to verify the calculations. It then authorises the finance function to pay the supplier. The purchasing and supply function should execute this task carefully and quickly so that suppliers are paid in accordance with the payment policy of the business.
- **Closing of the order.** Once the supplier has been paid, the purchasing and supply function must file all documents pertaining to the particular transaction or incorporate them into a system for future reference. This is a crucial part of the evaluation of a supplier's performance, and also constitutes an assessment of the purchasing and supply function's performance.

Critical thinking

Recall the case study of the soft drink industry (at the start of the chapter). Where in the purchasing process did the most crucial problems occur?

In the discussion of the purchasing and supply cycle, we have placed in perspective the principal purchasing and supply ac-

tivities, namely decisions regarding quality and quantities, choosing and managing suppliers, pricing, decisions regarding purchasing, and supply times. The next step is to examine these activities in greater depth.

23.3 Quality decisions as a purchasing and supply activity

23.3.1 The role of quality

The four main factors in each purchasing and supply decision are quality, supplier service, delivery and price. Quality is probably the most important of these factors. Even if the price and the service that a supplier offers are outstanding, material or services will not be bought from the supplier if the quality is in any way lower than required, because the material or service will not perform the function for which it was purchased.

Quality is an inseparable part of other purchasing and supply activities. Top quality is normally associated with high prices and vice versa. Quality also determines the number of suppliers. The higher the quality requirements, the fewer suppliers there will be to satisfy such requirements. Quality of materials also influences inventory holding or the quantity to be purchased. In the case of high-quality requirements, a reliable supplier that can meet the specification and deliver on time will be chosen. Smaller volumes of materials can therefore be kept in stock, because fewer materials will be rejected during inspection. In fact, continuous high quality is an absolute necessity in stockless systems such as **just-in-time (JIT)** and **materials requirements planning** (MRP), which are discussed in section 23.4.3.

The quality of purchased products and services rests on the various considerations discussed in the following section, namely:
- Determining the right quality for a given goal

- Describing quality so that both the buyer and seller understand it clearly
- Controlling quality to ensure that requirements are met

23.3.2 Determining the right quality

A buyer has a different perspective of the concept "the right quality" to that of a technical person. From a purchasing and supply perspective, the right quality can be defined as follows:

> **Definition**
>
> The right quality is that quality that is purchased at the lowest price, which satisfies a specific need and performs the function for which it was purchased.

For **engineers and designers**, technical considerations such as job performance and reliability are often the only factors that are important. It frequently happens that engineers and designers, without any commercial considerations, request the purchase of the highest or best quality materials or services, when lower quality materials or services would do the job just as well. Buyers are more attuned to commercial considerations such as the right quality, availability, price and delivery. A buyer should therefore have the right to question technical requirements, or to request that **specifications** be reconsidered on the strength of commercial considerations.

The best quality is therefore not necessarily the right quality. The right quality for a specific purchase is determined by balancing suitability (technical requirements), availability and cost (commercial requirements).

The **end-user** and/or the **marketing function** also often provide input on suitable quality, since the right quality materials not only increase the productivity of the user, but also influence the quality and price of the final product to be marketed. The quality of products is not only important for marketing, but also for public relations, because this influences the image the business wants to project, and will be decisive in determining which customers wish to associate with the business and its products. After-sales service, a policy on taking back materials or service of a poor quality, and the provision of guarantees by the supplier are important considerations that tie in closely with decisions pertaining to quality. Suppliers also play a vital role in determining suitable quality, because they are often in a position to recommend alternative materials or services.

> **Critical thinking**
>
> Will purchasers in the motor assembly industry query the quality of parts to be installed in the engine of a motor car?

23.3.3 Description of quality

Quality refers to measurable qualities, a condition or characteristics of materials or service, usually expressed according to grade, class, brand or specifications. It should be possible to describe the desired quality, otherwise there is no way the person requisitioning can communicate clearly with a buyer, and a buyer with a supplier, about what exactly is required. (For communication purposes, the description of quality is entered on the requisition and order.) The description of quality is also important because it serves as a measure for judging the quality of incoming materials by means of inspection or the evaluation of services performed. The following methods and forms should be noted:

- **Specifications are the most general method of describing quality.** A specification is a description of non-standard materials or services that are able to perform a certain function. Specifications for materials can be drawn up according to dimensions or physical features such as tolerance, work ability, uniformity and chemical composition. For services other dimensions will be used, such as the nature of the service and a step-by-step exposition of actions, timelines and required outcomes for each step. The purchasing and supply function should endeavour to prevent specifications being drawn up that are to the advantage of only one supplier, and that eliminate competition. A supplier can, for example, change an unimportant feature of material (for example the colour or name) to distinguish it from competing materials. If the user or buyer specifies the unique name or colour of the specific material, all competition (which is essential in the purchasing and supply process) is eliminated, even though the material performs exactly the same function as others competing in the market.

- **Standardisation is a further aid in describing quality.** It is, in effect, the process of making materials, methods, practices and techniques uniform. Standardisation can be set by a business or organisation, or nationally or internationally by an industry, and it has several advantages. If a business or organisation standardises materials, total inventory can be reduced, because fewer kinds and qualities are kept. Standardisation also improves collaboration between the user and buyer in a business, and communication between the buyer and supplier. Industrial and international standards make possible the mass production of products. Because many suppliers manufacture standard products, and standard materials can be bought everywhere, competition in the market is increased, and the purchasing and supply price of the product is reduced.
- Other **forms of quality description are market grades, brands, SABS (South African Bureau of Standards) standards, engineering drawings and samples.**

Critical thinking

What is the value of standardisation in a franchise group such as Steers? Has standardisation any value in a ladies' fashion boutique? If so, in what way?

23.3.4 **Control of quality**

It is imperative to control the quality of incoming materials and purchased services. Poor quality materials and services interrupt the manufacturing process, expose workers to danger, have a detrimental effect on the final product, and ultimately reduce the satisfaction of end-users and alter the perception they have of the business and its products.

Inspection is the normal process used to control quality. It is a method that ensures that the measurement, design, job performance and quality of materials or services received satisfy the standards or specifications on the order, and that goods or services are suitable for the purpose for which they have been ordered. Inspection is a technical process, and is not the task of purchasers, but that of the quality control function, or the function where purchased services are performed.

During inspection by quality controllers, samples of delivered materials or services are subjected to tests. However, inspection per se is not enough to guarantee the quality of incoming materials or services. If the purchasing and supply function buys from a supplier that has maintained top quality standards for years, it is actually unnecessary to inspect its products or services. In such a case, the business can negotiate a **supplier certification agreement** with the supplier. Based on agreed terms, the supplier and the buyer's quality control functions work together for a specific time, and the materials and operation processes are subject to intensive inspection for a certain period. After this, the supplier is certified, and it becomes responsible for quality assurance.

The SABS has a certification scheme where by enterprises are encouraged and supported in endeavours to establish and operate quality control systems, or quality assurance programmes. Part of the certification scheme of the SABS is the well-known ISO 9000 to 9004 and ISO 14 000 international standards. Because the establishment and operation of such programmes by suppliers is extremely costly, and the quality of materials or services is assured, buyers will be prepared to pay high prices particularly when high quality is crucial.

> **Critical thinking**
>
> Recall the case study of the soft drink industry (at the start of the chapter). Do you think that Sasol, PetroSA, Afrox and ABI have quality assurance programmes and implement ISO standards? Give reasons for your answer.

23.4 Deciding on purchasing and supply quantities

23.4.1 The need for inventory holding

If the operations function is 100% certain of the quantity of materials to be used in the manufacturing process, the marketing function is 100% certain about how many products are going to be sold, there are no supply problems in the supplier market, and the incoming materials completely satisfy quality requirements, then the purchasing and supply function can buy the exact quantity of materials required at a certain time.

Unfortunately, such a situation simply does not exist in practice. Because marketing and production or operations budgets are based solely on estimates, and the supplier market in South Africa tends often to be unreliable with regard to delivery and quality, the buyer has to purchase more materials than required to prevent a possible shortage when

they are needed, with the result that inventory holding becomes necessary. Inventory holding is therefore inextricably intertwined with the task of a buyer.

Pre-1994, during the sanctions era, it was normal practice for South African businesses to keep large stocks, especially those importing materials from abroad. After South Africa's readmission to normal world trade, however, the worldwide trend of keeping minimum inventory also took root in South Africa. The reason for this trend is that inventory holding generates considerable costs, and large amounts of operating capital are tied up in inventory. One of the main aims of contemporary approaches such as supply chain management and the concomitant enablers such as supplier alliances, e-procurement, JIT, MRP, **enterprise resource planning** (ERP), **efficient consumer response** (ECR), **automatic replenishment** (AR) and **quick response** (QR) is to limit **inventory holding** to the minimum.

If the holding of inventory is so unpopular, why should it be held? There are two major reasons for this:

- To ensure that the operations process (or the marketing process in a retailing organisation) can continue without interruptions resulting from shortages of materials
- To utilise cost savings through longer production runs and volume discounts

It is therefore clear that too little or too much inventory is undesirable, and that both have certain cost implications or disadvantages. Table 23.1 on page 572 provides a succinct summary of some of the implications of too little or too much inventory.

> **Critical thinking**
>
> Why should fuel companies keep more stock rather than less? Why should a retailer such as Edgars or Fruit & Veg not keep too large stocks?

Table 23.1: Implications of inventory positions

Disadvantages of too much inventory	Disadvantages of too little inventory
• Operating capital is tied up with the resultant opportunity and interest costs • Losses in terms of depreciation, obsolescence, damage and theft • Costs in terms of storage space (rental or interest), more warehouse staff and equipment, and bigger insurance premiums	• Higher unit prices as a result of smaller orders • More urgent orders with concomitant higher order and transport costs, and strained relations with suppliers • Cost of production or job interruptions and the accompanying strained relations with users or marketers in the business • Lost sales because of empty shelves in the retail organisation and the resultant negative influence on its image

23.4.2 Inventory costs

Certain costs increase when large quantities of stock are purchased, while others increase with the purchase of small quantities. It is necessary to categorise these cost elements and examine them more closely to determine optimal inventory quantity, that is, the inventory quantity that results in the lowest total cost of inventory.

Inventory-carrying costs are those involved in keeping inventory. They include the cost of storage, salaries of warehouse staff, insurance, property tax, obsolescence, wear and tear, theft, interest charges (for the financing of inventory), and opportunity costs (loss of income from investment in alternative profit-bearing projects, as capital has been invested in inventory). Larger order quantities cause larger inventory levels and therefore higher inventory-carrying costs. The opposite applies to small quantities and lower inventory levels.

Inventory-ordering costs are the costs of placing an order. Ordering costs include the salaries of purchasing and supply and expediting personnel, stationery, telephone and fax costs, on-line (e-procurement) costs, and postage. Larger purchasing and supply quantities result in fewer orders being placed and a decline in ordering costs.

Total inventory costs consist of the sum total of inventory-carrying costs and inventory-ordering costs. Ordering costs decline and carrying costs increase as order quantities increase, and ordering costs increase (because more orders have to be made) and carrying costs decrease as order quantities decrease. The influence of quantity on the two cost categories is indicated clearly in figure 23.2. The lowest total inventory cost is achieved where the two curves (carrying cost and ordering cost curves) intersect, in other words, when ordering costs are equal to carrying costs. The number of units opposite the lowest total inventory cost on the graph is the most **economic order quantity** (EOQ).

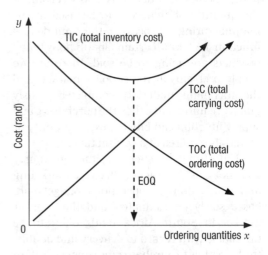

Figure 23.2: The economic order quantity

23.4.3 Inventory control systems

Inventory should be managed and controlled so that optimal inventory levels can be maintained. This means that inventory should be kept at such a level that the best service can be rendered to the user or customer at the lowest possible cost, and the quantities ordered each time should keep inventory at this level. Most inventory control systems are based on the principles of one of the systems described in sections 23.4.3.1 to 23.4.3.6.

23.4.3.1 The system of fixed order quantities

This system is based on the principle that each time new inventory is required, a fixed quantity (the EOQ) is ordered. The system is represented visually in figure 23.3.

The EOQ is ordered once inventory reaches a certain level (order point B) as a result of the use (or selling) of inventory items (A to B). Inventory is then replenished by ordering the EOQ to reach the maximum inventory level. The order level is determined in such a way that inventory does not become depleted during the delivery period of the order (lead time).

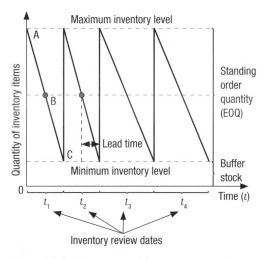

Figure 23.3: The system of fixed order quantities

The system is advantageous because attention is focused only on a specific item when the inventory level reaches the ordering point, and the same quantity is ordered every time. However, the system is unsuitable for items whose consumption or lead times are unreliable.

> **Applying the concept: The fixed order quantity system of a book publisher**
>
> A publisher may decide that when there are only 100 copies of a certain book in stock (level B) 3 000 copies need to be printed (that is, a fixed order quantity) to bring inventory up to level A. A buffer stock (for example, 50 books) is also kept as a precaution against unforeseen and exceptional circumstances.

> **Critical thinking**
>
> For which of the following situations will the **fixed order quantity** method be more suitable: a security gate manufacturer who delivers standardised security gates for large retail groups such as Makro and Builder's Warehouse or a retail shop such as Foshini?

23.4.3.2 The cyclical ordering system

According to this system, each item in the inventory is checked or reviewed at fixed intervals and is supplemented by an order to bring the inventory level to its maximum level again. Thus the ordering times are fixed, but the order quantity varies, as shown in figure 23.4 on page 574. The system is suitable for seasonal materials or materials used on an irregular basis, but where the acquisition of such materials can be planned far in advance on the basis of sales forecasts, for example in a clothing store. This system is used in grocery stores where, at the end of every week or month, stocktaking is done for each product on the shelves, and the order quantities

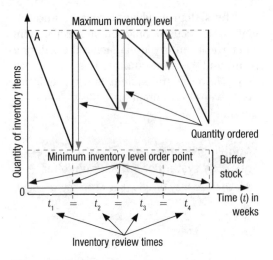

Figure 23.4: The cyclical ordering system

Critical thinking

Can MRP work if certain materials used in the production process need to be imported? What influence will the importation have on the inventory (stock) levels of the specific materials?

adjusted to the quantity on the shelves. Thus, for example, more cold drinks are ordered every week or month during summer than in winter.

23.4.3.3 The materials requirements planning (MRP) system

MRP is a computer-assisted system where the aim is to maintain minimum inventory levels. The system uses a computer to calculate the total need for materials that may be required by an operations process in a given period. The planned quantity of final products to be manufactured during the production or operations process, in the given period, is broken down into components and materials by the computer. It then determines the total need for each type of raw material and component, with due consideration for lead times, so that materials or components are received when the production process needs them. The advantage of the system is that inventory levels are low. However, the system works only if suppliers are extremely reliable with their delivery and quality. Contracts with suppliers are usually needed to keep this system going.

23.4.3.4 The just-in-time (JIT) system

This is in fact a production or operations scheduling system and not an inventory system. It virtually eliminates the holding of inventory. Its operation is based on re-quiring suppliers to deliver materials of the right quality to the business on the day they are needed and where they are needed – in other words, just in time. The system requires regular deliveries, and quantities should correspond exactly to needs. In other words, it is not the inventory system that determines the quantities to be purchased or to be delivered, but the operations (or production) system. Therefore, purchasing and supply has little or no influence on the quantities to be purchased. It is imperative for purchasing and supply to work closely with operations management, because the purchasing and supply function needs to be fully conversant with the changing needs of the operations system.

The JIT system works properly only if the supplier is extremely reliable and is integrated into the business's production or operations system. Supplier alliances are needed to make JIT work. The JIT system cannot satisfy all the needs of the business. Only materials used in the operations process are purchased according to the JIT approach. Requirements that do not relate to the manufacture of the business's final product, for example office and operations equipment and maintenance materials, obviously do not justify the use of the sophisticated JIT system and concomitant attention to the supplier base.

23.4.3.5 The quick response (QR) and automatic replenishment (AR) systems

QR is defined as a vertical strategy (in the supply chain) in which the manufacturer strives to provide products and services to its retail customers in exact quantities on a continuous basis with minimal lead times, resulting in minimum inventory levels throughout the retail apparel supply chain. QR can be regarded as the retail version of the manufacturing JIT concept – to deliver materials or merchandise to areas in the exact amount required at the precise time they are needed. With JIT the use of raw materials pulls raw materials into the production process. With QR merchandise is pulled by customer sales. In both cases information (about the production rate or the sales figures) is substituted with materials or merchandise.

AR is an integral part of any QR programme. AR can be defined as an exchange relationship in which the supplier replenishes or restocks inventory, based upon actual product usage and stock level information provided by the retail buyer. AR therefore provides the final customer (consumer) with the desired product and service in a timely fashion. The goal of AR is to manage inventory levels effectively. With AR, as already indicated, information is substituted for inventory or merchandise.[1]

23.4.3.6 The efficient consumer response (ECR) system

ECR was developed for the grocery industry and is based on the same principles as QR. ECR calls for the creation of a timely, accurate and paperless flow of information – relying heavily on electronic data interchange (EDI) and strategic alliances between supply chain members. The goal of ECR is to eliminate costs, such as inventory holding and ordering costs in an entire supply chain. The underlying objectives are to reduce cycle time (time from placing the order to receiving the goods) in

the supply chain, reduce inventories, avoid duplications in logistics costs and increase customer service.[2]

Critical thinking

Recall again the case study about the soft drinks industry. Do you think that Afrox and ABI keep sufficient stock of CO_2? Suppose they have kept two-weeks usage of CO_2. Do you think they could have prevented the crises in the consumer market? In view of the seasonal nature of demand for carbonated soft drinks, which inventory holding technique would you recommend to Afrox and ABI for CO_2?

23.5 The selection and management of suppliers

23.5.1 The importance of selecting the right suppliers

Selecting the right suppliers, particularly in the supply of strategic materials or services, is one of the most vital tasks of the purchasing and supply function, since effective purchasing and supply rely mainly on this. Competitive prices, reliable quality, timely deliveries, technical support, and good after-sales service are determined primarily by the choice of the right supplier. Hence, it is essential for the purchasing and supply function to make the effort and proceed systematically and objectively in selecting suppliers. An important consideration when making this choice is that a long-term relationship with suppliers of strategic products or services is necessary to ensure effective purchasing and supply at all times. Important components of such a relationship are honesty, fairness and frankness.

23.5.2 The selection process

Supplier selection is an ongoing process, because existing suppliers have to be constantly reconsidered with each new purchase, especially in view of changing circumstances and needs. Past performance of an existing supplier obviously counts a great deal in the selection process. However, the care taken in the selection process will be determined by the scope of the transaction, the availability of materials, their strategic value, and whether they are standard or custom made. Custom-made items are items for a specific purpose and are therefore not generally available in the market. Standard items, however, are freely available at more or less the same quality and price, and in this case the choice of suppliers is not particularly important.

The process starts with the compilation of a list of suppliers that may be able to satisfy the need. The list can be compiled from various sources, for example own supplier register, industrial advertisements, the Yellow Pages, trade guides, open tenders, shows and exhibitions. It is then reduced to a short list, after taking into account factors such as location, progressiveness, general reputation, and financial and technical ability. Suppliers on the short list are then requested to give a quote, or negotiations are conducted with them, to obtain the best value (in respect of price, quality, service and delivery) for the business. The final choice of a supplier is based on considerations such as past performance, quality, price, delivery, technical support, progressiveness and reliability.

Once the choice has been made, the next steps are the continuous evaluation of the performance of the supplier to ensure that it conforms to expectations, and the elimination of unsatisfactory suppliers. These will now be discussed in more detail.

23.5.3 Evaluating supplier performance

The objective evaluation of **supplier performance** is important for the following reasons:
- Ineffective or unreliable suppliers are identified.
- It leads to an improvement in supplier performance.
- It serves as a guideline for the development of suppliers.

Various methods can be used to evaluate the performance of suppliers, the most common being the weighted-point method.

With this method, weights are allocated to each factor taken into consideration. For the type of organisation indicated in table 23.2 the quality of purchased materials is the most important consideration. Therefore, a weight of four is assigned to it. If delivery is also important, but less than quality, it is assigned a weight of three. Depending on importance, price may receive a two and service a one. Every supplier's performance is rated out of ten in the different categories (quality, delivery, price and service) and each rating is multiplied by the specific weight in order to obtain a total for each factor. By

Table 23.2: Supplier performance evaluation by the weighted-point method

Assessment of weight	Quality (4)		Delivery (3)		Price (2)		Service (1)		Total
Suppliers	Rating	Performance	Rating	Performance	Rating	Performance	Rating	Performance	
Supplier A	8	32	7	21	6	12	5	5	70
Supplier B	7	28	3	9	6	12	1	1	50
Supplier C	9	36	6	18	5	10	9	9	73

adding the factor totals, an overall total for each supplier is obtained.

The supplier with the highest total has the best performance. This method is of particular importance in comparing suppliers. When only one supplier is used for particular materials or services, a different method can be used to make an assessment. For example, it could be made by purchasing and supply staff, users of the materials or services and the inspection function, using, for example, the categories "good", "satisfactory" or "unsatisfactory" with regard to quality, delivery, price and service. Then the purchasing firm can make a decision to continue using the supplier in the future or seek another supplier if the performance of the supplier is not acceptable.

23.5.4 Developing suppliers

Purchasing and supply functions may become involved in the development of suppliers for various reasons. Suppliers may be developed for affirmative purchasing purposes or to improve their performance as a result of performance appraisals, or if materials or service do not exist in the (local) market.

23.5.4.1 Affirmative purchasing

In the spirit of reconstruction and development, and setting right inequalities, there is increasing pressure on South African businesses to give disadvantaged suppliers who show potential an opportunity to enter the market. Large organisations can help these suppliers develop, over time, into fully fledged independent suppliers. Affirmative

purchasing and supply may be done in the following ways:

- When comparing quotations (prices) of the different suppliers, a certain percentage (see section 23.6.3) is subtracted from the quoted prices of independent disadvantaged suppliers in order to benefit them.
- Purchase specific pre-identified materials and services from disadvantaged suppliers with potential, and support such suppliers in adhering to the contract and executing orders. Support given to disadvantaged suppliers may be in the form of managerial and technical assistance, making facilities available, staff training, and advancing operating capital.
- Subcontract or outsource to disadvantaged suppliers products and services that were formerly produced by the business. Management of a business may, for example, decide to sell catering services to employees in the cafeteria, which then functions as a separate business, rendering services on a contract basis.
- Accord a certain preference percentage, when comparing prices, to other suppliers who, in turn, commit to making a certain percentage of their purchases from suppliers (second-tier suppliers) from disadvantaged groups.

23.5.4.2 Materials or service not available

If a firm has a need for a particular material or service, and such material or service is not available in the market, it can enter into a contract with a chosen supplier of another material or service to manufacture this material (product) or provide this service. Assistance to such a supplier may be in the form of staff training, the reconstruction or expansion of facilities, or the implementation of new facilities. A joint venture can be formed with the supplier. In any case a long-term agreement with such suppliers is a prerequisite.

23.5.4.3 Normal performance appraisal

Normal performance appraisals can contribute to the development of suppliers by pointing out their weaknesses, and they are thereby encouraged to perform better. This is an important factor in establishing successful long-term ties with suppliers.

23.5.5 Long-term relationships with suppliers

During the 1990s many new strategies developed in the supply of products and services. One of the most important developments was closer cooperation with suppliers in the form of strategic alliances or partnerships. Organisations have a variety of relationships with different suppliers. Some relationships are at arm's length, while other relationships are more involved. Every organisation, therefore, has various kinds of relationships with suppliers – from no involvement with suppliers of standard easy-to-get products or services, to high involvement with suppliers of strategic scarce materials or highly complicated, unique services. An alliance or a partnership is a high-involvement relationship. Attributes of strategic supplier alliances are trust and cooperation, interdependence, joint quality improvement efforts, information (and systems) sharing, risk and benefit sharing, and joint problem solving.

Critical thinking

Recall the case study of the soft drink industry (at the start of the chapter).
- Do you agree that CO_2 is a strategic material for ABI?
- Why can one make such a supposition?
- What kind of relationship should exist between ABI, Afrox, Sasol and PetroSA?
- Do you think that all the expectations and requirements of such a relationship were met in this case?
- Identify the cause of the problems in this case.

23.6 Pricing decisions

23.6.1 The "best" price

Price has traditionally been regarded as the decisive factor in awarding orders. However, low prices go hand in hand with higher costs in other areas, such as the costs and risks attached to low quality, and high inventory when low prices (as a result of quantity discounts) are linked to quantity. The right price is not necessarily the lowest one. The total or final costs should rather be seen as the decisive factor in awarding orders. In other words, price should be regarded as only one of the components of value, together with quality, delivery and cost of use. A buyer should always strive to obtain the highest value for the business.

On the one hand, the price paid for materials or services must be reasonable and should enable the purchasing enterprise to make its own product or service competitive in the market. On the other hand, a reasonable price should also be fair to the supplier to ensure that a supplier sells its materials or service at a price that will ensure its profitability and survival. The price should therefore be fair to the purchasing firm and the supplier in terms of profitability and value.

23.6.2 Price determination

The methods used to determine purchasing prices depend on the nature of the materials and the value of the transaction. **Published price lists** and available market information, including catalogues, brochures and advertisements in trade journals, are most suitable for the purchase of standard materials and orders of a low monetary value, for example when purchasing screws and stationery. Other methods of price determination are **quotations and tenders** (also called "bids" or "bidding"). When using quotations and tenders, suppliers are asked to make an offer. The purchaser calls for open tenders where the invitation to tender is published, and any supplier can make an offer. The trend, however, is to issue a request to tender to a number of known suppliers. These are the so-called **closed tenders** and are most suitable for purchasers with a complete list of suppliers.

Quotations are quick and informal and can be made by telephone, fax or electronic means. Quotations are used not only when standard materials are purchased, but are also suitable for non-standard or custom-made materials with a high monetary value, for example custom-made equipment that performs a unique function. **Tenders** go hand in hand with a drawn-out procedure that has to be followed to the letter. The modern trend is to limit the use of tenders to the minimum. Tenders are usually suitable for the purchase of custom-made materials with a high monetary value, when there is plenty of time for the process, and when there are many suppliers in the market in active and serious competition with each other, for example in the construction of buildings.

Tenders and quotations are also used as a basis for **post-tender negotiations. Post-tender negotiations** take place between purchaser and tenderer(s) once tenders have been considered and none of those received is acceptable, or where a supplier is chosen above another for certain reasons but the price or other conditions are unacceptable. Strong ethical conduct is a prerequisite in this type of negotiation. No information or any indication of any other tender should be made known during this type of negotiation.

Negotiation often gives a buyer the best results. However, it requires careful preparation by an experienced negotiation team if it is to be successful. Negotiation entails a personal meeting between buyer and seller with a view to reaching a compromise and concluding a deal. It is an expensive method and justified only in transactions with a high monetary value, where contract conditions are complex, when the execution of the contract stretches over a long period, and when business is conducted with the only suppliers in the mar-

ket (a monopoly) or a supplier in a strong market position.

Although tenders and negotiations have been discussed as pricing methods, it is important to emphasise that they are also used to determine quality, service and delivery of purchased materials or services.

> **Critical thinking**
>
> Why were tenders used as a method of selecting suppliers and determining prices for the Gautrain project?

23.6.3 Preferences in price comparison

Purchasers often adopt a policy of allocating a specified preference percentage to certain suppliers. This means that for price comparison purposes the supplier's price is reduced by, for example, 8%, because the material contains 80% local content (South African manufactured components). In other words, if a supplier enjoys preference because of local content, the price that it quotes is reduced by 8% before it is compared with the prices of other suppliers. Sometimes the preference with price comparison is enforced statutorily (by legislation), as is the preference for local content and black economic empowerment (affirmative purchasing). Preference can also be given to suppliers according to the purchasing and supply policy of the purchasing business, for example on the basis of fixed price contracts.

23.7 Timing of purchases

23.7.1 The "right" time to buy

The time at which purchases are made often determines the price paid for materials. In the same way, time and price determine the quantity to be purchased.

The aims of buying at the right time are:
- To ensure that the business is supplied on

an ongoing basis with the materials and services required for it to operate without interruptions
- To reduce the risk of price fluctuations
- To keep inventory holding at an optimal level

To realise these aims, a buyer should have a sound knowledge of the market and trends.

23.7.2 Factors influencing the scheduling of purchases

Various internal and external factors influence the time at which purchases (and obviously their quantity) should be made. **Internally**, business policy may prevent buyers from buying speculatively, so that they are unable to make use of bargain offers. Furthermore, the availability of funds in the business determines when products are purchased. Changes in the marketing and operations requirements may influence the time at which purchases are made, because most purchases are made for these functions. Physical facilities, such as storage space, is another factor that influences the timing of purchases.

The first **external factors** to determine the time of purchases are market conditions (supply and demand) and government regulations. During recessions, there is a favourable buyers' market, and materials can be bought at lower prices because of the decrease in demand for materials resulting from fewer economic activities. During these periods it is advisable to buy large quantities of materials. Obviously a business can benefit from such market conditions only if it has the necessary funds, and provided that its economic activities and demand for the final product or service are expected to increase. In a **boom** period, economic activities are high and the demand for suppliers' products increases. Prices increase and service to the purchaser tapers off. During such periods it is wise to buy early at lower prices. Buyers should, as far as possible, avoid making purchases when prices are high. If the boom is expected to level out (prices are expected to decrease) it is wise to buy at the last minute (within the limits of lead times) and in small quantities.

Lead times and the reliability of suppliers are additional external factors that determine the timing of purchases. Government restrictions are another consideration, in that they place limitations in particular on those organisations conducting business with foreign suppliers. A buyer in South Africa will, for example, have difficulty in obtaining permission to purchase materials overseas if South Africa's foreign money supply is limited or if the local suppliers' continued existence is at risk (for example the textile industry in South Africa).

> **Critical thinking**
>
> If petroleum companies in South Africa obtain information about a future meeting of crude oil producers in the Middle East and expectations are that these producers will decrease their barrel output in order to increase prices, what will the South African companies do? What will the advantages and disadvantages of their action be?

23.7.3 Market structures and the scheduling of purchases

Buyers make purchases in stable, unstable and structured markets. In **stable markets**, such as those for standard materials (for example equipment, chemicals, nuts and bolts), buyers purchase materials as needed to maintain optimal inventory levels, because in the short term, prices are not sensitive to fluctuations in demand and supply, and the products are widely available at more or less the same price.

In **unstable markets**, which are subject to major fluctuations in price and availability, as in the case of agricultural products, minerals and metals, the timing of purchases is a vital consideration. Here, buyers should purchase larger quantities during favourable periods and smaller quantities in less-favourable times. Successful purchasing and supply requires an in-depth knowledge of the market, as well as perfect timing.

Structured markets or commodity exchanges are found throughout the world, their aim being to facilitate international trade in materials such as grain, coffee, metals, minerals and wool. A commodity exchange is in fact a market where buyers and sellers meet and barter for a particular commodity (material). Commodity exchanges exist in two markets, namely the spot market and the futures market. Each commodity has two prices on a commodity exchange:

- A **cash price** determined by the existing market mechanism (supply and demand) and, in practice, the prevailing market price
- A **futures price** based on market conditions

Skilled buyers, by scheduling purchases in these two markets, are able to hedge against risk associated with large price variations. This ensures that commodities and materials are bought at competitive prices.

23.7.4 Policies for purchasing and supply at the right time

Four main policies affect the scheduling of purchases:

- **Scheduling purchases according to needs.** This is the most common policy, and entails purchasing materials when the business needs them, regardless of the price and market conditions. It is ideal for purchasing standard materials, but is sometimes also adopted by businesses that buy within unstable markets.
- **Advance purchasing.** This involves the purchase of more materials than required, the aim being to ensure future availability.

However, one disadvantage is that excessively high inventory levels lead to high inventory costs.

- **Speculative purchasing.** This entails purchasing materials that the business does not need in the near future, or may never need. Speculative buying is based on a knowledge of the market, and a buyer's anticipation that the price of materials is going to increase drastically in the future. The idea is to sell the purchased materials (which are not always part of the business's normal activities) at a profit when prices do rise. Another reason for speculative buying is the expectation that the business may develop a need for such materials sometime in the future.
- **Minimum purchases.** This entails scheduling purchases so that inventory is available only for the immediate needs of the business. Inventory is kept to a minimum and no buffer stocks are held. This policy is normally applied when prices of materials are in a downward phase. Of course, the business always runs the risk of running out of stock.

Critical thinking

Recall once again the case study of the soft drinks industry.
- What policy guidelines regarding timing of CO_2 purchases should ABI and Afrox have followed to prevent the problem of a CO_2 shortage described in the case study?
- What policy guidelines regarding timing are they most likely to have followed?

This concludes the discussion regarding purchasing and supply activities, but at this point it is important to emphasise once again that these activities should be executed in an integrated fashion. The next section deals with the strategy of **outsourcing** and two tools that buyers use to execute their task, namely **purchasing and supply research**, and negotiations.

23.8 The outsourcing decision

The outsourcing decision is actually a make-or-buy decision. When a firm decides to outsource a certain activity or process (or part of it), this becomes a purchasing issue. The materials (product), process or service is then purchased from an outside supplier.

> **Outsourcing** can be defined as the process of transferring a business activity, including the relevant assets, to a third party.

Organisations outsource when they decide to buy something they have been making in-house. For example, many organisations outsource services such as the cafeteria, cleaning and security services previously provided by internal personnel. The basic philosophy behind outsourcing is that organisations concentrate all their efforts and resources on core activities or core competencies, and buy all non-core activities or competencies from outside institutions or experts specialising in the specific activity or function. Often these institutions or experts can provide a better product or service at a lower cost.

Competencies are the skills, knowledge and technologies that an organisation possesses, on which its success depends. Only some activities performed by an organisation are core competencies. These core competencies underpin the ability of the organisation to outperform the competition, and they must therefore be defended and nurtured.[3]

Management of organisations should be cautious with respect to decisions as to what the core competencies are, and what activities are outsourced. Some organisations define core competencies and activities as "those things that we do best". Such an application has clear risks in that it may lead organisations to outsource (core) activities with which they are having trouble. These activities may be of significant value to the organisation both currently and in the future – thus contributing to the organisation's competitive advantage, for example if a university does not have enough competent academic personnel and the decision is made to outsource tuition or research.[4]

Insourcing is the opposite of outsourcing. Organisations can, for particular reasons – in particular, strategic reasons – decide to insource (provide or perform internally) a function or activity rather than buy it from an outside supplier.

The insourcing/outsourcing decision requires a wide variety of knowledge and technical skills, ranging from strategic thinking to an in-depth cost analysis. The cost analysis consists of a comparison of the costs of buying the product or service, and the cost of making the product or performing the service in the organisation. The discussion of the insourcing/outsourcing strategy will be

---

Applying the concept: Core competency and core activities at a university

The core activities of a university are the tuition it provides, the research it does and community projects. All other activities at a university are support or non-core activities. Often non-core activities – for example security, catering, printing, maintenance and logistics services, or parts of them – are outsourced. The core competency of a university (which make it better than competitors or give it a competitive advantage) should be in the tuition (academic programmes), research and community projects. However, the core competency can also lie in the mode of the service delivery (for example Unisa is an expert in distance education), the use of technology or the way in which the university is managed. Usually non-core competencies (those competencies at which the university lags behind, which are not core and which can be performed better by an outside institution) are outsourced.

Table 23.3: Main cost elements that should be included in the insourcing/outsourcing analysis

Costs to be included with insourcing	Costs to be included with outsourcing
Operating expenses • Direct labour • Fringe benefits • Direct materials Indirect labour Equipment depreciation Fixed overheads Engineering/design/research	Purchase cost Freight Inventory costs Administrative costs Relationship costs

concluded with table 23.3, which clearly indicates the costs that have to be considered regarding the insourcing/outsourcing decision.

23.9 Purchasing and supply research

Purchasing and supply research comprises the systematic collection and processing of information on the environment (internal and external) in which the purchasing and supply function operates, so that purchasing and supply decision making can be placed on an objective and scientific footing, and environmental risks kept to a minimum.

All research is costly, and purchasing and supply research is certainly no exception. Therefore, the benefits obtained from such research should be weighed up against the costs involved. Purchasing and supply research should be undertaken only in the areas of greatest risk to the effective performance of the purchasing and supply task. Also, such research is undertaken only in businesses that spend large sums of money on the purchasing of materials and services.

Purchasing and supply research can be organised in various ways. It may, for example, be undertaken by specialist researchers in an independent purchasing and supply research section. This is one of the more effective methods, but is also the most expensive. Another option is for buyers themselves to

conduct the research. This method is less expensive, and buyers have first-hand knowledge of any problems being experienced. The disadvantage, however, is that purchasers seldom have the time to do research over and above their daily purchasing and supply tasks.

The areas in which purchasing and supply research may be conducted are described in sections 23.9.1 to 23.9.3.

23.9.1 Research on materials and services

This type of research is mainly concerned with:

- The supply and demand of materials used by the business
- A forecast of the business's needs for materials, especially strategic materials
- The availability of the most important materials in the supply market
- Price trends in the supply market for the planning periods in question
- The development of new materials and services
- Substitute materials
- Cost-reducing strategies

This type of research is important because the needs of the market and technology are continually changing. The task of the purchaser is directly influenced by changes in the consumer market. The buyer may cooperate with marketing (in a cross-functional team) in conducting research in the consumer market. The areas to be investigated will be:

- Trends in the consumer market
- Supply and demand in the consumer market
- Competitive products, etc.

23.9.2 Research on suppliers

This is one of the most important fields of research. Information on financial stability, production capacity, and the progressiveness and performance of suppliers is indispensable in the choice of the right supplier.

23.9.3 Research on the purchasing and supply system

This type of research is concerned with the effective functioning of the purchasing and supply system, both internally and externally, with suppliers. Areas that merit research are the design of documentation, development of price indexes, the application of computers, and performance appraisal of the purchasing and supply function. This type of research is important when organisations decide to implement the supply chain management approach, which means an integration of systems with suppliers.

The above discussion emphasises the need for purchasing and supply research for effective decision making and the efficient performance of the purchasing and supply function. Extensive research is needed in all three areas before organisations can adopt new approaches to the purchasing and supply of materials and services.

Critical thinking

Recall once again the case study of the soft drinks industry. In what areas is ABI most likely to do purchasing and supply research, following the problems at the end of 2006?

23.10 Negotiations in purchasing and supply

Price negotiations were dealt with in section 23.6.2. However, negotiation with suppliers is conducted for other purposes as well. Negotiation is required for purchasers and suppliers to reach a common understanding about the assignment and execution of a contract, and includes considerations such as extent of cooperation, delivery, specifications (quality), prices, and conditions of payment. Negotiation is a comprehensive process and demands careful preparation, intelligent manoeuvres, and compromises.

Negotiation is used mainly in cases where:

- Unique or complex materials are purchased for the first time
- The supplier is in a strong position in the market
- There are few suppliers in the market
- There is price collusion between suppliers
- A buying transaction is accompanied by a service or maintenance contract, for example the purchase of a computer system
- Price increases are requested
- Long-term agreements and/or strategic alliances or partnerships are to be concluded with suppliers

The buyer should be part of the negotiating team and should therefore assist in preparing for negotiations. When making its preparations, the team should do the following:

- Firstly, the team should collect information on the economic forecast, conditions in the market, the legal considerations involved, and the financial position of the supplier. A sound knowledge of the materials required and possible substitute materials is also imperative.
- Secondly, the supplier's offer should be carefully considered and a cost analysis conducted.

- Thirdly, the strengths and weaknesses of the two negotiating teams should be weighed against each other and analysed prior to proceeding to the actual negotiations.

During the negotiating process, the two parties start at different levels and should move closer to each other through mutual concessions. Because various factors are involved in negotiations, one party may be more compliant about one aspect, and the other more compliant about another. The idea is not to obtain maximum concessions from the supplier, but to negotiate the maximum total value for the purchaser. In the process, the buyer should yield to some extent.

Negotiating tactics should not be used as a substitute for careful preparation or an experienced negotiating team. They can only be applied as a complementary psychological advantage and should not be overdone, otherwise there is no chance of a win–win situation. Also, negotiating tactics should be avoided when negotiating with long-term suppliers.

Other techniques, such as value analysis and the learning curve, can be applied during the preparatory phases and during negotiations to assist the buyer.

Critical thinking

Recall once again the case study of the soft drinks industry. What do you think were the nature and content of the negotiations between ABI, Afrox, Sasol and PetroSA during the last three months of 2006?

23.11 **Summary**

The discussion in this chapter concerned the purchasing and supply function. It was emphasised that the different purchasing and supply activities do not occur in isolation, but on an integrated basis.

In both chapter 22 and this chapter attention was focused on the integration of the purchasing and supply function with other functions of the business to enable the system to operate as a whole.

 Key terms

Advance purchasing	Negotiations
Automatic replenishment	Outsourcing
Developing suppliers	Post-tender negotiations
Economic order quantity	Published price lists
Efficient consumer response	Purchasing and supply cycle
Enterprise resource planning	Purchasing and supply research
Fixed order quantities	Quick response
Insourcing	Quotations
Inventory-carrying costs	Specifications
Inventory holding	Speculative purchasing
Inventory-ordering costs	Standardisation
Just-in-time	Supplier performance
Materials requirements planning	Tenders

? **Questions for discussion**

1. What are the logical steps to be followed in a purchasing and supply transaction? Illustrate and explain your answer.
2. What is the nature of quality decisions in purchasing and supply and what is the role of the supplier?
3. What would appear in a requisition and broad specifications for the following? Draw these up.
   a. *A truck for use by a neighbourhood nursery which also does some landscaping of gardens*
   b. *The training of staff by an outside training provider on a new computer system implemented by the firm.*
4. Why is inventory necessary and why should it be controlled?

5. What are the most common inventory control methods and the circumstances for their application?
6. What are the main issues in the selection and evaluation of suppliers?
7. What is the nature of pricing as purchasing and supply activity?
8. What are the influencing factors for the scheduling of purchases and the most important policy guidelines regarding the timing of purchases?
9. What is outsourcing, as viewed from a purchasing and supply perspective, and how does it work?
10. How is purchasing and supply research an aid for decision making?
11. How is negotiation an aid in concluding purchasing transactions?

References

1. Hugo, W.M.J., Badenhorst-Weiss, J.A. & Van Biljon, E.H.B., *Supply chain management: Logistics in perspective*, Van Schaik, Pretoria, 2004, p. 349–350.
2. *Ibid.*, pp. 350–352.
3. McIvor, R., "A practical framework for understanding the outsourcing process", *Supply Chain Management: An International Journal*, Vol. 5, No. 1, 2000, p. 24.
4. Lonsdale, C. & Cox, A., "Outsourcing risk and rewards", *Supply Management*, July, 1997, p. 33.

PART 4

Contemporary issues
IN BUSINESS MANAGEMENT

Chapter 1: The business world and business management **Chapter 2:** Entrepreneurship **Chapter 3:** The establishment of a business		Flows
Chapter 24: Contemporary management issues		Products
Chapter 4: The business environment		Services
Chapter 5: Introduction to general management **Chapter 6:** The basic elements of planning **Chapter 7:** Organising **Chapter 8:** Leadership **Chapter 9, 10, 11:** Human resources management **Chapter 12:** Controlling the management process	**Chapter 13, 14, 15 and 16:** Marketing and public relations management	Information
	Chapter 17, 18, 19: Financial management	Financial
	Chapter 20 and 21: Operations management	Resource
	Chapter 22 and 23: Purchasing and supply management	Demand

Customer satisfaction and value

Source: Adapted from: Mentzer, J. T. (ed.), *Supply Chain Management*, Sage, London, 2001 pp. 22–23.

CONTEMPORARY MANAGEMENT CHALLENGES IN BUSINESS MANAGEMENT

The purpose of this chapter

This chapter includes a number of contemporary challenges and management problems peculiar to the South African business environment to illustrate the increasing importance of sound management principles in the efficient and effective functioning of businesses, and to demonstrate the comprehensive field of study of this science. Three contemporary challenges in South African business management, namely productivity issues and productivity improvement, globalisation, and knowledge management are specifically discussed.

Learning outcomes

The content of this chapter will enable learners to:
- Place productivity problems in South Africa in perspective
- Identify misconceptions about productivity and productivity improvement
- Explain the importance of productivity improvement and the level of productivity in South Africa
- Explain ways of improving productivity in South Africa
- Identify the components of globalisation
- Identify and explain the advantages and disadvantages of globalisation
- Understand the three building blocks of the knowledge hierarchy
- List the benefits of knowledge management
- Explain the benefits of knowledge management

24.1 Introduction

In the introductory chapters of this book we discussed in detail the close relationship between a business and its environment, as well as the role of the business in satisfying the needs of society. Because of the important role of business in a market economy, there is a need for a science that can study ways and means of improving its functioning. These ways and means were elaborated on in previous chapters of this book. The discussion of general management and the environmental influences on it makes it clear that business management is not static but dynamic, because it has to deal with environmental change and management problems stemming from this change.

Business management is also multi-disciplinary and must continually keep track of developments in related disciplines that can be utilised to its advantage. The fact that different industries face different business and management problems further complicates this field of study. For example, South African businesses increasingly need international management skills. At the same time, businesses constantly need to increase their productivity to remain competitive. Small businesses, which provide 95% of all jobs in the USA, have their own management problems relating to their scope and size. Managers need to be aware of these problems.

An introductory work of this kind can provide only a framework for examining the numerous problems confronting management in all spheres of business. In this context, it serves no purpose to complicate this framework by including too many additional and advanced aspects related to business management. However, a number of contemporary issues and management problems peculiar to the South African business environment are included here to illustrate the increasing importance of sound management principles in the efficient and effective functioning of businesses and to demonstrate the comprehensive field of study of this science. Three contemporary issues in South African business management, namely productivity issues and productivity improvement, globalisation, and knowledge management, are briefly discussed.

24.2 The problem of productivity in South Africa

24.2.1 Definition of concepts

Few concepts in business management are as frequently misinterpreted as those of productivity and productivity improvement. Any discussion of the problem of productivity in South Africa therefore requires one to have perfect clarity regarding the meaning of these two concepts.

Productivity[1] can be defined as the ratio between goods and services produced (**output**) and the resources (**input**) used to produce them, to indicate the productive efficiency with which labour, capital, material, and other inputs are combined and used to produce goods and services of a specific quality for the satisfaction of customer needs.

Example

$$\text{Productivity} = \frac{Q_u}{Q_i}$$

where Q_u = quantity of outputs of goods and services

and Q_i = quantity of inputs in resources (labour, capital, materials, etc.) needed to produce Q_u

Productivity improvement from one period to the next is represented by an increase in the output/input ratio in the second period compared to the first.

Example

$$\text{Productivity improvement} = \frac{Q_{ut}}{Q_{it}} < \frac{Q_{ut} + 1}{Q_{it} + 1}$$

where Q_{ut} = quantity of output of goods and services in period t

and Q_{it} = quantity of inputs in resources in period t to produce Q_{ut}

Case study

The new golden age in the world?

The World Bank is predicting a new golden age of prosperity over the next two decades. During this age, the number of people living in dire poverty will nearly halve, developing countries will assume a vastly expanded role in the world economy, and a new middle class will emerge.

The bank warns in its Global Economic Prospects 2007 report, that Africa is at risk of being left further behind in this new golden age of growth. But if governments get things right by implementing reforms to strengthen the investment climate, as well as receiving increased funds for infrastructure, it could see incomes double. It predicts that despite population growth, the number of people living in dire poverty – below the $1 dollar-a-day poverty line – is likely to fall to 550 million from 1,1 billion today.

The World Bank warns that the remaining poor are likely to be more concentrated in sub-Saharan Africa. With demographic trends heavily influencing economic growth, the global economy will be increasingly powered by developing countries. It is ironic that these nations, which were once considered peripheral to the world economy, could be its engine for growth in the future. By 2030 the bank expects per capita incomes in the developing world of $11 000, which is roughly the level of the Czech Republic today. The share of developing countries will rise from one-fifth to nearly one-third, resulting in a substantial shift in world economic power.

With that growth, the bank expects a new massive middle class of 1,2 billion people by 2030 to emerge in developing countries, three times larger than it is today. Through their active participation in the global marketplace, they stand to drive profound political changes in their own countries as well as in the global economy.

There are many provisos to the bank's golden-age scenario, including widening inequality, growing tensions between business and labour, and new environmental pressures from pollution and global warming. But in the long term, the bank believes its predictions are sound.

For Africa as a whole, the bank's central scenario is that most of the continent will miss out on the golden age and be left further behind. What this points to is a significant deterioration of living standards in Africa relative to the rest of the world. The litany of factors holding the continent back is well known – Africa's slower per capita income growth, often due to strife; rising population growth; and poor governance and policy.

For SA, the implications of the report are to stay the current course on economic policy and push harder in opening up the economy to the opportunities that globalisation presents. If more South Africans are to participate in this golden age, the economy needs to continue to be reformed to improve the investment climate. SA has made only limited inroads into dire poverty since its first democratic elections in 1994. The message for SA thus has to be about the need to markedly improve the effectiveness of government on delivery.

Source: Business Day, 15 December 2006.

There are five basic ways in which productivity improvements can be achieved:
- Increased output is accomplished with fewer inputs.
- Increased output is produced with the same inputs.
- The same output is produced with fewer inputs.

- A smaller output is produced with even fewer inputs.
- A larger output is produced with more inputs, but the marginal increase in output is larger than the marginal increase in inputs.

From our definition of the concept of productivity, it is clear that an improvement in quality also implies a productivity improvement, even if a particular output/input ratio remains unchanged.

From the viewpoint of the individual business, the objective of productivity improvement is the optimum combination or maximum utilisation of all production factors in a specific business so that only economically unavoidable costs remain. Thus the primary goal of the business, namely maximising the return on invested capital, can ultimately be achieved.[2]

With reference to the above explanation of the concepts of productivity and productivity improvement, one may ask why so much emphasis is currently placed on higher productivity and therefore productivity improvement in South Africa. Will higher productivity not result in larger business profits only, without any advantages for the rest of the community? Does productivity in South Africa really compare as poorly as is claimed with productivity in other countries, and, if so, what can be done, especially by management, to increase productivity? After examining some of the misconceptions about productivity and productivity improvement, we will attempt to provide answers to these questions.

24.2.2 Misconceptions about productivity and productivity improvement

In section 24.2.1 we mentioned that there are many misconceptions about productivity and productivity improvement. Included among these are the following:

- **Productivity improvement will result in a decrease in job opportunities.** This is obviously not true. The foregoing definition of productivity indicates that productivity improvement can be achieved without affecting the number of job opportunities, because productivity can be increased through improved utilisation of any of the production factors. Even if the number of workers is increased, but the productivity of, say, capital and materials increases at an even higher rate, total productivity will still increase.
- **A productivity improvement programme is a one-off occurrence.** Productivity improvement is, in fact, a lengthy, ongoing process requiring continuous attention if progress is to be achieved and maintained.
- **A productivity improvement programme is the responsibility of one person, institution or sector.** Such an approach can at best be only partly successful. The best results in a productivity improvement programme can be achieved only with the full cooperation of the management team, workers, input suppliers, and, even, consumers.
- **Productivity is the same as production.** Production is merely the cumulative output of goods or services, while productivity is related to the input used to achieve the output.
- **Productivity and productivity improvement relate to only the manufacturing sector.** This is incorrect, because businesses in all sectors use inputs to produce outputs. By definition, the concept of productivity therefore applies to all organisations, and every organisation is more or less productive.
- **Productivity improvement is equated with harder work or longer working hours.** Productivity refers to the input/output ratio, while harder work and longer working hours relate only to inputs. Although all people should do a fair day's work, and idleness leads to low productivity, productivity in general does not mean harder work or longer work-

ing hours; it means working without wasting.

- **Productivity improvement benefits only employers.** There is a strong correlation between real remuneration and productivity, and therefore employers will pay employees more if they produce more. They cannot, however, pay them more than they are worth, because then they will eventually be forced out of business.
- **Productivity improvement increases work stress and reduces work satisfaction.** Research has proved this to be incorrect, because about two-thirds of both stress and dissatisfaction at work are linked to non-productive activities. The teaching of stress management skills often merely teaches people to be happy with such non-productive activities. It is far better in such cases to remove the non-productive factors and the resultant stress and dissatisfaction and replace them with satisfying, productive activities.

24.2.3 The importance of productivity improvement and the level of productivity in South Africa

Since it is impossible within the ambit of this section to give a full exposition of the importance of productivity improvement and the level of productivity in South Africa, we will focus on a few salient aspects only.

Basically, **economic growth** can be obtained in two ways:

- Through an **increase in resources consumed** (capital, labour, material, energy)
- Through **more productive utilisation** of these resources

In South Africa, productivity makes a very small contribution to overall economic growth (in some years it has even made a negative contribution). However, the converse applies to many of South Africa's trading competitors, for whom productivity growth is responsible for as much as 80% of economic growth. South Africa could achieve a much higher economic growth rate if productivity growth could be enhanced. Figure 24.1 shows that South African companies do not fare badly in productivity comparisons. The World Bank report from which figure 24.1 is taken found that South Africa's labour productivity is far higher than in Senegal and Kenya, the most productive low-income countries in sub-Saharan Africa.

According to figure 24.1:

- Labour productivity is higher in South Africa than elsewhere in Africa and is high-

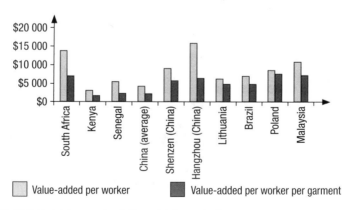

Figure 24.1: South Africa's labour productivity put into context

Source: World Bank, http://www.southafrica.info/doing_business/investment/incentives/world-bank (15 March 2007).

er than, or comparable to, other middle-income economies and the most productive areas of China.

- South Africa's labour productivity also compares favourably with other middle-income countries such as Lithuania, Brazil, Poland and Malaysia – all of which, other than Brazil, have higher per capita income.[3]

Productivity improvement is particularly important to the community because it plays a crucial role in economic growth. The better the productivity improvement, the higher the economic growth rate (see also figure 24.2). A high economic growth rate is essential to improving the standard of living of all South Africans, because it entails more job opportunities, combats unemployment, and allows more people to share in the economic prosperity being created.

It is theoretically possible to strip the rich of their wealth by decree. However, policies such as nationalisation cannot make the poor even moderately well-off. The emphasis should be on the improvement of South Africa's economic growth potential. The standard of living also cannot be permanently improved by means

of salary and wage increases – these must be accompanied by increased productivity. Cost-push inflation can be effectively combated by productivity improvements, because productivity enhancement means better utilisation of resources with further cost savings, resulting in a lower cost structure and inflation rate. It is also only through productivity improvement that South African manufacturing organisations can ensure that their products can compete in national and international markets.

Any reduction in a business's cost structure will inevitably have a favourable effect on its profits. Hence, profitability and productivity enhancement have a positive correlation – the greater the productivity improvement, the higher the profits achieved.

The following summarises the importance of productivity improvement: higher productivity creates the possibility of paying higher wages to employees, of declaring satisfactory dividends to shareholders, and of offering products and services at lower prices. Productivity improvement thus benefits the entire community and is hence also the community's responsibility.

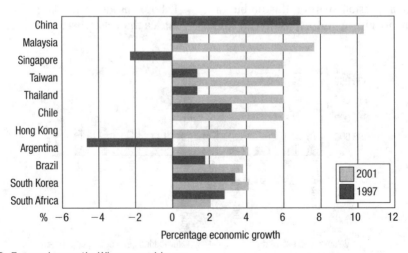

Figure 24.2: Economic growth: Winners and losers

24.2.4 Productivity improvement in South Africa

How can productivity improvement be stimulated in South Africa? In section 24.2.1 we mentioned five ways to increase productivity. Although theoretically correct, these methods are too simple and too vague to be of any real

value, and therefore a summary of the most important factors and techniques of productivity improvement is provided in table 24.1.

It is not possible, within the ambit of this section, to make a detailed analysis of all the different factors and techniques of productivity improvement provided in table 24.1. Therefore a few comments must suffice.

Table 24.1: Summary of the most important factors and techniques of productivity improvement

A. External factors and techniques for enhancing productivity

1. The attitudes of workers and management towards productivity enhancement
2. Economic and environmental factors enhancing productivity:

(a) The size of the market	(f) The tax structure
(b) Stability of the market	(g) Available training facilities
(c) The mobility of production factors	(h) Research and exchange of information
(d) The quality and availability of raw materials	(i) Technological innovation and mechanisation
(e) The availability of capital and credit	(j) Locality advantages

B. Internal techniques for enhancing productivity

1. Factory layout, machinery and equipment:

(a) The amount of capital per worker	(c) The maintenance of machinary and equipment
(b) Materials management	(d) Factory layout

2. Costing and cost reducing techniques:

(a) Cost control	(e) Break-even analysis
(b) Budgets and budgetary control	(f) Management by exception
(c) Opportunity cost analysis	(g) Organised cost-reducing programmes
(d) Incremental cost analysis	(h) Discounted cash-flow computations

3. Organisation, planning and control of production:

(a) Production planning and control	(e) Inventory control
(b) Classification, standardisation and specialisation	(g) Organised cost-reducing programmes
(c) Work study	(h) Discounted cash-flow computations
(d) Organisation and method study	

4. Personnel policy

(a) Cooperation between management and workers	(f) Wage incentives and profit-sharing schemes
(b) Selection and placement of workers	(g) Work environment and welfare services
(c) Vocational training	(h) Work methods
(d) Job analysis, staff evaluation and promotion	(i) Length of working day
(e) Supervision and discipline	(j) Number of shifts worked

Source: Van Niekerk, W.P., *Produktiwiteit en werkstudie,* © W.P. van Niekerk

24.2.4.1 Productivity awareness

Productivity awareness is a state of mind. It is the spirit of progress, of the continuous improvement of what already exists. It is the determination to perform better today than yesterday. It is the desire to improve the existing situation, irrespective of how good it may already be. It is the continuous attempt to implement new techniques and methods.

Is this state of mind present among South Africans? Unfortunately, the answer is generally "no". In the past, South Africans never needed to maintain a high level of productivity. The economy grew by using more labour, capital, raw materials and energy, which were readily available. Growth was not dependent on the better utilisation of inputs – hence, productivity was not part of the national culture.

The National Productivity Institute (NPI) actively promotes productivity, but the promotion of productivity is the responsibility of the population as a whole and of the economically active sector in particular. Productivity awareness should therefore form an integral part of education from an early age.

24.2.4.2 Training

Illiteracy does not promote productivity, and unfortunately, it takes many years to rectify the effects of poor schooling. Hence, management has a huge responsibility to train employees to meet the requirements of their jobs. In this regard, it has been claimed that insufficient investment in education and training is one of the major causes of low productivity.

Employees are increasingly realising that there is a positive correlation between training and remuneration, because trained workers are more productive and therefore better paid. However, it is common knowledge that in the past remuneration bore no relation to productivity performance (and this is so in some cases even today). This situation may be attributed mainly to the notion that workers could easily switch between different types of jobs – hence there was little specialisation. It is only now that South Africa is reaping the bitter fruits both of indifference in the selection, training and placement of workers and of bad planning for South Africa's future needs.

It is of critical importance that managers implement training to stimulate productivity. Four main factors in training increase the performance and resultant productivity of employees:[4]

- Employees require an adequate knowledge of tasks.
- Employees require skills to perform tasks.
- Employees need to be motivated.
- Management should provide opportunities for utilising other production resources effectively.

One of the most important issues in training is the motivation of employees to achieve higher performance. Unfortunately, many organisations in South Africa do not have productivity standards – the point of departure for productivity improvement – and, as a result, employees usually do not know what is expected of them in terms of increased performance. Even if they sometimes do know, the encouragement to live up to expectations is often lacking.

Today, trainers quantify the advantages of training in terms of higher productivity, which, although no easy task, is essential. The idea is to evaluate training (to measure its influence on productivity) rather than to confirm it (to determine whether it has taken place).

24.2.4.3 The implementation of new technology

Technological development and its successful implementation are significant factors that can contribute to productivity improvement. However, South African organisations do not make sufficient use of the advantages offered by improved technology – in many instances,

South African organisations are still struggling with the complexity of technology.

In South Africa, there is a large gap between the technology available and its utilisation in trading and manufacturing industries. There is therefore a pressing need for the selection of well-chosen technology and its appropriate implementation in order to bring about clear productivity advantages.

24.2.4.4 Government action

From the information provided in table 24.1, and the discussion of productivity improvement thus far, it is clear that government can, in various direct and indirect ways, influence the productivity performance of a country.

In order to be a positive influence on productivity improvement in South Africa, government should take the following actions:

- **Generally lower tax rates.** Excessively high tax rates have a negative impact on entrepreneurship and efficiency in the production of goods and services, and productivity is therefore reduced.
- **Create training facilities.** Training can make employers and employees more aware of the importance of higher productivity.
- **Link wage and salary increases.** Productivity improvements should accompany wage and salary increases in the public as well as related sectors.

- **Make training subsidies available.** Such action would help to establish a better trained labour force. See also the box below on South Africa's skills shortage.

If the above were attended to, South Africa would be assured of productivity enhancement.

24.2.4.5 Business management

In the final instance, the responsibility for productivity improvement lies with the management organisation, which should follow a holistic approach that includes all resources and activities (see table 24.1 in this regard). A major stumbling block, however, is the general shortage of properly trained managers.

To increase productivity in South Africa to desired levels, more and better managers are needed. The existing management echelon is too small to satisfy this need, and the solution is for all workers to be properly utilised. Development and promotion on merit should be accepted as healthy competition, because it is becoming increasingly necessary for management positions to be filled by candidates whose abilities fit the job description, and who will not be chosen on the basis of skin colour. The philosophy, outlook and form of management should be aimed at the optimal utilisation and exploitation of knowledge, ability and experience. Such an

---

World Bank report on South Africa's skills shortage

Most South African managers said worker skills were a serious obstacle to their operations and to growth. Despite South Africa's greater productivity, the cost of labour is high – more than three and a half times that of the most productive areas of China, two and a half times higher than in Brazil and Lithuania, and 75% higher than in Malaysia or Poland.

Wages are particularly high for highly skilled workers and managers. An additional year of education is associated with an 11% to 12% increase in wages in South Africa – compared to about 5% to 7% in developed countries.

The premium paid for education results in salaries for skilled workers and managers that are high by international standards. Although wages are similar for unskilled workers in Poland, managers' wages are over two and a

---

Source: http://www.southafrica.info/doing_business/investment/incentives/world-bank-151205.htm (15 March 2007).

approach will assist productivity improvement, because then the most suitable person will be appointed to the right post.

Critical thinking

The South African textile industry was under serious threat of being uncompetitive. Thousands of jobs were lost in this industry. What can this industry do to improve their productivity?

24.2.5 Final comments on productivity

A high real economic growth rate is essential to ensure a satisfactory standard of living for all South Africans, and this can come about only through sustained productivity improvement. This improvement is the responsibility of every member of the community, but it probably applies most to business management, which has the power to realise it through the application of healthy management principles.

24.3 Globalisation

24.3.1 Introduction

Globalisation is a term widely used, but it defies precise definition. From an economic perspective, **globalisation** may be described as the increasing interaction and integration of national economic systems through the growth of international trade, investment and capital flows – but globalisation also has social and cultural implications, which are not captured in this description.

Globalisation

Globalisation involves the growing interdependence among countries as reflected by increasing cross-border flows of goods, services, capital and know-how, thereby creating a whole new world order for firms around the world.

24.3.2 The components of globalisation

Globalisation has two components:
- The globalisation of markets
- The globalisation of production

24.3.2.1 The globalisation of markets

The globalisation of markets refers to the merging of historically distinct and separate markets into one integrated marketplace. Thus, it is argued that the tastes and preferences of consumers in different countries are beginning to converge in accordance with some global norm, thereby helping to form a global marketplace. Consumer products such as Coca-Cola, Levi's jeans, Apple iPods and McDonalds hamburgers are examples of this trend.

Lifestyle

We are not just connected with the rest of the world, we have assimilated parts or more of their culture and values, whether it was forced upon us or embraced willingly in the name of "lifestyle". As we look around us today, at the clothes and shoes we are wearing, the brands of make-up and perfume, and the fact that we use make-up and perfume, speaks volumes for the close-likeness of lifestyle, globalisation, westernisation and colonisation, all seemingly very much the same animal, evolving over time.

Although consumer products are gaining importance on global markets, industrial products still form the basis for world trade. Commodities such as aluminium, gold, oil, and wheat are traded in huge quantities on world markets. Rivalry between suppliers of these goods as well as particular consumer goods occurs on a global basis. For example, Coca-Cola's rivalry with Pepsi is not limited to the American or the European market – the competition is global.

24.3.2.2 The globalisation of production

The globalisation of production refers to the tendency of companies to source goods and services from locations all over the world to take advantage of national differences in the cost and quality of factors of production. In so doing, companies attempt to lower their overall cost structures and to improve the quality of their product offerings.

24.3.3 Causes of globalisation

Economies were previously isolated (and protected) from each other by barriers to cross-border trade, long distances, different time zones, language and cultural differences, and government regulation.

The majority of these economies are now actively involved in cross-border trade as a result of the following developments:[5]

- **Trade liberalisation and the easing of barriers to trade and investment by governments worldwide.** After World War II, nations committed themselves to removing barriers to the free flow of goods, services and capital. This goal was enshrined in a treaty known as the General Agreement on Tariffs and Trade (GATT). In 1995, GATT was replaced by the World Trade Organisation (WTO). The WTO is, similarly, a multinational institution with the goal of lowering trade and investment barriers. It also polices the global trading system and allows member nations to impose retaliatory tariffs on countries that do not abide by WTO rules. The WTO has 135 member countries, and it attempts to resolve trade disputes between member nations.
- **Rapid technological advances in communications.** Over the past 30 years, global communications have been revolutionised by developments in satellite, optical fibre and wireless technologies, the Internet and the World Wide Web. Lower communication costs, quicker response times, and the establishment of web-based electronic commerce (e-commerce) make it possible for businesses to expand their global presence at a lower cost than ever before. The web makes it easier for buyers and sellers to find each other, wherever they are located and whatever their size.
- **Rapid technological advances in transportation.** Advances in transportation have also contributed to globalisation. Commercial jet aircraft, on the one hand, have reduced the time it takes to get from one location to another in a different country, thus making it easier for business people to operate in locations all over the world. Containerisation, on the other hand, has significantly contributed to the lowering of costs of shipping goods over long distances, thus making it cheaper and easier to export goods to other countries.
- **The change from formerly centrally planned economies to freer market economies.** Today, many of the former communist nations of Europe and Asia share a commitment to democratic politics and free-market economics. Having been largely closed to western trade for many years, these countries now trade actively with other countries. The huge potential for trade with China has not been exploited fully, even though trade with China has increased over 15% per annum over the past 20 years.
- **The increasing importance of multinational enterprises worldwide.** During the 1960s global activity was dominated by large multinational businesses based in the USA. This has, however, changed quite remarkably, and Japanese, German, French and British companies currently compete actively in the global market. South African companies such as BHPBilliton, Anglo-American and SABMiller have invested in other countries, while a number of companies such as Sappi, Old Mutual, Liberty and Didata have exploited international capital markets through listings on foreign stock exchanges. Multinational companies have a pronounced effect on world trade.

The extent of the increase in world trade compared to growth in GDP is depicted in figure 24.3.

24.3.4 Measuring globalisation

One of the ways in which globalisation can be measured is in terms of the rising ratio of world trade to output (GDP). Figure 24.3 shows that world output expanded by 27% for the period 1990 to 2001, while world trade expanded by 83% over this same period.

Another measure of globalisation is for-

eign direct investment (FDI). According to Hill,[6] FDI occurs when a firm invests directly in productive facilities in a foreign country where an equity interest of at least 10% is regarded as a direct investment. In some countries, this minimum requirement could be as high as 25% or even 30%.

Compared with that in other developing countries, FDI in South Africa is small in value terms. The cumulative FDI in South Africa between 1994 and 1998 amounted to almost US$5 billion. In comparison, China, for example, received US$203 billion in the same

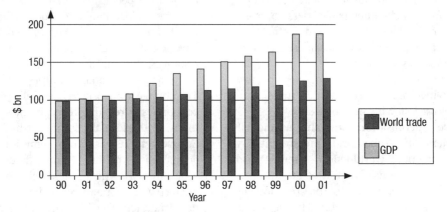

Figure 24.3: The growth of world trade and world output (GDP) 1990–2001

Source: http:/www.wto.org (World Trade Organisation) (15 March 2007).

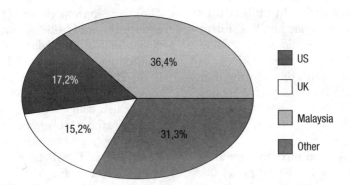

Figure 24.4: The sources of FDI in South Africa by country for the period 1995–1998

Source: Du Mhango, D., Industrial Development Corporation – Foreign Direct investment in South Africa: How has the policy towards FDI worked and how can it be strengthened? TIPS Forum 1999: Growth and Investment in South Africa http:/www.tips.org.za/node/954.

period, while India received US$12 billion. Between 1994 and 1998, 17,5% of FDI in South Africa went to telecommunications, 15,2% to "other sectors", 11,4% to energy and oil, 10,7% to motor and components, and 10,4% to food and beverages.

24.3.5 The advantages and disadvantages of globalisation

The **advantages** of globalisation include the following:

- The lowering of trade barriers allows businesses to market and sell their products internationally. The world as a whole becomes the market for a specific product or service – the market is not limited to a specific region or country.
- The lowering of investment barriers allows companies to base production in the optimal location from where world markets can be served.
- Many supporters of globalisation believe that increased cross-border trade and investments result in greater efficiency and therefore lower prices for goods and services. Because its proponents believe that globalisation stimulates economic growth, they argue that globalisation raises the income of consumers and that it creates jobs in countries that participate in the global system.

The **disadvantages** of global trade are as follows:

- Globalisation confronts companies with the challenge of having to compete internationally, whereas previously they had to compete with only local rivals. In addition,

globalisation raises questions as to how to invest, produce and compete in foreign markets while dealing with differences in culture, language and government regulations.

- Falling trade barriers often destroy jobs instead of creating jobs. Globalisation allows countries to move their production facilities to locations where wage rates are lower, thereby destroying jobs in the country of origin. People in developing countries, however, argue that jobs are destroyed because smaller local companies cannot compete with large international organisations. International competition eventually forces them to close down, with an accompanying loss of job opportunities.

The counter-arguments to these concerns are that the benefits of free trade exceed the costs, that free trade will eventually result in a more efficient system, and that the advantages of economies of scale, increased productivity, and the increased level of skills required to compete in a global economy should have a positive net effect.

24.3.6 Concluding remarks on globalisation

Since World War II there has been a significant lowering of trade and investment barriers,

---

Example

The Boeing Company's 777 jet airliner contains 132 500 major component parts that are produced all over the world by 545 suppliers in Singapore, Japan, Italy and other countries.

Source: Hill, C.W.H., *International business*, McGraw-Hill, New York, 2001, p. 6.

Africa's business boom is taking strain from skills shortages and globalisation

Domestic industries are experiencing difficulties in competing on a global scale due to a lack of skills. South African companies are finding it increasingly difficult to compete because they must deliver bigger volumes of goods to increasingly diverse customers. Growing competition from low-cost, emerging market countries such as India and China are making South Africa's companies struggle to be profitable.

Source: Business Times, 11 March 2007, p. 1.

which has resulted in a freer flow of products, services and capital. This has, in turn, resulted in a more integrated and interdependent world economy, through the process referred to as globalisation. Globalisation has two components, markets and production, and is measured by world trade in relation to world output and foreign direct investment. Although severe criticism is often directed at globalisation, its proponents believe that it results in greater efficiency, with a net benefit to the entire world.

> **Critical thinking**
>
> With South Africa's economy in a substantial upswing and with more and more products entering South Africa from emerging countries, what would be the best way for South Africa to keep its competitive edge?

24.4 Knowledge management

24.4.1 Introduction

Knowledge management emerged in the 1990s as an attempt by companies to harness the wealth of underutilised data, information and knowledge in their organisations. Traditionally, particular individuals and departments have secured their positions and status within the corporate hierarchy by hoarding information and knowledge.

However, the demands of a post-industrial economy, with its fast-changing and more competitive environment, have forced organisations intelligently to manage and use existing information and knowledge. Knowledge is today regarded as a new form of capital in what is referred to as "the knowledge economy". Organisations need to share and manage knowledge as a valuable resource in order to survive in this economy.

24.4.2 What is knowledge management?

Knowledge management is the process of identifying, collecting, storing, and transforming data and information into an intellectual asset that is available to all staff members. It aims to develop a solid base of intellectual capital by gathering and sharing the knowledge of individual staff members.

Companies introduce knowledge management in order to:

- Increase workplace efficiency
- Save time
- Reduce costs
- Retain, re-use and exchange knowledge

24.4.3 The knowledge hierarchy

Knowledge consists of the following three building blocks:

- **Data.** This is the most elementary building

Applying the concept: Knowledge management

Imagine being able to extract specific information about your business and its processes from filing cabinets, computer hard drives, websites, and people's minds. Now imagine depositing that information in a system that automatically organises it into logical subject areas, is easily able to be searched, and is accessible to whoever has approved access to it. Imagine that

the information is centralised, easy to understand, and can also be added to.

Imagine, also, improving your workplace environment by removing physical obstacles between people (partitions and filing cabinets) so that informal knowledge-sharing becomes the norm. Finally, imagine employees so encouraged by having the right information at their fingertips, that they are more than happy to follow set procedures and help collect, update and store your intellectual property.

block in the knowledge hierarchy. Data has the following characteristics:

- It represents facts, events or uncoded source-data.
- It has no meaning in itself.
- It simply exists, and has no significance beyond its existence.
- As a result of the lack of context, data requires human intervention and interpretation in order to extract even a minimal amount of usefulness from it.

Examples of data

- Student lists
- Statistics of populations
- Bank statements
- List of share prices

- **Information.** Data becomes information when it is categorised in a logical manner. In information, units of measure – such as time, distance, and magnitude – provide additional context not found in data alone. This is data that has been given meaning by way of a relational connection. Information embodies the understanding of a relationship of some sort, possibly cause and effect.

Examples of information

- The temperature dropped 15 degrees and then it started raining.
- The increase in earnings per share of 10% resulted in an increase in the share price.

- **Knowledge.** This is an organised body of information that forms the basis of insights or judgements. Information becomes knowledge when people use the information to make decisions or predictions. The human contribution therefore distinguishes knowledge from data and information. Nonaka and Takeuchi[7] make three observations in describing the similarities and differences between knowledge and information:

- Knowledge, unlike information, is about beliefs and commitment.
- Knowledge is a function of a particular stance, perspective, or intention.
- Knowledge, unlike information, is about action. It is always knowledge "to some end".
- Knowledge, like information, is about meaning. It is context-specific and relational.

Examples of knowledge

- If the humidity is very high and the temperature drops substantially, it is unlikely that the atmosphere will be able to hold the moisture, so it rains.
- Given that general market conditions remain the same, an increase in earnings will most probably result in an increase in the share price.

Source: Adapted from *Jakarta Post*, 8 June 2002.

24.4.4 The knowledge management process

The knowledge management process consists of four steps:[8]

- **Step 1: Identify existing knowledge.** Knowledge management starts by identifying what is already known. This includes the knowledge that resides in the minds of staff members, in reports, in data sets held throughout the organisation, or among regular suppliers and customers. The start of any knowledge management strategy is to be clear about where knowledge managers will begin.
- **Step 2: Reflect on existing knowledge.** Once the locations of the existing knowledge that resides in the organisation have been identified, the next step is to take stock of the knowledge. What is it that the people in the organisation know? How useful is that knowledge? Reflecting on current

knowledge provides the opportunity of summarising the existing knowledge into a form that can be easily shared with others. This also makes it possible to identify the gaps in the existing knowledge and to focus future knowledge-gathering efforts.

- **Step 3: Redistribute the knowledge.** A critical component of knowledge management is the creation of a system that ensures knowledge is shared with those who need it. The aim is to make the knowledge available wherever it is needed in the organisation.
- **Step 4: Apply the knowledge.** The most important reason for the initiation of knowledge management systems by organisations is to improve their perform-ance. Hence, the ultimate goal of identifying, reflecting upon, and sharing what an organisation knows is the application of that knowledge.

24.4.5 The benefits of knowledge management

The following benefits of knowledge management have been reported by companies of varying sizes:

- **Less frustration.** Staff members can access information themselves and do not need to rely on the availability of other people.
- **Better customer service.** Staff members know where to find the information that the customer needs.
- **Decreased vulnerability when staff leave.** The work processes of staff are documented so that others can pick up those tasks without confusion arising.
- **Increased competitiveness.** Management can see at a glance where the business is weaker or stronger.
- **Improved productivity.** Access to the right knowledge saves time that might have been wasted in looking for it.
- **Improved internal communication and teamwork.**
- **Possibility of automating some tasks.** This could occur when enough information about them has been gathered.

- **Improved market forecasting.** Knowledge management systems can provide forecasts on supply or economic problems, and companies can, accordingly, adjust inventory and other expensive processes to cope with these.

24.5 Summary

This chapter dealt with three contemporary issues in South African business management, namely productivity issues and productivity improvement, globalisation, and knowledge management.

 Key terms

Globalisation	Outputs
Inputs	Productivity
Knowledge management	

? Questions for discussion

1. Is there a link between the concepts of productivity, globalisation and knowledge management?
2. How can knowledge management help South African companies to become more competitive in the global market?

References

1. Mainly based on Republic of South Africa, President's Council, *Report of the committee for economic affairs on a strategy and action plan to improve productivity in the RSA*, Report PC 1/1989, Government Printer, Cape Town: National Productivity Institute, Productivity Focus, National Productivity Institute, Pretoria, 1991.
2. Van Niekerk, W.P., *Produktiwiteit en werkstudie*, Butterworth, Durban, 1978, p. 6.
3. http://www.southafrica.info/doing_business/investment/incentives/world-bank (15 March 2007).
4. Botha, F., "Verhoogde produktiwiteit deur motivering", *Volkshandel*, October 1980, p. 26.
5. Ball D.A., McCulloch, W.H., Frantz, P., Geringer,

J.M. & Minor, M.S., *International business*, 8th edition, McGraw-Hill Irwin, New York, 2002.

6. Hill, C.W.L., *International business*, 4th edition, McGraw-Hill Irwin, New York, 2003.

7. Nonaka, I. & Takeuchi, H., *The knowledge-creating company: How Japanese companies create the* *dynamics of innovation*, Oxford University Press (USA), 1995, pp. 57–58.

8. Sterndale-Bennett, B., "Defining knowledge management", *British Journal of Administrative Management (AMT)*, July 2001, p. 26.

Index